THE LITERATURE OF DEATH AND DYING

This is a volume in the Arno Press collection

THE LITERATURE OF DEATH AND DYING

See last pages of this volume for a complete list of titles

DEATH AS AN ENEMY

ACCORDING TO ANCIENT EGYPTIAN CONCEPTIONS

With a New Index

J[an] Zandee

ARNO PRESS

A New York Times Company

New York / 1977

Reprint Edition 1977 by Arno Press Inc.

Reprinted from a copy in
The Princeton University Library

THE LITERATURE OF DEATH AND DYING
ISBN for complete set: 0-405-09550-3
See last pages of this volume for titles.

Manufactured in the United States of America

Library of Congress Cataloging in Publication Data

Zandee, Jan, 1914-
Death as an enemy according to ancient Egyptian conceptions.

(The Literature of death and dying)
Reprint of the ed. published by Brill, Leiden, which was issued as no. 5 of Studies in the history of religions, supplements to Numen.
Includes bibliographical references.
1. Eschatology, Egyptian. 2. Death (Egyptian religion) I. Title. II. Series. III. Series: Studies in the history of religions, supplements to Numen ; 5.
BL2450.E8Z33 1977 299'.31 76-19597

ISBN 0-405-09591-0

DEATH AS AN ENEMY

STUDIES
IN THE HISTORY OF RELIGIONS

(SUPPLEMENTS TO *NUMEN*)

V

J. ZANDEE, THEOL. D.

DEATH AS AN ENEMY

LEIDEN
E. J. BRILL
1960

DEATH AS AN ENEMY

ACCORDING TO ANCIENT EGYPTIAN CONCEPTIONS

BY

J. ZANDEE, THEOL. D.

LEIDEN
E. J. BRILL
1960

Original Dutch text translated by Mrs W. F. Klasens

PRINTED IN THE NETHERLANDS

To the memory

OF MY FATHER
AND OF MY TEACHER
PROFESSOR A. DE BUCK

ACKNOWLEDGEMENTS

With the completion of this book I wish to state my sincere thanks to all those who have in any way contributed to it.

Foremost among these was my former teacher, the late Prof. Dr A. de Buck, under whose guidance the present book was prepared as a doctoral thesis for the Faculty of Literature and Philosophy of Leiden University. He spent many hours reading through and discussing the manuscript and I have profited not a little from his good advise. The years during which I had the privilege of being his pupil will always be among my best remembrances.

Prof. Dr H. P. Blok very kindly stood ready to take the place of Prof. de Buck after the latter's decease.

Prof. Dr J. Vandier, Curator in Chief of the Egyptian Department of the Louvre Museum, granted me access to unpublished papyri and permitted me to have a look at the Papyrus Jumilhac which he will publish in the course of 1960.

Dr P. Barguet, a scientific official of the Louvre Museum, placed his bureau at my disposal and gave in every respect indispensable assistance.

During a stay at Paris the help of Prof. Dr G. Posener was very valuable and the contact with Professors Clère and Malinine was important.

The Executive Committee of the International Association for the History of Religions fostered the publication of the present book in the series "Supplements to NVMEN." Especially helpful in this matter were the former chairman, the late Prof. Dr R. Pettazzoni, and the secretary, Prof. Dr C. J. Bleeker.

Mrs. W. F. Klasens-van der Loo made the translation into English in a most accurate manner. She was assisted by her husband Dr A. Klasens, Director of the Museum of Antiquities at Leiden.

Last, but not least, I desire to record the support of the Netherlands Organization for the Advancement of Pure Research (Z.W.O.) which enabled me to work for two months in the Louvre Museum in 1953 and subsidised the translation and the publication.

Without the most appreciated aid of the above mentioned persons and organizations it would have been impossible to finish the book. Therefore, the author wishes to express his deep gratitude to all of them.

CONTENTS

Acknowledgements VII
List of abbreviations and literature IX

CHAPTER I. GENERAL OUTLINE

Par. 1. The monistic and the dualistic conception of death . . 1
Par. 2. The texts 3
Par. 3. The way in which the dualistic conception of death occur in the texts 5
Par. 4. Traces of Sheol representations in Egypt 7
Par. 5. Views based on direct observation of death as a physical phenomenon 10

a. The decay of the body 10. — b. Being motionless 11. — c. Non-functioning of the senses and limbs 12. — d. Passing away and being carried off 13.

Par. 6. Death as absolute destruction 14

a. Death as such is perishing 14. — b. Being burnt (B.3) 14. — c. Cutting and slaughtering 16. — d. Other actions directed against the dead 17. — e. Total destruction as (a consequence of) punishment in the realm of the dead 18.

Par. 7. Dangers, which impend over essential parts of the personality (B.8) 19
Par. 8. Torment and torture 20
Par. 9. Dangerous places 24
Par. 10. The journey of the dead. 25
Par. 11. Judgment and sentence 31
Par. 12. Terms for sin 41

a. Words, which mean bad in a non-moral sense 41. — b. Words for disaster and misery 42. — c. Words for being bent 42. — d. Words for taboo 43. — e. *Ṯmś* = red (C.6.w) 43. — f. *Wn* = guilt (C.6.g) 43. — g. *Ḳn* = damage (C.6.s) 43. — h. Sin as rebellion against deity 43. — i. Sin as transgression 43. — j. *Sp* = case 44. — k. *ʾIsf.t* 44.

CHAPTER II. TERMS

A. Death in contrast with life 45
1. Total destruction 45

Chapter II. Terms, A

a. *3k̥*, to be destroyed 45. — b. *wn*, to pass 45. — c. *mt*, to die 45. — d. *n wn*; *tm*, not to be 48. — e. *n ḫpr*, not to become 49. — f. *ḥtm*, to perish 49. — g. *si*, to perish 50. — h. *śki*, to perish 50. — i. *š3y*, fate 51.

2. Passing away 52

a. *ii*, to come 52. — b. *isi*, to pass away 52. — c. *w3i*, to be far 52. — d. *pri*, to go forth 53. — e. *mni*, to land 53. — f. *ḫ3ʿ*, to leave 53. — g. *ḫpi*, to go away 54. — h. *sm3 t3*, to land 54. — i. *šm*, to go away 54.

3. Terms for decomposition. 56

a. *imk*, transitoriness 56. — b. *inp*, to consume 56. — c. *isi*, to be light, to fall into decay 56. — d. *ʿḫm*, to dry up 57. — e. *fnṯ*, to become maggoty 57. — f. *fd.t*, sweat of the corpse 57. — g. *rwi*, to perish 57. — h. *rḏw*, fluid of the corpse 57. — i. *hb*, to decay 58. — j. *ḥw3*, to consume 58. — k. *ḫśḏ*, to go bad 59. — l. *ẖnn*, to decay (of the corpse) 59. — m. *s3b*, to flow away 59. — n. *snṯ*, products of decomposition 59. — o. *śnśn*, to smell bad 59. — p. *śṯi*, smell 60.

4. Deterioration of the body and loss of the functions of life 60

a. *i3rr*, blindness(?) 60. — b. *id*, to be deaf 60. — c. *ʿ.t*, part of the body 60. — d. *ʿnḫ*, ear 61. — e. *brd*, to be stiff (?) 61. — f. *nk*, to copulate 61. — g. *nḏmy.t*, sexual desire 61. — h. *r3*, mouth 62. — i. *rwḏ*, tendon 62. — j. *rd*, foot 62. — k. *ḥr*, face 63. — l. *ḫrw*, sound 63. — m. *ẖ.t*, belly 63. — n. *ẖ3.t*, corpse 63. — o. *śmḫ*, to forget 63. — p. *śṯi*, to impregnate 64. — q. *šp*, blind 64. — r. *šdn*, to close 64. — s. *k̥ś*, bones 64. — t. *k̥rf*, to be bent 64. — u. *tp*, head 65. — v. *tḫni*, to injure (the eyeball) 65. — w. *ḏ.t*, body 65.

5. Encroachment on the complete continuance of life . . . 66

a. *3b.t*, relatives 66. — b. *ib*, to suffer thirst 67. — c. *itmw*, want of breath 67. — d. *ʿwg*, to dry up 67. — e. *ʿḫm*, to desiccate 67. — f. *wʿi*, to be alone 67. — g. *wś*, to be in want 68. — h. *wšr*, to dry up 68. — i. *fdk̥*, to cut off (breath) 68. — j. *mw*, water 68. — k. *mn*, to suffer 68. — l. *nwḫ*, to be scorched 68. — m. *ḥwʿ ib*, to be sad 68. — n. *ḥk̥r*, to suffer hunger 68. — o. *snw*, to suffer 70. — p. *śin*, to hurry 70. — q. *śʿr.t*, shortening of the time of life 70. — r. *śrf*, warm breath 71. — s. *g3w*, to be narrow 71. — t. *t*, bread 72. — u. *ṯ3w*, breath, air 72.

6. The world reversed 73

a. *iwty.w*, digestion products 73. — b. *wśš.t*, urine 74. — c. *ḥś*, excrements 74. — d. *śḫd*, to go upside down 75.

7. To be bound and imprisonment 78

a. *imy rd*, foot-iron 78. — b. *ink̥*, to fetter 79. — c. *inṯ.(t)*, to fetter 79. — d. *m3r*, tie 79. — e. *mḏ.t*, cattle halter 80. — f. *nṯ.t*, tie, 80.

Chapter II. Terms, A

— g. *ḫtr*, bond 80. — h. *ḫtm*, to close 80. — i. *ś3r*, bond 80. — j. *śfḫ*, to loosen 81. — k. *šśm*, strap(?) 81. — l. *ḳ3ś*, bond 81.

8. Death as sleep 81

a. *wrḏ*, to be tired 82. — b. *b3n*, to sleep 82. — c. *b3gi*, to be tired 82. — d. *m3ʿ*, to be extended 83. — e. *nmʿ*, to sleep 83. — f. *nni*, to be tired 83. — g. *śb3gi*, to make tired 84. — h. *śḳd*, to make asleep 84. — i. *śgnn*, to soften 84. — j. *śḏr*, to sleep 84. — k. *ḳd*, to sleep 85.

9. To be snatched away 85

a. *ini*, to take away 85. — b. *iṯi*, to take away 86. — c. *ʿw3*, to rob 87. — d. *nḥm*, to take away 87. — e. *ḫnp*, to rob 87. — f. *šd*, to take away 87. — g. *ṯ3i*, to take away 87.

10. The realm of the dead as a place of darkness 88

a. *iḫḫ.w*, darkness 88. — b. *wš3.w*, night, evening, darkness 88. — c. *śnk.(t)*, darkness 88. — d. *knḥ.w*, darkness 88. — e. *kkw*, darkness 89. — f. *grḥ*, night 91.

11. The netherworld 91

a. *3kr*, name of the god of the earth 91. — b. *ʾImn.t*, the West 92. — c. *ʾIgr.t*, the domain of silence 93. — d. *Nwn*, primeval ocean 94. — e. *nn.t*, subterranean realm of the dead 94. — f. *smy.t*, netherworld 94. — g. *šṯy.t*, realm of the dead 95. — h. *Gb*, god of the earth 95. — i. *t3*, earth 96. — j. *d3.t*, netherworld 96.

12. Snakes as animals of the earth. 97

a. *ʿ3 ḥry ḫ.t.f*, big one, which is on its belly 98. — b. *Nḥb k3.w*, name of a snake 98. — c. *r3*, worm 100. — d. *rrk*, a snake 100. — e. *hki*, a snake 100. — f. *ḥf3w*, snake 101. — g. *ḥnwy.t*, a snake 102. — h. *ḥnb3*, a snake 102. — i. *s3 t3*, son of the earth 102. — j. *k3*, a snake 102. — k. *ḏdf.t*, snake, worm 102.

13. Tomb and funeral 102

a. *im.t*, tomb 102. — b. *is*, grave 103. — c. *ḥ.t*, house 103. — d. *ḥ3.t*, grave 104. — e. *ḫr.t*, grave 104. — f. *ḥmw*, dust 104. — g. *ḳrś*, funeral 105. — h. *ḳd*, to build 107.

14. Mummy bandages 108

a. *ʿfn.t*, bandages 108. — b. *ʿnn*, bandage 108. — c. *wt*, mummy bandages 108. — d. *ṯs.t*, tie 108.

15. Death as horror 109

a. *nri*, to fear 109. — b. *nḥ3 ḥr*, wild of face 109. — c. *ḥrw*, terror 109. — d. *śnḏ*, to fear 110. — e. *śd3*, to tremble 110. — f. *šfšf.t*, fright 110. — g. *ḳ3 ḫrw*, high of voice 110. — h. *dnyw.t*, shouting 110.

Chapter II. Terms, A

16. Death as affliction 110

a. *i3kb*, to cry 111. — b. *nhm*, to cry 111. — c. *rmi*, to cry 111. — d. *hwt*, to lament 111. — e. *hmhm.t*, shouting 112. — f. *ḥ3*, to mourn 112.

B. Dangers of the hereafter 112

Introduction 112

1. Gates, which the dead has to pass 114

a. *ˁ3*, door 114. — b. *ˁrr.t*, gate 115. — c. *r3 n d3.t*, gate of the *d3.t* 116. — d. *rw.t*, gate 117. — e. *ḥnḥn*, to keep off 117. — f. *ḫśf*, to keep at bay 118. — g. *śb3*, gate 120. — h. *śbḫ.t*, gate 121. — i. *śmi*, reporter 124. — j. *šnˁ*, to keep off 124. — k. *tkn*, to approach 125.

2. Deprivation of liberty 125

a. *inṯ*, to put in irons 125. — b. *iḥ*, rope 126. — c. *ˁb3.wt*, fetters 126. — d. *ˁntt*, to fetter 126. — e. *nwḥ*, rope 126. — f. *nṯṯ*, to tie 126. — g. *ḫ3.w*, ropes 127. — h. *ḫnr*, to lock up 127. — i. *s3w*, to guard 128. — j. *śwš.t*, snares 130. — k. *śnḥ*, to bind 130. — l. *śśnḥ*, to bind 131. — m. *śdf*, fetter 131. — n. *śḏ3.wt*, sealing 131. — o. *ḳ3r.t*, bolt 131. — p. *ḳ3ś*, to bind 132. — q. *ṯṯ*, fetters 132. — r. *ḏḥr.t*, strap 132. — s. *ḏdḥ*, to arrest, to lock in 132.

3. Burning 133

a. *3m*, *3mw.t*, *ś3m*, to burn, burning 133. — b. *3śb*, to burn 134. — c. *ˁḫm*, to extinguish 134. — d. *w3w3.t*, fire 134. — e. *wbd*, to burn 134. — f. *whm*, to burn 134. — g. *bḫḫ.w*, flame 134. — h. *bś*, flame 135. — i. *pˁ.w*, fire 135. — j. *mw n śḏ.t*, fire-water 135. — k. *nwḫ*, to be burnt 135. — l. *nbi*, flame 135. — m. *nfw.t*, red-hot breath (of a snake) 136. — n. *nḫ*, flame 136. — o. *nś*, flame 136. — p. *nśb*, to lick 137. — q. *nśr.t*, flame 137. — r. *rkḥ*, to burn 137. — s. *hwt*, fire 137. — t. *hh*, glowing breath 137. — u. *ḫ.t*, fire 138. — v. *śś*, to burn 139. — w. *śti*, to burn 139. — x. *śḏ.t*, fire, flame 139. — y. *šm*, heat 141. — z. *ḳrr*, to burn 141. — aa. *t3*, fire 142. — bb. *tk3*, flame 142. — cc. *ḏ3f*, to burn 142.

4. To cook 142

a. *ˁḫ*, coal-basin 142. — b. *wḫ3.t*, cauldron 143. — c. *pfś*, cook 144. — d. *pśi*, to cook 145. — e. *mˁḳ*, to roast 145. — f. *ḫry.t*, furnace 145. — g. *ḫnf.t*, cooking-pot for flesh 145. — h. *kty.t*, cauldron 145. — i. *ṯnm*, kettle 146. — j. *dwfy*, cauldron 146.

5. Bloody punishments and mutilation of the body 147

a. *i3ṭ*, to mutilate 147. — b. *iw*, to chop off 147. — c. *inin*, to cut off 147. — d. *isp*, to hew 147. — e. *ˁ3b.t*, offering 147. — f. *ˁḏ*, to chop, *ˁḏ.t*, slaughter 148. — g. *wbn*, gaping wounds 148. — h. *wḥś*, to slaughter 148. — i. *bḥn*, to cut to pieces 148. — j. *bśk*,

Chapter II. Terms, B

to cut out 149. — k. *fdḳ*, to cut to pieces 149. — l. *rḫś*, to slaughter 149. — m. *hb*, to penetrate (of knives) 149. — n. *ḥnṯi*, to cut to pieces 149. — o. *ḥśb*, to slaughter 149. — p. *ḥśḳ*, to chop off (the head 149. — q. *ḥdḳ*, to chop off 150. — r. *ḫry.t*, slaughter 150. — s. *sw3*, to chop off (the head) 150. — t. *sf*, to cut off, knife 150. — u. *sft*, to slaughter 151. — v. *sn*, to cut off 151. — w. *snf*, blood 151. — x. *śiḳ*, to chop off 152. — y. *śpd*, sharp 152. — z. *śm3*, slaughter 152. — aa. *śt3.w*, wounds 153. — bb. *śʿ*, to chop off, *śʿ.t*, carnage 153. — cc. *śʿd*, to chop off 154. — dd. *śdi*, to take away (parts of the body out of the body) 154. — ee. *ḳf*, knife(?) 156. — ff. *tbś*, to pierce 156. — gg. *tḫś*, to slaughter 156. — hh. *dm*, to cut 156. — ii. *dn*, to cut 157. — jj. *dr*, to remove 157. — kk. *dś*, knife 157. — ll. *dšr.w*, blood 158. — mm. *ḏnḏn*, to chop off (the head) 158.

6. To be devoured 158

a. *ʿm*, *śʿm*, to devour 158. — b. *ʿnḫ m*, to live on 159. — c. *wnm*, to eat 160. — d. *swr*, to drink 160. — e. *śẖb*, to devour 160. — f. *dp*, to consume 160. — g. *dnm*, eating worm 160.

7. Dangerous places 160

a. *i3b*, left, eastern 161. — b. *i3t*, chamber of torture 161. — c. *in.t*, valley 161. — d. *ʿr*, pool 162. — e. *w3.t*, road 162. — f. *mʿḏ*, slaughtering-block 166. — g. *nm.t*, slaughtering-block 166. — h. *nḫ3*, name of a channel 167. — i. *ḥ3d*, fish-trap, pit 168. — j. *ḥtmy.t*, place of destruction 169. — k. *ḫb.t*, place of judgment 170. — l. *ẖ3s.t*, name of a well 171. — m. *ś.t bin.t*, evil place 171. — n. *š*, pond 171. — o. *š3ʿ.t* 172. — p. *ḳ3b*, bend 172. — q. *ḳrr.t*, cave 173. — r. *tpḥ.t*, cave 173.

8. Dangers which threaten essential parts of the personality 173

a. *3ḫ*, spirit 174. — b. *ib*, heart 174. — c. *b3*, soul 176. — d. *rn*, name 179. — e. *ḥ3ty*, heart 180. — f. *ḥk3*, magical power 181. — g. *ẖ3.t*, corpse 182. — h. *šw.t*, shadow 182. — i. *k3*, soul 184.

9. Words for seizing 184

a. *3m*, to seize 184. — b. *iti*, to seize, to snatch away 185. — c. *mḥ*, to seize 185. — d. *nḏr*, to seize 185. — e. *ḫfʿ*, to seize 186.

10. Words for ruin and destruction 186

a. *mt m wḥm*, to die for the second time 186. — b. *ḥtm* (causative *śḥtm*), to destroy 188. — c. *ḫmi*, to throw down walls 189. — d. *śḫr*, to fell 190. — e. *śkśk*, to destroy 190. — f. *ḳn*, to kill 190.

11. Raging against the dead 191

a. *3.t*, rage 191. — b. *3d.w*, fury 191. — c. *nšni*, rage 191. — d. *ḫnnw*, disturbance 191. — e. *ḏnd*, fury 191.

12-16. Beings to be feared 192

Chapter II. Terms, B

12. Animals 192

a. *ꜣpd*, bird 192. — b. *ꜣd*, crocodile 192. — c. *iʿr.t*, uraeus 192. — d. *ibw*, kid(?) 193. — e. *ibkꜣ* 193. — f. *ʿꜣ*, ass 194. — g. *ʿpšꜣy.t*, grasshopper 194. — h. *ʿẖm*, a demoniacal animal 194. — i. *wnš*, wolf 194. — j. *bik*, falcon 194. — k. *miwty*, cat 194. — l. *mśḥ*, crocodile 194. — m. *rw*, lion 195. — n. *rm*, fish 195. — o. *rri*, pig 195. — p. *rḫty* (dual), a kind of insect 195. — q. *šꜣ*, boar 195. — r. *Śmty*, name of a snake in the netherworld 195. — s. *ktt*, ichneumon-fly 195. — t. *gbgꜣ*, kind of bird 195. — u. *ṯsm*, dog 196. — v. *db*, hippopotamus 197.

13. Men 197

a. *ꜣḫ*, spirit 197. — b. *mt*, dead one 198. — c. *nty.w iwty.w*, who are there and who are not there 199. — d. *rmṯ*, men 199. — e. *s*, man 200.

14. Demons I; names, which indicate a function 200

a. *iꜣy.w*, torturers 200. — b. *imnḥ.w*, slaughterers 200. — c. *iry*..., keeper of ... 200. — d. *irr.w ir.t.śn*, who do their (evil) deeds 201. — e. *isfty.w*, evil-doers 201. — f. *ʿb.w*, heapers-up of corn 201. — g. *ʿḥꜣ.w*, fighters 201. — h. *ʿḏty.w*, slaughterers 201. — i. *wpwty*, messenger 202. — j.*wrš*, guard 203. — k. *mꜣśty.w* (other spelling *mꜣś.w*) 204. — l. *nb.w dꜣ.t*, lords of the netherworld 204. — m. *nhś*, watchman 204. — n. *ḥnṯ.w*, slaughterers 204. — o. *ḫꜣty.w*, slaughterers 205. — p. *ḫꜣk.w ib*, rebels 205. — q. *smꜣ.wt*, gang 205. — r. *snṯ.w*, rebels 205. — s. *śbi*, rebel 206. — t. *ṯsty.w*, enemies 206. — u. *ḏrḏr.w*, strangers 206.

15. Demons II; a choice from names, which specify the essence. 206

a. *ʿḥꜣ ḥr*, combative of face 206. — b. *wr*, great one 206. — c. *nʿḫ*, strong one 207. — d. *nwn*, with tumbled hair 207. — e. *nwt.k nw* 207. — f. *nbḏ*, evil one 208. — g. *ḥśꜣ ḥr*, savage one of face 208. — h. *štꜣ ḥr*, hidden one of face 208. — i. *ḳꜣ ḫrw*, high of voice 208. — j. *km ḥr*, black one of face 208.

16. Gods 209

a. *ʾItm* 209. — b. *Bꜣ pf* 209. — c. *Bꜣbꜣ* 209. — d. *Wśir*, Osiris 210. — e. *nṯr*, god 212. — f. *Ḥr ḫnty Ḫmw* 212. — g. *Ḥr dꜣti* 213. — h. *Ḫnsw* 213. — i. *Ḥrty* 213. — j. *Śrḳ.t* 214. — k. *Śḫm.t* 214. — l. *Śtš*, Seth 214. — m. *Św* 215. — n. *Śsmw* 215. — o. *Ḏḥwty*, Thoth 216.

17. The use of the term *ḫfty*, enemy 217

a. Demons as enemies, who waylay the dead 217. — b. Enemies as opponents in a law-suit 219. — c. The enemies of the dead as opponents of Osiris 221. — d. Sinners as enemies of Re or of Osiris 223. — e. *Ḫfty* as devil 224.

Chapter II. Terms, B

18. Instruments of torture 224

a. *3b*, branding-iron 225. — b. *wśr.t*, torturing-post 225. — c. *mnỉ.t*, mooring-post 225. — d. *śmś.t*, device of decapitation 226. — e. *d3s.wy*, torturing-posts 226.

19. Terms for hunting. 226

a. *ỉ3d.t*, net 227. — b. *ỉbṯ.t*, bird-trap 230. — c. *ỉśś*, to catch, *ỉśś.t*, trap-net 230. — d. *ʿmʿ3.t*, boomerang 231. — e. *ʿḥ*, net 231. — f. *wḥʿ*, to catch (fish), catcher 231. — g. *wsf*, fisherman 232. — h. *nḏḥ*, to catch with the lasso 232. — i. *rtḥ*, to catch 232. — j. *ḥ3m*, to catch (fish) 232. — k. *śpḥ*, to catch with the lasso 233. — l. *śḫty*, fowler 233. — m. *grg*, setter of traps 234. — n. *ḏśf*, to catch 234.

20. Categories of people, who take an unfavourable position in the hereafter 234

a. *ỉ3d*, wretched one 234. — b. *ỉwty.w*, whose who are not 234. — c. *ỉmy.w Wśỉr*, who are in Osiris 325. — d. *ỉmn.w ḥr.w.śn*, hidden ones of face 235. — e. *ỉmnty.w*, western ones 235. — f. *ỉḫm.w*, who are destroyed 235. — g. *ỉḫmty.w*, see *wḏb.w* 235. — h. *ʿ3m.w*, Asiatics, see *Nḥś.w* 235. — i. *wḏb.w*, riverains 235. — j. *mḥy.w*, drowned ones 236. — k. *Mḏ3.w*, see *Nḥś.w* 237. — l. *nnty.w*, denizens of the *nn.t*, the counter-heaven 237. — m. *Nḥś.w*, negroes 237. — n. *rḫy.t*, men 240. — o. *ḥtrty.w*, see *wḏb.w* 240. — p. *ḫrw*, "enemy" 240. — q. *Ṯmḥ.w*, see *Nḥś.w* 240. — r. *d3ty.w*, denizens of the *d3.t* 240. — s. *ḏwy.w*, enemies 240.

21. Sundries 241

a. *3r*, to press hard 241. — b. *ỉỉ r*, to come towards somebody in a hostile way 241. — c. *ỉw*, to be without a ship 241. — d. *ỉrỉ r*, to act against 241. — e. *ỉh*, to suffer 242. — f. *ỉśḳ*, delay 242. — g. *ʿ*, document 242. — h. *ʿw3*, robbery, outrage 243. — i. *ʿnn*, to twist 243. — j. *wḫd*, to suffer 243. — k. *wd*, to hit 243. — l. *pnḳ*, to bail out 244. — m. *pḥ*, to attack 244. — n. *m33*, to see 244. — o. *mr*, painful 245. — p. *mdś*, sharp, painful 245. — q. *nḥm*, to take away 246. — r. *nḳʿ*, to cut out (the heart) 246. — s. *nkn*, damage 247. — t. *rmn tp*, to take the head away(?) 247. — u. *h3ỉ*, to be brought down, to land in 247. — v. *hp*, to hurry 247. — w. *ḥsỉ*, to come to meet inimically 248. — x. *ḥk3*, to charm 248. — y. *ḥd*, to damage 248. — z. *ḫbḫb*, to trample down 248. — aa. *ḫpr r*, to happen to 248. — bb. *ḫr*, to fall 248. — cc. *ḫśf*, to approach 249. — dd. *sbn*, to be brought down 249. — ee. *śḫ3*, to remember (somebody in an evil way) 249. — ff. *śḫm m*, to have power over 249. — gg. *śḏ*, to break 249. — hh. *śdb*, calamity 249. — ii. *śpt*, annoyance 250. — jj. *śnṯ*, to fight 250. — kk. *ḳnḳn*, to strike 250. — ll. *ḳ3* (*ʿn.t*), to stretch (the nail) 251. — mm. *ḳ3.t*, toil 251. — nn. *thỉ*, to affect 251. — oo. *ḏ3ỉ*, to put oneself in the way inimically 252. — pp. *ḏw.*(*t*), disaster, evil 253.

Chapter II. Terms, B

Excursus: To escape and to be saved from dangers 253

Introduction 253. — a. *wb3*, to open 254. — b. *prỉ*, to escape 254. — c. *pẖr*, to go round (something) 254. — d. *nwḏ*, to recede 255. — e. *nhỉ*, to escape 255. — f. *nḥm*, to save 255. — g. *nḏ*, to save 255. — h. *ḫm*, to recede 255. — i. *ḫrỉ*, to be far 256. — j. *ḫśf*, to put off (demons) 257. — k. *s3w*, to beware 257. — l. *św3*, to pass 257. — m. *śśḏ3.t*, protecting spell 259.

C. Judgment and execution 259

1. To lodge a complaint 259

a. *ỉṯỉ*, to bring (into court) 259. — b. *ʿ3p*, rebuke 259. — c. *bṯ*, to let down 259. — d. *mtr*, to give evidence 259. — e. *rḳỉ*, to rebel 259. — f. *ḥwỉ mtr r*, to give evidence against 260. — g. *ḥmśỉ r*, to testify against 260. — h. *śỉʿr*, jemds. böses Tun berichten dem... 260. — i. *śỉw*, to accuse 261. — j. *śʿḥʿ*, to set up 261. — k. *śmỉ*, to accuse 261. — l. *śrḫw*, plaintiff 261. — m. *śḫśf*, to oppose 262. — n. *śḫnš*, to make stinking 262. — o. *śḏwỉ*, to slander 262. — p. *šn ḫ.t r*, to be at law with 263. — q. *grg*, lie 263. — r. *ṯsỉ bt3*, to reproach with guilt 263. — s. *ḏbʿ*, to reprimand 263.

2. The judgment 263

a. *wpỉ*, to divide 263. — b. *wḏʿ* (*mdw*), to judge 264. — c. *wśḫ.t*, hall 268. — d. *mḫy*, counsel 268. — e. *mḫ3.t*, scales 269. — f. *nhp*, to judge 269. — g. *ḥśb*, to count 269. — h. *ḫmʿ*, extirpating of sin 271. — i. *ḫśr*, to drive away, to dispel 271. — j. *śpḫ3*, to acquit 271. — k. *śm3ʿ ḫrw*, to justify 271. — l. *śḏm mdw*, to hear the case 272.

3. Denominations for judges of the dead 272

a. *ỉʿn*, baboon 272. — b. *ʾInp*, Anubis 272. — c. *nb.w m3ʿ.t*, lords of truth 273. — d. *nb.w ḫ.t*, lords of offerings 273. — e. *Ḫnty ʾImnty.w* 274. — f. *śr*, high official 274. — g. *šny.t*, courtiers 274. — h. *ḳnb.t*, council 274. — i. *ḏ3ḏ3.t*, council 274.

4. To condemn and to sentence 278

a. *ỉp*, to count; *śỉp*, to assign 278. — b. *wḏ*, to assign 280. — c. *nỉś*, to call 280. — d. *rdỉ*, to deliver up (to a punishment) 280. — e. *š3m*, to cover 281. — f. *ṯnw.t*, counting 282.

5. To punish 282

a. *ỉss*, to punish 282. — b. *nỉk*, to punish 282. — c. *nḏ*, to punish 284. — d. *ḫśf n*, to punish somebody 284. — e. *śswn*, to punish 284. — f. *ḏw.t*, evil 285. — g. *ḏ.t*, eternity 285.

6. Sin 286

a. *ỉw*, sin 286. — b. *ỉwy.t*, sin 286. — c. *ỉrỉ r*, to act against 286. — d. *ỉsf.t*, sin 286. — e. *ʿw3*, robbery 287. — f. *ʿb*, mischief, sin 287.

Chapter II. Terms, C

— g. *wn*, guilt 287. — h. *wš3 ḫrw*, to pour out voice 287. — i. *bỉn*, bad 288. — j. *nỉ.t*, sin 288. — k. *nḏy.t*, wickedness 288. — l. *ḫww*, wicked actions, sin 289. — m. *ḫbn.t*, crime 289. — n. *ḫ3b.t*, sin 290. — o. *ḫ3k*, to rebel 290. — p. *sp*, guilt 290. — q. *śḫ3ỉ*, to denude 291. — r. *šnṯ.t*, slander 291. — s. *ḳn*, "Böses, Schaden", "Übeltat" 291. — t. *ḳnỉ*, to be dissatisfied 291. — u. *try.t*, sin 292. — v. *thỉ*, to trespass 292. — w. *ṯmś.w*, evil, crime, injustice 292. — x. *ṯs ḏw*, bad spell 293. — y. *ḏw*, evil in a moral sense, sin 293. — z. *ḏ3.t*, transgression 294.

7. Sinner 294

a. *ỉsfty.w*, sinners 294. — b. *ʿpp*, Apophis 294. — c. *mś.w Bdš.t* 294. — d. *nỉk*, the evil being to be punished 295. — e. *rḳw*, enemy 295. — f. *ḫfty*, enemy 296. — g. *śbỉ*, rebel 296. — h. *kywy*, the others 296. — i. *ḏ3ty.w*, opponents 296.

CHAPTER III. REPRESENTATIONS OF THE NETHERWORLD IN DEMOTIC LITERATURE

CHAPTER IV. PUNISHMENT IN THE HEREAFTER ACCORDING TO THE COPTIC TEXTS

The river of fire, ιερο ⲛ̄ ⲕⲱϩⲧ, ιαρο ⲛ̄ ⲭⲣⲱⲙ. 307
The realm of the dead, ⲁⲙⲛ̄ⲧⲉ. 310
Gates, ⲣⲟ, ⲡⲩⲗⲏ. 316
Realm of the dead, netherworld, ⲛⲟⲩⲛ. 318
Tartarus, ⲧⲁⲣⲧⲁⲣⲟⲥ. 319
The hell, ⲅⲉϩⲉⲛⲛⲁ. 320
Fire, ⲕⲱϩⲧ, ⲥⲁⲧⲉ. 320
Prison, ϣⲧⲉⲕⲟ. 323
Darkness, ⲕⲁⲕⲉ. 324
Punishment, ⲕⲟⲗⲁⲥⲓⲥ. 326
Demons and punishing angels 328
Enemy, ϫⲁϫⲉ. 332
Serpent, ⲇⲣⲁⲕⲱⲛ, ϩϥⲱ (*ḥf3w.t*) 333
To seize, ⲁⲙⲁϩⲧⲉ (*mḥ*, B.9.c) 335
Grief, ϩⲓⲥⲉ (*ḥsy*) 336
To cry, ⲣⲓⲙⲉ (*rmỉ*, A.16.c) 336
To devour, ⲱⲙⲕ̄ (cf. B.6) 337
The sun in the netherworld 337
To count, ⲏⲡⲉ (*ỉp*, C.4.a) 338
To tie up, ⲥⲱⲛϩ̄ (*śnḥ*), ⲙⲟⲩⲣ (*mr*), cf. B.2, particularly B.2.k . 338

Chapter IV. Coptic texts
To shorten, ⲥⲃⲟⲕ. 338
Trident, ϣⲗⲓϫ. 339
Flogging, ⲙⲁⲥⲧⲓⲅⲟⲓⲛ. 339
Scroll, ⲭⲉⲓⲣⲅⲣⲁⲫⲟⲛ. 340
Sword, ⲥⲏϥⲉ. 340
Path, ϩⲓⲏ. 341
Bad smell, ⲥϯ ⲃⲱⲛ. 341

Summary 342

Corrections and Additions ---- 345
Index of References ---- 377

LIST OF ABBREVIATIONS AND LITERATURE

AcOr: Acta Orientalia ediderunt Societates Orientales Batava Danica Norvegica, Lugduni Batavorum.

M. Alliot, Les rites de la chasse au filet, aux temples de Karnak, d'Edfou et d'Esneh, Revue d'Egyptologie, Tome cinquième, Le Caire, 1946, pp. 57-118.

E. Amélineau, Etude sur le Christianisme en Egypte au septième siècle, Paris, 1887.

Amduat: Les Textes des tombes de Thoutmosis III et d'Aménophis II, par M. Paul Bucher, Tome Premier, Mémoires publiés par les membres de l'Institut Français d'Archéologie Orientale du Caire, Tome Soixantième, Le Caire, 1932, quoted to the tomb of Tuthmosis III, with number of hour and line, e.g., I. 235 = 1st hour, line 235.

H. P. Blok, Eine magische Stele aus der Spätzeit, AcOr VII, 97-113.

B.D. = E. A. Wallis Budge, The Book of the Dead, The Chapters of coming forth by day, 3 vols., Text, Translation, Vocabulary, London 1898, quoted to page and line of page.

BIFAO: Bulletin de l'Institut Français d'Archéologie Orientale, publié sous la direction de M. Pierre Jouguet, Le Caire.

Book of the Gates, see B.S.

Divisions:

Entrance Hall, B.S. Pl. V; Budge 1st division (pp. 80-85); Cenotaph Seti I 1st division.

1st division, B.S. Pl. IV, III; Budge 2nd division (pp. 86-99); Cenotaph Seti I 2nd division.

2nd division, B.S. Pl. III, II; Budge 3rd division (pp. 100-118); Cenotaph Seti I 3rd division.

3rd division, B.S. Pl. II, VIII, VII; Budge 4th division (pp. 119-138); Cenotaph Seti I 4th division.

4th division, B.S. Pl. VII, VI, V; Budge 5th division (pp. 139-157); Cenotaph Seti I 5th division.

Judgment Hall of Osiris, B.S. Pl. V; Budge 6th division (pp. 158-167); Cenotaph Seti I Pl. LV; Horemheb, ed. Davis-Maspero Pl. LIII, LIV.

5th division, B.S. Pl. XVIII; Budge 6th division (pp. 168-189); Cenotaph Seti I 7th division; Champollion, Notices 501, 502, 503; E. Lefébure, M.M.A.F.C. III, 1, Pl. XXX, XXXI.

6th division, B.S. Pl. XIX; Budge 7th division (pp. 192, 193); Cenotaph Seti I 8th division; E. Lefébure, M.M.A.F.C. III, 1, Pl. XXXII-XXXIV.

7th division, Budge 7th division (pp. 190, 191, 194-218); Cenotaph Seti I 6th division; E. Lefébure, M.I.F.A.O. II, 2, Pl. XI seq.

8th division, B.S. Pl. XV, XIV, XIII; Budge 8th division (pp. 219-236); Cenotaph Seti I 9th division.

9th division, B.S. Pl. XIII, XIV; Budge 9th division (pp. 237-258); Cenotaph Seti I 10th division.

10th division, B.S. Pl. XI, XII; Budge 10th division (pp. 259-278); Cenotaph Seti I 11th division.

11th division, B.S. Pl. X, IX; Budge 11th division (pp. 279-300); Cenotaph Seti I 12th division.

12th division, B.S. Pl. IX, XV; Budge 12th division (pp. 301-306); Cenotaph Seti I "Final Scene".

B.S.: The Alabaster Sarcophagus of Oimenephtah I, by J. Bonomi and S. Sharpe, London 1864. The Book of the Gates has been quoted to the plates of this edition.

Budge, Hom.: E. A. Wallis Budge, Coptic Homilies in the dialect of Upper Egypt, London 1910. Coptic Texts edited with introductions and English translations, Vol. I.

E. A. Wallis Budge, Coptic Biblical texts in the dialect of Upper Egypt, London 1912. Coptic Texts Vol. II.

Budge, Apocr.: E. A. Wallis Budge, Coptic Apocrypha in the dialect of Upper Egypt, London 1913. Coptic Texts Vol. III.

Budge, Martyrdoms: E. A. Wallis Budge, Coptic Martyrdoms in the dialect of Upper Egypt, London 1914. Coptic Texts, Vol. IV.

Budge, Miscell.: E. A. Wallis Budge, Miscellaneous Coptic Texts in the dialect of Upper Egypt, London 1915. Coptic Texts, Vol. V.

E. A. Wallis Budge, The Egyptian Heaven and Hell, Reprinted, Three Volumes in one, London, 1925.

C.T.: The Egyptian Coffin Texts, ed. by A. de Buck and A. H. Gardiner, The University of Chicago Oriental Institute Publications, Chicago, 1935 seq.

C.d.E., Chron. d'Eg.; Chronique d'Egypte, Bruxelles.

Franz Cumont, Lux Perpetua, Paris 1949.

W. Erichsen, Demotisches Glossar, Kopenhagen 1954.

W. Erichsen, Demotische Lesestücke I, Literarische Texte, Leipzig 1937.

A. Erman und H. Grapow, Wörterbuch der Ägyptischen Sprache, Leipzig 1925.

R. O. Faulkner, The man who was tired of life, J.E.A., Vol. 42, 1956, pp. 21-40.

H. Frankfort, The Cenotaph of Seti I at Abydos, Vol. I Text, Vol. II Plates. 39th memoir of the Egypt Exploration Society, London 1933.

A. H. Gardiner and K. Sethe, Egyptian Letters to the dead, mainly from the old and middle kingdoms, London 1928.

F. Ll. Griffith, Stories of the High Priests of Memphis, Oxford 1900.

JEA: The Journal of Egyptian Archeology, London.

Jb.E.O.L.: Jaarbericht van het Vooraziatisch-Egyptisch Gezelschap "Ex Oriente Lux", Leiden.

JNES: Journal of Near Eastern Studies. Vol. IV, January 1945, Number 1, Chicago. Miriam Lichtheim, The Songs of the Harpers, pp. 178-212, Plates I-VII.

P. Lacau, Fragments d'Apocryphes Coptes, M.I.F.A.O. IX, Le Caire 1904.

P. Lacau, Sarcophages antérieurs au Nouvel Empire, 2 vol., 1903-1906, Catalogue Général du Musée du Caire.

E. Lefébure, Les Hypogées Royaux de Thèbes, Première Division, Le Tombeau de Séti Ier, Annales du Musée Guimet, Tome Neuvième, Paris 1886.

E. Lefébure, Les Hypogées Royaux de Thèbes, Seconde Division, M.M.A.F.C., Tome Troisième, 1e Fascicule, Paris 1889.

L. Th. Lefort, S. Pachomii Vita, Bohairice scripta, Louvain 1953, Corpus Scriptorum Christianorum Orientalium, Vol. 89. Scriptores Coptici Tom. 7. Vol. 107, Tom. 11, Interpretatus est L. Th. Lefort, Louvain 1952.

L. Th. Lefort, S. Pachomii Vitae, Sahidice Scripta, C.S.C.O., Vol. 99, 100, Louvain 1952. Scriptores Coptici, Ser. III, Tom. 8.
Louvre 3292, ed. Nagel: Un papyrus funéraire de la fin du nouvel empire (Louvre 3292, inv.), par M. G. Nagel, B.I.F.A.O. XXIX, 1929, pp. 1-128, Plates I-VIII.
L.Q.: B.I.F.A.O. XLI, 1942. A. Piankoff, Le Livre des Quererts. Ier tableau (avec 9 planches) pages 1-11, Pl. I-IX.
XLII, 1944, Seconde-Cinquième Division, pages 1-62, planches X-LXXIX.
XLIII, 1945, Sixième Division, pages 1-50, planches LXXX-CLI.
E. Lüddeckens, Untersuchungen über religiösen Gehalt, Sprache und Form der ägyptischen Totenklagen. Mitteilungen des Deutschen Instituts für ägyptische Altertumskunde in Kairo, Bd. 11, Heft 1 und 2, Berlin 1943.

G. Maspero, The Tombs of Harmhabi and Touatânkhamanou. Theodore M. Davis' Excavations: Bibân el Molûk, London 1912.
Charles Maystre et Alexandre Piankoff, Le Livre des Portes, Le Caire; Ministère de l'éducation nationale, Mémoires de l'Institut Français du Caire, sous la direction de M. P. Jouguet, I, Texte; 1e fasc. 1939; 2e fasc. 1944; 3e fasc. 1946.
MIFAO: Mémoires publiées par les membres de l'Institut Français d'Archéologie Orientale du Caire.
MMAFC: Mémoires publiées par les membres de la mission archéologique Française au Caire.
G. Möller, Die beiden Totenpapyrus Rhind, Leipzig 1913.
P. Montet, Les scènes de la vie privée dans les tombeaux égyptiens de l'ancien empire, Publications de la faculté des lettres de l'université de Strasbourg, fascicule 24, Strasbourg, 1925.
W. Max Müller, Die Liebespoesie der alten Ägypter², Leipzig 1932.

E. Naville, Textes relatifs au Mythe d'Horus, recueillis dans le Temple d'Edfou, Genève et Bâle, 1870. (= Mythe d'Horus).
E. Naville, Papyrus Funéraires de la XXIe dynastie, Le Papyrus hiéroglyphique de Kamara et le Papyrus hiératique de Nesikhonsou au musée du Caire, Paris 1912.
E. Naville, Das ägyptische Todtenbuch der XVIII. bis XX. Dynastie, 3 vols., Berlin 1886.
N.T.T.: Nederlands Theologisch Tijdschrift, ed. H. Veenman en Zonen, Wageningen.

A. Piankoff, Le Livre du Jour et de la Nuit, avec un chapitre sur l'écriture énigmatique par E. Drioton, Le Caire 1942. Institut Français d'Archéologie Orientale, Bibliothèque d'Etude, T. XIII.
G. Posener, Les criminels débaptisés et les morts sans noms, Revue d'Egyptologie, Tome cinquième, Le Caire 1946, pp. 51-56.
Pyr.: Die Altägyptischen Pyramidentexte, von Kurt Sethe, Erster Band, Leipzig 1908, Zweiter Band, Leipzig 1910.

Revue d'Egyptologie publiée par la société Française d'égyptologie, Le Caire.
F. Robinson, Coptic Apocryphal Gospels, Cambridge 1896; J. Armitage Robinson, Texts and Studies, contributions to biblical and patristic literature, Vol. IV.

Sachau, Festschrift Ed. Sachau, see Gotthold Weil.

C. E. Sander Hansen, Der Begriff des Todes bei den Ägyptern, København, 1942; Det Kgl. Danske Videnskabernes Selskab, Historisk-Filologiske Meddelelser, Bind XXIX, Nr. 2, pp. 1-32.

Schmidt, Sark.: Valdemar Schmidt, Sarkofager, Mumiekister, og Mumiehylstre i det gamle Ägypten, Typologisk Atlas, København 1919, quoted to number of figure.

K. Sethe, Übersetzung und Kommentar zu den altägyptischen Pyramidentexten, 4 vols., Glückstadt no date.

Henri Sottas, La préservation de la propriété funéraire dans l'ancienne Egypte, Paris 1913; Bibliothèque de l'école des Hautes Etudes, Sciences Philologiques et Historiques, 205e fascicule.

J. Spiegel, Die Idee vom Totengericht in der ägyptischen Religion, Leipziger Ägyptologische Studien, Heft 2, Glückstadt und Hamburg 1935.

Urk.: Urkunden des Ägyptischen Altertums, herausgegeben von Georg Steindorff.

Urk. I, Erster Band, Urkunden des Alten Reichs I, bearbeitet von Kurt Sethe, Leipzig 1903.

Urk. IV, Urkunden der 18. Dynastie, bearbeitet von Kurt Sethe. Historisch-Biografische Urkunden, Zweite Auflage, Leipzig 1930. Urkunden des Äg. Alt., vierte Abteilung.

Gotthold Weil, Festschrift Eduard Sachau zum siebzigsten Geburtstage, Berlin 1915; pp. 103-112, A. Erman, Zwei Grabsteine griechischer Zeit.

W. Wolf, Die Bewaffnung des altägyptischen Heeres, Leipzig 1926.

Z.Ä.S.: Zeitschrift für ägyptische Sprache und Altertumskunde, herausgegeben von G. Steindorff.

CHAPTER ONE

GENERAL OUTLINE

Par. 1. The monistic and the dualistic conception of death

Kristensen [1]) showed that the Egyptians have answered the question of the relation between life and death in two ways. It has been his life-work to investigate the monistic view. Death is considered the necessary condition for eternal life. Without death no victory over death. Death becomes the foundation of eternal life, life in its potential form [2]). The Egyptian orientated himself to nature for this monistic conception. There is a rhythm in vegetation: plants and crops mature and die down, but they spring up again from the seed which has been put into the earth and has died. After each setting the sun rises in the East through its own spontaneous power. This resurrection from death points to the fact that the secret of spontaneous life lives under the earth in the realm of the dead. Kristensen himself shows [3]) that this monistic conception stands in contrast with a dualistic one, in which death is considered the enemy of life. This dualistic view is the primary one, sprung from the natural fear of death in mankind. The monistic conception is a faith based on religious reflection. This faith being strong in Egypt does not alter the fact that utterances, which show fear of death, occur in the texts. They even form the background against which the pronouncements about resurrection and life must be seen. The care of the dead presupposes fear of death as complete destruction [4]). In the inscriptions on tombs the passer-by is hailed as follows: "You who loves life and hates death" [5]). Also in the Egyptian the natural human reaction is present that death is hateful. He wishes to die at an advanced age (A.5.q., pp. 70-71). The doctrine of Ptahhotep says that an obedient

---

1) *Het Leven uit de Dood*[2] (*Life from death*), p. 7.
2) Op cit., p. 17.
3) Op. cit., p. 17.
4) Gardiner, *The attitude of the ancient Egyptians to death and the dead*, p. 13.
5) C. E. Sander-Hansen, *Der Begriff des Todes bei den Ägyptern*, p. 22.

son "reaches a high age and becomes venerable" [1]). As an ideal age he himself wishes to become a 110 years old [2]).

The Egyptian considered death the enemy of the good life on earth, which he loved and knew how to enjoy with a gay meal accompanied by play and dance. "I am the master of the light, I detest dying" the dead says [3]). "As regards death, may you be able to elude him" is said to him as a wish [4]). Concerning death all sorts of terms of fear and fright are used (A.15). Gates in the realm of the dead strike terror into those who must pass them; a name like "mistress of terror" for such a gate proves this (A.15.a). Spirits and dead are afraid of Osiris as the king of the realm of the dead (A.15.d).

In the "*Lebensmüde*" the soul cannot hold out any hope of a life after death. The construction of costly sepulchral monuments is of no avail (A.1.d, p. 49; A.13.g, p. 106). For these are going to be destroyed and the funeral offerings are not kept up. Everything aims at life on earth. Dying (p. 107) is only destruction and brings mourning. The funeral (A.9.f, p. 87) does not ensure eternal life, but goes together with sadness. Therefore the best advice the soul can give is "carpe diem" [5]). The same negative attitude is observed in the songs of the harpers.

According to the song of Antef the funeral is a being dragged to the land that loves silence (p. 53) [6]). Also in these songs the following advice is given: Celebrate a gay day, follow your heart! (A.1.c, p. 47, A.2.i, p. 56, A.2.e, p. 53). At the funeral (A.2.c, p. 53, A.2.f, p. 53) the widow clasps the mummy's feet as if she wants to retain her husband and is full of doubt about the effect of the funereal ritual. The wailing-women (A.1.a, p. 45) deplore (A.9.b, p. 86) death as being only loss. The call of death (A.1.c, p. 47) is enexorable. When death says: "Come" one simply has to go. Death is a robber who snatches the child away (A.9.e, p. 87) from the arms of its mother. The realm of the dead is a place to which one goes but from where nobody ever returns (A.2.i, p. 55, A.11.b, p. 93). Man loves life on

---

1) Dévaud, 590.
2) Janssen, *On the ideal lifetime of the Egyptians*, *OMRO*, *NR* XXXI, pp. 33-34.
3) B.D. 85; Naville II, 192.
4) C.T. I. 284. g.
5) De Buck, *Kernmomenten*, p. 23.
6) Op. cit., p. 25.

earth. He is afraid of dying young, of passing away, before a normal time of life has gone by (A.5.q). On a tomb-stone for a young girl we read a lamentation about her early death (A.5.q, p. 71).

The fear of death may take various forms. Death as such is feared in contrast with life (A). The realm of the dead is a gloomy place (A.10), where no life is possible. Death is compared with sleep; they resemble each other in that both put motion and consciousness aside. Normal life has been eliminated (A.8). The state of being motionless is also meant, where the dead is called one who is bound (A.7). The body decays and the senses no longer function (A.3, A.4). Death is being snatched away from life (A.9), and is accompanied by wailing (A.16), whilst the tomb is a place of terror (A.13).

A more reflected view assumes that salvation from death is possible in the beyond. A place is there where man may continue his life and where fertile fields yield him abundance of food [1]). Nevertheless the fear of death is not suppressed, for many dangers may impend over man (B). On his journey through the realm of the dead he has to pass gates, from where the keepers may repel him (B.1) [2]). Demons want to harm him (B.12-B.16). He may be burnt by fire (B.3) or be slashed to pieces with knives. There are numerous dangerous places, where he may be tortured (B.7) and which he must try to pass (B. excurs.). The demons may perform many a disagreeable action against him, they may put him in irons, seize him and beat him (B.2, B.9), which may result in total destruction (B.10), or at least may bring about suffering (B.21). Consequently the texts know of names for the dead which point to a sad fate (B.20).

The fear of death may also have an ethical strain, viz. that man expects to have to appear before a judge of the dead, who may condemn him on account of sins committed by him (C). He may be accused (C.1) before a court of justice (C.3), be condemned (C.2 and 4) and be punished (C.5). That the ethical view has played a prominent part is proved by the many terms for sin (C.6).

Par. 2. The texts

The texts where these conceptions are to be found, are, of course, in the first place the spells of the dead in the Pyramid Texts from the

---

[1]) *Ḥtp*-fields, B.D. 110.

[2]) Kees, *Totenglauben*, p. 429 sqq.

Old Kingdom, the Coffin Texts from the Middle Kingdom and the Books of the Dead from the New Kingdom. Among the Coffin Texts especially the *Zweiwegebuch* should be mentioned. For the New Kingdom the so-called "*Livres*" [1]) are of importance, the books that describe the journey of the sun through the realm of the dead. This literature shows the imminent dangers of the netherworld and how sinners are punished. The *Zweiwegebuch* is a guide for the other world. A black-coloured pathway (the lowermost) and a blue waterway (the uppermost) lead along a pool of fire, which the dead has to avoid [2]). Along the roads all kinds of dangers are imminent. Magical spells make it possible for the dead to overcome them and to charm the demons. Near the red strip of fire in the middle one reads [3]): "This is the pool of fire called *ʿȝtyw*. There is not a single man who falls into the fire." These texts are partly orientated towards the Re-religion, just as, in the Pyramid Texts, the Pharaoh wants to be with Re in heaven: "His (Re's) protection is my protection. Everything that is going to happen against me, may happen in the same way against him" [4]). The contents are partly directed to Osiris: "There are two plots of land in the field of *Ḥtp* among those who know. I take care of Osiris. I am an administrator of the fields on Thoth's side. I am the foster-mother of Osiris among those who make offerings. I am the pure one, who cooks for Osiris every day" [5]). Kees [6]) points to the fact that the *Zweiwegebuch* stands between the Pyramid Texts and Am-Duat.

The "*Livres*" deal with a subterranean realm of the dead. The sun travels along a river from West to East and passes 12 divisions corresponding to the 12 hours of the night. According to the Book of Gates they are separated by gates. Such gates, guarded by serpents, also already occur in the *Zweiwegebuch*. Usually the wall is divided into three registers, in the *ḳrr.t*-book even into five. The middle register is a river. Towers along the bank drag the sunboat on. The direction of travelling is in the Book of Gates, e.g., from right to left.

---

[1]) A. Piankoff, *Les différents "Livres" dans les tombes royales du Nouvel Empire*, *Ann. Serv.*, 40, 1940-'41, pp. 283-289.

[2]) Kees, *Totenglauben*, p. 430 sqq.

[3]) B 1 Bc 237; C.T. VII, Spell 1166.

[4]) Lacau, *Sarc.* I, 192, 30; C.T. VII, Spell 1055.

[5]) B 1 Bc 256; C.T. VII, Spell 1159.

[6]) Op. cit., p. 443.

The upper register is the right-hand bank, the lower register the left-hand one. In the upper register, that is on the right hand, there are usually pictured the righteous, who have a favourable fate. In the lower register, on the unfavourable left side, are the damned, who are punished [1]). The righteous see Re temporarily, as long as he is in their division, but complain as soon as Re goes away and leaves them in the dark (A.16.d). The unjust do not see Re at all (B.21.n). They remain in the darkness of death. Especially in this lower register many of the horrors of the realm of the dead are represented and described. It is an extremely important source of information about the Egyptian conceptions of hell. The punished sinners are called enemies of Re as well as of Osiris (B.17.d). Apophis also, as the principal enemy of Re and chief devil, is punished. In the Book of Gates his punishment of Atum is represented (B.17.e).

Par. 3. The way in which the dualistic conceptions of death occur in the texts

It is not always equally easy to conclude from the texts what the Egyptians thought about death as an enemy. They do not like to write about it. Unfavourable utterances about death are preferably not laid down in inscriptions or written down. From such a record an evil influence may emanate towards the person involved. Therefore the texts do not directly describe circumstances which are unfavourable to the dead. This is the reason why, for instance, the Pyramid Texts offer relatively little material. They want to describe a favourable fate of the dead. So these texts talk about the king's ascension and his resurrection and relate how he joins the company of Re.

Thus much of the material dealt with here is in the negative form: "Rise, N.N., you will not die" (A.1.c) [2]). So from these negative spells it must be deduced what is actually feared. Many spells begin with the title: "Spell in order not to . . ." and there follows some unpleasant fate in the hereafter, which must be averted. "Spell in order not to go upside down in the realm of the dead" (A.6.d) [3]).

A fate detrimental to the dead is also to be found in what a man

---

[1]) Cf. S. Morenz, *Rechts und links im Totengericht*, *ZÄS* 82 (1957), pp. 62-71.
[2]) Pyr. 792. c.
[3]) C.T. Spell 224; III. 211. a.

wishes his enemies, e.g., in the inscriptions directed against tomb robbers [1]): "Truly, my Majesty shall forbid that they will be at the head of the spirits in the realm of the dead, but (order) that they shall be bound and fettered as condemned ones of King Osiris and their town god" (B.2.k) [2]).

Names of demons, of gates and other dangerous places are mentioned, in order that the dead may know them and may have power over them. A labyrinth of dangerous roads is, it is true, outlined and described, but beside it is written: "As regards those who know them, they find their ways" (B.7.e). According to the inscriptions the purpose of these spells is to escape dangers (B.excurs.). After mentioning the demons the dead says: "I have power over them, they have no power over me" [3]). From places like these, which want to avert dangers, we may deduce which are the menaces of the hereafter.

Punishment and torture are also mentioned there where the judgment of sinners is described. This is especially the case in the so-called "*Livres*". The kings have the victory of the sun-god over his enemies represented in their tombs (18th dyn. sqq). Herewith they glorify the sun-god, designate themselves as his servants and participate in his triumph. Under such circumstances representations of judgment scenes are not dangerous for the dead himself. The texts make it clear enough that the king stands on the right side.

The punishments of the hereafter are also applied to Seth and his gang as opponents of Osiris and to Apophis as enemy of Re. In the *ḳrr.t*-book human trespassers are punished as enemies of Re or of Osiris (B.17.d). In the Book of Gates the unjust, who are punished, are those who sinned on earth against Re or Osiris. But also Apophis is punished there (C.7.b), as the chief one of those who opposed Re. Like the human trespassers he is represented in the lower register among the punished. A document like the Papyrus Jumilhac [4]) deals with Seth as enemy of Osiris. He is punished by Anubis, just as in

---

[1]) H. Sottas, *La préservation de la propriété funéraire dans l'ancienne Égypte*, p. 36 sqq; p. 96.

[2]) Urk. I. 305. 17-18.

[3]) C.T. II. 162. g. h.

[4]) Non-edited papyrus in the Louvre. We have to thank Prof. J. Vandier for the perusal of it. His edition went to press.

the Book of Gates Apophis, the enemy of Re, is punished by Atum. So henceforth punishments, applied to Seth and Apophis, will be described as punishments of sinners.

Par. 4. Traces of Sheol representations in Egypt

It is generally known that with the Semites the dualistic conception of death prevails. The Babylonians call the netherworld *irṣit la tāri*, land without return [1]), "where dust is their nourishment and mud their food." The Old Testament knows the שְׁאֹל, where the dead lead a shadowy existence. With the Egyptians, on the other hand, there was a belief in resurrection from death. "Its power could be broken. And it was the source of eternal life for mankind. According to the Egyptians man becomes in death the peer of the gods. Again and again he identifies himself with the victors of death, more especially with Re and Osiris. "I am the sun-god, Re, Tum, Chepera" reads a common formula in the texts of the dead. The identification of the dead with Osiris even goes so far that finally the name of the God becomes a common indication, a title of each person deceased. "Osiris N.N." is the deceased who possesses the power of resurrection which Osiris has. The mystery of eternal life is identical for men and gods in every respect" [2]). Such conceptions seem to exclude a Sheol representation. With the Egyptians, as far as the historical data go, the belief in a resurrection and a new life are always connected with death.

Nevertheless there are found utterances now and again, which make us think of a negative view. In the Pyr. Texts the king has to pass doors, before he may begin his ascension. These doors open to him, but they keep the *rḫy.t* at bay. In early dynastic representations [3]) the *rḫy.t*-birds represent a group of people, which rebels against legal authority. In the Pyr. Texts by *rḫy.t* the common people are meant, who, in contrast with the king, are not allowed to go to heaven. In variants of Pyr. 1726.a.b foreign peoples take the place of

---

[1]) Carl Bezold, *Babylonisch-Assyrisches Glossar*, p. 69 b.

[2]) Kristensen, *Het leven uit de dood* (*Life from death*), pp. 40, 41.

[3]) Quibell, *Hieraconpolis*, I, Pl. XXVI, c. the *rḫy.t*, carried along on standards; the South conquers the North. The *rḫy.t* are the inhabitants of the Delta, hence the common people, the rabble.

the *rḫy.t*. When these are not allowed to go to heaven, another sad fate is fixed for them. If the Pyr. Texts still contain further indications of a Sheol, these *rḫy.t* could be considered to be its population (B.1.f).

In the Pyr. Texts staying in the earth, which is defined as the god of the earth *3kr*, Geb or written with the word *t3* (A.11.i), stands in contrast with the ascension. The dead hopes to escape from the earth and not to be seized by the gods of the earth, so that he is in the heavens with Re. The doors of Geb must be opened to him, so that the ascension may begin. The avertion for Geb even remains as long as the C.T. In an ascension text we read that the mouth of the earth is opened to the king, so that he may ascend to heaven (A.11.a.h.i). This ascension is the king's privilege. Consequently it is necessary that men remain locked up in Geb's realm. That immortality and ascension are for the king only and not for the people appears from Pyr. 604, e-f. "Take N.N. by his arm, take N.N. to heaven, that N.N. may not die on earth among men" (A.1.c).

In some places of the Pyr. Texts staying with Osiris is also opposed to staying with Re in the heavens, Pyr. 145.b: "Re-Atum has not given you to Osiris, he (Osiris) has not counted your heart, he has not taken possession of your heart" (B.16.d). Osiris bears sway over the "hidden ones of place", Pyr. 2023.a (A.11.j), that is to say he is king over those who are locked up in the netherworld. In Pyr. Neith 779 it concerns Osiris and *Ḫrty*, a god who is akin to him. There it says: "I have claimed him (the king) from *Ḫrty*. I do not deliver him to Osiris, I open to him the gate that keeps at bay" (B.16.i). This gate reminds one of the doors which keep the *rḫy.t* from ascension. Staying with Osiris is a possibility contrary to the ascension.

The use of the verb *śḫd*, to walk upside down, fits in with the subterranean realm of the dead, Pyr. 323.a (A.6.d): "It is N.N.'s horror to walk in darkness, b, he cannot see walking upside down" [1]).

This passage reminds one strongly of a Sheol. He who does not ascend to heaven, finds himself in a subterranean, dark realm of the

---

[1]) For the meaning of *n m33.f*: B.D. 85, Nav. II, 191, 2-3: I abhor evil, I cannot see it. C.T. VI. 136. k: He abhors that which is not; he cannot see evil. The same phrase as in Pyr. 323. a occurs C.T. VI. 189. e-f: (His) horror is going away by night, N.N. cannot see walking with the head down. That is to say he cannot bear it.

dead. In *sḫd* there is thought of a reversed world [1]). He who formerly walked on the earth, now walks with his feet against the bottom of the flat disk of the earth, as it were against a ceiling, head down. This is the only place in the Pyr. Texts, where *sḫd* occurs, which is not astonishing, because the Pyr. Texts preferably speak about the positive side of the death of the king, that is to say his ascension.

There are many spells in the C.T. for preventing this *sḫd*. The stars Orion and *Spd* must carry the dead to heaven and save him from the state of the dead, who walk upside down (A.6.d) [2]). This is the fate of the dead in the West, which, contrary to heaven, is considered a horrific place. Instead of being with his feet against the ceiling the dead wants to walk upright. These spells for not walking upside down are often connected with a charm not to eat excrements. The idea was that, in walking upside down, the products of digestion flowed down and that the mouth served as the anus. In the later "*Livres*" *sḫd* has become a punishment for the godless. Then a shift in the use of the word has taken place. Whereas *sḫd* in the Pyr. Texts is the general fate of men, who do not ascend to heaven like the king, in the "*Livres*" it is a special punishment for the unjust beside other chastisements, like being tortured or burnt. In the C.T., however, the older conception is still present. In the texts that should prevent people from walking upside down or eating excrements, ascension is frequently set against this undesired fate. This also points to the fact that the conception of a subterranean realm of the dead was connected with walking upside down, the counterpart of this realm being the ascension. "I do not go with my head down for you, . . . oh these great ones, oh these distinguished gate-keepers of this big heaven . . . I walk on this road on which you are walking. I land in heaven, for it is the place where I like to live" [3]).

The netherworld is dark (A.10.e). The horrors of this gloomy place are described in B.D. 175 in the dialogue between Atum and Osiris. What Osiris regrets reminds one strongly of a Sheol-conception. Osiris complains: "Oh Atum, whereto do I go? There is no

---

[1]) The use of *nn.t* (*nw.t*, Wb. II. 213. 7) the "counter-heaven", taken as realm of the dead and determined with the sign of heaven reversed (B.20.1) also fits in with being reversed.

[2]) C.T. I. 188 d. sqq.

[3]) C.T. Spell 220. III. 201. k. sqq.

water, there is no air, it is very deep, dark and extensive." Further Osiris wails about the fact that ordinary life is extinguished. There is no sexual intercourse, one cannot eat and drink there normally. Just as in a Sheol one leads a shadowy life there.

Although in many texts the West is considered the normal realm of the dead it is sometimes also taken in an unfavourable sense: "May you not go on the roads of the western ones, who go on them, they do not return [1]) may you go on these roads of the eastern ones, among the followers of Re" [2]). Only he who is with Re participates in the resurrection and full life.

Although the texts differ in regard to the position of the *d3.t*, the latter is sometimes connected with a subterranean realm of the dead. In Pyr. 1014 *3kr* is a variant of *d3.t*. In the Book of Gates II, middle register, B.S. Pl. III, 12-15, the gods, who carry the boat of the earth, who raise the boat of the *d3.t*, are mentioned. *D3.t* is here parallel to *t3*. The Pyr. Texts state that the gate of the *d3.t* is opened to the king, so that he may sail to heaven (A.11.j). Pyr.871.c says that the king first comes to the deceased, "those who are in Nun", but he does not remain there, he sails to heaven (A.11.d). *D3.t* and *Nwn* are a Sheol here, a dark subterranean realm of the dead, where the inhabitants lead a gloomy existence. There must have been a view that this was the fate of all the dead. Therefore it must be denied emphatically that the king participates in it. Contrary to common mortal men he does not remain in the realm of the dead, but he sails to heaven.

Par. 5. Views based on direct observation of death as a physical phenomenon

a. The decay of the body

One of the first phenomena which occur immediately after death and is much abhorred by mankind is the decomposition of the body. Many spells want to undo this. The terms used for decay and decomposition are *ḥw3* (A.3.j), *imk* (A.3.a), *isi* (A.3.c), *rwi* (A.3.g), *hb* (A.3.i) and *ẖnn* (A.3.l). The decomposition of the body should be

---

1) Cf. Babylonian *irṣit la tāri*, land without return.
2) Pyr. 2175; A.11.b.

checked, because the dead needs his body in order to be able to continue his existence, hence mummification. "Flesh of N.N., do not waste away, do not decay, do not become bad in smell." (A.3.j) [1]). If his body decays the king cannot sail to heaven. His body is of gold, the everlasting substance of the gods [2]). B.D. 154 tells us in detail how the dead will not decay and that his body will not be eaten by worms (A.3.j). The occurrence of fluid from the dead body, *rḏw* (A.3.h), *fd.t* (A.3.f) is denied. By *rḏw* the secretion is meant which a corpse shows when decaying. In Pyr.1283.a.b. *fd.t* and *rḏw* are parallels (A.3.a), in C.T. I. 295.b *rḏw* and *ḥwȝȝ.wt* (A.3.h). Oil has to give vital strength to the dead and has to stop the fluid from his corpse. (A.3.f) [3]). No cadaverous smell may arise (*śṯi*, A.3.p; *śnśn*, A.3.o). C.T. I. 304, b.c. is a spell for preventing the smell becoming bad (A.3.p). The corpse (*ẖȝ.t*, A.4.n) may not decompose, but must last for the sake of the survival of the dead.

b. Being motionless

One of the phenomena of death is that the body does not move any more, has become a thing [4]). In this respect death tallies with sleep. Words for sleeping may be used as analogous terms for death (A.8). The rigidity of the stiffened body makes death to be considered as being bound (A.7). Resurrection from death is like awakening from sleep, like rising after lying down (*śḏr*, A.8.j). In Pyr.721.d (*ḳd*, A.8.k) the aversion to death is expressed as "he detests sleep, he hates fatigue." Also verbs of being tired (*bȝgi*, A.8.c, *nni*, A.8.f, *wrḏ*, A.8.a) are used as equivalents of being dead. About the resurrection of Osiris from death it is said: "A tired god is waking up." (A.8.c) [5]). In C.T. I. 306.a *nni* and *śḏr*, being tired and sleeping are parallels. Both mean lying motionless in death (A.8.f). In B.D. 45, where *wrḏ*, being tired, comes near to *ḥwȝ*, to waste away, death also must be meant (A.8.a).

The impossibility of moving is like being bound by fetters. This

---

1) Pyr. 722.
2) Pyr. Neith 653.
3) Pyr. 1800, 1801.
4) J. P. Sartre says about the dead, *L'être et le néant*, 42e éd., p. 629: Ils sont réduits à la seule dimension d'extériorité.
5) Pyr. 2092. a.

does not refer to the bandages of the mummy, but to a metaphor for stiffening through death. In Pyr.349 (A.7.l): "N.N. comes to you, that he may be released from his bounds and break away from his fetters" is on a par with the sequel: "N.N. did not die a death." Re's "being fettered" as his setting stands in contrast with his rising (*pri*) (A.7.c) [1]. In the line: "The bonds (*ḫtr*) that are on my mouth are driven away" (A.7.g) we must not think of mummy linen either but of the stiffening of the lips through death. It is said of Horus, who revives the dead like his father Osiris, that he unties his cattle halter (*mḏ.t*, A.7.e). Being motionless in death is being tied up like an animal, which may not run away. Rising is undoing the bonds of death (*sfḫ*, A.7.j).

c. Non-functioning of the senses and limbs

This also belongs to the symptoms of death that are perceived immediately. Certain spells are intended to make the body function again. The sensory perception is deranged, the mouth is silent (*gr*, A.11.c), the eye is blind (*šp*, A.4.q), the ear is deaf (*id*, A.4.b). One of the names for the realm of the dead is *Igr.t*, which is connected with the verb *gr*, to be silent (A.11.c). The interrupted functions of the body are restored by a spell, C.T. Spell 455 (A.4.h): "My eyes and ears are opened . . ., the bonds that are on my mouth are opened." "I do not grow blind, I do not become deaf" (A.4.q) [2]. The eyesight is restored: "My face is opened" (A.4.k). B.D. 42 makes the body function again by identifying the parts of the body with gods: "There is no part of the body on me free from a god" [3]. The dead can walk again as before: "I go on my feet" (A.4.j). His body, decayed and fallen to pieces in consequence of death, is composed again: "Receive your head, collect your bones, collect your limbs, shake the dust from your flesh" (A.4.u) [4]. Burial in the earth without mummification is presumed. The fingers bent by death, are straightened out again (A.4.t). The dead also regains his mental faculties. He is able to remember what he had forgotten (A.4.o). The spells about suffering hunger and

---

1) Pyr. 285. c.
2) C.T. V. 223. g.
3) Naville II, 116.
4) Pyr. 654.

thirst may also be mentioned in this connection. The body does not function any longer. The dead cannot eat and drink any more, he goes hungry (A.5.n) and is consumed with thirst (A.5.e.h). Opposed to these are spells which make it possible for him to take food and be satisfied. Food offerings serve for this purpose, consisting of the usual diet of bread and beer. Before being able to partake of these a resurrection must have taken place first. The son who comes to the grave with the food revives his father: "Rise from your left side, turn on your right side.... I have grown barley. I have reaped spelt. I have made offerings for your feasts" [1]). After the resurrection the body can function again and eat the food. Without this resurrection the body is powerless and suffers hunger and thirst.

d. Passing away and being carried off

All over the world these metaphors are used for dying. It is a departure from the land of the living, a being taken away by the invisible hand of fate. Being taken away and brought back in the Pyr. Texts [2]) are equivalents for dying and reviving (A.9.b). The same is the case with the series "to go away and return, to sleep and to wake up, to land and to revive" (A.2.i). The verb *šm* in Egyptian is used for going away, e.g., in *šm n.k* = go away. The verb *ii* is not only to come but also to return. In B.D. 179, a spell for going away yesterday and returning tomorrow, the deceased has left death behind and has arisen from death. That by "going away" death is meant appears from a similar line of the same chapter: "I died yesterday and return today." Here *mt* takes the place of *šm* (A.2.i). Sometimes, however, *ii* is parallel with *mt*, so that going away means dying and not returning (A.2.a). Who or what takes man away, is often not mentioned. The moment and the cause of death are unverifiable. In the wisdom of Ani [3]) we read: "His fate comes to take him away." In another place [4]) personified death itself is the subject: "Who carries the child away which is still on its mother's lap." Man fears death as a being taken away from earthly life against his will. As a farewell for ever the dead also regrets the being separated

[1]) Pyr. 1747, 1748.
[2]) Pyr. 1459. b.
[3]) VII. 12.
[4]) V. 2-4.

from his relatives. There is a sequence of spells for being reunited with one's relatives (A.5.a) [1]).

Par. 6. Death as absolute destruction

a. Death as such is perishing

Death is opposed to life (A.1.c). "When he wants you to die, you die; when he wants you to live, you live" [2]). Dying is not-to-be, ceasing to exist [3]). The name is a person's essence. If his name perishes, he himself does not exist any more. "He shall not die, his name shall not perish" [4]). Only by resurrection the dead is freed from this non-being: "Get up, do not perish, do not go down" [5]). *Tm* and *śki* "not to be" and "to perish" are parallels here. The alternative of resurrection is staying in transiency (A.1.d). Also the use of the term *śki* points to a conception of death as absolute destruction (A.1.h). In B.D. 46 *śki* stands in contrast with "to live", *ʿnḫ.Śki* is parallel with *ḥtm* in Pyr. 764b: "You shall not go down, you shall not perish in eternity." In a rubric of a spell of the Book of the Dead [6]) it is said of somebody who performs the prescribed ritual *n śk.n.f n mt.n.f m wḥm*, he does not perish, he does not die for the second time. *Śki* and *mt m wḥm* are both terms for total destruction. *Mt m wḥm* is the second death. What part of man still survives in the hereafter, his *b3*, his *šw.t*, is destroyed too after his first, his bodily death. Only the performance of the right ritual can save him from this. Decay of the body also may bring about one's ruin [7]).

b. Being burnt (B.3)

Like many peoples the Egyptians also have the conception of a hellfire, where one may end up or into which one may be thrown as

---

[1]) C.T. Spells 131-146.

[2]) Pyr. 153. c.

[3]) Whoever is in miserable circumstances on earth, is dead, even though he still lives. Piankhi calls the inhabitants of a town which he besieges: "You who live in death" (Urk. III, 24, 4 and 6). In a *satire des métiers* it is said about the hardships of an officer's career: "He is dead, while he is still alive" (Lansing IX, 8, ed. A. Erman and H. O. Lange, *Det Kgl. Danske Videnskabernes Selskab. Hist.-fil. Medd.* X, 3, p. 86).

[4]) Pyr. 1812. c.

[5]) Pyr. 1299. c.

[6]) B.D. 136 A.

[7]) B.D. 163.

a sinner. The idea of this punishment by fire is not eternal torture, but total destruction. What is burnt ceases to exist. In the *Lebensmüde* his soul has given him the advice of seeking death by fire [1]). The man does not want to accept this. Death by fire would mean total destruction and the soul itself cannot survive without its corpse. In the *Zweiwegebuch* the pool of fire in the middle is a danger threatening everybody who has to make the journey through the realm of the dead. In the tombs of the kings fire is a punishment, which falls upon sinners and to which they are condemned by a judge of the dead. Nine serpents burn Chepri's enemies (B.3.a) [2]). Enemies of Re are burnt (*š3m*, B.3.a). It is said to one of the two demons, who want to deprive the dead of his magical power: "Backwards, flame" (B.3.l) [3]). A serpent must burn with its fire those who have sinned against Osiris (B.3.u): "Horus says to the *ḫty*-serpent: "Oh fire, great of flame, this one, on whose mouth my eye is and whose convolutions my children guard, open your mouth, open your jaws. Place your flame in my father's enemies, that you may burn their bodies and that their souls may be burnt by this glowing breath which is on your mouth, by the blaze that comes from your belly" [4]). The snake has to execute this burning with his fiery breath. The essential elements of the personality, the corpse and the soul, must be consumed by fire. This is the absolute destruction of the one punished. In the *ḳrr.t*-book [5]) we read near those punished: "These enemies of Osiris, who are under the flames, whose bodies are burnt." Without a body as essential element of the personality nobody can continue his existence. It is said about a place of destruction (*ḫb.t*) [6]): "Whose flame is not against you." It concerns a pool of fire, where the impious will land, but not the just. Their destruction takes place by burning. In the realm of the dead there is a gate, "which repeats the cutting, which burns the rebels" (B.3.e) [7]). In Am Duat [8]) the same (B.3.a) is said about a gate: "The cutting one, which burns

---

[1]) De Buck, *Kernmomenten*, p. 21.
[2]) Am Duat VI, 216, 217.
[3]) C.T. V. 319. a.
[4]) Book of Gates VIII, lower register, B.S. Pl. XIV, 35-48.
[5]) L(ivre des) Q(ererts) CI. 6.
[6]) Book of Gates II, upper register, B.S. Pl. II, 55; B.3.aa.
[7]) B.D. 146.
[8]) Am Duat VIII. 226.

the dead who are in it" (*dś ś3m mt.w*). As a punishment of Seth is mentioned (B.3.v): "His corpse is burnt, his soul does not exist, his children who live on earth are extirpated." That his descendants are also exterminated shows that Seth should completely cease to exist.

c. Cutting and slaughtering

One of the most usual punishments in the realm of the dead is that the victims are belaboured with knives and swords, are maimed, stabbed or beheaded. Pictures in the texts represent demons with swords and knives. Just as burning with fire cutting into pieces means one's total destruction. Re triumphs over his enemy Apophis: "Your sacredness arises, which is in the earth. Apophis has been slaughtered in his blood" (B.5.o) [1]. Seth, who killed Osiris, is extirpated in his turn: "Osiris N.N. bring for you him who wanted to slaughter you (*śm3*) in cut condition" (*š'*) (B.5.bb) [2]. "Don't give me to this slaughterer (*śm3y*), who slaughters bodies (*śm3*) . . . who chops up many corpses (*ḫb3*), who lives on slaughtering (B.5.z) [3]. Executioners of Osiris are mentioned [4], "who hack off heads (*ḥśḳ*) and cut off necks (*sn*), who take along with them souls and spirits to the slaughtering-block of him who eats raw flesh" (B.5.p). It is said to enemies of Osiris: "Your corpses are cut to pieces" (B.5.bb) [5]. Beside enemies of Osiris it is written: "Oh you who are put on the head, bleeding ones, whose heart has been pulled out, who are in the place of destruction" (B.5.w) [6]. "Oh you who must be destroyed (*ḥtmtyw*), oh you who must be beheaded (*ḥśḳ*), enemies of Osiris, whose necks do not exist" [7].

The dead says about his enemies: "I destroy their glory (*bḥn*, to cut to pieces, B.5.i). The dead says to demons: "May I not fall, on account of your knives" (B.5.kk) [8]. These terms for cutting to pieces also refer to the victim's total destruction. The corpse, the soul,

---

[1] *ḥśb*; Book of Gates X, upper register, B.S. Pl XI, 14-16.
[2] Pyr. 1337. d.
[3] B.D. 154; 400. 14-401. 2.
[4] C.T. III, 296. a. b.
[5] L.Q. CXVIII. 2.
[6] L.Q. XXV. 1.
[7] B. 5. b; L.Q. IX. 1.
[8] C.T. IV. 322. d.

the spirit or the shadow are mutilated and without these essential parts the dead cannot continue his existence. The corpse is completely cut to pieces or the heart is torn out. The person struck bathes in his blood. He herewith ceases to exist. Verbs like *ḫr*, to be brought down, or *ḥtm*, to be destroyed, also point to total destruction in this connection. Verbs for cutting are used in the lower registers of the Book of Gates and the *ḳrr.t*-book, where it concerns the destruction of the enemies of Re and Osiris.

d. Other actions directed against the dead

If the dead is devoured by a demon, he ceases to exist. His vital strength passes into him who devours him. A tormenting devil lives on (*ʿnḫ m*) his victims (B.6.b). The dead asks Atum for help: "Save me from this god, who lives on slaughter-cattle" (B.6.b) [1]. This concurs with the terms of par. 6.c: the dead is slaughtered first and eaten up afterwards. The 42 judges of B.D. 125 are called: "Those who live on the evil ones whom they guard" (B.6.b) [2]. Already in the Pyr. Texts a demon, *Ḫrty*, occurs, who lives on the hearts of men (B.6.b) [3]. In the Book of Gates [4]) it is said of punishing demons, who destroy sinners: "They live on southern ones, they subsist on northern ones" (B.6.b). The dead keeps a demon off with the words: "Do not eat me" (B.6.c) [5]. Other demons eat and destroy (*wnm*, *ḥtm*) the souls, which are on earth (B.6.c) [6]. The names *ʿm b3* (devourer of souls) and *ʿm šw.t* (devourer of spirits) occur (B.6.a). From the use of verbs like *ḥtm*, to destroy, and from the fact that essential parts of the person are eaten up, (*b3*, *šw.t*), it appears that the devouring also causes absolute destruction of the dead.

The verb *nkn*, to damage, also points to destruction of the dead. It stands in contrast with *ʿnḫ*, to live and is parallel with *šʿ.t*, blood-bath (B.21.s). A sinner is destroyed by breaking his bones (*śd ḳs.w*, B.21.gg).

[1]) C.T. IV. 312. b. c.
[2]) B.D. p. 249. 11, 12.
[3]) Pyr. Neith 665.
[4]) Book of Gates IX, lower register, B.S. Pl. XIII, 14-16.
[5]) B.D. 40; 109. 7.
[6]) C.T. II. 254. p.

e. Total destruction as (a consequence of) punishment in the realm of the dead

The punishments, which in the "*Livres*", usually in the lower register, are applied to sinners, cause their extirpation, as the result of the above-mentioned treatments of cutting and burning. Osiris as judge of the dead destroys those who sin against him: "Oh Osiris, who destroys his enemies" (*ḥtm*, B.10.b) [1]). The destruction of these enemies is attained by destroying their souls (*b3*, B.10.b) [2]). Without the *b3* nobody can continue to exist. Opponents in the realm of the dead are belaboured with knives. They do not get offerings and belong to destruction (*ḥtm*, B.10.b) [3]). Without offerings they cannot live. A cumulation of terms of destruction is used in order to underline the complete destruction of Osiris' enemies (B.10.b) [4]): "Oh great snakes, gate-keepers of the place of destruction (*ḥtmy.t*), keep watch over these enemies of Osiris. I rest (Re says) in the beautiful West in order to arouse their places of judgment (*nm.t*) against them, in order to destroy their souls (*ḥtm b3.w*), in order to wipe out (*sin*) their shadows, to destroy (*śk ẖ3.t*) their corpses, to take away their glory (*3ḫ.w*)." The verb *ḫmi*, originally "to overturn walls" is also used for the destruction of man (B.10.c). Apophis, as enemy of Re, is felled (*śḫr*, B.10.d). Damage is done (*ḳn*) to the dead on the slaughtering-block (B.10.f). So they are killed off there and hewn to pieces.

The result of all the tortures and torments applied to the sinners, is that they "do not exist". About enemies of Osiris, who are punished in one of the lower registers of the Book of Gates, it is said [5]): "You do not exist (*n wn.ṯn*), your *b3* is destroyed. He does not live on account of what you have done against my father Osiris" (A.1.d). Not to live, not to exist are parallels and are the consequence of the destruction of the *b3* as constituent part of the personality. In Am Duat [6]) *tm*, to perish, not to be, is the result of burning (A.1.d). The enemies of Osiris are assigned to destruction and counted out to non-existence[7])

[1]) L.Q. XXII. 3.
[2]) L.Q. XXII. 8-9.
[3]) C.T. I. 208. b.-d.
[4]) L.Q. IX. 4.
[5]) Book of Gates VIII, lower register, B.S. Pl. XIV, 20-24.
[6]) Am Duat IX. 99.
[7]) L.Q. XXV. 1-2.

Ḥtm and *tm* are parallels. Time and again in the "list of punishments" of L.Q. there is spoken about the non-existence (*nn wn*) of sinners as the result of cutting into pieces and burning. Such an expression is used in Am Duat [1]: *N ḫpr.ṯn*, you shall not become (about enemies of Osiris, A.1.e).

Summarising we may say that especially in the lower registers of the books on the walls of the tombs of the kings of the New Kingdom terms for burning and cutting up are used, actions, which result in the complete destruction of the dead.

Par. 7. Dangers, which impend over essential parts of the personality (B.8)

The Egyptian distinguished various parts of the human personality which are essential to his imperishableness [2]. If one or more of these "substances of the soul" are impaired, man ceases to exist. Many spells have to prevent this. The *3ḫ*, spirit, represents a glorified situation. The dead says to a demon: "Do not take away my glory" (B.8.a) [3]. The element that moves freely is the *b3*-soul bird. This *b3* fetches drinkingwater for the corpse and holds the symbol of the air to its nose. Without this *b3* the corpse perishes and man cannot continue his existence. Some spells prevent the *b3* being locked up and hindered in its movements (B.8.c) [4]. Demons can take souls and spirits with them to the slaughtering-block (B.8.c) [5]. Executioners of Osiris want to destroy the *b3* by cutting the latter to pieces (B.8.c) [6]. In L.Q. soul-birds are represented in fire-basins, in which they are burnt (B.8.c). To punished enemies of Osiris it is said: "You do not exist, your *b3* is destroyed, it does not live" (B.8.c) [7]. The destruction of the *b3* is the ruin of man himself. The *b3* may be eaten up (B.8.c) [8].

---

1) Am Duat XI. 77.
2) J. Sainte Fare Garnot, *L'anthropologie de l'Égypte ancienne*, *Anthropologie religieuse*, ed. C. J. Bleeker, *Studies in the history of religions*, *Suppl. to NVMEN* II, 1955, pp. 14-27.
3) C.T. V. 51. g.
4) B.D. 91.
5) C.T. III. 296. b.
6) Am Duat III. 141.
7) Book of Gates VIII, lower register, B.S. Pl. XIV. 20-22.
8) B.D. 163.

The enemies of Osiris do not have a *b3*, the latter being taken away from their corpse (B.8.c) [1]. Without *b3* the *ẖ3.t* also has to perish. In L.Q. XXXVII, 4 reversed *b3*-birds are mentioned, whose corpses (*ẖ3.t*) do not exist (B.8.g). The shadow is destroyed: "Extirpate the shadow of those who must be destroyed" (B.8.h) [2]. Together with the shadow the person himself perishes. In L.Q. the shadows (*šw.t*) as well as the souls are pictured in cauldrons. The name (*rn*) is on a par with its bearer. C.T. Spell 411 protects the name, so that a person does not forget it or that it is taken away from him (B.8.d). Many spells have to further that a person keeps his magical power (*ḥk3*, B.8.f). A crocodile wants to devour somebody in order to usurp his magical power. The dead wants to keep the disposal of his heart (*ìb*, B.8.b, *ḥ3ty*, B.8.e). He wishes to get his own heart back. The heart is the seat of the intellectual faculties. Through them he is able to remember what he had forgotten. His heart must not be cut from his body [3]. It must not testify against him in the judgment of the dead. The heart may also be burnt by fire [4].

When these powers of the soul are destroyed, a man dies for the second time (*mt m wḥm*, B.10.a). From C.T. V. 175, a.b. it appears that "dying for the second time" is the same as losing the *ḥk3*. The first death is the bodily death. After this death a man may continue to live by the powers of his soul (*b3*, *šw.t*, *ḥk3*). If also these are destroyed it means his end for ever. This is the fate of the enemies of Re and Osiris, the sinners who are enemies of the god. By cutting up or death by fire, means to absolute destruction, also these powers of the soul are struck.

Par. 8. Torment and torture

Various actions directed against the dead, torments and tortures are described by the texts. Some of these are the same as those used on earth against criminals: "You are not counted, you are not locked in, you are not imprisoned, you are not put in irons, you are not guarded, you are not put in the place of judgment, in which the rebels

[1]) L.Q. XXXIV. 4.
[2]) Am Duat V. 45. 46.
[3]) C.T. III. 296. h. i.
[4]) L.Q. XCVIII. 8.

are placed" (B.2.s) [1]). This is the complete series of punitive measures which are applied to a criminal from the apprehension until the sentence. About the just it says: "Your power does not reach their sealing" (*śḏ3y.t*) [2]). Being sealed perhaps means being in confinement here. The people confined are watched by gaolers (*s3w*, B.2.i). Demons in every shape and form serve as such (B.12). The Lord of the universe has given the power of watching his enemies to controllers (*ỉry.w śỉpw*) [3]). Not always the terms of locking up allude to prison. *Ḫnr*, to lock up, may also be figuratively used for death. The rigidity of death is a being imprisoned, the idea being at the same time a being kept in a subterranean realm of the dead, a being hindered in the liberty of action. Against this the dead identifies himself with a bird in order to be able to leave the grave and to fly freely, where he wants (B.2.h) [4]).

Among the terms for infernal punishments there are also many for tying and fettering. The enemies of the gods are represented with their hands tied to their backs, as is the case, for instance, with conquered foreigners as enemies of the king. This binding sometimes precedes further chastisements with fatal outcome. In L.Q. beheaded persons in shackles are represented. Sinners are also tied up to poles, where they are tortured.

In the Book of Gates I, lower register, B.S. Pl. IV, 18-19, where the punished are, it reads: "You are bound (*k3ś*, B.2.p), your arms are not pulled apart." The arms are tied behind the back. About people, who have sinned against Osiris, it is said (B.2.p): "Who act against Osiris in a hostile way, who rebel against the overlord of the *d3.t*, ties for your arms! Your fetters are painful" [5]). These notions are already old. From a charter of the Old Kingdom it appears that Osiris as judge in the realm of the dead punishes sinners (desecrators of the graves) (B.2.k): "Truly, my majesty will order that they shall not be at the head of the spirits in the realm of the dead, but that they shall be bound and fettered (*śnḥwy*; *nṯṯwy*) as condemned by Osiris and their town god." The idea is that in the

[1]) C.T. I. 70. b-d.
[2]) Book of Gates III, upper register, B.S. Pl. VIII. 11-14.
[3]) B.D. 17; Urk. V. 78. 15; C.T. IV. 321. e.
[4]) C.T. II. 230. a. sqq.
[5]) Am Duat VII, 29-33.

hereafter the same happens to criminals as on earth. Apophis, as an enemy of Re, is put in irons [1]). That the punishment begins with fetters and after that results in total destruction, appears from C.T. IV. 12. b: "The destructors do not put straps on me" (*ḥtm.w*; *ḏḥr.wt*).

These demons bind their victims first and then bring them to ruin (B.2.r). In the Book of Gates V, B.S. Pl. XVIII, 3, enemies of Re are tied to torture-posts (*wśr.t*, B.18.b). These are called the torture-posts of Geb, perhaps in connection with the unfavourable part for the dead, which Geb plays as god of the earth, who keeps the dead imprisoned (A.11.h). In L.Q. the *mnỉ.t* (mooring posts) are used in a similar way (B.18.c). The enemies of Osiris are tied to them (*ḳ3ś*). In B.D. 180 these posts are called the place of the punished. This is the punishment for those, who have sinned against the mysteries of Osiris [2]). The *d3s.wy* (B.18.e) are also such torture posts [3]). The inscription to it states that those, who are tied to them, cannot free themselves. So it concerns an eternal punishment.

Close to the terms for tying are those which are derived from hunting. The enemies of the gods are caught like cattle with a lasso or like birds and fishes in a net, to be killed afterwards. C.T. Spell 343 and B.D. 153 deal with being caught in a net (B.19.a). The net is thought of as a fishing-net with floats and weights, which give it a vertical position. The net, however, catches birds, because it is stretched between heaven and earth. This net is intended for the spirits [4]), which, as we know, are represented in the shape of birds. It here concerns an ascension of the spirit. The net wants to draw him into the realm of the dead of Khenty Imentyu. That it regards here a net stretched in the air also appears from C.T. III. 296. f, where the net of Shu is mentioned. The idea of the bird-trap (*ỉbṯ.t*, B.19.b) is being locked up in the earth, so that the dead cannot move freely. The dead may be caught with the boomerang by demoniacal gods (B.19.d). This means definite destruction for these dead, for the demons do this—just as in the cannibal texts—in order to appropriate the *ḥk3* and the *3ḫ.w*, the magical power and the mental strength of the dead. The dead may also be caught with a lasso (B.19.h.k), just

---

1) *ʾInṯ.t*, C.T. V. 245. c; Book of Gates X, upper register, B.S. Pl. XI. 20.
2) L.Q. XCVIII. 2.
3) L.Q. LXV. 9.
4) C.T. IV. 355. a.

as it happens to cattle destined for slaughter [1]). C.T. IV. 300. b deals with a demon "a god, who throws a lasso over the evil-doers in order to fetch them to his slaughtering-block." Being caught with a lasso is the action that precedes eternal destruction. Judging the just and unjust [2]) the sun-god says: "I take care of those who are in the netherworld, I catch enemies with the lasso for the place of perdition" (*ḫtmy*). The just receive a favourable fate. The sinners are caught and made away with.

A group of words indicates that demons try to get somebody in their power. The fear of death as something to which one is entirely delivered, is laid down in them. The dead may be seized. He prays: "Save me from the claws of him who takes for himself what he sees" (B.9.b, *iṯi*). In this connection *nḏr* (to seize) is a much used term: "There is no god who seizes N.N., there is no opponent who puts himself in the way of N.N." (B.9.d) [3]). The dead fears to be seized by demons and be hindered in his ascension. Gate-keepers threaten him, but the dead says: "I am not seized, I am not repelled from the gates" [4]). This is a passage from the *Zweiwegebuch*. Along these roads the dead has to pass dangerous gates.

The fear exists that demons get the dead in their power (*śḫm m*; (B.21.ff). The texts very often use this term and so numerous spells serve for preventing man being at the mercy of evil beings: "The messengers of Osiris have no power over me" [5]); "the *d3.t*-denizens have no power over me" [6]).

Demons come to the dead (*ii r*) with inimical intentions; they act against him (*iri r*, B.21.b). "Do not come against me" [7]). "N.N. has risen against those who act against him" [8]). "You have power over those who act against you in the realm of the dead" [9]). The dead charms a demon by saying: "He does not attack me" (*pḥ*, B.21.m). "There is nobody who comes to meet me" [10]). Demons also may

[1]) P. Montet, *Les scènes de la vie privée*, p. 152.
[2]) L.Q. XI. 8.
[3]) Pyr. 1237. a, b.
[4]) C.T. VII, Spell 1061; B 1 L, 393; B.9.d.
[5]) C.T. V. 331. g-i.
[6]) C.T. V. 332. a.
[7]) C.T. V. 50. c; *m iw r.i.*
[8]) B.D. 172; 445. 8, 9.
[9]) C.T. III. 230. c.
[10]) *Ḫśf*, C.T. II. 252. f.

stop the dead with evil intentions on his journey to the realm of the dead. About the gate-keepers he says: "Let them not put themselves in my way as enemies" (*ḏ3i͗*, B.21.oo). Demons rage and rave at their victims (B.11). "N.N. is not surrounded by your fury, oh gods" (*ḏnd*, B.11.e) [1]).

Certain parts of the body are tortured. Without doubt here the treatment of criminals by a court of justice on earth is taken as an example, "N.N. is one of those ... who are not led before high officials, who are not sentenced, who are not condemned ... N.N. is not impoverished. His finger-nails are not stretched. None of the bones of N.N. has been broken" [2]). The arms are turned the wrong way round (B.21.i). The condemned is struck (*ḳnḳn*, B.21.kk). Parts of the body or strength is taken away from him (*ʿw3*, B.21.h; *nḥm*, B.21.q).

In connection with these bodily punishments the demons are called "painful" (*mr*, B.21.o; *mdś*, B.21.p), "painful of fingers" (*mr.w ḏbʿ.w*) [3]), "painful of rage" (*mdś 3d*) [4]).

All the evil that may be caused to the dead, is recapitulated under the name *ḏw.t* (B.21.pp), e.g., the sentence and punishment before Osiris [5]): "Nothing evil will happen against me in this land, in this hall of the double truth".

Par. 9. Dangerous places

There are many places in the realm of the dead where the dead has a great deal to suffer. He is put on a slaughtering-block and killed like a piece of cattle (*nm.t*, B.7.g; *mʿḏ*, B.7.f). He may fall into pools, which are usually full of flames (*š*, B.7.n.; *ʿr*, B.7.d; *nḫ3*, B.7.h; *ẖ3s.t*, B.7.1). As a punishment he is put into a burning division of hell (*ḥ3d*, B.7.i). The netherworld is full of sinister caves (*i͗n.t*, valley, B.7.c; *ḳrr.t*, B.7.q; *ṯpḥ.t*, B.7.r). There are places of judgment where he is slaughtered or completely destructed in another way (*ḫb.t*, B.7.k; *ḥtmy.t*, B.7.j). To the punishment by burning the possibility belongs of putting the dead into cauldrons or copper basins. Under

---

1) Pyr. 1501. b.
2) Pyr. 1041 sqq.; B. 21. 11.
3) C.T. IV. 303. b.
4) C.T. VII, Spell 1144; B 1 Be 191.
5) B.D. 125; 252. 7, 8.

them a fire is burning and he is roasted (B.4, *wḥ3.t*, *ḥry.t*, *ḳty.t*, *ʿḫ*, *ḫnf.t*, *ṯnm*, *dwfy*). Certain spells help the dead to pass these dangerous places and their demoniacal guards (B, excurs. *św3*; *pẖr*, to go round something; *nhi*, to escape). He deters demons by ordering them: "Retreat!" (*nwḏ*, B. excurs, d; *ḥm* B, excurs, h). He invokes gods kindly disposed towards him, in order to save him from these dangers (*nḥm*, B, excurs. f; *nḏ*, B, excurs, g).

Par. 10. The journey of the dead

It is a general feature of humanity to represent dying as a departure, a journey to another country. According to the Persian religion the souls of the just as well as the unjust go along roads, on which they have all sorts of adventures. In doing so the soul has to pass the Činvat bridge, which is as narrow as the edge of a knife. The sinners fall from it and land in hell. The just go to heaven to Ahura Mazda. The Egyptian religion also considers the fate of the dead a journey, the covering of a distance. Dying is going away, leaving the world of the living (*šm*, A.2.i).

The Egyptian makes long voyages by boat along the Nile. Also the dead does so and he "lands" in the other world (*mni*, A.2.e; *sm3 t3*, A.2.h). In this term the funeral voyage to the necropolis on the western bank of the Nile and sailing with Re in his boat also play a part. Boats and oars were sent along with the dead in the tomb with a view to this voyage.

The numerous texts that are connected with the ascension, also relate to the idea of a journey. The dead king invokes four beings, who should not stop him, but must help him in his ascension. In these texts a ladder is often mentioned, along which the dead climbs to heaven [1]: "Hail to you, daughter of Anubis, who is near the windows of heaven, friend of Thoth, who stands near the rungs of the ladder. Let N.N. through, that he may pass (*iwn w3.t N. św3.f*). Hail to you, ostrich, who is near the bank of the *nḫ3*-lake, let N. through, that he may pass", etc. . . . A spell of the ladder of heaven [2]) says: "Who makes you ascend? . . . Who draws you? . . . Why do you

---

1) Pyr. 468, 469.

2) C.T. Spell 629; VI. 249. q sqq.

ascend? (answer) I ascend on Shu. I climb up on the god of light..... Who introduces you to this sovereign, who is there (Re)?" In this ascension the dead has to conquer all sorts of obstacles. Spells, which have been sent along with him on the walls of his tomb, must prevent their harming him. Pyr. 498.b is directed against four winds, which put themselves in the way of the dead and which stretch their hands towards him so that he incurs the risk of not reaching Re. For the sun-god is the aim of his journey to heaven [1]: "N.N. comes to you, his father Re, after having traversed Shu (*š3ś.n.f Šw*) ...... He has rounded *Ḥḫw* four times." The dead has passed some dangerous beings before [2]: "N.N. has passed this *Ḥnʿ*, who is in Nun. N.N. has passed this raging one, who is within the reach of the *3ḫ.t*, who strikes every god."

Especially the so-called *Zweiwegebuch* mentions roads, along which the dead must go in order to reach a beatific region. Along these roads many dangers impend over him. Demons may seize him. He may turn into a by-road and land into a pool of hell-fire. The actual *Zweiwegebuch*, a black road by land and a blue road by water, is only part of the whole complex. Sometimes a whole labyrinth is mentioned. It is often said that the roads are situated in the Memphitic hereafter *R3-śṯ3.w* (B.7.e, p. 165).

Where do these roads lead? Sometimes they lead through the realm of the dead to the place where Osiris is: "I have come in order to see Osiris, that I might live on his side" [3]. Sometimes Osiris is located in heaven: "To be in the heaven of Osiris" [4]; sometimes in the *Ḥtp*-field: "Spell, to be in the *Ḥtp*-field among the followers of Osiris, among the followers of Thoth, every day. It is the place of a spirit, which does not die in eternity. As regards anybody, whose plot is in the *Ḥtp*-field, he sees Osiris every day. He is not kept at bay by the evil-doers, the gate-keepers" [5]. The dead goes to Osiris, that the wounds afflicted to him by Seth may be cured and that he may obtain a fate favourable to himself: "I open ways in Ro-setau. I relieve Osiris' sufferings" [6]. This train of thought also occurs in

[1] C.T. VI. 149. a-d.
[2] C.T. VI. 149. e. f. The dead traverses the sky.
[3] C.T. VII, Spell 1131; B 1 Be. 6.
[4] C.T. VII, Spell 1036; B 2 L. 481.
[5] C.T. VII, Spell 1162, 1164; B 1 Be. 259, 260.
[6] C.T. VII, Spell 1086; B 1 Be. 303; cf. B 1 L. 448.

other places, e.g., C.T. Spell 228, III. 268-276, where the dead asks a gate-keeper of Osiris to let him pass in order to cure Osiris and consequently be born again himself. About Ro-setau it is said: "As regards anyone who is there, he sees Osiris every day" [1]). "Osiris, rise in your strength and your vigour, alive, in salvation and health, your power is in Ro-setau" [2]).

That the purpose of the journey is to serve Osiris also appears from C.T. VII, Spell 1085; B 1 Be.311. 312: "Go in peace, in order to attend at the court of Osiris and to pass all gates." The dead hopes to participate in the offering made to Osiris [3]): "Spell in order to be in Ro-setau and to live on the extra offering on Osiris' side." Also outside the *Zweiwegebuch* the purpose of the journey of the dead is to obtain admittance to Osiris: "To enter freely the hidden gates. He is not kept off from Osiris" [4]). In B.D. 147 the spirit of the dead approaches through seven gates without being kept off from Osiris. The gates of the netherworld open to the dead. He goes to Osiris in order to state the condition of his son Horus to him [5]).

Beside a stay with Osiris being with Re also is set as a purpose to the journey in the *Zweiwegebuch*. It is mentioned especially at the end. There are also pictures there of boats, in connection with which we must think of the sun-boat. The dead identifies himself with Re, in order to emphasize his request of being let through: "Make me pass in peace. Re proceeds. The way is paved for me. He sails. He proceeds. Re's protection is my protection" [6]). "I have inherited the *3ḫ.t* of Re, for I am Atum . . . It is said to me: "Inherit the *3ḫ.t*. Prepare the way for Re, that he may let himself down" [7]). The dead holds a conversation with the gate-keepers and asks them to let him pass: "I am not kept off from Re. I do not go into the valley of darkness. I do not enter the pool of the criminals" [8]). So the result of the spell is that the keepers of the gates the dead has to pass let him through, so that he may reach Re. "I open the *3ḫ.t* for Re.

[1]) C.T. VII, Spell 1087; B 1 Be. 309.
[2]) C.T. VII, Spell 1085; B 1 Be. 315.
[3]) C.T. VII, Spell 1085; B 1 L. 440.
[4]) B.D. 137 A; 309. 5.
[5]) P. 122; C.T. Spell 312; C.T. IV. 84. a; p. 120; C.T. IV. 74. f; 77. a.
[6]) C.T. VII, Spell 1167; B 1 Be. 241; B 5 C. 268.
[7]) C.T. VII, Spell 1174; B 1 Be. 269.
[8]) C.T. VII, Spell 1099; B 1 L. 484.

I have made his boat. I adore Re. I am not without a ship. I am not kept off from the *3ḫ.t*. I am Re. Praise be yours, Re, lord of the *3ḫ.t*. I save Re from Apophis. I enhance Re by what I have done for him. I chase the clouds away that his beauty may be seen. I am the great one, who is in his eye, who sit kneeling down in the big boat of Khepri. I descend into your boat. I sit down on your throne" [1]). In the Pyr. it is a common theme that the earth opens its gates, so that the dead may leave the netherworld in order to meet Re and sail to heaven (p. 117). Also elsewhere in the C.T. and in the B.D. this train of thought is further followed up (p. 121). The gates of the netherworld are opened, the dead comes to places where the sun rises, namely *iw Nśiśi* and the *3ḫ.t*. He joins Re (p. 120 sq).

When somebody made a journey and travelled from one town to the other, he had to pass gates, through which the gate-keepers could let him pass or not. Also in the spells of the dead that are related to a journey, gates are mentioned, mostly with demoniacal gate-keepers, who may keep the dead at bay. Knowledge of the spell concerned enables him to impose his will on the gate-keepers (B.1, p. 114 sqq). When the dead sets off through the netherworld to Osiris "the gates of the roads of *'Imḥ.t*" are opened to him [2]). So here gates occur together with roads. The *Zweiwegebuch* also mentions that demoniacal gate-keepers do not keep the dead at bay, when he approaches Osiris: "He sees Osiris every day. He is not kept off by the evil-doers, the gate-keepers" [3]). When he is on his way to the *3ḫ.t* of Re, the dead says [4]): "I am not seized. I am not kept off from the gates" (*n nḏr.i n ḫśf.i ḥr ʿrr.wt*; see *šnʿ*, B.1.j; *ḫśf*, B.1.f). A spell in the *Zweiwegebuch* serves "to pass all gates" [5]). The dead addresses himself to the gate-keepers and the result is that they let him pass [6]): "Let me pass (literally: Prepare the way for me, *ir n.i w3.t*), door-keeper of this big war-ship." The dead arrives at a "gate, burning of front, hidden of back" [7]) and then says: "I have come.

[1]) C.T. VII, Spell 1099; B 1 L. 489-502.
[2]) C.T. IV. 97. g; p. 120.
[3]) C.T. VII, Spell 1164; B 1 Be, 260; *nbḏ.w*; *iry.w ʿrr.wt*, variant *nb.w ʿrr.wt*, lords of the gates.
[4]) C.T. VII, Spell 1061; B 1 L. 393.
[5]) C.T. VII, Spell 1085; B 1 Be. 312.
[6]) C.T. VII, Spell 1085: B 1 Be. 322.
[7]) C.T. VII, Spell 1132; B 1 Be. 12.

I have power over my ways" [1]). At the end of the *Zweiwegebuch* [2]) four gates are pictured. The names of the gate-keepers are inscribed in them. The dead knows them and may pass unhindered. The unjust are not let through. One out of a sequence of six gates is called [3]) "gate of darkness". On the doors the word for flame (*śḏ.t*) is written. About such a gate (*ʿrr.t*) it is said: "Which lives on evil ones, who do not know how to pass it" [4]). If the gates let the just pass, he is freed at the same time from evil-doers [5]): "Hail to you, gates (*śbḫ.wt*), hidden of name, sacred of places, save me from all evil injuries of the powers that are before you, till I come before the Lord of the universe." The dead is admitted and may approach Re freely. It is important that the dead on his journey knows how to "pass" dangerous places safely. Therefore the verb *św3* is often used in spells (B. excurs, 1). Thus it already occurs in the Pyr. Texts. The dead goes unscathed along dangerous places (*pr b3 pf*, *š wr*, pp. 171, 172) and sails to heaven. The *Zweiwegebuch* is full of them. Many demons, who are on the roads of the realm of the dead, are pictured there. Next to these spells are written, which the dead has to recite in order to charm them. When the dead reaches a gate, he says that he comes from a sacred town, e.g., Abydos [6]), which gives him authority to be let through. He says at the gate [7]): "Hu, who speaks in the darkness, belongs to me, he who is rich in hours, who opens the ways, that I may pass to you along them by saying my name." "Make me pass in peace," the dead says [8]), and near a demon, who stands near a turn in the road, it is written: "Who watches the twist of this pond" [9]). The waterway runs along a red coloured strip, near which it is written [10]): "Spell in order to pass the way of the flame." The spell should help the dead not to land in a pool of fire. C.T. Spell 650 is an address to a river of fire (*itrw n ḫ.t*) to pass it [11]):

---

[1]) C.T. VII, Spell 1132; B 1 Be. 16, 17.
[2]) C.T. VII, Spells 1100 sqq.; B 1 L, 504 sqq.
[3]) C.T. VII, Spell 1107; B 1 L. 529.
[4]) C.T. VII, Spell 1108; B 1 L. 534.
[5]) C.T. VII, Spell 1125; 456. a. b.
[6]) C.T. VII, Spell 1135; B 1 Be. 69.
[7]) C.T. VII, Spell 1136; B 1 Be. 77-80.
[8]) C.T. VII, Spell 1167; B 1 Be. 241.
[9]) C.T. VII, Spell 1168; B 1 Be. 242; *iry ḳ3b*, see *ḳ3b*, B. 7. p.
[10]) C.T. VII, Spell 1157; B 1 Be. 251.
[11]) C.T. VI. 272. f-p.

"Let me pass . . . Then it will say: On which of these roads do you pass safely? Then you will say: the (road in the) middle is the right one. Then it will say: Pass along the one you like. I shall go. Beware of what he will say to you."

Before arriving at a place desired the dead has to cross a river or canal. For this purpose he needs a ship or a ferry-man has to take him across. In the Pyr. a winding canal occurs, situated in the East [1]). He has to cross this before he may begin with his ascension [2]). Also the *ʾI3r.w*-fields are associated with it [3]). It is an area abounding in waters. When the water level is favourable, the *mr nḫ3* also fills with water [4]).

In order to reach the *ʾI3r.w*-fields the dead has to cross a stream. For this purpose he appeals to spirits, who fill the part of ferry-men [5]). In doing so he asks for the ferry-boat of Re. All this is to be read in a spell for having the disposal of a ferry-boat. There also the "gates" [6]) of the *ʾI3r.w*-field which the dead has to pass, are mentioned (p. 121). In the *Ḥtp*-field itself too the dead may still travel. He sails on its waters and approaches its towns [7]). C.T. Spells 395-398 deal with the ferry-boat that has to take people across. "Spell in order to bring the ferry-boat" [8]). For this purpose the ferry-man is summoned with the order: "Bring me this" (i.e., the ferry-boat with its belongings) [9]). The ferry-man *M3-ḥ3.f* ("he who looks behind him") and the newly arrived get into conversation, from which it appears that the latter is engaged in making a journey [10]): "Where do you go?" "I am on my way to *Wrś*." The destination of the journey is "the eastern side of heaven" [11]). "Do you know the road on which you have to go?" "I know the road on which I have to go . . . I am going to the

---

1) *mr nḫ3*, a.o.: 340, d; the "turns" *ḳ3b.w*, 2061. c.
2) 1162. c; B.7.h p. 167.
3) Pyr. 340. c.
4) Sethe, *Kommentar Pyr.* II, p. 44.
5) B, introduction, p. 112.
6) Cf. C.T. IV. 49. p: N.N. knows the hidden roads and the gates of the *ʾI3r.w* field.
7) C.T. V. 339. a.
8) C.T. V. 68. b.
9) C.T. V. 121. c. d.
10) C.T. V. 68. e.
11) C.T. V. 80. b; 103. e.

ʾI3r-w-field" [1]). "Do you intend to cross to the place where the glorious god (Re?) is?" "Truly, this glorious god says: "Did you ferry a man to me, who could not count his fingers [2]) ?" In C.T. V. 151.f the *Ḥtp*-field and the *ʾI3r.w*-field are both mentioned; in 158.e the islands of the *ʾI3r.w*-field; after that Hathor holds out her hand to the dead to take him to heaven. In order to be ferried the dead must have the disposal of passage-money (154.c) and as a "test" he must be able to count on his fingers [3]). He must also be able to name the parts of the boat, as these are identified with gods [4]). In this way the dead obtains power over the boat. In connection with this voyage the dead does not wish to be without a ship (B.21.c, *iw*, p. 241).

Finally concerning the roads the dead has to cover, we may also think of the funeral procession and the funerary voyage, e.g., in the mastabas, where "the glorious roads to the West, on which the venerable walk" are mentioned, where further "uniting oneself with the earth" (i.e., the burial, see p. 163) is mentioned. This road to the place of burial is indicated with the word *mtn* in the passage Urk. IV 1084.15: "May the *ḥś3.t*-cows take you across, may the roads be flooded with their milk, may you join the caves which are in eternity."

Par. 11. Judgment and sentence

To the conceptions about the hereafter also those of the judgment of the dead belong. Ethical considerations play a part here [5]). Man is judged according to his actions. He may be condemned on account of offences against his fellow-men, but also on account of sins against a god and cultic transgressions [6]). One of the most well-known places in literature, where this judgment of the dead occurs, is B.D. 125 [7]).

---

1) C.T. V. 105. b. e. h.
2) C.T. V. 115. a-d.
3) C.T. V. 115. d. e. f; 154. e sqq.
4) C.T. V. 125. a. sqq.
5) J. Spiegel, *Die Idee vom Totengericht in der ägyptischen Religion*, 1935, p. 15.
6) For sin as a crime against men and transgression against God, see J. Spiegel, *Totengericht*, p. 22.
7) Cf. J. Spiegel, *Totengericht*, p. 51 sqq.

The dead appears before Osiris and his 42 [1]) executioners in the hall of the double truth. His heart is balanced against the truth [2]) (C.2.e). A monster, "Devourer of the dead" [3]), is ready to eat him, if the sentence is unfavourable. The dead justifies himself by his "confession". The latter is partly negative: he clears himself from sins: "I bring you the truth and chase evil away for you. I did not do any sins against men ... I did nothing that the gods detest. I did not make any servant suspected with his superiors ... I made nobody suffer from hunger ..." [4]). For another part his defence is positive [5]): "I have pacified the god with that which he favours. I gave bread to the hungry and water to the thirsty" [6]). After in this way having acquitted himself from the 42 sins before the 42 judges the dead hopes to escape the sentence.

This well-known chapter of the judgment of the dead does not stand by itself. Already from the Old Kingdom something similar is known. The expressions used are strictly juridical. Before a court of justice a complaint is lodged against the perpetrator. Re [7]) or Osiris usually act as chief justice. Reminiscences of the lawsuit between Seth and Osiris show their influence. The dead has an opposing party (*ḫfty*, B.17.b) and expresses the wish that the decision may be in his favour. He has a counsel (C.2.d). The judge gives a verdict. If it happens to be unfavourable, the person condemned is assigned to punishment. As it here concerns a judgment on actions, it is not astonishing, that many terms for "sin" are used (chapter I, Par.12). Pyr. 1041 (C.1.a) is a spell in order to prevent somebody being summoned in the realm of the dead before a king or a high official. *Iṯi* is used here in the meaning of "to bring before the court". The dead says of somebody who treats his grave well, he will see that no

---

1) "Hier scheint die Vorstellung mitzuspielen, dass jedes Mitglied des Totengerichts mit der Untersuchung einer Sündengattung speziell befaszt ist", J. Spiegel, *Totengericht*, p. 67.

2) Cf. J. Spiegel, *Totengericht*, p. 68.

3) Naville I, Pl. CXXXVI, Ag; cf. B.D. Budge, 16. 10.

4) B.D. Budge, p. 249. 15-250. 9.

5) The individual case is measured by the general order, J. Spiegel, *Totengericht*, p. 70.

6) B.D. Budge, p. 261. 1, 2.

7) According to J. Spiegel, *Totengericht*, pp. 17, 41, the idea of the judgment of the dead and the norm of justice is originally connected with Re. Osiris, as judge of the dead, is secondary with respect to Re.

reproach (*ʿ3p*) arises against him with the god (C.1.b). So people, who had done something against each other on earth, could make a charge against each other before the judge of the dead and were each other's opponents (*ḫfty*). There are many spells for preventing somebody's own heart taking action against him as a witness before the judge of the dead. The heart is the carrier of the intellectual functions. It has the power of recollection. It is also able to remember somebody's sins and to memorise them before the judge of the dead. The dead wants to prevent his own heart lodging a complaint against him. For this purpose the following terms are used: *Ḥmśi r*, to give evidence against (C.1.g), *śḫnš*, to make stinking (C.1.n), *śḫfḫf*, to oppose (C.1.m), *rḳi*, to rebel (C.1.e), *bṯ*, to desert (C.1.c), *grg*, to speak lies (C.1.q), *ḏbʿ*, (to raise) a rebuke (C.1.s). Also the following words are used for making a charge against somebody in the judgment of the dead: *Śiʿr*, to let (somebody's guilt) approach (C.1.h), *śmi*, to accuse (C.1.k), to "set up" a judgment (*śʿḥʿ*), i.e., to lodge a complaint (C.1.j). In the Pyr. the dead has a prosecutor (*śrḫ.w*, C.1.l) against him before the ferry-man. Consequently the latter only puts the just across, so that the journey to heaven may begin. The dead may be "slandered" (*śḏwy*, literally "to make bad" [1]) (C.1.o). A formal legal term is used, when a god or goddess is refused to go to law (*šn ḫ.t r*) against the dead, in which Osiris is thought of as a judge in a subterranean realm of the dead (C.1.p). That it here concerns sins committed during life on earth appears from B.D. 163 (C.1.r): "Spell in order not to allow that he is reproached for his guilt, which he had on earth" (*ṯsi bt3*) [2]).

The dead appears before a judge, who judges him. The latter makes a judicial decision (*wpi*, literally "to divide", C.2.a). The wisdom of Ani (VII.11) says that already on earth one should go to law against an enemy, even if the god will judge later in the judgment of the dead (*p3 nṯr wp.t p3 m3ʿ*). The term that is by far the most used for judgment of the dead through all periods is *wḏʿ* (*mdw*). This already occurs regularly in the inscriptions against tomb-robbers of the Old Kingdom (C.2.b). When somebody damages the tomb, he will litigate with him before the great god. The god will enter into

---

[1]) Cf. the use in the "negative confession" of B.D. 125: "I have not slandered a servant with his superior." J. Spiegel, *Totengericht*, p. 61; B.D. Budge, p. 250. 8.

[2]) B.D. Budge, p. 411. 1, 2.

judgment with him who does something against the tomb [1]). In this judgment sentence is pronounced [2]) according to the norm of *mꜣꜥ.t* [3]). This idea of justice always plays a part in the judgment, up to B.D. 125. If the dead wins the suit and obtains judgment against the defendant, he may annoy, as a ghost, the tomb robber still living on earth [4]). On the other hand he may intercede for him who treats the tomb well [5]). The just dead is acquitted by Osiris: "You are justified on the day of judgment" [6]). Is it supposed that his judgment of the dead takes place immediately on the day of decease?

The gods which mostly act as judges of the dead are Re and Osiris. Sometimes these two are even combined [7]), probably because both of them are eligible [8]). In C.T. IV. 94.1 there is thought of Re. There the judgment takes place in the "big house of the judge, which is in Heliopolis." In the later "*Livres*" especially Re is looked upon as a judge of the dead, whose journey through the realm of the dead is described. About Re it is said: "He judges those who are on earth" [9]). Judgment takes place according to works [10]). Re judges the enemies of Osiris, "he gives them their bad place in the region of doom on account of these things which they have done". As a just king Re stands up for the weak and humiliates the proud: "To sail by this great god . . . in order to judge in the West, in order to make the great one a small one among the gods who are in the netherworld" [11]). To the same effect four baboons act, judges on the boat of Re, which (C.2.a) divide between the unhappy and the brute [12]). The judgment is twofold; the righteous have a favourable fate, the sinners are condemned, "in order to put the spirits in their places and to deliver

---

1) Urk. I. 226. 6, *wḏꜥ.f mdw ḥnꜥ ỉrty.fy ḫ.t r.ś.*

2) Urk. I. 256. 4.

3) The idea of justice is connected with the sun-god, J. Spiegel, *Totengericht*, p. 22.

4) Urk. I. 260. 12 sqq.

5) Urk. I. 261. 8.

6) C.T. I, 268, d, *hrw wḏꜥ mdw*, cf. *hrw śḏm mdw*, Pyr. 1027. c, the day of hearing; *hrw ḥśb ḳd.w*, the day of counting the characters, C.T. I. 181. e (C.2.g).

7) B.D. 180; 470.14.

8) In B.D. 125, the psychostasy for Osiris, are formulations, which originally refer to Re, J. Spiegel, *Totengericht*, pp. 51, 52.

9) L.Q. XL. 3.

10) L.Q. CXX. 5-6.

11) Book of Gates, I, middle register, B.S. Pl. IV. 17-18.

12) *Wpỉ*, B.D. 126; 269. 7.

the dead to their sentence" [1]). The *3ḫ.w* are the righteous, the term *mt*, the dead, is often used for condemned dead.

Ḥśb ḳd.w, counting the characters, is also a term for the judgment of the dead (C.2.g). "Your sin is driven away, your guilt is wiped out by those who weigh with the scales on the day of counting the characters" [2]). In the judgment the dead is acquitted of guilt. For the latter expressions are used like *śpḫ3* (C.2.j) and *śm3ʿ ḫrw* (C.2.k). *Śḏm mdw*, to hear a person, also belongs to the lawsuit (C.2.l).

A double judgment, a favourable fate for the righteous and an unfavourable one for the sinners is mentioned in the following places: Book of Gates IV, lower register, 2nd figure, B.S. Pl. VI. 26-29. Here beings are pictured, who carry a rope, on which the hieroglyph for *ʿḥʿ.w*, time of life, is drawn. The inscription going with it reads: "Who carry the time of life in the West. They are the ones who fix the time of life, who decide on the days of the souls which are in the West, who deliver up to the place of judgment." The righteous arrive in the West, the normal realm of the dead, the sinners land in the place of destruction (*ḫtmy.t*). About a gate (*śbḫ.t*) in the second hour of the *Livre de la Nuit* it is said: "The first gate, mistress of shudder, high of walls, superior, mistress of the trampling down, which repels the raving one (*ḫśf.t nšny*), which saves the robbed (*nḥm.t ʿw3*). The unfavourable fate which falls upon the sinner, is expressed by "to repel" (*ḫśf*), the favourable one, which is destined for those treated unjustly, by *nḥm* (to save). About the 15th gate in B.D. 146 it is said, that it seizes the enemy by his coil (snake), but extends its hand to the tired one (Osiris). The gates exercise a critical function. They let only the qualified—the righteous—pass.

Judgment takes place according to works. Beatification is a reward for serving god, impiety is liable to be punished by hell. "The jubilants, who are in the netherworld, they exult at Re in the West. They exalt Harakhte. Those who knew Re, while they were on earth, who made offerings to him, rest on their seats. Their glory is in the sacred place of the West. They say to Re: Welcome Re, now that you are near the netherworld. Praise be yours, now that you enter

---

[1]) Book of Gates I, middle register. B.S. Pl. IV. 17-18.
[2]) C.T. I. 181. c-e.

the sacredness of the *Mḥn*-snake (the snake that lies protectingly around the cabin of Re's ship). Re says to them: Offerings belong to you, oh beatified ones. I am content with what you have done for me, when I rose in the East of heaven and when I went down into the sanctuary of my eye" [1]). Beatitude in the hereafter is a reward for serving the god during life on earth. This serving is indicated by the word *rḫ* = to know, which is more than an intellectual knowing and comes near to loving the god. The just are rewarded by the same as what they have done on earth. They made offerings to Re. Now they themselves receive offerings for the dead, which are essential for their survival. For the beatified the word *ḥtpy.w* is used, cf. Book of Gates I, upper register, B.S. Pl. IV. There also they are men who have served Re and have offered to him. In this place there is a pun with the verb *ḥtp*, to be content [2]). Perhaps this word means "offerer" in connection with *ḥtp* = offering [3]). The beatified do the same things in the hereafter as during their life on earth, that is to say they praise Re. The times of the rising of the sun and its setting are the opportunities for extolling the sun-god. The expression "praising Re at sunrise and sunset" often occurs [4]). The beatified are rewarded, because they have taken the part of Osiris [5]); "To speak words through this great god to the gods who are in this field, . . . the *ḥtpty.w*" (cf. *ḥtpy.w* in Book of Gates IV; *ḥtpty.w*, Book of Gates I). Offerings and strength belong to you. "You save Osiris from those who do this, who perform robbery against him." In this retaliation reward and punishment are in accordance with the deeds accomplished during life on earth. Those who have sinned against Re, are tied to torture-posts (*wśr.t*) [6]). The inscription to it reads: "Oh gods, who are behind the *wśr.t*-posts, who are behind Geb, the prince, seize the enemies, watch over the evil-doers. May they not escape from your hands, may they not get clear of your fingers. Oh enemies, be con-

---

1) Book of Gates, IV, upper register, B.S. Pl. VII. 1-VI. 17.

2) *Ḥtp.w n.ṯn ḥtpy.w ḥtp.n.ỉ m ʾir.t.n.ṯn*, Book of Gates, upper register, B.S. Pl. VI. 12-14.

3) Wb. III. 195. 3.

4) Cf. *Belegstellen* Wb. I. 292. 11. B.D. 15A praises Re at his rising, 15B at his setting.

5) Am Duat VI, 7-17.

6) Book of Gates V, middle register, B.S. Pl. XVIII. 12-42; E. Lefébure, M.M.A.F.C. III, 1, Pl. XXX. 26-Pl. XXXI. 43.

sidered to be exterminated, as Re has ordered, when he founded *'Igr.t* for his corpse, when he created the *d3.t* for the parts of his body. He assigns you to your slaughter. He counts you out to what you have done in the great hall of Re." The idea is: they are treated just as badly as they have treated Re. In the upper register of the same gate the reward of the just is described. Their fate in the hereafter also is similar to their behaviour on earth: "Those who offered incense to their gods and performed purifications for their kas, who did not keep any spirit off from his breath (= life) and any dead from his libations, they are in their offerings. Their gods and their kas approach them. Their portions belong to them. They go in to their offering cakes in the hall, which feeds its gods" [1]. Those who have acted well on earth by offering to the gods and the dead, are rewarded in the same way. They also obtain their funerary offerings.

The text continues: "Those who did the truth, when being on earth, who fought for their gods, they are called to rejoicing. Those who lived on justice, their justice will be to their credit before the great god, who extirpates evil" [2]. Osiris says to them: "You are just, oh *m3ʿty.w*, you have peace by what you have done, like the figures that are behind me" [3]. Those who have done justice, now also receive *m3ʿ.t*. They are justified. Confer *śip.f ṯn n ir.t.n.ṯn*, he counts you out to what you (the sinners) have done, with *śip.tw n.śn m3ʿ.t.śn* and *ḥtp.ṯn m ir.t.n.ṯn*. *Śip* is *vox media*, to count somebody to a punishment or favourable fate, to blame or credit a person for something. In both cases also *ir.t.n.ṯn* is used. The judgment takes place according to works. Also in the "*Livre de la nuit*" the just are rewarded in the hereafter with the same as they did on earth [4]. "Those who were on earth, while offering frankincense to the gods, who are in the *d3.t*, they are in the retinue of this god. Meals are given to them. They will not be repelled from the gates of the lords of offerings (*śb3.w nw nb.w ḫr.w*). Your head-gear is removed, your bandages are loosened. Your bread is not cut down."

---

[1]) Book of Gates V, upper register, E. Lefébure, M.M.A.F.C. III, 1, Pl. XXX. 1-11.

[2]) Book of Gates V, upper register, E. Lefébure, M.M.A.F.C. III, 1, Pl. XXX. 23-XXXI. 30.

[3]) Book of Gates V, upper register, E. Lefébure, M.M.A.F.C. III, 1, Pl. XXXI, 30-34.

[4]) XIth hour.

The idea of retaliation as punishment of the god during life on earth, the nature of the punishment being in accordance with that of the crime, occurs in the wisdom of Ptahhotep [1]): "Do not be anxious as a man. God punishes with the same. If somebody thinks of living on it, he is without bread in his mouth." The idea is: If somebody is worried about his daily bread, God punishes him with hunger. In the lower register of the Book of Gates Atum punishes those who have sinned against Re [2]). First their sins are enumerated. They have thrown a (slanderous) testimony and poured out their voices against Akhte [3]). They are punished with the same as what they have done wrong: "The giving of evidence (*ḥwỉ mtr*) belongs to you in an evil way. Your slander (*wš3.w*) belongs to you in an evil way (*bỉn*). The inspection with my father (*śỉp*) belongs to you" (C.1.f), Book of Gates I, lower register, B.S. Pl. IV, 28-32. The punishment is of the same nature as the sin.

The dead must appear before a court of justice. The terms most used for it are *ḳnb.t* (C.3.h) and *ḏ3ḏ3.t* (C.3.i). Re and Osiris have such a council with them and each god can have one [4]). That *ḏ3ḏ3.t* already occurs in the Old Kingdom, points to the high age of the representation of the judgment of the dead. The king [5]) must first justify himself before a court of justice and after that he may sail to heaven (C.3.i). Tomb-robbers are threatened with a judgment in the council of the great god [6]).

In the bible the view occurs that the pious themselves help judging God's enemies, who are also their enemies. "You shall trample upon the wicked, for they shall be dust under the soles of your feet on the day I am about to make, says the Lord God of Hosts" [7]). "And I saw thrones and seated on them were those to whom judgment was committed" [8]). "I give power over the heathens to him who conquers and he shall rule them with a rod of iron" [9]). "He who

---

[1]) 99 sqq.
[2]) *Ḏ3ty.w* from *ḏ3ỉ*, to put oneself in the way in a hostile manner.
[3]) Akhte = Re; *ḥwỉ mtr*; *wš3 ḫrw*.
[4]) *Ḏ3ḏ3.t n.t nṯr nb nṯr.t nb.t*, C.T. IV. 333. f.
[5]) Pyr. 1776. a.
[6]) Urk. I. 202. 9.
[7]) Malachi 4: 1-3.
[8]) Rev. 20: 4.
[9]) Rev. 2: 26.

conquers, I will grant him to sit with me on my throne" [1]). "Or do you not know that the saints will judge the world?" [2]). "Truly, I say to you, you, who have followed me, will also sit on twelve thrones in the re-birth, when the son of man will sit on the throne of his glory in order to judge the twelve tribes of Israel" [3]). This theme that the beatified, who are acquitted in the judgment of the council, will now in their turn also judge over other dead, is found in the Egyptian texts too. The following description occurs about the spirits (*3ḫ.w*), who receive their regular funerary offerings: "They are the ones who judge at this gate [4]), who interrogate those who are in it. Re says to them: Hail to you, gods, council of judges [5]), which judges the dead [6]), but puts the divine son (Horus) on his throne. Your justice belongs to you" [7]). To that they reply to Re: "We execute the judgment over the dead [8]). We protect the spirits." The *mt.w*, the condemned dead, stand in contrast with the beatified *3ḫ.w*, both used proleptically here of those who will become dead and spirits after the judgment. The just, who, as a reward for their justice regularly receive funerary offerings, form themselves a council of judges to assist Re. They condemn the unjust. Near a picture of twelve men the following description occurs [9]): "The souls of the people (*rmṯ.w*) who are in the *d3.t*. Who spoke the truth on earth. Who held the way of life of the god in esteem. Re says to them: Well-being for your souls, breath for your noses. Estates belong to you in the *ʾI3r.w*-field. Your (towns) of the just belong to you. Your seats belong to you, in order to be like a council (*ḳnb.t*, C.3.h), where those who are in me, judge." Here it regards people, who have been just on earth and who have served Re. They obtain a happy fate in the hereafter. They reap their *ʾI3r.w*-fields. Now they themselves are in their turn a council for judging others. They are

---

1) Rev. 3: 21.
2) Cor. 6: 2.
3) Matth. 19: 28.
4) *Ntśn wḏʿ r śbḫ.t tn*, C.2.b.
5) *Ḏ3ḏ3.t n.t wḏʿ y.w*.
6) *Wḏʿ.w*.
7) Book of Gates VI, lower register, E. Lefébure, M.M.A.F.C. III, 1, Pl. XXXIV, 31-41; Cenotaph Seti I, Vol. II, Pl. LX.
8) *ʾIw ir.n wḏʿ.w mt.w*.
9) Book of Gates IV, middle register, 2nd figure, b.S. Pl. VI. 31-39.

suitable for it, for judging is exercising *m3ʿ.t* and during their life on earth they have always practised *m3ʿ.t*. The *nb.w m3ʿ.t*, owners of justice, should perhaps also be taken as righteous dead, who are now judges themselves (C.3.c). The same is the case with the *nb.w ḫ.t* (or *ḫr.t*), the owners of offerings. So it occurs frequently in the Book of Gates that those who have offered on earth, now receive funerary offerings themselves. Only the just receive these offerings and so they are *nb.w ḫ.t*, who also judge over the dead (C.3.c). Atum has a council with him [1]), which punishes Apophis. The members of that council regularly receive offerings. They are just, who may participate in the judgment.

They also sit on the council that destroys the enemies of Re [2]), who live on the immaterial offering of justification (*m3ʿ ḫrw*). The *imy.w ḫt Wśir* (B.16.d) are also such figures. They annihilate [3]) those who perform bad deeds against Osiris. It is said to them just as to the beatified dead: "Breath for your nose, ... hearing for your ears, ... your offerings belong to you on earth." So they are just men, who, as a reward for their righteousness, regularly receive funerary offerings.

They may, as friends of Osiris, punish the latter's enemies. They have, already on earth, always chosen the side of Osiris against the latter's enemies. Also in the C.T. it is said that the dead is in the retinue of Osiris. There he is among the *iry.w ʿ.wt*, the keepers of the chambers who a.o. appear in B.D. 92 and who, together with Osiris, execute the judgment of the dead [4]): "I am among the followers of Osiris [5]), with those who are in the retinue, the keepers of the chambers (of) Osiris, who are on the throne in the hidden room." Already in the Pyr. Texts the idea occurs that the righteous judges together with Re. There it concerns the person of the king, to whom it is said at his ascension [6]): "Sit down on your wonderful throne, that you may judge together with the two Enneads" [7]). Also in Pyr. 1168.c the king participates in the judgment of the dead, "he hears the people"

---

1) Book of Gates II, lower register, B.S. Pl. III.
2) Book of Gates IV, lower register, B.S. Pl. VI. 38-40.
3) Am Duat III, 197; 201. 202.
4) C.T. VI. 176. h-j.
5) *Wnn.i m.m imy.w ḫt Wśir.*
6) Pyr. Neith 765.
7) *Wḏʿ.k mdw*, C.2.b.

(C.2.l). The dead judges together with Re in the latter's boat [1]). A few passages from the *Lebensmüde* also give the impression of regarding the participation of the just, who is with Re, in the judgment over the godless [2]): "Truly, he who is yonder, will be a living god, whilst he punishes the sin of him who commits it; truly, he who is yonder, will stand in the sun-boat."

After having passed sentence the condemned is assigned to punishment. The verb *śip* is very common here (C.4.a), although in itself it is a *vox media* and may also be used in a favourable sense, e.g., of just people [3]): "Their righteousness will be counted out to them." The verb *rdỉ* is used of being delivered to punishment (C.4.d). It may also have the meaning of "to retaliate" [4]): "This evil spell . . . may it not be retaliated upon me" [5]).

Finally the punishment is executed. From the verb *nỉk* (C.5.b) the identical name for Apophis is derived, as the evil one, who has to be punished. The verb *śswn*, to punish (C.5.e), originally means to destroy. Thus it is often close to *ḥtm*. In L.Q. XLI. 7 it is parallel with *wd r ḥtm.t*, to bring ruin upon. Compare also the following passage [6]): "I punish my enemies . . . in the place of destruction (*ḥtmy.t*)."

Punishment is considered to be everlasting (C.5.g). The sinners do not escape their judges (*n prỉ*). In the Book of Gates the netherworld (*d3.t*) is called: "of a lasting nature" (*mn.t śḫr.w*), which means that what is decided there, is irrevocable.

Par. 12. Terms for sin

a. Words, which mean bad in a non-moral sense.

Ḏw (C.6.y) is also used for the unpleasant smell (*śṯỉ*) of a corpse (Wb. V. 547. 1), of disaster or disease, which befall somebody (Wb. V. 546. 15), of bad dreams or restless sleep (Wb. V. 546. 7) and of unfavourable days (Wb. V. 546. 2). *Bỉn* stands in contrast with *nfr* (C.6.i), in the sense of unpleasant, e.g., of the complaints of old age

[1]) C.T. II. 140. b, C.2.b. Idem Pyr. 273 (C.2.b).

[2]) *Lebensmüde* 142-144.

[3]) Book of Gates V, upper register, B.S. Pl. XVIII. 19. 20; E. Lefébure, M.M.A.F.C. III, 1, Pl. XXXI. 27. 28.

[4]) B.D. 105; 216. 14.

[5]) *N rdỉ n.ỉ.*

[6]) L.Q. XXXVII. 8.

(p. 288). It is used for milk having become sour (Wb. I. 443. 9), for miserable circumstances (Wb. I. 443, 1). Terms like *dw* and *bin* describe sin as that which is depraved or ugly. From there they have got a moral meaning.

b. Words for disaster and misery.

To these the following terms belong: *'Iw* in the meaning of misery (C.6.a). People with a dismal fate in the realm of the dead are called "the sufferers of the West" [1]). A passage from the wisdom of Ptahhotep [2]), where the calm and the hot-tempered one are opposed, reads: "If you are a man of influence, you have to inspire awe for you by knowledge and by speaking quietly. Do not give any orders, unless it is suitable. He who is hot-tempered in speaking gets into misery" [3]). *'Iw* stands in contrast with *mnh* in the following passage from the wisdom of Ptahhotep [4]): "Seek all excellence for yourself, till your management is without evil." *Mnh śhr.w* means "efficient of management" and is used of the king, who rules the country well. Where it stands in contrast with *mnh*, *iw* means that something does not yield any result [5]).

'b (C.6.f) is used in the meaning of disaster beside *śdb*, damage [6]). These terms express that he who sins is in a miserable position, brings misery on himself, has no success.

c. Words for being bent.

Hbn (C.6.m) is written with the bent arm in Pyr. 1041. d. *Hbn hrw* is the opposite of *m3' hrw*. The first means "crooked of voice", the second "straight of voice". *M3'* is originally straight of direction and gets a moral meaning afterwards. The meaning "crooked" is more clear in *h3b.t* (C.6.n), derived from the verb *h3b*, to be crooked. *H3b* is determined by a sickle. *H3b.t* is the thread of the red crown, thus called on account of the bent form. In a moral sense it is used,

---

[1]) C.T. I. 189. b; Wb. I. 48. 10, *hry iw* = *der Bedrückte.*
[2]) Prisse XI. 11. 12.
[3]) *Iw štm 'k.f n iw.t.*
[4]) Prisse VI. 4. 5.
[5]) Wb. II. 85. 26. J. Zandee, *De hymnen aan Amon van Papyrus Leiden* (The hymns to Amon from Papyrus Leiden) *I* 350, p. 61.
[6]) C.T. III. 293. b.

for instance, in an autobiography [1]: "I never said anything to anybody in an evil, bad and wicked manner" (*ḏw, ỉw, ḫ3b*).

d. Words for taboo.

Herewith sin is described as something that lies in a fenced off and protected field, which man may not touch, which he must respect. *Ḫww* (C.6.l) is connected with *ḫwỉ* = to protect, which sometimes also has the meaning of "respected" or "sacred" [2]). This fits in with the idea of taboo; that which is protected, must be respected.

The term *ṯry.t* (C.6.u) is probably connected with *twr* = to respect. Also this fits in with the idea of taboo, the sinful is the domain on which man may not tread, which he must respect.

e. Ṯmś = red (C.6.w).

The words *ṯmś.w* for sin and *ṯmś* = red may be connected with each other. Here red is considered an unfavourable colour.

f. Wn = guilt (C.6.g).

This occurs beside *śrḫ* = reproach. It means something with which may be found fault.

g. Ḳn = damage (C.6.s).

This word is also used in connection with famine. It is sin as a defect, a word, which in English too has a moral meaning.

h. Sin as rebellion against deity.

To this points the terms *rḳw* (C.7.e) and *śby* (p. 296). In the "*Livres*" punished sinners, who have rebelled against Osiris or Re during their life on earth, are continually mentioned. Apophis is considered the chief devil and the principal of the rebels against Re. Also *ḫfty*, enemy (of the god. B.17.d), belongs to this category.

i. Sin as transgression.

Tḥỉ (C.6.v) is "to commit a transgression." It is also used of overstepping a limit. (Wb. V. 320. 12). Cf. Wb. 5. 320. 14, to cross some-

---

[1]) Urk. I. 204. 9.
[2]) Wb. III. 245. 5-9.

body's way = to become unfaithful to somebody. The latter is close to *ḏ3i* (Wb. V. 514, 14-17) = to put oneself in somebody's way as an enemy, sometimes together with a substantive for "way". From this *ḏ3y.t*, recalcitrance, transgression is derived [1]). A sin is a transgression of the code of morals.

j. Sp = case.

Sp is a *vox media* and means case, sometimes character. Without an adjective for "evil" going with it it may also be used in the meaning of "guilt". In an autobiography somebody enumerates his good deeds and says: "My *sp* has not gone in it", i.e., "I have not been deficient in it" [2]).

k. ʾIsf.t.

The most usual term for sin is *ʾisf.t* (C.6.d). It is often opposed to *m3ʿ.t* and parallel with *grg*, lie. The king restores order by ascending the throne. The sun in rising chases darkness away. About both it is said that they bring *m3ʿ.t* instead of *ʾisf.t*, order instead of disorder, chaos.

The etymology of *ʾisf* is "to wear out". *ʾIsf.t* is determined with the sign for a strip of cloth. Sethe thinks of a connection with the word *śsf*, "*dünnes Gewebe*" [3]). The causative is *śisf* [4]), which stands in parallelism with *śḥtm*. "My lord, who destroys the lie, (*śisf grg*), who creates the truth, who creates everything that is good, who destroys everything that is evil" [5]). *ʾIsf.t* would mean literally: "What is worn out, what is flimsy".

---

1) Wb. V. 518. 3 sqq, see p. 294 and cf. *ḏ3ty.w*, opponents (C.7.i).
2) Urk. IV. 484. 8.
3) Pyr. 265. c and commentary of Sethe on this. See also Sethe. Dramat. Texte, p. 216.
4) Wb. IV. 40. 5 inserted as *śis*.
5) The eloquent Peasant, B 1, 241. Read *śḥtm bw nb ḏw*.

CHAPTER TWO

TERMS

A. Death in contrast with life

In the following death is treated as a general phenomenon, as a fate, which hangs over everybody. Death is feared as a destruction: man ceases to exist. His body decays. The relations experience the death of their relative as a being snatched away. The realm of the dead is a place of darkness. So it does not concern here special dangers of the realm of the dead or punishments, which strike the one and not the other, but it regards death as destroying full life on earth. It may happen, however, that, what was at first considered as everybody's fate, was deemed afterwards a punishment for the godless only. In that case also these data from the texts are dealt with under A.

*A.*1. *Total destruction. Terms which describe death as a ceasing to exist, a being destroyed totally.*

A.1.a. *3ḳ*, to be destroyed.

The passing away is lamented, the dead is deplored. His dying is a loss. The wailing-women sing at the funeral: "Woe, woe, hail, hail, hail, hail. Lament indefatigably. Alas, what a loss (*3ḳy.t*). The good shepherd has gone away to the land of eternity" [1]).

A.1.b. *wn*, to pass.

The inevitability of death is described as follows [2]): "Think, oh heart, of this day of death, may it be placed in the heart of one who has a funeral, for truly, there is nobody, who gets past it (*wn*); the strong and the weak together, who sails to the north and to the south in his time of life, lands after that on the bank."

A.1.c. *mt*, to die.

Only in the eyes of the *Lebensmüde* death is something favourable, especially because he is convinced that he will be well of in the here-

---

[1]) Tomb of Neferhotep, time of Eye, E. Lüddeckens, *Totenklagen*, p. 112.

[2]) M. Lichtheim, The songs of the harpers, J.N.E.S. IV, Pl. I, 1-2.

after with Re: "Today death is in my eyes as when a sick person gets well, as going out after illness" [1]).

For him, who loves life on the contrary, death is an undesired situation which stands in contrast with the good life on earth (*ʿnḫ*). The texts which are sent along with the dead into his tomb, deny with the greatest emphasis that he has died. These texts have a magical effect. By denying death they annihilate him and revive the dead. In the meantime these texts show that death as an absolute destruction is feared. Some examples of this follow:

Pyramid Texts: "N.N. has not died a death" [2]). "Rise, N.N., you will not die" [3]). "N.N. is the successor of Re. He does not die" [4]). Pyr. 1477 is a warning of the sun-god to Seth, who wants to kill Osiris: "Did you act against him, did you think that he would die? He does not die. N.N. lives eternally." The king does not remain dead, no more than Osiris after the attacks of Seth. "He will not die, his name will not perish" [5]). From this place it appears that *mt* is "non-being", "ceasing to exist". "Take N.N. by the arm, take N.N. to heaven, that N.N. may not die on earth among men" [6]). Immortality is only for the king, not for the common people.

Coffin Texts: The shortest form is the simple denial of being dead: "I do not die" [7]). Death is undone by an ascension. "You cross to the offering fields among your brothers, amidst those—that is to say those people—who say: You died a death. I let not die you dying with a death, oh great one of sleep, great one of fatigue" [8]). "N.N. returns to life after dying like Re every day" [9]). From a resurrection text: "Stand up, rise to life, do not die" [10]). "Spell in order to return to life after death . . . I repeat life after dying like Atum, every day . . . I revive after dying" [11]). The dead is identified with Osiris or with the sun-god, so that he rises like them. "N.N. has passed the night like this great one who has fallen on his side . . ., whom the two women (Isis and Nephthys over Osiris) have mentioned. This N.N. does not remain dead . . . (title) in order not to remain dead" [12]). Death is considered something unfavourable, where it is

1) *Lebensmüde*, 130, 131.
2) Pyr. 350. b.
3) Pyr. 792. c.
4) Pyr. 1464. c.
5) Pyr. 1812. c.
6) Pyr. 604. e. f.
7) C.T. III. 349. e.
8) C.T. I. 300. b-f.
9) C.T. V. 263. a.
10) C.T. I. 207. b.
11) C.T. V. 290. a; 291. k. n.
12) C.T. VI. 304. h. j. m. o.

put on a level with ruin and destruction and is rejected as such: "I do not fall, I do not go under, I do not perish, I do not die" [1]).

In a later text the intercourse with a deceased person in the realm of the dead is opposed to the ascension: "Atum promises me his goodness. He saves me from *Nḥbk3.w*. He makes me land in the *3ḫ.t* of heaven. I do not die in the realm of the dead. He treats my soul with respect. He makes my corpse glorious. He makes my body live again [2]) (*ḏd n.ỉ Tm nfr.w.f św3ḏ.f wỉ m.ʿ Nḥbk3.w rdỉ.f s3ḥ.ỉ t3 m 3ḫ.t n.t p.t nn mt.ỉ m ẖr.t nṯr try.f b3.ỉ s3ḫ.f ẖ3.t.ỉ sʿnḫ.f ḥʿ.ỉ m wḥm*)."

The summons of death is inexorable. Therefore he is feared. Nobody can avert him: "As regards death, "Come" is his name (pun upon *mt* and *mỉ*). All whom he calls to him come immediately. Their hearts are afraid from fear of him. There is nobody who will see him among god and men. Great ones are with him like poor ones. There is nobody who repels his evil from himself" [3]). The same denomination of death is mentioned in a harper's song from the 19th dynasty [4]): "Remember this day of "Come", in order to draw you to the West."

Against death being so alarming the advice is given to enjoy life: "Celebrate a very happy day." The soul of the *Lebensmüde* gives the same advice: Funerary offerings are of no avail. The fate cf the dead in the hereafter is sad. "Listen to me. Behold, listening is good for a man. Follow a beautiful day. Forget trouble" [5]). This point of view of "Carpe diem" also occurs in the Antef song [6]), where at the same time the opinion of the soul of the *Lebensmüde* is given that funeral liturgy is of no avail: "Rejoice, in order to make your heart forget the funeral liturgy (the spells of glorification said by a priest). Live for pleasure as long as you live. Put myrrh on your head. Dress yourself in linen." "Celebrate a gay day. Do not get tired of it" [7]). Thus in these younger texts human feelings are more voiced, from

---

[1]) C.T. VI. 134. i.

[2]) Louvre 3865. IV. 2-4 (not edited).

[3]) Erman, *Zwei Grabsteine Griechischer Zeit*, *Festschrift Sachau*, p. 110.

[4]) M. Lichtheim, The songs of the harpers, J.N.E.S. IV. p. 203.

[5]) *Lebensmüde* 67.

[6]) W. Max Müller, *Liebespoesie* XII. 9; M. Lichtheim, The songs of the harpers, p. 192, 193.

[7]) W. Max Müller, *Liebespoesie* XIV. 2.

which it appears that death is feared on account of its hardness and of extinguishing full life.

A.1.d. *n wn*; *tm*, not to be.

Death is considered a not-to-be, a total ceasing of existence. This is the case in a Pyramid Text, where it is said, that the dead king rises and where this not-to-be is denied: "Get up, do not perish, do not go under" [1]). The same usage occurs in the C.T., where *tm* is also parallel with *śki*, to perish: "I do not go under, I do not perish in this land to all eternity" [2]). "Osiris N.N. does not perish" [3]). Tomb robbers, who make survival impossible, are threatened themselves with eternal destruction: "As regards any priest of the dead and any man who will disturb it (the tomb), he shall not exist, his son shall not exist on his seat" [4]). In order to escape eternal destruction the dead identifies himself with a god and then says: "I shall not perish" (*nn tm.i*) [5]).

In the tombs of the kings of the New Kingdom wrong-doers are punished in the netherworld with total destruction, so that they do not exist any more. About those, who are chastised by Atum, it is said: "Your souls belong to non-being" [6]). If the substances of the soul which are essential to survival, are damaged, man himself also perishes. About enemies of Osiris, who are burnt by the fire of a snake: "You are not, oh non-beings" [7]). Horus punishes the enemies of his father Osiris. About the latter it is said: "You do not exist. Your soul is destroyed. It does not live in consequence of what you have done against my father Osiris" [8]). The not-to-be is not inherent to death in this case, but is inflicted as a punishment. Uraeus snakes destroy the dead, but they do not harm the king. "King N.N. knows them, he sees their shape. He does not perish through their flames" [9]). About punished enemies of Osiris in the netherworld it is said:

---

[1]) Pyr. 1299. c.
[2]) C.T. Spell 540; VI. 136. s.
[3]) C.T. VI. 163. h.
[4]) Middle Kingdom, Beni Hassan, Sottas, *La Préservation de la Propriété funéraire*, p. 53.
[5]) B.D. 8; 30. 9.
[6]) Book of Gates I, lower register, B.S. Pl. IV. 37-III. 38.
[7]) Book of Gates VIII, lower register, B.S. Pl. XIV. 33, 34.
[8]) Book of Gates VIII, lower register, B.S. Pl. XIV. 20-24.
[9]) Am Duat IX. 99.

"Oh enemies of the ruler of the *d3.t*, Osiris, who is in the West, behold, I assign you to destruction, I count you out to non-existence" [1]).

The thought of total destruction is also present there where complaints are raised about the uselessness of the care for the funeral. Tomb monuments go to ruin and consequently the possibility of survival for the one buried there comes to an end. In the song of king Antef [2]) it reads: "The gods who once were, rest in their pyramids; the noble ones and the spirits are also buried in their pyramids . . . Their places do not exist anymore. What has become of them? Their walls have gone to ruin, their places do not exist, as if they never had been." The same pessimism is present where it is suggested that a past generation has perished for ever [3]): "Generations pass by since the time of the god. Descendants come in their places."

A.1.e. *n ḫpr*, not to become.

This term has the same meaning as A.1.d. About enemies of Osiris, who are destroyed, it is said in the tombs of the kings: "You do not become" [4]). Compare with this what the annals say about defeated enemies of the king [5]): "He who fled was one who was placed on his side (i.e., killed) like those who have not come into being." So the king destroys the rebels and they become as if they had never existed. Also in the Bible this saying occurs [6]): "And they (the Edomites) shall become as if they had never existed."

A.1.f. *ḥtm*, to perish.

Ḥtm means to destroy, to exterminate, and may be applied to death, which destroys life. Usually also this term stands in the negative form as something the dead does not want to suffer. Meaning and usage are close to the term *śkì*, A.1.h.

A dead, who is in a happy position in the hereafter, says [7]): "I do not perish there to all eternity." "If you think that this N.N. descends in order to purge himself beside this *ʾIśnw*, the lord of destruction,

---

[1]) L.Q. XXV. 1-2.

[2]) M. Lichtheim, The songs of the harpers, 192, 193; W. Max Müller, *Liebespoesie*, Pl. XII. 4.

[3]) M. Lichtheim, op. cit., 195; W. Max Müller, *Liebespoesie* I. 2.

[4]) Am Duat XI. 77.

[5]) Urk. IV. 7. 6; cf. 6. 14, "his gang was not existing", *m tm.t ḫpr*.

[6]) Obadja 16, וְהָיוּ כְּלוֹא הָיוּ.

[7]) C.T. III. 359. c.

this N.N. will repel him like this tom-cat" [1]). "He has given me the beautiful West, which destroys the living" [2]). "The Ennead that watches, may they give awakening to Osiris N.N.; he does not perish to all eternity" [3]).

A.1.g. *sỉ*, to perish.

Pyr. 145. a: There is no seed of a god, which has perished, one who belongs to him, and thus you also shall not perish, one who belongs to him.

A.1.h. *śkỉ*, to perish.

Compare for the use *ḥtm*, A.1.f. The deceased does not go down in death. He rises, he sails to heaven, so it is said in spells for the dead. But the background of this is the fear that death means destruction. In an ascension text we read: "You will not go down. You will not perish to all eternity" [4]). About enemies of the dead, who are thrown into the water and drown, it is said: "Your enemies perish, they perish" [5]). When the dead king is received among the gods, he is safe from destruction: "Put me among the gods, who do not know destruction, that I may land among them. He cannot go down, he cannot perish" [6]). "You do not perish, your *kꜣ* does not perish, you are a *kꜣ*" [7]).

In inscriptions of spells for the dead and rubrics it is said that he, who knows the spell, will not go down. "Spell in order not to perish and to be alive" [8]). *Śkỉ* stands in contrast with *ꜥnḫ*. "He who performs this ritual, does not go down. He is a sacred god. No evil hurts him . . . he does not die for the second time" [9]). A rubric of a spell from the C.T. reads: "Not to go down to all eternity" [10]).

About the body or the separate parts of the body it is said, that they do not perish. In order to be able to survive the body also has to remain intact. For this purpose parts of the body are identified

---

1) C.T. VI. 316. r; 317. a.
2) B.D. 32; 100. 3.
3) B.D. 168; 432. 1.
4) Pyr. 764. b.
5) Pyr. 2186. a.
6) Pyr. 1760. Parallelism of *ḥtm* and *śkỉ* also C.T. I. 295. a and B.D. 89; 190. 14.
7) Pyr. 149. d.
8) B.D. 46; 120. 11.
9) B.D. 136 A; 300. 4.
10) C.T. Spell 258; III. 371. a.

with gods [1]). In the *ḥtp*-field the dead lives in abundance. He says: "My heart does not perish there" [2]). "I do not perish, my name does not get lost" [3]). "My corpse is lasting, it does not perish, it does not go to pot in this land to all eternity" [4]). "Spell in order not to allow somebody's corpse perishing in the realm of the dead . . . and to make his flesh and bones safe from the worms" [5]). "It is the arms of N.N., which support Nut as those of Shu, while his bones are of bronze and his body is imperishable" [6]).

In a text, in which the dead is identified with the scribe of Hathor, *śkỉ* is parallel with *tm* (A.1.d) = not to be: "I do not perish, I do not go down in this land to all eternity" [7]). Cf. C.T. VI. 134. i, where *Śkỉ* is parallel with *ḫr*, to fall, *mt*, to die and a verb, which should probably be read *snsn* and which C.T. VI. 173. m is parallel with *whn* = to devastate. A ritual funeral bewares of destruction: "To take his place in the coffin, to be buried in the western necropolis, to remain on earth in health, without going down to all eternity" [8]). *Śkỉ* is used transitively in the following passage: The great Bastet, the mistress of Bubastis, destroys him who destroys the structure of the tomb to all eternity. His son shall not be after him to all eternity" [9]).

A.1.i. *š3y*, fate.

Death is the fixed fate of mankind: "His fate of death is coming, in order to fetch him" [10]). Death as such is called "fate", e.g., in the songs of the harpers: "The good fate has set in" [11]). No alteration of the days which are measured out takes place. Fate checks them accurately and makes somebody die, when his day has come: "Fate counts his days" [12]). "Fate does not stop counting his days and his appropriate time, nothing is added to them" [13]). Nevertheless some-

---

1) Pyr. 149.
2) B.D. 110; C.T. V. 346. a.
3) C.T. IV. 93. p-q. Of the name also Pyr. 1812. c; C.T. II. 253. g.
4) B.D. 154; 402. 2.
5) B.D. 163; 410. 16.
6) Pyr. 1454.
7) C.T. VI. 136. s.
8) Urk. IV. 146. 17-147. 3.
9) Sottas, *Préservation*, p. 158.
10) Wisdom of Ani VII. 12.
11) W. Max Müller, *Liebespoesie* I. 2, M. Lichtheim, Songs of the harpers, p. 195.
12) M. Lichtheim, op. cit., 195; W. Max Müller, *Liebespoesie* I. 16.
13) M. Lichtheim, op. cit., p. 203, tomb of Paser; Pl. III. 11-12.

times the idea occurs that a god grants somebody a longer life than was originally allotted to him [1]).

A.2. *Passing away.*

The dead leaves the world of the living. He goes to another country. He leaves his relatives on earth behind.

A.2.a. *ii*, to come.

The deceased has left his world behind him and now arrives in the realm of the dead. In a spell, serving as a defence against demons, who hasten somebody's death, it says [2]): "You cut off the head, you cut off the neck of your male and female enemies, who bring your death near, who hasten your coming, who say to the god on the day of judgment: "Fetch him." *'Ii* is parrallel here to *mt*.

A.2.b. *isi*, to pass away.

A Pyramid Text says about the king's dying and resurrection [3]): "It is N.N. who goes (passes away, dies); it is N.N., who comes (returns, revives)." In the same way the term *isi* is used in the C.T. with, as a contrast, *ii*, to return. *'Isi* means to die, *ii* to return to life. In a text concerning re-birth it says [4]): "I was conceived in the night, I was born in the day-time. I passed away yesterday and returned today" [5]). Compare also the following places [6]): "I am the scribe of him who passes away and returns." "I died yesterday. I have returned tomorrow, I have risen today" [7]). *'Isi* alternates with *mt* [8]). So it is an equivalent of dying.

A.2.c. *w3i*, to be far.

The relative experiences the death of the beloved as a being left behind by him. The dead has gone far away. A widow says so in a

---

[1]) G. Thausing, *Der Ägyptische Schicksalsbegriff*, M.D.A.I.K. Bd. 8; C. J. Bleeker, *Die Idee des Schicksals in der altäg. Rel.* NUMEN II p. 28; J. Zandee, *De hymnen aan Amon* (The Hymns to Amon), p. 56, 58. In B.D. 71. 20, 21, Naville II, p. 153 we read: "He gives . . . many days to my days of life, etc. . . . till I pass away." Cf. Ps. 61: 7; 2 Kings 20: 6.

[2]) C.T. I. 72. b-73. b.

[3]) Pyr. 1193. b.

[4]) C.T. VI. 86. e.f.

[5]) Cf. VI. 89. a.b., 90. j. k, 91. e.

[6]) C.T. VI. 90. i.

[7]) C.T. VI. 100. c.e.

[8]) In VI. 89. a there is a variant *sbi*, to pass by.

lamentation at the funeral when holding the mummy [1]): "You good father, my being far from you, how is that?

A.2.d. *prỉ*, to go forth.

Man must arrange his tomb in time. Before he sets out on his journey, he must know the place of his destination [2]): "Do not leave your house, when you do not know the place where to rest."

A.2.e. *mnỉ*, to land.

The well-known "euphemism" for dying, "to land", should probably also be classified under the category of dying as setting on one's journey. This time the image is a voyage by ship. In the *Zweiwegebuch* at the end of the blue waterway it says [3]): "Spell in order to be in the *Ḥtp*-field among the followers of Osiris, among the followers of Thoth, every day. They eat bread among the living. They do not "land". There is air in their noses. It is the place of the spirit which does not "land"". "He does not land" occurs also in other places as an equivalent of "he does not die" [4]). Sometimes there is thought yet of landing in the literal sense of the word: to arrive somewhere. The dead says [5]): "I am one who was well off on the earth with Re, who landed safely with Osiris." In one of the songs of the harpers preference is given to a happy life on earth over going away to the realm of the dead [6]): "Celebrate a happy day, oh god's father . . . Place song and dance before you. Despise all evil (the unpleasant) things, remember the joy, till this day comes on which one lands in the land that loves the silence."

A.2.f. *ḫ3ʿ*, to leave.

The relations experience the decease of somebody whom they loved, as a being left by him. The widow clasps the mummy. She cannot give up her husband to the grave and says [7]): "I am your sister, Merit-Re. You great one, do not leave Merit-Re. Your character was good. You good father, my being far from you, how is that? I go alone and behold, I walk behind you. You who liked to

---

[1]) E. Lüddeckens, *Totenklagen*, p. 109, tomb of Neferhotep.

[2]) Wisdom of Ani, IV, 11, 12.

[3]) C.T. VII, Spell 1162; B 1 Be 259.

[4]) C.T. VI. 293. n. Cf. C.T. V. 380. b.

[5]) C.T. IV. 308. b. c. (B.D. 17).

[6]) M. Lichtheim, The songs of the harpers, 195; W. Max Müller, *Liebespoesie* I. 6-9.

[7]) E. Lüddeckens, *Totenklagen*, p. 109, 110, tomb of Neferhotep.

talk to me, you are silent, you do not talk." Two maid-servants lament: "He leaves his servants" [1]). Lamentation of a wife: "Said by his beloved wife; *Nb-t3wy*, deceased, do not leave, do not leave, you great one, do not leave me" [2]). Lamentation of a son: "Do not leave, do not leave, you my good father, do not leave" [3]), E. Lüddeckens points to the fact [4]) that these lamentations, notwithstanding the belief in the funeral ritual, give a pessimistic impression.

A.2.g. *ḫpi*, to go away.

Dying is "To go away to the beautiful West" [5]). *Ḫpy.t* occurs as an equivalent of dying (*mt*) and is something detested by men [6]): "Oh you that hates dying." In this way the surviving on earth are hailed by the dead from his tomb-stone and invited to repeat the offering formula. That we have here an equivalent of *mt* appears from similar invocations, where *mt* takes the place of *ḫpy.t*: "Who loves life and hates death" [7]).

A.2.h. *sm3 t3*, to land.

After death the dead makes a journey. He must cross a river to land in the domain of Re. In a spell of the ferry-boat it reads: "Come, make me land near the large town, near Re" [8]).

A.2.i. *šm*, to go away.

The *Wörterbuch* gives as the meaning [9]) of *šm* "*fortgehen, auch im Sinne von abscheiden, sterben, auch mit dem Zusatz m ḥtp*". *Šm*, to go away, in contrast with *ii*, to come, indicates death as a going away from this world to another place. In a series of parallels for dying and resurrection it says [10]): "You are going away and you return. You sleep and get awake. You land and you revive. Get up." B.D. 179 [11]) is a "spell in order to go away yesterday and to return today." Compare [12]): "I died yesterday and returned today." From the

[1]) Op. cit., p. 114.
[2]) Op. cit., p. 121.
[3]) Op cit., p. 156.
[4]) Op cit., p. 171.
[5]) Lacau, *Sarc.* I. 217. 27; C 28085; C.T. VII, Spell 1117.
[6]) Urk. IV. 439. 12. Also Leiden V. 38, 18th dyn.
[7]) Urk. VII. 14; cf. Urk. IV. 965.
[8]) C.T. Spell 775; VI. 409. f.
[9]) Wb. IV. 463. 8.
[10]) Pyr. 1975. a.
[11]) B.D. Budge, p. 468. 14.
[12]) B.D. Budge, p. 469. 5.

parallelism it appears that *šm* is a synonym of *mt*. Death is a departure to a foreign country, resurrection is a return to life. Some more examples of this usage: "To go away today, to return tomorrow" [1]. "(My) going away is like (my) returning and v.v., like Re, who sleeps in the night, after he has turned round" [2]. "Osiris, deceased, you have perished and arisen in your name of father of the gods, you have gone away and have returned, you have fallen asleep and got awake. Chase away the fluid of your corpse" [3]. *Tm*, *šm* and *śḏr* are equivalents of dying; *ḫpr*, *iw* and *rś* for resurrection.

Sometimes it is denied emphatically that going away is dying, e.g. in the phrase: "Truly, you have not gone away dead; you have gone away alive" [4]. In the songs of the harpers the going away is often mentioned in a very pessimistic tone. The mourning relatives grieve over the fact that they had to take leave from the dead for ever. Sometimes the texts express themselves "in a Babylonian way", when the realm of the dead is mentioned as the place where one arrives, but from where one does not return [5]. "The great shepherd has gone away, he marches past us. Come that you may see us" [6]. From a lamentation of men at a funeral [7]: "Would that this day became eternity [8], in beholding you. For look, you go to the land which mixes people" [9]. In the very pessimistic song of king Antef it says [10]: "There is nobody who returns from there, that he may tell about their circumstances and may mention their situation and may satisfy our wish, till we go to the place to where they have gone." "Behold, nobody is allowed to take his possessions with him. Behold, there is nobody who has gone, who has returned" [11]. Death is going away in the absolute sense, one has to leave behind everything one

---

1) C.T. VI. 86. i.
2) C.T. VI. 91. m. n.
3) C.T. Spell 785; VI. 414. j-l.
4) Pyr. 134. a; C.T. VI. 380. e.f.; E. Lüddeckens, *Totenklagen* 29, Antefoker, time of Sesostris I.
5) *Irșit la târi.* Cf. Pyr. 2175. a, p. 93.
6) E. Lüddeckens, *Totenklagen*, p. 97.
7) Op. cit. 102.
8) The speakers want to keep the dead with them.
9) That is to say all people are alike in death.
10) M. Lichtheim, The songs of the harpers, p. 192, 193; W. Max Müller, *Liebespoesie*, XII. 8.
11) Op. cit., XIV. 2.

possesses. While in texts mentioned before *ii*, to return, stands in contrast with *šm*, to go away, as to survive after death, this is denied here. "Remember the day, on which you are drawn to the land . . . there is no return" [1]). Now that death is taken so dismally as a going away from the land of the living, the advice of the "*carpe diem*" is connected with it [2]): "There is nobody who has gone away and who returned. Celebrate a gay day."

Finally the term *šm*, to go away = to die is used in the following passage from the wisdom of Ani: "Direct your attention to the road of going away" [3]). That is to say: Think of death. In the sequel the advice is given: Prepare your tomb.

A.3. *Terms for decomposition.*

As soon as death has set in, the body begins to decay. This strikes terror into man and fills him with disgust. Spells have to check the putrefaction of the body. According to the Egyptian conceptions man cannot continue to exist without his body.

A.3.a *imk*, transitoriness.

A total destruction in the dust of the earth is denied [4]): "N.N., your transitoriness, the sweat of your corpse, the fluid of your corpse, your dust do not exist, oh N.N."

A.3.b. *inp*, to consume.

In a spell, which must check the transitoriness of the corpse, a pun has been made upon the name Anubis. Identification with this god must avert the danger. "Do not decompose in this your name of Anubis" [5]).

A.3.c. *isi*, to be light, to fall into decay.

B.D. 154 [6]) is a "spell not to let the corpse decay". The dead identifies himself with Khepri [7]), "who does not perish". For Khepri is the very sun in its first phase, in its rising. That this spell relates to the decay of the body appears there [8]) where the dead says to Osiris: "I have come in order to treat you (medically), that you may treat my flesh."

---

1) Op. cit., 196; W. Max Müller, *Liebespoesie* I. 23, Neferhotep I.
2) Op. cit., p. 203, Paser, Pl. III. 12.
3) Wisdom of Ani IV. 13.
4) Pyr. 1283. a. b.
5) C.T. VI. 384 p.
6) B.D. Budge, p. 398. 15.
7) B.D. Budge, p. 399. 3.
8) B.D. Budge, p. 399. 1,2.

A.3.d. *ʿḫm*, to dry up.

This is a term, which must define the decay of the body, the shrivelling. It occurs in combination with other words, which indicate the situation in the realm of the dead as an unpleasant one. "He does not suffer, he does not go upside down, he does not dry up"[1]).

A.3.e. *fnṯ*, to become maggoty.

There are spells, which prevent the decaying of the body and the being consumed by worms. About a part of the body it is said [2]): "It does not become maggoty" [3]).

A.3.f. *fd.t*, sweat of the corpse.

Oil is taken to the dead in order to revive his body. "I fill you with it, that it may tie your bones together, . . . that it may undo your bad sweat" [4]).

A.3.g. *rwỉ*, to perish.

"Spell in order not to let the corpse perish" [5]). About Osiris it says: "His destruction does not exist" [6]).

A.3.h. *rḏw*, fluid of the corpse.

Occurrence of fluid of the corpse as a phenomenon of decomposition is rejected. "Fluid from your corpse does not exist. Your products of digestion do not exist" [7]). "I detest the fluid of the corpse. I do not eat it" [8]). "I expel my fluid of the corpse" [9]). That *rḏw* means fluid from the corpse, a secretion of fluid from the body, corpse sweat, appears from C.T. Spell 764, a resurrection text. The dead is put on a par with Osiris, whose son Horus collects the parts of his body [10]). The dead loosens his ties [11]). The text continues [12]): "Shake the secretion that is on your flesh on the earth." *ʾIry ỉf.w.k* shows that *rḏw* is something like *fd.t*, sweat of the corpse. "He has shaken

[1]) C.T. VI. 161. e. f.

[2]) C.T. VI. 385. f, Spell 755.

[3]) Cf. Spell 756, C.T. VI. 386. b, do not become maggoty in this your name of "worm", pun upon subst. and verb *fnṯ*.

[4]) Pyr. 1800-1801. c.

[5]) Louvre 3283, VI. 1, *r3 n tm rdỉ.t rwỉ ẖ3.t*, unedited.

[6]) Louvre 3283, VI. 6, *nn rwyt.f*, unedited.

[7]) C.T. I. 295. b.

[8]) C.T. III. 141. e. f. *Rḏw* "*als Bezeichnung für etwas Faules, Verwesenes, vor dem es einen ekelt . . . bei* Lacau, *Textes Religieux* XXIII. A 74", H. P. Blok, AcOr VIII, 197.

[9]) C.T. IV. 64. b.

[10]) C.T. VI. 394. c.

[11]) C.T. VI. 394. m.

[12]) C.T. VI. 394. o.

off the fluid of his corpse [1]). Compare C.T. II, Spell 96 [2]): "For I am this great *b3* of Osiris . . ., which Osiris had made from the fluid of his corpse, coming from his body."

A.3.i. *hb*, to decay.

"You decay in the earth" [3]). According to the Commentary of Sethe this is said about the corpse that decays in the earth, in contrast with the soul which meets Re.

A.3.j. *ḥw3*, to consume.

The decaying of the body in the earth is opposed to the resurrection [4]): "Flesh of N.N., do not consume, do not decay, do not become bad of smell . . . You shall not tread on the excrements of Osiris." "N.N. is one of those four beings procreated by Atum, generated by Nut, who do not consume and thus N.N. will also not consume, who do not perish and thus N.N. will also not perish, who do not fall from heaven on earth and thus N.N. also will not fall from heaven on earth" [5]). The body of the dead is of gold like that of a god and so it consists of imperishable material. "Rise on your bones of bronze and on your limbs of gold, for this body of yours belongs to a god. It does not perish, it does not decompose, it does not consume" [6]). Isis and Nephthys protect the dead, like they do Osiris [7]): "They prevent the streaming on earth of your digestion products in this name of yours of leopard (pun upon *ś3b*)." B.D. 45 is a "spell in order not to consume in the realm of the dead. Tiredness (bis) is in Osiris. Tiredness of limbs is in Osiris. They are not tired. They do not consume . . . I am Osiris. He who knows this spell does not consume in the realm of the dead of Osiris" [8]). A close connection between the dead and Osiris, who does not perish in death, also exists in a series of Coffin Texts: "That someone does not consume in the realm of the dead" [9]). About the limbs of Osiris it is said [10]): "They do not consume and do not perish." "The tears of the god are (my) digestion products" [11]). "A part of the body of me, it does

1) C.T. VI. 396. n.
2) C.T. II. 77. a-d; 78. a.
3) Pyr. 285. a.
4) Pyr. 722. a-d.
5) Pyr. 2057, 2058. a-d.
6) Pyr. Neith 653.
7) C.T. I. 304. b, cf. C.T. VI 384. q; 386. e.
8) B.D. Budge, p. 120. 4.
9) C.T. Spell 755; VI. 384. h.
10) C.T. VI. 384. k.
11) VI. 385. d. See also 384. o: "Do not decay in this your name of *Ḥ3*" = Spell 756, 386.a, with pun upon *ḥw3* and the name *Ḥ3*.

not consume, it does not perish" [1]). In B.D. 154 we find a detailed description of the entire process of decomposition, about which it is denied that the dead participates in it [2]): "Then I shall not decompose, like you have done against any god, goddess etc. . . ., who will perish, whose *b3* ascends after having died and descends after being decayed. He perishes. All his bones perish. Oh you, who slaughters bodies, who slackens bones . . . , behold the bad water (fluid of the corpse), it smells, it perishes, it becomes maggots . . . Your body belongs to you [3]), you do not consume, you do not become maggoty, you do not smell, you do not suppurate [4]), you are not becoming maggots . . . I do not perish."

A.3.k. *ḫśḏ*, to go bad.

About the flesh (body) of the dead it is said: "It does not go bad, it does not consume, it does not decay" [5]). The same verb is used for the going bad of beer at the funerary offering [6]).

A.3.l. *ẖnn*, to decay (of the corpse).

A passage from B.D. 154 reads: "I do not decay. I am not destroyed by my cadaverous smell, I am not mutilated [7]), my eye does not perish" [8]).

A.3.m. *s3b*, to flow away.

S3b is a verb, which is used for the flowing away of the cadaverous sweat or digestion products. "Do not flow on the earth [9]) in this your name of jackal" [10]). "Do not let your digestion products, which are in it, flow out in this your name of jackal" [11]).

A.3.n. *snṯ*, products of decomposition.

This word is parallel to *rḏw*. "The *snṯ* of Osiris is hidden" [12]).

A.3.o. *śnśn*, to smell bad.

"You do not smell, you do not suppurate, you are not becoming maggots" [13]).

---

[1]) C.T. VI. 385. e.

[2]) B.D. Budge, p. 399. 11 sqq.

[3]) B.D. Budge, p. 401. 5.

[4]) *im*? Wb. I. 76. 1; or for *imk.k* as in Pyr. 722.b?

[5]) C.T. VI. 108. g.

[6]) C.T. VI. 380. m.

[7]) Read *i3ṯ*.

[8]) B.D. Budge, p. 401. 12.,

[9]) About sweat of the corpse.

[10]) C.T. VI. 384. q, cf. C.T. I. 304. b.

[11]) C.T. VI. 386. e.

[12]) L.Q. CVIII 9, parallel with *ḥ3p rḏw*.

[13]) B.D. 154; 401. 6.

A.3.p. *śṯi*, smell.

In a text, which describes the unpleasant smell of a corpse in decomposition, it says: "How disgusting is your smell, how unpleasant [1]) is your odour, how great is your smell" [2]).

A.4. *Deterioration of the body and loss of the functions of life.*

The functions of the body are interrupted by death. Certain texts must undo this. In an inscription of a tomb there is a nearly complete enumeration of the parts of the body, which are revived [3]): "Your eyes are given back to you, in order to see, your ears, in order to hear words. Your mouth speaks words, your feet go. Your arms and shoulders serve you, your flesh is strong. Your veins are sweet. You rejoice at all your limbs. You count all your limbs, while they are healthy. There is no evil at all in you. Truly, your heart is with you. Your former heart belongs to you. You ascend to heaven."

A.4.a. *ἰ3rr*, blindness (?).

C.T. Spell 226 deals with the making undone of defects of the body, arisen in consequence of death. "They chase away the blindness (?) of your sight, the bend (?) of your limbs. They open your blinded (?) eyes. They straighten your bent fingers" [4]).

A.4.b. *ἰd*, to be deaf.

"My ear is not deaf" [5]).

A.4.c. *ʿ.t*, part of the body.

The dead gets his body, which has fallen apart by death, back: "The parts of my body are brought to me" [6]). C.T. Spell 761 is "a spell in order to unite the parts of the body of a spirit for him in the realm of the dead" [7]). This is connected with the resurrection of Osiris. For the dead is invoked: "Wake up, wake up, Osiris N.N., wake up" [8]). *Ḥʿpy* says to the dead, whose body has fallen apart like that of Osiris, but which is protected by the four sons of Horus [9]): "I have fastened the extremities of your body." There is thought here of the body which is not yet preserved by mummification and the skeleton of which falls apart in the long run.

---

1) *ἰ3b*, at the left, gets the meaning of "unfavourable", cf. p. 172, Pyr. Neith 763 of *pr b3 pf*.

2) Pyr. 1780. b.

3) Urk. IV. 114. 10-115. 5.

4) C.T. III. 255. a; 256. a. b.

5) B.D. 154; 401. 14.

6) C.T. V. 328. h.

7) C.T. VI. 391. a.

8) C.T. VI. 391. b.

9) B.D. 151; 385. 3.

A.4.d. *ʿnḫ*, ear.

A spell makes the ears of the dead function again [1]): "My ears are opened."

A.4.e. *brd*, to be stiff (?).

E. Lüddeckens connects this word, which is unknown for the rest, with an Arabic word, which means "to chill", and the hebrew בָּרָד, hail. In that case it would refer to the stiffening and chilling of the body in death. Attendants of the corpse at the funeral say: "The good man, who loved the truth, who abhorred the lie, is stiffened." "Stiffened is the one who was the sober-minded one of his town, the silent one of his place" [2]).

A.4.f. *nk*, to copulate.

The dead fears that he will not be able to satisfy his sexual desire anymore. Osiris complains with Atum about the sad situation of the realm of the dead [3]): "No sexual desire is indulged in." At the bier of her deceased husband the widow laments [4]): "Would that I might lie down, that I might be the bier which carries you." According to Kees' explanation the wife wants to have sexual intercourse, which is not possible in death. It is also thought that in the *i3rw*-fields, where full life is restored, one feels sexual desire again [5]): "Make him exercise sexual desire there." C.T. Spell 576 is a spell in order to be able to copulate again [6]): "My phallus is *B3b3* . . ., there is sperm in my mouth . . . N.N. has the disposal of his desire . . . N.N. possesses procreating power, so that he creates. My sperm is the sperm of this one and the other. As regards everyone who will know this spell, he copulates in this land by day and night." The dead repels anybody who would make sexual intercourse impossible for him [7]): "He who took the intercourse with my wife away from me, when it was there."

Getting back the sexual power [8]) also belongs to the restoration of the functions of life after death [9]): "Sperm is in his phallus."

A.4.g. *nḏmy.t*, sexual desire, see *nk*, to copulate, A.4.f.

---

[1]) C.T. V. 327. h; *ʿnḫ.wy.i*, ideographically *mśḏr.wy* may also be read.
[2]) Op. cit., p. 124.
[3]) B.D. 175; 458. 11.
[4]) H. Kees, Z.Ä.S. no. 62, p. 78, line 3-4, "*rechter Klagelied*"
[5]) C.T. V. 209. n.
[6]) C.T. VI. 191. c. e. g. j-l.
[7]) C.T. VI. 234. a.
[8]) C.T. III. 74. c. = Pyr. 1061. b.
[9]) ' Breath is in his nose."

A.4.h. *r3*, mouth.

The funerary ritual of the opening of the mouth not only refers to the mouth, but must also enable the dead to exercise again all the functions of his body, which death has eliminated. Spells of the dead state that the deceased again has the disposal of his power of speech. "My mouth is opened. I see with my two eyes" [1]). Opening one's mouth, in order to be able to eat, is mentioned beside the restoration of other functions of life [2]). "My eyes are opened, my ears are unclosed by (*'Imy*) *ḫnt irty*. The ties, which are on my mouth, are opened. What is in my behind is carried off by *Ḫnty irty*. I go out in the day. I eat with my mouth. I have motion with my behind." Digestion is normal again.

The dead must have the disposal of his mouth again, if it were only for being able to utter his magical spells and to work by his magical power. Some spells are directed against demons, who prevent his doing this. B.D. 90 is a spell, directed against demons, who put a gag into somebody's mouth, in order to disable him to speak [3]).

Also C.T. Spell 698 deals with this topic [4]): "To keep off him who is in the realm of the dead, who comes in order to close somebody's mouth. Oh bowman of Shu, who closes the mouth . . ., your eye is broken."

A.4.i. *rwḏ*, tendon.

The dead again obtains the command over them: "My tendons, which are in Letopolis, are brought to me" [5]).

A.4.j. *rd*, foot.

The dead fears that he cannot use his feet or that demons will hinder his going. "You do not take away the going of these feet of mine . . . You have no power over these feet of mine" [6]). C.T. Spell 365 should bring about the normal use of the body [7]): "I have descended into the land of the Silent One . . . My bones are drawn out, my limbs are stretched. I go on my feet like Osiris."

---

[1]) B.D. 55; 127. 3-4.

[2]) C.T. Spell 455; V. 327. h-m.

[3]) *Ḫtm r3*, to close one's mouth, J. Zandee, Ch. 90 of the Egyptian Book of the Dead, N.T.T. VII, 193-212.

[4]) C.T. VI. 322. a-d.

[5]) C.T. V. 328. f.

[6]) C.T. III. 305. b, f.

[7]) C.T. V. 26. a. h. i.

A.4.k. *ḥr*, face.

When dying the eyes grow dim. Certain spells should restore the eyesight. "My face is opened," that is to say I can see again [1]). Re says to the spirits in the netherworld [2]): "Opening for your face." The dead can see again: "The cloudiness is chased away from the face of Osiris N.N." [3]).

A.4.l. *ḫrw*, sound.

The shadows in the realm of the dead do not have the disposal of the complete human voice any longer, but can only produce a whispering or buzzing sound. In a description of a division of the realm of the dead it is said [4]): "In this cave a sound is heard like that of many bees . . . their souls which call to Re" [5]). "As the voice of people who are crying" [6]). "In this cave a sound is heard like the howling of a tom-cat" [7]). "The squeaking of a nest of birds" [8]).

A.4.m. *ẖ.t*, belly.

The belly is the seat of desire, of passion and it is full of magical power (*ḥkȝ*). Therefore it is very important for the dead that his belly does not perish in death. "He has chased away his dust. He has saved his belly" [9]).

A.4.n. *ẖȝ.t*, corpse.

The corpse is the body of the dead. It must not become decomposed, for it is indispensable to his survival. There are spells for preventing the body from decaying. "They prevent the smell of your corpse becoming bad in this name of yours of *Ḥr ḫȝty*" [10]). "Spell in order not to let the corpse decompose" [11]). "My corpse does not perish" [12]).

A.4.o. *śmḫ*, to forget.

Death means interruption of the spiritual functions. Man loses his memory. "I count them out to the *Tiȝ.w*, who have forgotten

---

1) B.D. 44; 119. 13.

2) Book of Gates VI, lower register. E. Lefébure, M.M.A.F.C. III, 1, Pl. XXXIII. 3.

3) B.D. 135; 295. 3.

4) Am Duat VIII. 15. 16.

5) Cf. O.T., Pedersen, Israel, I, p. 180; Jes. 8: 19; 29: 4, the spirits of the dead, *rᵉfāʾim*, squeak.

6) Am Duat VIII. 35, 36.

7) Idem 182.

8) Idem 212.

9) C.T. VI. 223. i. j.

10) C.T. I. 304. c. d.

11) Louvre 3283 VI. 1. See A.3.g.

12) Louvre 3283 VI. 3, *nn šm n ẖȝ.t.i*, unedited.

their essence" [1]. "I am the one who remembers for himself what I had forgotten about it (i.e., about my magical power)" [2]. "Mistress of the two countries, secure for me my magical power. It calls to my mind what I had forgotten" [3]. B.D. 25 is a spell to give memory. "Be my name given back to me in *pr wr*. May I remember my name in *Pr-nśr*." Only when somebody in the realm of the dead can remember his name, he is himself [4].

A.4.p. *śṯi*, to impregnate.

Through death sexual power is destroyed. The dead wishes to have it restored. "It is this *b3* of Osiris, the bull of the West, to whom impregnation on earth is given" [5]. "To me my *b3* belongs, that I may impregnate with it" [6].

A.4.q. *šp*, blind.

"I do not become blind. I do not become deaf" [7].

A.4.r. *šdn*, to close.

Eyes closed by death are opened again [8].

A.4.s. *ḳś*, bones.

Spells about collecting the bones point to the decay and the falling apart in the earth of the body not mummified. "It (the oil) ties your bones together. It unites the parts of your body for you. It collects your flesh for you. It loosens your bad sweat on earth" [9]. It belongs to the restoration of the decayed body that the bones are given back. "My bones, which are in Busiris, are brought to me" [10].

A.4.t. *ḳrf*, to be bent.

In dying the parts of the body contract and stiffen. There are spells for removing this condition and for making the parts of the body stretch themselves again. "They stretch for you your bent fingers" [11]. Feet bent in consequence of death are straightened again [12].

---

1) C.T. II. 254. o. The *Tì3.w* are dead who have an unfavorable fate. Cf. Pyr. 2083. d; *ḫm ḏ.t* = to be senseless. *Tì3.w* is perhaps related to *tì3*, tooth-ache Wb. V. 251. 5-9.

2) C.T. V. 364. b.

3) C.T. V. 368. c. d.

4) Cf. *ìb*, B.8.b.

5) C.T. VI. 72. h. i.

6) Idem 74. c.

7) C.T. V. 223. g.

8) B.D. 26; 89. 12.

9) Pyr. 1801. b sqq. See also Pyr. 1908. b; Pyr. Neith 479; 729.

10) C.T. V. 328. e.

11) C.T. III. 256. b.

12) B.D. 26; 89. 13

A.4 u. *tp*, head.

The Pyr. Texts preserve memories of a way of burying without mummification, in which the body fell to pieces and the head became detached from the trunk. "Receive your head. Collect your bones. Collect your limbs. Shake the dust from your flesh" [1]. "Receive your head for you. Your teeth belong to you. Your hair belongs to you" [2].

The skull detached from the spine, is put in its place again and the eyes are placed back into the eyesockets. "Spell to give somebody's head back in the realm of the dead. My head is tied on for me by Shu. My neck is fixed for me by Tefnet on this day, on which the heads of the gods are fastened to them. My eyes are given back to me, that I may see with them. I receive my spine from Ptah-Sokaris" [3]. Later texts think of the wilful cutting off of the head by a demon [4]. To the dead as Horus it is said: "You are Horus . . . to whom the head is given back after being chopped off. Your head will not be taken away afterwards. (Your) head is not taken from you to all eternity" [5].

A.4.v. *tḫnỉ*, to injure (the eyeball).

"Spell in order to land, in order not to let it (the eyeball) be injured" [6].

A.4.w. *ḏ.t*, body.

It is of importance that somebody's body remains intact. "Man does not continue to exist, if his body is destroyed. The rebel is threatened that he will have no grave and that his corpse will be thrown into the water. An adulteress is punished by being burnt, while her ashes are cast into the river" [7]. Spells undo the decomposition of the body. Man needs his whole body in order to be able to live eternally. The deceased saves his body from death like Osiris. "I have come that I may save my body . . ., that I may sit in the residence of Osiris, that I may dispel the sufferings of the sick god . . . I appear and I am strong like Osiris. I am born with him, while I am young" [8].

---

1) Pyr. 654. b.; cf. Pyr. 639. a. b; 828. a; 835. a; 572. c; 75. a.
2) Pyr. Neith 766.
3) C.T. Spell 532; VI. 126. a-h.
4) See vbs like *šˁ*, *šˁd*, B.5.bb, cc.
5) B.D. 166; 421. 4 sqq.
6) B.D. 165; 418. 7.
7) De Buck, *Kernmomenten*, p. 22.
8) C.T. Spell 228; III. 272. d.e; 274. b-276. c.

A.5. *Encroachment on the complete continuance of life.*

Tomb inscriptions describe how, after a ritual burial, life is restored. From these positively worded descriptions can be deduced what is feared: decay of the body, suffering hunger and thirst. The spell must prevent this. "You go in and out, rejoicing in the favour of the lord of the gods. You are buried in the western necropolis, having become a living soul. Truly, he has the disposal of bread, water and air [1]). It happens that you live [2]). Your soul shall not leave your corpse . . . You have the disposal of water. You breathe air. You drink from your heart's desire. Both your eyes are given back to you in order to see, your ears, in order to hear. Your mouth speaks. Your feet go . . . You count all the parts of your body, while they are healthy . . . You receive cakes, which come from the god" [3]).

What is feared is not death as a total destruction, but as a decline of life, a distressful existence, in which man has to suffer hunger and thirst, is cut off from the intercourse with his relatives and is lonely.

A.5.a. *3b.t*, relatives.

Death is a being separate from one's relatives. Some spells aim at re-uniting relatives [4]). "To give my relations back to me" [5]). My father, my mother, my brothers and sisters, my town, my relatives, all of them have been given back to me" [6]). "To me my relatives, my father and my mother are given back" [7]). In a pessimistic view of the realm of the dead it is said about the dead: "They do not wake up in order to see their brothers. They do not see their fathers and their mothers. They miss their spouses and their children" [8]). As something favourable is said about the dead: "He joins his father and mother" [9]). In a prayer to Amon-Re it reads: "You make me descend to the beautiful West that I may join my father and mother" [10]).

---

1) The *b3* moves freely in order to fetch food from the earth.

2) Urk. IV, 114; the restoration of full life.

3) Urk. IV. 113-115.

4) M. S. H. G. Heerma van Voss in *Pro Regno Pro Sanctuario*, pp. 227-232; C.T. Spells 131-146.

5) C.T. II. 151. d.

6) C.T. III. 52. d.

7) C.T. VI. 406. o.

8) Tomb stone of Ta-imhotep, *Zwei Grabsteine Gr. Zeit*, A. Erman, *Festschrift Sachau*, p. 108.

9) E. Lüddeckens, *Totenklagen*, p. 146, 19th dyn.

10) Urk. IV. 445. 9. 10.

A.5.b. *ib*, to suffer thirst.

The dead cannot drink any more. He suffers thirst. One who died young, complains: "I am thirsty, though there is water on my side" [1]). See *ḥḳr*, to suffer hunger, A.5.n.

A.5.c. *itmw*, want of breath.

See also *g3w*, A.5.s and *ṯ3w*, A.5.u. A torture of death is that breath is cut off. At first this is a general phenomenon, which belongs to death as such, later it becomes a punishment for the impious. As such *itmw* occurs in the tombs of the kings [2]). Four women put on their head are represented. The inscription near it reads: "Truly, you are in want of breath. You come into the place of destruction."

A.5.d. *ʿwg*, to dry up.

It is feared that one is in want of drinking water in the realm of the dead. "You do not perish. You are not flooded (too much water). You do not dry up (too little water)" [3]). "Spell in order to drink water and not to dry up by fire . . . I do not dry up, I am not burnt" [4]). "I am the one who does not dry up" [5]).

A.5.e. *ʿḫm*, to desiccate.

In a spell for having the disposal of water it says: "I am not scorched, I do not desiccate" [6]). It is feared about death that one cannot eat or drink any more, so that the body dries up.

A.5.f. *wʿi*, to be alone.

Death means loneliness. Demoniacal watchmen keep everybody at bay who wants to keep the dead company. On a stele of one who died young, from the Greek period, it reads [7]): "The keepers of this gate keep all people away from me, (from me) who was not in the time of the being alone. My heart was content with seeing many, for I loved gaiety." Especially for a small child, who is afraid when it is alone, it must be torture. Also on the tomb of Neferhotep such a complaint of loneliness occurs [8]): "You who were rich in people, you are in the country that loves loneliness."

---

[1]) Erman, *Festschrift Sachau*, p. 104.
[2]) L.Q. XXXIV. 5, 3rd *ḳrr.t*, lower register, 2nd tableau.
[3]) C.T. V. 10. g.
[4]) B.D. 63 A.
[5]) B.D. 63 B.
[6]) C.T. V. 12. d.
[7]) Erman, *Festschrift Sachau*, p. 106.
[8]) E. Lüddeckens, *Totenklagen*, p. 112.

A.5.g. *wś*, to be in want.

About the belly it is said: "It is not in want to all eternity" [1]).

A.5.h. *wšr*, to dry up.

"I do not suffer thirst. My lips do not dry up" [2]).

A.5.i. *fdḳ*, to cut off (breath).

"Breath is not cut off from my nose" [3]).

A.5.j. *mw*, water.

In the realm of the dead there is want of water and one suffers thirst there. A spell must prevent this. "Spell in order to have the disposal of water" [4]). In a funerary lamentation it says [5]): "Woe be to you who are mine, who liked to be drunk is in the land that is without water. The lord of many granaries has gone away. He passes by the singers." This fits in with a conception of the realm of the dead as a barren desert.

A.5.k. *mn*, to suffer.

In a lamentation about death as a nuisance it says: "Would that my heart cooled down in its grief" [6]).

A.5.l. *nwḫ*, to be scorched.

This is a term for drying up for lack of water. See *ʿwg*, A.5.d. and *ʿḫm*, A.5.e.

A.5.m. *ḥwʿ ỉb*, to be sad.

In the *ḥtp*-field one is safeguarded against this [7]): "My heart does not perish there and is not sad there" [8]).

A.5.n. *ḥḳr*, to suffer hunger.

As the functions of life stop through death it is feared that the dead cannot take food any more and must go hungry. Contrary to this are conceptions of a happy place in the hereafter, where the dead has plenty. Magical actions and spells restore to the dead the disposal of his mouth and he eats his fill of food offerings. What is feared for the dead is denied in a spell. The spell has to remove the undesired situation. "This land, into which N.N. goes, N.N. is not thirsty there,

---

[1]) Louvre 3283 VII. 5, *nn wś.ś r nḥḥ ḏ.t*, unedited text.
[2]) C.T. V. 19. a. b; idem C.T. V. 22. c.d.
[3]) C.T. II. 117. k.
[4]) C.T. V. 8. a; idem B.D. 58.
[5]) E. Lüddeckens, *Totenklagen*, p. 134.
[6]) Erman, *Festschrift Sachau*, p. 109.
[7]) B.D. 110; 225. 11, 12 = C.T. V. 346. a.
[8]) Literally "short", the opposite of *3w ỉb*.

N.N. does not suffer hunger to all eternity" [1]). In *t3 pf* one should not think of a heavenly hereafter. The dead does not go hungry and thirsty, because of the fact that the goddess *'Ipìì* refreshes him with her milk. In the Pyramid Texts there are certain sequences of spells, which deal with the nutrition of the dead. [2]) "Hunger, do not come against N.N. [3]) . . . N.N. does not suffer hunger on account of Horus' wheaten bread, which he has eaten, which . . . has prepared for him that he may be satisfied by it, that he may regain his normal condition through it. N.N. shall not suffer thirst on account of Shu. N.N. shall have no hunger through Tefnet. *Ḥpì*, *Dw3.mw.t.f*, *Ḳbḥ-śn.w.f* and *'Ims.tì*, they shall chase away this hunger which is in the body of N.N., this thirst, which is on the lips of N.N." [4]). The sons of Horus, who watch over the intestines of the dead, take care of his satiation. "The hunger of N.N. comes from the hand of Shu, the thirst of N.N. comes from the hand of Tefnet. N.N. lives on the morning bread that comes in its time. N.N. lives on that on which Shu lives. N.N. eats from that from which Tefnet eats" [5]). The phenomenon to which these conceptions reach back, is that the dead lies down motionless. He does not eat or drink any more. He suffers hunger. The hereafter is a desert, a land of emptiness and barrenness. Is that why Shu as the god of emptiness makes him suffer hunger? The spell wants to give satiation to the dead, either by letting him stay in a place comparable to the *ḥtp*-fields of B.D. 110, a fertile region in the hereafter, or by mentioning the provision with funerary offerings. Against suffering hunger is set having abundance" [6]). In a text [7]), in which it is mentioned that the dead has ointment, clothes and food, the passage occurs: "This N.N. rubs himself with oitnment, is dressed, lives on . . . May you give his food from what your father Geb has given you, under which you are not hungry, under which you are not perishable." In a text, which also deals with the food offering to the dead it says [8]): "You give me bread, when I go hungry, you

[1]) Pyr. 382. a. b.
[2]) Commentary Sethe, p. 36.
[3]) Or: Do not come to fetch N.N.
[4]) Pyr. 551 sqq., *Spruch* 338.
[5]) Pyr. 553, *Spruch* 339.
[6]) For instance *bʿḥ.t*, Pyr. 555. b.
[7]) Pyr. 1512 sqq.
[8]) C.T. III. 19. a-d.

give me beer, when I go thirsty." Other similar texts read: "I do not suffer hunger, my lips do not parch. I quench my thirst with this great liquid of my father Osiris" [1]). "N.N. is not hungry, he is not thirsty" [2]). After that funerary offerings are mentioned. Bread, barley etc. are given to the dead. "What N.N. detests is hunger. He does not eat it. What he detests is thirst. N.N., bread is given to him by the lord of eternity" [3]).

A.5.o. *snw*, to suffer.

The decay of the body in death is deemed to be a suffering. Horus says about the decomposition of the corpse of his father Osiris: "I am Horus, Osiris N.N., I do not permit you to suffer" [4]). Compare the passage: "Your bones do not perish, your flesh does not suffer" [5]). In a text, in which Isis and Nephthys take care of Osiris, it reads: "May you not suffer" [6]). In a text for preventing an unpleasant fate in the realm of the dead, it is said about the dead: "He does not suffer, he does not go with the head downwards" [7]).

A.5.p. *śin*, to hurry.

Death is an infringement on life. Man clings to his existence on earth. He fears to die before the appointed time. Certain spells must prevent a premature death. "Let an early death have no power over me" [8]). "To remain on earth, not to die a hasty death. This is his salvation" [9]). "I shall not die a precipitate death" [10]). "I shall not land hurriedly" [11]). "My horror is dying before I have become old, before I have come to venerableness" [12]).

A.5.q. *ś‛r.t*, shortening of the time of life.

A premature death is feared. "He has heard out of the mouth of the keepers that this father of mine, who is in the West, has created

---

[1]) C.T. V. 19. a-d.
[2]) B.D. 178; 463. 14.
[3]) Idem 466. 4.
[4]) Pyr. 1753.
[5]) Pyr. 725. a; cf. 617. a; 637. a.
[6]) Pyr. Neith 833.
[7]) C.T. VI. 303. o. p; Spell 674. Idem VI. 161. e.
[8]) De Buck, *Pro Regno Pro Sanctuario*, pp. 79-85; The fear of premature death in Ancient Egypt, Pl. III. 23.
[9]) Op. cit. III. 27.
[10]) C.T. I. 164. i; Spell 38.
[11]) C.T. I. 165. a.
[12]) C.T. Spell 40; I. 173. i.

me in order to fetch me, in order to reduce my days in this land of the living, before I have educated my children, before I have brought up my offspring, before I have reached my time" [1]). Oh you who takes years away, who reduces days, do not take away my years, do not reduce my days. I am Horus, the lord of the *d3.t*" [2]). An enemy, who shortens somebody's time of life and takes away his food, is repelled: "He who brings the days of my death nearer, who reduces the days of my life, his blood belongs to the inhabitants of heaven, his blood belongs to the dwellers on earth" [3]). "N.N. has saved himself from those who did this against him, who took away his food from him, when it was still there, who took away his evening-meal, when it was still there, who robbed the air from his nose, who reduced the days of N.N.'s life" [4]). "He took me to this house, when my days were there. He made my years approach (i.e., he shortened), when my . . . was on earth" [5]). On a tomb-stone of a girl who died young, the following complaint of her early death is written [6]): "I praise your *k3*, lord of the gods (Osiris), while I am still a child (she is now already with the king of the realm of the dead). This harm was done to me, when I was still a child without guilt, oh you who speaks and it happens. I sleep in the valley in my youth. I am thirsty although there is water on my side. I have been pushed away as a young girl, when it was not yet time. I turned away from my house in my childhood, when I was not yet satiated with it (i.e., with the house)."

A.5.r. *śrf*, warm breath.

A phenomenon of death is that man does not breathe out warm air any more. It belongs to the restoration of life, that the warm breath returns. The retaining of somebody's life is coupled to the life of the cosmos: "The winds of the heavens go to perdition, when the warm breath, which is in your mouth, goes to perdition" [7]).

A.5.s. *g3w*, to be narrow.

The dead fears oppression of the throat, suffocation. In dying

1) C.T. I. 167. a-g, De Buck, *Pro Regno Pro Sanctuario*, p. 83.
2) C.T. V. 330. f-i.
3) C.T. VI, 234 b-e; De Buck, op. cit., p. 81.
4) Pyr. 290. c sqq.
5) C.T. V. 334. j-m.
6) A. Erman, *Festschrift Sachau*, p. 104; Leiden S.A. 3, Greek period.
7) C.T. VI. 108. k. l.

breath stagnates. Spells have to prevent this. "Nut seizes your arm, that you may not suffocate, that you may not sigh, that you may not . . ." [1]). In a spell for living on air it reads: "My throat is not oppressed" [2]). The dead complains: "My throat is narrow" [3]).

A.5.t. *t*, bread.

In order to make him not suffer hunger, spells are sent along with the dead, which enable him to eat bread. "Spell in order to eat loaves in the realm of the dead. I have come as *Npr* . . . I have gone into the house of *Ḥw*. What I ask him is given to me" [4]). *Npr* is the corn-god. *Ḥw* is the god of command, who is also related to food. This spell is akin to the spells for having the disposal of air [5]), for having the disposal of water [6]). Also Spell 165 is a spell for eating bread [7]). "Spell for eating loaves from the altar of Re, to make food offerings in Heliopolis." From the oldest periods food and drink offerings have been sent along with the dead, to effect that he is not in want and that life in its fulness is continued.

A.5.u. *ṯ3w*, breath, air.

When dying man gets oppressed. About the realm of the dead the conception prevailed that there was want of air. Certain spells must accomplish that a person has the disposal of breath. "Breath is not taken away from my nose" [8]). "N.N. breathes air. There is nobody who takes it away from him" [9]). "Spell for having the disposal of air in the realm of the dead. The opening of my nose is opened in Busiris" [10]). "To inhale air in the water (the primeval ocean is the realm of the dead) . . . The doors of the gates are opened that the winds may pass . . . The winds enter . . . There is air in my nose. It is Seth who says to me, who lets me know: Be provided with life and breathe air in the water" [11]). Seth is connected with the air. As god of the wind he gives breath to the dead. C.T. Spells 630-635 are spells for giving somebody's breath back in the realm of the dead. "Air is given to Osiris N.N., because he knows it. N.N. does not mean the air, the name of which men know. He only speaks about the air which is in the house of Seth . . . N.N. is *'Isṯ.ti*, the lord of

[1]) Pyr. 903. a.
[2]) B.D. 38 A; 103. 11.
[3]) B.D. 41; 111. 5.
[4]) C.T. Spell 371; V. 33. d. e; 34. a. b.
[5]) C.T. Spells 162; 355; 373.
[6]) C.T. Spells 353; 356; 359; 361; 362.
[7]) C.T. III. 5. a.
[8]) C.T. III. 298. c.
[9]) C.T. VI. Spell 663; 289. a.
[10]) C.T. V. 1. a. d.
[11]) C.T. V. 35. a. k. l. p. q.

the air. N.N. knows the air in this his name of Seth *'Isṯ.ti* [1]). "To become air, to inhale air in the realm of the dead, in the *'I3r.w*-field" [2]). "Osiris N.N. has descended. He has smelled air. He has inhaled *m3ʿ.t*. Osiris N.N. has inhaled air" [3]). The title of Spell 633 reads: "That there may be air in somebody's nose in the realm of the dead." Also here Seth, as god of the wind, is connected with the giving of breath: "There is air in the nose of N.N. as in (that of) Seth" [4]). Isis, hovering like a bird over Osiris, blowing air to him with her wings and reviving him, is thought of in the passage [5]): "Osiris N.N., Isis has come. She makes breath go out. She wants him to enter into the cavities which are in your head, that you may live (again)." Also the Book of the Dead knows various spells for giving breath to the dead. "Spell for giving air in the realm of the dead" [6]). In order to attain his object the dead identifies himself with the god of the air Shu. Also B.D. 58 and 59 are spells for breathing air. In B.D. 59 it is Nut as the goddess of the sycomore, who gives water and air.

A.6. *The world reversed.*

The realm of the dead is situated on the under-side of the disk of the earth. People there walk with their feet against the ceiling. This has the unpleasant consequence that digestion goes in the reverse direction, so that the excrements arrive in the mouth. The netherworld is a שְׁאֹל.

A.6.a. *iwty.w* [7]), digestion products.

The denizens of the realm of the dead eat their own excrements. The following passages go back to this conception. Name of a demon: "Who swallows digestion products" [8]). Name of a mummy, who watches over the second gate in the Book of Gates: "Who eats digestion products" [9]).

---

[1]) C.T. VI. 252. c-e. g. h.
[2]) C.T. Spell 631; VI. 253. g. h.
[3]) C. T. Spell 632; VI. 255. a-d.
[4]) C.T. VI. 255. k. l.
[5]) C.T. Spell 777; VI. 410. a-c.
[6]) B.D. 55; 126. 15.
[7]) The word *iwty.w* is related to *iwy.t* which occurs in the passage "the Western desert (the necropolis) . . ., which conceals what is perishable." N. de Garis Davies, A. H. Gardiner, The Tomb of Amenemhēt, Pl. XXX, c.
[8]) C.T. IV. 320. a.
[9]) Book of Gates, 2nd gate, B.S. Pl. III.

About executioners of Osiris it is said: "You are those who watch over souls. You live on their digestion products. You breathe on their decayed matters" 1).

A.6.b. *wśš.t*, urine.

Certain spells must guard against a dead drinking urine. "In order not to eat excrements, not to drink urine in the realm of the dead . . . I do not drink urine for you" 2). The dead eats his normal food offerings. He does not eat filth and does not drink urine. He has no motion through his mouth, so that his excrements arrive there (because he goes with his head down), but his *anus* functions regularly. "My four offering loaves are in Heliopolis. Three offering cakes are in the *'I3r.w*-field. I detest ordure. I do not eat it. I do not smell it. The urine, I do not drink it, but I eat with my mouth and I have motion with my anus" 3). "I detest ordure. I do not eat it. I do not drink urine. I do not go upside down" 4). See further *śḫd*, A.6.d. and *ḥś*, A.6.c.

A.6.c. *ḥś*, excrements.

The spells not to eat excrements are closely connected with the spells for not going with the head downwards (A.6.d). C.T. Spells 173-218 deal with it.

Spell 173: "In order not to eat excrements, not to drink urine. What I detest is what I detest, I do not eat (it). Excrements are my horror, I do not eat them. Satiation of the *k3* 5), it does not go into my mouth. I do not eat it with my mouth . . . for I shall not eat excrements for you, I shall not drink urine for you, I shall not descend for you with my head downwards" 6). In this spell the eating of excrements is connected with going with the head downwards. Gods are threatened, if the dead has to eat excrements. "Backwards, excrements. Your name is not excrements. Re is your name. *'Iḥy* is your name. When you say I must eat this, Re will eat tortoises (the tortoise is the enemy of Re)" 7). In Spell 174 the eating of excrements is opposed to eating normally with the mouth 8): "I detest the

---

1) Book of Gates, middle register, B.S. Pl. VIII. 24-27.
2) C.T. Spell 173; III. 47. a. b; 48. a.
3) C.T. Spell 174; III. 60. a-h.
4) C.T. III. 75. i-l.
5) *Ḥtp k3*, circumscription for excrements.
6) C.T. III. 47. a-48. b.
7) C.T. V. 30. a-e.
8) C.T. III. 60. c-h.

excrements, I shall not eat them. I shall not smell them. I shall not drink the urine. I eat with my mouth. I have motion with my *anus*." Spell 181: "I detest the excrements. I do not eat them. Truly, I do not drink urine. I do not go with my head downwards" [1]).

The dead also does not wish to touch digestion products with his hands or feet. They make somebody impure. "The excrements are my horror. The satisfaction of the *k3*, I am not disturbed by it. I do not approach it with my hands. I do not tread upon it with my foot-soles" [2]). Instead of excrements the dead eats normal bread [3]). "I live on bread in the *Ḥtp*-field."

The spells not to eat excrements also occur in the Book of the Dead. "My horror is my horror. I do not eat it. My horror are the excrements. I do not eat them. The horror of my *k3*, it does not go into my belly . . . I live on, I have the disposal of loaves" [4]).

The wish not to eat excrements occurs in food- and offering-texts. The dead has abundance of food. In the funerary cult food-offerings are made to him regularly. He is not in want and need not eat his own excrements. "In order not to eat ordure . . . I descend on the bank. I eat and feed in the *Ḥtp*-field . . . I live on that on which you live. I have plenty of that of which you have plenty . . . My loaf consists of white wheat . . . What I abhor is ordure. I do not eat it. I do not drink urine. I do not go with my head downwards . . . I respect (= fear) the ordure . . . I dread the urine . . . My abundance is in the *Ḥtp*-field. My superabundance is in the gods . . . What I abhor is ordure. I do not drink the urine, its sister. Every god who says that I must eat what I abhor, he shall eat it with me" [5]).

A.6.d. *sḫd*, to go upside down.

Many spells must prevent somebody going with the head hanging down. The term occurs only a few times in the Pyramid Texts. "It is the horror of N.N. to walk in darkness. He cannot see (= bear) the going upside down" [6]).

This is the reversal of earthly existence. Instead of living in the light and going over the earth on one's feet, one here goes in darkness with the feet turned upwards.

---

[1]) C.T. III. 60. c-h. [2]) C.T. III. 80. a-g. [3]) C.T. III. 81. d. e.

[4]) B.D. 82; 179. 12-16. See also B.D. 102, 214. 10-12; 124, 243. 13. 14.

[5]) C.T. Spell 581; VI. 196. n. o. w. 197. a. e. p-s. 198. d. j. n. o. p.

[6]) Pyr. 323. a. The same passage C.T. VI. 189. e.

In the C.T. there are many spells to prevent somebody going with the head downwards. A son says to his deceased father [1]): "They (Orion and *Śpd*) save you from the wrath of the dead who come with their head turned down. You are not among them. You shall not descend to the slaughter-cattle of the first of the decade among the sufferers of the West." The going upside down belongs to the terrors of the West, like a שְׁאֹל, a dark realm of the dead. Gods of heaven like Orion and *Śpd* should snatch the dead away from it and apparently take him to heaven. Something similar is also meant in the following passage [2]): "You go on your feet. Do not go upside down. You go out to the gates from the depths of the earth." Contrasted with the going upside down is going on one's feet. The spell must bring about the restoration of the normal functions of the body. A variant of *ḫr rd.wy* is the old perfective of *ʿḥʿ*, to get up. "In order not to go upside down. If I go upside down, he goes upside down [3]) . . . A great one stands upright . . . I go upright, I do not go upside down" [4]).

Going upside down belongs to a whole complex of conceptions, according to which one has not the normal use of the parts of one's body. In contrast with this the dead wishes to go normally on his feet, to breathe normally through his nose. All this fits in with the conception of a שְׁאֹל, where normal life has become impossible. "I do not go upside down among the ones going upside down. I go on my feet like Nefertem. I smell air with my nose like Khonsu, the lord of food. I see the road with my eyes" [5]). The wish not to go with the head down, often goes together with the desire not to eat excrements [6]). The title of a spell reads: "Not to go upside down. Not to eat excrements" [7]). "I go on my feet. I do not go upside down. I abhor ordure. I do not eat (it). The urine spares me like Re sleep and Atum death" [8]). When a person walks upright he eats and urinates in a normal way [9]): "Not to eat ordure. I am these two gods, who ascend to heaven like falcons and I ascend on their wings, which descend to the earth as snakes and I descend on their coils [10]). I do

[1]) C.T. I. 188. d-189. b. *Ḫr iw*, Wb. I. 48. 10, *der Bedrückte*.
[2]) C.T. I. 59. f-60. c. The dead leaves the subterranean realm of the dead.
[3]) Formula for the threat of a god.
[4]) C.T. V. 28. d-e; 29. d. f. g.
[5]) C.T. VI. 162. r-u.
[6]) See *ḥś*, A.6.c.
[7]) C.T. II. 291. j. k.
[8]) C.T. III. 194. e-j.
[9]) C.T. Spell 197; III. 116. a.-118. g.
[10]) Cf. C. T. Spell 674; VI. 302, b-303. r.

not eat ordure for you [1]). I do not walk bent for you. I walk upright. My phallus is united with me. My *anus* is united with me. I eat with my mouth. I have a motion with my *anus*. On which do you live, is what they say, viz. those who are there (the dead)? Two fields are blocked for me in Busiris. Two fields are opened to me in *Ỉrw*." The dead lives on the corn that these fields yield. In 117.d *ḳś* is a synonym of *śḫd*. The old perfective of *ʿḥʿ* in 117.e is opposed to it just as to *śḫd* in other places. In a spell not to eat excrements [2]) *ḳś* and *śḫd* are parallels ."I am protected against the being bent. I do not go, after having been put on my head" [3]). Also the following passage suggests that in going with the head down the mouth serves as *anus*: "Spell not to go with the head down; that somebody may have the disposal of his foot. I eat with my mouth. I have motion with my back-part" [4]).

As opposed to the going upside down and eating ordure it is said that the dead eats normally and has abundance of food. "My bread is in the field of abundance . . . I do not drink urine for you. I do not eat excrements for you. I do not go upside down for you. I live on red spelt there . . It is Isis who gives me water" [5]).

In the Book of the Dead chapter 189 is a spell in order not to go with the head downwards [6]). "Spell in order not to let somebody go upside down and not to let him eat ordure. To speak words by N.N. What I abhor is what I abhor, I do not eat it. The excrements are my horror. I do not eat them. The motion, no evil happens to me on account of it. It does not fall into my belly. I live on seven loaves" [7]). "I do not walk for you with the head down" [8]). In this text the receiving of regular food offerings stands in contrast with the eating of excrements. The same is the case in C.T. Spell 661 [9]): "Spell in order

---

[1]) Only in the ms. S 6 C, 117. c there follows: "I do not go upside down for you."

[2]) C.T. Spell 202.

[3]) C.T. III. 128. i. j. See also C.T. II. 60. a; 310. d sqq.; III. 48. b; 75. 1; 79. c; 85. g; 125. a; 126. k; 130. a; 133. c; 139. i; 142. d. e; 143. a; 146. e; 148. b; 153. a; 154. d; 168. e; 173. e; 197. a; 201. k; 202. h; V. 251. a.

[4]) C.T. Spell 574; VI. 183. f. g; 184. e. f.

[5]) C.T. VI. 13 h. j-14. d. g.

[6]) B.D. Budge, p. 492. 7.

[7]) Cf. C.T. VI. 288. h.

[8]) B.D. Budge, p. 494. 8.

[9]) C.T. VI. 287. g-i. k. l.

to receive loaves in Heliopolis . . . I do not eat filth. I do not drink urine. I do not go with my head down . . . I am a great one in P, a master of bread in Heliopolis" and in C.T. Spell 580 [1]): "In order not to go with the head down. Back, *Śrdy* and *Śp3y*! Do not set upon N.N. . . . N.N. does not eat ordure for you and does not drink urine. N.N. lives on the two *ḫnm.t* loaves which come from the altar of Re . . . N.N. does not live on that on which *Ḥ3-t3* lives. N.N. does not go upside down for you."

In B.D. 101, a spell for the ferry-boat of Re, the following passage occurs [2]): "Oh Re, in this your name of Re, if you pass those who are there, who are turned with the head down, you will put Osiris N.N. on his feet. If you fare well, he fares well." Here *śḫd* is not a punishment for the godless, but a fate, which strikes all dead. It is temporarily suspended when Re, on his voyage, passes through the netherworld, just as in the Book of Gates those who are in the dark, revive temporarily, when Re travels through their division. Consequently we have a שְׁאוֹל representation in B.D. 101: going on the head as a sad fate for everyone after death.

In the later "*Livres*" the term *śḫd* also occurs. There it is not a general fate, which threatens every dead, but a punishment for sinners. "Oh you who go with the head down, tied ones, who are in the place of destruction (hell)" [3]). In Am Duat Re's enemies are represented upside down in the divisions of hell in the fire [4]). In the Book of Gates Apophis is pictured with his head down [5]).

A.7. *To be bound and imprisonment.*

When death sets in the body stiffens. Man cannot move any more and go where he wants. This is the cause of considering death as a being fettered or an imprisonment.

A.7.a. *imy rd*, foot-iron.

The dead frees himself from fetters, which hinder him in the ascension. N.N. flies like a bird to heaven, away from people . . .

---

[1]) C.T. VI. 195. a-c. e. f. m. n.

[2]) B.D. Budge, p. 212. 16-213. 3.

[3]) L.Q. Pl. XXIV, 9, lower register; idem XXXIV. 3; XXXVI. 7; XCIX. 7, B.I.F.A.O. XLIII, p. 15, n. 7; CXXXV. 7.

[4]) Am Duat XI. 76.

[5]) Book of Gates, lower register, B.S. Pl. III. 10. *śḫd.k*.

"N.N. frees himself from the foot-iron that is on earth. N.N. frees himself from the hand-iron" [1]). "Horus comes to you, he loosens your ties, he throws off your halters, Horus takes away your "foot-iron", the gods of the earth do not seize you" [2]). As *imy rd* is on a level with words for ties, it must mean something like it. In the C.T. *imy rd* is determined with the sign for man or god. So it is personified there. It is not an object, but a person, a being hostile to the dead, who tries to seize him by his foot. "There is not a single "waylayer", who will overturn N.N. There is not a single "waylayer" who will come after me" [3]). "His "waylayer" does not exist. N.N. has come today from the *3ḫ.t* of heaven" [4]). In the C.T. there is thought of a hostile being, who holds the dead. Especially from the Pyramid Texts it becomes clear that these spells mean that the dead does not remain bound to the earth, but ascends to heaven.

A.7.b. *inḳ*, to fetter.

In the ceremonial of the opening of the mouth the wailing-women lament the sad fate of the dead. He lies down stiff. He cannot move any more. The mummy bandages too cramp the liberty of his actions. "He, who willingly opened his legs to go, is fettered, bound and checked." "He who was rich in garments, who liked to dress, now lies down in a garment of yesterday" [5]). In the latter passage there is thought of the mummy bandages.

A.7.c. *inṯ.(t)*, to fetter.

At his setting the sun-god is tied with the bonds of death. "You see Re in his being tied" [6]).

A.7.d. *m3r*, tie.

The second half of Pyr. Spell 222 is an ascension text. The king arises with the sun-god Atum. In this connection it is said [7]): "You cut the ties of the netherworld and stand as a king over the places of the primeval ocean. You ascend with your father Atum. The ties are loosened for you." According to Wb. II. 30. 10 and the *Belegstellen* the M.K. versions of this Pyramid Spell determine the word *m3r* with the rope or the bow-string. It is not the word *m3r*, distress,

---

[1]) Pyr. 1484. See also 211. a; 322. a; 417.b; 1236. b; *iry rd*, Pyr. Neith 750, parallel with *iry* ʿ.

[2]) Pyr. 2202.

[3]) C.T. VI. 165. g. h.

[4]) C.T. VI. 396. q. r; Spell 766.

[5]) E. Lüddeckens, *Totenklagen*, p. 112.

[6]) Pyr. 285. c.

[7]) Pyr. 207. b. d.

as Sethe sees it, but a word for tie. *Wḏ*ʿ is used for the cutting of ties [1]). Here is a representation like Pyr. 349-350 [2]), where the dead bursts the ties of death and stands up in order to go to heaven.

A.7.e. *mḏ.t*, cattle halter.

The rigidity of death is a being tied up. Resurrection is like an animal freeing itself from the halter (*mḏ.t*), with which it is tied up. "Horus comes to you, that he loosens your ties, that he bursts your chains" [3]).

A.7.f. *nṯ.t*, tie.

The rigidity of death is finished. The body functions again. "Oh bull, discern (?) your ties; oh bull, make your ties being loosened" [4]). Cf. 114.a, where the body is collected again. See *ḥtr*, A.7.g.

A.7.g. *ḥtr*, bond.

The bonds of death are broken. The mouth speaks again. "The bonds which are on my mouth, are chased away" [5]). "Loosened are the bonds which are on my mouth" [6]).

A.7.h. *ḫtm*, to close.

The dead does not want to be shut up in the realm of the dead. "May your doors not be closed behind me" [7]). In the Book of Gates the dead are shut up in divisions of the netherworld. They revive during the time Re is there, after which they are in darkness again. It does not concern here a punishment for sinners, for these do not see the sun at all. The dead as such are shut up in a dark realm of the dead. Re says to mummies in chapels [8]): "I have opened your chapels, . . . after I have found you mourning, and closed your chapels behind you." At the gate of each division it reads: "This door is closed after this god having entered." Then those who are in their divisions of the realm of the dead, lament.

A.7.i. *ś3r*, bond.

Loosening the bonds of death occurs in a resurrection text, in which the shaking off of dust and the collecting of bones is also mentioned. Here there can also be thought of loosening the mummy bandages. "Your bonds are loosened for you, like those of Horus, who is in his house, your ties are loosened for you like for Seth,

1) Wb. I. 404. 8.
2) See *ḳ3ś*, A.7.l.
3) Pyr. 2202.
4) C.T. II. 112. b. c.
5) C.T. II. 115. b.
6) C.T. V. 327. i.
7) B.D. 72; 160. 12. Idem Louvre 3148 IX. b. 3.
8) Book of Gates II, upper register B.S. Pl. III. 11-16.

who is in the *T3ḫb.t*" [1]). About the resurrection of Osiris it is written [2]) "Your bonds are loosened."

A.7.j. *śfḫ*, to loosen.

In a spell for getting back one's relatives it is said that the father, the mother and other relatives of the dead rise and are re-united with him. "But when this father of his is given back to him and the mother of N.N. has been loosened for him . . . then cakes are offered, then this boat of Re is navigated" [3]). The gods are threatened in case they do not fulfil the wish of the dead. The metaphor is that the mother is tied with the bonds of death.

A.7.k. *šśm*, strap (?).

In the resurrection the ties of death are broken. "Your straps are loosened" [4]).

A.7.l. *ḳ3ś*, bond.

The dead rises and ascends to heaven. "He comes to you, he comes to you [5]), that he is loosened from bonds and untied from fetters. He has freed N.N. from *Ḫrti*. He does not surrender him to Osiris. N.N. has not died a death. He has become *3ḫ* in the *3ḫ.t*. He has become lasting in the *Ḏdw.t*" [6]). As appears from the use in texts like Pyr. 1363, where a burial in the earth without mummification is meant, *ḳ3ś.w* does not concern the mummy bandages, but the rigidity of death. Likewise there occurs the following passage in a resurrection text [7]): "Rise . . . You remove all your bonds. Your being watched is withdrawn for you." *Ḳ3ś* here concerns the bonds of death. Staying in the tomb is imprisonment.

A.8. *Death as sleep* [8]).

Sander-Hansen here speaks of a *pars pro toto* for death. "Ὕπνος and θάνατος are twins. Death and sleep concur in many respects: in

---

[1]) Pyr. Neith 743. Idem 664. For the reading *T3ḫb.t* see Pyr. 2184. b. and E. Edel. Z.Ä.S. No. 79 (1954), pp. 86-90.

[2]) Pyr. Neith 833.

[3]) C.T. II. 191. c. d. 196. d. 197. a. 198. b.

[4]) Pyr. 2114. b.

[5]) Gods announce the dead to Re.

[6]) Pyr. 349. a-350. c.

[7]) C.T. VI Spell 764; 393. q-394. m. n.

[8]) C. E. Sander-Hansen, *Der Begriff des Todes*, II. b. De Buck, *De godsdienstige opvatting van de slaap* (The religious conception of sleep).

lying down without motion, the unconsciousness. The ancients saw congeniality in them: full life was suspended. The position of the corpse, on its side or squatting, was the position of sleep [1]). Turning to the other side is awakening, resurrection.

A. 8. a. *wrḏ*, to be tired [2]).

The title of a spell reads: "In order not to allow to be tired of heart in the realm of the dead" [3]). About the dead Osiris it is said: "Tiredness, tiredness in Osiris, tiredness of limbs in Osiris. They are not tired. They do not waste away" [4]). The deceased does not remain dead: "Osiris N.N. does not hasten. He does not become tired in this country for ever" [5]). The dead Osiris is called *wrḏ ỉb*, tired of heart [6]). *Wrḏ* as an equivalent of death occurs in the *Lebensmüde* [7]). "I alight, after you have got tired" (i.e., are deceased), the soul says to the man. In a song of the harpers [8]) it is said about the dead: "How tired is this just, noble one."

A. 8. b. *b3n*, to sleep.

"How near is sleep, how far is the passing away" [9]). *Ḳd* is favourably used here of a sleep, from which one can wake, *b3n* is unfavourable. "This great (Osiris) lies down, while he has passed away" [10]). "Oh N.N., great of sleep, great of lying down. This great one lies down, while he has passed away" [11]).

A. 8. c. *b3gỉ*, to be tired [12]).

About the resurrection from death it is said: "Osiris wakes up. A tired god awakes" [13]). About a goddess it is said, that she saves Osiris from tiredness and the dead likewise [14]). About a demon, who waylays the dead, it is said: "He who caused your damage rejoices. Let him not come, lest he sees your tiredness" [15]). Whom those, who are in tiredness, fear" [16]). The dead, who in the Book of Gates [17])

---

1) De Buck, op. cit.
2) Wb. I. 337. 3, *vom Tod sein.*
3) C.T. V. 45. a.
4) B.D. 45; 120. 5.
5) B.D. 133; 290. 3.
6) Wb. I. 338. 7.
7) *Lebensmüde* 153.
8) M. Lichtheim, J.N.E.S. IV. 195; Max Müller, *Liebespoesie* I, 1-2.
9) Pyr. Neith 661.
10) Pyr. 735. a; *ỉb3n*, old perfective with prosth. *ỉ*.
11) Pyr.; Neith 737; cf. Pyr. 894. b.
12) Wb. I. 431. 2, *seit Pyr. oft bildlich tot sein.*
13) Pyr. 2092. a.
14) C.T. III. 349. b. c.
15) C.T. IV. 73. a. b.
16) C.T. IV. 320. d (B.D. 17).
17) Book of Gates VII, lower register, Budge, The Eg. Heaven and Hell II, p. 210; E. Lefébure, *Le Tombeau de Séti Ier*, II. 12. 13.

lie on a bench of snakes, are called *imy.w b3g.w*. The netherworld "hides the tired one" [1]). In this passage "tired one" is equivalent to dead.

A.8.d. *m3ʿ*, to be extended.

About 12 mummies, who lay on a snake-shaped bench, it is said [2]): "Who are extended on their sides and who lie in their places."

A.8.e. *nmʿ*, to sleep.

The *Wörterbuch* [3]) also gives "*im Todesschlaf liegen*" and *nty nmʿ* = "*der Tote*" [4]). In a lamentation of a dead it reads [5]): "Her protector sleeps."

A.8.f. *nni*, to be tired.

The dead are spoken of as the tired ones. "Oh tired one, oh tired one, who sleeps, oh tired one in this place, which you do not know" [6]). In the tombs of the kings condemned in the netherworld are represented watched by Atum with the inscription *nni.w* [7]). In the *Livre de la Nuit* they are pictured in a swimming position [8]). It is said about them: "Tired ones, swimmers, you swim with *ḥʿpy*, you land with *ḏfy.t*" [9]). Offerings are made to them. They are between the *isfty.w* and the *m3ʿty.w*. Do they form, as drowned ones, an intermediate class between sinners and just? In the *Lebensmüde* the *nny.w*, who die on the bank and who do not get a normal burial, also occur [10]). The soul speaks of the worthlessness of a ritual funeral: "Their altars are empty like those of the tired ones, who die on the dike without any descendant on earth. The water takes its part and the sun likewise. The fish of the banks speak to them." About Apophis it is said [11]), that he lives "on tired ones". After that the text continues: "May I not be tired on account of you. May I not be beaten by you." The tired ones are caught in the net [12]). The M.K. version says in

---

1) B.D. 146; 353. 14; 354. 14.

2) Book of Gates VII, lower register, Budge, The Eg. Heaven and Hell II, p. 214; E. Lefébure, *Le Tombeau de Séti Ier*, II. 10.

3) Wb. II. 266. 8.

4) Wb. II. 266. 9.

5) E. Lüddeckens, *Totenklagen*, p. 116. Tomb of Neferhotep.

6) C.T. I. 306. a.

7) Book of Gates I, lower register, B.S. Pl. IV. 14.

8) 2nd hour, 5th register.

9) Idem, 9th hour. Cf. *mḥw*, B. 20. i.

10) *Lebensmüde* 63.

11) B.D. 7; 29. 8.

12) B.D. 153 A; 390. 11.

the spells of the net [1]): "Do not catch (?) me in this net (?) of yours, in which you catch the tired ones."

Sometimes *nnỉ* gives the impression of being an equivalent of death as eternal destruction [2]): "I am not tired, I do not perish." In a spell not to arrive on the slaughtering-block *nny.w* are demons, who are kept off. "He has fastened a knot against the tired ones on his two thighs on this day of the cutting off of sadness" [3]). The M.K. version of this passage is different [4]): "He (Re) fastens a knot against my tiredness on his knees." Re makes a magical knot, in order to protect the dead with it against tiredness [5]).

A.8.g. *śb3gỉ*, to make tired.

"The one who has been made tired (against his will)" [6]).

A.8.h. *śḳd*, to make asleep.

"Who makes the soul sleep" is the name of a demon [7]).

A.8.i. *śgnn*, to soften.

To demons it is said: "Oh you who slaughter bodies, who soften bones" [8]).

A.8.j. *śḏr*, to sleep [9]).

In parallel sequences for dying and resurrection it reads: "You go away and return, you sleep and wake up, you land and revive" [10]). In the following passage there is probably a contrast between the king, who sails to heaven and the people who remain dead. "The *mẖn.t* belonging to it is on you, who lie down; (but) to you the doors of heaven are opened" [11]). "I am the one who wakens my father, when he sleeps" [12]). That is to say I make him rise from the dead. The dead speaks about his resurrection and says: "Truly, I live (again), after having fallen asleep" [13]). The dead are called "the

---

1) C.T. VI. 3. e. g; 4. a; 17. e; 37. n; 43. n.
2) C.T. VI. 63. a.
3) B.D. 50 A; 121. 14, cf. 122. 10.
4) C.T. VI. 261. e.
5) Tiredness is death in an unfavourable sense.
6) Pyr. 260. b.
7) C.T. V. 211. c.
8) B.D. 154; 399. 16-400. 1.
9) Wb. IV. 391. 20, *schlafen* = *tot sein*, 21 + m, *im Sarge, im Grabe ruhen.*
10) Pyr. 1975. a. b.
11) Pyr. Neith 751, 752.
12) C.T. V. 79. a.
13) B.D. 41; 111. 6.

sleeping ones" in the tombs of the kings, where, in the kingdom of Osiris, they are in an adoring attitude before him [1]). In the Book of Gates it is said about 12 mummies who lie down on a snake-shaped bench, that they are "extended on their sides and lie in their places" [2]). One who died young says: "I sleep in the valley in my youth" [3]).

A.8.k. *ḳd*, to sleep.

A resurrection spell, addressed to a dead king, reads: "You who hates sleep, who is made tired, rise!" [4]) About the deceased king it says: "He abhors sleep, he hates tiredness" [5]). About Osiris, rising from the dead: "Osiris, he hates sleeping. He abhors tiredness" [6]). The same idea is expressed in a Pyramid Text [7]): "The horror of N.N. is the earth. N.N. does not enter Geb, so that his *b3* perishes and he sleeps in his house on earth, so that his bones are severed." Here with *ḳd* is thought of the body which rests in the grave in the earth and decays there. About 12 mummies, which sleep on a bench, it is written: "Who are behind Osiris, the sleeping ones" [8]).

A.9. *To be snatched away* [9]).

Death snatches somebody away from life on earth and takes him away from his relatives.

A.9.a. *ini*, to take away.

The verb *ini* may not only mean "to bring", but also to carry off as a prize [10]). It is used in C.T. Spells 38 and 39, where a son utters the fear of being taken away to the realm of the dead by his deceased father. "He said that I should be taken (away) at your command" [11]). "Do you (the deceased father) say that I must be taken away to this

---

[1]) *Livre de la Nuit*, 8, lower register.

[2]) Book of Gates VII, lower register, Budge, The Eg. Heaven and Hell II, p. 214; E. Lefébure, *Le Tombeau de Séti Ier*, II. 10.

[3]) Erman, *Festschrift Sachau*, p. 104.

[4]) Pyr. 260. b.

[5]) Pyr. 721. d; 1500. c; C.T. I. 292 .d.

[6]) C.T. IV. 383. d-f.

[7]) Pyr. 308. b. sqq.

[8]) Book of Gates VII, lower register, Budge, The Eg. Heaven and Hell II, p. 210; E. Lefébure, *Le Tombeau de Séti Ier*, II. 10-12.

[9]) H. Grapow, Z.Ä.S. 72, p. 76, 77, *Der Tod als Räuber*; C. E. Sander-Hansen, *Der Begriff des Todes*, I. d, *die Trennung von Angehörigen und Besitz*. P. Derchain, *La mort ravisseuse*, Ch. d. E. Tome XXXIII, No 65, pp. 29-32.

[10]) Wb. I. 90. 20.

[11]) C.T. I. 158. c.

isolated country where you are?" [1] "... that this father of mine, who is in the West, has created me in order to fetch me, in order to bring my days in this land of the living nearer (= to shorten" [2]). In a letter of a widow to her deceased husband it is written that she rather prefers the father taking his son to him than the latter being reduced to slavery: "I would prefer your taking him who is here, to you, on your side" [3]).

A.9.b. *iṯi*, to take away.

Death takes somebody away from life on earth. "To be taken away and to be brought back" are equivalents of dying and reviving. "N.N. is the uraeus that comes out of Seth, that is taken away and is brought back, and thus N.N. is taken away and brought back" [4]). A deceased comes and fetches a living one and takes him along to the realm of the dead. Herewith a deceased threatens anyone who robs his grave. "As concerns anyone who will enter this tomb on his own account, I will seize him like a bird" [5]). A demon of death takes somebody away. About Osiris as king of the realm of the dead it is said: "To whom everything is brought, for whom everything is fetched" [6]). To the boat of a demon it is said: "Have you come in order to take mine away, to leave me behind crying?" [7]). Somebody asks a demon not to take him away. "Do not take me away" [8]). "Oh great one, do not take me away, do not eat me, may I not be eaten on the day of yesterday, may I not be captured on the day of today" [9]). A book of wisdom says, that somebody's "fate of death comes to fetch him" [10]). Dying is generally called "being taken away", without it being indicated by whom. In a spell, which must prevent somebody being taken to the East, as being an unfavourable place. it reads: "If I am taken away, if I am taken across to the East . . ." [11]), '*Iṯi* here means "to be taken away by death." Danger is averted by threatening with disturbing the cosmic order: "Then an inflammation will arise in the eye of *Ṯb* (sun eclipse)" [12]). The relations mourn for a dead: "The shepherd is taken away to the country of eternity" [13]).

1) C.T. I. 162. g.
2) C.T. I. 167. b. c.
3) Gardiner-Sethe, *Letters to the dead*, Pl. I. A., line 8.
4) Pyr. 1459. b. c.
5) Urk. I. 122. 14, 15; idem 202. 6.
6) C.T. II. 116. w.
7) E. Lüddeckens, *Totenklagen*, p. 104.
8) B.D. 40; 110. 5.
9) C.T. VI. 33. c. d.
10) Ani VII. 12.
11) C.T. VI. 144. h.
12) C.T. VI. 145. c.
13) H. Kees, Z.Ä.S. 62, p. 76, *Ein Klagelied über das Jenseits*.

A.9.c. *ʿw3*, to rob [1]).

Death is feared as a being snatched away and a being taken along to a place of torture. In case this occurs to somebody he threatens with disturbance. "When I go away to the slaughter-place of the gods, where they ask to give account . . . then an inflammation arises in the eye of the *Ḥtm*-bird, before I am snatched away" [2]). In a spell for having power over his enemy, it says: "I am not snatched away" [3]). A demon is threatened: "He who lives on his snatching, backwards, back, backwards!" [4]).

A.9.d. *nḥm*, to take away.

Servants lament to their deceased master: "The shepherd of us both has been taken away from me" [5]).

A.9.e. *ḫnp*, to rob [6]).

Death snatches the child away from its mother: "Death comes. He robs the child that is in the embrace of its mother, as much as the man who is old" [7]). Death as a robber is unrelenting. He does not respect anybody. He is inescapable. He cannot be influenced by a bribery gift.

"He robs the son frcm his mother, more than the old one, who goes about in his neighbourhood. All afraid ones plead before him and he does not incline his ear to them. He does not come to those who plead to him. He does not hear who praises him. He does not look as if he gets bribery presents of all things" [8]).

A.9.f. *šd*, to take away.

In the *Lebensmüde* the soul denies the value of a ritual funeral and says about it: "It is taking somebody away from his house and throwing him on the desert plateau" [9]).

A.9.g. *ṯ3i*, to take away.

"Save me from this god, who takes souls away" [10]). "When your angel of death comes to take you away" [11]).

---

[1]) P. Derchain, *La mort ravisseuse*, Ch. d. E. Tome XXXIII, no. 65, pp. 29-32. According to Derchain the terms *ʿw3* and *ḫnp* only refer to a premature death.

[2]) C.T. VI. 145. e-146. d.

[3]) C.T. VI. 193. f.

[4]) C.T. VI. 293. r. s.

[5]) E. Lüddeckens, *Totenklagen*, p. 114, tomb of Neferhotep.

[6]) P. Derchain, *La mort ravisseuse*, Ch. d. E., Tome XXXIII, no. 65, pp. 29-32.

[7]) H. Grapow, Z.Ä.S. 72, p. 76, wisdom of Ani V. 3.

[8]) Erman, *Festschrift Sachau*, p. 110.

[9]) *Lebensmüde*, 58, 59.

[10]) C.T. IV. 319. e.

[11]) Wisdom of Ani IV. 17 sqq.

A.10. *The realm of the dead as a place of darkness* [1]).

In the realm of the dead everything that gives colour to the existence on earth, is wanting. It is a dark place, where the light of the sun does not penetrate. Sander-Hansen points out [2]) that the passers-by of a tomb should lament "him who is in the dark". The dead hates sleep and does not love darkness. The house of the inhabitants of the West is deep and dark. There are neither door nor window in it, no light for lighting . . . The sun does not rise there, but the dead lie in the dark all days. On the other hand in the Amarna hymns the night is compared with death.

A.10.a. *iḫḫ.w*, darkness.

One of the 42 judges in B.D. 125 [3]) is called "fiery of foot, who comes from the darkness". The name of a bearded mummy, a watchman of the 12th gate in the Book of Gates, is *iḫḫy* (B.S. Pl. IX. 3).

A.10.b. *wšꜣ.w*, night, evening, darkness.

"I rest in the *dꜣ.t*. I have power over the darkness" [4]).

A.10.c. *śnk.(t)*, darkness [5]).

A child, who died young, says about the sad fate of the dead [6]): "The darkness which a child abhors, how close is it to me, while the breast is still in my mouth." In the realm of the dead men are in gloomy divisions, which are only temporarily lighted when the sun-god passes. They are pictured in chapels with a snake above them, which watches over them. Re says to them: "I have opened your chapels, that my light may enter your darkness, after I have found you mourning and your chapels closed behind you" [7]).

A.10.d. *knḥ.w*, darkness.

The *Ḥtp*-field is a happy place in the hereafter, where one is not tortured by the darkness of death. Somebody, who is there, says: "I am the moon, I have devoured darkness" [8]).

A.10.e. *kkw*, darkness.

The realm of the dead is the reverse of life. It is dark there. Men

---

[1]) See E. Hornung, *Nacht und Finsternis im Weltbild der Alten Ägypter* (1956).
[2]) *Der Begriff des Todes*, p. 13, II. b.
[3]) B.D. Budge, p. 256. 10.
[4]) B.D. 180; 472. 6.
[5]) Wb. IV.176.9.
[6]) Erman, *Festschrift Sachau*, p. 106.
[7]) Book of Gates II, upper register, B.S. Pl. III. 11-16.
[8]) C.T. V. 371. f. g.

go with their feet upwards and their heads hanging down. Demons torture there with fire. "N.N. abhors to walk in darkness. He cannot see (= bear) the going upside down . . . May N.N. not be delivered to your flame, oh gods" [1]). In the texts of which the *Zweiwegebuch* forms a part, dark places are mentioned again and again. A boat is represented there, in which a seat is placed [2]). Above it heaven with a sun-disk is drawn, under it a black-edged part. The inscription going with it states that the upper part is the seat of a *3ḫ ʿpr*, who goes to heaven. About the lower part it is said: "This is the place of a spirit, which has fallen into the fire, which enters darkness, which cannot ascend to the heaven of Re-Hor-Smśw, in the retinue of Re-Hor-Smśw." It occurs more than once in these texts that darkness is indicated in black. A twofold fate is possible for the dead. Either he may be with Re in heaven or in a subterranean realm of the dead, which is dark. With the latter again a torture with fire is connected. The *Zweiwegebuch* also shows the picture of the *ʿrry.t kkw*, the gate of darkness, which is shut by a fiery door, on which the word *śḏ.t*, flame, is written. The *ʿrry.t* is black, the door is of a red colour. The inscriptions to it state: "I enter you, oh thunder-storm, covering of Re . . . I have come, oh Re . . . I am near you" [3]). The dead overcomes the darkness to be with Re in heaven. "I come to you, oh great lord among those who enter the vault of heaven. Save me from the claws of him who takes for himself what he sees. May the glowing breath of his mouth not take me . . . lest I enter the darkness" [4]). The darkness is the residence of demons, from whom one hopes to be snatched away to heaven. About a place with demons it is said: "It is a secluded place, which is in the darkness. A fire is around it, containing this fluid of Osiris' corpse. He who places himself in *R3-śṯ3w* is hidden, since he has fallen into it" [5]). The darkness is a dangerous place in the hereafter and a spell must serve for "showing the way in the darkness" [6]).

---

1) Pyr. 323. a-d.
2) Cairo 28085, Lacau, Sarc. I. 216-217, 20-26; C.T. VII, Spells 1115, 1116.
3) Cairo 28085, Lacau, Sarc. I. 216, 17-18; C.T. VII, Spells 1112, 1113; B 1 L, 539-543.
4) Cairo 28085, Lacau, Sarc. I. 215. 13; C.T. VII, Spell 1106; B 1 L, 527.
5) Lacau, Sarc. I. 212. 67; C.T. VII, Spell 1080; B 2 L, 580.
6) C.T. IV. 65. b.

The dead hopes that he does not arrive in the darkness, or that the latter may be lighted by gods who are kindly disposed to him. "You light, you chase darkness away" [1]. The dead having protested his innocence says: "Osiris N.N. does not go to the valley of darkness" [2]. Consequently staying in the darkness is a punishment for sin.

In the tombs of the kings the darkness is the residence of the dead. They revive temporarily, as long as Re shines there. The darkness is also the place to which the enemies of Osiris are sent as a punishment. They never catch sight of the sun. "The hidden apartment is in darkness, till the apparition of this god takes place" [3]. "You are those enemies of Osiris, those who do not see my light, whom I have put in the darkness of the place of destruction. I have made them watched" [4].

In a dialogue between Atum and Osiris the realm of the dead is described as a gloomy place, where all life is extinguished. "Oh Atum, where do I go? There is no water. There is no air. It is very deep, dark and extensive." "No sexual desire is satisfied." Atum answers: "I have given glory instead of water, air and sexual desire, and contentment instead of bread and beer" [5]. The same terminology is used in a wife's lamentation about the hereafter beside a husband's bier [6]: "The wailing-women say: the house of the residents of the West, it is deep and dark. There is no door and no window in it. There is no light for lighting, no north wind for making the heart glad. The sun does not shine there. They lie in darkness every day." This is an absolutely negative description of the realm of the dead, corresponding with the semitic שְׁאל-conception. In the same passage it reads: "The shepherd has been taken away to the country of eternity, to the place of infinity. Those who are in the West, are hidden. Their condition is miserable. One hesitates to go to them. Nobody tells of his circumstances. He is resting in his one place. He is in darkness for ever." A dead is lamented, because he is lonely now and stays in a country of darkness. "Woe to you, who were

---

1) B.D. 127 A; 271. 5.
2) B.D. 130; 279. 14.
3) Book of Gates, gate 1st division. B.S. Pl. IV, 1. 2.
4) L.Q. Pl. CI. 6.
5) B.D. 175; 458. 7 sqq.
6) H. Kees, Z.Ä.S. 62, p. 76, *Ein Klagelied über das Jenseits.*

rich of people. He passes all his relations. He has hurried to the eternal land of darkness, where there is no light," a lamentation reads beside a funeral procession [1]). It is striking that the people who lament at the funeral procession sing of this negative side of death, as if the funerary ritual with which they are occupied, is of no use. In a lamentation about death from the tomb-stone of Ta-imhotep [2]) it says: "What are all the years on earth? As regards the West, it is a land of sleep, oppressing darkness, the residence of those who are there. Sleep is their shape." Death is like the night, in which one sleeps. Life is totally extinct.

A.10.f. *grḥ*, night.

In the tomb darkness reigns. The dead wants to leave it, "to go out into the day." "I abhor going out into the night. I go out in daytime" [3]). In the tomb a candle is lighted in order to light the darkness [4]): "Going out into the day, returning in the night to your tomb falls to you. There a Horus-eye is lighted for you, till the sun rises beaming over your breast." The passage from a funerary lamentation: "Your night is beautiful to all eternity" [5]), concerns the night of death.

A.11. *The netherworld.*

The dead sojourn under the earth. The realm of the dead was also localised in the West, the place where the sun sets. The realm of the dead is the domain of silence. The primeval ocean too, on which the earth floats, was conceived as netherworld and realm of the dead.

A.11.a. *ȝkr*, name of the god of earth.

ȝkr is connected with the earth as appears from the expression "the *ȝkr* of Geb (the god of the earth)" [6]). In the Pyramid Texts the dead king hopes to escape the gods of earth and to ascend to heaven. "You are not seized by the *ȝkr.w*" [7]). "The *ȝkr.w* do not seize you" [8]) it reads in an ascension text. "My soul is not seized by the *ȝkr.w*" [9]). "To you are opened the two doors of *ȝkr*, to you are opened the two doors of Geb" [10]). The dead leaves the earthly realm of the dead

---

1) E. Lüddeckens, *Totenklage*, p. 135.
2) Erman, *Festschrift Sachau*, p. 108.
3) C.T. VI. 86. c. d.
4) Urk. IV. 148. 12 sqq.
5) E. Lüddeckens, *Totenklagen*, p. 130.
6) C.T. II. 28. a.
7) Pyr. 658. d.
8) Pyr. 2202. c; idem C.T. I. 280. f.
9) C.T. I. 398. a.
10) Pyr. 796. b.

by a gate, which leads to heaven. In the Pyramid Texts the subterranean is a gloomy realm of the dead. A happy hereafter only exists in heaven with Re. In later texts, e.g. in those of the tombs of the kings of the New Kingdom also under the earth a favourable fate is possible for the dead.

A.11.b. *ʾImn.t*, the West.

Usually this is thought of as the normal realm of the dead in a not unfavourable sense. In the Book of Gates [1]) it is said about certain gods: "They are the ones who fix the time of life, who decide on the days of the souls that are in the West, who assign to destruction." *ʾImnt.t* here stands as a favourable place in contrast with the *ḥtmy.t*. In tomb inscriptions going to the West is considered to be something good. At the funeral it is said to the dead [2]): "To the West, to the place where your desire is." In the songs of the harpers they sometimes complain of death and "*carpe diem*" is advised. However, in the same kind of literature there also occurs a polemic against this point of view as taken by thc Antef-song. The good life in the realm of the dead, after a ritual funeral of course, is commended [3]). The harper says to Neferhotep: "He is a god, who lives for ever, as an extolled one, in the West . . . I have heard these songs, which are in the tombs from of old, what they say in order to glorify life on earṯh and to belittle the realm of the dead . . . The country of eternity, quarrel is its horror. There is nobody who prepares himself against his fellow-creature . . . As regards the time of what is done on earth, it is a dream. One says: Welcome, safe and sound, to him who reaches the West."

But the West may also be seen as a dangerous place, where demons threaten somebody. Four spirits are invoked who [4]) perform an action inimical to the dead. They are invoked as "these four, who are in the West" [5]), but the variants read "these four spirits who are on the slaughtering-block." The term *nm.t*, slaughtering-block, here stands as a variant of *ỉmn.t*. The West is a place of terror. From the point of view of the Re-religion the West is regarded as unfavourable.

---

[1]) Book of Gates IV, lower register, B.S. VI. 26-29.
[2]) E. Lüddeckens, *Totenklagen*, p. 28.
[3]) M. Lichtheim, J.N.E.S., IV, p. 197; Gardiner, P.S.B.A., XXXV, p. 165-170.
[4]) C.T. VI. 152. j.
[5]) C.T. VI. 152. f.

"May you not go on these roads of the western ones. Those who go on these, do not return. May you go, N.N., on these roads of the eastern ones among the followers of Re" [1]).

A.11.c. *'Igr.t*, the domain of silence.

In the realm of the dead there is silence. It is the domain of silence. Silence is one of the phenomena which occur when death has set in and in that case it stands as *pars pro toto* for being dead [2]). From the verb *gr*, to be silent, the name *'Igr.t* for the realm of the dead is derived. Sometimes it is parallel with *d3.t*. To the just, who obtain a favourable place in the realm of the dead, it is said [3]): *'Igr.t* opens its arm for you (to receive you) that you may enter the sanctity of Osiris." Just as about a human dead the view also prevails about Re, that he has a *b3* in heaven and a corpse in the earth. About condemned sinners it is said: "Oh enemies, may you be counted out to the cutting off, as Re has ordered against you, when he founded *'Igr.t* for his corpse and created the *d3.t* for his body" [4]). The realm of the dead is called the domain where there is silence. "Sharp are the steps of those who are in it on account of the rage of the town of silence, the domain of rest" [5]). From the word *3.t*, rage, it appears that this silence is thought of as something unfavourable. "He assigns me to these four gate-keepers of the district of silence" [6]). About going to the realm of the dead it is said: "Bury me near this strong *i3.t* among those, who are in silence (= the dead)" [7]).

"I have descended to the land of the Silent One (the god of the realm of the dead)" [8]). "It (the wind) saved him who-was-in-the-belly (Horus as a child) from the taciturn ones (evil spirits of the netherworld as the country of silence)" [9]). *Śgr.w* is a denomination for the dead [10]). A woman, who clasps the mummy of her husband, laments:

---

[1]) Pyr. 2175. a-d.

[2]) C. E. Sander-Hansen, *Der Begriff des Todes*, II. c, p. 14.

[3]) Book of Gates VI, lower register, E. Lefébure, M.M.A.F.C. III, 1, Pl. XXXIII. 23-25; Cenotaph Seti I, Vol. II, Pl. LIX.

[4]) Book of Gates V, middle register, E. Lefébure, M.M.A.F.C. III, 1, Pl. XXXI. 34-39.

[5]) Pyr. Neith 718.

[6]) C.T.V. 333. g. h. Idem Sethe, *Lesestücke*, p. 72.11.

[7]) C.T. II. 125. d. e.

[8]) C.T.V. 26. a. [9]) C.T.V. Spell 464; 338. a.

[10]) *Livre de la Nuit*, 8th gate, A. Piankoff, *Le Livre du Jour et de la Nuit*, Le Caire, 1942, p. 66, cf. p. 42.

"You who liked to talk to me, you are silent, you do not speak" [1]). The god of the realm of the dead is called the lord of silence. Somebody states in a "negative confession": "I have not been loud of voice in the house of the lord of silence" [2]). In the texts it is sometimes difficult to trace whether the place of burial or the realm of the dead is meant. So for instance in a passage, where a wife laments at the bier of her husband: "How oppressing is going to the land of silence. The vigilant one becomes a sleeper. He who did not fall asleep during the night, now lies down tired all days" [3]). The day of the burial is the day on which one "lands in the domain that loves silence" [4]).

A.11.d. *Nwn*, primeval ocean.

Nun, the primeval ocean, is thought of as realm of the dead. This conception is very close to that of a netherworld, as the primeval ocean extends under the disk of the earth. First the king comes to the deceased, but he does not remain in the subterranean realm of the dead, he sails to heaven: "Those who are in Nun, fear you" [5]). The gods welcome the king, who has left Nun, in heaven: "Come, resident of Nun, Atum says. Come to us, they say viz. the gods with regard to Osiris" [6]).

A.11.e. *nn.t*, subterranean realm of the dead.

The denizens of the netherworld are called "who are in *nn.t*" [7]).

A.11.f. *smy.t*, netherworld.

In the introduction to the Book of Gates, middle register, B.S. Pl. IV. 18. 19, there are represented two men with staffs between them, which are crowned by animal's heads. The inscription to it reads: "Re says to the *smy.t*: Become light, oh *smy.t*, shine, oh you that are like two men." So the *smy.t* is a dark netherworld. But it is also said about the *smy.t* that it awards him who has made offerings to the dead.

---

[1]) E. Lüddeckens, *Totenklagen*, p. 110.

[2]) Urk. IV. 1031.9; cf. Eloquent Peasant, Sethe, *Lesestücke*, 20.12.

[3]) H. Kees, Z.Ä.S. 62, p. 76.

[4]) M. Lichtheim, *The songs of the harpers*, 195; W. Max Müller, *Liebespoesie*, I. 9.

[5]) Pyr. 871. c.

[6]) Pyr. 1525.

[7]) Pyr. 166. c.

A.11.g. *šty.t*, realm of the dead.

This is the normal realm of the dead in contrast with hell. A text from the tombs of the kings [1]) reads: "You ruin my enemies' souls. You assign them to destruction. They do not see the realm of the dead."

A.11.h. *Gb*, god of the earth.

The god of the earth, Geb, is taken in an unfavourable sense as one who keeps the dead imprisoned. "The earth speaks to you, the gates of *ꜣkr* are opened to you, the doors of Geb are opened to you" [2]). The earth, which otherwise holds on to its prey, sets the king free. After that he ascends to heaven. The reverse is meant in C.T. Spell 619, where the dead summons the watchmen of Re's chapel to let him pass and threatens them in case they do not do so [3]). "If you do not let me pass, in order that I pass, I'll put the western ones in Geb, the father of the gods. The *bnw.t*-bird announces that the light rises, the great one gets up and the Ennead speaks, but the earth does not open itself. Geb does not speak. Re is not high in the sky." It seems to be the idea here that the earth remains closed, the dead remain imprisoned in it. Re does not arise. He also remains caught in the earth. Geb is a dreaded realm of the dead, which holds on to what it has seized once. About Geb it is said [4]) that he cuts out hearts. The dead wishes to leave the earth. "Geb has opened the gate to me, that I may go out" [5]). From the view-point of the Re-religion Geb is considered unfavourable. From that of the Osiris-religion Geb may also be seen as a favourable god of the earth. Aversion from Geb appears from the following places: "He has passed the seats of Geb" [6]). I.e. he has raised himself above him, he is superior to him [7]). "It is a lie when you say that you live on the bread of Geb. You abhor it, you do not eat it" [8]). The doors of heaven are opened to me. Geb, the monarch, opens his jaws to me, that he may open my eyes, which are closed" [9]). The earth sets the dead free. He can use his eyes again [10]).

[1]) Book of Gates IV, lower register, B.S. Pl. VI. 35-38.
[2]) Pyr. 1713. a.
[3]) C.T. VI. 231. d-k.
[4]) Pyr. Neith 834.
[5]) C.T. II. 75. a.
[6]) C.T. I. 37. d.
[7]) C.T. II. 162. d., I have outstripped the strong ones, *ḫnti*.
[8]) C.T. Spell 225; III. 232.b.; 234. a-c.
[9]) B.D. 26; 89.10-12.
[10]) Cf. C.T. III. 253. a.

A.11.i. *t3*, earth.

The earth must set the dead free, so that he can sail to heaven. For the belief, which is directed to heaven and Re, the earth is a gloomy realm of the dead. "N.N. abhors the earth. N.N. does not enter Geb, lest his *b3* perishes" [1]). In an ascension text it reads: "The mouth of the earth is opened to you. Geb speaks to you" [2]). "The earth opens its mouth to you. Geb opens his jaws to you" [3]). "She (the goddess of heaven Nut) raises you to heaven. She does not throw N.N. to earth" [4]).

A.11.j. *d3.t*, netherworld [5]).

Sometimes *d3.t* is close to Geb or *3kr* as the earth from which the dead wishes to escape. "The earth speaks, the gate of the *d3.t* (variant *3kr*) is opened. The gates of Geb are unlocked to you" [6]). The dead leaves the earth and sails to heaven [7]). Staying in the *d3.t* is seen as a sad fate, where Horus helps those who are there. "You (Horus) open the face of those who are in the *d3.t*" [8]). Rising to heaven is opposed to staying in the *d3.t* "You ascend to heaven. You open the netherworld in all shapes you want. You are daily invited to the offerings-table of *Wnn-nfr*" [9]). "Rising to heaven, opening the netherworld amidst the indefatigable ones. They make offerings and bring cakes" [10]). The *d3.t* is a prison, from which the dead knows how to free himself.

Opposed to a dark fate under the earth is the staying in heaven as something desirable. The same thought is at the root of C.T. Spell 655: "To go out, to enter, to descend among the followers, to leave the *d3.t*, to know the ways . . . I go out . . . The thing stopped up is opened. The darkness is lighted. You go out into the day. You have power over his (read: "your") enemies" [11]). The *d3.t* is populated with menacing demons, whom the dead repels. "Create fright of me, that the gods of the *d3.t* may fear me" [12]).

---

1) Pyr. 308. b. c.
2) Pyr. 2169. a.
3) C.T. I. 11. a. b. Idem C.T. VI. 95. h.
4) Pyr. 2171. b.
5) About localising the *d3.t*, Sethe, commentary on *Spruch* 216 Pyr. *Anhang*; *Die Lage der d3.t*.
6) Pyr. 1014.
7) Cf. Pyr. 1986. b.
8) C.T. I. 255. d.
9) Urk. IV. 497. 11-13, (=1219. 15).
10) Urk. IV. 1085. 10.
11) C.T. VI. 275. h- j.m.v; 276. a. b.
12) C.T. IV. 69. c. e. Cf. C.T. IV. 72. d.; 73. f.; 74. d. e.; 83. i.

Especially the *d3.t št3.t*, the hidden *d3.t*, is held to be something unfavourable. The sun-god, on his journey through the realm of the dead, says: "I pass the hidden *d3.t*" [1]). The *d3.t št3.t* is pictured under the throne of Osiris, where there are two monsters [2]). About two demons in a chapel, guarded by a snake, it is said: "Gods, who are in the hidden *d3.t*, in the West" [3]). About the sun-god it is said that he created the *d3.t* in order to hide his body in there (*śšt3*) [4]). The dead in the netherworld are called "the hidden ones". They have disappeared from the sight of the living hidden away under the earth. "Those who are in the West, are hidden. Their position is miserable" [5]). The dead in the netherworld glorify the sun-god, when he passes. "The hidden ones praise you (Re)" [6]).

The circumpolar stars give light to the dead, who are in darkness. They are the ones "who open the sight to those hidden of place" [7]). The denomination "hidden" of the netherworld further occurs in the Book of Gates [8]), where Re says to those who pull his boat: "May you smooth the way to the caves hidden of contents." Those whose place is hidden, are the denizens of the subterranean realm of the dead, over whom Osiris reigns. "Oh N.N., how beautiful is this, how great is this what your father Osiris has done for you. He has given you his seat that you may order those hidden of place. You lead their glorious ones. All spirits serve you" [9]). Compare the following Pyramid Text: "I come to you, hidden of places, that I may lead you to heaven . . . he is hidden. I cannot find him (the dead)" [10]).

A.12. *Snakes as animals of the earth.*

The snake is an animal of the earth. It lives in a den and hisses over the earth. Also outside Egypt the snake is considered a chthonic

---

[1]) L.Q. CXIV. 6. [2]) Schmidt, Sark. 698. [3]) Schmidt, Sark. 700.

[4]) Zandee, *De hymnen aan Amon van Pap. Leiden* I 350, p. 81 (The hymns to Amon of Pap. Leiden).

[5]) H. Kees, *Ein Klagelied über das Jenseits*, Z.Ä.S. 62, p. 76.

[6]) Book of Gates VIII, middle register, B.S. Pl. XIV. 19. 20.

[7]) C.T. II. 147. f.

[8]) Book of Gates IV, middle register, B.S. Pl. VI. 14. 15.

[9]) Pyr. 2022. a-2023. b.

[10]) Pyr. Neith 767. See further Pyr. 134; 656. d.; 747; 873; 1953; 1955; 1641, parallel with *ỉmy.w ỉs.w*, who are in the tombs.

animal. In the tombs of the kings the snake is a symbol of the earth. The travelling of the sun through the netherworld is represented as if the sun is drawn through a big snake. Closely connected with the fear of the earth as realm of the dead is the fear of snakes, who have the earth as a residence. Many spells bear upon preventing the dead being bitten by snakes. Charms, which were used by living people as preventive against snake bites, may also be applied in behalf of the dead.

A.12.a. *ʿ3 ḥry ẖ.t.f*, big one, which is on its belly.

This is a big snake, which is feared by the dead. It is represented in the 4th division of the *ḳrrt*-book over the whole width of the register [1]). As an animal of the earth it houses in the darkness of the realm of the dead. The inscription to it reads: "This great god (Re) enters the twilight. This great god passes the den of the big one, which is on its belly, whose head is in darkness and whose behind is in darkness, whose den the gods, spirits and dead do not approach and whom nobody passes except this great god, who is in heaven."

A.12.b. *Nḥb k3.w*, name of a snake.

This snake is sometimes conceived as being favourable, sometimes as unfavourable for the dead. In a favourable sense *Nḥb k3.w* is used in C.T. Spell 762 [2]): "You are *Nḥb k3.w*, the son of Geb, whom his mother *Rnnwt.t* (determined by the snake) has given birth to. You are truly the *k3* of each god who has the disposal of his heart. You have risen, Horus has saved you. He has provided you with the *k3* of all gods. There is no god whose *k3* is not in you." As son of the god of earth and the goddess of fertility *Nḥb k3.w* is a creator-god, on whom the other gods are dependent as regards their vital strength (*k3.w*). There is a pun with the element *k3.w*, which occurs in the name. *Nḥb k3.w* is the vital strength of all gods and the vital strength of the gods is in him. The dead is identified with this powerful primordial god.

B.D. 17 also puns upon the name [3]): "I spend eternity like *Nḥb k3.w* (*śki.i nḥḥ mi Nḥb k3.w*).

---

[1]) L. Q. XXXIX. 1.

[2]) C.T. VI. 392. g-n. See also the article ,,Nehebkau" in H. Bonnet, *Reallexikon der Ägyptischen Religionsgeschichte*, pp. 510, 511. N. is a primordial god, who is at the beginning of chronology. He grants vital strength and fertility.

[3]) C.T. IV. 311. b.

According to H. Kees [1]) *Nḥb k3.w* "*der die Eigenschaften bestimmt*", is a snake, a primordial god and a chthonic competitor of Atum. *Nḥb k3.w* helps the dead on his journey to heaven. "The circumpolar stars come to you in a bent attitude. *Nḥb k3.w* accompanies you to the *š3r.w*. Sit down on your wonderful throne and judge with the two Enneads" [2]). C.T. Spells 84-87 [3]) are spells, which make it possible for the dead to change himself into *Nḥb k3.w*. The result is that he receives plenty of offerings. Spell 85 reads [4]): "N.N. is the *nʿw*-snake, the bull of *Nw.t*. N.N. is the great one of Atum, who devours seven uraei. Osiris N.N. is high, Osiris N.N. is exalted like *Nḥb k3.w*. N.N. comes to you, gods, who grant dignity, who take away glory. To become like *Nḥb k3.w*." As appears from the identification with the *nʿw*-snake *Nḥb k3.w* is also thought of as a snake. At the same time there is made a pun upon *nḥb k3.w*, to grant dignities [5]), which is here opposed to *nḥm 3ḫ.w*, to take glory away. Compare Pyr. Texts 161.b and 311.a, where *nḥb k3.w* contrasts with *nḥm k3.w*. See also Pyr. Texts 2040 a.b.: "N.N. orders, grants dignity, indicates places." The context of Spell 682 places the dead Pharaoh in a high position. He gives orders to the gods. The meaning is: he gives the gods indications and establishes their rank and position. They are subservient to him. This fits into the picture of a primordial god, as H. Kees wants to conceive *Nḥb k3.w*. C.T. Spell 87 makes the dead lord of the Ennead. He is not liable to magical power. Spell 88 is a similar spell, but there the dead identifies himself with Re. However that may be, the dead puts himself on the same footing as *Nḥb k3.w* as a powerful god, who occupies a leading position in respect of other gods. By this position of authority he knows how to overcome dangers.

In an unfavourable sense *Nḥb k3.w* is taken in the following places. Atum, as ichneumon, kills the *Nḥb k3.w* snake, which is dangerous to the dead [6]). "This is the nail of Atum, which was on the dorsal vertebra of *Nḥb k3.w*. Fall, turn round." "He (Atum) saves me from *Nḥb k3.w*." [7]).

Another Pyramid Text reads: "A fire goes out to *3kr* (the earth).

---

[1]) *Götterglaube*, p. 55, A. 4.
[2]) Pyr. Neith 765.
[3]) C.T. II. 49 sqq.
[4]) C.T. II. 51. d-j.
[5]) Wb. II. 291. 9.
[6]) Pyr. 229. a-c.
[7]) Louvre 3865 IV. 2-3, *św3ḏ.f wỉ m-ʿ Nḥb k3.w*.

Nḥb k3.w is burnt by the poison of the monster" [1]). This passage agrees with other spells against snakes, which have to be destroyed. *Nḥb k3.w* forms part of the group of 42 executioners of Osiris, which occurs in B.D. 125 [2]).

Nḥb k3.w is looked upon in a twofold way. He is a mighty snake-demon. He stands in close connection to gods of the earth and to fertility. He takes a leading position in respect of other gods. Either the dead identifies himself with him, in order to appropriate his power, or he charms him, when he fears danger from him. This tallies with the double aspect of the earth: favourable, because the earth is the source of fertility and potential life; unfavourable as far as it is the dark netherworld.

A.12.c. *r3*. worm.

"Not a single worm eats me" [3]).

A.12.d. *rrk*, a snake.

This often occurs in spells for averting snakes.

"Spell in order to avert the *rrk* . . . Oh *rrk*, *šmty* (in the tombs of the kings a snake on feet) of Shu, messenger of Bastet, may I not be given to him who eats the one cut up" [4]). "Spell to keep *rrk* at bay" [5]). "It is a keeping off of the *rrk*-snake, which destroys the *k3.w*." [6]) "To keep the *rrk*-snake off in the realm of the dead" [7]). "To keep the *rrk*-snake at bay, to cut his veins in two. To repel the snake which destroys the *k3.w* (vital strength). Oh cutter of the head, cutter of the neck, this mate of Osiris' enemies. Oh *ḥnb3*-snake, which has neither arms nor legs [8]), do you rejoice in this, what is on your mouth (poison), what your mother Selkis has given you (the scorpion also works with poison)? May your mother go out against you. Recede on account of what you have seen, villain!" [9]).

A.12.e. *hkì*, a snake.

"*Hkì*-snake, go away . . . You should not do your work on N.N." [10])

[1]) Pyr. Neith 717.
[2]) Naville II, p. 308, no 40.
[3]) B.D. 164; 418. 3-4.
[4]) C.T.V. 41. a-d.
[5]) C.T.V. 42. f; VI. 205. h.; 261. a.
[6]) C.T.V. 44. c.
[7]) C.T.V. 44. h.; see also C.T.V. 283.b.; 286. a.
[8]) Cf. Genesis the curse against the snake, which has to go on its belly.
[9]) C.T. Spell 436; V. 287. a-289. b.
[10]) Pyr. 429. a-c.

A.12.f. *ḥf3w*, snake.

This word occurs in many charms against snakes. "Not to die on account of a snake" [1]. "To keep a snake off in the realm of the dead" [2] "It is on account of not permitting that snakes eat him in the hereafter, but it means that he eats all snakes" [3]. "To keep snakes at bay, which are in a pond in the realm of the dead, which eat from it, which drink from it. On your faces, you who are in the West" [4]. "That a woman may not be eaten by a snake, which Atum (as ichneumon) has bitten. It has filled his mouth (i.e., that of Atum). It twists a coil. Coolness in the town, heat in the country, do not seize this N.N. Seize him who seizes her" [5].

In the *Ḥtp*-field, where the dead leads a beatified life, he is safeguarded against snakes. "There is not a single fish, not a single snake" [6]. The representation in the Book of Gates of snakes as guards of the gates of the netherworld goes back to the *Zweiwegebuch*. Pictures are found there of fiery gates with snakes. Near such a gate it is written: "The mouth of their snakes protects it" [7]. There the dead hopes to be secured from snakes: "Smooth for me the way that is wide, which is not surrounded by snakes" [8]. At the end of the waterway it reads: "These are the snakes which watch over the gate-structures" [9]. Beside a snake at the end of the black road it says: "It is he who is under this convolution. It is the guard of the twist of this pool" [10]. Also the Book of the Dead knows spells against snakes: "Spell in order to keep a snake off" [11]. "Spell that N.N. may not be bitten by a snake in the realm of the dead" [12]. "On your faces (or "a face on you"), oh snakes, oh worms, make me pass" [13].

---

[1]) C.T. II. 373. d.
[2]) C.T.V. 31. e.
[3]) C.T.V. 33. b. c. See also C.T.V. 38. a.
[4]) C.T. Spell 686; VI. 315. a-c.
[5]) C.T. Spell 717, partly = Pyr. 425; VI. 346. a-g.
[6]) C.T.V. 355 (X).
[7]) C.T. VII, Spell 1139; B 1 Be, 122; B 1 P, 572; B 5 C, 453.
[8]) C.T. VII, Spell 1139; B 1 Be, 126.
[9]) Lacau, Sarc. I. 191. 24; C.T. VII, Spell 1052.
[10]) Lacau, Sarc. I. 194. 46. 47; C.T. VII, Spell 1069.
[11]) B.D. 33.
[12]) B.D. 34.
[13]) B.D. 136 B; 302. 15.

A.12.g. *ḥnwy.t*, a snake.

"Oh biting one, which is in its den, great of fright. Bend, retract your arm" [1]).

A.12.h. *ḥnb3*, a snake.

"Oh *ḥnb3*-snake, which has neither arms nor legs" [2]).

A.12.i. *s3 t3*, son of the earth.

"Truly the *s3-t3*-snake has fallen with its vertebra beneath it" [3]). In the tombs of the kings the *s3-t3* is a terrifying snake [4]).

A.12.j. *k3*, a snake.

In a snake spell from the Pyramid Texts, originally meant for living ones, it says: "A *k3*-snake has fallen on account of a *śḏḥ*-snake, a *śḏḥ*-snake has fallen on account of a *k3*-snake" [5]). "I have averted the trembling for you, great *k3*-snake" [6]).

A.12.k. *ḏdf.t*, snake, worm.

"No snakes come against him in their shape" [7]).

About the decomposition of a corpse, which is consumed by worms, it is said: "Let not a single worm pass. Let them not come against me in their shape" [8]).

A.13. *Tomb and funeral.*

The tomb is spoken of in two ways. On the one hand with appreciation: the funerary ritual, the tomb-structure and the funerary cult are indispensable to survive. But the texts also speak of the tomb as a dark place, which man wishes to leave in order to see the sun. The tomb is the repository of man's mortal remains. He wishes his bones to reassemble themselves and that he may rise from death.

A.13.a. *ỉm.t*, tomb.

The tomb is an unfavourable place of residence, which man wants to leave. "Spell that somebody may open his grave" [9]). From the context it becomes evident what the meaning is. The dead does not

---

1) L.Q. III. 5.
2) C.T. V. 288. a.
3) Pyr. Neith 717.
4) L.Q.Pl. IV. 2, 1st *krr.t*.
5) Pyr. Neith 716=Pyr. 430. a.
6) C.T.V. 286. c.
7) Louvre 3283. VI. 13, *nn ỉỉ.n ḏdf.wt r.f m ḫpr.w.śn*
8) B.D. 154; 400. 12-14.
9) C.T. Spell 754; VI. 383.h. For *ʾim.t* cf. *ỉmy.t*, C.T. I. 283.h.

wish to remain in the grave. The parts of his body—they have fallen apart through death—are collected, as was the case with Osiris. He revives, his body functions again.

A.13.b. *is*, grave.

The grave is spoken of in an unfavourable sense, when the dead says, that he wants to shake off the dust of earth and will rise from the dead. "Truly, those who are in the graves, have risen, the hidden ones of place. Wake up, rise, with your hands on your offerings" [1]). "Those who are in their graves rise. Your bandages are loosened. Shake off the dust which is on your face" [2]). Especially those parts of the dead which serve to move freely must be able to leave the grave. "Spell in order to open the tomb to the *b3* and the shadow" [3]).

The grave is taken in a favourable sense as the place where the body is kept whole. A certain spell should be beneficial to a good funeral. "Those who are in their graves, are merciful to you. The owners of a funeral open to you. They bring you the parts of your body, which were far from you" [4]). Enemies of the dead are threatened with their burial being undone. "I chase them away from their graves" [5]). Nevertheless the dead hopes not to remain always locked up in his grave, but to leave it in order to receive offerings. "To come out of the gates which are in the graves, a coming forth in the day" [6]). The grave is also favourably regarded as the eternal house of the dead, where Osiris cares for him. "Those who accompany the funeral procession, say: "To the West, to his place of eternity, to his grave of the necropolis, his eternal house . . . To be buried in the western necropolis, in the grave-yard of the lord of eternity, in the favour of the lord of the gods" [7]).

A.13.c. *ḥ.t*, house.

The grave is the house where the dead lives. He wants to be able to leave it in order to see the sun. In this case the grave is regarded pessimistically. "He goes out and enters his house, in order to be able to see the sun disk of the day" [8]).

---

[1]) Pyr. 1641. a-c.

[2]) Pyr. 1878. a. b.

[3]) B.D. 92; 194.12. For the reverse, to open the grave, so that the *b3* may go into it, to join its corpse, C.T. Spell 242, see p. 106.

[4]) C.T. I. 57. b-d. See NVMEN III, p. 81-96, A. Hermann, *Zergliedern und Zusammenfügen.*

[5]) C.T. I. 400. c.

[6]) C.T. V. 327. a. b.

[7]) Urk. IV. 1200. 4-8.

[8]) Urk. IV. 1183. 15.

The grave is also regarded optimistically. It is the place where the funerary offerings are made, where the one buried lives. In a spell for protecting the tomb-structure it reads [1]): "To build the house, that is in the water. To discover the inundation (to give free course to)." After that passages follow, in which gods provide the tomb with all kinds of food: "*Šsmw* and Sokaris, who is in *Pḏw*, bring offerings." The tomb being neglected ought to be prevented: "If he does not order and does not pay attention to its building, the houses are destroyed and the lower houses are all overturned" [2]). The songs of the harpers contain passages, in which life on earth is glorified. Sometimes they also take the traditional view, in which the fate of the dead in the hereafter is represented as being favourable. In the realm of the dead, in his tomb the dead continues to exist. "Your heart is glad in the realm of the dead, you join (your) grave in peace. The gods of the *d3.t* say to you: welcome to your *k3* in peace" [3]).

A.13.d. *ḥ3.t*, grave.

The dead leaves the grave. "You have assembled your bones. You have restored the parts of your body. You have shaken off your dust. You have loosened your bonds. You have opened the grave. You have opened the doors of the coffin" [4]). The dead rises. As regards the doors of the coffin we may think of the picture of doors on the coffin, which already occurs in the Old Kingdom (1st dynasty).

A.13.e. *ḥr.t*, grave.

This is used in a favourable sense in the wish: "May I rest in the tomb that I have made myself" [5]). The grave is the place that ensures the survival of the dead.

A.13.f. *ḫmw*, dust.

In the Egyptian texts there are reminiscences of a funeral without mummification, directly into the earth without more. The corpse decays, the bones are scattered. This dreaded fate must be undone. The dead shakes the dust off and rises. "Rise, shake off your dust,

---

[1]) C.T. Spell 571; VI. 170. g.h.
[2]) C.T. VI. 171. a.; 173. k-n.
[3]) M. Lichtheim, J.N.E.S. IV. 206.
[4]) Pyr. 2008. a.b.; 2009. a.
[5]) Urk. IV. 10. 9.

remove the dirt which is on your face [1]). Loosen your ties, they are not ties, they are the curls of Nephthys" [2]). "Rise, receive your head, assemble your bones, collect the parts of your body, shake off the dust of the earth which is on your flesh" [3]). "Your dust does not exist" [4]). The dead arrives in the netherworld. Osiris welcomes him and invites him to be greeted as a king. "Be jubilant when seeing him, having come today from the land of life to his place of justification." The dead comes like somebody who has conquered death. In this connection it is said of him: "He has chased away his dust" [5]).

A.13.g. *ḳrś*, funeral.

By *ḳrś* the ritual funeral is understood with everything belonging to it. For instance, *ḳrś* is also a word for coffin. It is comprehensible that the texts hardly ever speak of the funeral as of something that the dead shuns. It is the totality of the rites which bring about his immortality. Therefore somebody prays to Amon-Re: "Grant that my grave may exist for ever" [6]). If the grave remains undamaged, life is secured. The Egyptian wants a well-executed funerary ceremonial. "May she give a fine funeral in the western desert" [7]). The mummy and the grave are under the protection of Anubis. "An offering to the dead, which the king gives and Anubis, the lord of the good funeral, that he be buried in peace in the necropolis" [8]). "How gladdening is this which has happened to him. He fixed his place of arranging his tomb. He filled his heart with Khons in Thebes. He makes him reach the West" [9]). Also the songs of the harpers sing of the good side of the funeral. "Oh divine father, your soul proceeds. Your sarcophagus comes nearer. Anubis lies his hands on you. The two sisters protect you. Purification is performed for you again. You are distinguished by an eternal work: the stone statue of a god in his exact form" [10]). One may think here of the representations, where Anubis takes care of the mummy, of the priest with

---

1) Cf. C.T. I. 71. a.b.: "No sand is put on your face, lest it might be too heavy for you."

2) Pyr. 1363. a-c. Idem C.T. III. 248. a-e.

3) Pyr. 654. a-d. See A. Hermann, *Zergliedern und Zusammenfügen*, NVMEN III, p. 85, note 26.

4) Pyr. 1283. b.

5) C.T. VI. 223. i.

6) Urk. IV. 446. 8.

7) Urk. IV. 414. 2.

8) E. Lüddeckens, *Totenklagen*, p. 21; Cairo 1808.

9) Op. cit. p. 100, 18th dynasty.

10) M. Lichtheim, J.N.E.S. IV. p. 198, Pl. II. 9.

the Anubis mask, who accepts the corpse, of the wailing-women, who play the part of Isis and Nephthys and who, by their songs, resuscitate the dead as their brother Osiris [1]), of the statue in the tomb, a body in which the dead can continue to exist.

How highly the funeral ritual was valued, also appears from the fact that the grave of enemies, sinners or other evil beings should be disturbed. Without a grave, mummy and funerary cult they are doomed to destruction. Sinners are punished by violation of their graves by certain demons, about whom it is said [2]): "They are the ones who bare the corpses and who make the mummy bandages into a ball for the enemies, whose punishment is ordered in the *d3.t*." Seth is punished with the loss of a ritual funeral [3]). Tomb robbers are threatened on the monuments and in spells. "N.N., place a flame and throw fire against him who will raise his hand against the grave of Osiris N.N." [4]). From this sharp threat it appears how much value was set on the grave remaining intact. He who desecrates somebody's grave does not get a ritual funeral himself. "As concerns anyone who will do damage to my statue, he shall not follow the king of his time. He shall not be buried in the western desert. The time of his life on earth will not be fulfilled" [5]). The tomb robber is threatened with an early death and non-survival for want of a ritual funeral.

In the dialogue between the *Lebensmüde* and his soul the funerary ceremonial is deemed to be problematical. In the background is a period of decline, in which the tomb monuments were neglected and the funerary offerings did not take place [6]). The soul rejects the orthodox point of view of the man that the funerary ceremonial gives eternal life. The man stands up for a good funeral. The corpse remains intact and the *b3*-bird can alight upon it [7]). "I shall make him reaching the West like one who lies in his pyramid and of whose

---

[1]) C. J. Bleeker, *Isis and Nephthys as Wailing Women*, NVMEN V, p. 14.

[2]) Am Duat X. 11.

[3]) Pap. Jumilhac, XV. 24.

[4]) B.D. 163; 412. 4-6.

[5]) Urk. IV. 401. 16-402. 2.

[6]) G. Posener, *Littérature et Politique dans l'Égypte de la XIIe Dynastie*, p. 10.

[7]) Cf C.T. Spell 242, III. 327. a, a spell in order to achieve that the tomb may be opened, so that the *b3* can join "its" corpse. "Spell to open a gate for the *b3*." "Open to me, that I may see my corpse."

funeral a relative takes care. I shall make a hiding-place for your corpse, that it does not suffer of cold. I shall drink water at the well, so that you may make another soul, which is hungry, jealous. But if you drive me so (prematurely) into death you will not find a place in the West, upon which you can alight" [1]). The *Lebensmüde* also pleads for a good maintenance of the tomb by the heir. "So have patience, my soul, my brother, till there will be a heir, who will make offerings and will take care of the grave on the day of the funeral and who will spread the bed of the netherworld" [2]). The care of the tomb cult of the deceased father was entrusted to the eldest son [3]). In view of this alone somebody wishes to have a son. C.T. Spell 700 is probably one which must help somebody who died childless, to get male descendants after his death. "That somebody may be among the living . . . If somebody has no son, he will beget one afterwards with the daughter of the phoenix" [4]).

The soul of the *Lebensmüde* has its doubts about the latter's pleading for a good funeral. The ritual is of no avail. The tomb monuments are destroyed. The funeral itself is only sadness and lamentation for somebody who passed away. "My soul opened its mouth to me, that it might give an answer to what I had said: if you recall the funeral, it means sadness and bringing tears by putting somebody in a sad mood" [5]).

At the end of the conversation they seem to come to an agreement. The soul acknowledges the meaning of a good funeral and promises to render the indispensable services to the dead. "Whether you want me to stay here, after you have rejected the West, or whether you want to reach the West and want your body to be buried and me alighting after your having died, we will stay together" [6]).

A.13.h. *ḳd*, to build.

In the conversation with the *Lebensmüde* the latter's soul points out the uselessness of tomb constructions. "Those who have built with granite, who constructed halls in beautiful pyramids as a

---

[1]) *Lebensmüde* 41-51.
[2]) *Lebensmüde* 52-55.
[3]) *S3 mr. f*, taken over by the *ḥm-k3*-priest.
[4]) C.T. VI. 333. a. i. j.
[5]) *Lebensmüde* 55-57.
[6]) *Lebensmüde* 151-154.

beautiful work, as soon as the builders have become gods, it happens that their offering stones are empty" [1]).

A.14. *Mummy bandages.*

These are necessary for preserving the body, it is true, but nevertheless the dead wishes to free himself from them in order to rise from death and to be able to move freely.

A.14.a. *ʿfn.t*, bandages.

When the sun-god appears in the netherworld, the dead throws off the mummy bandages in order to be able to see the sun. "Your head-cloths are unfolded, . . . your bandages are loosened, my light is for you" [2]).

A.14.b, *ʿnn*, bandage.

The dead wishes the mummy bandages to be loosened in order to be free to execute the functions of his body. "The bandages which are on my intestines, are opened" [3]).

A.14.c. *wt*, mummy bandages.

The mummy bandage is thrown off, so that the dead may rise. "Loosening of your bandages" is said to the dead in the netherworld [4]). In the Book of Gates [5]) four mummies are represented with their heads free, *wt3.w*, wrapped like mummies, derived from *wt*. It is said to these "hidden of arm": "Your needs belong to you, . . . your heads are bared, your arms are hidden. Breath belongs to your noses, loosening to your bandages." The arms of the mummies are still wrapped up, but their heads are stripped of bandages. It is a beginning of resurrection, which is considered to be something better than mummification. The latter remains an impediment to the free motion of the body.

A.14.d. *ṯs.t*, tie.

"Your ties are loosened" [6]). Cf. *ḳ3ś*, A.7.1; perhaps not mummy bandages, but the ties of death.

---

[1]) *Lebensmüde* 61-63.

[2]) Book of Gates VI, middle register, E. Lefébure, M.M.A.F.C. III, 1, Pl. XXXIV. 40-43; Cenotaph Seti I, Pl. LIX; C. T. III. 350. a, the wrapping of the dead, may I not go in there.

[3]) C.T. II. 115. c.

[4]) Book of Gates VI, lower register, E. Lefébure, M.M.A.F.C. III, 1, Pl. XXXIII. 10. 11; idem Pyr. 1878. a.

[5]) Book of Gates II, middle register, B.S. Pl. II, 46-51.

[6]) Pyr. 593. b.

A.15. *Death as horror.*

The fear of death is expressed in representations of terrifying beings in the hereafter, who scare people. Certain spells are directed against this.

A.15.a. *nrỉ*, to fear.

The dead undoes the fright which a dangerous god strikes into him. "He seizes your fright, lord of the light" [1]). A gate in the netherworld, which the dead has to pass, is called "mistress of fright" [2]). A goddess with snake-heads and snakes in her hand, standing in a fiery gate, says [3]): "I am the gate-keeper with mysterious faces, with many names in the *d3.t*, who strikes fear into the spirits." Of a vulture-goddess, who personifies terror, it is said [4]): "Frightful one, mistress of the dew (= divine power), who makes a slaughter." Near the pictures of snakes is written [5]): "Oh *nš3y*-snake, destroying of eyes, which the denizens of the netherworld fear when they see it."

A.15.b. *nḥ3 ḥr*, wild of face.

This is an epitheton of demoniacal beings who inspire fear: of the messengers of Osiris [6]); of a demon at a fiery gate [7]); of one of the 42 judges of Osiris [8]). In one of the books from the tombs of the kings, which describe the netherworld, it is said about a snake: "Oh wild one of face, which is in its den, to which those who are in the *d3.t* assign the souls of the place of destruction" [9]).

A.15.c. *ḥrw*, terror.

A snake, which terrifies the dead, is called "great of terror" [10]). The name of a snake, which watches over a division of the realm of the dead, is: "Master of terror" [11]). The dead wants to be protected against demons: He is saved from the terror of the evil-doers, which is in the whole country" [12]).

---

1) C.T. VI. 150. h.i.
2) *Livre de la Nuit*, ed. A. Piankoff, p. 36, 1st gate (Seti I).
3) Schmidt, Sark, 697.
4) B.D. 146; 356. 10-12.
5) L.Q. XI. 5.
6) C.T. III. 304. f.
7) C.T. VII, Spell 1090; B 1 L. 466.
8) B.D. 125; 253.16; variant 253.4 *nḥ3 ḥ‘.w*, wild of limbs.
9) L.Q. III. 7. 8.
10) L.Q. III. 5.
11) Louvre 3292, ed. Nagel, N. 9.
12) B.D. 163; rubric, 414. 15. 16.

A.15.d. *śnḏ*, to fear.

About a demon in the realm of the dead it is said: "Whom they fear who are in tiredness (i.e., the dead)" [1]). Demons "frighten" [2]) the dead. A gate in the realm of the dead is called: "Mistress of fear" [3]). Horus says to his father Osiris: "The spirits are afraid of you, the dead are frightened of you" [4]). A gate-keeper with the head of a crocodile and snakes in his hands is called: "Mistress of fear" [5]). A goddess with the head of a lion in Am Duat is somebody "who makes the spirits fear" [6]).

A.15.e. *śdȝ*, to tremble.

"I have repelled the trembling for you, great *ḳȝ*-snake" [7]), the dead says. A gate in the realm of the dead is called: "Mistress of trembling" [8]). In the realm of the dead gates are dangerous places, which are watched by demons.

A.15.f. *šfšf.t*, fright.

The name of a gate in the netherworld is: "Great of fright" [9]).

A.15.g. *ḳȝ ḫrw*, high of voice.

In C.T. Spell 653 demoniacal guards, whom somebody has to pass, are represented near the bends of a river. One of these guards frightens by his loud roaring. "This is this guard of his, whose name is: high (loud) of voice" [10]).

A.15.h. *dnyw.t*, shouting.

About the 10th gate in B.D. 146 [11]) it is said: "With noise, which makes somebody wake with a start, crying at the top of his voice, frightful one, mistress of fright. It does not remove what is in it." This gate intimidates by roaring.

A.16. *Death as affliction.*

The realm of the dead is a dark and gloomy place. Those who are there, grieve. At the most this grief temporarily turns into joy,

---

[1]) C.T. IV. 320. d.; B.D. 17.
[2]) C.T. I. 229. a, causative *śśnḏ*.
[3]) *Livre de la Nuit*, 9th gate.
[4]) Book of Gates III, lower register, B.S. Pl. VIII. 10.11.
[5]) Schmidt, Sark. 694.
[6]) Am Duat II. 61, read: *śśnḏ.t*.
[7]) C.T. V. 286. c.
[8]) B.D. 141, 1st gate.
[9]) *Livre de la Nuit*, 4th gate; Book of Gates, 9th gate, B.S. Pl. XIII. 5.6.
[10]) C.T. VI. 274. e.
[11]) B.D. Budge, p. 354. 4.

when they catch sight of the sun on its nightly journey through the realm of the dead. But the godless do not see the sun at all. All this fits in with a שְׁאֹל-conception of the hereafter.

A.16.a. *i3kb*, to cry.

When Re, on his journey, through the realm of the dead, has left their division and they are in darkness again, those who are there, cry. "They lament on account of the great god, when he has passed them" [1]). In the 5th hour of Am Duat the Memphitic conception of the netherworld of Sokaris is described. The sun does not come there. It is a sad place. "The waters of those who cry, the gods who are in *'Imḥ.t*, along whom the boat (of Re) does not pass. The *d3ty.w* do not dispose of their water, which is in this necropolis. Their water is against those who are in there like fire" [2]). "I have lighted the darkness . . . Those who are in their darkness, praise me. Those who grieve, rise for me" [3]). All these quotations point in the same direction. Without Re spreading his light the netherworld is a gloomy place full of crying.

A.16.b. *nhm*, to cry.

This does not happen in the *Ḥtp*-field, being a paradise in the hereafter. "There is no clamour there at all, there is not a single evil thing there" [4]).

A.16.c. *rmi*, to cry.

Punished enemies of Re are called *rmy.w*, crying ones [5]). The dead has overcome a sad fate in the realm of the dead: "You have exercised your power against your enemies, the crying has died down" [6]). "Do not permit . . . him to remember the crying" [7]).

A.16.d. *hwt*, to lament.

Whenever in the Book of Gates Re has left a part of the realm of the dead, the denizens are left lamenting. So, e.g., it reads in the first division (B.S. Pl. IV. 1): "This door is closed, after this god having

---

[1]) Book of Gates II, lower register, B.S. Pl. II. 52-54.
[2]) Am Duat V. 238.
[3]) B.D. 80; 177. 9-10.
[4]) C.T. V. 349. f; 350. a.
[5]) L.Q. XLVIII.5; cf. B.I.F.A.O. XLII. 40.
[6]) C.T. I. 313. a.
[7]) C.T. III. 33. b-34. a. In C.T. Spell 615, a spell in order "to join a god", it reads: "I am cheered up. My tears are carried off" (VI. 227. h.i.). This must refer to annulling the fate of death as something sad.

entered. Then those who are in their divisions lament, when they hear that this door falls to." When Re is not present, the dead are in sadness and lamentation. The realm of the dead is a cheerless place.

A.16.e. *hmhm.t*, shouting.

People, painfully punished in the realm of the dead by demons shout. "He who knows the punishers of the enemy, passes them (safely). He does not come to their roaring (that is to say what they have caused). He does not fall into their "traps" [1])." The boat of Re does not come to the domain of Sokaris, but is pulled past it. In this place the wailing of the dead who are there, is heard. "A sound is heard in this desert after this great god has passed them like the roaring of the sky, when it rages (the thunder)" [2]).

A.16.f. *ḥ3*, to mourn.

He who does not sail to heaven with Re, stays under the earth in a sad realm of the dead, a view which also occurs in the Pyramid Texts. "They mourn with their hair before this great god in the West. They return to this gate. They do not enter heaven" [3]).

B. Dangers of the hereafter.

Introduction.

The hereafter as such is not conceived as a dark realm of the dead. There is a possibility to escape from death there. In the Pyramid Texts the dead king is able to sail to heaven. There is a region of fertile fields washed by water. A ferry-man takes one across to it. It is an archipelago, where the dead ploughs and sows. The corn grows high there. He is not in want there. The texts speak about the *'I3r.w*-field or the *Ḥtp*-field. Sometimes this domain is thought of as being in *'Imḫ.t* [4]), a netherworld where Osiris is king. It is said about it: "You rejoice at your ploughing your plot of the *'I3r.w*-field. Your subsistence arises as that which you have grown. Harvest comes to you in abundance."

The Pyramid Texts localise the *'I3r.w*-field in the East, near the place where Re rises. "Re has purged himself in the *'I3r.w*-field.

---

1) Am Duat III. 25-27.
2) Am Duat V. 197-199.
3) Book of Gates XI, lower register, B.S. Pl. IX. 42-46.
4) Urk. IV. 116. 13-15.

N.N. has purged himself in the *ʾI3r.w*-field. The hand of N.N. is the hand of Re. Nut, take his hand. Shu, raise him" [1]). Here is thought of the sunrise.

The same in Pyr. par. 526, where in connection with *śḫ.t ʾI3r.w* "early in the morning" (*m tp dw3*) is used. Also the Coffin Texts [2]) associate the *ʾI3r.w*-field with the eastern part of heaven. "If you think of crossing to the eastern part of heaven, in order to do what do you cross?" "That I may assume the government of the towns and that I may take charge of the fortresses." "Do you know the road along which you have to go?" "I am going to the *ʾI3r.w*-field." In another spell the *ʾI3r.w*-field is associated with heaven. [3]) "What are they, those two domains (?) where you go?" "The *Ḥtp*-field and the *ʾI3r.w*-field" . . . "The ponds of *ʾI3r.w* are flooded. Green are their ponds with me. Hathor, do give me your hand, that you may draw me to heaven." The *ʾI3r.w*-field and the *Ḥtp*-field are practically identical. In a Pyramid Text, where the *ʾI3r.w*-field and the *Ḥtp*-field are mentioned together, they are localised in the sky among the circumpolar stars [4]): "Cross the sky to the *ʾI3r.w*-field, settle down in the field of foods among the circumpolar stars in the retinue of Osiris."

So there is, after all, something to be said for it, with R. Weill [5]), to localise the *śḫ.t ʾI3r.w* in the East, but not, like he does, the *śḫ.t ḥtp.t* in the West. Nowhere the texts state clearly that the *śḫ.t ḥtp.t* is in the West, but they rather place it in the sky.

In Memphis the conception of *R3-śṯ3.w* is it being a place of beatitude. The *Zweiwegebuch* describes how two roads, one by sea and one by land, lead through it. On this journey to the place of the beatified, however, the dead is exposed to all kinds of dangers. Between the two roads is a pool of fire. The dead has to take care not to land there. The spells of the book help him with this.

On his journey through the realm of the dead he has to pass dangerous places and demons or gates, which are guarded by deterrent keepers.

---

1) Pyr. *Spruch* 253; 275. b-f.
2) C.T. V. 103. e-104. a; 105. b. h; Spell 397.
3) Spell 398; C.T. V. 151. e.f; 158. e; 159. a-d.
4) Pyr. 749. c-e.
5) *Le champ des roseaux et le champ des offrandes*, Paris, 1936.

Especially in later texts, like those from the tombs of the kings, these dangers have taken the shape of infernal punishments, to which the dead is exposed after being condemned. Just as *sḫd*, to go with the head down, was at first a danger which threatened each dead, but which became a punishment for sinners in the tombs of the kings, so also, e.g., the fire, a dangerous place in the *Zweiwegebuch*, which one must and can avoid,—has become a punishment of hell in the tombs of the kings. So in this group of conceptions it is not always possible to distinguish sharply between dangers, which are imminent to everybody and punishments for sinners.

B.1. *Gates, which the dead has to pass.*

In the hereafter the dead has to pass several gates in order to reach the ultimate object. They are a hindrance, which he has to overcome. He may be stopped at the gate. Usually the gate-keepers are demoniacal beings, who wish to hurt or kill him, when he approaches them. Only forced by a powerful charm they will let him pass and the doors will open. Sometimes it is said that the gate lets only just people through, but keeps sinners at bay. The texts that deal with the gates, give the necessary knowledge to somebody for being admitted and reaching one's destiny: to be with Re in the heavens or in the realm of Osiris.

B.1.a. *ʿ3*, door.

During his ascension the dead has to pass doors. By his spell the doors are opened and he may proceed unhindered. "To you both the doors of heaven are opened just as to Horus of the gods. To you both the doors of *Ḳbḥw* are opened as to the eastern Horus . . ., to you the doors of heaven are opened, to you the gates of the *3ḫ.t* are unlocked as to Horus of the gods" [1]).

iry ʿ3, door-keeper.

The gates are watched by keepers. They are demons armed with knives, or snakes, which want to keep off the dead. They perform the function of judges, who let the just pass, but keep the sinner at bəy or condemn him.

In an ascension text it says [2]): "He finds before him *Šṯṯ*, the caller,

---

1) C.T. VI. 353. o.p; 354. a.

2) Pyr. 1157. a-c. See further Pyr. 520. a = Pyr. Neith 818; Pyr. 1201. a; 1252. a.

the door-keeper of Osiris, who detests the taking across." The idea here is a ferry-man who has to put the dead across and who must make the ascension possible for him. The judicial function appears from a text from the Book of the Dead [1]: "Oh gate-keepers, oh gate-keepers, guards of their gates, who gulp down the souls, who devour the corpses of the dead, along whom one passes in their judgment of the place of judgment, who make the soul of a spirit be led to excellence." Consequently a sinner is condemned, a just man let through.

In the funerary texts numerous invocations occur, which serve to charm gate-keepers. "Gate-keeper of the great house, open to me" [2]. Here gate-keepers in a subterranean realm of the dead are referred to. The dead refers to his good qualities in order to be let through. "That his goodness may be in the heart of the door-keepers" [3]. "There is no grief caused by your gate-keepers against me" [4]. The dead makes himself announce as a powerful one to a gate-keeper and in this way he hopes to be let through: "Oh Wr, enter, say to *ʾIʿb-sšw*, the door-keeper of Osiris, that I have come, that I am glorious, that I am strong . . . that I have come in order to save my body" [5]. The dead asks to be admitted to a happy destination. "Gate-keeper of *Mdw-tꜣ.f*, open to me. Make room for me, let me pass that I may sit in the place where I want, as a living *bꜣ*" [6].

B.1.b. *ʿrr.t*, gate.

This occurs as synonym of *śbḫ.t* (B.1.h) [7]. It is a place, where people are tortured in the hereafter. "Gate, burning of front, hidden of back. Somebody is there, while being bound. It is something wonderful" [8]. A drawing of demoniacal animals goes with it [9]. In the *Zweiwegebuch* *ʿrr.t* is a division bordered with black, red or blue. "Gate of the darkness, gate of the fire" [10]. *ʿrr.t* is not a gate-

[1]) B.D. 127 A; 272. 2-6.
[2]) C.T. IV. 343. a.
[3]) Louvre 3292, ed. Nagel, L. 6-7.
[4]) Op. cit. P. 7.
[5]) C.T. Spell 228; III. 268. a.b; 270. b.g.; 272. d.e.
[6]) B.D. 189; 493. 6 sqq.
[7]) C.T. IV. 72. e; 74. f.
[8]) *Zweiwegebuch* B 1 Be. 12; B 1 P, 468; B 5 C, 348; C.T. VII, Spell 1132.
[9]) C.T. VII, Spell 1132; B 5 C. 348.
[10]) C.T. VII, Spell 1036; B 2 L. 488. 489.

structure but a space [1]). A title of the *Zweiwegebuch* reads: "To pass all gates" [2]). In B.D. 136 A we read: "Osiris N.N. announces Re at the gates" [3]). Just as in the texts from the tombs of the kings this refers to gates in the netherworld, which Re passes on his journey. "The gate-keepers are not unacquainted with him" [4]). So they do not trouble him. The dead hopes, on his journey through the realm of the dead, to pass the gates safely. "I pass their gates. They extol when they see me" [5]). In B.D. 144 and 147 seven *ʿrr.t* occur. With each are three figures, in the gate a gate-keeper with a knife in his hand, *iry ʿrry.t*, a guard, *s3w*, with a ram's head and a *śmi*, one who announces, also with a knife in his hand. B.D. 147 says [6]): "To speak words in approaching the seven gates. This spirit enters into this gate without being kept off from Osiris. He is made to be among the excellent spirits . . . As regards each spirit for whom this is done, he will be there as lord of eternity, one body with Osiris." When somebody is kept off by the gate-keepers, he does not obtain a favourable fate in the hereafter. When he can pass the gate, a beatified life near Osiris is waiting for him. The same idea occurs in Papyrus Louvre 3292 [7]): "Spell to see the gate by N.N. He says: Hail to you, this gate of the great god, which no evil-doers enter, which no living ones see . . . You receive Osiris N.N. in peace. He joins your customs. You open to him these doors of yours. I enter there as I like to." Sinners are kept at bay. Only the just enter through the gate.

B.1.c. *r3 n d3.t*, gate of the *d3.t*.

The dead may go in and out freely through the gate of the netherworld. "Seven cups are permanently with you, giving you a good quality, a good life, good breathing, good exit and good entrance through the gate of the *d3.t*, while you do what you like in the West to all eternity" [8]).

---

1) "*Gebiet*", S. Schott, *Die Schrift der verborgenen Kammer in Königsgräbern der 18. Dynastie*; *Nachr. d. Ak. d. Wiss. i. Göttingen, I, Phil.-Hist.Kl.* 1958, Nr. 4, p. 345.

2) C.T. VII, Spell 1085; B 1 Be. 312.

3) B.D. Budge, p. 299. 6.

4) B.D. Budge, p. 299. 9.

5) B.D. 127 A; 273. 8. 9.

6) B.D. Budge, p. 362. 8 sqq.

7) Ed. Nagel, P. 1-7.

8) Louvre 3148, III. 10.11, *ḥn.wt* 7 *mn ḥnʿ.k ḥr rdi.t n.k ḳi.w nfr.w ʿnḫ nfr snsn nfr pr nfr ʿḳ nfr r r3.w nw d3.t iw.k ḥr ir.t mr.k m imnt.t ḏ.t.*

B.1.d. *rw.t*, gate.

In the Pyramid Texts *rw.t* is a gate, which may keep the dead locked up in the earth. He wishes this gate to open in order to be able to sail to heaven. In a resurrection text it reads: "The earth speaks to you, the gate of *ȝkr* opens to you, the doors of Geb are opened to you" [1]). The gate of *Ḫnti mn.wt.f.* is opened to you [2]). "This is a Horus-god, who guides the dead to heaven [3]). Also here it concerns an ascension. "I have claimed him from *Ḥrty* [4]). I do not deliver him up to Osiris. I open to him the gate, that repels" [5]). The gate may also remain closed, so that the dead is imprisoned in the earth.

In a N.K. text it reads: "As regards this big gate of the realm of the dead, which is hidden to man, to which the spirits do not know the way, which the dead do not cross, along which the sun disk passes in order to see both countries, from *Ỉgr.t*, to this one Osiris N.N. approached ... He addresses these gate-keepers: Open your doors to me, for I have power over them. I have already had business with you, as I have descended in the sun-boat. I have made all good offerings to him who is in his boat" [6]). The text is very closely connected with the Book of Gates. Two mummy-shaped beings and four snakes watch over the gate. Such figures also occur as guards in the Book of Gates. The dead does not want to share the sad fate of those who must always remain in the netherworld and who revive only temporarily when the sun passes. He wants to have a place in the sun-boat in order to get through the gates of the realm of the dead together with Re.

B.1.e. *ḫnḫn*, to keep off.

The dead sets value upon the fact that he may move freely in the hereafter. He fears that he might be imprisoned somewhere or be kept at bay. He wishes that his *bȝ* is able to move in order to provide him with food. Certain spells must prevent the *bȝ* being hampered in its movements. "You go in and you go out. You are buried in the western necropolis. You become a living *bȝ*. Truly, it

---

1) Pyr. 1713. a.
2) Pyr. Neith 757.
3) Pyr. Neith 807=Pyr. 1764.
4) Unfavourable god of the dead, akin to Osiris.
5) Pyr. Neith 779.
6) Louvre 3292, ed. Nagel, N. 1-4.

(the *b3*) has the disposal of bread, water and air. It transforms itself into a phoenix, a swallow, a falcon or a heron, as you like. You cross in the ferry-boat. You are not kept off. You sail the waters. It happens that you revive" [1]). Not being kept off here refers to not being rejected by the ferry-man who has to put him across a river in order to reach a place like the *ḥtp*-fields, where there is abundance of food. The text continues [2]): "You eat cake on the side of the god near the big staircase of the lord of the Ennead (Re). You make yourself comfortable there near the place where he is amidst the first council. You walk about among them. You join the followers of Horus. You ascend and descend without being kept off. You are not kept off from the gate of the netherworld. The two wings of the doors of the *3ḫ.t* are opened to you . . . You join the hall of the double truth. The god who is in there, speaks to you. You sit down in *'Imḥ.t*. You stride along in the town of the Nile inundation." The journey of the dead continues. He arrives in the surroundings of Re. After that he wants to go to Osiris, the king of the netherworld. He expects to be acquitted by the judgment in the hall of the double truth. On his way to the *d3.t* he has to pass gates again, where he may be kept at bay. The "being kept at bay" is a being hampered in attaining the ultimate aim: the entrance to a happy place in the hereafter.

B.1.f. *ḫśf*, to keep at bay.

There are doors, which the dead has to pass in order to be able to sail to heaven. He may be kept at bay there. "Go and stand near the doors that keep people at bay" [3]). "The two doors of *Ḫnty Ỉmnty.w* which keep man at bay, are opened to you" [4]). The *rḫy.t*, the *profanum vulgus*, as opposed to the king, is not admitted to the ascension. So they have to remain in a subterranean realm of the dead. The dead may be hindered in the free admittance to the realm of the dead. He expresses the wish that this may not happen. "It is brought about that he is powerful among these gods. He is not kept at bay, he is not turned away from the gates of the *d3.t*" [5]).

---

1) Urk. IV. 113. 5-114. 1.

2) Urk. IV. 115. 17-116. 12.

3) Pyr. 655. b.; C.T. I. 289. f.

4) C.T. VI. 104. b. Cf. Pyr. 1749. b and C.T. VI. 104. j, *pr.k r p.t*, ascension text; Pyr. Neith 766, 767, "Oh Neith, the doors which keep people at bay are opened for you. . . . . I conduct you to heaven."

5) B.D. 144; 333. 1-3.

Also without there being any talk about a gate *ḫśf* is used for keeping the dead off, so that he cannot reach a favourable place in the hereafter [1]). "I am a follower of Re . . . I am not kept off from Re. I am not kept off by him who acts with both his arms. I do not go into the valley of darkness. I do not enter the pool of malefactors"[2]). Being kept off here means being prevented from being in the neighbourhood of a god. The dead arrives in a place of horror.

The dead wishes that the gate-keepers of the netherworld do not keep him at bay. He wants to enter the *d3.t* in order to join Osiris. He also wants to leave it in order to receive his offerings. "My soul be alive near the lord of eternity (Osiris). The gate-keepers, who watch over the gates of the *d3.t*, will not keep him off. May he go out when the offerer calls in my tomb of the necropolis. May he rejoice at bread. May he have plenty of beer. May he drink water at the drinking-place [3]) of the river. May I go in and out like the glorious spirits of the dead, who have done what their gods praise" [4]).

The dead wants not to be hampered in his movements. He wants to see Re, to be with Osiris in the hall of judgment, to be able to enter the netherworld freely for that purpose, but also to be able to leave it, in order to cross to the *Ỉ3r.w*-fields, where he may live on a rich harvest. "You see Re daily. Your face sees the sun, when it shines. Cakes are given to you in Heliopolis. You let yourself down in the hall of the double truth. *Ỉmḥ.t* opens its gates to you. You venerate the god who is on his seat. You are not repelled from the door-posts. You cross in the ferry-boat, as you wish. You plough in the *Ỉ3r.w*-field" [5]). Not being kept off refers to free passage for the *b3*. "Those who watch over their hearts, do not keep me at bay . . . Open ways to my *b3* and my shadow" [6]). The dead rises. He does not remain in the earth. "*3kr* does not keep me off" [7]). He has free admittance to Re. "You come to meet Re . . . You are not kept at bay" [8]).

---

[1]) Also the verb *šnʿ* is used in this sense.

[2]) *Zweiwegebuch*, C.T. VII, Spell 1099; B 1 L, 482-485; B 3 L, 651-654; "*Torhütergespräche*" B.D. 130.

[3]) The *b3* is represented in the Theban tombs while scooping water from a pond with its hands, e.g., Userhet.

[4]) Urk. IV. 430. 9-15.

[5]) Urk. IV. 520. 2-11.

[6]) C.T. VI. 67. g.j.

[7]) C.T. VI. 95. 1.

[8]) C.T. VI. 107. k; 108. b.

B.1.g. *šb3*, gate.

The dead wishes that the gates are opened to him and that he has free passage. These gates may be in the earth or give admittance to heaven.

The earth should set the dead free, that he may travel with Re along heaven" [1]). Geb has opened the gate to me, that I may go out" [2]). The gates of the netherworld must open to the dead, that he may obtain free admittance to Osiris. "They fight against the gates of the *d3.t* for N.N." [3]). The dead goes in and out freely through the gate of the netherworld in order to join Re. "May you go in and go out in the West, may you stride freely through the gate of the *d3.t*. May you adore Re, when he rises in the *3ḫ.t*. May you honour him when he sets in the *3ḫ.t*. May you receive offerings, may you be contented with offering-loaves from the altar of the lord of eternity" [4]). The dead prays to demoniacal gate-keepers, that they open the doors of the *d3.t* to him, that he may sail to heaven [5]) "To open a gate in the *d3.t* for Osiris N.N. Archers (?) of Shu, who are in the light, let N.N. pass. Open to him a gate in the land of the *d3.t*. N.N., truly, to him belongs the entire earth. To open a gate to somebody in the land of the *d3.t*."

The realm of the dead is considered favourably. The dead is received there with joy [6]). "There is a sound of jubilation in the realm of the dead. The inhabitants of the *d3.t* say "welcome", so they say to Osiris N.N. Those who are in their graves rejoice in Osiris N.N.: you are the great god who is in heaven among the gods. Osiris N.N. descends. The gates of the roads of *Ỉmḥ.t* are opened to you." The gates of the realm of the dead open, that the dead may sit down in the sun-boat and ascend with Re [7]). "The gates of *Ỉmḥ.t* open to me to the beautiful roads on this day to the island of the just, to the place where the horizon dwellers are. I go out there through the sacred gate." The dead is, as Osiris, under the protection of the goddess of heaven Nut. She has to open her gates to him, that he may join Re in his boat. "Open to me. I am Osiris. Do not close your (Nut's) gates against me, that I may cross the heavens, that I may join the

1) C.T. II. 81. c-83. b.
2) C.T. II. 75. a.
3) C.T. IV. 74. f. Cf. 77. a.
4) Urk. IV. 1063. 13-1064. 3.
5) C.T. Spell 645; VI. 265. i-n.
6) C.T. IV. 97. a-g.
7) C.T. Spell 341; IV. 344. c-e.

lustre, that I may repel Re's horror in his boat" [1]. C.T. Spell 752 is an ascension text. The dead wishes to be near Re. "Spell, in order to enter the West among the followers of Re, each day. Oh gods, gate-keepers of ... who watch over this gate of ascending to heaven, open to me, that I may inhale the air which is in the water ... My seat is in the boat (of Re)" [2]. Here it concerns keepers, who are near a gate which gives admittance to heaven. Gate-keepers of heaven are also mentioned in the following passage: "Gate-keepers of the upper heaven, open ways to my *b3* and my shadow" [3]. On the way to heaven the gate is a critical point: gate-keepers could refuse the passage to the dead.

The dead has free passage. "To you both the doors of heaven are opened by Re ... To you the gates in the earth are unlocked by Geb" [4]. Heaven and earth are separate fields, railed off by gates. If the gates of the netherworld remain closed, the dead cannot sail to heaven.

In B.D. 127 A [5] gate-keepers, who may sentence somebody, occur. The dead wants free passage of them in heaven and on earth. "Open the gates to him. May the earth open its cave to him .... Open to me the gate to heaven, the earth, the *d3.t*. I am the *b3* of Osiris." In order to be admitted to the *İ3r.w*-field the dead has to pass a gate first [6]. The gate-keeper [7] only lets him through if he knows the spell concerned.

B.1.h. *sbḫ.t*, gate.

The dead makes a journey through the netherworld. In doing so he has to pass gates. These are watched by demoniacal gate-keepers. The spells related to this, help the dead to pass the gates safely. The dangers that arise near these gates, are described in C.T. Spell 336, a M.K. version of B.D. 17. "The first gate, called "Beware of the fire", it is its flame that watches over it. Fifty yards beside it exist of fire ... It made gods like a prey" [8]. The gate is connected with fire, which threatens the passer-by. It is said to the keeper of this gate [9]: "Oh you, who guides its horn, whose name is "he who

---

1) C.T. VI, Spell 644; 264. e-j.
2) C.T. VI. 381. p; 381. a-c. g.
3) C.T. VI. i. j.
4) C.T. I. 75. b.h.
5) B.D. Budge, p. 272. 3; 272. 9; 273. 7.
6) C.T. V. 181. a.
7) C.T. V. 181. b.
8) C.T. IV. 327. a-c.g.
9) C.T. IV. 327. h-l.

is in the hidden place", open to me, let me pass. Behold, I have come, oh Atum, who is in the palace, sovereign of the gods. Save me from this god, who lives on slaughter-beasts." Atum is called to assistance to save the dead from the demon who watches over the gate. The gate-keeper is summoned by the dead to open the gate to him and to let him pass. About the third gate it is said: "The third gate, he has called it the gate of the bodies . . . One cannot approach it at all. Four "schoinoi" (a measure) of fire flames are around it . . . It does not spare him who enters it . . . who is in his cave . . . Let me pass, . . . oh lord of the Ennead, save me from these slaughterers" [1]). This gate is also dangerous on account of the fire which surrounds it. A god is asked for protection against demons.

Also in C.T. Spell 312 it is described how the dead travels through the netherworld. "Truly I am the one who reports the condition of Horus to Osiris to the *d3.t*" [2]) On this journey he is menaced. The spell is aiming at the demons not doing him any harm. "You will be there as Lord of the universe. The gods of the *d3.t* fear you" [3]). He also has free passage through gates, which might have kept him off. "Create fear of me, so that the gods of the *d3.t* stand in awe of me and the gates beware of me" [4]). Presumably he will be let through. Ways are opened, so that they are cleared for N.N." [5]).

The *Zweiwegebuch* also knows the passing of gates. "Hail to you, gates, hidden of name. Save me from all who cause me harm, which is evil to the living, who are before you, till I come before the lord of the universe" [6]). Men, who kill Apophis with a spear, are pictured [7]). "The spearmen make him fall" the inscription near it reads. After that the boat of Re is pictured. So here there are already representations as in the later Book of Gates: a gate, the boat of Re and the punishment of Apophis, in which *śbḫ.t* is also a space behind the gate, where the judgment of Re's enemy is executed.

B.D. 145 and 146 deal with the passing of gates. The latter are represented in the vignettes. In the gates are demoniacal keepers, armed with knives. The title reads [8]): "Beginning of the gates of

---

[1]) C.T. IV. 329. c-330. e.g.h.
[2]) C.T. IV. 78. a.
[3]) C.T. IV. 72. c.d.
[4]) C.T. IV. 69. c.e.f.
[5]) C.T. IV. 83. f.
[6]) Cairo 28085, Lacau, Sarc. I. 218. 40; C.T. VII, Spell 1125.
[7]) Idem 41-50; C.T. VII, Spell 1127.
[8]) B.D. Budge, p. 334. 7.

the *Ỉ3r.w*-field of the house of Osiris." So somebody has to pass these gates in order to reach the *Ỉ3r.w*-field. "You are greeted by Horus, oh first gate of the tired one of heart. Let me pass. I know you. I know your name. I know the name of the god who watches over you" [1]). The composition of these spells is: invocation of the gate, order to let the dead pass, declaration that he has power over the gate on account of knowing the name and that he is entitled to pass, because he is pure. The formula *wn n.ỉ*, let me pass, already occurred in C.T. Spell 336; IV. 327. i.

The name of the gate says something about the essence of it [2]). "Mistress of trembling, high of wall, superior one, mistress of trampling down. Which announces words, which keeps the dead off. Which saves the robbed one who comes from afar" [3]). The gate fulfils a judicial function, keeps the godless at bay, but let the just pass. Also the *śbḫ.wt* of the *Livre de la Nuit* have similar names. They are "burning of fire", "from which one is not saved", "along which one cannot pass" [4]), "sharp of knives, which make the enemies of the tired one of heart [5]) tremble" [6]). In B.D. 145 and 146 there are 21 gates in total. From the 11th gate onwards the keeper [7]) is no longer mentioned, but there is only the formula: "I do know what is in it."

The term *śbḫ.t* also occurs in the Book of Gates, where the gates are watched by snakes. *Śbḫ.t* is the gate-structure with the doors as well as the space behind it, e.g., of the 2nd gate: to approach by this great god to this gate of entering this division (B.S. Pl. II. 7)". The first *śbḫ.t* is the gate-structure, the second the "division", the space behind the gate, in which the dead are. Free passage for the dead is also asked for in the following spell: "Open to me both the doors in heaven and on earth (ascension together with the sun), like you do for gods and goddesses. Make Anubis open the gates of the *d3.t* to me" [8]).

---

[1]) 334. 9. sqq.
[2]) B.D. Budge, p. 334. 11-13.
[3]) Idem *Livre de la Nuit*, ed. A. Piankoff, p. 35, 1st gate.
[4]) 2nd gate.
[5]) Osiris
[6]) 3rd gate.
[7]) *S3w; ỉry ˁ3*
[8]) Louvre 3865 III. 11, *wn n.ỉ ˁ3.wỉ m p.t m t3 mỉ ỉrr.k n nṯr.w nṯr.wt mỉ wn n.ỉ ʾInpw n3* sbḫ.wt *n.t t3 d3.t*, unedited.

B.1.i. *śmi*, reporter.

This is a gate-keeper, who announces (*śmi*) the dead at the gate [1]. He may be represented as a demon, armed with knives.

B.1.j. *šn*ʿ, to keep off.

The dead does not want to be kept off by gate-keepers on his journey through the realm of the dead. For this purpose the term *šn*ʿ, to keep off, is used. "Who knows this book, no evil thing has power over him. He is not kept off from the gates of *Imnt.t*" [2]. Here the West is the normal realm of the dead, to which the dead wishes to be admitted, but entering of which the gate-keepers may refuse him. The just are let through. "They are not kept off from the gates of the lords of the offerings" [3] (they are admitted to the just who receive normal funerary offerings). "He is not kept off from any gate of the West" [4].

To be kept off may also be the gate-keepers of the netherworld preventing the dead (or his soul) leaving the realm of the dead, in order to go and relax on earth. "May my *b3* go out. May it have abundance on earth. May it walk through its garden according to its wish. May I assume shapes. May I go out in day-time. May I cool myself under my sycamore-trees. May I drink water as I want to. May I not be kept off by the gate-keepers from the gates of the West" [5] It is the function of the *b3* to leave the grave and to move freely on earth in order to fetch food from there, which does the dead good. If the *b3* is kept off at the gate of the realm of the dead, this is not possible for him (compare *ḫnr b3*). "May they (certain gods) give to assume shapes, as his heart suggests in each form he wants; to go out as a living *b3*, without being kept off from the gate of the *d3.t*" [6].

In B.D. 72 the *nb.w k3.w*, the lords of food, are invoked, variant *nb.w ḫ.t*, lords of the offerings, *nb.w m3*ʿ*.t*, lords of the truth. These are justified dead, who have done no evil on earth and who now have a favourable fate in the hereafter. They may or may not admit

1) B.D. 144; 147; 181.
2) B.D. 181; 477.13-15.
3) *Livre de la Nuit*, 10th gate, ed. A. Piankoff, p. 74.
4) B.D. 125; 268. 11.
5) Urk. IV, 65. 1-9. It is also possible that the point is to keep the *b3* off from its return to the realm of the dead. It becomes not quite clear from the context what is meant exactly. Cf. p. 106, C.T. Spell 242.
6) Urk. IV. 1014. 16. 17.

to their gates other dead, who land in the netherworld. To be let through means participation in the same favourable fate as theirs, i.e., to receive funerary offerings too. "May I not be chased away from the *mśk.t*. May the rebels have no power over me. May I not be repelled from your gates. May you not shut your doors behind me"[1]).

The verb *šnʿ* is also used in a general sense, without concerning a gate. The way to ascension is free. "You will not be kept off by the "breakers" (demons)" [2]). "I come to you (Re), that I may be with you, to see your sun disk every day, without my being imprisoned, without my being kept off" [3]).

B.1.k. *tkn*, to approach.

About a gate it is said: "One cannot approach it at all" [4]). So this gate is dangerous for the dead.

B.2. *Deprivation of liberty.*

The dead fears that he will be checked in his liberty of action. He might remain locked up in his tomb or in the realm of the dead, so that he does not see the sun. In a general sense the realm of the dead is conceived as a prison. The dead asks liberty of action especially for those elements of his personality which must be able to function freely, in order to secure his continuance. His *b3* may not be locked up, otherwise it would not be able to get food for him. In the realm of the dead there is fear of demons, who seize somebody and then take him in custody. Also confinement and imprisonment are punishments for sinners. Tomb robbers are put in irons like thieves. In the tombs of the kings of the New Kingdom the enemies of Re and Osiris are imprisoned and fettered. These punishments are applied especially to Apophis as the head of all rebellion against Re.

As chief devil he undergoes the same punishment of deprivation of liberty as human sinners.

B.2.a. *inṯ*, to put in irons.

The dead takes the part of Re and so he is not put in irons like Apophis. "I am the one, who saves Re from the raging of Apophis. I do not fall into his iron" [4]). Near destructors of Apophis it is

[1]) B.D. Budge, p. 160. 11-13.
[2]) C.T. I. 182. d.
[3]) Louvre S.N. 173, VIII. 6 = B.D. 15; 41. 2.
[4]) C.T. IV. 329. g.
[5]) *Zweiwegebuch*, B. 1 L, 474; B 2 L, 639; C.T. VII, Spell 1094.

written: "They fell Apophis, while he is put in his irons . . . Then this great god passes, after his bonds are tied" [1]. About a snake as enemy of Re it is said: "You are in your fetters" [2]. About the punishment of Apophis: "His fetters are fastened by these gods" [3]. A derivation is *ỉnty.w*, "the fetterers". They are four gods, who stand near Apophis. In their left hand they have the noose of the rope with which they bind Apophis [4].

B.2.b. *ỉḫ*, rope.

In the Book of Gates [5] this is a rope, with which an inimical snake is tied. "They watch over the rope of the being to be punished, who is in the hand of the hidden of corpse. The gods are placed in his circle near the gate of *Ḫnty Ỉmnty.w*. These gods say: Darkness for your faces, *W3mmty*, destruction for you, oh children of *Bdš.t*. The hand of the hidden of corpse, it achieves (your) evil by means of the rope of the being to be punished."

B.2.c. *ʿb3.wt*, fetters.

About Apophis, who is punished as Re's enemy, it is said: "Apophis is in his fetters" [6].

B.2.d. *ʿntt*, to fetter.

About sinners as enemies of Re: "I deliver you to *ʿḥ3*, while you are fettered" [7].

B.2.e. *nwḥ*, rope.

About the children of Horus, who punish Apophis, it is said: "Their ropes are in their fingers" [8]. The dead says to demons: "Do not tie me to your poles" [9].

B.2.f. *nṯt*, to tie.

For Urk. I. 305. 17. 18 see *śnḥ* (B.2.k). About sinners, who are tied to poles [10]: "Behold, I put you in irons. I count you out to the keepers." Those who rebelled against Osiris, are punished: "Irons

---

1) Book of Gates, X, upper register, B.S. Pl. XI. 11-13; 18-20.
2) C.T. II. 386. a.
3) C.T. V. 245. c.
4) Book of Gates X, upper register, B.S. Pl. XI. 7-14.
5) Book of Gates X, upper register, B.S. Pl. XI. 34-44.
6) Book of Gates X, upper register, Champollion, *Notices*, II. 532.
7) L.Q. XLVIII. 6-7.
8) Book of Gates, middle register, B.S. Pl. IX. 29-30.
9) B.D. 180; 473. 8.
10) L.Q. XCVIII. 3.

for your hands, tying for your bonds" [1]). About the children of *Bdš.t*, who rebel against Re, it is said: "Geb watches over your bonds" [2]). So they are locked up in the earth.

B.2.g. *ḫ3.w*, ropes.

About the punishment of Apophis: "The ropes of this rebel are in the hands of the children of Horus" [3]).

B.2.h. *ḫnr*, to lock up.

The dead rejects being locked up and being checked in his liberty of action. "A god does not lock me up. I am a human falcon. I depart as a man and I return as a man" [4]). This spell runs counter to the phenomenon of a dead missing liberty of action. The dead identifies himself with a falcon in order to fly out freely, like this bird, wherever he wants.

He who sins against Osiris, is locked up as a punishment. "I am a god . . ., who locks up those who rebel against him" [5]). The dead himself rejects being locked up. "I am not locked up in the dignity of well-provided spirit" [6]).

The dead wants to see the sun-god in the netherworld. "Those who are in the *d3.t*, have gone out, to meet you, in order to see this beautiful image of yours. I come to you. I am with you to see your disk, every day. May I not be locked up. May I not be kept at bay. My limbs are renewed by seeing your beauty as all your favourites, for I am one of those who were agreeable to you on earth. I have reached the country of eternity. I have united myself with the land of eternity, for you are the one who has allotted it to me, my lord" [7]). According to this sun-hymn only those who have served Re on earth have the liberty of communicating with him in the hereafter and in this way renewing life. Those who have sinned against Re, are locked up and consequently prevented of seeing him.

It strikes us that the danger of locking up holds good especially for the "forces of the soul", particularly for the *b3*, but also for others, the shadow (*šw.t*), the magical power (*ḥk3*) and also the corpse (*ẖ3.t*). The rejection of being locked up corresponds with

---

1) Am Duat VII. 32-33.
2) Book of Gates X, upper register, B.S. Pl. X. 45. 46.
3) Book of Gates XI, middle register, B.S. Pl. IX. 25-27.
4) C.T. II. 230. b-e.
5) C.T. IV. 94. f.h.
6) C.T. IV. 119. e.
7) B.D. 15; 40. 15. sqq.

the wish to move freely, to leave the grave, to find the way to heaven and to join Re. "Smelling the lovely breath of the northern wind, to change oneself into . . ., to see the sun disk early in the morning without the *b3* being locked up" [1]). The dead does not want to be checked in his ascension. "I ascend to heaven and descend to the earth. I am not kept off from the road. The keeping at bay of my *k3* is not executed. My *b3* is not locked up. I am amidst those praised among the honoured ones" [2]).

To demoniacal helpers of Osiris it is said: "May you have no power over my being locked up, over the guarding of my *b3*, my shadow, my spirit and my magical power" [3]). Keeping the dead imprisoned makes him not able to join Re. "Truly, take my *b3*, my spirit, my magical power and my shadow to the place where Re is, every day, to the place where Hathor is, every day" [4]). Instead of being locked up the dead asks free admittance for his soul. "Opened be a way to my *b3*, my magical power, my shadow. It has the disposal of its foot" [5]). "In order not to keep off the soul of a woman, that it goes in and out, like it wants in the realm of the dead" [6]).

B.2.i. *s3w*, to guard [7]).

This term is used for somebody being kept imprisoned by demons. "My soul is not guarded by the chamber-keepers of Osiris" [8]). It here concerns the *b3*, which is checked in its liberty of action. Apophis, as enemy of the sun, is watched. "Bull of the *ḥḥ*-gods, who watch over Apophis, may Apophis retreat for you" [9]). "This night . . . of guarding the rebels (of Re)" [10]). There are "revisors", to whom the lord of the universe has given *3ḫ.w* "in order to keep his enemies imprisoned"; "from whose guarding one does not escape" [11]). Officers of the court keep punished sinners imprisoned. About a gate-keeper it is said that he "will watch over malicious ones" [12]).

---

1) Urk. IV. 938. 3-6.
2) Urk. IV. 1193. 14-1194.1.
3) C.T. VI. 70. b.
4) C.T. VI. 80. f.g.
5) C.T. VI. 82. a.
6) C.T. VI. 73. a.; Spell 493.
7) Wb. III. 416. 19, *Personen bewachen, bes. auch Feinde, Gefangene, dasz sie nicht entfliehen.*
8) C.T. I. 362. d.; 364. a.
9) C.T. II. 13. c.d.
10) C.T. IV. 282. c.; 284. a.; Wb. III. 418. 6, *iri s3w.t, gefangen halten.*
11) C.T. IV. 322. a.c. = B.D. 17.
12) C.T. II. 55. c.

In the *Zweiwegebuch* a red-coloured demon is pictured near a turn in the black pathway. One has to try to pass him safely. He who lands in the dangerous place near the turn, is seized by him. "His name is protector of the two gods. He is the guard of this twist. He is the one who watches over him who lands there" [1]). The term *s3w* is used of somebody who guards a gate-structure in the netherworld. "I know you. I know your name. I know the name of the god who watches over you" [2]). So these "guards" are near the gates behind which they may lock up the dead. "It is an equipped spirit which watches the gate of the house, with many faces" [3]). In the late "*Livres*" also these guards often occur. In the Book of Gates they are snakes, represented on the gate. In this way the snake on the first *śbḫ.t* [4]) is called: *S3w smy.t*. Further it is said of him: "He is on this door. He opens to Re." Sia says to the guard of the *smy.t*: "Open your gate to Re." Such snakes also occur in the Book of the Caves. "Oh snake, who is in his hole, door-keeper of those who are in it, who do not escape from his guarding" [5]). The condemned in the netherworld are eternally kept imprisoned by the guard. Snakes are invoked. They are "gate-keepers". They belong to Osiris. Re places them in "hell". They exercise the watch over the enemies of Osiris. They are the ones "from under whose fingers one cannot escape" [6]). "One of them is your guard, who destroys the souls of the *śḏby.w*, from under whose hand the souls cannot escape" [7]). An inscription near people with jackal's heads in the Book of Gates [8]) reads: "Your portions belong to you, oh gods in this pond, which you watch. Your subsistence consists of your pond. Your offerings consist of what (you) guard, oh jackals, who rest near your pond." Compare the beginning of B.D. 125 [9]) of the 42 judges of Osiris: "Who live on the bad ones, who are watched (literally bad guarding)." The

---

[1]) Cairo 28083; Lacau, Sarc. I, 192. 33; C.T. VII, Spell 1059; B 2 L. 518; B 1 L. 385. 386.

[2]) B.D. 145; 334. 10. 11.

[3]) *Zweiwegebuch*, B 1 Be. 34; B 1 P. 491: B 5 C. 371; C.T. VII, Spell 1134.

[4]) Book of Gates, B.S. Pl. IV. 20. 1. 2.

[5]) L.Q. XI. 1. 2.

[6]) L.Q. VIII. 5.

[7]) L.Q. XXXIV, 6, lower register, 2nd *tableau*.

[8]) Book of Gates, upper register, B.S. Pl. VIII. 30-35.

[9]) Naville II. 277.

judges of the dead, who watch over the condemned, eat them. In the Book of Gates enemies of Re are represented on torture posts. Gods like Re, Shu and Atum stand near them as "guards" [1]).

In an ascension text the dead wants to move freely and not be held by a demon [2]). "It is the one who watches over you, who sets you free. It is the one who has laid his hand on you, who let his hand hang downwards (i.e., who sets you free)." The text mentions that the doors of heaven and earth are opened in order to let the dead pass freely. It is possible that the demons, who hold the dead, belong to the netherworld. They must set him free in order to let him be with Re in heaven. In B.D. 17 [3]) it is said of Isis: "She chases my guards away."

Especially about the heart or the soul (*b3*), whose liberty of action the dead values, it is said that it is kept in custody by demoniacal gate-keepers "who guard hearts in the inundation" [4]). Demoniacal helpers of Osiris "watch over all the souls" [5]). The dead says: "I am not guarded by those who watch over souls" [6]). Also about posts it is said that they "watch over" them. "Let your two columns and your two pillars not guard me, oh Re" [7]).

B.2.j. *św š.t*, snares.

Executioners in the netherworld fetter their victims. "Tying together belongs to your snares" [8]).

B.2.k. *śnḥ*, to bind.

Tomb robbers are threatened [9]): "Truly, my majesty shall forbid them to be at the head of the spirits in the realm of the dead, but (he shall command that) they shall be bound and fettered like condemned ones of king Osiris and of the god of their town." *H̱r mdw*, under the word, is something like "under the sentence", condemned. This place is very important, because here it appears that the representation of Osiris as subterranean judge of the dead, who tortures

---

1) Book of Gates V, middle register, B.S. Pl. XVIII. 4; E. Lefébure, M.M.A. F.C. III, 1, Pl. XXX. 23; XXXI. 30. 31. 46.

2) C.T. Spell 225; II. 216. a.b.

3) Naville II. 72.

4) C.T. VI. 67. h.

5) C.T. VI. 70. a.

6) C.T. VI. 132. i.

7) C.T. VI. 165. b. The function of these columns is not clear. They may exercise an unfavourable influence on the dead. In C.T. Spell 417 the dead says that he comes and goes among them. This is a spell in order not to go with the head downwards.

8) Am Duat V. 54-56.

9) Urk. I. 305. 17. 18 (Sottas 96).

the condemned and ties them, already occurs in the Old Kingdom and consequently it is not a later formation of the "theology" of the "*Livres*". In the *ḳrr.t*-book enemies of Osiris are pictured with their hands tied to their backs, inscription to it: "In order to bind and fetter your enemies" [1]). Re says to two goddesses with hyena's heads [2]): "Watch over those . . . fetter and tie their bodies. They say: Let their souls not escape, let their shadows have no power on account of this great thing, which they have done." In the Book of Gates sinners are tied in punishment. The inscription reads: "You are bound and fettered with strong tendons. I have ordered against you that you be bound. Your arms are not taken apart" [3]). Anubis punishes Seth by tying him hand and foot and by robbing him afterwards of his male power [4]).

B.2.1. *śśnḥ*, to bind.

About a gate in the *Zweiwegebuch* it is said [5]): "Somebody is in there while he is bound."

B.2.m. *śdf*, fetter.

About the fetters with which Apophis is bound: "They seize the fetters of this *Ḏwy*-snake" [6]). "Behold, fetters are put on the savage one of face" [7]). Near half of the 16 gods, who hold the fetters of Apophis, *śdfy.w*, the fetterers is written.

B.2.n. *śḏ3.wt*, sealing.

About the beatified gods, the just dead, who have served Re, it is said [8]): "You have rest. Your enemies are destroyed. Your glory does not reach to their places of residence. (Your) power does not reach to (their) sealing." There is a strict separation between the blessed and the condemned. Being locked up is a punishment especially for the doomed.

B.2.o. *ḳ3r.t.* bolt.

The dead asks of the gate-keepers of the netherworld, to be let through just as Re on his journey through the realm of the dead [9]): "Open your roads, open your bolts to me."

---

1) L.Q. IX. 6.
2) L.Q. CXXXIII. 7.
3) Book of Gates I, lower register, B.S. Pl. IV. 15-19.
4) Pap. Jumilhac III. 18.
5) C.T. VII, Spell 1132; B 1 Be. 12; B 1 P. 468; B 5 C. 348.
6) Book of Gates X, upper register, B.S. Pl. XI. 27-29.
7) *Ibidem*, 30-32.
8) Book of Gates III, upper register, 1st figure, B.S. Pl. VIII. 9-14.
9) B.D. 180; 474. 2.

B.2.p. *ḳ3s*, to bind.

About punished sinners in the netherworld it is said: "You are bound. Your arms are not taken apart" [1]. In the "*Livres*" the punished are often pictured as prisoners with their arms tied to their backs. Those who sinned against Osiris, are punished in the netherworld. "Those who act inimically against Osiris, who rebel against the overlord of the *d3.t*, bonds for your arms, binding for your fetters" [2]. About the enemy of Re, whom he conquers on his journey: "The enemy has fallen. His arms are bound" [3]. "The gods of the South, the North, the West and the East have put him in irons" [4]. Selkis is pictured above Apophis. The inscription to it reads: "Selkis fetters him" [5]. The same occurs in the Book of the Dead: "You are put in irons by Selkis" [6]. The children of Horus punish Apophis: "They put their bonds on" [7]. Human sinners and the mythical enemy of Re, Apophis, are punished in the netherworld in the same way.

B.2.q. *ṯt*, fetters.

In a snake spell it is said about the *m3fd.t*-cat, which kills snakes: "The hand of the great one, which fetters, which is in the house of life. He who is seized by it, does not live. He who has been beaten by her, his head is not tied on" [8].

B.2.r. *ḏḥr.t*, strap.

About demons, who want to fetter the dead, it is said: "The destructors do not put straps on me" [9]. He fortifies himself against them by identifying himself with a falcon.

B.2.s. *ḏdḥ*, to arrest, to lock in.

The dead is not struck by punishments which are applied to men who have sinned against a god. "You are not counted, you are not locked in, you are not imprisoned, your are not fettered, you are not watched, you are not placed in the place of judgment, in which

---

1) Book of Gates I, lower register, B.S. Pl. IV. 18. 19.
2) Am Duat VII. 29-33.
3) B.D. 15; 36. 8.
4) B.D. 39; 106. 4. 5.
5) Book of Gates X, upper register, B.S. Pl. XI. 21. 22.
6) B.D. 39; 105.12.
7) Book of Gates XI, middle register, B.S. Pl. IX. 37. 38.
8) Pyr. 672. b.c.
9) C.T. IV. 12. b.

the rebels are put" [1]). Just as *ḫnr ḏdḥ* also is used for locking up the *b3*. "Spell in order to save somebody from those who eat souls, who are locked up in the *d3.t*. He is not taken to any prison." "He is saved from the enemy, from the evil being that is in the *d3.t*, the souls are not locked up" [2]).

B.3. *Burning.*

In the hereafter the dead is threatened with fire. In the *Zweiwegebuch* the pathway and the waterway lead along a red strip in the middle. This is a pool of fire, which the dead has to avoid. The notion of a fiery hell is wide-spread in Egypt. The fire means total destruction for the dead.

B.3.a. *3m*, *3mw.t*, *s3m*, to burn, burning.

In the *Zweiwegebuch* the blue road leads along a "pond of fire" [3]). One has to avoid this place, otherwise one is burnt. About a goddess it is said: "She has been placed behind Osiris to burn his enemies" [4]). In B.D. 17 [5]) demons occur "who burn the souls of his enemies."

Especially in Am Duat *3m* is used as a punishment of the godless. About 9 snakes, which protect the body of Khepri: "You burn the enemies of Khepri" [6]). About a snake: "The flame of the *ʿnḫ-irw*-snake is against them (the enemies of Osiris), that he may burn them" [7]). Compare with this what is said of the uraeus, which destroys the enemies of the king: "The uraeus, which is on your head, punishes them . . . It burns by its flame those who are on their islands. It cuts off the heads of the Asiatics [8]). What they do is burning corpses of dead by the red-hot breath of their mouth daily" [9]). Burning is a punishment for those who have sinned against Re: "They are the ones who burn fire in order to burn Re's enemies" [10]). About a gate: "The cutting one, which burns the dead that are in there" [11]). Cutting and burning form a cumulation of punishments. This accentuates the total destruction of the godless. This combination also occurs in the passage: "They cause the burning of the enemies like that which is on the point of their knife" [12]).

1) C.T. I. 70. b-d.
2) B.D. 164; 418. 1. 2.
3) C.T. VII, Spell 1152; B 1 P. 336; B 1 Be. 236.
4) C.T. IV. 262. a.
5) Naville II. 74.
6) Am Duat VI. 216. 217.
7) Am Duat VII. 22.
8) Urk. IV. 613. 15-614. 1.
9) Am Duat V. 63.
10) Am Duat II. 192-194.
11) Am Duat VIII. 226.
12) Am Duat III. 148-150.

B.3.b. *3sb*, to burn.

The name of a demon is [1]): "Burning of face, who goes out retreating."

B.3.c. *ʿḫm*, to extinguish.

A hell of fire burns the enemies of Osiris: "The fire of their flame is not extinguished" [2]).

B.3.d. *w3w3.t*, fire.

A uraeus in the netherworld is called: "Mistress of the flame" [3].) Enemies of Osiris are burnt. "The flame which is at the head of its kettle, is against you" [4]). About a place where godless can be burnt: "This pond consists of flames" [5]).

B.3.e. *wbd*, to burn.

In a gate in the realm of the dead the unjust are punished. This gate is called: "Which repeats the cutting, which burns the rebels, mistress of all gates" [6]). Cutting up and burning are again connected here. It is said to the enemy of the sun about *Śḫm.t* "She burns your limbs" [7]).

B.3.f. *whm*, to burn.

A snake is called: "Which is in its burning" [8]).

B.3.g. *bḫḫ.w*, flame.

The entrance to heaven is blocked by fire [9]). "The phallus of *B3by* has left. The wings of the doors of heaven are opened . . . The way goes over the blaze under that which the gods scoop (water to extinguish the fire)" [10]). About Khons as a demon it is said: "I am the flame, the lord of the hearts" [11]). About the *ḥ3d.w*, hell divisions, it is said that they are "red-hot", *bḫḫ.w* [12]). The name of a gate is *bḫḫy*, the burning one [13]). About a fire-spitting goddess, who stands near a *ḥ3d*, a hell division, it is said: "The flame which comes from the mouth of her who is at the head of her slaughter-place, is against you" [14]).

---

1) B.D. 17; C.T. IV. 270. b.
2) L.Q. CXVIII. 8.
3) Am Duat IX. 74.
4) Am Duat XI. 77.
5) Book of Gates II, upper register, B.S. Pl. II. 43. 44.
6) B.D. 146; 354. 11; 11th gate.
7) H. P. Blok, AcOr, VII. 98, 100.
8) C.T. II. 276. a; 379. a.
9) Pyr. 502. a.b.
10) See commentary of Sethe.
11) C.T. IV. 66. n.
12) Book of Gates III, lower register, 3rd figure, B.S. Pl. VII. 51.
13) Book of Gates VIII, B.S. Pl. XV.
14) Am Duat XI. 77.

B.3.h. *bś*, flame.

About a fire-demon in the *Zweiwegebuch* [1]) it is said: "*Bśw* is his name". The eighth gate of B.D. 146 [2]) is called "burning of flame". About uraei it is said: "They swallow their flame, after this great god has passed" [3]).

B.3.i. *pʿ.w*, fire.

The second gate of the *Livre de la Nuit* and the eighth gate of B.D. 146 are called "sharp of fire" [4]).

B.3.j. *mw n śḏ.t*, fire-water.

In the netherworld is a pool of fire, from which the spirits cannot drink: "Oh this place, in which there is water, of which the spirits cannot dispose, because its water is of fire and whose upper side is in the quality of fire-water, so that one does not drink its water . . . there is no quenching of their thirst" [5]).

B.3.k. *nwẖ*, to be burnt.

The dead identifies himself with a *nʿw*-snake, in order to safeguard himself against dangers and now he is somebody "who is not burnt by fire" [6]). He says: "I am not parched, I am not burnt" [7]). "I do not desiccate, I am not burnt" [8]).

B.3.l. *nbỉ*, flame.

About a gate in the realm of the dead it is said: "There are four schoinoi (a measure) around it with fiery flames" [9]). To one of the (two) *rḥty* or *mrrwty*, who want to take away the magical power from the dead it is said: "Backwards, flame" [10]). A demon is called: "Face of flames" [11]). About another demon, who tortures the dead: "He who is in the two flames is the guard of this field" [12]). One of

---

[1]) C.T. B 1 L. 413; Lacau, Sarc. I. 194. 61; C.T. VII, Spell 1071.

[2]) B.D. Budge, p. 353. 3. 4.

[3]) Am Duat IX. 100.

[4]) B.D. Budge, p. 353. 4.

[5]) Louvre 3283 II. 3-7; B.D. 149, Naville II, no. 85, *ỉ ś.t tn nty ỉw mw m ẖnw.ś nn śẖm.n 3ḫ.w ỉm.ś ḫr nty mw.ś m ḫ.t ḥr.t.ś m ỉrw mw n śḏ.t śḥtm mrw.t* (read with B.D. 149 *n mrw.t tm śwr mw.ś*) *nn ʿḫm n ỉb.śn.*

[6]) C.T. II. 54.j. k.

[7]) C.T. V. 12.d.

[8]) B.D. 63 A; 133. 7. 8.

[9]) C.T. IV. 329.h.

[10]) C.T. V. 319.a.

[11]) Am Duat III. 83; *Livre du Jour*, 3rd register, of one of the 6 opponents of Apophis, ed. A. Piankoff, p. 15.

[12]) Am Duat II. 200, 201.

the 42 judges in B.D. 125 is called: "Flame, which goes out going backwards" [1]).

B.3.m. *nfw.t*, red-hot breath (of a snake).

A snake demon is repelled. His weapons aim at each other. "Your red-hot breath is against your slaughtering and *vice versa*" [2]). Also here burning and slaughtering are combined.

B.3.n. *nḥ*, flame.

A snake protects the mummy of Atum. "It places its fire in those who rebel against you" [3]).

B.3.o. *nś*, flame.

The king is not exposed to the dangers of a dark realm of the dead. "N.N. shall not be delivered to your flame, oh gods" [4]). About a gate of hell, wrapped in flames, it is said: "It is its flame, which removes from it" [5]). In a spell for going in and out of the fire it reads: "The *gmm.w* of the great one do not burn me" [6]). In B.D. 125 [7]) one of the 42 judges is called "thriving of flame". Re says to the uraeus-snakes, which guard a pond: "Your portions belong to you, uraei in this pond, which you watch. The flame of your glowing breath is in my enemies. Your flame is in those who harm me" [8]). In the netherworld the fire of the snakes burn those who have sinned against Re. It is said likewise to a snake: "Oh *Śśy*-snake, powerful of flame, which puts fire into those who are near it" [9]). About torture of enemies of Osiris by a fire-spitting goddess at the head of a hell-division: "The flames of her, who is at the head of her hell divisions, are against you" [10]). Around a pond of fire in the realm of the dead red-coloured flames are drawn. Here the word *nś* is written in red. In there are four massive black-coloured bodies. It here concerns doomed ones in a hell-blaze [11]).

---

1) Compare B.D. 17, C.T. IV, 270.b, name of one of the 7 spirits: "Burning of face, who goes out, going backwards". Of twisting flames? See Wb. III. 354. 1, of poison, which pervades the body.

2) C.T. V. 286.e.

3) Am Duat VII. 49.

4) Pyr. 323. d.

5) C.T. IV. 327.b.

6) C.T. III. 337.f.

7) B.D. Budge, p. 254. 1.

8) Book of Gates III, upper register, 3rd figure, B.S. Pl. VII. 49-53.

9) L.Q. XI. 6.

10) Am Duat XI. 77.

11) Louvre I. 3297.

B.3.p. *nśb*, to lick (of a flame)[1].

It is used of the burning *3ḫ.t*-eye of Horus, which, as a demon, "devours" all male and female dead[2]. "The licking one" is the name of a fiery gate in the Book of the Dead[3]. In the Book of Gates it is the name of a flame[4].

B.3.q. *nśr.t*, flame.

This is the name of a female fire-demon, which burns the enemies of Osiris[5]. A god in Am Duat is called "painful of flame"[6].

B.3.r. *rkḥ*, to burn.

The 8th gate in B.D. 146 is "burning of flame, sharp of blaze, quick of hand, slaughtering, without one being able to ask after it, along which one does not pass for fear of the suffering which it causes"[7]. A demon "*Ỉ'rty*, burns them" (enemies of the overlord of the *d3.t*)[8]. A uraeus is called "mistress of the fire"[9].

B.3.s. *hwt*, fire.

A demon is called "who comes from its blaze"[10]. "Who is on his fire" is the name of a judge of Osiris[11].

B.3.t. *hh*, glowing breath.

The dead keeps a demon at bay. "The glowing breath of your mouth does not rage against me"[12]. *Hh* is the glowing breath which a demon blows and with which he scorches his victims. It often occurs with fire-spitting snakes. About one of the four schoinoi (measure of distance) round a gate-structure it is said: "The third is the fiery breath of the mouth of Sekhmet"[13].

To demons who set traps for birds and who take souls away, lock the shadow in and put it into the place of judgment, it is said: "Let your glowing breath not attack him. Let your testimony have no power over him"[14]. Demons are kept at bay: "He (Osiris N.N.) is not taken away by the red-hot breath of your fury"[15]. Apophis

---

1) Wb. II. 234. 12 of a cow, which licks a calf.
2) C.T. IV. 107.a.
3) B.D. 146; 350. 9; Wb. II. 234. 16.
4) Book of Gates VII, lower register, Budge, The Eg, Heaven and Hell II, p. 215, 216; E. Lefébure, *Le Tombeau de Séti Ier*, II. 12.
5) B.D. 17; C.T. IV. 260.c.
6) Am Duat I. 176. 177.
7) B.D. Budge, p. 353. 3-6.
8) L.Q. XCIX. 1.
9) Am Duat IX. 76.
10) C.T. II. 73.a.
11) B.D. 17; C.T. IV. 268.c.
12) C.T. II. 225.c. d.
13) C.T. IV. 329.k.
14) C.T. Spell 494; VI. 76.d. e.
15) B.D. 130; 283. 13. 14; C.T. VII, Spell 1099; B 1 L. 501; B 2 L. 669.

must be punished. "May the glowing breath of the netherworld go out against you" [1]). A tomb robber is chastised by a demon. "Oh you who sleeps in his corpse, whose glowing breath becomes a flame, which burns in the sea, by which burning the sea rises, come, place a flame, throw a fire against him who will raise his hand against the tomb of Osiris N.N." [2]).

B.3.u. *ḫ.t*, fire.

The name of a gate in the netherworld is: "Beware of the fire" [3]). "50 yards beside it are full of fire" [4]). About one of the four schoinoi (measure of distance) around the gate it is said: "One is of fire" [5]). The later notions of burning gates in B.D. 145 and 146 and in the Book of Gates tally with this. Such a gate in B.D. 146 is called: "The burning one, the mistress of the flames, the rejoicing one, which asks to give to it. There is no one entering it, while his head is there" [6]) One does not go through this gate without his head being cut off.

In the hereafter the dead should avoid dangerous rivers and pools of fire. In his coffin a map is sent along with him, that he may know the way [7]). He says to the river: "Hail to you, river of fire, lord of power, great of glory, greater than his lord, . . . Let me pass . . . Then he says: Pass safely" [8]). About the curved line, drawn around a figure sitting in an island, it is said: "It is his river" [9]). Seated in the boat of Re the dead may avoid a dangerous pool of fire. "Spell in order to sail in the big boat of Re, to pass the circle of fire" [10]).

The dead wishes to escape from the fire: "I come from this fire intact. I am not treated violently" [11]).

Ḫty is the name of a fire-spitting snake [12]). This snake breathes its fire against the enemies of Osiris. "Horus says to the *Ḫty*-snake: Oh fire, great of flame, this one on whose mouth my eye is and whose convolutions guard my children, open your mouth, open your jaws. Place your flame into the enemies of my father, that you burn their corpses and that their souls be burnt by this glowing breath, which is on your mouth, by the glow, which comes from your

---

1) Book of Gates II, lower register, B.S. Pl. III. 21. 22.
2) B.D. 163; 412. 1-6.
3) C.T. IV. 327.b.
4) Idem 327.c.
5) Idem 329.i.
6) B.D. 146; 351. 12 sqq.
7) C.T. VI. 271, map.
8) C.T. VI, Spell 650; 272.d. f. i. j.
9) C.T. VI. 274.f.
10) B.D. 136 B; 300. 16-301. 1.
11) C.T. VI. 342.r. s.
12) Book of Gates VIII, lower register, B.S. Pl. XIV. 35-48.

belly" [1]). Total destruction through death by fire is the punishment of sinners. This also appears from the *Lebensmüde*. The soul advises the man to burn himself, so that he will not survive [2]). "Behold, my soul deceives me, but I do not listen to it. It pulls me to death before I have come to him, throws (me) into the fire in order to burn me." The soul gives a bad advice. It is determined in the *Lebensmüde* with the sign for enemy. Suicide by burning would mean the definite end of the man. The latter prefers the usual funeral ritual, which secures his survival.

B.3.v. *śś*, to burn.

Seth is punished by death through fire. As a criminal he is destroyed up to and including his descendants [3]). The enemies of Osiris are "burnt of corpse" [4]). Punished ones in the netherworld are called *śśy.w*, burnt ones [5]).

B.3.w. *śti*, to burn.

Demons punish the sinners. "They light the fire . . . of the enemies" [6]). Snakes destroy the enemies of Osiris. "Names of the uraei, which burn for Osiris, who is at the head of the *d3.t*, with the flame that is on their mouth. They swallow their flame, after this great god passed them" [7]). The name of the 2nd gate of the Book of Gates is: "It burns for Re" [8]).

"Burning of face" is the name of a demon [9]) and of a snake on a gate [10]). The name of a snake, guard of chapels, in which the beatified dead are, is *Śty*, the burning one [11]).

B.3.x. *śḏ.t*, fire, flame.

This word is the most usual for the infernal fire. It thus occurs in the whole of the *Zweiwegebuch*. The inscription near the red strip in the middle, along which the two ways lead, reads [12]): "It is a pool of

---

1) The name of the snake is derived from the word *ḫ.t*.
2) De Buck, *Kernmomenten*, p. 21; ed. Faulkner 11-13.
3) Pap. Jumilhac XV. 25.
4) L.Q. CI. 5. 6.
5) *Livre de la Nuit*, I, 5th register, ed. A. Piankoff, p. 38, cf. pp. 35, 61, 66.
6) Am Duat III. 147.
7) Am Duat IX. 100.
8) Book of Gates II, B.S. Pl. III.
9) Am Duat III. 80
10) Book of Gates VIII, B.S. Pl. XV.
11) Book of Gates II, upper register, B.S. Pl. III. 9.
12) C.T. VII, Spell 1166; B 1 Be. 237.

fire, called *ʿ3tyw*; there is not a single man who falls into the fire. May he be kept off from it." "*M3ʿ.t* belongs to this god, who is in the fire, who has not placed the just in himself" [1]). The idea here is a twofold judgment: the sinners are brought to the judgment, but the just are not.

Under a fiery gate it is written: "The flame is that which has not power over him" [2]). Above a boat, with the chapel of Re in it, a pond of fire is pictured. The text reads: "The northern bank of the *ḫ3*-lake, its width is endless, its outline, consisting of flaming fire, is a million cubits" [3]). From what follows it appears that this fire is directed against the dead's enemies and protects him in this way. More than once gates of hell are pictured, doors with the inscription *śḏ.t*, sometimes with snakes near it as in the Book of Gates. The dead has tc pass these. The colour of the doors is red [4]). Near the fiery doors are gate-keepers. The spells beside them, which contain the name of the gate-keeper, enable the dead to pass them [5]). In the red road under such gates of fire it is written: "Oh flame, backwards! You that burns there, I shall not be burnt. I wear the *nmś* and the white crown" [6]). This spell enables the dead to avert the dangers of the fire. The crowns give him protection.

In the blue road it is written: "Spell in order to pass to the road of the flame" [7]). The road leads along a red partition with five names of flames in it, among which *śpd ḥr*, sharp of face. A byroad turns downwards, to the red strip in the middle. Near it is written [8]): "It is the road which is in the chapel. You must not go on it." This spell shows the whole meaning of the *Zweiwegebuch*, viz., to help the dead in order that he does not land in the pool of fire. "*Iknty* [9]), who utters his roaring like a flame . . . he lives on fire. That which is on his mouth, is a spell in order to pass him."

---

[1]) C.T. VII, Spell 1142; B 2 L. 515; B 1 Be. 169.
[2]) C.T. VII, Spell 1138; B 1 Be. 116.
[3]) Cairo 28085; Lacau, Sarc. I. 220. 58; C.T. VII, Spell 1129.
[4]) C.T. VII, Spell 1135; B 1 Be. 47; B 1 P. 503; B 5 C. 384; B 1 L. 464, 465 etc.
[5]) Cairo 28085; Lacau, Sarc. I. 215. 14-16; C.T. VII, Spells 1108-1110; B 1 L. 533-538.
[6]) C.T. VII, Spell 1091; B 1 L. 470; B 2 L. 629.
[7]) C.T. VII, Spell 1157; B 1 Be. 251; B 1 P. 339.
[8]) C.T. VII, Spell 1156; B 1 Be. 248.
[9]) C.T. VII, Spell 1110; B 1 L. 537. 538.

A spell against the fire reads: "I have extinguished the flame. I have cooled down the heat. I have made silent that which is in its redness, the blaze that divides the gods and unites them" [1]). "Spell in order to go into and out of the fire . . . I have gone into and out of the fire. The gods of light do not cut me". "To go out of the fire after the great god" [2]). C.T. Spell 610 is "a spell in order to go out of the fire . . . N.N. is *Hdd*, who is in the middle of his eye, who goes into and out of the fire . . . N.N. has not taken an oath with the lord of eternity" (and therefore he does not land in the fire, in virtue of moral purity) [3]).

Some of the 42 judges of Osiris work with fire. One of them is called "embracer of flames" [4]), another "whose eyes are a flame" [5]). A similar demon occurs in C.T. Spell 653, a guard near the river, which the dead must try to pass safely. "It is this guard of his, the lord of disturbance, whose face is a fire, whose eyes are a fire is his name" [6]).

In Am Duat a pool of fire occurs, which one has to avoid [7]). "The water of the mourning ones, the gods who are in *'Imḥ.t*, along which the boat does not pass. The denizens of the netherworld have no power over their water, which is in this necropolis. Their water is like a fire against those who are in there." It here concerns punished sinners. They do not see Re on his journey through the netherworld.

The enemies of Osiris are burnt in the netherworld: "These enemies of Osiris, who are under flames, whose bodies are burnt" [8]).

B.3.y. *šm*, heat.

About four fiery divisions near a gate: "The second is fire" [9]). One from a series of gates in the realm of the dead is called: "Which announces dawn in its time, which is hot the whole day, mistress of strength" [10]).

B.3.z. *ḳrr*, to burn.

One of the five persons, armed with lances, in the procession of the sun-god, "he burns with his heart" [11]).

---

1) C.T. I. 378.a-380.a.
2) C.T. Spell 246; III. 337.a. d. e; Spell 247; III. 339.a.
3) C.T. VI. 224.u. f. t.
4) B.D. 125; 252. 13.
5) B.D. Budge, p. 253. 16.
6) C.T. VI. 274.i.
7) Am Duat V, lower register, 238.
8) L.Q. CI. 6.
9) C.T. IV. 329.j.
10) B.D. 146; 357. 7.
11) *Livre du Jour* I.

B.3.aa. *t3*, fire.

About an eye, which menaces the dead, it is said: "Its flowing breath does not take her along. Its flame does not attack her" [1]). About certain gods it is said: "May they grant that Osiris N.N. has cooling in the place of the fire" [2]). In the Book of Gates it is said of a place of destruction in the netherworld "the flame of which is not against you" [3]). Here it concerns a pool of fire, destined for the godless, it is true, but not for the just. One of the 42 judges of Osiris is called: "Fiery of foot, who comes from the darkness" [4]).

B.3.bb. *tk3*, flame.

About a gate in the realm of the dead: "The point of its flame crosses the earth from heaven" [5]). Apophis is punished: "A flame is fired against him from the houses of Sepa" [6]). A demon is called "face of flames" [7]). Other punishing demons are called: "Burning heads" [8]). About a uraeus it is said: "Its flame is on its mouth" [9]), All these denominations point to gates or demons in the hereafter. threatening the dead with fire.

B.3.cc. *d3f*, to burn [10]).

A gate in the realm of the dead is called *d3f.t* [11]). Another is named "fiery of burning" [12]).

B.4. *To cook.*

A special form of torture by fire is the victim being cooked or roasted. This may take place in cauldrons, as it is also known from mediaeval representations of hell.

B.4.a. *ʿḫ*, coal-basin.

Birds, as a symbol of enemies of the god, are burnt in a coal-basin [13]).

---

1) C.T. VI. 74.m. n.
2) B.D. 168; 430. 5.
3) Book of Gates II, upper register, B.S. Pl. II. 55.
4) B.D. 125; 256. 10.
5) C.T. IV. 327.d.
6) C.T. V. 245.b.
7) Am Duat III. 89; snake of the 4th gate in the Book of Gates, B.S. Pl. VII. 61.
8) Am Duat V, lower register, 211.
9) *Livre du Jour*, 4th register, ed. A. Piankoff, p. 27.
10) Wb. V. 522. 12, *Feinde verbrennen.*
11) *Livre de la Nuit*, 2nd gate.
12) B.D. 146, 8th gate; 353. 4.
13) Kees, *Tieropfer*, p. 85; Edfou VII, p. 124.

"They become baked in your fire-basin." The dead rejects to be used as an offering. "Your offerings of mine are not made to them who are set over their coal-basins" [1]). The dead fears a hunter who catches fish and birds. He does not want to be burnt in the latter's coal-basin. By knowing the name of the coal-basin he knows how to charm this instrument. In this way he does not share the fate of the godless, who are roasted like fish and birds. He says to the catcher: "I know the coal-basin, in which you cook" [2]). In the *Livre de la Nuit* [3]) condemned in hell are mentioned, in which the *ʿḫ.w*, the burnt, are written with the fire determinative.

S. R. K. Glanville states that in the demotic papyrus containing the history of Onchsheshonqy the following passage occurs concerning the punishment of Harsiesi [4]): "Pharaoh caused to be built an altar of earth at the gate of the palace (and) he caused Harsiesi, son of Ramose, to be placed (in) the furnace (*ʿḫ*) [5]) (of) copper, together with all his people and with all the people who had agreed to the vile plan (against) pharaoh." As a commentary Glanville adds to this: "The word *ʿḫ* = ⲁⲓ̣ϣ is found in Rylands IX, 13/11 in the same kind of context. The use of the article *p3* before *ʿḫ* suggests to me that "the furnace" was a recognised form of punishment." So being burnt in an oven was also a form of capital punishment in the administration of justice.

B. 4. b. *wḥ3.t*, cauldron.

Pyr. Spells 273 and 274 contain the well-known cannibal texts. The dead eats gods in order to avail himself of their powers. These gods are tortured and killed by tormenting devils. Among them is the god of the wine-press, *Šsmw*, who also occurs in B.D. 17 [6]) as an executioner in the service of Osiris. The entire description tallies with the later punishments of hell in the netherworld. The idea of this cannibal spell must have been that in the hereafter the tormenting devils made the dead eat the spiritual power of those whom they torture. In the later funerary literature demons occur who live on

---

1) B.D. 17; C.T. IV. 309.a.
2) C.T. VI. 40.h.
3) *Livre de la Nuit*, VI, 5th register, bottom.
4) B.M. 10508, IV, 3-5. B.H. Stricker, O.M.R.O. XXXIX (1959), p. 59.
5) "Not cauldron", S.R.K.G.
6) Urk. V. 57.

men [1]), on hearts [2]) and on their magical power [3]). The dead does the same in the Pyramid Texts [4]). He is on a par with those demons who appropriate the forces of those tortured by them. About certain demons, who cook the gods, it is said: "They are the . . ., who lay a fire for him with the shanks of the eldest of them, near the cauldrons, which contain them" [5]). The dead eats gods who are rich in magical power [6]), after they have been cooked for him in cauldrons [7]): "It is the great one of heart, the northern one of heaven, who makes cauldrons ready for me against them on the feet of their wives. Fire is placed for me near the cauldrons."

By his spell the dead wants to prevent his being tortured by the demons of Osiris [8]): "I do not land in their cauldrons." The determinative indicates the form ◡ or ▽ (Pyr. Ծ). "May N.N. not land in their cauldrons" [9]).

The cauldrons also occur in the *ḳrr.t*-book as a punishment of the enemies of Osiris. "These two uraei . . . in the place of destruction, place your fire under these cauldrons, in which the enemies of Osiris are" [10]). "You are enemies of Osiris. *K3.t* throws her fire, *G3g3y.t*, she stokes the cauldron" [11]). To demons in the netherworld it is said: "Destroy the shadows of those who ought to be exterminated in your cauldrons" [12]). A god, who punishes the enemies of Osiris, is called: "Who is at the head of his cauldrons" [13]).

B.4.c. *pfś*, to cook.

In the spells about the fishing- or bird-net in which the dead may be caught, it also concerns the possibility that he is cooked as a fish or bird caught. The spell prevents this by letting the dead know the name of the cooking apparatus. "The coal-basin, on which you cook . . ., this, where you cook him . . ., this big offering table, on which you cook and place him . . ., this great one is the one for whom you cook him and place him" [14]).

---

1) C.T. V. 29.a.
2) *ỉb.w*, B.D. 124; 244. 15.
3) *ḥk3.w* C.T. IV. 347.g.
4) Pyr. 403. c; 410.c.
5) Pyr. 405.a. b.
6) C.T. VI. 178.j.
7) C.T. VI. 179.l. m.
8) B.D. 17: C.T. IV. 305.b.
9) C.T. IV. 323.d.
10) L.Q. XCVII. 8-XCVIII. 1.
11) L.Q. CXIX. 7. Further final scene L.Q., B.I.F.A.O. XLIII, p. 48; L.Q. LI, 3rd register, 3rd tableau; XCIX. 5; CXVII. 6.
12) Am Duat V. 45 sqq.
13) Am Duat XI. 79 and 93.
14) C.T. VI. 40. h (cf. 8.f.); j. l. n.

B.4.d. *pśi*, to cook.

The rise of Re is preceded by the destruction of his enemies. "It is *nśm.f*, who cooks the enemies of Re in the early morning" [1]).

B.4.e. *mʿḳ*, to roast [2]).

About 9 snakes, which in the netherworld punish the enemies of Khepri, it is said [3]): "It is what they do in the *dȝ.t*, roasting of the . . ." Above enemies of Osiris it is written: "He roasts them by roasting for himself" [4]).

B.4.f. *ḥry.t*, furnace.

More than once a picture of this occurs in the *ḳrr.t*-book, a basin supported by arms,  , in which parts of the enemies of Re are burnt, viz. the head, the heart, the shadow, the *bȝ* etc.; sometimes the latter are, moreover, placed upside down in it. "The *ḥry.t* is as follows: Arms come from the place of destruction. They raise you, great fire, to which the heads of enemies are counted out. *Ỉʿrty*, lord of the flame (a uraeus god, pictured beside it), he places fire into you" [5]). "Re says about this *ḳrr.t*: Oh uraeus god, . . . this god, great of shapes, burning of fire, flaring up (?) of flame in the furnace which you guard, to which the heads and the hearts of my enemies are counted out, who rebel against me, there is no extinguishing (?) for the fire that is in it. Place your flame, put your fire into all my enemies" [6]).

B.4.g. *ẖnf.t*, cooking-pot for flesh.

Herein a charmed snake is cooked. "Flesh-pot of Horus, crawl into the earth" [7]).

B.4.h. *kty.t*, cauldron.

In a cannibal text it is said about the god *Šsmw*: "He cooks a meal of them in his cooking-place in the evening" [8]).

In the spells about the net in which the dead is caught like a fish or bird to be cooked afterwards as spoils of the chase, the cauldron of *Šsmw* also occurs. The dead knows it and so has power over it.

---

1) Am Duat XII, 98.
2) Wb. II. 50. 3, *auch von der Bestrafung der Bösen.*
3) Am Duat VI, lower register 222. 223.
4) Am Duat VII. 24, compare III, 140, lower register, *ỉr.t mʿḳ*.
5) L.Q. LI, 5th *ḳrr.t*, 3rd register; LXVI. 7.
6) L.Q. LXVII. 7 sqq.
7) Pyr. 245.b. See also commentary Sethe. 8) Pyr. 403.b.

"For I know the name of the woman, in whom he cooks them [1]), it is the cauldron, which is in the hand of *Šsmw*" [2]). "This cauldron, in which he cooks, it is the cauldron, which is in the hand of *Šsmw*" [3]). The dead fears *Šsmw* as a demon, who sheds the blood of the dead. For Pyr. 403. b compare C.T. VI. 179. i: "A meal is cooked of them for me in this cauldron of the evening." Khons and *Šsmw* slaughter and cook *ḥkꜣ*-gods for the dead, that he may live on them. In the netherworld is a cauldron, in which the dead may be cooked. "You are a cauldron. You cook on the coal-fire. You are respected in the *dꜣ.t*" [4]). It here concerns demons, "who are in their kettles" [5]). "To them a portion on earth is made as an offering as to him who does not fall into their cauldrons" [6]). A goddess, who guards a fiery division of hell, is called: "Who is at the head of her cauldrons" [7]). Re addresses two demons, who torture dead ones in the netherworld: "Re says to this *ḳrr.t*: Oh two goddesses, great of fire, who set fire to their cooking-places with the bones of the foreigners [8]), who burn the souls, the corpses, the bodies and the shadows of my enemies, behold, I pass you. I harm my enemies. You are permanent in your *ḳrr.t*. Your fire is in your cauldrons" [9]).

B.4.i. *ṯnm*, kettle.

The dead prays to Re: "Save me from these kettles, sharp of fingers" [10]). "May I not sit in your kettles" [11]). As appears from the determinatives they are cauldrons, in which sinners are cooked as a punishment.

B.4.j. *dwfy*, cauldron.

In the *ḳrr.t*-book the burning of enemies of Osiris is mentioned. "Oh uraeus, which is at the head of its flame, which puts fire into its cauldron, which contains the heads of the enemies of Osiris and the hearts of the enemies of *Dꜣty*, put your flame into your cauldron, burn the enemies, who are in the *dꜣ.t*" [12]). "The enemies of the overlord of the *dꜣ.t* are destroyed. Their heads have fallen into their cauldrons" [13]).

---

1) *šw* = *šn*, viz. *rm.w*, fish, C.T. VI. 7.g.
2) C.T. VI. 8.d. e.
3) C.T. VI. 32.g. h.
4) C.T. VI. 206.d. e. f.
5) B.D. 17; C.T. IV. 309.b.
6) B.D. 168 A; 423. 5. 6.
7) Am Duat XI. 77; 84.
8) Cf. Pyr. 405.b to light fire with the *ḫpš.w*.
9) L.Q. LXXV. 1-4.
10) C.T. IV. 303.a.; B.D. 17.
11) C.T. IV. 323.a-c.
12) L.Q. XCVII. 7-8.
13) L.Q. XCVIII. 6.

B.5. *Bloody punishments and mutilation of the body.* [1])

In drawings in books about the hereafter, like the *Zweiwegebuch*, the Book of Gates or Am Duat, demons are pictured, who, with knives in their hands, hold themselves ready to wound the dead bloodily or to slaughter him. The dead fears that he may be cut to pieces. The spells should prevent his. He does not want to be slaughtered as an enemy of Osiris. For these are treated as offering cattle. They are bound, thrown down, belaboured with the slaughtering-knife. The heart is torn out and they are sacrified. Certain spells must prevent the head being cut off. Just as burning also this cutting to pieces or slaughtering brings on the total destruction of man.

B.5.a. *i3ṯ*, to mutilate [2]).

The dead rejects that he is injured in the hereafter: "I do not perish, my brains are not destroyed, I am not mutilated" [3]).

B.5.b. *iw*, to chop off.

Re says, in the netherworld, to enemies of Osiris: "Oh you who must be destroyed, oh you who must be beheaded, enemies of Osiris, whose heads are chopped off, whose necks do not exist . . . Behold, I pass above you. I assign you to your evil. I assign you to the non-being" [4]). Chopping off of the head means total destruction. In B.D. 71 "to cut off the neck" (*iw nḥb.t*) is parallel with "to chop off the head" [5]).

B.5.c. *iṅin*, to cut off.

A demoniacal snake is called "cutter of the neck" [6]).

B.5.d. *isp*. to hew [7]).

"The heart of Seth is hewn to pieces" [8]). "I come in order to see my father Osiris, to hew the heart of Seth to pieces" [9]). "The heart of the narrow one of throat is hewn to pieces" [10]).

B.5.e. *ʿ3b.t*, offering.

The dead fears to be slaughtered by demons as an offered animal. A spell must undo this. "There are made no offerings of me by the chamber-keepers of Osiris" [11]).

---

[1]) A. Hermann, *Zergliedern und Zusammenfügen*, NVMEN III, p. 84, note 19.

[2]) For the meaning see C.T. II. 276.b, mutilation of the mouth; V.110. h, damage to a boat.

[3]) B.D. 154; 401. 13.

[4]) L.Q. IX. 1. sqq.

[5]) B.D. Budge, p. 158. 7-8.

[6]) C.T. V. 287.c.

[7]) Of parts of a ship with an axe.

[8]) C.T. IV. 85.q.

[9]) B.D. 9; Nav. II. 19.

[10]) C.T. VI. 47.b.

[11]) C.T. VI. 132.d.

B.5.f. *ʿḏ*, to chop, *ʿḏ.t*, slaughter.

The verb occurs in a passage, where Anubis punishes Seth. He chopps Seth's head off, so that the latter is covered with blood [1]). Usually the substantive *ʿḏ.t*, slaughter, is used for a bloody punishment of sinners. A goddess with a knife in her hand, tortures enemies of Osiris in the netherworld. "She makes your slaughter, she executes your slaughter" [2]). Re punishes his enemies in the realm of the dead. "He assigns you to your slaughter. He counts you out to what you have done (or: "He punishes you on account of what you have done") in the big hall of Re" [3]).

B.5.g. *wbn*, gaping wounds.

In the spells of the net it occurs that the dead, as a fish or bird caught, is belaboured with a knife, causing wounds. The spell should prevent this. "N.N. has escaped from the gaping wounds" [4]). "He shoots and he catches in the place of this gaping wound, from which I have escaped" [5]).

B.5.h. *wḥś*, to slaughter.

The tenth hour of Am Duat is called: "The raging one, which slaughters the rebels" [6]). The 18th gate of B.D. 146 is called: "Which slaughters the rebels at night" [7]).

B.5.i. *bḥn*, to cut to pieces.

The dead hopes that he may not suffer this fate. On the contrary, he wishes to do it himself to his enemies in the realm of the dead. "May I not be delivered to him who eats those cut to pieces" [8]). "I am not cut to pieces by the day" [9]). The dead says of his enemies: "I cut their glory to pieces" [10]). He executes the divine judgment to the enemies of Osiris: "I have cut your rebels to pieces for you" [11]). To punished ones in the netherworld it is said: "You are cut to pieces in the place of destruction" [12]). The name of the place where this happens, indicates that the cutting to pieces aims at total destruction.

---

1) Pap. Jumilhac XX. 6.
2) Am Duat XI. 78.
3) Book of Gates V, middle register, B.S. Pl. XVIII. 37-40; E. Lefébure, M.M.A.F.C. III, 1, Pl. XXXI. 39-43.
4) C.T. VI. 21.p.
5) C.T. VI. 47.c.
6) Am Duat X. 2.
7) B.D. Budge, p. 357. 4.
8) C.T. V. 41.d.
9) C.T. II. 112.f.
10) C.T. I. 402.b.
11) C.T. IV. 90.m.; 97.j.
12) L.Q. XCVIII. 4.

B.5.j. *bśk*, to cut out.

Horus punishes the followers of Seth: "You cut (their hearts) out. You tear their hearts out" [1]). "Horus, who is in his house, has sailed over Seth like Geb, like the *rpw*, who cuts out hearts" [2]).

B.5.k. *fdk*, to cut to pieces.

Śḫm.t punishes the enemy of the sun: "She cuts the soles of your feet to pieces" [3]). The sun-god triumphs over his enemy. "Re continues to exist, Apophis is cut to pieces" [4]).

B.5.l. *rḫś*, to slaughter.

About a demon who threatens the dead, it is said: "Oh that he might be slaughtered with knives and wounded (?) in his body" [5]). *Rḫś* is used of the slaughtering of cattle [6]).

B.5.m. *hb*, to penetrate (of knives).

The dead wishes that demons will not harm him. "May their knife not penetrate me" [7]). Horus says to enemies of Osiris, who are punished: "Be there penetrating (of knives) for your shadows" [8]). "My brains are not pierced (by knives)" [9]).

B.5.n. *ḥnti*, to cut to pieces.

The enemies of Osiris are punished. "He cuts it (part of the body of Osiris' enemy) to pieces for Osiris, that he (Osiris) may make him overlord of those who cut to pieces" [10]).

B.5.o. *ḥśb*, to slaughter [11]).

Re triumphs over Apophis in the netherworld. "Your sacredness (of the chapel in the sun-boat) arises, which is in the earth. Apophis has been slaughtered in his blood" [12]).

B.5.p. *ḥśk*, to chop off (the head).

The dead wishes to be saved from the executioners of Osiris. "Save me from the fishermen of Osiris, who chop off heads and cut off necks, who take souls and spirits along to the slaughtering-block of him who eats raw flesh. My head is not chopped off, my neck is

---

1) Pyr. 1286.b.
2) Pyr. Neith 833. 834.
3) H. P. Blok, AcOr VII, 98, 100; Wb. I. 583. 7, „*den Bösen zerhacken*".
4) Berlin P 3050. IV. 8.
5) C.T. Spell 756; VI. 386.f.
6) Inscriptions of slaughtering scenes in the mastabas, P. Montet, *Scènes de la vie privée*, p. 153.
7) C.T. IV. 322.d.; B.D. 17.
8) Am Duat XI, 76
9) B.D. 154; 401. 14.
10) Pyr. 966.e.
11) Wb. III. 168. 4.
12) Book of Gates X, upper register, B.S. Pl. XI. 14-16.

not cut off. My name is not known among the spirits" [1]). The dead threatens a demon: "As regards each cutter of heads who puts himself in my way" . . . [2]). A ritual funeral protects against dangers in the hereafter: "I rejoice in a funeral. The head-chopper has no power over me" [3]). A spell tries to prevent the dead being taken to a place of torture by a threat. "When I go away to the slaughter-house (*ḥ3.t ḥśḳ*) of the gods and they call me to account there, truly the horns of *Ḫpr* will butt" [4]).

In the *ḳrr.t*-book four beheaded ones are pictured with their heads chopped off before them. Their hands are tied to their backs. This is already to be seen of conquered foes on the Narmer-palette. The inscription to it reads: "Oh beheaded ones, who have no head, who are in the place of destruction" [5]). *Ḥśḳ* is used pregnantly here in the meaning of beheaded ones, while the verb in itself means to chop off. About punished enemies of Osiris it is said: "You are beheaded. You do not exist" [6]). From this it is evident that the beheading means the total destruction of man.

B.5.q. *ḥdḳ*, to chop off.

Somebody's nose is chopped off, so that he cannot breathe. The text must prevent this. "The breath is not cut off from my nose (by a green stone at the throat, which works as a charm). It (the nose) is not chopped off" [7]).

B.5.r. *ḫry.t*, slaughter.

Demons, who threaten the dead, are called: "Lords of the slaughter" [8]). About uraei, which lighten the darkness for Osiris: "It is the flame that is on their mouth, which causes slaughter in the *d3.t*" [9]).

B.5.s. *sw3*, to chop off (the head).

The dead will take care that he who separates him from his relatives, is punished: "N.N. will let his head chop off on the slaughter-block of Khnum" [10]).

B.5.t. *sf*, to cut off, knife.

In a picture of the *ḳrr.t*-book three goddesses cut with knives

---

[1]) C.T. III. 295.h.; 296.a-e.
[2]) C.T. IV. 126.d.e.
[3]) C.T. VI. 264.p. q.
[4]) C.T. VI. 145.e.; 146.a. b.
[5]) L.Q. XXIV, 8, 2nd *ḳrr.t*, 5th register, bottom.
[6]) Book of Gates VIII, lower register, B.S. Pl. XIV. 20. 21.
[7]) C.T. II. 117.k.
[8]) C.T. IV. 11.d.
[9]) Am Duat IX. 97.
[10]) C.T. II. 205.a.

into people who are bound and beheaded. It concerns a punishment of sinners. "Oh *ʾIgr.t* of the cut ones, who is at the head of the place of destruction, triumphing *ʾIgr.t*, sharp of knives . . . *ʾIꜣy.t*, great of digestion products . . . with the blood of the sinners, who cut the heads of the enemies off . . . their shadows are blood-covered" [1]. The first of the women is called "ruining of cutting". About punishing demons in the netherworld it is said: "They cause the burning of the enemies like that which is on the point of their knife" [2]. Enemies of Osiris are punished in the realm of the dead: "The knife of her, who is at the head of her knives, is in you" [3].

B.5.u. *sfṯ*, to slaughter [4].

In the chapters of the catching-net the dead refuses to be caught or slaughtered like a bird (or fish). "For I know the name of this man who slaughters. It is the knife that is in the hand of *Šsm.w*" [5]. *Šḫm.t* punishes the enemy of the sun. "She chops off your fingers" [6].

B.5.v. *sn*, to cut off.

Demoniacal monkeys threaten somebody in the realm of the dead with cutting his head off. "Oh female baboons of his who chop off the heads, N.N. may pass you in peace, after he has tied his head to his neck" [7]. The following passage regards a judgment: "Oh these seven spells, which carry the scales in this night of the counting of the *wḏꜣ.t*-eye, which chops off heads, which cuts off necks, which takes hearts away and robs hearts, which brings slaughter about in the isle of fire, I know you, I know your name" [8]. Apophis is punished in the realm of the dead. The Ennead of Re says to him: "Your head be cut off, oh Apophis. (Your) coils may be cut off" [9].

B.5.w. *snf*, blood.

In the netherworld sinners are punished. A picture shows people with the head down. Their torn out hearts stand before them. From a wound in the breast blood is flowing. The inscription to it reads: "Oh you placed on your heads, bleeding ones, whose hearts have

---

1) L.Q. CXXXII. 4, 6th *ḳrr.t*, 3rd register, 1st tableau.
2) Am Duat III. 148-150.
3) Am Duat XI. 77.
4) In slaughtering scenes in the mastabas, P. Montet, *Scènes de la vie privée*, p. 167, 169, 173.
5) C.T. VI. 8.b. c.
6) H. P. Blok, AcOr VII. 98.
7) Pyr. 286.b.
8) B.D. 71; 158. 5-10.
9) Book of Gates II, lower register, B.S. Pl. III. 17-19.

been torn out, who are in the place of destruction" [1]). To enemies of Osiris it is said: "Your blood be shed" [2]). About a goddess in the netherworld it reads: "She lives on the blood of the dead" [3]). To enemies of Re and Osiris it is said: "Be silent, be deaf to Osiris N.N. It is what this god does, great of slaughter, great of terror. He bathes in your blood. He laps your blood" [4]). About four beings standing on their head, guarded by a god, it is said: "Their blood is on their corpses" [5]).

B.5.x. *śiḳ*, to chop off.

Sinners are punished in the netherworld. The picture shows heads chopped off and a goddess with a knife. "Chopping off for your heads" is written beside it [6]).

B.5.y. *śpd*, sharp.

Knives or flames, with which the dead is threatened, may be sharp. To executioners in the realm of the dead it is said: "Sharpness for your knives" [7]). Re says to snakes, which kill the enemies of Khepri: "Sharpness belongs to your knives" [8]). A gate in the realm of the dead is called "Sharp of flames" [9]). The name of the 2nd gate of the Book of Gates is "Sharp of flame" [10]). The name of the second gate of the *Livre de la Nuit* and of the 8th gate of B.D. 146 is "Sharp of fire". In the *Zweiwegebuch* is a red-coloured, and consequently fiery place, along the blue waterway. One of the five flames therein is called "Sharp of face" [11]). A place of torture in B.D. 17 is called "Sharp of fingers" [12]). The attribute sharp of places in the realm of the dead means that they can inflict painful injuries to the dead. It is especially used of fiery gates, which burn the passer-by.

B.5.z. *śmꜣ*, to slaughter.

An unnamed enemy waylays the dead, just as Seth waylaid Osiris. "He has come against you, when he thought of slaughtering you" [13]). "Osiris N.N., fetch for you him who wanted to slaughter you. Let him not escape from your hand. Osiris N.N., fetch him who wanted

---

1) L.Q. XXV. 1.2nd *ḳrr.t*, lower register.
2) L.Q. CXVIII. 3.
3) Am Duat V. 63.b.
4) B.D. 134; 293. 1 sqq; *bʿbʿ snf*, Pyr. 1286.c.
5) L.Q. XLIX. 7.
6) Am Duat XI. 76.
7) Am Duat V. 52. 53.
8) Am Duat VI. 215. 216.
9) Am Duat VIII. 223.
10) Book of Gates II, B.S. Pl. III.
11) C.T. VII, Spell 1154; B 1 Be. 246.
12) C.T. IV. 303.a.
13) Pyr. 944.a.

to slaughter you, perform his execution. Osiris N.N., fetch for you him who wanted to slaughter you in a cut condition (thrice)" [1]. *Śm3* is now applied in its turn to Seth and his gang. Horus is the one "who will slaughter Seth, the enemy of his father Osiris" [2]. The dead asks to be safeguarded against a demon: "(to Osiris) Do not deliver me to this slaughterer, who is in his . . ., who slaughters the bodies, who causes inflammation, the hidden one, who cuts many corpses to pieces, who lives on slaughter . . . Do not deliver me to his fingers, let him not have power over me" [3]. A name of a demon in the realm of the dead is: "Who slaughters his enemies" [4]. In the netherworld are persons armed with lances, one of whom is called: "Who slaughters with his tongue" [5].

The dead does not want to be looked upon as an enemy of Osiris. In that case he would be taken to Osiris as a victim like Seth and his gang.

Enemies of a god are slaughtered and offered to him. Sacrificial animals take the place of enemies.

B.5.aa. *śṯ3.w*, wounds.

The dead asks Re for protection: "Save me from those who inflict wounds" [6]. There is a demon, "who inflicts injuries, without being seen" [7].

B.5.bb. *šʿ*, to chop off, *šʿ.t*, carnage.

About executioners in the realm of the dead, who punish the enemies of the Lord of the universe, it is said that they are the ones "who cause slaughter in their chambers of torture" [8]. Chamber-keepers of Osiris, demoniacal helpers, are called "who execute slaughtering on their slaughtering-blocks" [9]. The dead threatens with cosmic disturbance in case he would be slaughtered: "If I am taken along and ferried across to the East, that an offering of me may be made like an evil slaughtering . . ., I shall swallow the phallus of Re" [10]. He does not want to be slaughtered like a sacrificial animal.

---

[1]) Pyr. 1337.b-d.
[2]) C.T. II. 213.b.
[3]) B.D. 154; 400. 14 sqq.
[4]) Am Duat III. 41.
[5]) *Livre du Jour*, 1st register, ed. A. Piankoff, p. 7.
[6]) B.D. 17; C.T. IV. 303.a.
[7]) C.T. IV. 314.d. e.
[8]) B.D. 17; C.T. IV. 322. b. Apophis tries to devour the eye of Horus, but the flame of the eye penetrates into his body. To the sun-god is said "It cuts into your limbs"; H. P. Blok, AcOr VII, 98.
[9]) C.T. VI. 132.e.
[10]) C.T. VI. 144.h-145.a. d.

The dead is somebody "to whom his head is given back, after it has been chopped off" [1]). The dead has to pass gates in the hereafter. He charms dangerous gate-keepers by calling their name. "They chop off the nose and the lips of him who does not know their names" [2]). As a wish to a helping god it is uttered: "May he save me from the evil slaughtering, which men, gods, spirits and dead think of executing against my *b3*" [3]). Osiris, as executioner, is called "Lord of the slaughter" [4]).

To enemies of Osiris in the netherworld it is said: "Your corpses are cut to pieces" [5]). Re orders their execution: "The majesty of this god orders that the slaughtering of those, who struck his (Horus) father Osiris, is executed" [6]). The dead says to the 42 judges of Osiris: "I shall not fall on account of your slaughter" [7]). Horus fights Seth and his gang. He makes a slaughter among them by beheading them [8]).

The dead wants to be safeguarded against this punishment: "There is not made a slaughter by the two great ones of the reckoning" [9]). B.D. 41 is "a spell in order to keep the slaughter off, which is made in the realm of the dead" [10]).

B.5.cc. *šʿd*, to chop off.

B.D. 43 [11]) is "a spell for not letting somebody's head being cut off from him in the realm of the dead. I am the one, . . . to whom his head is given back, after it has been cut off. The head of Osiris is not taken away from him". The rubric of B.D. 163 [12]) indicates the consequences of applying the ritual: "He does not die on account of the slaughter of Seth." In both cases the dead identifies himself with Osiris. No more than in the case of Osiris the attacks of Seth have a chance of success with him.

B.5.dd. *šdi*, to take away (parts of the body out of the body).

In the oldest times the heart was removed from the body when

---

1) C.T. V. 62.a.
2) C.T. V. 182.f.
3) C.T. VI. 93.d. e.
4) C.T. II. 116.v.
5) L.Q. CXVIII. 2.
6) Am Duat XI. 76.
7) B.D. 125; 260. 1.
8) Pap. Jumilhac XXII. 9-11.
9) Louvre 3283 VII, 4, *nn šʿ.tw in wr.wy nty ḥsb*.
10) B.D. Budge, p. 110. 9. C.T. Spell 704 has the same title; VI. 335. m, "To keep off slaughtering in the realm of the dead."
11) B.D. Budge, p. 116. 15 sqq.
12) B.D. Budge, p. 414. 13.

mummifying it. An artificial heart was put in its place. The texts on the heart scarab refer to this. Texts like B.D. 27 and 28 must prevent somebody's heart being taken away from him. In later periods they left the heart in its place, but the use of the heart scarab was maintained [1]).

Apophis is considered to be a demon and the chief sinner and so he is punished as such. He is sentenced by taking his heart away [2]). "It is the gods who tear your heart out" [3]). Apophis is tied and slaughtered like a sacrificial animal. The taking away of the heart out of the body was a certain part of it [4]). Enemies of the gods are slaughtered like sacrificial animals and on the other hand sacrificial animals represent the enemy of a god. The same happens to the enemies of the king. The latter, like Osiris, has left his son Horus at his death on earth. His son punishes his enemies as followers of Seth. They are slaughtered and sacrificed for the king. "They have left Horus behind in his garment. He punishes the followers of Seth. They are seized. Their heads are chopped off. They are slaughtered. You cut them out. You tear their hearts out. You drink their blood"[5]). This does not refer to taking the heart away as part of the normal mummification, but it concerns a bloody punishment here. *Šd ḥ3ty* as a punishment for the unjust occurs in a description of the netherworld, where the drawing shows tied persons with the head downwards whose heart is torn out from their breast [6]). The inscription to it reads: "Oh bleeding ones, turned with the head downwards, whose hearts have been torn out in the place of destruction." The tearing out of the heart was a punishment, which the king applied to a conquered foe [7]). "I seized the evil one. He was tied with his bonds. I tore his heart out . . . I tore his heart away out of his left side." That *šd* means a.o. to tear out violently also appears, e.g., from

---

[1]) Sethe, *Mélanges Maspero*, M.I.F.A.O. LXVI, 1935, p. 113 sqq; A. de Buck, J.E.O.L. III, no. 9, p. 17.

[2]) B.D.39; 105. 11.

[3]) Wb. IV. 561. 7, *Körperteile aus dem Körper herausnehmen, bes. vom Herausnehmen des Herzens.* In slaughtering scenes: L. Klebs, *Die Reliefs des Alten Reiches*, pp. 121, 126, picture 99; Montet, *Scènes de la vie privée*, p. 167.

[4]) In the mastabas it concerns the slaughtering of cattle for the funerary offering.

[5]) Pyr. 1285.c-1286.c.

[6]) L.Q. XXV. 1.

[7]) Wb. *Belegstellen* IV. 561. 7, Theb. T.

the *Mythe d'Horus* [1]), where Horus changes himself into a lion and with his claws tears the kidneys out of the bodies of his enemies.

B.5.ee. *kf*, knife (?).

First the dead has secured strength for himself, a.o. by identifying himself with gods. Now he is able to frighten demons. "The carriers of knives do not come to me. They do not deliver (me) (to) the gods of the wine-press. Your fright is placed against the carriers of knives" [2]). "The knife has no power over me" [3]).

B.5.ff. *tbś*, to pierce.

Four uraei in the netherworld punish Apophis as enemy of Re. "The four uraei, which hastily pierce the enemy of the flame, when they sail before the flame (i.e. Re)" [4]).

B.5.gg. *ṯḫś*, to slaughter.

This verb is used [5]) for slaughtering sacrificial animals and for killing Seth [6]), for instance in the passage [7]) "I have marched out, I have killed off Seth." It also occurs in an enumeration of evil things, of which the dead says that they will not happen to him in the hereafter [8]). "I sat down next to the god. I am content. There is nothing evil in me. I am not slaughtered by the two great ones of the reckoning. I do not land in the place (of the judgment). My ears are not deaf. My head is not chopped off. My tongue is not taken away. My skin is not slaughtered [9]). Nothing bad is done against my belly. It is not destroyed. It does not suffer want in eternity."

B.5.hh. *dm*, to cut.

C.T. Spell 246 is a spell to go in and out of the fire. The dead says: "The gods of light do not cut me" [10]). In the rubric of B.D. 163 it is said of him who keeps to the ritual: "He is not cut" [11]). The third gate of the *Livre de la Nuit* is called "Sharp of knives" [12]).

---

1) *Mythe d'Horus* XVIII. 2. 2) C.T. Spell 469; V. 396.a-c; cf. VI. 319.q.
3) C.T. II. 133.f. 4) *Livre du Jour*, 2nd register, ed A. Piankoff, p. 10.
5) Wb. V. 328. 4. 6) Wb. V. 328. 5.
7) Dend. 4495, temple of Osiris.
8) Louvre 3283 VII. 3-5, *iw.i śndm.n.i ḥnʿ nṯr iw.i hry ib nn ḫ.t nb.t ḏw.t ḫr.i nn šʿ.tw.i in wr.wy nty ḥśb nn h3.i m ḫnt ś.t nn śḫi mśḏr.wy.i nn ḥśḳ tp.i nn iṯ.tw nś.t.i nn ṯḫś mśk.i nn ir.tw ḫ.t nb.t ḏw.t r ẖ.t.i nn śk.ś nn wś.ś r nḥḥ ḏ.t*
9) Flayed? The other *Belegstellen* give no rise to this translation.
10) C.T. III. 337.e.
11) B.D. Budge, p. 414. 12.
12) 3rd *śbḫ.t*.

B.5.ii. *dn*, to cut.

In the realm of the dead the slaughtering-block is "that which cuts the soul to pieces" [1]). The dead keeps a demon at bay: "N.N. is stronger than he who cuts the heads off" [2]). In the tombs of the kings women with knives are pictured, who punish godless in the realm of the dead. They are the ones "who cut the heads of the enemies off" [3]). The same occurs when earthly enemies of the king are exterminated. About the uraeus on the forehead of the king it is said: "It cuts off the heads of the Asiatics" [4]). The third hour of Am Duat and the third hour of the *Livre de la Nuit* are called: "Which cuts the souls." About demons in the *ḳrr.t*-book it is said: "They cut the *b3* to pieces"[5]). "*Nmty* cuts their limbs off" [6]).

B.5.jj. *dr*, to remove.

Thoth removes the head of the enemies of the king in the realm of the dead. "Sharpen your knife, Thoth, the sharp one, the cutting one, which removes heads, which cuts out hearts, that it may remove the heads and cut out the hearts of those, who will put themselves inimically in the way of N.N., when he comes to you, Osiris" [7]). To enemies of Osiris in the realm of the dead it is said: "Your head is cut off" [8]). "Your souls are taken away, ... your shadows are taken away" [9]). A gate is called: "The cutting one, who takes away (extirpates) its enemies" [10]).

B.5.kk. *dś*, knife, cutting.

In the *Zweiwegebuch* demons are pictured with knives in their hands in order to cut with them him who passes them. In the vignettes of the Book of the Dead gate-keepers are represented with knives in their hands. The dead king calls to Thoth for assistance to cut his waylayers with a knife. "Whet your knife, Thoth" [11]). "I am the sharp knife that is in the hand of Thoth," says another text [12]). About demons of Osiris it is said: "Their knives have no power over me" [13]). "May I not fall on account of your knives" [14]), a dead says, who

---

1) C.T. IV. 301.a.
2) C.T. IV. 67.h.
3) L.Q. CXXXII. 6. 6th *ḳrr.t*, 3rd. register, 1st tableau.
4) Urk. IV. 614. 1.
5) L.Q. CXXVIII. 3.
6) L.Q. XXXVI. 3.
7) Pyr. 962.a.b.; 963.a. b. See also Pyr. 1286.a.
8) L.Q. CXVIII. 2.
9) L.Q. CXVIII. 3. 4.
10) Am Duat VIII. 219.
11) Pyr. 962.a. See B. 5.jj. *dr*.
12) C.T. III. 337.g.
13) B.D. 17; C.T. IV. 305.a.
14) C.T. IV. 322.d.

wants to be safeguarded against the threatening of demons. "Truly, my spell is more useful than his knife" [1]). In the spells which should prevent the dead being caught by a net, he fears the knife, with which birds and fish are slaughtered. "This knife, with which he cuts it (fish or bird), the knife that is in the hand of *Šsm.w*" [2]). *Šsm.w*, the god of the wine-press, is feared on account of the bloody punishments, which he executes. The name of the fourth gate in B.D. 146 is: "Powerful of knives, mistress of the two lands, who hurts the enemies of the tired one of heart" [3]). In passing the gate the danger of the dead being belaboured with knives there is imminent. About snakes, which punish the enemies of Khepri, it is said: "You cut their shadows" [4]).

B.5.ll. *dšr.w*, blood.

A demon is called: "Lord of the blood, fresh of slaughter-places" [5]). The name occurs in the *ḳrr.t*-book: "Great of secret, lord of the blood, fresh of slaughter-places" [6]).

B.5.mm. *d̲nd̲n*, to chop off (the head).

The dead says: "I have chopped off the head of your (Osiris') enemies for you" [7]). About the punishment of Apophis it is said: "Your head is cut off" [8]).

B.6. *To be devoured.*

The dead may be eaten by demons in the hereafter.

B.6.a. *ʿm*, *sʿm*, to devour.

The dead says to a demon: "Your name is devourer" [9]). Another demon is called: "Devourer of millions" [10]). The monster near the scales of Osiris, which is ready to eat those who are found too light, is called "Devourer of the dead" [11]). To a demon, "Devourer of asses" it is said [12]): "Oh you, who devours evil-doers, who takes

---

1) C.T. V. 49.c.

2) C.T. VI. 32.e. f.

3) B.D. Budge, p. 351. 5. 6.

4) Am Duat VI. 217.

5) B.D. 17; C.T. IV. 316.c. Perhaps also to be translated: "Red of slaughter-places", cf. w*3d.t*, WB. I. 268.16, for the red crown. Cf. also w*3d*.w, raw flesh, Wb. I. 268. 4. Does it concern slaughter-places, which time and again are provided with fresh meat?

6) L.Q. LXXXVII. 1.

7) C.T. IV. 90. 1.

8) B.D. 39; 106. 13.

9) C.T. V. 51.e. Idem keeper 4th gate Book of Gates, B.S. Pl. VII. 56.

10) C.T. IV. 315.d.; B.D. 17.

11) Wb. I. 184. 9. Idem about a demon in Am Duat, II. 57. 58.

12) B.D. 40; 109. 15.

away while robbing . . . I am no evil-doer." About the 42 executioners of Osiris who punish the godless it is said that they "swallow up their blood" [1]). One demon is called "Devourer of shadows" [2]), another "Devourer of corpses" [3]). The dead asks for protection against a demon: "May you save Osiris N.N. Prevent him being taken away by his enemies, who swallow the souls" [4]). So these demons are especially aiming at those parts of the personality which are essential for survival, *šw.t*, *ẖ3.t* and *b3* [5]).

B.6.b. *ʿnḫ m*, to live on.

Demons and tormenting devils "live on" their victims. The king is saved from such a demon. "I have saved you from *H̱rty*, for he lives on the hearts of men" [6]). The dead identifies himself with a demon and says: "I am a god, who lives on men" [7]). There is a fiery gate in the *Zweiwegebuch*, "which lives on the evil ones who do not know how to pass it" [8]). The idea is that the keeper of the gate devours somebody. The dead fears to be slaughtered as a piece of cattle and to be eaten by a demon and he asks Atum for protection: "Save me from this god who lives on slaughter beasts" [9]). The 42 judges of Osiris are called: "Who live on the evil ones whom they guard. Who swallow their blood on this day of the punishment before *Wnn-nfr*" [10]). The dead asks of them: "Save me from *B3b3*, who lives on intestines" [11]). Apophis "lives on tired ones" [12]) (i.e., dead ones). A punishing demon "lives on hearts" [13]). There are "gods . . . who are in *R3-sṯ3.w* who live on the bodies of . . ." [14]). In the Book of Gates it is said about certain gods: "They live on southern ones, they subsist on northern ones" [15]). The dead hopes not to be delivered to a demon "who lives on slaughtering" [16]). In Am Duat [17]) demons occur, who live on the immaterial food of the lamentations, uttered by condemned sinners who are tortured

1) B.D. 125; 249. 12.
2) B.D. 125; 253. 2; B.D. 17; C.T. IV. 314.b.
3) B.D. 17, Naville II. 64; B.D. 127 A; 272. 3.
4) B.D. 163; 412. 11.
5) *ʿm b3*, Am Duat VII. 152.
6) Pyr. Neith 665; cf. Neith 668; Pyr. 662.d.
7) C.T. V. 29.a.
8) C.T. VII, Spell 1108; B 1 L. 534.
9) C.T. IV. 312.b. c.
10) B.D. 125; 249. 11-12.
11) B.D. 125; 260. 11.
12) B.D. 7; 29. 8.
13) B.D. 124; 244. 15.
14) Louvre 3177 b,*nṯr.w. . . . . .nty.w m R3-sṯ3.w ʿnḫ.w m ḥʿ.t.*
15) Book of Gates IX, lower register, B.S. Pl. XIII. 14-16.
16) B.D. 154; 401. 1-2.
17) Am Duat XI. 80. 81.

by them. "They live on the lamentations of the enemies (of Osiris) and on the roaring of the souls and of the shadows which are given to them in their divisions of hell."

B. 6. c. *wnm*, to eat.

A demon with a slaughtering-block is called: "Who eats raw flesh" [1]). One of the 42 judges of Osiris bears the name of "Eater of blood" [2]), another "Eater of intestines" [3]). To a demon, named "Devourer of asses", the dead says: "Do not eat me" [4]). Especially about the *bꜣ* it is stated that it is eaten up. The dead delivers those who threaten him, to demons. "I count them out to . . . those who eat the soul, that they may eat their souls and destroy those who are on earth" [5]). A certain text is a "spell in order to save somebody from those who eat souls" [6]).

The dead himself becomes a demon who eats his opponent in the hereafter: "Who is found by N.N. on his way, he eats him, body and bones" [7]).

B. 6. d. *swr*, to drink.

The dead keeps a demon at bay: "Your blood is drunk" [8]).

B. 6. e. *śḫb*, to devour.

In Am Duat a snake occurs "which devours the shadows" [9]). A keeper of the second gate of the Book of Gates is called "Gulper of blood" [10]). Keepers of the gates "devour souls" [11]).

B. 6. f. *dp*. to consume.

There is a demon "savage of face", "from whose mouth fiery breath comes in order to consume souls" [12]).

B. 6. g. *dnm*, eating worm.

In the realm of the dead there are worms which eat up corpses [13]).

B. 7. *Dangerous places.*

There are all kinds of places in the realm of the dead, where the dead must be very careful. Some of them are divisions of hell, where he may be tortured or burnt. There is a block, on which he may be

---

1) C.T. III. 296.b.
2) B.D. 125; 254. 5.
3) B.D. 125; 254. 7.
4) B.D. 40; 109. 7; 110. 5.
5) C.T. II. 254.o. p.
6) B.D. 163; 411. 1.
7) Pyr. 278a., cf. 407.c.; 444.e.; Neith 659.
8) C.T. V. 51.a.
9) Am Duat VI. 153.
10) Book of Gates, B.S. Pl. III. 3.
11) B.D. 127 A.; 272. 3.
12) B.D. 163; 411. 16.
13) Wb. V. 467. 12; B.D. 163; 411. 4.

slaughtered like a piece of cattle. He goes along roads of which he must know the right direction. Along these roads demons or pools of fire wait for him. He must be able to pass these safely. The spells which deal with this, should give him information about it and impart the necessary knowledge to him in order to escape these dangers.

B.7.a. *i3b*, left, eastern [1]).

The dead does not want to land in unfavourable places in the East. "Osiris N.N., do not go to these eastern lands, do go to the western countries on the roads of the followers of Re" [2]). Messengers announce him to Re. C.T. Spell 548 serves not to take a person across to the East. In case this happens the dead threatens with cosmic disturbance. "When I am taken along, when I am taken across to the East . . ., an inflammation in the eye of *Ṯb* (= *Tbi*?, name of the sun-god) is caused . . ., before I am taken across to the East." There an "evil slaughter" against the dead is executed. [3]) In B.D. 176 the eastern country occurs in an unfavourable sense. "Spell not to die for the second time . . . I detest the eastern country. I do not enter the place of judgment. To me nothing is sacrificed of that which the gods abhor, for I am the one who passes pure" [4]).

B.7.b. *i3ṯ*, chamber of torture.

This word is connected with *i3ṯ*, to mutilate, B.5.a. In B.D. 17 revisors are mentioned, "who execute slaughters in the chambers of torture" [5]). "May I not enter in your chambers of torture", the dead says [6]).

B.7.c. *in.t*, valley.

If the dead does not know his spell, he lands in the realm of the dead in a valley as a place of horror. ". . . the two doors of the

---

[1]) For the meaning *i3b*, unfavourable, see *śṯi*, A.3.p.; *š wr*, B. 7.n.; *pr b3 pf*, B. 16. b.; See also Morenz, *Rechts und links im Totengericht*, Z.Ä.S. 82 (1957), pp. 63-65. M. takes his point of departure in the passage Bibl. Aegyptiaca VII. 2 and 16: "Amun judges the earth with his fingers and speaks to the heart. He judges the guilty and assigns him to the East (*ḫ*ʿ(*w*)) and the just to the West" (translation R. A. Caminos). According to M. *ḫʿ.w* is the place where the sun rises (*ḫʿi*) and where he in cosmic battle annihilates his enemies. Seth is punished too on the "secret place of slaughter of the East" (*ḫb.t št3.t n.t i3b.t*, Pap. Salt 825, IV. 7). See Wb. III. 242. 9, *ḫʿw*, „*Strafort für die Bösen.*" H. P. Blok, AcOr VII, 110: „*Im Osten der Welt also befindet sich die göttliche Richtstätte*".

[2]) Pyr. 1531.a.b.

[3]) C.T. VI. 144.a.h.; 145.c.; 146.e.; 145.a.

[4]) B.D. Budge, pl 460. 13-16.

[5]) C.T. IV. 322.b.

[6]) C.T. IV. 306.a: 323.b.

3ḫ.t. The name of their keepers is this, which is written down (that is to say in the text and which the owner of the text consequently knows). As regards anyone who does not know their words, he falls into the *ỉnn.wt* (a kind of traps or snares?) of the valley there. But as regards anyone who will know their words, he passes there" [1]). "I do not go into the valley of darkness" [2]). The "valley of the net" is mentioned here [3]). Apparently this net is set up in the valley and he who passes the valley, may land in it. A goddess helps the dead with his ascension and takes care that he does not land in a valley. "My mother *Śpd.t* makes my way. She builds a staircase to this very large territory of *Nnmw.t*, that I may go out of the valley of the mountain of *Sḥsḫ*" [4]). A place in the realm of the dead where there are condemned ones, is "the valley of those who go with their heads downwards" [5]).

B.7.d. *ʿr*, pool.

"Beware of the pool that belongs to the spirits" is said as a warning to the king [6]). The pool is a place where there are condemned dead. "The pool that belongs to the dead, you run away from it" [7]). "Horus has chopped off their heads to heaven like birds and their thighs to the pool like fish" [8]). As opposed to *p.t*, heaven, *ʿr* is a pool in the netherworld, where enemies are punished.

B.7.e. *w3.t*, road.

Passing away to the hereafter is conceived as setting out on a road. This road may be considered as being favourable. In the mastabas of the Old Kingdom the transportation of the corpse at the funeral is a going on the beautiful roads to the West. In the other world are also roads. They lead to the *d3.t*, the netherworld. They may be full of dangers. The text has as its aim to avoid these dangers or to know the roads, so that the dead will not lose his way. In order to prevent this maps are sent along with him, for instance of the pathway and the waterway in the *Zweiwegebuch*. The road leads to

1) *Zweiwegebuch*, B. 1 Be. 7. 8, C.T. VII, Spell 1131.
2) *Zweiwegebuch*, B. 1 L. 485, C.T. VII, Spell 1099.
3) C.T. IV. 353.d.
4) C.T. Spell 469; V. 389.i-k.
5) Am Duat XI, lower register, Bucher, p. 77.
6) Pyr. 771.c. In Pyr. Neith 761 this is an apposition to *š wr*, see B. 7.n.
7) C.T. I. 284.f. g.
8) B.D. 134; 292. 10-12.

a place, where the ascension begins, or the going along a road regards the ascension itself and the going to join Re. The funeral is being led along a road to the necropolis in the West. "May he be led by his kas to his pure places, may his hand be taken by the great god. May he be led on the glorious ways to the West, on which the venerable walk. May he unite himself with the earth, cross the heavens. May the western desert hold out both its hands to him in peace, in peace near the great god" [1]). There is thought of an ascension in the following passage: "May he walk on the glorious roads, on which the venerable walk . . . May he be near the great god, the lord of heaven, among the venerable" [2]). In the following places there is also a connection with the ascension. "Go away to the *3ḫ.t* . . . Re has given you your beautiful roads, which are in there. The gates of heaven are opened to you" [3]). The dead goes to heaven as the morning-star, the gates of the *d3.t* open and the dead joins Re. "To become the morning god. The roads of the *d3.t* are opened to this N.N., the gates which are in the *3ḫ.t* are opened to her . . . N.N. is the only star that belongs to the *3ḫ.t*. Her father Re has given the whole sky to her" [4]). Along the roads of the *d3.t* (here netherworld?) and through gates the dead reaches the (eastern) *3ḫ.t*, to rise there with Re as morning-star. In a text, in which the dead is put on a level with Re, going along the roads is likely to regard an ascension. "Guard of the roads, leave the road free for me, that I may pass along it" [5]). It here concerns a guard along the road, who may keep the dead at bay. He can move freely in heaven and on earth; "Heaven and earth come to me. Their great ones, the upper gods, come to me. They open the glorious roads to me" [6]). Along hidden roads the dead approaches a gate, which is probably thought of as lying in the East, in order to rise there with Re: "To speak words by the western souls. The late Osiris N.N. has come along secret roads. He has reached the gates of Nun. He has approached the gate of ascending to heaven with knowledge of pulling, instructed in rowing. His sceptre is given to him, that he may strike with it. He announces Re, in the front of the boat" [7]).

---

1) Junker, Gîza II. 58.
2) l.c.
3) C.T. Spell 763; VI. 393.b. f. g.
4) C.T. Spell 722; VI. 350.f. g. h. q. r.
5) C.T. VI. 270.r. s.
6) C.T. VI. 135.b-d.
7) C.T. Spell 780; VI. 411.g-n.

So the dead has to go along "the roads of the *dꜣ.t*", along "secret" roads to a gate (in the East?), in order to rise there with Re (the gates of Nun are the place where Re rises from the primeval ocean). This gives the impression that man, immediately after his death, first has to travel, not without dangers, before he may rise with Re. Unfortunately C.T. Spells 747 and 748 have gaps and are therefore difficult to understand. It is clear, however, that they deal with the guidance of somebody along the roads of the *dꜣ.t* [1]), in order to effect that he is not assaulted by a demon there, "do not seize her on the road, ignorant one" [2]), so that he is eventually in the heavens with Re [3]). Spell 625 also belongs here [4]): "Oh this great council of heaven, you introduce me among you as one of you . . .; evil-doers, open the two doors to me . . . May the dark roads be broad for me." The dead wishes to go unhindered along dark roads, to go to heaven afterwards.

C.T. Spells 758-760 belong to a remarkable figure [5]). A god seated on a throne with a crown of snakes, his head in full face, is surrounded by four ovals, which represent roads. The way around it is the *mḥn*-snake, which usually twists itself protectingly around Re in his chapel. The four roads are dangerous. They are "fiery roads" [6]). There is a demoniacal guard [7]) and there are gates which lead astray [8]). Round the four roads is the *mḥn*-snake [9]). The dead does not want to be kept away from Re [10]). The dead says: "I know the dark roads along which Hu enters together with Sia [11]), like dark snakes, behind which and before which light is spread. I enter among the two of them under the hidden road which is on the crown of Re. I know these hidden roads, where the cat enters every day [12]). Prepare the roads for me, open the gates to me, oh you that are in the *mḥn* . . . I know the roads of *mḥn*" [13]). "He who knows the name of these roads of his, enters the *mḥn*. He who knows this spell, does not perish to all eternity" [14]). The purpose of the spell is to know the dangerous

---

[1]) C.T. VI. 377.a.
[2]) C.T. VI. 377.g.
[3]) C.T. VI. 378.m.
[4]) C.T. VI. 242.a. b. d. h.
[5]) Drawing C.T. 386.
[6]) C.T. VI. 387.b.
[7]) C.T. VI. 387.c.
[8]) C.T. VI. 387.e.
[9]) C.T. VI. 387.j. k., the *mḥn*, which surrounds the roads of fire.
[10]) C.T. VI. 388.h.; I am not kept off from Re within his *mḥn*.; so the seated figure is Re.
[11]) C.T. VI. 388.j.
[12]) C.T. VI. 388.p.
[13]) C.T. VI. 389.a. d.
[14]) C.T. Spell 760; VI. 390.k. l.

roads, full of fire, which the *mḥn*-snake encircles, and in this way to come within the circumference of the *mḥn*-snake and to be protected by it like Re.

Sometimes the roads which do lead to Re, are not the point at issue, but the road he has to travel himself. "He crosses the vault of heaven. He crosses the sky. He goes in peace along the beautiful roads, on which the venerable go" [1]).

In an ascension text the dead goes along beautiful roads to the two *ḥtp*-fields of Osiris, where he is satiated [2]). "To knit a ladder to heaven . . . For me a beautiful way is paved to these two excellent plots of the dumpalm . . . For which purpose do I come here? I come to place the portion of the only one in the two *ḥtp*-fields of Osiris."

On the bottom of the wooden sarcophagus, where also the *Zweiwegebuch* is to be found, a labyrinth of roads is drawn, which lead through the realm of the dead. Beside it there are spells, which help somebody to know these roads, so that he cannot lose his way on them. "It is the spell of the road. These roads are as follows: The one of them, which meets the other, leading in another direction. As regards him who knows them, they find their ways. The height of their walls of fire-stone is in *R3-st3.w*" [3]).

C.T. Spell 649 reminds one of the *Zweiwegebuch*. A map with rivers is drawn [4]). First there is a gate, after that pictures of demoniacal guards. In between are spells, which must help somebody to pass these. "Open the road to me, I am . . . Make me pass safely," the dead says to the guards. Also in Spell 619 such passage spells occur [5]). "Prepare the way for me, that I may pass. If you do not prepare the way for me (i.e., let me through), so that I pass, I'll place the western ones in Geb, the father of the gods . . . Oh Re, watch over the roads against those, who pass. Block the roads for those who go out before me." The dead have to pass gates, where others are hold up. Apparently also here it concerns a journey through the *d3.t*, which should be brought to a happy conclusion before the ascension. "Oh great one of harvest (?, cultivation, ploughing?) in the midst of the

[1]) C.T. V. 166.a. b.

[2]) C.T. Spell 629; VI. 248,a.d.; 249.d. e. Emendation of *ỉỉ.n.ỉ* into *ỉỉ.n.k*.

[3]) C.T. VII, Spell 1182; B 1 Be. 291 sqq.

[4]) C.T. VI. 271.

[5]) C.T. VI. 231.c. d. e. s.; 232.a. e. f. g. h. i.

d3.t, prepare for me the way, that I may pass. Behold, it has come to meet me. The beautiful West has come to meet me. It says: Oh son of the bull, welcome in heaven."

B.7.f. *mꜥḏ*, slaughtering-block.

"N.N. will make his head being hewn off on this slaughtering-block of *Ḫnmw*" [1]).

B.7.g. *nm.t*, slaughtering-block.

Nm.t is a block, on which an animal is slaughtered [2]). It is used of sacrificial animals. "May you eat the shins, may you taste of the piece of meat, may you receive a double rib of the slaughtering-block" [3]). One of the dangers in the realm of the dead is, that somebody is killed on such a slaughtering-block. There are many spells for preventing this. "Not to come on the slaughtering-block of the god . . . I am not taken to the slaughtering-block of the god. I am not led to the slaughtering-block of the god" [4]). In the realm of the dead there is a demon "the lord of the blood, whose slaughtering-blocks are well-provided" [5]). About such demons the dead says: "I shall not descend on their slaughtering-blocks" [6]). Anubis protects the dead. "He saves you from the *m3šty.w*, the messengers of the hidden slaughtering-block" [7]). In a spell about not taking the heart away it reads: "I detest the slaughtering-block of the god" [8]). The dead says: "I am not fetched by the slaughterers to the slaughtering-block. Their offerings of me are not made" [9]). This terminology is borrowed from the offering scenes. Man is offered as enemy of the god. He is slaughtered like a piece of cattle. His heart is pulled out of his body like that of a sacrificial animal [10]). The spell has to prevent this. "I am not taken to the slaughtering-block of the god . . . There is not made a bloody sacrifice out of me by the chamber-keepers of Osiris, who make massacres on the slaughtering-blocks. I do not come on their slaughtering-blocks. I am not brought on the slaughtering-block of the god . . . My soul and my shadow escape

---

[1]) C.T. II. 205.a.
[2]) H. P. Blok considers it to be a sandy hill, AcOr VII, 98, 103-113.
[3]) Pyr. Neith 771.
[4]) C.T. II. 131.d.; 132.a. c.; C.T. IV. 12.a.; C.T. VI. 261.a.; Spell 640.
[5]) B.D. 17; C.T. IV. 316.c.; of *Ḥry-š.f* C.T. V. 257.g.
[6]) B.D. 17, Naville II. 68.
[7]) C.T. I. 196.d.
[8]) C.T. V. 57.d.; idem B.D. 28; 91. 16.
[9]) C.T. V. 224.f.
[10]) See *šdi*, B. 5.dd.

from it . . . for I am this well-provided spirit, who knows his spell, who does not come on the slaughtering-block of the god" [1]).

Especially the soul of the dead is in danger of being destroyed on the slaughtering-block. This would be for him the definite impossibility of continuing to exist. There is a separate title: "Not to take somebody's soul to the slaughtering-block of Shu" [2]). The dead fears a demon "who throws a lasso around his enemies in order to fetch them to his slaughtering-block, which cuts the souls to pieces" [3]). Cattle are first caught with a lasso and after that bound and slaughtered.

In the tombs of the kings of the New Kingdom sinners are killed in the netherworld on slaughtering-blocks. "The way of the executioners of the slaughtering-block is paved against you (that is to say they are turned loose against you), so that you are beheaded" [4]). "I put the enemies (of Osiris) on their slaughtering-blocks" [5]). A fire-spitting goddess with a knife in her hand is pictured near a division of hell. She is the one "who is at the head of her slaughtering-block". She tortures the enemies of Osiris [6]). From the word *nm.t* *nmty*, executioner of the slaughtering-block, is derived as a nisbe. "The executioners of the slaughtering-block of the god have no power over me" [7]). "Oh executioners, who belong to the slaughtering-block, who take care that damage is done to the dead . . . punish the enemies" [8]).

B.7.h. *nḫ3*, name of a channel.

This channel is one of the impediments on the way to heaven, which the dead king has to pass. "Raise N.N., lift him up to the *nḫ3*-channel" [9]). The determinative is a curved channel. Its "bends" are mentioned [10]). So it is a winding stream. Wings, a ferry-man or poles help the dead over it. The *nḫ3*-channel belongs to the conception of the river of the dead, also known from other religions, which somebody has to pass, before he reaches a beatified place.

---

[1]) C.T. Spell 535; VI. 132.b. d-g. j. l. m.

[2]) C.T. VI. 152.a.

[3]) C.T. IV. 300.b.; 301.a.=B.D. 17.

[4]) Book of Gates IX, middle register, B.S. Pl. XIII. 29-XII. 31.

[5]) L.Q. III. 6.

[6]) Am Duat XI. 77; 87.

[7]) C.T. III. 335.h.

[8]) Am Duat V. 37-39. 43. 44.

[9]) Pyr. 1760.a.= Neith 2; see also 1376.c.; 1382.a.; 1441.a.; 1541.a.; 1574.c.; 1737.a.; 2172.c.

[10]) Pyr. 2061.c.

B.7.i. *ḫ3d*, fish-trap, pit.

Ḥ3d originally means a fish-trap, woven from flexible branches. This word also occurs in B.D. 113 [1]), where *Śbk*, at the command of Re, must catch into a fish-trap the hands of Horus, which have been thrown into the water. Re says [2]): "Oh bring me *Śbk* of the two marsh-fields, that he may catch them (the hands of Horus)." *Śbk* answers [3]): "I have "trapped" them into the fish-trap in the two marsh-fields. In this way the fish-trap came into being." As a device dangerous for the dead *ḫ3d* still occurs in the original meaning in C.T. Spell 474. This is one of the spells for escaping the net [4]): "Catcher, captor, hidden of fingers, take this net of yours away, this hidden one of yours which catches food. Live on the fish-traps [5]) of Re, on the traps of *Ỉmyḫnt-wr*. This N.N. has escaped from them." Also in B.D. 17 there is thought of a fish-trap as appears from the determinatives. "May I not land in your fish-traps" [6]). "May I not sit in their fish-traps" [7]). "Hidden one of shape, which the god *Ḥmn* has given, is the name of the fish-trap" [8]). Seth is punished on account of his enmity with Osiris. He is fettered and placed under Osiris as being conquered and a fish-trap is put over him [9]).

Much more often, however, we have to think of something else than of the original meaning, namely of a fiery pit, also in connection with the Coptic ϩιειτ, ϩιτ [10]). In Am Duat [11]) such pits are represented in the shape ∩, with fire-dots in it and a demon standing near it. Parts of the dead are burnt in them. The enemies of Osiris are punished. "I order that they fall into their "fish-traps" and be counted out to their cauldrons" [12]). In connection with the parallelism with *wḥ3.t* we must think here of fiery pits or ovens. "He who knows them (the punishing ones of the enemy), he does not fall into their "fish-traps" [13]). Enemies of Osiris are punished in the netherworld. "You go upside down. You do not rise after you have fallen into your "fish-traps" [14]). From what follows it appears that there are flames

1) C.T. II, Spell 158.
2) C.T. II. 351.b. c.
3) C.T. II. 353.b. c.
4) C.T. VI. 21.i-m.
5) Determinative 
6) C.T. IV. 323.d.
7) C.T. IV. 324.a.
8) Naville II. 73. 74.
9) Pap. Jumilhac VIII. 19. 20.
10) Wb. III. 36. 4-6.
11) Am Duat XI, Bucher Pl. X, XI.
12) L.Q. CXVII. 9.
13) Am Duat III. 27
14) Am Duat XI. 77.

(*ꜣm*, B.3.a). Near each of the six divisions is a goddess, "who is over her fish-traps". Demons live on the lamentation of those, who are in there. The tormented ones are tortured by the fire. So it here concerns real fiery divisions of hell. There is also cumulation of punishments. The tormented ones are, moreover, put on their heads. Also in the Book of Gates such divisions of hell are drawn, in which enemies of Osiris are punished. Osiris says: "Come to me, my son Horus, save me from those who act against me. Assign them to him who is set over the destruction. He is the one who watches over "fish-traps" [1]). Four divisions of hell are pictured with a guard beside them. The inscription near it reads: "They who are at the head of their "fish-traps". Horus says to these gods: "Seize the enemies of my father. Snatch (them) away to your "fish-traps", on account of this painful thing they have done against him who has procreated me." Horus says to the guards of the "fish-trap": "(Your) fiery fish-traps are guarded on the command of Re."

B.7.j. *ḫtmy.t*, place of destruction.

This word is derived from the stem *ḫtm*, to destroy, to perish (A.1.f). The term already occurs in the Pyramid Texts. Any god, who hinders the dead king in his ascension, will be imprisoned in "hell" for ever [2]), to him the doors of the "Destroying One" will not be opened. Sethe also translates by "*Hölle*" and sees in it the same word which is later used in the tombs of the kings. In another place in the Pyramid Texts this "hell" is conceived as being personified [3]): "The "Destroying One" has raised you", that is to say, has set free Osiris. These places are important because they indicate that the representations of hell, worked out in detail in the later tombs of the kings, are already known in the Pyramid Texts. But the matter is not entered further into, because everything is focused on the ascension of the king. Only a few places, which deal with the punishment of sinners, mention it incidentally. But also these few places show that beside the conception of a kingdom of heaven also that of a dark subterranean realm of the dead as a place of punishment was present.

In the tombs of the kings the following passages occur. Sinners

---

1) Book of Gates III, lower register, B.S. Pl. VIII. 20-25; Pl. VII. 44-49; 50-52.
2) Pyr. 485.c. 3) Pyr. 1329.a.

are punished as enemies of Re. "Hail to you, Re, you are powerful, Re. Your enemies belong to the place of judgment" [1]). About sinners as enemies of Osiris: "I count them out to the place of destruction" [2]). "You are the enemies of Osiris, who are in the place of destruction" [3]). In the Book of Gates there are pictured beings who bear symbols of the lifetime (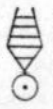). "They are the ones, who fix the lifetime, who define the days of the souls that are in the West, who assign to destruction" [4]). The idea here is a judgment of the dead. The just continue to live in the West as the normal realm of the dead. The sinners go to the place of judgment. Accordingly it is said of the enemies: "They do not see the *šṯy.t*" [5]), where *šṯy.t*, like the West, must be considered a favourable place. A place in Am Duat [6]) is remarkable, where it is said of the sun-god on his journey through the realm of the dead: "You light the darkness. You make the place of destruction breathe." Here also those who are in "hell", catch sight of the sun. Usually the judgment in a division of hell is irrevocable. Those who are there do not see Re, when he travels through the realm of the dead.

B.7.k. *ḫb.t*, place of judgment.

Ḫb.t is a locality, where the dead is executed. He may be placed in it. He wants to open it to escape from it. "You are not locked in. You are not imprisoned. You are not guarded. You are not placed in the place of execution" [7]). Bird-catchers, who take the soul away, obtain the attribute "who put down in the place of execution" [8]).

The word *ḫb.t* is connected with the verb *ḫb*, to execute [9]). An inscription in the *Zweiwegebuch* above the second part of the black road, directly under a red piece in the middle, reads: "I am the great name... I go to the way of the truth. What I detest is the place of execution. My protection is the protection of *Ḥr Śmśw*" [10]). The dead

---

1) Book of Gates I, lower register, B.S. Pl. III. 40-43.
2) L.Q. VIII. 8; IX. 1.
3) L.Q. CXX. 2.
4) Book of Gates, IV, lower register, B.S. Pl. VI. 26-29.
5) Book of Gates, IV, lower register, B.S. Pl. VI. 37. 38.
6) Am Duat I. 234.
7) C.T. I. 70.b-d.
8) C.T. VI. 73.g.
9) Urk. V. 87. 13; Wb. III. 252. 7; H. P. Blok, AcOr VII, 105.
10) C.T. VII, Spell 1172; B 1 Be. 262.

wants to evade this slaughtering-place. "I am the one who opens the place of execution" [1]). "I do not enter the place of execution of the denizens of the netherworld" [2]). "You walk quickly past the place of execution" [3]). The gang of Seth is punished in the same way as man in the netherworld. The dead says about it: "I have placed them in this place of execution, south of *Śp3* and north of *Ḥnn*" [4]). One of the 42 judges of Osiris is called "Who comes from the place of execution" [5]). There the victims are belaboured with a knife. "Let their corpses be saved, let they save them from the place of execution of the mutilating ones who are in the evil hall" [6]).

B.7.l. *ẖ3s.t*, name of a well.

Four men are represented on the brink of a well in the realm of the dead [7]), where there is a uraeus. The inscription near it reads: "They stand on the brink of this well. There is a living uraeus in this well. The water of this well consists of fire. The gods of (this) territory and the souls of (this) territory do not descend to this well on account of the fire of this uraeus . . . Your fire, your glowing breath and your flame is against the souls, when they approach in order to transgress against Osiris." The fire of the well mentioned here is mortal for sinners.

B.7.m. *ś.t bỉn.t*, evil place.

Of a place in the realm of the dead where there are condemned, it is said: "The enemies are in their evil place" [8]).

B.7.n. *š*, pond.

On his journey to heaven the dead has to pass a dangerous pond. He must take care that he does not land there. "Beware of the lake" [9]). "N.N. passes the house of this *b3* (also a dangerous place mentioned more than once). He escapes the fury of the big lake" [10]). "Beware

---

1) C.T. II. 72.b.

2) C.T. IV. 62.q.

3) C.T. IV. 353.c.; variant 366.j: "The place of execution escapes me."

4) C.T. VI. Spell 595; 213.k.

5) B.D. 125; 255. 5.

6) B.D. 164 (Leps.); 416. 14. Cf. 416. 8 about the bones: "Save them from the evil hall", *ḫ3 bỉn*, Wb. III. 221. 21, *Totb. Sp. als Bez. der Richtstätte für die Bösen, die Hölle.*

7) Book of Gates VII, lower register, Budge, The Eg. Heaven and Hell, II, pp. 215, 216; E. Lefébure, *Le Tombeau de Séti Ier*, II. 11-13.

8) L.Q. CXX. 5.

9) Pyr. 136.a.

10) Pyr. 334.a.

of the big lake" [1]). "Beware of the big lake, this pool, which belongs to the spirits, this *ḫnś*, which belongs to the dead. Beware of these people of the house of that *b3* (*pf* unfavourable, "*iste*"), who are on the doing evil (*ḫr.t ḏ3.t*, to oppose inimically) in this their name of inimical women. May they not lead you to the house of that *b3*. It is evil, it is painful, it causes loss and it is "left". You are escaping it an escape. You consider it to be unfavourable. Hasten to the prosperous one of heart, the brother of Sokaris, his beloved. May he leave the road free to you with those who are on it" [2]). *Š wr* here occurs in a series of dangerous places, which the dead has to evade. They give the impression to be populated with dead, who have an unfavourable fate and who try to draw the dead king to them. Apparently they are deceased, who do not participate in the ascension. A place from the C.T. comes close to it [3]): "The pool of the dead, evade it. Leave off from the road to it."

The enemies of the dead king arrive in *š wr*. This is their downfall. "They fall for you in *š wr*" [4]). The dead himself hopes to be spared from it. "*Š wr*, I do not see it" [5]). In the *Zweiwegebuch* the black pathway goes round ponds and the blue waterway leads past estates. Among them there may be dangerous pools. "I do not enter the pool of the criminals" [6]). Dangerous ponds are mentioned in the following passage: "The ponds of the destroying one, may I not fall into it" [7]). In B.D. 17 a demon occurs: "The guard of the bend of the fire-lake" [8]).

B.7.o. *š3ʿ.t*.

This must be a place of judgment. "It is not allowed that you descend into the big *š3ʿ.t* among those who quarrel with the god, who destroys the robbery before the face of him who commits it" [9]).

B.7.p. *ḳ3b*, bend.

The roads which lead through the realm of the dead, have dangerous twists, where demons lie in wait for the passer-by. They frequently occur in the *Zweiwegebuch*. *B3b3* is a demon, "who guards this bend of the West" [10]). In a lake there is a dangerous bend [11]). A demon is

---

[1]) Pyr. 872.d.; 885.a.; 1752.c.
[2]) Pyr. Neith 761 sqq. = Pyr. 1931.
[3]) C.T. I. 284.f-h.
[4]) C.T. I. 291.f.
[5]) C.T. IV. 39.c.
[6]) C.T. VII, Spell 1099; B 1 L. 485.
[7]) C.T. III. 3.b.
[8]) C.T. IV. 313.d.; 314.a.; Naville II. 64.
[9]) C.T. I. 196.i.; 197.a. b.
[10]) B.D. 17, Naville II. 64.
[11]) C.T. IV. 313.d.

there with a dog's head, "who watches over the twist of the fire-lake" [1]).

B.7.q. *ḳrr.t*, cave.

This is a place of residence of the dead in the netherworld. The *ḳrr.t*-book describes the journey of the sun along it. When Re has passed, in the Book of Gates, a division of the netherworld, the dead lie in darkness again and their caves close behind them. Nagel translates *ḳrr.t* as prison in Louvre 3292, S. 15. The *ḳrr.wt* are no divisions of hell, it is true, but with respect to heaven these places in the netherworld are unfavourable. To Re, who travels through the netherworld, it is said: "According to your wish the *d3.t* belongs to you, which you have made hidden for those, who are in their caves. According to your wish heaven belongs to you, which you have made hidden for those who are near it" [2]).

B.7.r. *ṯpḥ.t*, cave.

This is a place of residence in the netherworld, something like *ḳrr.t*. In a favourable sense it is used in the following passage [3]): "I am taken to the cave of Khenty Imentyw. I am sitting on the banks of Ageb. I am among the rejoicing ones." "Open the door of the cave for those who are in Nun, open the territory of water for those who are in the light" [4]). *Ṯpḥ.t* must also here be a favourable place, where the dead likes to sojourn.

Unfavourable, as place of residence of demons, it is used: "Then N.N. passes those who are in their caves, the keepers of the house of Osiris" [5]).

B.8. *Dangers which threaten essential parts of the personality.*

Man continues to live in the hereafter by certain forces of the soul, the *b3* and the *k3*. Also the *šw.t*, the shadow, and the *ẖ3.t*, the corpse, are indispensable parts of the personality. Further the dead exists by his *ḥk3*, magical power. His heart, *ib*, *ḥ3ty*, may not fail him. If these constituent parts of the personality are hurt, the dead cannot continue to exist. Affection of these powers of the soul is one of the dangers of the realm of the dead.

---

1) C.T. IV. 314.a.
2) Book of Gates VIII, upper register, B.S. Pl. XIV. 49-53.
3) C.T. II. 253.d-f.
4) C.T. VI. 170.a. b.
5) C.T. IV. 84.f.

B. 8. a. *3ḫ*, spirit.

As *3ḫ* the dead leads a glorified survival. Reciting certain spells of the dead at the funeral by a priest is called *s3ḫ*, to make into an *3ḫ*. So the *3ḫ* only plays a part after death. It is represented by a tufted ibis. That the dead becomes an *3ḫ* is in itself no guarantee for a happy fate in the hereafter, for also the *3ḫ* may be tortured. A gate in the netherworld is called: "Which cuts the glory of the spirits to pieces" [1]).

There are demons there, "who take souls and spirits along to the slaughtering-block of him who eats raw flesh" [2]). To such a demon the dead says: "Do not take my glory away" [3]). To beings, who want to snatch the *b3* away, it is said: "I do not deliver my glory" [4]). "This N.N. does not give his glory to the messengers of Seth" [5]).

Tomb robbers are threatened that they will not even reach the status of *3ḫ*: "Those who will do something harmful to your monuments, . . . my majesty will prevent that they join the spirits in the realm of the dead" [6]).

B. 8. b. *ib*, heart.

Beside getting back other parts of the body it is also necessary that the heart functions again. "Oh N.N., collect your bones for you, gather your limbs for you, make your teeth white for you, receive your own heart, shake off this earth which is on your flesh" [7]). The context shows that is does not concern here an intentional taking away of the heart, but a desiccation in consequence of a burial in the earth. "Your *3ḫ* belongs to you in you, your *b3* belongs to you behind you, your own heart belongs to you" [8]). "I am Nephthys. I have come (to you), that I seize you and that I give your own heart back to you" [9]). This giving back of the heart and putting it in its place again often occurs in the texts [10]). Perhaps there is still a reminiscence here of the time that, when mummifying, the heart was taken from the body [11]). Possession of the heart is indispensable for the

---

[1]) Am Duat VIII. 25 [2]) Am Duat VIII. 225. [3]) C.T. III. 296.b.
[4]) C.T. V. 299.d. In V. 311.e. f.; this stands parallel with: "I do not deliver my magical power." [5]) C.T. VI. 294. 1.
[6]) Urk. I. 304. 17-305. 4, 6; Sottas 93. [8]) Pyr. Neith 742.
[7]) Pyr. Neith 738, 739. [9]) Pyr. 1786.b.; cf. 2097.c.
[10]) Pyr. 828.c.; 1892.a.; B.D. 101; 213. 6. "Then you will give back N.N.'s heart to him." [11]) See *šdi*, B. 5.dd.

deceased, in order to be able to continue full life after death. A spell serves "to give somebody's heart back to him" [1]. "Your heart is brought back to you in your body, like Horus brought the heart of his mother" [2].

With the functioning of the heart and also with the possession of the magical power the wish of getting back his power to remember is very closely related. Death is forgetting the existence on earth. To continue the latter, one must be able to remember his past. C.T. Spell 572 is a spell to bring somebody's magical power back to him, in the realm of the dead [3]. The dead gets his *ḥkꜣ* back, like Horus his and now "it is said to him, what he knew and what he had forgotten" [4]. He has got his memory back. "I remember what I have forgotten" [5]. For this purpose it is indispensable that the heart functions well. "My heart is not ignorant of its place. It remains in its spot" [6]. So the heart is the seat of the spiritual faculties. Now the dead is able to say: "I know my name. I am not ignorant of it" [7]. By the memory the identity of the personality is safeguarded during his earthly existence and in the hereafter. He who remembers his name in the hereafter is the same he was on earth. Compare Spell 716 [8]: "To me is named (I am reminded of) what I have forgotten." Horus helps his deceased father Osiris. "Hail to you, my father Osiris. Behold, I come (to you). I am Horus . . . I give you back your heart in your body, that you may remember what you had forgotten" [9]. The dead wishes: "May my heart not be forgetful" [10].

Further there are spells that somebody's heart does not remember its sins and gives evidence of it before the judge of the dead. "Oh my heart, I am your lord. Be never far from me. (Come) to me, my own heart. You are in my body. Do not rebel against me" [11]. "Spell in order not to let somebody's heart give evidence against him. This heart of mine does not fail me" [12].

---

1) C.T. V. 332.h.
2) C.T. I. 80. 1.m.
3) C.T. VI. 174.h.
4) C.T. VI. 175.c.
5) C.T. VI. 175.f.
6) C.T. VI. 176.f.
7) C.T. VI. 176.g.
8) C.T. VI. 345.n. See also A. 4.o. *śmḫ*.
9) C.T. I. 265.a. b. e. f.
10) C.T. III. 296.k.
11) Louvre 3148 V. 1, *ỉ ỉb.ỉ ỉnk nb.k n wꜣ.k r.ỉ rꜣ nb* (*lac.*) *n.ỉ ỉb.ỉ ḏś.ỉ ỉw.k* (*m*) *ẖ.t.ỉ nn rkỉ.k r.ỉ r.ỉ*. Cf B.D. 27 and 30B; *Buch vom Atmen* B.D. Budge, p. 513. 16; J. E. O. L. No. 9, p. 19, art. de Buck.
12) C.T. II. 126.d.; 128.d.

So there are spells, which serve to prevent somebody losing his heart through death. The heart is indispensable and must function well. But even if somebody has got his heart back, it might be taken away from him again or be injured in the realm of the dead. A punishing goddess in the netherworld is called "Who destroys the heart" [1]). To gods in the realm of the dead it is said [2]): "Hail to you, lords of eternity, who prepare infinity. Do not take this heart of mine away, do not seduce this breast of mine" [3]). The dead is assured: "Your heart belongs to you. It is not robbed by the road-keepers" [4]). "Your heart belongs to you. It is not taken away among those who are in revolt" [5]).

B.8.c. *b3*, soul.

The *b3* is a power of the human soul, incarnated in a bird. While the corpse is resting in the earth, the *b3* can move freely, to fetch food for man. The functioning of the *b3* may be menaced. There are spells to prevent the *b3* being imprisoned [6]). The *b3* must be able to go to heaven freely. "Gate-keepers of the upper heaven, open the roads to my *b3*, my *3ḫ* and my shadow. It brings *m3ʿ.t* to Re" [7]). The dead asks for free passage for the forces of his soul. "A way is opened to my *b3*, my *3ḫ*, my magical power, my shadow, that it may enter freely with Re in his chapel" [8]). Demons may hinder the *b3* in its freedom of action and in that case the *b3* cannot fulfil its task of bringing elements of life to the corpse. So these demons are adjured not to do this. "Keepers of the limbs of Osiris, who watch over all souls, who lock up the shadows of all male and female dead, have no power over my locking up and over the guarding of my *b3*, my shadow, my spirit and my magical power" [9]). The doors of heaven open to the *b3* and the *iry.w ʿ.wt Wśir* do not lock him up [10]). A spell prevents the soul being imprisoned: "His *b3* is not seized, his shadow is not caught" [11]).

Worse still than being hampered in his liberty of action is the *b3*

---

1) Am Duat VII. 101.
2) B.D. 27 = C.T. Spell 715; VI. 344 n-p; 344. j., "who takes hearts away".
3) The aim of Spell 715 is to prevent his heart rebelling against him in the judgment.
4) C.T. I. 210.b.
5) C.T. I. 212.d. e.
6) B.D. 91.
7) C.T. VI. 67.i-k.
8) C.T. VI. 69.a. b.
9) C.T. VI. 69.c-70. b.
10) C.T. VI. 71.a. b. f.
11) C.T. VI. 89.m. n.

being threatened with total destruction. He may be slaughtered. In the netherworld there are demons, "who take along souls and spirits to the slaughtering-block of him who eats raw flesh" [1]). A spell aims at letting the *b3* and the shadow escape from the slaughtering-block of a god. "I am not watched by the keepers of souls. My *b3* and my shadow escape from it" [2]). Spell 553 is a spell not to take somebody's *b3* to the slaughtering-block of Shu [3]). There is a slaughtering-block, which cuts souls to pieces [4]). A spell serves "not to have somebody's soul taken away from him. Oh power, come and say to him who has sent you: Truly, my spell is more excellent than his knife" [5]). The satellites of Osiris cut the *b3* to pieces [6]).

The *b3* is burnt. A female demon does this. "She is behind Osiris, in order to burn the souls of his enemies" [7]). These enemies of Osiris are sinners, who are punished in the netherworld. "Oh souls of Osiris' enemies, shadows of Osiris' enemies, against whom the two snake-goddesses throw fire" [8]). In the *ḳrr.t*-book soul birds and shadows are represented in fire-basins, in which they are burnt. By the fire the soul is entirely destroyed.

For destroying the *b3* the verb *ḥtm* is used. "He who knows this spell, his *b3* is not destroyed for him to all eternity" [9]). In a punishment of the enemies of Osiris in the netherworld it reads: "You do not exist. Your *b3* is destroyed. It does not live" [10]). Destruction of the *b3* is on a par with total ruination. "Ruin to your souls, beheading for your shadows" [11]). As occurs so often, the *b3* and the *šw.t* are mentioned here together. In fiery divisions of hell in the netherworld [12]) souls are represented with a punishing goddess beside them. In a spell against scorpions and snakes [13]) it reads: "You are the one who has spoken words against the four bricks of enamel, which are in Heliopolis [14]).

1) C.T. III. 296.b.
2) C.T. VI. 132.i. j.
3) C.T. VI. 152.a.
4) C.T. IV. 301.a.
5) C.T. Spell 384; V. 49.a-c.
6) Am Duat III. 141.
7) C.T. IV. 262.a.; B.D. 17, Naville II. 74.
8) L.Q. CXVII. 3-4.
9) C.T. IV. 338.m.
10) Book of Gates VIII, lower register, B.S. Pl. XIV. 20-22.
11) Am Duat VII. 34. 35.
12) Am Duat XI. 76, Bucher Pl. X.
13) Louvre 1039.
14) J. Monnet, *Les Briques Magiques*, Rev. d'Ég. VIII (1951), p. 162.

They will strike your head. They will break your vertebrae. They will destroy your *b3*."

The *b3* is eaten. A spell of the Book of the Dead serves [1]) "to save somebody from those who eat souls, who are locked up in the *d3.t.*" "He who knows this spell is somebody whose *b3* *ʿb-š* (a crocodile) does not swallow up" [2]). The dead makes his enemies in the hereafter harmless. "I count them out to . . . those who eat the soul, that they eat their souls and destroy those who are on earth" [3]).

The *b3* must be able to join the corpse, in order to bring life to the corpse. The dead fears that his *b3* is taken away, so that his corpse has to perish also. About certain gods it is said [4]): "Who make the souls approach the mummies." This is the normal situation. The *b3* now "sees its corpse. It rests on its mummy" [5]). B.D. 89 is "a spell to make the *b3* join its corpse" [6]). When this happens the dead will live for ever. "Without ever perishing . . . It happens that you live again. Your soul shall not leave your corpse. Your *b3* is divine with the gods" [7]). The corpse perishes, when the *b3* does not bring him any elements of life and then the whole personality decays. Sinners in the netherworld are punished by it. "You are enemies of Osiris, who have no *b3*. You are dark, from whose corpses your souls are taken away" [8]).

The soul is destroyed totally, does not exist any more. Seth is punished by the fact that his corpse is burnt and that his soul is destroyed [9]). About punished sinners in the netherworld it is said: "Your souls belong to the non-being" [10]).

The *b3* may be punished by going on the head. In the *ḳrr.t*-book the souls of Osiris' enemies are drawn in this way. The inscription to it reads [11]): "Oh soul of Osiris' enemies, who go upside down in the place of destruction, whose corpse is not seen."

The dead hopes that no other being will have power over his *b3* [12]), that his soul will not be taken into custody [13]). The souls of beheaded ones are tortured in a subterranean realm of the dead.

---

1) B.D. 163; 411. 1.
2) Am Duat VII. 152.
3) C.T. II. 254.o. p.
4) B.D. 89; 190. 6.
5) B.D. Budge, p. 190. 13.
6) B.D. Budge, p. 189. 4.
7) Urk. IV. 1218. 1. 9-11, cf. 114. 2.
8) L.Q. XXXIV. 4-5.
9) Pap. Jumilhac XV. 25.
10) Book of Gates I, lower register, B.S. Pl. IV. 37-Pl. III. 38.
11) L.Q. XXXVII. 2-3.
12) C.T. I. 196.h.
13) C.T. IV. 178.m.

"Whose soul does not escape from the earth" [1]. To punishing-demons it is said: "You are these gods who deliver the souls to the slaughter-place" [2]. Am Duat mentions the "delivering of souls to the place of destruction" [3].

B. 8. d. *rn*, name.

The name is an essential element of the personality, in which somebody continues to exist. Affection of the name is an injury to the bearer of it. The dead wishes for himself: "May my name not be unknown among the spirits" [4]. Demons must not know his name, because then they would get power over him and might use the name with evil intentions [5]. "Oh Neith, when they ask my name of you, you must not mention to them my name".

Some spells aim at somebody remembering his name. This is necessary in order to survive in the hereafter and to be identical with one's own personality. "To remind somebody of his name in the realm of the dead. May my name be given back to me in *pr wr*" [6]. "I know my name . . . I do not forget it, this name of mine . . . Do not seal my name up . . . I have cut off him who will take my name from me" [7]. In a threat of tomb robbers it reads [8]: "He will not be commemorated by his relatives. His offerings are not made to him. No water is poured out to him. No funerary offerings are made to him on the *w3g*-feast. His name will not exist. The ritual of his funeral is not performed in the necropolis." The non-existence of the name of the tomb robber is the total non-existence of himself. The name of the dead continues to exist among the relatives on earth and through his name he himself survives. "My name does not perish in eternity in this country" [9]. Nearly the same passage occurs in a tomb inscription: "The name of a strong one is based on what he has achieved. He does not perish in this country in eternity" [10]. It is a consolation to a dying man, that "his name will be lasting on (his) monument" [11]. The name of an opponent is erased on his tomb-structure. As a consequence he has no eternal life, no offering cult

1) L.Q. CXXXIV. 9-CXXXV. 1.
2) L.Q. XXXIII. 3.
3) Am Duat VI. 224. 225.
4) C.T. III. 296.e.
5) Pyr. Neith 771; Pyr. 1939, 1940.
6) C.T. Spell 410; V. 234.a-c.
7) C.T. Spell 411; V. 236.e. g.; 237.a.; 238.e.
8) Sottas, p. 49, 9th and 10th dyn.
9) C.T. II. 253. g.
10) Urk. IV. 2. 5-6.
11) Urk. IV. 518. 14.

etc. [1]). "He who will oppose against me shall not live, my opponent will not inhale any air. His name will not be among the living ones." The remembrance of a criminal is wiped out. It is injurious to him that people do not remember him in their prayers any more. "Without his name being remembered in this temple, like one does to (one's) equal, resisting an enemy of his god" [2]).

There is a close connection between the name and the *k3* [3]). "N.N. is healthy together with his flesh. He is doing well together with his name. N.N. lives together with his *k3*" [4]). The mummy, the name and the *k3* are parts of the personality, in which the dead king survives [5]). The *k3* is bearer of the king's name in the protocol. In Ptolemaic texts *k3* may be read as *rn*. According to the *Wörterbuch* *k3* is rendered by *rn* in demotic [6]). To the close relation between *k3* and *rn* also points a place in the Coffin Texts [7]). "My *k3* is high, it has repeated my name. I do not die." Is it the idea that the *k3* is a duplicate of somebody's being? In that case, indeed, *k3* and *rn* approach each other. The *k3* and the name lead an existence somewhat independent of the person. Outside his body man lives in his *k3* and his name. In order to assure his survival they may not be affected.

B. 8. e. *ḥ3ty*, heart.

The dead fears that his heart will be taken away from him. Spells must prevent this. "Not to take somebody's heart away from him ... I detest the slaughtering-block of the god. May this heart of mine not be taken away to the fighter in Heliopolis" [8]). "The heart of N.N. be not taken away. His heart be not taken away" [9]). "Not to let somebody's heart be taken away from him in the realm of the dead" [10]). The dead addresses himself to a demon: "Have you come (to fetch) this heart of mine of the living? I do not give my heart to

---

1) G. Posener, *Les criminels débaptisés*, Rev. d'Eg. V, p. 55.
2) Op. cit., p. 54.
3) H. W. Obbink, *De magische betekenis van de naam* (The magical meaning of the name), pp. 13-16; H. Kees, *Totenglauben*, p. 69.
4) Pyr. 908.a. b.
5) Comparison with Pyr. 338.a shows that *k3* and *rn* are used in the same way.
6) Wb. V. 86. 13. , *k3* is a term for "name" since the 22nd dyn., *Wb.* V. 92, 18 sqq.
7) C.T. III. 350.e-g.
8) C.T. V. 57.a. d.; 58.b. Idem C.T. V. 297.b.
9) Pyr. 748.d.
10) C.T. V. 54.a.

the *ḫpp.w*" [1]). In B.D. 17 a demon occurs "who robs hearts" [2]). B.D. 30 is a spell "in order not to let somebody's heart be kept off from him in the realm of the dead" [3]). Further the wish is uttered that his heart gives no evidence against him in the judgment.

The heart may be tortured by fire and destroyed in the realm of the dead. "Their hearts are brought to the flame" [4]). About executioners of Re it is said: "They are the ones who throw hearts (of enemies of Re) into the fire" [5]).

B.8.f. *ḥk3*, magical power.

In order to be able to survive the dead must have the disposal of his magical power. Demons threaten to rob him of this. Certain spells must prevent this. "Oh my dorsal vertebra, which makes your spell in connection with this magical power of mine, do not let this crocodile take him away who lives on magical power" [6]). Another spell is a defence against demons "who come in order to take the magical power of this N.N. away from him." "I do not deliver this magical power of mine to you" [7]). In a spell to make a demon not snatch away somebody's *b3*, *3ḫ.w* etc., it reads: "Protect my magical power" [8]). "As regards any god or goddess . . . who will repel my magical power" [9]); "I do not give my magical power to the *mrwty*. They find me provided with my magical power . . . My magical power is not attacked" [10]). To demons who threaten to take the *b3* away, the dead says: "Bring me my *b3*. Save my magical power for me" [11]). B.D. 31 is a "spell to keep a crocodile at bay, which comes to snatch the magical power of N.N. away from him in the realm of the dead." The dead says: "I live on my magical power . . . This magical power of mine, do not take it (away from me), oh crocodile, which lives on the magical power." To the dead his magical power is indispensable. He can keep demons at bay with it. He sails to heaven by it [12]).

The *ḥk3* is connected with preserving one's memory. When somebody has his *ḥk3*, he remembers his name and his heart stays

[1]) C.T. V. 54.c.; 55. a. b.
[2]) C.T. IV. 314.c.
[3]) B. D. Budge, p. 501. 5.
[4]) L.Q. XCVIII. 8.
[5]) Am Duat II, 195. 196.
[6]) C.T. Spell 342; IV. 347.f. g.
[7]) C.T. V. 319.n. b.
[8]) C.T. V. 52.b.
[9]) C.T. V. 263.c. g.
[10]) C.T. V. 311.f. g.; 312.a. b. h.
[11]) C.T. V. 299.b.
[12]) C.T. V. 271.c.

in its place. "Spell to bring somebody's magical power to him in the realm of the dead . . . You bring the magical power of Horus to him as his great protection and in this way you bring this magical power of this N.N. to him in any place, where he is . . . This magical power of mine, come to me . . . I remember what I had forgotten" [1]. "To remember the magical power. My heart, rise in your place, remember what is in you. I have remembered all my magical power, which is in this belly of mine" [2].

B.8.g. *ẖ3.t*, corpse.

Also the corpse may be struck by an unhappy fate. The corpse respectively the mummy remaining intact is necessary to survive. On a coffin three signs for *ẖ3.t* are pictured in an oval with red dots, a fiery division of hell [3]. Above it are a fire-spitting snake and a goddess with a knife. The corpse is burnt in hell. The dead does not wish this fate. "*Ḫmyt* does not cut his corpse all to pieces" [4]. In a book about the realm of the dead a text to *b3*-birds, placed on their heads, reads [5]: "Whose *ẖ3.t* does not exist. Which do not come from the earth." Here it concerns a total destruction of the corpse.

It is of importance that the body is well preserved. B.D. 154 is a spell in order not to let the corpse decay. "My corpse is lasting" [6]. For that purpose the funerary ritual must be performed in the right way. "The corpse of N.N. is buried (ritually)" [7].

B.8.h. *šw.t*, shadow.

The judgment on the shadow is usually mentioned beside that of the *b3*. See also B.8.c., *b3*. The shadow is, just as the *b3*, threatened with being locked up. The function of the shadow seems to have been the same as that of the *b3*: to move freely, to fetch food for the dead, while the corpse remains on the spot. About punished sinners in the netherworld it is said [8]: "Whose souls do not leave the earth, whose shadows do not rest on their corpses." Here there is the same link between *šw.t* and *ẖ3.t* as between the *b3* and the corpse. In the

---

1) C.T. Spell 572; VI. 174.h.; 175.a. b.; 175.k. f.
2) C.T. Spell 657; VI. 278.g. o. p. r.
3) Schmidt, Sark., 871.
4) Am Duat, Abr. Thutmoses III, 26, Bucher, p. 88.
5) L.Q. XXXVII. 4.
6) B.D. Budge, p. 402. 2.
7) C.T. IV. 49.s.
8) L.Q. XXXIII. 9-XXXIV. 1.

Pyramid Texts *b3* and *šw.t* occur together in a passage [1]), where the dead has obtained the qualities of gods: "Behold, their *b3* is with N.N., their shadows are with their comrades." Also in the Book of the Dead *b3* and *šw.t* occur together. B.D. 92 is a spell to open the grave for the *b3* and the *šw.t* [2]). The dead has the disposal of his feet. He goes out into the day. The *b3* and the *šw.t* [3]) are not locked up. So they form the elements of the dead moving freely. In a hymn to Amon it reads [4]): "You pave the way to my *b3*, my spirit and my shadow . . . you make my tomb to be open for ever."

Also here the main thing is the liberty of action, the not being bound to the grave, so that the *b3* and the shadow may act in the interest of the dead on earth.

The shadows are represented in a fiery division of hell [5]). A fire-spitting snake and a goddess with a knife are standing near it. Enemies of Osiris are fettered in the netherworld for punishment [6]). The inscription to it reads: "Destruction for your souls, detention for your shadows". The punishment is that the shadow is hampered in its liberty of action. A demon is called: "Devourer of shadows" [7]). To snakes, which punish the enemies of Khepri it is said: "You cut their shadows" [8]). That the shadow is tortured with knives, also occurs elsewhere in Am Duat [9]): "Entering (of knives) for your shadows," thus Horus to the enemies of Osiris. The representation shows shadows in a fiery division of hell and beside it a goddess with a knife. In a book about the netherworld four women, pictured with their heads downwards, are addressed [10]): "Oh enemies, who have no shadow, who are not, who walk with their heads downwards, for whom living souls function as their shadows." Loss of the shadow means the end of existence. What the meaning of the last line is, is not quite clear. Do others take the place of their *šw.t*?

Sinners are punished in the realm of the dead: "Destroy the shadows of those who should be destroyed and who should be punished in your cauldrons" [11]). In the *ḳrr.t*-book the shadows are

---

1) Pyr. 413.c., cf. C.T. VI. 182.b.: "Their shadows are with (*ḫr*) their lord."
2) B.D. 92 = C.T. Spell 499.
3) The C.T. also mention *3ḫ* and *k3*.
4) Urk. IV. 446. 6-8.
5) Schmidt, Sark. 871.
6) Am Duat VII, 34, 35.
7) B.D. 125; 253. 2.
8) Am Duat VI. 217.
9) Am Duat XI. 76.
10) L.Q. XXXIV. 3-4.
11) Am Duat V. 45 sq.

pictured, just as the souls, in cauldrons. The inscription to it reads: "Your souls and your shadows are destroyed" [1]). In B.D. 149 the *šw.t* is not mentioned beside the *b3*, but beside the *3ḫ*. It there refers to the *i3.wt*, divisions in the realm of the dead. Division k [2]) mentions the place of the *Ḳ3ḥ.w*-gods, demons, who take the spirits away and who have power over the shadows, which eat raw flesh and excrements.

B.8.i. *k3*, soul.

It strikes us that in this series the *k3* fails. A demon is punished [3]), "the evil one, who ruins the kas." In C.T. Spell 586 [4]) demons occur, who do damage to the *k3*, or a demon, who does damage to the kas. But in the representations of hell of the tombs of the kings the *k3* is not punished beside the *b3*, the *šw.t* etc. Perhaps this throws some light on the nature of the *k3*. The *k3* is not a human soul, but a being of higher order than mankind which guides him as a genius, who in this way is not affected by demons, but on the contrary defends him against them.

In the above-mentioned quotations from the C.T. it could be possible that a demon is referred to, who violates the "genius" of man.

The difference in function between the *b3* and the *k3* appears from Papyrus Westcar [5]): "Your ka quarrels with (fights against) your enemy. Your *b3* knows the ways which lead to the gate of *Ḥbś-b3gy*" [6]). The *k3* is a guardian spirit, which fights against somebody's enemies. The *b3* moves freely between the grave and the upper world and so knows the ways.

B.9. *Words for seizing.*

The fear of death expresses itself in the thought that one is seized by a demon like one powerless.

B.9.a. *3m*, to seize.

"My soul is not seized by the swine" [7]). "I am not seized by the gods of the earth" [8]). In a spell, which must prevent the dead being caught in a net, it reads: "Do not seize me, do not catch me, do not

---

1) L.Q. XCVIII. 5.
2) Naville II. 412.
3) C.T. V. 41.i.; 42. d. e.
4) C.T. VI. 206. 1.p.; 207.c.; 208.a.
5) Sethe, *Lesestücke*, 30. 5-6.
6) A demon, who watches the gate of the realm of the dead.
7) C.T. I. 397.b.
8) C.T. II. 112.e.

do against me what you like" [1]). The dead inspires his waylayers with awe by saying: "Those who are, stand in awe of me; those who are not, respect me. You do not seize me. You do not catch me" [2])

B.9.b. *iṯi*, to seize, to snatch away.

In the *Zweiwegebuch* the dead asks for protection against a demon, who threatens him in the realm of the dead: "Save me from the claws of him, who takes for himself what he sees. May the glowing breath of his mouth not take me away" [3]). The name of the third gate in Am Duat is *iṯ.wt*, "the seizing one" [4]). For the "snatching away" of the heart, see *ib*, B.8.b, *ḥ3ty*, B.8.e. For dying, being taken away as such, see A.9.b.

B.9.c. *mḥ*, to seize.

"May I not be seized. No single god may subdue me" [5]).

B.9.d. *nḏr*, to seize.

A spell denies that the dead is seized hold of by a demon. "There is no god, who seizes N.N. There is no opponent, who puts himself in N.N.'s way" [6]). The fear exists to be caught by demoniacal gate-keepers. The dead wishes to be let through freely. In the *Zweiwegebuch* it says: "I am not seized. I am not kept off from the gates. I am equipped with *Rwty*" [7]). The godless are seized, the just let through. "When this (ceremonial) is done for him, he goes in and out. He is not kept at bay. He is not seized" [8]). In the Book of Gates a snake is punished as an enemy of Re and a devil. "Seize the N.-snake. Do not let him loose, till I have passed you . . . watch (him), that my coming into being may arise" [9]). The snake must be seized hold of and destroyed, that he does not hinder Re in his rise.

The dead is not seized by bird-catchers, "for N.N. knows the name of the fingers which seize him" [10]). When he knows them he has power over them and can make them harmless.

"I am not seized by the gods of the earth" [11]). The dead is not seized hold of in a subterranean realm of the dead. "She is not seized" [12]). About the *b3* it is said: "You are not seized. You are not locked up

---

[1]) C.T. VI. 40.d. e. [2]) C.T. VI. 40.p.; 41.c.

[3]) C.T. VII, Spell 1106; B 1 L. 527; Cairo 28085, Lacau, Sarc. I. 215. 13.

[4]) Am Duat III. 1. [5]) C.T. III. 317.o. [6]) Pyr. 1237.a. b.

[7]) C.T. VII, Spell 1061; B 1 L, 393, above the black road; B 1 Be, 270; Lacau Sarc. I. 193. 35. Idem B.D. 144; 330. 12. [8]) B.D. 137 A; 309. 6-8.

[9]) Book of Gates IV, middle register, B.S. Pl. VI. 20-27.

[10]) C.T. VI. 22.c. [11]) C.T. VI. 46.g. [12]) C.T. VI. 74.k.

by all who belong to heaven and earth" [1]). "His *b3* is not seized, his shadow is not caught" [2]). Especially about those powers of the soul, for which it is of importance to be able to move freely, it is denied that they are taken hold of.

B.9.e. *ḫfʿ*, to seize.

The soul is not hindered in its liberty of action. "My *b3* is not seized by the gods of the earth" [3]). The dead denies that he is seized by Shu, taken as a demon. "I am not seized by Shu" [4]). The fear of Shu also appears from the passage: "Both my eyes belong to the grip of Shu and to the embrace of the darkness" [5]). Evil forces in the realm of the dead do not harm him: "I am not seized by my arms. I am not seized by my hands" [6]).

B.10. *Words for ruin and destruction.*

According to the Egyptian belief there are all sorts of possibilities for surviving in the hereafter. However, these possibilities may be affected. The soul or the corpse may be injured. What part of the dead continues to exist may be subject to punishment in the realm of the dead. Demons may destroy it. As a consequence man is doomed to eternal destruction. He dies for the second time.

B.10.a. *mt m wḥm*, to die for the second time.

This is a circumscription of the eternal judgment in the realm of the dead. Compare with this the term ὅ θάνατος ὅ δεύτερος in the Revelation of John, 2 : 11; 20 : 6; 21 : 8. Many spells have as a title: "Not to die for the second time" [7]). "He who knows this spell does not die for the second time" [8]). "He makes the soul of Osiris N.N. live. He does not die for the second time to all eternity" [9]). The second death is the eternal judgment, in which the *b3*, the *ḥk3* or other essential parts are destroyed. C.T. Spell 402 has the title: "Not to die for the second time, to give somebody's magical power back to him" [10]). Consequently the contents of the text is that the dead gets his *ḥk3* back. "Truly, this magical power is of mine brought to me, this magical power of mine is united with me in each place where

1) C.T. VI. 84.e.
2) C.T. VI. 89.m. n.
3) C.T. I. 398.a.
4) C.T. II. 112.e.
5) C.T. II. 45.c.
6) B.D. 42; 113. 6.
7) C.T. III. 396.g.; V. 261.a.
8) C.T. II. 47.b.
9) B.D. 168; 431. 13. 14.
10) C.T. V. 175.a. b.

it is" [1]). To die for the second time is remaining deprived of the eternal force of the soul, the *ḥkꜣ*, in the realm of the dead after the death of the body. C.T. Spell 423 has as a title: "Not to die for the second time" [2]). We find in the text a.o.: "N.N. lives (again) after death like Re every day. N.N. lives (again) after death. As regards any god and goddess, etc. . . . who will keep off the magical power from N.N., a fire goes out against them . . . from the eye of Re" [3]). To die for the second time means that the dead cannot make use of his magical power in the hereafter. So he cannot live again. After his bodily death also eternal survival is made impossible for him.

C.T. Spell 548 is a spell "not to take somebody across to the East" [4]). The manuscript T 2 L has as a variant: "Spell not to die for the second time in the realm of the dead." The East may be conceived as a place unpleasant for the dead (B. 7. a). To the dangers which threaten the dead, belongs that a slaughter is made against him [5]), that he has to go to a chamber of torture where parts of his body are cut off [6]). To die for the second time is, after the bodily death, to be punished by a sentence in the hereafter, with, as a consequence, total destruction. C.T. Spell 458 reads as follows: "I do not die in the West. The messengers of Osiris have no power over me. I am Horus, the son of Osiris . . . I do not die for the second time" [7]). Having already arrived in the realm of the dead one may still die another time, viz. when he is punished by an eternal sentence by the executioners of the judge of the dead. The second death is torture by the keepers of the netherworld.

In Spell 767 a favourable fate of the dead in the hereafter is described. He has inherited the *ꜣḫ.t*. Osiris gives him his *kꜣ*. "N.N. lives . . . He has taken eternity. He has completed infinity. N.N. does not die for the second time" [8]). From the contrast it is evident that the second death is to be struck by a sentence in the hereafter, so that one does not continue to exist for ever. Spell 787 (B.D. 44) reads: "Not to die for the second time. N.N.'s face is opened. N.N.'s heart is in its place. My crown is with me. I am Re, who protects himself. N.N. is not destroyed. Live! I have appeared as king of the gods. I do not die

---

1) C.T. V. 175.g. h.
2) C.T. V. 261.a.
3) C.T. V.263.a-c. g.; 264.a.
4) C.T. VI. 144.a. b.
5) C.T. VI. 145.a.
6) C.T. VI. 145.e.
7) C.T. V. 331.d. f-j, jj.
8) C.T. VI. 399.d . f . g.

for the second time" [1]). To die for the second time has as an equivalent in the text *ẖm* = to be destroyed. So it means to be struck in the hereafter by an eternal sentence, which may happen on account of somebody not disposing of his forces any more, e.g., because the heart does not function any longer. The opposite is living and rising with the sun-god. Spell 438 is a spell in order to live again after dying [2]). A variant of this title is: "Not to die for the second time in the realm of the dead" [3]). The text describes that the dead is received favourably in the hereafter, sails in the sun-boat of Re and continues: "I open my mouth. I eat life. I live on the wind. I repeat life after having died like Atum every day" [4]). Repeating life is rising like the sun-god from death and partake of the elements of life (air). Dying for the second time is not participating in the resurrection from death. Also Spell 267 is a spell in order not to die for the second time. There we read o.a. [5]): "Nut has given birth to you at the births of Re. Powers go out from Heliopolis, great ones, *nʿw*-snakes, which are in the *3ẖ.t*, I remain, I live like Thoth." Each morning the dead is reborn from the goddess of heaven, Nut, just as the sun. To die for the second time is that he does not participate in this, that he is excluded from resurrection and survival after death.

B.10.b. *ḥtm* (causative *śḥtm*), to destroy.

This verb is used for the destruction of evil-doers in the netherworld. The dead conquers gods, spirits and dead, who want to do him evil in the hereafter. "It is Thoth, who places your arm against them and your knife into them. You keep them off from yonder ways among the possessors of offerings (they do not get offerings). They belong to the destruction which is in the *d3.t* among the evildoers" [6]).

As judge of the dead Osiris destroys those who have sinned against him. "Oh Osiris who destroys his enemies, lord of the dead, ruler of the spirits" [7]). "Osiris, . . . whose words destroy his enemies, . . . who drives his enemies away, who destroys the souls of those who rebel against him" [8]). A snake-enemy of Re is killed in the nether-

---

[1]) C.T. VI. 415.h-q.
[2]) C.T. V. 290.a.
[3]) C.T. V. 290.d.
[4]) C.T. V. 291.i-k.
[5]) C.T. III. 398.a-d.
[6]) C.T. I. 208.b-d.
[7]) L.Q. XXII. 3.
[8]) L.Q. XXII. 8. 9.

world: "One calls to them that he may be destroyed" [1]). "You destroy the enemies of Re" [2]).

The causative *sḫtm* is used in the same sense. Enemies of Osiris are destroyed by snakes in the netherworld at the command of Re [3]). Re says: "Oh great snakes, sons of the earth, gate-keepers of the place of destruction, watch and repel these enemies of Osiris. Behold, I pass by your caves. I rest in the beautiful West, in order to let arise their places of judgment against them, to destroy their souls, to erase their shadows, to destroy their corpses, to take away their *3ḫ.w*." The punishment of the enemies of Osiris is, that they be exterminated thoroughly. The destruction of each part of their personality is mentioned separately. They are thrown into the absolute not-to-be. The same punishment is applied to sinners in Am Duat [4]): "Destroy the dead".

B.10.c. *ḫmi*, to throw down walls.

The dead fears demons who try to destroy him in the realm of the dead and who want to make any survival impossible for him. In order to prevent this he utters his spell against them. In a resurrection text a demon is kept at bay. The latter tries to call the risen one back to his grave. "He who will attack you (*ḫmiw.ty.fy*) shall not live, he who will call to you has receded. For it is not your name" [5]). "N.N. is not destroyed. He who will destroy him, does not exist" [6]). In the *Zweiwegebuch* a plan of a house is drawn, which is inhabited by a demon, a giant, who waits for his prey in ominous darkness. The spell should help the dead to pass it unhampered, for the demon would totally destroy him. "Picture of a house . . . It is the place of the destroyer (*ḫm*). He who puts himself within the reach of it sees an equipped spirit. The way to pass it, when he sails there. It is a man of countless (sc. cubits) in length. He is in darkness. He is not seen" [7]). The dead says of demons: "The keepers of the room do not ruin me" [8]). "Those who do evil, do not destroy me" [9]). "There is not a single waylayer, who will destroy N.N." [10]). "Men, gods, spirits and dead

[1]) Book of Gates VII, upper register, Budge, The Eg. Heaven and Hell, p. 204; E. Lefébure, *Le Tombeau de Séti Ier*, II. 12.
[2]) B.D. 127 A; 271. 4.
[3]) L.Q. IX. 4-6.
[4]) Am Duat V. 44.
[5]) Pyr. Neith 744.
[6]) Pyr. 309.c.
[7]) C.T. Spell VII, 1146; B 1 Be. 213-219.
[8]) C.T. VII, Spell 1169; B 1 Be. 244.
[9]) B.D. 85; C.T. IV. 63.c.
[10]) C.T. VI. 165.g.

have no power to repel me and to destroy me" [1]). "N.N. is not destroyed" [2]). The substantive *ḫmy.w*, destroyers, is used of demons. "My stick is in my hand, so that I have power over the great destroyers" [3]). One of the 42 judges of Osiris is called *ḫmy* [4]). A spell should deter these executioners. "He has given the fear of me to those who are set over the destruction" [5]). The text continues: "I am not brought to the slaughtering-block of the god. The destroyers do not apply their leather straps to me." This connection indicates that it concerns a total destruction of the dead.

B.10.d. *śḫr*, to fell.

This verb is nearly everywhere used of destroying the enemies of Osiris. This does not always take place in the hereafter, but it may also regard the destruction of the enemies of Osiris in general. Horus says to Osiris: "I come after I have felled your enemies for you" [6]). The same happens to the enemies of Re, that is to say Apophis or people, who have sinned against Re during their life on earth. "What Atum does for Re, is making the god *3ḫ* and felling the rebel" [7]). In the Book of Gates beings occur, about whom it is said: "Who felled the enemies of Re" [8]). About a council of gods in the netherworld, a college of judges, which protects Osiris, it is said: "What they do in the *d3.t* is felling the enemies of Osiris" [9]). So it here concerns a punishment of sinners in the netherworld. They are destroyed for ever.

B.10.e. *śkśk*, to destroy.

The 12th gate in B.D. 146 is called: "Which destroys those who come early in the morning" [10]).

B.10.f. *ḳn*, to kill [11]).

To the gods of the *d3.t* as punishing demons it is said: "You kill the enemies of Osiris" [12]). There are executioners in the netherworld, "who take care of (doing) harm to the dead" [13]). To them it is said: "Harm belongs to your slaughtering-blocks" [14]).

---

1) C.T. VI. 269.p.
2) C.T. Spell 787; VI. 415.m.
3) C.T. II. 117.n.
4) B.D. 125; 255. 11.
5) C.T. IV. 11.d.
6) B.D. 173; 452. 14.
7) Book of Gates II, lower register, B.S. Pl. III. 8. 9.
8) Book of Gates VII, upper register, Budge, The Eg. Heaven and Hell, II, p. 204; E. Lefébure, *Le Tombeau de Séti Ier*, II. 11. 12.
9) Am Duat IX. 93-94.
10) B.D. Budge, p. 355. 3.
11) Wb. V. 44. 6.
12) Am Duat II. 256. 257.
13) *Ḳn.t*, harm, Wb. V. 48. 14. Am Duat V. 38. 39; V. 63.
14) Am Duat V. 53. 54.

B.11. *Raging against the dead.*

The inimical activity of demons, to which the dead is exposed in the hereafter, is described as a raging of a god against him.

B.11.a. *3.t*, rage.

By this word the threatening of the grim realm of the dead is described. "*Śpd.t* ascends, while she is clad with (?) her sharpness . . . Sharp are the steps of those who are in her, on account of the rage of the town of silence, the territory of rest" [1]).

B.11.b. *3d.w*, fury.

The lords of the kas are invoked: "Save me from the fury of this country of the righteous" [2]).

B.11.c. *nšnỉ*, rage.

This is a term for a hostile action, which a demon or a god exercises over somebody. A spell must undo this, "It is N.N., who chops off the rage of any god, any spirit, any dead, who will oppose N.N. in an inimical way, in these shapes of his" [3]). Demons rage against the dead and keep him off from Re: "Osiris N.N., detests rage . . . Osiris N.N. is not kept off from Re" [4]).

B.11.d. *ẖnnw*, disturbance.

Certain spells must prevent damage being done to the dead. "Come in all your shapes. There is no part of your body which is harmed" [5]). "My white crown is Sekhmet, my red crown is *W3ḏy.t*. I am not harmed" [6]). The southern and northern Egyptian crown protect the dead. No harm is done to him. "Nephthys punishes those who harm me" [7]). "Osiris N.N., behold, you are avenged. You live. You move each day, while no harm is done to you" [8]). *H̱nnw* as something evil, which is done to somebody in the hereafter, also occurs in B.D. 42 [9]).

B.11.e. *ḏnd*, fury.

"N.N. is not surrounded by your fury, oh gods" [10]). An epitheton of Khonsu is: "Who sends out fury" [11]). A demon is conjured: "Oh raging one, long of names, your *b3* is snatched away [12]). C.T. Spell

[1]) Pyr. Neith 718.
[2]) B.D. 72; 160. 2.
[3]) C.T. VI. 300.i. j.
[4]) B.D. 130; 279. 11.
[5]) C.T. VI. 158.e. f.
[6]) C.T. Spell 757; VI. 386.h-j.
[7]) B.D. 17, Naville II. 72.
[8]) Pyr. 1610.a. b.
[9]) B.D. Budge, p. 114. 9.
[10]) Pyr. 1501.b.
[11]) C.T. IV. 65.j.
[12]) C.T. V. 49.e; 50.a.

551 is an ascension text. The dead goes to his father Re [1]), after having passed through the sky [2]). Earlier he has bathed ritually in sacred ponds, which enables him to ascend [3]), because he has become purified [4]). On his way to heaven he safely passes certain demons, who cannot harm him [5]): "N.N. has passed this "Raging one", who is within the reach of the *3ḫ.t*, which keeps off every god." This raging god hinders everybody in his ascension.

The tenth hour of Am Duat is called: "The raging one, who slaughters the rebels" [6]). So sinners, who have to be punished in the netherworld, are struck here by the rage of the gods.

B.12 - B.16. *Beings to be feared.*

A great number of beings are feared by the dead as waylayers in the realm of the dead. They may be classed under the following categories.

B.12. *Animals.*
B.13. *Men.*
B.14. *Demons I*; *names which indicate a function.*
B.15. *Demons II*; *a choice from names which specify the essence.*
B.16. *Gods.*

B.12. *Animals.*

B.12.a. *3pd*, bird.

"Their (of the denizens of the *d3.t*) birds do not let themselves fall upon me" [7]).

B.12.b. *3d*, crocodile.

"Osiris N.N. does not go on the road of the crocodiles. Osiris N.N. detests the crocodiles. He does not reach them. Osiris N.N. descends into your boat, oh Re" [8]).

B.12.c. *iʿr.t*, uraeus.

In the netherworld the uraeus occurs as a fire-spitting snake, which threatens the dead. "These 7 uraei, from which one has to be saved" [9]). About a gate in the netherworld it is said: "The border

1) C.T. VI. 149.a.
2) C.T. VI. 149.b. c.
3) C.T. VI. 149.g; 150.a.
4) C.T. VI. 150.b.
5) C.T. VI. 149.f.
6) Am Duat X. 2.
7) C.T. V. 332.c.
8) B.D. 130; 283. 15-284. 3.
9) C.T. IV. 66.d.

with ornaments consists of uraei ... As regards each god, who knows his protection against Sekhmet, he is safe from you, basin of these snakes" [1]). These gates with snakes, already known in the C.T., now also occur in the New Kingdom. In the Book of Gates 10 uraei are pictured near the "uraeus pond" [2]). They are "living uraei". "They cry out, after Re has approached them. Souls recede. Shadows perish on account of hearing the voice of the uraei." In Am Duat it is said about uraei [3]): "Spirits and dead do not pass them." That is to say they cannot get past them without being killed. Uraei serve for the punishment of sinners in the realm of the dead. "Oh these nine uraei [4]), whose flames (come) out of their mouths, in order to burn the enemies of Osiris." They kill their prey with their poisonous breath. In the Book of Gates a fiery well is pictured with a uraeus in it [5]). The inscription to it reads: "There is a living uraeus in this well. The water of this well consists of fire. The gods of (this) domain and the souls of (this) domain do not descend to this well on account of the fire of this uraeus."

B.12.d. *ỉbw*, kid (?).

The dead approaches a gate-keeper in the realm of the dead. "I come to you, *ỉbw Wr.t*, gate-keeper of the fighting-place of the gods, who will keep watch over the malicious ... I have power over my enemies" [6]).

B.12.e. *ỉbk3*.

A demon in the shape of a pig (?). It is not clear, which part he plays [7]). He occurs in B.D. 65 [8]). "I have seen *'Ibk3*, while he is put in shackles and *'Iwmś*, while he is put in custody." The dead moves freely when these beings are loosened. In C.T. II. 116.a the loosening of *'Ibk3* is mentioned. In C.T. Spell 107 *'Ibk3* is a pig. Perhaps it is a form of Seth, who is also pictured as a pig and with whom the name *'Iwmś* (lie) would fit in.

---

[1]) C.T. IV. 327.t; 328.b. c.

[2]) Book of Gates III, upper register, 3rd figure, B.S. Pl. VII. 46-48.

[3]) Am Duat IX. 98.

[4]) L.Q. I, 1st *ḳrr.t*, upper register, L.Q. IV, 4. Cf. 16 uraei in the gate of Book of Gates X, B.S. Pl. XII.

[5]) Book of Gates VII, lower register, Budge, The Eg. Heaven and Hell, II, p. 215; E. Lefébure, *Le Tombeau de Séti Ier*, II. 11. 12.

[6]) C.T. Spell 89; II. 55.b. c.; 56.b.

[7]) J. Zandee, N.T.T. V, pp. 280-283. [8]) Naville II. 140, 141; B.D. 65. 7-8.

B.12.f. *ʿ3*, ass [1]).

In a text which aims at furthering the nourishing of the dead, he charms two asses of Shu, which threaten him [2]). "Backwards, on your faces, you two asses of Shu, who draw Shu to heaven . . . Prepare the way for N.N., that he ascend and descend on it."

B.12.g. *ʿpš3y.t*, grasshopper.

"Spell in order to keep a grasshopper at bay" [3]).

B.12.h. *ʿẖm*, a demoniacal animal.

The dead identifies himself with a god who lights the dark. He keeps demoniacal animals at bay. "I have lighted the darkness. I have felled the *ʿẖm.w*. Those who are in their darkness, extol me" [4]). In a spell, addressed to Re, it reads: "Prepare my spirit in order to drive the *ʿẖm.w* back" [5]).

B.12.i. *wnš*, wolf.

"Wolf, do not enter its territory" [6]).

B.12.j. *bik*, falcon.

"My soul is not seized by the falcons" [7]).

B.12.k. *miwty*, cat.

This is a demon with the head of a cat, to whom sinners are delivered for punishment. It is said to four enemies of Re, who are, as a punishment, put on their heads in the netherworld: "I make you be counted out to *miwty*, from whose guarding one does not escape" [8]).

B.12.l. *mśḥ*, crocodile.

A spell serves "to repel a crocodile, which approaches in order to take somebody's magical power away from him. Backwards! . . . Do not come against me as one who lives on my magical power" [9]). So the demoniacal crocodile is after somebody's magical power" [10]). Spell to repel a crocodile, which comes in order to take away the magical power of a spirit in the realm of the dead" [11]). A crocodile eats somebody hide and hair and in this way gets hold of the latter's *ḥk3*. In this respect there is similarity with the cannibal texts [12]).

---

1) For Apophis as an enemy of the sun in the form of a donkey, see H. P. Blok, AcOr VII, Pl. II, p. 109.

2) C.T. Spell 662; VI. 287.o. p.; 288.a.

3) B.D. 36.

4) B.D. 80; 177. 9.

5) Louvre 3292, ed. Nagel, T. 15.

6) Pyr. 1351.a.

7) C.T. I. 397.b.

8) L.Q. XLVIII. 7.

9) C.T. IV. 346.a-f.

10) Cf. C.T. IV. 347.g.

11) B.D. 32; 98. 6. 7.

12) See also C.T. VI. 205.h.

B. 12. m. *rw*, lion.

"Backwards, lion, white of mouth, with flat-squeezed head. Recede for my power" [1]). "Backwards, lion, back *Pḥwy*, let the god pass" [2]).

B. 12. n. *rm*, fish.

A fish is something repulsive for the dead. About the *Ḥtp*-field, where there is nothing of the distress of the realm of the dead, it is said: "In there there is not a single fish, not a single snake" [3]). The denizens of the *d3.t* have no power over the dead. He says: "Their fishes do not eat me" [4]).

B. 12. o. *rri*, pig.

"Spell in order to keep a pig at bay" [5]).

B. 12. p. *rḥty* (dual), a kind of insect.

"Spell in order to keep the *rḥty* at bay" [6]). The word *rḥty* is determined with two insects.

B. 12. q. *š3*, boar.

"My soul is not seized by the boars" [7]).

B. 12. r. *Šmty*, name of a snake in the netherworld.

I is a snake on legs. The name is connected with the verb *šm* = to go. It is terrifying. One withdraws before its bad smell. Souls of evil ones are counted out to it [8]).

B. 12. s. *ktt*, ichneumon-fly.

"The ichneumon-fly is coming. He who is bitten by the ichneumon-fly, dies" [9]).

B. 12. t. *gbg3*, kind of bird.

There are various spells to keep this bird away from the dead [10]). C.T. Spell 688 reads: "To keep the *gbg3*-bird off . . ., the scribe of the court of justice of 30 . . . N.N. sits before Re. He makes you fall (?) before the double Ennead. This N.N. says this name of yours, which he has learned on *'Iw Nšiši*, (your name) of bull of the two *gbg3*-birds. Your writing-reed is broken. Your two palettes are

---

1) B.D. 17, Naville II. 71.
2) Pyr. 1351.b.
3) C.T. V. 355.x.
4) C.T. V. 332.b.
5) C.T. Spell 440; V. 293.a.
6) C.T. Spell 439; V. 292.a.
7) C.T. I. 397.b; cf. C.T. II. 42.b, boars live on the desert; Wb. IV, 401. 7, *š3* = Seth-animal.
8) Book of Gates IX, upper register, B.S. Pl. XII. 32-39.
9) C.T. V. 281.c. Cf. Pyr. 1772.c.
10) C.T. V. 269.a; III. 144.d; IV. 385.b; V. 26.b; 277.a.

smashed. Your books are destroyed, on account of what you thought of doing against N.N. Backwards, black bird, equipped with gluttony . . . Backwards, black bird, which comes from the Great Bear, which speaks in behalf of its father" [1]). In other similar spells there is also time and again talk of the destroying of the writing-materials of the *gbg3*-bird. The text cited makes the impression that the bird is the registrar of a court of the gods, before which the dead is condemned and where Re is in control. The dead destroys the writing-materials of the bird, so that the latter cannot write down a damning evidence. The court of 30 also occurs in C.T. Spell 277 [2]), where the dead is identified with Thoth (the ibis) and where it, just as the latter, has judged objectively on Horus and Seth. Concerning the *m'b3y.t* one may think of a court of gods in the hereafter. The *gbg3*-bird performs a similar part as Thoth, who writes down the issue of the jurisdiction. Also Spell 425 may be interpreted in this sense. "To keep the *gbg3*-bird at bay. Hail to you, bull of bulls with him, who looks after the truth. Oh these two *gbg3*-birds. I come to you, that I break your ink-pot, that I smash your palette. Pave the way for me to the place, where the great god is" [3]). This great god may be Re, the president of the court at Heliopolis. The *gbg3*-bird must not hinder free admittance to Re by a damning evidence.

B.12.u. *ṯsm*, dog.

In the *Zweiwegebuch* there is a demon, who must be passed on one of the two roads. "Dog's face, hidden of shape, is his name" [4]). The *Zweiwegebuch* is full of such demons, wholly or partly in the form of an animal. They are drawn along the roads, often armed with a knife. They threaten the dead who pass. The dead asks for salvation from a demoniacal animal. "Oh Atum . . . save me from this god, who lives on slaughter beasts, whose face is like that of a dog and whose shape (literally skin) like that of a man, who guards this twist of the fire-lake" [5]). Jackal-like gods in the realm of the dead are invoked: "Oh you nine gods, great of silence in the western country, who are keepers of the souls, lords of foods in the West, whose face is made like that of a dog in order to lick rotten and putrified things" [6]). The picture shows 9 shapes with a dog's head. [7])

1) C.T. VI. 318.a-o.
2) C.T. IV. 21.b.
3) C.T. V. 269.a-g.
4) C.T. VII, Spell 1171; B 1 P. 365.
5) B.D. 17; C.T. IV. 311.c-314.a.
6) L.Q. V. 3-4.
7) L.Q. I, 2nd register

B.12.v. *db*, hippopotamus.

In the *Zweiwegebuch* a demon with the head of a hippopotamus peers at the wayside. "Hippopotamus' head, alert in the attack" [1]). "Hippopotamus' head, raging with fury" [2]). The same figure occurs in the later Book of the Dead as one of the *śmi.w* of the 5th *ʿrr.t*, which one has to pass. Compare C.T. B 1 L. 388 with B.D. 144 [3]).

B.13. *Men.*

The dead may influence life on earth in a favourable, but also in an unfavourable sense. As ghosts they may cause calamities [4]). In the netherworld malevolent spirits of the dead may do harm to those who arrive there.

B.13.a. *3ḫ*, spirit.

The *3ḫ* may be conceived as a haunting dead. In a threat of tomb robbers it says: "I shall make all living ones, who are on earth, fear the spirits that are in the West, of which one is afraid" [5]). Another text intimidates desecrators of graves by the following words [6]): "All who will enter my grave in their impurity and who have eaten what an eminent spirit (*3ḫ iḳr*) detests, . . . I shall seize his neck like that of a bird, putting fear into him, so that the spirits which are on earth, see it and fear for an eminent spirit." Consequently an *3ḫ* can punish somebody on earth. A widower reproaches the spirit of his wife, that it makes him meet with accidents. He writes a letter to her on this subject [7]): "To the excellent spirit of Ankhiry. What crime have I done against you, that I have come into this bad situation in which I am? What have I done against you? What you have done is that you have laid your hand upon me, although I have done nothing wrong against you." The spirit of the dead makes itself felt on earth. "To lay one's hand on" must have an evil meaning [8]).

---

1) C.T. VII, Spell 1170; B 1 Be. 263; B 1 P. 361.
2) C.T. VII, Spell 1062; B 1 L. 388; Lacau, Sarc. I. 193. 41.
3) B.D. 144; 328. 11; 147; 360. 14. 15.
4) Gardiner-Sethe, *Egyptian Letters to the dead*, London, 1928, p. 11.
5) Urk. I. 260. 17.
6) Letters to the dead, X. n. 2, 4-6.
7) Letters to the dead, VII, 1-3; Leiden 371.
8) Cf. Erman, *Denksteine aus der thebanischen Gräberstatt*, 1098, Turin, Stele 102: I sinned against the mountain-peak and it punished me, while I was in its hand.

As a ghost the *3ḫ* can harm somebody [1]). A wife writes to her deceased husband, the priest Antef, that he should help a member of the female staff and should punish those who harm her [2]). "As concerns this servant *'Imiw*, who is ill, you do not fight for her night and day with any man who treats her in a hostile way nor with any woman, who treats her in a hostile way." The spirits of the ancestors are invoked by somebody alive, in order to destroy his enemies who may be alive or spirits of the dead [3]). "Rouse your father *'Ii* against B., rise, hasten against him . . . Rise against them with your fathers, your brothers, your friends. Fell B. and A., the son of 'ai." In this way a son invokes the spirit of his deceased father.

Not only on earth, but also in the realm of the dead the spirits may threaten somebody. In the *Ḥtp*-field he is safeguarded against it: "I am stronger and more competent than the spirits. They have no power over me" [4]). Thoth helps the dead against spirits which assault him. "As regards any god, any spirit, any dead, who will oppose this dignity of yours . . . it is Thoth who places your hand against them" [5]). The dead finds that he has left evil spirits in the realm of the dead behind him. "I have passed the spirits" [6]). They wait for him along the paths of the *Zweiwegebuch*, "these spirits which keep watch over this road" [7]). He wants to be saved from any male and female spirit which will keep off his magical power [8]).

B.13.b. *mt*, dead one.

Other dead may do harm to a deceased person in the hereafter. "Your sceptre, your staff, your nails, which are on your fingers, are the knives that are on the arms of Thoth . . . You strike your arm against the dead, against the spirits, which will lead you to *Ḫnty 'Imnty.w*" [9]). In the Pyramid Texts the idea prevails that only the king sails to heaven but that the other dead stay in a subterranean realm of the dead, which is ruled by Osiris. On this journey to heaven they might waylay him. To the deceased king it is wished: "May you look down on Osiris, when he commands the spirits" [10]). "N.N. has

[1]) In IV.a, 3-4 it says that the spirit of the deceased father protects his daughter against robbers of his inheritance. So there the spirit helps.

[2]) Letters to the dead, 12th dyn. VI. A. 2-4.

[3]) Op. cit. I.a, 9-11, 6th dyn.

[4]) C.T. V. 343.a.b.

[5]) C.T. I. 207.e; 208.b.

[6]) C.T. II. 50.i.

[7]) C.T. VII, Spell 1149; B 1 Be. 232.

[8]) C.T. V. 263.d. g.

[9]) Pyr. 1999.b-d.

[10]) Pyr. 251.b. c.

torn away your boundary-marks, oh dead. N.N. has overturned your boundary-stones, opponents, assistants of Osiris" [1]). In the realm of the dead there is a pool, which one has to avoid, in which there are spirits and dead [2]). The deceased is provided with a charm against "any male and female dead, who will keep off his magical power" [3]).

The dead may also harm the living on earth. In medical papyri diseases are ascribed to the influence of the dead [4]). "Oh Isis, great of magical power, set me free, undo me from all evil, bad and red things, from the blow of a god and the blow of a goddess, from a male and female dead, from a male and female being, which will oppose me inimically." Also in the "Letters to the dead" a bad influence is attributed to a male or female dead [5]).

In the later literature the *mt.w* are the punished sinners in the realm of the dead, while the beatified are called *nṯr.w*. In this way the terms occur in the Book of Gates. "You purge yourself, Re, in your sacred pond, in which you purge the gods, who do not approach the souls of the dead" [6]). Another division deals with jackals, which are in the pond of life. "They are in the surroundings of this pond, to which the souls of the dead do not approach, because it is "taboo" to be in there" [7]). Re travels through the netherworld "in order to put the spirits in their places and to deliver the dead to their sentence" [8]).

B.13.c. *nty.w iwty.w*, who are there and who are not there.

The dead keeps beings in the hereafter, who threaten him, at bay. "My glory is my power . . . I chase away those who are there. I punish those who are not there" [9]).

B.13.d. *rmṯ*, men.

The dead asks for help against those who assault him. "Save me . . . from all evil things, devised to be done against me by people, gods, spirits and dead" [10]). About the happy sojourn in the *Ḥtp*-field it is said: "I know the depths of the snakes, so that I am saved from men and gods" [11]). Thus the word *rmṯ* regularly occurs in sequences

---

1) Pyr. 1236.a. b. 2) Pyr. Neith 761, 762. 3) C.T. V. 263.d.
4) Ebers I. 13-16; Sethe, *Lesestücke*, 47. 19-48. 3. 5) IV. A. 5. Cf. *wpi*, C. 2.a.
6) Book of Gates III, upper register, B.S. Pl. VIII, 36-VII. 40.
7) Book of Gates III, upper register, 2nd figure, B.S. Pl. VIII. 26-29.
8) Book of Gates I, middle register, B.S. Pl. IV. 17-20.
9) C.T. Spell 149; II. 252.a. d. e.
10) B.D. 148; 365. 7-11. 11) C.T. Spell 467; V. 375.a. b. (B 3 L).

of beings, who may do evil to the dead. "Oh men, gods, spirits, powers, uraei, see me, fear me" [1]). These are conquered by the spell [2]). Also at people, inimical to the dead, the pronouncement is aimed: "Oh people, male and female, I truly pull a brick from the grave of my father, that I may stop up your mouth with it" [3]).

B.13.e. *s*, man.

One spell serves to make the *b3* keep a man at bay who is annoying for the dead [4]): "Go, my soul, that this man may see you." The dead passes him unhindered. "The sem-priest, the first of the house of Thoth, will make the heart of this man forgetful, till I have passed him. It cannot speak" [5]). The idea of the spell is that the man can say nothing evil to the dead. For this purpose his memory is deranged.

B.14. *Demons I*; *names, which indicate a function.*

B.14.a. *i3y.w*, torturers.

An exact translation of this word is not possible. They punish Apophis in the realm of the dead. "The torturers are against you, so that you are destroyed" [6]).

B.14.b. *imnḫ.w*, slaughterers [7]).

These are demons, who slaughter or cut somebody. C.T. Spell 750 is a spell "to keep the *imnḫ.w* at bay. Oh these *imnḫ.w* of the lord of life, who make an offering of child's flesh to the lord of life, go away from Osiris N.N. Do not make an offering of her, go away from her. Behold, she will let him (the lord of life) know that she slaughters his enemies for him. Osiris N.N., you have gone away alive. You have not gone away dead" [8]).

B.14.c. *iry . . .*, keeper of . . .

In the *Zweiwegebuch* the dead must pass all sort of demoniacal beings, who are also pictured, either armed or not with knives. Their names are sometimes combined with *iry* . . . "who belongs to", after which the name of the place where they are, follows. In this way there are the *iry.w ʿ.t*, the keepers of the room [9]); the *iry r3*,

---

[1]) C.T. VI. 201.d-f.
[2]) Cf. C.T. VI. 203.a; 93.a. e; 269.p.
[3]) C.T. Spell 461; V. 334.a-c.
[4]) C.T. Spell 99; II. 94.d.
[5]) C.T. II. 95.g; 96.a. b.
[6]) Book of Gates IX, middle register, B.S. Pl. XII. 31. 32.
[7]) WB. II. 84. 2 *mnḫ*, to slaughter.
[8]) C. T. Spell 750; VI. 379.k-t; 380.a-e. See also C.T. VI. 195.i; C.T. IV. 303.b; III. 285.a.
[9]) C.T. VII, Spell 1169; B 1 Be. 244.

keeper of the opening of the door and the *iry ḳ3b*, keeper of the bend (in the road) [1]). Further there are the *iry.w w3.wt*, keepers of the road, who take away the heart of the dead [2]). There are demons who seize somebody by a leg or an arm, *iry rd*, *iry* ʿ [3]). The dead is not left to them. There are also "keepers of hearts, *iry.w ib.w* [4]). See also *iry* ʿ*3* and *iry śbḫ.t*. B.1.a.

B.14.d. *irr.w ir.t.śn*, who do their (evil) deeds.

Demons who may harm the dead, are charmed. "Those who do (evil) deeds have no power over the destroying of my heart's desire in the two countries as a whole. I eat their magical power. I devour their glory. My strength is with me against them. Their glory is in my arms" [5]).

B.14.e. *isfty.w*, evil-doers.

These occur as demoniacal gate-keepers. "Evil-doers, open to me the two doors" [6]).

B.14.f. ʿ*b.w*, heapers-up of corn [7]).

These are demons, with "pitch-forks", who treat the dead badly. To the *b3* it is said: "May you not be among the heapers-up of corn (carriers of pitch-forks), among the guards, who belong to the parts of the body" [8]).

B.14.g. ʿ*ḥ3.w*, fighters.

They are beings, inimical to the dead, who take the heart away [9]).

B.14.h. ʿ*ḏty.w*, slaughterers.

About a helping god the dead says: "He prevents my being among the slaughterers of Osiris" [10]). "You are far from me, slaughterers of Osiris. You have no power over these feet of mine" [11]). The context is that the dead prefers a favourable fate with Re in the heavens as opposed to a sojourn with Osiris in the netherworld. Osiris is a god of the realm of the dead, who, by means of his executioners, tortures the deceased.

---

1) Lacau, Sarc. I. 192. 31; 33; C.T. VII Spells 1057. 1059,
2) C.T. I. 210.b.
3) Pyr. Neith 750.
4) C.T. VI. 67.g.
5) C.T. VI. 181.h-l. Cf. Pyr. 298.b; 414.b.
6) C.T. VI. 242. d.
7) Wb. I. 176. 15.
8) C.T. VI. 84. g.
9) B.D. 28; 92. 1; A. de Buck, J.E.O.L., no. 9, p. 20.
10) C.T. Spell 221; III. 206.d.
11) C.T. III. 305.e. f.

B.14.i. *wpwty*, messenger [1]).

The messengers are a group of servants of Osiris, who want to seize the dead. Their threatening attitude is connected with the unfavourable part that Osiris may play in the Pyramid Texts as ruler of the subterranean realm of the dead. "N.N. has passed the messengers of Osiris (safely). There is no god, who seizes N.N." [2]). Osiris says: "The country where I am, is full of messengers with grim faces, who are not afraid of god nor goddess. I shall send them upwards and they shall fetch the heart of anyone who will do evil deeds" [3]). They help Osiris as judges of the dead and punish the unjust. They hinder the dead from making use of his magical word. "Oh savage ones of face, messengers of Osiris, who close the mouths of the spirits over what is in them. You have no power over the closing of this mouth of mine. You do not take away the going of these feet of mine" [4]). Also other gods than Osiris have such messengers, who want to take away the heart of the dead. "Backwards, messenger of whatever god. Have you come to take away this my heart of the living ones? This my heart of the living ones will not be given to you" [5]). The dead says to Osiris: "Oh Lord of the Atef-crown, . . . save me from your messengers, who do damage, who cause punishment, who are not lenient" [6]). Another text states: "The messengers of Osiris have no power over me" [7]).

In a passage where man is urged to be prepared to die, the *wpwty* is an angel of death, who comes and fetches man. "When your messenger comes to fetch you, he finds you prepared. Do not say: I am too young for being taken away" [8]). In the netherworld four goddesses occur, with whose work Osiris is satisfied. They are "the female-messengers of him who hides his name" [9]). A *wpwty* as demon is mentioned in a passage of the Book of the Dead: "He is not bared by the messenger, who affects, who exercises mutilation over the whole earth" [10]). The messengers form a court of judges with Osiris. "To approach to this spirit by the gods of the *d3.t*, the messengers

1) E. Suys, *Les messagers des dieux*, Egyptian Religion II (1934), pp. 123-139.
2) Pyr. 1236.d; 1237.a.
3) Chester Beatty I. 15. 5. A. de Buck, J.E.O.L., no. 9, p. 21.
4) C.T. Spell 236; III. 304.f-305.b.
5) B.D. 29; 93. 4-7; C.T. V. 54.b-55.b.
6) B.D. 125; 262. 3-6.
7) C.T. V. 331.g. h. i.
8) Wisdom of Ani IV. 17 sqq.
9) L.Q. XCIV. 5.
10) B.D. 163; 414. 11.

of the great god (Osiris). Salutation of this spirit by this court of justice, when they approach him. He proceeds with them to this sacred place, where this sacred god is" [1]). *Wpwty.w* is here parallel with *ḳnb.t*. The picture shows that they take the deceased by the hand. They carry signs of life, so they have no evil intentions towards the just dead.

Also Seth has his demoniacal helpers, who may harm man. "N.N. does not give his glory to the messengers of Seth, who lives on his plunder" [2]).

The dead himself has such an officer of the court, who punishes men or gods inimical to him: "Khensu is my messenger, sent out to punish" [3]). The ushabti is called in aid against a *wpwty*, who wants to put somebody at work in the hereafter: "In this way you will speak to each messenger, who will come for N.N." [4]).

The wailing-women at a funeral ascribe it to a *wpwty* that the dead is snatched away. "Oh *nšm.t*-boat of the followers of the messenger of the snake, savage of face. You have come in order to take mine away" [5]).

B.14.j. *wrš*, guard.

By his magical power the dead deters demons. "He has filled his belly with magical power. As a consequence he has quenched his thirst, and has made his keepers tremble like a bird" [6]).

In the Pyramid Texts the guards do not play an unfavourable part. There they belong to a group of courtiers, who welcome the king in heaven and who present him with tokens of esteem. "The great ones rise for you. The guards sit down for you" [7]). "The great ones flock together for you. The guards get up for you" [8]). "The guards dance for you" [9]). "The guards of Buto pay homage to him. The guards of Hieraconpolis clothe him with dignity" [10]). According to the latter text it here concerns dignitaries, who play a part in the coronation. In a few places the *wrš.w* are, as appears from the determinative, wailing-women [11]).

---

1) Schmidt, Sark. 700.
2) C.T. VI. 294. 1. Next Seth is styled as a power, which is behind corpses. Seth and his messengers harm the *3ḫ* or the corpse.
3) C.T. VI. 179.g.
4) C.T. VI. 1.j.
5) Lüddeckens, *Totenklagen*, p. 104.
6) C.T. I. 137.d; 138.a-c; I. 90.d; 118.c.
7) Pyr. Neith 661.
8) Pyr. 656.e.
9) Pyr. 1947.a.
10) Pyr. 1013.b.
11) Pyr. 744.b.

B.14.k. *m3śty.w* (other spelling *m3ś.w*).

In the *Zweiwegebuch* there are pictured beings who are called thus. They squat, have animal's heads and carry reptiles in their hands. Is their name connected with the word *m3ś.t*, knee, and are they called thus on account of their squatting position? They are demons, dangerous to pass. The dead charms them: "Be weary, oh *m3śty.w*, with mysterious faces (on account of the animal's heads)" [1]). One of them is called: "Who eats his fathers", another: "Who eats his mothers." When the dead knows the right spells, he passes them unhindered and reaches *R3-śṯ3.w* safely. "As regards anyone who is seen there (in *R3-śṯ3.w* as the end of the road) alive, he does not go under to all eternity, because he knows the spell to pass the *m3śty.w*, the keepers of the gates" [2]). It is said about them: "It is Geb, who has put them in *R3-śṯ3.w* round his son Osiris for fear of his brother Seth, that he may not harm him" [3]). The part of the *m3śty.w* is protecting Osiris. They help him against Seth. They punish him who is, like Seth, ill-disposed to Osiris. They are to be compared with the *ỉmy.w ḫt Wśỉr* or the *ỉry.w ʿ.wt Wśỉr*. About Anubis, the protector of the dead, it is said: "He saves you from the *m3śty.w*, the messengers of the hidden slaughtering-block" [4]).

B.14.l. *nb.w d3.t*, lords of the netherworld.

The dead is fearless of judges in the realm of the dead. "Osiris N.N. is undaunted with the lords of the netherworld" [5]).

B.14.m. *nhś*, watchman.

A spell for keeping demons off: "N.N. is loud of voice in the *3ḫ.t* like the great one. On your faces, oh watchmen!" [6]).

B.14.n. *ḫnṯ.w*, slaughterers.

These are executioners, who torture the sinners. In the Book of Gates they punish Apophis. They are represented with four snake's heads and with a rope and knife in their hands, the rope being for tying up the slaughter-beasts, the knife for killing them off [7]). A gate-keeper in the realm of the dead is called "Cutter of the rebel to

[1]) C.T. VII, Spell 1183; B 1 Be. 293.
[2]) Cairo 28085; Lacau, Sarc. I. 211. 58. 59; C.T. VII, Spell 1076; 212. 66, 68; C.T. VII, Spells 1079-1081.
[3]) C.T. VII, Spell 1099; B 2 Bo. 155 sqq.
[4]) C.T. I. 196.d.
[5]) B.D. 168; 431. 6. 7.
[6]) C.T. VII, Spell 1181; B 1 Be. 287.
[7]) Book of Gates X, upper register, B.S. Pl. XI.

pieces" [1]). Demons, who threaten the dead, are called: "Slaughterers, strong of arm" [2]). They hinder the dead on his flight to the *3ḫ.t.* They keep the *b3* off.

B.14.o. *ḫ3ty.w*, slaughterers.

These are demons who operate with knives in the hereafter. The dead repels a god, who wants to do him evil and of whom even the demons are afraid. "Recede far, you whom the slaughterers respect" [3]). The determinative is a knife. The demons do no damage to the king. "For you the slaughterers fall on their faces" [4]). "A slaughterer does not bend over N.N." [5]). These slaughterers are sometimes placed among the stars: "You call to the slaughterers. You guide those who do not go under" [6]). They are to punish sinners in the realm of the dead: "The slaughterers, who are in the slaughter-place of Osiris, they bring about your slaughtering" [7]). They are pictured with knives in their hands before condemned ones. The dead says: "The slaughterers will not overtake me" [8]). Further in the Book of the Dead "the slaughterers of Sekhmet" are mentioned [9]).

B.14.p. *ḫ3k.w ib*, rebels.

The term would mean being cunningly or ill-disposed [10]). "Beware of the rebels" [11]). Demons are deterred: "I have put your fear in those who are on earth like those of Horus among the gods . . . I have put your rage among the rebels" [12]).

B.14.q. *sm3.wt*, gang.

The gang of a hostile being can do no harm to the dead any more, because it is imprisoned. "His (of the *ḫfty*) gang is locked up for her" [13]). The term *sm3.wt* may be thought of as being the "gang" of Seth.

B.14.r. *snṯ.w*, rebels.

"I am not kept off by the rebels" [14]).

---

1) B.D. 145; 337. 11; B.D. 146; 351. 14.
2) C.T. VI. 77.a.
3) Pyr. 1265.c; 1274.a.
4) Pyr. 1535.b; C.T. I. 290.h; 291.a.
5) Pyr. 748.c.
6) C.T. VI. 107.e. f. Pyr. 1726.c also places the *ḫ3ty.w* among the stars. *Niś r* in unfavourable sense also Pyr. Neith 744: "He who will attack you, shall not live, he who will call you, has receded. Parallel of *ḫm.*
7) L.Q. XXV. 2.
8) B.D. 149; 372. 5.
9) B.D. 145; 348. 9.
10) Wb. III. 363. 11. 12.
11) C.T. I. 249.b.
12) C.T. VI. 327.d. i.
13) C.T. VI. 74.p.
14) C.T. IV. 115.f.

B.14.s. *śbỉ*, rebel.

A spell must prevent the *b3* being threatened by rebels. "A feast of the rebels is not celebrated against you" [1]). They are not allowed to do any harm to the dead. "The rebel who comes by night, the robber of the early morning, is kept off for you" [2]). "Let the rebels have no power over me" [3]).

B.14.t. *ṯsty.w*, enemies.

The dead is terryfying like the thunder-god. His enemies stand in awe of him. "I have heaped up the rain-clouds. I have made noise. The enemies give praise to me" [4]).

B.14.u. *ḏrḏr.w*, strangers.

In a metamorphose text, where the dead changes into a swallow, he states that he is safe for certain demons: "Strangers have no power over N.N." [5]).

B.15. *Demons II; a choice from names, which specify the essence.*

The denominations indicate in which respect the demons are terrifying for the dead.

B.15.a. *ʿḥ3 ḥr*, combative of face.

It is asked of the nightly hours to let the dead go to the eastern horizon in order to rise with Re. On his way he wants to be saved from demons: "That N.N. may pass by the frontier guards of the combative ones of face" [6]). Also in a council of judges in the realm of the dead these combative ones of face occur [7]).

B.15.b. *wr*, great one.

A demon, who catches dead in a net is invoked. "Oh god, who sees what is caught in it. It is the great one, who sits in the dark. Praise to you, great one" [8]). "This great god, to whom he (the *wdp.w*, servant) brings, it is this great one, who sits in the darkness, who is not seen, whose voice is not heard" [9]). That he is tall of stature and lives in the dark gives him his ominous character.

---

1) C.T. II. 109.c. Cf. C.T. VI. 145.a "to celebrate a feast of the rebels with me like an evil slaughter". The meaning might be that somebody is put to death in a bloody way by the rebels.

2) C.T. I. 268.g-i.

3) Louvre 3148 IX. b. 3, *nn śḫm śbỉ.w ỉm.ỉ.*

4) C.T. V. 379.a. b.

5) C.T. Spell 678; VI. 305.e; *ḏrḏr.w* with the determinative for god.

6) Pyr. 269.b.

7) Book of Gates VI, middle register, E. Lefébure, M.M.A.F.C. III, 1, Pl. XXXIV. 41.

8) C.T. VI. 36.g-i.

9) C.T. VI. 45.g. h.

B.15.c. *nʿḫ*, strong one.

Orion gives his scepter to the dead. Now he can chase demons away with it. "I make the strong ones tremble with it" [1]).

B.15.d. *nwn*, with tumbled hair.

They are unfavourable beings who have to pass the dead. "I keep the beings with tumbled hair off, gods, let me through, that I may pass" [2]). Another text has [3]) as a variant *ḫ3ty.w* [4]). *Nwn* means to let the hair hang tumbled down as a token of mourning. It is used of beings, who welcome the king in heaven [5]). *Nwn* occurs beside *sps*, which has the same meaning. The dead identifies himself with *sps* and *nwn*, in order to confer a position of authority upon himself. "I am *sps*, who comes from his *3ḫ.t*. I am *nwn*, who goes out by his power" [6]). Also in C.T. Spell 624 [7]) *nwn* and *sps* occur beside each other. There it concerns the strength of the dead, which reaches heaven and earth and also his redness. There are no bounds to his steps. Perhaps the dead identifies himself with a raging demon, in order to make an impression. *Sps* in the original meaning "with tumbled hair", as a token of mourning, still occurs in the passage: "Shu has comforted (?) the "mourners" [8]).

B.15.e. *nwt.k nw*.

This is a demoniacal opponent of the dead [9]). He is "door-keeper of the secret desert." This fits in with a connection with a hunter. A Pyramid Text [10]) reads: "It is your nails which cut the house of *nwt.k nw* to pieces, oh Neith, see what I have done for you. I have saved you from him who belongs to your leg. I have not abandoned you to him who belongs to your arm. I have protected you against your enemy." It here concerns the ascension after the release from the grave. *Nwt.k nw* represents death, which keeps somebody imprisoned. "I do not deliver you to *nwt.k nw*" [11]). Compare further: "The evil . . . that *nwt.k nw* has done" [12]).

---

[1]) C.T. Spell 469; V. 390.f.

[2]) C.T. Spell 257; III. 368.a-c.

[3]) S 1 C[a].

[4]) B.14.o.

[5]) Pyr. 1005.c.

[6]) C.T. Spell 513; B.D. 179; C.T. VI. 98.d; 99.a. b.

[7]) C.T. VI. 240.k; 241.c.

[8]) C.T. IV. 155.f.

[9]) Pyr. Aba 561 sqq., determinative of hunter. See also C.T. I. 282.h; I. 80.k.

[10]) Pyr. Neith 748-751.

[11]) Pyr. Neith 665.

[12]) Pyr. 1639.c; 851.b.

B.15.f. *nbḏ*, evil one.

The *nbḏ* plays a part like Apophis. He attacks the boat of Re. "I am the one, who keeps this *nbḏ* off, who comes to set the boat of Re aflame" [1]). The dead himself is in the boat of Re and safe from *nbḏ* [2]). "*Nbḏ* does not attack him." The dead goes safely along the black road in the *Zweiwegebuch*: "The smell of a god is on me. The evil one does not attack me" [3]). "I have seen that he keeps the evil one at bay, who destroys the kas in the house where the executioners are" [4]). "Brighten my heart in the moment that *nbḏ* makes himself felt" [5]). "*Nbḏ* does not attack him. The gate-keepers are not unacquainted with him" [6]).

B.15.g. *ḥś3 ḥr*, savage one of face.

A tutelary deity is invoked: "Come to Osiris N.N. Save him from the power of *ḥś3 ḥr*, who has power over hearts, who takes limbs away, from whose mouth fiery breath comes to consume souls" [7]). Is a snake meant here? [8]).

B.15.h. *št3 ḥr*, hidden one of face.

The dead deters a demon, who waylays him: "What is on the flame, is against the hidden one of face" [9]).

B.15.i. *ḳ3 ḫrw*, high of voice.

A demon frightens by the loud roaring he utters. "If you think that this N.N. will purge himself beside this *Mnš*, high of voice, evil of seed, then N.N. will keep him at bay" [10]).

B.15.j. *km ḥr*, black one of face.

A demon, "black of face, who is in the time that he makes himself felt" [11]). In a spell against snakes and crocodiles it reads: "Backwards, black one of face, do not make your glory sharp against me" [12]). To a demon it is said: "Backwards, black one of face, known by his smell (?), who is in the house of the necropolis, disturber . . ." [13]).

---

[1]) *Zweiwegebuch*, C.T. VII, Spell 1099; B 1 L, 502, 503.

[2]) B.D. 136 A; 299. 8.

[3]) C.T. VII, Spell 1169; B 1 Be, 244, *Zweiwegebuch*, 3rd part black road.

[4]) C.T. V. 41.i.

[5]) Louvre 3865, 4, *śndm.k n.i ib.i m 3.t n.t nbḏ* (2nd century A.D.).

[6]) B.D. 144; 331. 12.

[7]) B.D. 163; 411. 14-16.

[8]) L.Q. CV. 5 determined with snake.

[9]) C.T. VI. 150.k.

[10]) C.T. VI. 317.b. c.

[11]) C.T. IV. 268.d; B.D. 17.

[12]) C.T. VI. 205.i. j. k.

[13]) C.T. VI. 293.o-q.

B.16. *Gods*.

B.16.a. *'Itm.*

In the tombs of the kings of the New Kingdom it is Atum, who punishes the enemies of Re. He watches over the condemned. He is pictured with sinners before him, who have to be punished [1]). The inscription near it reads: "What Atum does for Re ... To place the evil in his enemies." Atum keeps watch over the torturing-posts of Geb [2]). The *Livre du Jour* says: "Atum, he fells the enemies of Re" [3]).

B.16.b. *B3 pf.*

In the Pyramid Texts "the house of *b3 pf*" is mentioned [4]). It is a place which the dead avoids. *B3 pf* means "that ba", in which *pf* has the same unfavourable meaning as Latin *iste*. About this house it is said: "It is bad, it is painful, it causes loss and it is unfavourable" [5]). So *b3 pf* can do evil to the dead. Another Pyramid Text states: "N.N. has passed the house of *b3 pf*" [6]). Also in C.T. the denomination occurs. "May they not take you along to the house of *b3 pf*" [7]). "Go to the doors of the house (*ḥ.t*) of *b3 pf*" [8]). Funerary offerings are mentioned, "which *b3 pf*, which is in its redness, has given to you" [9]). In this place the term is not used in an unfavourable sense. It is the denomination of the sun-god, which also occurs elsewhere [10]). H. W. Fairman, in virtue of information of B. Grdseloff, mentions some more places, where *b3 pf* occurs [11]) viz. in the tomb of *Mrś'nḫ* III, Gizah, on a statue of queen *Ti'3* (both unpublished) and in Brugsch, Thesaurus, 28. The first two places mention a *ḥm-nṯr* of *B3 pf*. In the third place *B3 pf* is determined as a god. So *B3 pf* has been taken as a god.

B.16.c. *B3b3.* [12]).

He is the eldest son of Osiris [13]). As a demon he occurs in B.D. 17 [14]): "He keeps watch over this bend of the West." He is near a turn of a road through the realm of the dead and threatens those who get past it. To the 42 judges in B.D. 125 the dead says: "Save me from

1) Book of Gates I, lower register, B.S. Pl. IV. 8-10.
2) Book of Gates V, middle register, B.S. Pl. XVIII. 8.
3) 3rd register.
4) Neith 762.
5) Neith 763.
6) Pyr. 334.a.
7) C.T. I. 284.i.
8) C.T. I. 273.c.
9) C.T. III. 258.a.
10) Pyr. 854.a; C.T. V. 318.a.
11) *Ann. du Serv.* 43, p. 309.
12) Ph. Derchain, *Bébon, le dieu et les mythes, Revue d'Égyptologie* IX (1952), p. 23-47.
13) C.T. V. 12.e.
14) Naville II. 64.

B3b3, who lives on intestines" [1]). The study of Derchain shows that he is pictured as a baboon. He carries knives in his hands [2]). He is called [3]): "This *B3b3*, the bull of the baboons. What he sees, does not live." He is a demon, who kills what he meets on his way (by his mere look?). The dead identifies himself with this demon, to intimidate in this way certain beings, who threaten him. *B3b3* has his demoniacal character beside all kinds of traits of a different nature, such as god of the male fertility and guard of the boat of Re. A Pyramid Text says [4]): "One can only live when one is unknown to him." In a tomb of a king from the New Kingdom the gods are beseeched to keep the messengers of *B3b3* at a distance [5]). He is identified with Seth [6]).

B.16.d. *Wśir*, Osiris.

Sometimes Osiris is represented as a demoniacal god in the realm of the dead. In the Pyramid Texts the dead wishes to be with Re in the heavens and not in the realm of the dead with Osiris [7]): "Re-Atum has not delivered you to Osiris (the dead = Seth), he (Osiris) has not counted your heart. He has not taken possession of your heart." Also in the C.T. Osiris sometimes is of a demoniacal nature. "Osiris, the lord of the slaughter, great of fright, to whom everything is brought, for whom everything is fetched" [8]). "I have spoken to you, Osiris, that you might turn what has gone from your mouth against me" [9]). Osiris has to take back an evil spell, which he has uttered against the dead. In the later literature Osiris has only his threatening side for those who have sinned against him and whom he condemns as a judge.

The texts also know all kinds of demons who are in the service of Osiris as executioners. The dead wants to pass safely "those who are in their caves, the keepers of Osiris' house" [10]). He fears "the slaughterers of Osiris, painful of fingers" [11]). The "descendants of Osiris" [12]) are executioners who take away somebody's face. Also "the fishermen of Osiris" [13]) are demons.

1) B.D. 125; 260. 10. 11.
2) In Derchain figure I.
3) C.T. VI. 297.c-e.
4) Pyr. 516. c, in Derchain, op. cit., p. 41.
5) Derchain, op. cit., p. 42.
6) Derchain, op. cit., p. 43.
7) Pyr. 145.b.
8) C.T. II. 116.v. w.
9) C.T. IV. 71.c. d.
10) C.T. IV. 84.f.
11) *Ỉmnḥ.w*, C.T. IV. 303.b; *ʿḏty.w Wśir*, C.T. III. 206.d; III. 305.e.
12) C.T. III. 323.a.
13) C.T. III. 295.h.

The dead invokes the *imy.w ʿ.t* of Osiris and says to them: "Do not lock my *b3* up, do not guard my shadow" 1). The dead calls them: "Who guard spirits, who lock up spectres of the dead, who do evil against me" 2). Most of the *mss.* of Naville have the reading *imy.w ʿ.t*, with the determinative of flesh. Others read *iry.w ʿ.t Wśir*. This term is now here determined with the sign for flesh, now there with the house. The meaning is respectively: "Guards of the parts of Osiris' body" and "chamber-keepers of Osiris". In the Pyramid Texts 3) they open the doors of heaven to the king. So there they are gate-keepers 4). A C.T. 5) reads: "My soul is not guarded by the chamber-keepers of Osiris." Also here the determination varies. A variant has *iry.w ʿrr.wt*, gate-keepers. Their function is clear: they are servants of Osiris, who may keep the soul of the dead imprisoned. C.T. Spell 491 is a spell to make the *b3* and other forces of the soul move freely 6): "Guards of the parts of Osiris' body 7), who watch over all souls, who keep the shadows of all male and female dead imprisoned, have no power over my detention." "You are not locked up 8) by the guards of the parts of Osiris' body" 9). In this connection also the *iry.w št3.w* of Osiris are mentioned 10). Another passage reads 11): "The guards of the limbs of Osiris do not lock him up. The guards of the limbs of Osiris have no power over the locking up of my *b3* and my magical power" 12). The blood-thirsty character is evident from the following text: "There are not made offerings of me by chamber-keepers of Osiris, who make a slaughter on their slaughtering-block. I do not come on their slaughtering-blocks. I am not taken to the slaughtering-block of the god" 13). Although their name is spelled differently, it is nevertheless clear which is the part played by the *iry.w ʿ.wt* of Osiris. Osiris is looked at from his demoniacal side. These servants help him to ill-treat the dead. More especially it is their task to lock the forces of the soul so that these cannot save the dead in the hereafter.

1) B.D. 92; 195. 11.
2) B.D. Budge, p. 195. 16.
3) Pyr. 1151.a.
4) Determinative signs of flesh.
5) C.T. I. 363.d-364.a.
6) C.T. VI. 69.e; 70.a. b.
7) Only determined with signs of flesh.
8) Subject *b3*, *św.t* etc.
9) C.T. VI. 71.f = B.D. 92.
10) C.T. VI. 72.e.
11) C.T. VI. 81.b.
12) Variants *iry.w ʿ.wt* with the determinative of house and *iry.w ʿrr.wt*, gate keepers.
13) C.T. VI. 132.d-g.

A similar group form the *imy.w ḫt Wśir*, those who are behind Osiris. They are mentioned a.o. in Am Duat [1]). There all kinds of punishments are mentioned [2]), which they let criminals endure, e.g., cutting the souls to pieces. They exterminate those who sin against Osiris [3]). Further on it is said about them, that there is breath for their noses, that they receive offerings and do not descend into destruction. They give the impression to be themselves righteous dead, who are acquitted in the judgment, to have become followers of Osiris, as they actually were already during their life on earth, and now may judge on other dead. If certain ceremonies are fulfilled the dead "will be an excellent spirit in the realm of the dead on New Year's day like the followers of Osiris" [4]). So the just dead is going to belong to the *imy.w ḫt Wśir*. These may also help the dead. "The nine of them who are behind Osiris, may they make Osiris N.N. have power over his enemies" [5]). The followers of Osiris are represented with knives in their hands. They are involved in the punishment of Seth, who has been drawn under Osiris in a *ḥ3d* [6]). They help Osiris at the judgment. "Oh nine of Osiris, who judge on the *d3.t* of Osiris, who are behind him . . ." [7]). A similar part play the *imy.w ḫt Wśir* in the Book of Gates [8]). They are called there "who are in their coffins" and they are "keepers" of souls.

B.16.e. *nṯr*, god.

The dead asks for protection against a god not called by his name, who threatens him in the realm of the dead. "Save me from this god, who takes away souls, who swallows decayed things, who lives on digestion products, who belongs to the dark, who is in the darkness, whom those who are in tiredness (the dead), fear" [9]). See also *nṯr* in the sequence *rmṯ nṯr.w 3ḫ.w* etc., B.13.d. One has to take into account that *nṯr* is also used of deified dead in the hereafter [10]).

B.16.f. *Ḥr ḫnty Ḫmw*.

This god is a demon, who threatens the dead. "Save me from

---

1) Am Duat III. 100.
2) Am Duat III. 139-150.
3) Am Duat III. 197 sqq.
4) B.D. 155; 402. 14. 15.
5) B.D. 168; 431. 7-8.
6) Pap. Jumilhac. X. 16.
7) L.Q. VI. 4.
8) Book of Gates III, middle register, 2nd figure. B.S. Pl. VIII. 23-25.
9) B.D. 17; C.T. IV. 319.e-320.d.
10) E.g. Book of Gates II, upper register of twelve mummies in chapels; B.S. Pl. III; Wb. II. 358. 3; 359. 13.

this god, hidden of stature, whose two eyebrows are the arms of the scales, on this day of settling the account of the robbery before the Lord of the universe. Who throws a lasso around the evil-doers in order to pull them to the slaughtering-block which cuts souls to pieces. Who is that? It is Horus, the first of Letopolis. Other reading: It is Thoth. It is Nefertem, the son of the great Sekhmet; *ʾIn-ʿ-f*" [1]). It here concerns a demon, who punishes the dead. Also Thoth as maintainer of the law may be considered here.

B.16.g. *Ḥr d3tỉ.*

This god is involved in the punishment of Osiris' enemies in the netherworld. "Their slaughtering is ordered every day by the majesty of *Ḥr d3tỉ*" [2]). According to a Pyramid Text he is a star in the sky [3]). About him it is said: "You are seated on your wonderful throne, about which the dead are astonished." The deceased king is in the heavens as a star just as *Ḥr d3tỉ* and takes a position of power in respect of other dead [4]).

B.16.h. *Ḫnsw.*

The demon Khensu catches gods and men for the deceased king, that he may eat them. "It is Khensu, who kills the lords, while he cuts their throats for N.N." [5]). In order to impress more the gods in the hereafter the dead identifies himself with the demon Khensu and says [6]): "I am Khensu, who sends out rage, who burns hearts." In his quality of Khensu it is said about the dead: "The bread of N.N. consists of men. I have offerings, consisting of children . . . Who lives on hearts" [7]). So Khensu is a demon, who devours people alive. The dead makes Khensu his helper. "My messenger is Khensu, sent out for punishing" [8]). Khensu slaughters and cooks the *ḥk3*-gods. The dead eats them and lives on their *ḥk3*. Khensu gives the impression of being a cannibalistic demon, who devours his victims in order to appropriate their magical power.

B.16.i. *Hrty.*

This is a ram-god. He is close to Osiris and is not well-disposed to the dead. "I have claimed him from *H̱rty*. I do not deliver him to Osiris. I open to him the gate which repels" [9]). "I have saved you

---

1) B.D. 17; C T. IV. 298.a-302.e.
2) Am Duat XI. 78.
3) Neith 746.
4) Pyr. 1734.b; 1258; 1207; 1134.
5) Pyr. 402.a.
6) C.T. IV. 65.j.
7) C.T. IV. 67.o. p. s.
8) C.T. VI. 179.g.
9) Pyr. Neith 779.

from the hand of *Ḥrty*, for he lives on the hearts of men. I have not delivered you to your opponent" [1]). The dead king is snatched away from *Ḥrty*, who might procure him a sad fate in the netherworld. It seems to be a local Osiris [2]).

B.16.j. *Śrḳ.t.*

This scorpion-goddess watches in the *Zweiwegebuch* over a twist of the black pathway [3]). She punishes Apophis in the netherworld and fetters him [4]). A text mentions the fetters of Selkis [5]).

B.16.k. *Śḫm.t.*

She is present in dangerous places in the realm of the dead, which the dead has to pass. She is near a gate. "As regards any god, who knows his protection against *Śḫm.t*, he is safe for you, basin of these snakes" [6]). About a fiery river near a gate in the realm of the dead it is said: "The third (river) is the fiery breath from the mouth of *Śḫm.t*" [7]). The knife of those who are before *Śḫm.t* is mentioned [8]). As raging lion-goddess she punishes the enemies of Re in the realm of the dead. "You stand in front of the boat of your father, felling the malicious one (Apophis)" [9]).

B.16.l. *Śtš*, Seth.

Seth waylays man in the realm of the dead. The dead is put on a par with Osiris and Seth treats him as inimically as his brother. When after somebody's death his relatives are given back to him, he is delivered from what Seth has done to him, "releaseḍ from the fatigue-duty of Seth" [10]). The dead says: "Seth has no power over me" [11]). This occurs in a passage, where the dead is put on a level with Osiris. A goddess is invoked: "Who saves Osiris from fatigue (= death), may you save me from fatigue. I know your name. I do not die" [12]). No more than Seth had power over his brother Osiris he will have it over the dead. It is said to the dead: "Seth is in fear when he sees you. He knocks his rebellion down" [13]). Seth threatens

---

1) Pyr Neith 665.

2) Pyr. 349.b-350.a; 445; 545.a; 1264.c; 1308.a; 1547.b; 1557.d.

3) C.T. VII, Spell 1176; B 1 Bc. 275; Lacau, Sarc. I. 193. 45; C.T. VII. Spell 1069.

4) Book of Gates X, upper register, B.S. Pl. XI. 21; A. Klasens, *A magical statue base*, p. 104.h. 9-10. B.D. 39; 105. 12; see above p. 132, B.2.p. *ḳ3š*.

5) C.T. IV. 90.g.

6) C.T. IV. 328.b-d.

7) C.T. IV. 329.k.

8) C.T. IV. 67.i.

9) B.D. 164; 415. 4. 11. 12. See also H. P. Blok, AcOr VII, pp. 98, 103, 108; Pl .II.

10) C.T. II. 151.e.

11) C.T. Spell 251; III. 349.f.

12) C.T. III. 349.b-e.

13) C.T. I. 249.c-e.

the dead like he threatened Osiris, but Horus helps him. "He (Horus) has effected that Thoth makes those who are behind Seth, recede for you" [1]). The dead escapes from Seth. "N.N. has avoided the ways. of Seth" [2]). He has to protect himself against the gang of Seth. About the parts of his body, which are identified with gods, it is said: "They strike the gang of Seth for you" [3]). Seth has no hold on the dead: "He does not die on account of the massacre of Seth" [4]). What Seth has done to the dead is undone: "*Dwn-ʿ.wy* has hidden his arms behind me to chase away the damage done by Seth" [5]). This occurs in a spell for fastening the head, which has been struck off by Seth.

B.16.m. *Św.*

The god of the air, Shu, may be dangerous for the dead. "He crosses the *ḥsꜣ*-water, the wall of Shu is turned over" [6]). The wall of Shu, according to Sethe the air, is an obstacle in the ascension [7]). The dead fears the grip of Shu [8]). He says: "I am not trapped by the net of Shu" [9]). In a text, which deals with the restoration of the functions of the body it reads: "Truly, Shu goes out without my flesh" [10]). Just like Osiris and Seth also Shu has a group of executioners with him, "the torturers of Shu" [11]). Shu is represented as a demon, who kills somebody off. There is a spell "not to take somebody's soul along to the slaughtering-block of Shu", or "not to fall on the slaughtering-block of Shu" [12]).

B.16.n. *Šsmw.*

This is the god of the wine-press [13]). He is a demon who squeezes the heads of the condemned out like grapes. The god *Šsmw* slaughters men and gods for the deceased king, who eats them. "*Šsmw* slaughters them for N.N." [14]). "*Šsmw* comes to you with grape-juice" [15]). He also occurs in the C.T. as a blood-thirsty god: "*Šsmw* near his knives

---

1) Pyr. 575.b.
2) Pyr. 1236.c.
3) B.D. 151; 382. 11.
4) B.D. 163; 414. 13.
5) C.T. VI. 126.j. k.
6) Pyr. 1121.b.
7) See also Pyr. 208.a, the bones of Shu.
8) C.T. II. 45.c.
9) C.T. III. 296.f.
10) C.T. V. 329.a.
11) B.D. 90; 191. 12.
12) C.T. Spell 553; VI. 152.a.
13) S. Schott, Z.Ä.S. 74, p. 88, *Das blutrünstige Keltergerät.* H. P. Blok, AcOr VII, p. 108.
14) Pyr. 403.a.
15) Pyr. 1552.a; see also Pyr. 545.b; 1770 = Pyr. Neith 6.

in his shape of slaughterer" [1]). The dead does not wish to be abandoned to gods like this one. "They do not deliver (me) (to) the *Šsmw*-gods" [2]). "The *Šsmw*-gods fear your" [3]). Part of the net, with which the dead may be caught, is called "leg of *Šsmw*" [4]). Also in the M.K.-version of the spells of the bird-net *Šsmw* occurs. Also there he is a demon, who executes bloody punishments. "It is the knife that is in the hand of *Šsmw*" [5]). "It is this cauldron that is in the hand of *Šsmw*" [6]). Because he knows the name of these instruments, the dead has power over them and escapes. In a cannibalistic text, where the dead eats gods, in order to appropriate their magical power, it is *Šsmw*, who slaughters them for him. "It is *Šsmw*, the red one (blood) of the beam, who slaughters them for me" [7]). So *Šsmw* is a slaughtering-demon, who kills his prey with knives, so that there flows blood.

B.16.o. *Ḏḥwty*, Thoth.

Thoth exercises a judicial function. "Sharpen your knife, Thoth, the sharp one, the cutting one, which removes the heads . . . It will remove the heads . . . of those who will oppose N.N." [8]). The knife of Thoth is sometimes thought of as being the crescent of the moon. These traits of Thoth as a god, who causes painful wounds and who belabours his victims with a knife, occur in the texts frequently [9]). He obtains the same predicate as the knife with which he works, viz. "the cutting one": "Thoth, the cutting one, who has sprung from Seth" [10]). "The knives which are on the arms of Thoth, the cutting one, who has sprung from Seth" [11]). These passages allude to the unnatural birth of Thoth from the knee of Seth, after the latter being made pregnant by Horus [12]). Demons, who threaten the deceased, are deterred by this blood-thirsty Thoth: "Thoth, the son of the stone, who has sprung from the two eggs (?), beheads them" [13]). In this text there follows immediately a passage, which would fit in very welll with this character of Thoth: "He bathes in your blood. He feasts on your redness (= blood)". Sometimes Thoth is the helper

1) C.T. I. 123.b.
2) C.T. V. 396.b.
3) C.T. V. 396.d.
4) B.D. 153 A; 391. 3-4.
5) C.T. VI. 8.c.
6) C.T. VI. 8.e.
7) C.T. VI. 179.h.
8) Pyr. 962.a-963.b.
9) H. Kees, *Zu den ägyptischen Mondsagen*, Z.Ä.S. 60, p. 1-5.
10) Pyr. Neith 753.
11) Pyr. 1999.c.
12) H. Kees, *Götterglaube*, p. 184.
13) B.D. 134, Naville II, p. 345.

of Seth against Osiris [1]). He is also responsible for the missing part of the damaged moon-eye [2]). With a view to this dangerous character of Thoth it is possible that the dead states that Thoth does him no harm. "I proceed and I go out to *'Inśw* (a name of Thoth). I have power over him" [3]). The strict character of Thoth has a favourable side, when it directs itself against evil-doers. He takes the part of the just, he punishes the sinner. He justifies Osiris. He makes up the difference between Horus and Seth. As god of the moon he is close to Osiris. "Book in order to give air to the tired one of heart by the activity of Thoth, who keeps the enemies of Osiris at bay . . . I am Thoth, who justifies Osiris against his enemies . . . I am Thoth, I have satisfied Horus. I have set the two comrades at rest in the moment of raging" [4]). In a spell against tomb robbers it reads: "Who speaks evil against these writings, Thoth will be a quarrelling companion for him" [5]). "I am Thoth, the lord of the truth, who justifies the injured, who helps the wretched" [6]). Thoth, as god of the moon, being connected with the cosmic order, may be maintainer of *m3ʿ.t*.

B.17. *The use of the term ḫfty, enemy.*

Death is feared as an enemy. This fear finds expression in representations of enemies, who waylay the dead in the hereafter. The enemies may be of a different nature.

a. Demons as enemies, who threaten the dead.
b. Enemies as opponents in a law-suit.
c. The enemies of the dead as opponents of Osiris.
d. Sinners as enemies of Re and Osiris.
e. *Ḫfty* as devil.

B.17.a. Demons as enemies, who waylay the dead.

All sorts of demons threaten the dead as his enemies. Often a spell, against this danger, states: "His enemy has no power over him" [7]). Enemies, who threaten the king in his ascension, are repelled.

---

1) Pyr. 163.d. H. P. Blok, AcOr VII, p. 108.
2) H. Kees, *Götterglaube*, p. 184; C.T. II. 298. a.
3) C.T. V. 363.e. f.
4) B.D. 182; 480. 10. 11; 481. 15. 16; 483. 5-7.
5) Sottas, p. 161.
6) B.D. 183; 488. 15. 16.
7) C.T. II. 47.d; V. 328.b; 329.e.

"Your enemies perish. They perish. If they fly out against you, they will be thrown into the lake. They are thrown into the sea" [1]).

Many funerary spells give power to fight the enemies. The god "from whom I have sprung, may he make me have power over my enemies, who are in heaven and on earth. I have chased them away from their tombs. I have upset their buildings. I have chased them away from their seats. I punish their rank. I damage their magical power. I destroy their glory. I assign them to (a punishment), as he who arose spontaneously has ordered to be done against my enemies, namely the dead, the living, who are in heaven and on earth, who will damage my plants in my field, who will not raise me, who will not proclaim for me the way to the *hny*-boat" [2]). Here the enemies are of various kinds: demons and spirits of the dead, but also people living on earth. They try to damage the grave of the dead with the laying-out around it. This would be disastrous for his survival. He, on his part, threatens them with disturbing their graves. It is stated that the dead has power over his enemies, so that they cannot harm him. "You have power over your male and female enemy. You have power over those who act against you in the realm of the dead. You have power over him who orders to act against you in the realm of the dead" [3]).

As the masculine as well as the feminine forms, *ḫfty* and *ḫft.t*, occur in the sequence *mt*, *mt.t* etc., who are charmed in magical texts, it is evident that it concerns demoniacal beings, who will do harm to the dead [4]). The enemy is charmed by uttering a spell over his statue. This imitative magic is executed on statues of enemies. What one wants to attain in reality is performed symbolically. "May you destroy and exterminate him, this enemy. May you place him under your feet for ever. To speak words over the statue of an enemy, made of wax" [5]). The dead is happy, when his enemy cannot harm him any more. "Her enemy has fallen for her" [6]). "I have power over my enemies, who are in *ʾIw Nšiši*. I pass safely" [7]). The dead leaves the netherworld, where his enemies waylay him. "The darkness

---

[1]) Pyr. 2186.a. b.
[2]) C.T. I. 400.a. b. c. d.; 401.a-c; 402.a-e; 403.a-c; 404.a-c; 405.a.
[3]) C.T. Spell 225; III. 230.a-232.a.
[4]) Cf. C.T. I. 12.e-13.d.
[5]) C.T. I. 156.d-157.a.
[6]) C.T. VI. 74.o.
[7]) C.T. VI. 270.w. x.

is lighted. You go out into the day. You have power over your enemies . . . Your arm has power over your enemies" [1]). The enemies rob the offerings of the dead. A demon is invoked to fight them. "Oh devourer of millions, oh ass, oppose yourself to these enemies of Osiris N.N., who will go to meet her in order to take her bread away from her" [2]). The dead devours his enemies, like a demoniacal god pieces of meat. "His enemies are his pieces of meat. The enemies of his *k3* are the pieces of meat of *B3by* in this night of sleep (?). He has power over him" [3]). Gods conquer the deceased's enemies for him. "All gods make you appear. They fell your enemies for you on this beautiful day" [4]). Geb helps the dead like he has helped Osiris. "Listen what your father Geb has done for you. He has placed your enemies under you for you" [5]). Servants, who carry the coffin at the funeral, say the same: "Words spoken by the servants: I throw your enemies under you" [6]). The dead has helpers, who save him from his waylayers. "My followers kill my enemies for me" [7]). Certain rites give him protection. "If this ritual will be done for him, Re is his protection. Then none of his enemies will know him in the realm of the dead, in heaven, on earth, everywhere, where he goes" [8]).

B.17.b. Enemies as opponents in a law-suit.

The dead appears before a court of justice consisting of gods. He is there together with his opponents, who litigate with him. Against these enemies the case is decided in his favour. Here there may be thought of the law-suit between Osiris and Seth before the court of justice of Re in Heliopolis.

The "Letters to the dead", some of which go back as far as the Old Kingdom, mention spirits of dead, who behave in a hostile way towards the surviving. Sometimes the spirit of a deceased is invoked in order to fight this inimical dead. They litigate before a court of justice consisting of gods in the hereafter. A mother calls for the help of the deceased son against an enemy, who lodges a complaint against her before a court of justice of gods [9]). "Make

---

1) C.T. VI, Spell 655; 276.a. b. h.
2) C.T. Spell 656; VI. 276.l-p.
3) C.T. VI. 289.j-l.
4) C.T. VI. 326.l. m.
5) C.T. Spell 761; VI. 391.d. e.
6) E. Lüddeckens, *Totenklagen*, 66 (Rekhmara).
7) B.D. 17, Naville II. 72.
8) Rubric B.D. 148; 366. 11-14.
9) A. Piankoff, J. J. Clère, *A letter to the dead on a bowl in the Louvre*, J.E.A., XX, pp. 157-169.

an obstruction against the male and female enemy with an evil character against your house, your brother, your mother". The son in his turn has to give evidence against this plaintiff before the court of justice. "Be for yourself the (most) praised one of my male and female dead. You know that he said to me: I will lodge a complaint against you and your children. Lodge a complaint against it. Behold, you are in the place of justification." So the one dead must fight the other who waylays somebody alive [1]).

A litigation takes place against the dead. He hopes to emerge from it victorious. "May you justify the soul of N.N. against his enemies in heaven and on earth in these 7 councils, the councils of Osiris" [2]). Here Osiris is president of the court. Such a law-suit is also mentioned in a text, which serves for becoming a human falcon, for beatifying somebody in the realm of the dead and for making somebody have power over his enemies [3]). "My claim is admitted in the council on account of what has been done against me unjustly by my enemies . . . I am a human falcon . . . I go and I come, so that I shoot at my enemy as a human being. I have gone to battle with him in the council of *Ḫnty ʾImnty.w*. In the night I have been judged with him on the side of those of his who are in the realm of the dead. His lawyer, who is in the council, is standing there, with his hands at his face, after having seen that I am justified . . . I have appeared as a great falcon. I have seized him with my claws." The dead identifies himself with a falcon. As such he has the strength to conquer his enemies. The latter loses a lawsuit in the council of the judges of the dead. His lawyer makes a gesture of despair, when he sees that the case is lost. A victory in a lawsuit is also mentioned in the following passage from the Book of the Dead [4]): "The great red crown is given to me. I go out against this enemy of mine in the daytime. I fetch him. I have power over him. He is delivered to me. He is not taken away from me. He has the worst of me in the council." Compare with this the following passages. "I seek my enemy (in order to beat him). It is given to me that he has the worst of me in the council" [5]). "Somebody goes out against his enemy in the realm

---

[1]) Cf. *wḏʿ mdw*, C.2.b.
[2]) C.T. V. 227.g. h.
[3]) C.T. Spell 149; II. 228.b; 229.a; 230.c; 232.c. d.; 233.a-235.a; 236.b. c.
[4]) B.D. 179; 469. 15-470. 2; C.T. VI. 193.j-m.
[5]) C.T. VI. 86.g. h.

of the dead" [1]). "I ascend, I descend against this enemy. He has been delivered up to me, while he has been defeated by me" [2]). Also in this connection "his lawyer, who is in the council" is mentioned [3]). "I go out (victoriously) against this enemy of mine. I come from the council today, after I have been heard with him" [4]).

The dead speaks like Horus: "I am tried. I am justified, I have power over my enemies" [5]). "My purification is the purification of Horus, after he has bound his enemy, after he has been justified against him who speaks to him (= litigates?)" [6]). In the judgment the dead's case is decided in his favour. "Oh Osiris N.N., rise, descend into the council. You are justified to your enemies, to those who act against you, who hate you. On this day there will be a decision between you and them" [7]). "Life is given to him for his nose, justification against his enemies" [8]). "That somebody may have power over his enemy (identification with gods follows in order to strengthen his position) . . . My power is that of Thoth. He (the dead) goes on his feet. He speaks with his mouth in search of his enemy. He has been given up to N.N. in the council. He is not taken away from him. N.N. has power over him. He (the enemy) has the worst of him" [9]). "I go out against my enemy in the daytime. I have power over him. He has been given up to me. He is not taken away from me. He has got the worst of me in the council. The great place, which is on the sceptre of the gods has given him to me. He belongs to my claws as a lion. He belongs to my grip as a crocodile. The way is paved for me, that I may lead my enemy away . . . I am the lord of the violent ones. I am not robbed . . . It is effected that I go out on this day against my enemy. I lead him away. I have power over him" [10]).

B.17.c. The enemies of the dead as opponents of Osiris.

In the myth of Osiris there is a conflict between this god and his enemies, the gang of Seth. The dead is identified with Osiris and knows, like he does, how to conquer his enemies.

1) C.T. VI. 86.j.
2) C.T. VI. 91.g. h.
3) C.T. VI. 91.j.
4) C.T. II. 57.a-c. See also C.T. II. 62.a-c; II. 66.c; C.T. VI, Spell 577; B.D. 10 and 11.
5) B.D. 138; 314. 4. 5.
6) C.T. VI. 119.k-m; read *ḳ3ś* instead of *ḳ3ḥ*?
7) C.T. I. 8.d-9.c.
8) B.D. 178; 467. 11.
9) C.T. Spell 569; VI. 168.a. e; 169.a-i.
10) C.T. Spell 577; VI. 192.a-193.b. e. f. k-m.

Just as Osiris by his mother Nut and his father Geb the dead also is protected from his enemies. "Osiris N.N., your mother Nut has expanded over you . . . She has made you be a god. Your enemy does not exist in your name of God. She has saved you from all evil in her name of *Ḫnm.t wr*" [1]). "Listen what your father Geb has done for you. He has placed your enemies under you for you" [2]).

The dead is put on a par with Osiris. He now has a position of authority and conquers his enemies. "You stand in the two chapels before the jackal-gods. You strike your hand against your enemies, whom Anubis, who is in the chapel, has given to you, because he institutes you, oh Neith, as *Ḫnty ʾImnty.w*" [3]). As Osiris the dead overmasters the gang of Seth. Horus and Thoth assist him in this, as they also do in the myth of Osiris. "He (Horus) has effected that Thoth makes those who are behind Seth, recede for you" [4]). "Horus has made you seize your enemies. There is no one of them who can withdraw from you" [5]). "He (Horus) has given the gods, your enemies, up to you. Thoth brings them to you" [6]). "I am Thoth, the son of your son, seed of your seed. I have taught you in the inside of the sun, that I should glorify you and should fell your enemies for you, so that they are placed in the slaughter-place of Hermopolis" [7]). "My son Horus has saved me with his mother Isis from this enemy, who has done this against me" [8]). "Osiris N.N. deceased, Horus has saved you, he has destroyed the jaws of your enemies" [9]).

The gang of Seth threatens the dead, but is made harmless. "I am the one, who opens your way, who fells your enemy for you, who slashes his gang to pieces for you, who comes against you, your food and your dignity" [10]). Like Osiris the dead is protected against the gang of Seth. In a spell of a staff, which gives protection, it reads: "Spell of a staff. What stands, stands behind Osiris. A staff stands behind Osiris. It beats the enemies, the gang (of Seth). Sharp one of

---

[1]) Pyr. 1607.a-1608.a.

[2]) C.T. Spell 761; VI. 391.d. e.

[3]) Pyr. Neith 730.

[4]) Pyr. 575.b. For Thoth as helper against Seth see Pyr. 635.c; 16.b; 651.b; 1336.a. b; 1658.b; 1979.c; in co-operation with Horus 956.b; 1570.b; commentary of Sethe III. 179.

[5]) Pyr. 579.b.

[6]) Pyr. 1979.c.

[7]) C.T. I. 231.c-232.a.

[8]) C.T. III. 260.g.

[9]) C.T. Spell 783; VI. 413.j. k.

[10]) C.T. I. 193.b-d.

front, great one of strength, which cuts the enemies of Osiris, put your arm protectingly behind me . . . that I become justified . . . I am his child" [1]). Isis says to the dead as Osiris: "I have placed your enemies under your soles" [2]). Also in the myth of Osiris the latter's victory over Seth is thus formulated that Seth is placed under him [3]). "Horus has brought you Seth: He has given him to you, while he is bent under you" [4]).

B.17.d. Sinners as enemies of Re or of Osiris.

This usage is especially found in the *Livres*. There the "enemies" are those who have sinned against Re or Osiris on earth and who have to expiate these in the realm of the dead by hellish punishments. *Ḫfty.wt* is the name of four women, represented in a lower register. They have been condemned because they have sinned against Osiris [5]). In the Book of Gates [6]) in the so-called "Judgment hall of Osiris" four enemies are pictured under the throne of Osiris. The inscription going with it reads: "His enemies are under his feet. Gods and spirits are before him. He sends his enemies to their destruction. He carries out their slaughter". Gods and spirits are the just dead, who have a happy fate in the realm of the dead. The enemies are the sinners who are condemned. A lower register of the Book of Gates deals with a punishment of sinners [7]). It is said about them: "These enemies are thus . . ." After which a description follows of their punishment by Horus. They are destroyed by the *Ḫty*-serpent. Sinners are punished in hell as enemies of the sun-god. Re says to condemned [8]): "You belong to this one who destroys my enemies." Now the term "enemy of Re" occurs already earlier than in the tombs of the kings. This denomination is used for mythical enemies of Re of the same nature as Apophis. When later in the netherworld punished sinners are called in the same way, they are put on a par with these mythical enemies of Re. A Coffin Text mentions "this day, on which the enemies of the Lord of the universe are destroyed" [9],

---

1) C.T. Spell 646; VI. 266.b-h.k.
2) B.D. 151; 382. 14. 15.
3) Pap. Jumilhac XX. 10.
4) Pyr. 1632.a.
5) L.Q. XXXIV. 3.
6) B.S. Pl. V; H. Frankfort, *The Cenotaph of Seti I at Abydos*, Vol. II, Pl. LV. Th. M. Davis' Excavations, Bibân el Mulûk, The Tombs of Harmhabi and Touatânkhamanou by G. Maspero, Pl. LIII.
7) Book of Gates VIII, lower register, B.S. Pl. XV. 9. 10.
8) L.Q. L. 2.
9) C.T. IV. 284.b; B.D. 17.

or there is talked of "the council which punishes the enemies of Re" [1]). The sinners who are punished in the texts from the tombs of the kings, are essentially identical with the cosmic enemies of Re.

They try to disturb the world-order, which is established by the sun-god in his regular course. "Oh Re, those enemies of Osiris N.N. thought that they could take the great white crown of your head... they thought that they would disturb the truth...." [2]). The enemies of the dead are also here the enemies of Re. They try to disturb *m3ʿ.t*, the cosmic order, which is established by Re. Also the sinners in the Book of Gates are punished, because they have not effected *m3ʿ.t*. Disturbance of the cosmic and the ethical order is the same, according to the Egyptian view. The part which the sinners have played towards Re and the punishment which is meted out to them, are essentially the same as the point at issue regarding the mythical enemies of the sun-god.

B.17.e. *Ḫfty* as devil.

Apophis, the enemy of Re, is punished in the netherworld [3]). Like other condemned sinners he is represented with the head downwards. Atum stands before this scene and executes the sentence. The inscription reads: "Atum says to these gods, who bear *ʿnḫ*- and *w3s*-signs, who lean on their *ḏʿm*-sceptres: "Ward off the enemy from Akhty. Make a slaughter in the flesh of the malicious one." Apophis is punished in the same way as the sinners, the enemies of Re. In B.D. 39 Apophis is called *ḫfty n Rʿ* time and again. Apophis is the chief devil. In punishing evil he also meets with judgment just as in the Revelation of John Satan is also condemned. That *ḫfty*, in contrast with *nṯr*, may have our meaning of "devil", also appears from some other places. "Greatness of heart is a gift of god, but he who indulges his passion, belongs to the devil" [4]). In a medical text it says: "A worm has stung into this belly of mine, whether god has done it, or the devil" [5]).

B.18. *Instruments of torture.*

In the netherworld there are devices with which the dead may be tortured.

---

1) C.T. IV. 304.b.
2) C.T. VI. 277.q-s; 278.d.
3) Book of Gates II, lower register, B.S. Pl. III. 28-Pl. II. 35.
4) Wisdom of Ptahhotep 247-248.
5) Ebers 19. 7 sq. = Sethe, *Äg. Lesestücke*², 48. 20.

B.18.a. *3b*, branding-iron.

In a chapter of the Book of the Dead, which deals with gates, where all kinds of tortures await the dead, it is said about one of these gates: "It loves the fire, which purifies the branding-irons. It loves the cutting off of heads" [1]). Apparently the passer-by may be marked with a branding-iron at this gate. The branding-iron was used in order to brand a mark of property into cattle or slaves [2]). Sometimes it is also applied as a means of punishment, e.g., by Anubis, who chastises Seth. After Seth has changed himself into a leopard, Anubis puts a glowing branding-iron on him everywhere, so that scorching-marks arise [3]). This is an aethiological myth, which explains how the panther comes by his spots.

B.18.b. *wśr.t*, torturing-post.

In the Book of Gates [4]) poles are pictured in the shape of the *wśr*-sign, with two condemned tied with their backs to them. They are called the *wśr.t*-posts of various gods, Re, Atum, Shu etc. In the text we read: "To approach the *wśr.t*-posts of Geb by this great god, to which the enemies (of Re) are counted out after the judgment in the West." The sinners are condemned to this punishment by the judge of the dead. "Sia says to this great god, when he approaches the *wśr.t*-posts of Geb . . .: Great god, behold, you approach the *wśr.t* of Geb. Atum says to the *wśr.t*-posts: Watch over the enemies, seize the rebels." The *wśr.t*-posts of Geb also occur in the Book of the Dead [5]) in a connection, which is not clear: *Mk št3.w śb3.w ḥr wśr.t twy n.t Gb.*

B.18.c. *mnì.t*, mooring-post.

This object is also used as torturing-post [6]). Re speaks to the cave of the two mooring-posts on his journey through the realm of the dead [7]). "Oh hidden one of arm (a goddess), who is put over the two mooring-posts, who watches over the enemies of Osiris, you have delivered the enemies of Osiris. You have tied them to the two

1) B.D. 146; 357. 2. 3. For *3b.t* compare Pyr. 675.b.

2) Wb. I. 6. 18; Luise Klebs, *Die Reliefs und Malereien des neuen Reiches*, I. 70.

3) Papyrus Jumilhac XI; play on *3b*, branding-iron and *3b*, panther.

4) Book of Gates, V, middle register, E. Lefébure, M.M.A.F.C. III, 1, Pl. XXX. 13-26. See H. P. Blok, AcOr VII, p. 103, 104.

5) B.D. 12; C.T. Spell 452; V. 321.a. b.

6) Wb. II. 73. 8.

7) L.Q. XCVII. 5. 6.

mooring-posts." The enemies of Osiris are sinners, who are punished in the realm of the dead. They are addressed in the following way: "Oh you who are tied to the posts, watched by the posts, you are these burnt ones, bound on account of the evil they have done against the mysteries of the great god" [1]). It here concerns people, who are punished on account of a cultic transgression. The dead asks that he may be saved from this punishment: "Save me from the mooring-posts of those who tie to their mooring-posts. Do not tie me to your mooring-posts. Do not put me in the place of the punished ones" [2]).

B.18.d. *šmś.t*, device of decapitation. 

A picture of this occurs in Am Duat [3]). This device is also mentioned in a Pyramid Text [4]): "Your mouth is closed by the instrument of torture, the mouth of the instrument of torture is closed by the panther-cat."

B.18.e. *d3s.wy*, torturing-posts.

A goddess in the netherworld holds a post in each hand, to which a kneeling enemy is tied with his back. The inscription to it says [5]): "This goddess is like this: In guarding the enemies of Re, who are counted out to the two *d3s*-posts, which are in her and which do not let loose what has been given to them. Re ... says to this cave: Oh slaughterer, who is in the place of destruction, who watches over my own enemies, whom I have placed in the darkness, ... you have knotted with both your arms, counting for you ... the two *d3s*-posts, which are in the earth, that they may count my enemies." This is a complete conception of hell. It concerns a dark place, where those who have sinned against Re and who are condemned, are tortured.

B.19. *Terms from hunting.*

The punishments or dangers of the realm of the dead are represented as a being caught like an animal in hunting.

---

[1]) L.Q. XCVIII. 2-3.
[2]) B.D. 180; 473. 6 sqq.
[3]) Am Duat VIII, middle register, Bucher Pl. VII; Capart Z.Ä.S. 36, p. 125.
[4]) Pyr. 230.c with commentary of Sethe.
[5]) L.Q. LXV. 9-LXVI. 6.

B.19.a. *i3d.t*, net [1]).

The chapters B.D. 153 A and B deal with the fact that the dead may be caught in a net. According to Naville [2]) A concerns the catching of birds and B the catching of fish, but it remains to be seen whether this distinction must be made so sharply.

B.D. 153 A reads: "Spell in order to escape the net. Oh catcher, who catches. Oh catcher, who catches his prey, who goes about in the stream [3]). Do not catch me with this net of yours, in which you catch these tired ones [4]). Do not trap me in your snares, in which you catch the "birds of passage" [5]), the floats of which reach to heaven and the weights to the earth" [6]). A.o. a fishing-net with floats is mentioned here, which draw the net up, and the counter-weights, which pull the bottom down, so that the net takes a vertical position. However, the net is spread between heaven and earth, so that it may catch the souls of people, who fly about like birds or who are on their way from the earth to heaven. A similar view is also found in some Coffin Texts. "Spell not to land in the net that catches" [7]). "Hurry, rise (Osiris N.N.), seize the tail of the big cow, the companion of Anubis, which knows the roads to the West. Those who travel along the heavens, make you travel along, who cross the vault of heaven, who turn *t3 ḏśr*. Travel hastily along the slaughter-place [8]). Hasten past the net, the net of *Ḫnty 'Imnty.w*, which catches, the floats of which are in heaven and the weights on earth, which is made for these spirits, which have gone to their *k3*, which have not failed. Then you will cool down by the cool waters of the son of Re" [9]). "May I not be caught in the net of Shu" [10]). Here also it seems to concern a fishing-net, which has been suspended between heaven and earth and which might be able to catch the

[1]) M. Alliot, *Le rite de la chasse au filet aux temples de Karnak, d'Edfou et d'Esneh*, *Revue d'Égyptologie* V (1946), pp. 57-118; *Les auxiliaires de chasse du tueur d'oiseaux*, *Bull. de la Soc. Fr. d'Ég.*, VI, 1951, pp. 17-24.

[2]) *Papyrus Funéraires de la XXI Dyn.*, 1912, pp. 37, 38, Papyrus Nesichons, Pl. XXVII, XXVIII, near 153 A is the vignette of a bird-net, near 153 B that of a fishing-net.

[3]) This makes one think of fishing.

[4]) *nni.w* = the dead.

[5]) Wb. III. 343. 8. It is not certain whether they are indeed birds.

[6]) A fishing-net.

[7]) C.T. IV. 348.a.

[8]) The net is meant.

[9]) C.T. Spell 343; IV. 351.c-356.b.

[10]) C.T. III. 296.f.

spirit of the dead, which flies to the West along the heavens. The net of Shu also reminds us of spirits of the dead, which fly through the sky, but which are caught by a net like fish swimming in a stream. So it regards fishing and bird-catching at the same time.

C.T. Spells 473-481 are the older version of B.D. 153. No more than in the texts from the New Kingdom it is clear there, what is exactly meant, bird-catching or fishing. The conceptions are mixed up. Several terms for net are used, e.g., *i3d.t*, determined with the clap-net for bird-catching [1]), *ibṯ.t* with the same determinative [2]), *iss.t* [3]) and *ḏśf* [4]). In Spell 473 the words *i3d.t* and *iss.t* are used. Sometimes here is thought of the bird-net. The dead charms the net by saying, that he knows the parts. He says a.o.: "For I know the name of my peg which is in it" [5]). This is a part of the bird-net [6]).

Just as in B.D. 153 also here the "tired ones" are mentioned [7]), The *ḫty.w t3*, "the marchers through the country", do not seem to be here "birds of passage", which are caught, but demons, who want to catch the dead and who are kept off. At least he says to them [8]): "They are coming, the "marchers through the country". Do not catch me into your nets, in which you catch the tired ones. Come, "marchers through the country", for I know your name." In the following spell [9]), however, they are the *ḫty.w t3* who are caught and there, indeed, it could be birds of passage. "Do not catch N.N. in this net (trap?) of yours, in which you catch the "birds of passage".

The many parts that are enumerated [10]) must be rather thought of as being the complicated bird-net with its rods and draw-cords than of the simple drag-net for fishing. The trap-layers and fowlers [11]) are only involved in fowling.

'I3d.t is, however, a general term, which is used for the bird-net as well as for the fishing-net. "*Le mot i3d.t s'appliquait a tout ce qui*

---

1) C.T. VI. 37.h.

2) Determined with the legs and the earth, as if it is an object jumping up from the earth.

3) C.T. VI. 3.a, determinative a wooden scaffolding for a trap.

4) Determined with knife, rope and knot, consequently a snare.

5) C.T. VI. 6.f.

6) Wb. II. 132. 14.

7) C.T. VI. 3.e. g., name for dead ones with an unhappy fate.

8) C.T. VI. 3. h-4.c.

9) C.T. Spell 474; VI. 17.f.

10) C.T. VI. 4.g sqq.

11) C.T. VI. 23.i.

était en filet, quels qu'en fussent la forme et l'usage, à un engin pour la chasse aux canards, à un sac à larges mailles qui servait à transporter les gerbes du blé, au vêtement transparent dont les favorites du Pharaon couvraient, sans les voiler, leurs charmes" [1]). So *i3d.t* may be used for the drag-net in fishing as well as for the clap-net in fowling.

In the mastabas *gw3 i3d.t* is used as term for the drawing together and dragging ashore of the fishing-net [2]) and this term also occurs in the Spells 473-481 of the Coffin Texts. "N.N. knows the territory, where it (the net) is drawn together" [3]). "Do not draw me together on the sides of it, in the middle of it" [4]). It is said expressly that fish are caught in it: "For I know the name of this man, who descends, that he may catch fish in it" [5]). Just as in B.D. 153 floats and weights are mentioned, which keep the net in a vertical position: "For I know the name of the floats at the top and the weights at the bottom"[6]). *'I3d.t* is sometimes determined as a drag-net, an oval sign with two projections, by which the drawcords at the extremities must be meant [7]). Also where a boat is mentioned we have to think of fishing. "For I know the name of the boat in which she catches." "This boat, in which she catches, it is this big ship" [8]). The parts of the boat are mentioned, such as the steering-oar, the pole to push-off and the oars.

The conclusion based on the Coffin Texts is that all sorts of nets are mentioned here, for fishing as well as fowling, while beside the most usual word net, *i3d.t*, also terms for bird-trap, snare and clap-net are used. The dead fears to be caught in traps by demons and to be consumed afterwards as their victim, as happens with caught fish or birds. "Catcher, poacher, hidden one of fingers, take this net of yours away, this hidden one of yours, which catches food. Live on the bow-nets of Re, on the traps of *'Imy-ḫnt Wr*. N.N. has escaped them" [9]). Also M. Alliot is of the opinion that in the chapters of the Book of the Dead 153 A and B and 154 we must think of fowling as well as fishing. In this way the members of the gang of Seth are caught. He points out that the vignettes show bird- as well

[1]) Montet, *Scènes de la vie privée*, p. 34.
[2]) Montet, op. cit., p. 34.
[3]) C.T. VI. 9. d; 19.a; 24.m.
[4]) C.T. VI. 30.b.
[5]) C.T. VI. 7.g. Cf. 19.c; 32.c; 40.a.
[6]) C.T. VI. 10.c. Cf. 17.g; 18.g; 31.g.
[7]) C.T. VI. 29.b.
[8]) C.T. VI. 10.f; 38.t; 39.f.
[9]) C.T. VI. 21.i-m.

as fishing-nets [1]). The dead is not caught together with the gang of Seth [2]). "This is the net of the strong catcher. It closes and does not let loose." A net is pictured, in which enemies as birds are caught, but in the continuation also fish are caught. "It catches marsh-birds. He takes along in it catch and prey, many fish, countless. He takes along in it fishes, that is to say Troglodytes and birds, that is to say the Beduins (fish and birds mixed) [3]).

The helpers of Osiris hunt Seth and his followers as a hunter with catching-nets and bow and arrow [4]).

B.19.b. *ỉbṯ.t*, bird-trap.

In the spells directed against the net, the dead also rejects being caught in a bird-trap. "For I know the name of the ropes, these four ropes, which are in this bird-trap of *Sbk*" [5]). Also the *ỉbṯ.ty.w* are mentioned, the fowlers, "who take away the souls, who lock the shadows up" [6]). The dead is saved from them. There is also a version of a spell from the New Kingdom against the bird-trap. "Spell to escape a bird-trap" [7]). About the demons invoked, who threaten the dead, it is said: "They can catch birds and fishes, which go into the water" [8]). "Do not set up against me, do not lead me to your nets, let me free, that I may go on earth" [9]).

B.19.c. *ỉśś*, to catch, *ỉśś.t*, trap-net.

C.T. Spell 477 is "another spell to escape from the trap-net" [10]). In C.T. Spell 480 we read: "Do not lead me away in this trap-net of yours, in which you seize the tired ones, in which you lead away the "birds of passage" [11]). The weights and floats are mentioned, by which we have to think of the drag-net again [12]). In B.D. 153 A the verb *ỉśś* occurs. "Do not catch me in these trap-nets, into which you catch the "birds of passage" [13]).

---

[1]) Rev. d'Eg. V, pp. 113, 114.

[2]) Op. cit., pp. 79-80.

[3]) Op. cit., p. 80; determinative bird-trap. The translation "he takes from it with him" also deserves consideration.

[4]) Papyrus Jumilhac XIV. 23 sqq.

[5]) C.T. Spells 473; 481; VI. 7.b.c. Cf. 17.h *ỉbỉ* and 21. 1; 37.h spelled *ỉb.t-t3*.

[6]) C.T. VI. 73.e. f; 75.l-n.

[7]) Louvre 3283, V. 1, *r3 n pr.t r rw.ty ỉbṯ.t*.

[8]) Idem V. 3, *rḫ.śn m ḥ3m rsf nty šm m ẖnw mw*.

[9]) Idem V. 4-5, *ỉmỉ grg r.ỉ ỉmỉ ỉn wỉ n ỉ3d.t.ṯn mỉ n.ỉ w3.t šm.ỉ m t3*.

[10]) C.T. VI. 34.a.

[11]) C.T. VI. 43.m-44.a.

[12]) C.T. VI. 44.n. o.

[13]) B.D. Budge, p. 390. 11-12; C.T. VI. 17.f.

B.19.d. *ʿmʿ3.t*, boomerang.

There is a spell which has to prevent the dead being caught with a boomerang by demons. "To keep the boomerang off. Backwards, quick, hasty boomerang, messenger of the gods, which the gods let go from the banks of the *nḫ3*-lake, to meet their children . . ., to take away their magical power, to take away their glory . . . I have withdrawn from you (i.e., I have escaped you)" [1]. *ʿmʿ3.t* is determined with a bent stick, hence the meaning boomerang and not only club [2]. In C.T. Spell 62 [3] it is described how the dead hunts on birds with a boomerang in a watery country. "Waterbirds come to you and m.—animals, placed on your roads, after you have thrown your boomerang at them. There are a thousand of them, which have fallen on account of its buzzing, (thousand) of geese." The dead hits snakes with it, which waylay him [4]. So *ʿmʿ3.t* is a typical hunting term.

B.19.e. *ʿḫ*, net.

The dead escapes it. "You hurry along the valley of the net" [5].

B.19.f. *wḥʿ*, to catch (fish), catcher.

A goddess is invoked by the dead for protection: "Save me from the catchers of Osiris" [6]. The term also occurs in B.D. 153 A [7] and 153 B [8] and in the M.K. version [9]. In the spells for escaping the net, the "catchers" are conjured not to catch the dead [10]: "Oh these four catchers of the drag-net, . . ., do not oppose N. inimically with this net of the drag-net." The catchers are called "hidden of fingers" [11]. The dead charms them by saying that he knows their names [12].

---

1) C.T. Spell 418; V. 252.a-253.a; 254.b. c; 256.b.

2) See about this term P. Montet, *Scènes de la vie privée*, pp. 18-20. Gardiner, Egyptian grammar, 3rd ed. 1957, sign list T, 14 p. 513, states that the bent stick is used in the sense of throw-stick as well as in the sense of club, a foreign weapon of war. W. Wolf, *Die Bewaffnung des altägyptischen Heeres*, Leipzig, 1926, p. 7 note 3, says: "*Das Wurfholz, für das man das Zeichen des gekrümmten Stockes fälschlich gehalten hat, ist in Ägypten niemals als Kriegswaffe, sondern stets nur als Jagdwaffe benutzt worden.*" So Wolf sees in the sign of the bent stick only a foreign weapon. Gardiner l.c. points out that the combination of the bent stick with the bird G 41 makes the value "throw-stick" for the sign T 14 plausible.

3) C.T. I. 269.c-j.

4) C.T. VI. 316.e.

5) C.T. IV. 353.d.

6) C.T. III. 295.h.

7) B.D. Budge, p. 390. 5-6.

8) B.D. Budge, p. 396. 1.

9) C.T. Spells 473-481.

10) C.T. VI. 20.e. h.

11) C.T. VI. 20.q.

12) C.T. VI. 22.o.

They are the *3kr.w*, who are before Atum, who are before Geb [1]. The dead says to them [2]: "Oh catchers, children of their father, who catch and go about in the valley, do not catch N.N. in this net of yours, with which you catch the tired ones." Compare with this the denomination of Horus, who catches the enemies of the king [3]: "The catcher, who goes out into the night."

B.19.g. *wsf*, fisherman.

This one stands on a level with the *śḫty* [4], the fowler, as a being who threatens the dead.

B.19.h. *nḏḫ*, to catch with the lasso.

The dead wishes not to get entangled into a lasso lest he should be kept off from his ascension. "On whose back no lasso has fallen, on whose arm nothing bad has fallen" [5].

B.19.i. *rtḫ*, to catch.

An inscription in a Ptolemaic temple [6] mentions that the king catches his enemies in a net. It there regards "a book to catch people". The description mentions a bird-trap, consisting of two halves [7].

B.19.j. *ḥ3m*, to catch (fish) [8].

B.D. 153 B is a "spell in order to escape from the fishing-net" [9]. In the Middle Kingdom version of spells like these we read [10]: "Do not catch me into this net of yours, in which you catch the "birds of passage"." In inscriptions on Ptolemaic temples [11] *ḥ3m* is used of catching the enemies of the king like birds in a net. "Be caught in the night." That it here regards birds appears from the text [12]. "That I may bring you hundreds of thousands (of birds), which alight. He brings you all birds of *Ḳbḥ.w*."

---

1) C.T. VI. 23.a, so gods of the earth.
2) C.T. VI. 17.c-e.
3) M. Alliot, *Les rites de la chasse au filet*, Rev. d'Eg. V. 73.
4) C.T. VI. 27.a.
5) Pyr. 1021.c.
6) M. Alliot, *Les rites de la chasse au filet*, Rev. d'Eg. V. 60.
7) Op. cit., p. 71.
8) See under *i3d.t*, net, B.D. 153; C.T. III. 296.f; IV. 348.a; 354.b.
9) For fishing-net it here reads *ḥ3m ftft*, literally "which catches the jumpers"; it concerns fishes which jump up in the net.
10) C.T. VI. 37.l-m.
11) M. Alliot, *Les rites de la chasse au filet*, Rev. d'Eg. V. 61.
12) Op. cit., p. 71.

B.19.k. *śpḥ*, to catch with the lasso.

The dead fears that he will be caught with the lasso like a cow to be brought to a slaughter-place. In a Pyramid Text it is used in a cannibalistic passage. God and men are caught for the dead king. He eats them and appropriates their strength in this way. "It is the seizer of the skull, who catches them with the lasso for N.N. "[1]). In B.D. 17 a demon occurs, "a god, who throws a lasso around the evil-doers, in order to take them to his slaughter-place" [2]). Here it is a punishment for evil-doers. A god, who protects the dead, says [3]): "Who comes to catch with the lasso, I shall not permit you to catch with the lasso. Who comes to hit, I shall not permit to hit, but I shall hit (you), I shall catch (you) with the lasso." The dead is safe from this danger: "He is divine, his corpse is complete, he is saved from the place of judgment, he does not catch him with the lasso" [4]). Apophis is punished by it in the netherworld. "He places the lasso of *Nikt* (a punishing goddess) around his feet" [5]). There is a twofold judgment of the dead. The just are protected, sinners are punished. "I take care of those who are in the netherworld. I catch enemies with the lasso for the place of destruction" [6]). The "enemies", who have sinned against the god, are caught with the lasso and taken to a slaughter-place as cattle.

B.19.l. *śḫty*, fowler.

It is a punishment for Seth that in the realm of the dead he becomes the prey of fowlers [7]). Also in B.D. 153 B [8]) and in the Middle Kingdom version, C.T. Spells 473-481, fowlers occur. "Oh catchers, oh children of their fathers, trap-setters and fowlers in the valley, do not catch this N.N. in your nets" [9]). In a spell for obtaining a ritual funeral it reads [10]): "N.N. you are one of these catchers [11]), who are before the trap-setters, who go to *Ṯnn.t*." Is the dead represented here as a helper of the demoniacal catchers, so that they will not harm him?

---

[1]) Pyr. 401.a.
[2]) C.T. IV. 300.b.
[3]) B.D. 151; 383. 4.
[4]) B.D. 165; 419. 7.
[5]) Am Duat VII. 79-80.
[6]) L.Q. XI. 8.
[7]) Papyrus Jumilhac XV. 20.
[8]) B.D. Budge, p. 396. 1.
[9]) C.T. VI. 23.g-j. Cf. 27.b.
[10]) Spell 549; C.T. VI. 147.b-e.
[11]) Wb. V. 534. II. See *ḏꜥr*, to look for, Wb. V. 539. 13. Perhaps the name indicates a certain function: "searchers", who hunt up the prey.

B.19.m. *grg*, setter of traps.

These setters of traps also occur in the spells of the net. "Oh children of their fathers, trap-setters and fowlers of the valley, do not catch this N.N. in your nets, do not ensnare N.N. in your nets, do not catch N.N. in this net of yours, in which you catch the tired ones, in which you ensnare the "birds of passage", for N.N. knows it up to the floats at the top and the counter-weights at the bottom" [1]). The terms *grg* and *sḫt* are used for catching birds with a trap or clap-net. The words floats and weights belong to the fishing-net.

B.19.n. *ḏśf*, to catch.

Also this term occurs in the spells of the fishing-net [2]). As a substantive it is determined by a knife, rope and knot [3]). Thus it might be a snare or a trap, in which birds are caught. The dead sets himself loose of it and ascends to heaven. "I am the one, who loosens "bonds" (*ḏśf.w*) . . ., I ascend to heaven among the gods" [4]).

B.20. *Categories of people, who take an unfavourable position in the hereafter.*

This part deals with persons, who have a sad fate in the realm of the dead. Sometimes it appears from the denominations, e.g., *iḫm.w*, who have been destroyed. Sometimes it is connected with their nature and character, e.g., concerning the *rḫy.t*, who as such form a lower grouping, or where it concerns non-Egyptians. It is not always easy here to tell these denominations apart from those for dead in general (A), as, e.g., B.20.c.d.e.

B.20.a. *i3d*, wretched one.

This is a denomination of condemned sinners in the realm of the dead [5]).

B.20.b. *iwty.w*, those who are not.

Thus the dead over which Osiris as king holds sway, are called. "I am Osiris, the bull of the West, the king of those who are not" [6]). In the Book of Gates surveyors occur. They stake plots out, in which the products for composing the food offering for the dead is grown. Only the just do receive such plots. "You are in harmony with those who are. You are not in harmony with those who are not" [7]). The

1) C.T. VI. 23.h-o.
2) B.D. 153 A; 390. 5.
3) C.T. VI. 37.h.
4) C.T. VI. 15.b-d.
5) L.Q. L. 1.
6) C.T. IV. 94.a.
7) Book of Gates IV, upper register, B.S. Pl. VI. 31. 32.

idea is: they give a favourable fate to the just in the realm of the dead, not to the unjust.

B.20.c. *imy.w Wśir*, who are in Osiris.

Here Osiris himself is the realm of the dead. In this case the dead are called: "Who are in Osiris" [1]. Their fate is mirthless, for it is a boon for them when they are shone upon by the sun when Re comes.

B.20.d. *imn.w ḥr.w.śn*, hidden ones of face.

Also this is a denomination for the dead [2]. Such a denomination probably indicates that their faces are wrapped, e.g., in mummy bandages, in consequence of which they cannot see.

B.20.e. *imnty.w* western ones.

This is a nisbe-form of *'Imn.t*, the West as realm of the dead. As far as this unfavourable place is conceived as the place where there is no full life any more, also the fate of those who stay there, is considered pessimistically. The dead king reigns like Osiris, the ruler of the subterranean realm of the dead. "You command the western ones, for you are the one, whom Osiris has placed on his throne, that you may guide the western ones" [3].

B.20.f. *iẖm.w*, who are destroyed [4].

This is a denomination of four sinners, enemies of Re, who are punished in the netherworld. They are placed with their heads downwards and are watched by a god with a cat's head. The inscription going with it reads: "Who are destroyed, blood-stained ones, crying ones, swollen ones, drowned ones, whose headdress does not exist among the spirits, to whom the eye of Horus is not near, whom *T3y.t* does not see, I deliver you to *ʿḥ3*, while you are fettered. I make you be counted out to *Miwty*, whose guarding one does not escape" [5].

B.20.g. *iẖmty.w*, see *wdb.w*.

B.20.h. *ʿ3m.w*, Asiatics, see *Nḥś.w*.

B.20.i. *wdb.w*, riverains.

In the *Livre de la Nuit* [6] there are pictured three groups of punished

[1] L.Q. a.o. XLVII. 5. [2] B.D. 80; 177. 11. [3] Pyr. Neith 733. 734.

[4] Wb. I. 125. 13, *auslöschen, annullieren*. Perhaps this word should be derived from *ẖm* = not to know, the meaning could be "those who do not know"; "unconscious ones". Cf. Wb. I. 125. 14-16.

[5] L.Q. XLVIII. 5-7. [6] 3rd gate, lower register, ed. A. Piankoff, p. 46.

ones, *wdb.w. iḫmty.w*, *ḥtrty.w*, all written with the land determinative. They are standing bending forward with their hands at their hair. Do they tear their hair in despair? They are on the banks of the wadi, along which the sun-boat is pulled.

B.20.j. *mḥy.w*, drowned ones.

These occur in the Book of Gates [1]. *'Imy Nw* says to them: "Oh drowned ones, who are in the water, swimmers, who are in the stream, see Re, who enters his boat, great of mystery. He takes care of the gods. He takes care of the spirits. Well then, get up, tired ones. See Re. He takes care of you. Re says to them: Exit for your heads (= your head above the water), oh sinking ones. Movement of the arms for your arms, oh overturned ones. Circulation for your legs, oh swimmers (= movement of arms and legs in swimming). Air for your noses, oh oppressed ones. May you dispose of your water. May you be content with your libations. Your gaits belong to Nun, your steps to the stream. Your souls, which are on earth, they are satisfied with their life. Their destruction does not exist. Their offerings consist of the offerings of the earth. Offerings are made to them on earth as to one, who has the disposal of his offerings on earth, together with (?) the one, whose soul is not in the earth." A similar passage occurs in Am Duat [2]. The picture shows swimmers in various attitudes. "Horus says to the drowned, the overturned, those lying on their backs (these are the attitudes of the three groups in the drawing), who are in Nun, denizens of the netherworld: Oh drowned ones, who are dark in Nun, whose arms are at the height of their faces, oh you whose faces are overturned in the netherworld, whose dorsal vertebrae are in the water, oh you, who float on Nun, as persons lying on their backs . . . breath belongs to your souls. They are not oppressed. Swimming-movements belong to your arms, they are not hindered. You go by way of Nun on your feet. You come from the water. You descend into the *hnhn*-water. You swim in the great Nile. You land on its bank. Your body does not decay. Your flesh does not go bad. You inhale what I have assigned to you. You are these who are in Nun, the drowned ones".

To gods in the realm of the dead it is said: "Keep watch over your

---

[1]) Book of Gates VIII, middle register, B.S. Pl. XIV. 25-55.
[2]) Am Duat X. 79 sqq.

bank, place water near the drowned who are in Nun. Make them land on the banks of your stream" [1]). In the *Livre de la Nuit* [2]) three persons called *mḥ.w*, occur.

Drowned ones may be the same here as "who are in Nun", a denomination, which occurs in the above passages and which may be found now and then as term for the dead. Nun is the realm of the dead. It is possible, however, that the texts cited have still another meaning. In the *Lebensmüde* the soul speaks of the drowned ones, who die on the bank. Also there they are called "tired ones" [3]), whose offering stones are empty. They have not had a ritual funeral. They do not receive funerary offerings. So they lack the complete survival after death. The passages from the Book of Gates and Am Duat give the impression that they fight this. They give the possibility that also for the drowned ones, who have not been buried ritually and for whom consequently the worst threatens, a favourable fate will still be possible in the realm of the dead.

B.20.k. *Mḏ3.w*, see *Nḥś.w*.

B.20.l. *nnty.w*, denizens of the *nn.t*, the counter-heaven.

They occur in the *Livre de la Nuit*, in the Kingdom of Osiris [4]). In the Pyramid Texts they people a subterranean realm of the dead. The dead king holds sway over them just as Osiris, the king of the netherworld, rules his subjects. "Those who are in the "counter-heaven" (as netherworld) belong to N.N." [5]). Their fate is less favourable than that of the king who is their superior.

B.20.m. *Nḥś.w*, negroes [6]).

In the *Livre de la Nuit* condemned ones occur in the lower register [7]). Among them are also foreign peoples: negroes, Nubians, Lybians

[1]) Am Duat V. 20. [2]) 3rd hour. [3]) See A.8.f.

[4]) 1st gate, 5th register, ed. Piankoff, p. 38; 9th gate, kingdom of Osiris, ed. Piankoff, p. 61; cf. 8th gate, ed. Piankoff, p. 66. [5]) Pyr. 166.c.

[6]) This is a geographical indication for inhabitants of Nubia. In the Old Kingdom they are still Hamitics. Only in later periods the *Nḥś.w* are negroes. H. Junker, *The first appearance of the negroes in history*, J. E. A. VII (1921), pp. 124. 125. For *Nḥś.w* as denizens of the banks of the Nile in lower Nubia and part of Middle Nubia, distinct from the *Mḏ3.w* as inhabitants of the hilly country in the desert, see G. Posener in Z.Ä.S., vol. 83 (1958), pp. 38-43.

[7]) 5th gate, 5th and 6th register. The foreign peoples have been represented kneeling, hands being tied on the back; the Egyptians, *rmṯ*, and the *rmṯ-dšr.t* stand upright, their hands being untied. So the Egyptians have a more favourable position than the foreigners have; ed. A. Piankoff, p. 51.

and Asiatics. They are the classic enemies of Egypt. In the Pyramid Texts doors occur, which keep certain persons off, so that they cannot sail to heaven like the king. It is these doors "which keep the Libyans at bay" [1]), "which keep the Phoenicians off" [2]). In these texts the residence of the king in heaven is considered analogous to the palace on earth. Also in heaven the king is in a place where his enemies cannot reach him. This involves that they have no part in the celestial happiness like the king. Sethe has devoted a study to the foreign peoples becoming involved in the Egyptian judgment of the dead [3]). He there deals with a passage from the introduction of B.D. 125 according to the Book of the Dead of Ani. Anubis speaks to a council of judges, consisting of the four sons of Horus. "Anubis said to his side (i.e., the gods on his side): The voice of a man, who comes from Egypt, who knows the way to us and our town. I am satisfied (with him). I smell his scent like that of one of you. He says to me: I am Osiris Ani, deceased, I have come here to see the great gods." Sethe remarks: As here especially an Egyptian is mentioned, also other nationalities arrive there. It is not said in this place, what happens to them. However, it might be concluded from this introduction to B.D. 125 that with Anubis an Egyptian has some advantage over foreigners who apparently do not know the way to the town of the realm of the dead. Further Sethe also points to a conversation with a door-keeper in B.D. 125. Thoth is mentioned there as interpreter of an Egyptian, who has to translate the words of the one arrived for the door-keeper. Sethe assumes that there were also interpreters for other nations. In virtue of the texts quoted by Sethe, it may be assumed that according to the Egyptians also foreign peoples were involved in their conceptions about the hereafter.

In contrast with the *Livre de la Nuit* the Book of Gates does know a favourable fate for non-Egyptians in the realm of the dead. There the way of thinking seems to be more cosmopolitic in the spirit of the Amarna-songs, which say that Aton has placed a Nile in the

---

[1]) Pyr. Neith 736.

[2]) Pyr. Aba 538.

[3]) In Studies presented to F. Ll. Griffith, 1932, pp. 432-433, *Kosmopolitische Gedanken der Ägypter des Neuen Reichs in Bezug auf das Totenreich.*

heavens also for foreigners. The passage concerned [1]) is, it is true, in a lower register, where usually the punishments in the netherworld are described, but here also foreigners experience the favour of Re. Horus is pictured with Egyptians (*rmṯ*), Asiatics, negroes and Libyans. "Horus says to this herd of Re, which is in the netherworld, namely Egyptians and foreigners [2]): May you do well, herd of Re, which has sprung from the Great One, who is in heaven. Air for your noses, loosening of your bandages. You are the tears of my *3ḫ.t*-eye in your name of people." Here is a universalism, which considers the whole *genus humanum* as a creation of Re. That men are the herd of the god is a thought, which occurs also elsewhere in Egypt and which is older than Amarna. Well-known is a passage from Papyrus Westcar, where a perilous test is not carried out on a man, because one does not do such a thing to the "cattle" of the god [3]). That mankind (*rmṯ*) has arisen from the tears (pun with *rmỉ*) of the god, is also a well-known conception, a.o. in the *Zweiwegebuch*, where the Lord of the universe says: "I have created the gods from my sweat, mankind is the tears of my eye" [4]). With puns upon the names of foreign peoples these are involved in the favourable actions of Re in the text of the Book of Gates. "The water of creation is great, so you say in your name of Asiatics [5]). Sekhmet is fallen to their share. It is she who protects their souls." Sekhmet is the goddess of the Asiatics. Also these have a *b3*, which warrants a normal existence after death. "You are those against whom I have struck. I rest in an infinity of many, which have sprung from me in your name of negroes. They have fallen to Horus. He is the one who protects their souls" [6]). The somewhat pantheistic thought that Re manifests himself in the millions of his creatures is also known from

---

[1]) Book of Gates IV, lower register, 1st figure, B.S. Pl. VII. 1-VI. 11. In E. Lefébure, *Le Tombeau de Séti Ier*, Paris 1886, II, 4-5, the foreigners are pictured with features and cloths, which are characteristic for them, the *Nḥś.w* as negroes.

[2]) *Dšr.t*, the red country, the foreign country in respect of the "black" country, the cultivated land of Egypt.

[3]) Westcar VIII. 17 = Sethe, *Lesestücke* 31. 2. See about this W. Spiegelberg in Z.Ä.S. 64, pp. 89. 90; A. M. Blackman in J. E. A. XVI, p. 67. Instructions for Merikare, Pap. Petersborough 1116 A. ed. Golenischeff, 131.

[4]) Lacau, Sarc. I. 28085. 221. 59; C.T. VII, Spell 1130.

[5]) Pun *ʿ3 mw n śḫpr* and *ʿ3m.w*; *mw n śḫpr* = seed?

[6]) Pun *nn ḥw.n.ỉ r.śn* and *nḥśy*.

elsewhere [1]). "I have looked for my eye. You have arisen in your name of Libyans. Sekhmet falls to them. She is the one, who protects their souls" [2]). This is an allusion to the legend of the sun-eye, which was in a foreign country.

B.20.n. *rḫy.t*, men.

They occur in the Pyramid Texts as the ordinary people, who are not admitted to heaven like the king [3]). The name *rḫy.t* must probably be connected with the *rḫy.t*-birds, pictured on a predynastic sceptre-head from Hieraconpolis [4]). In the uppermost of three registers dead *rḫy.t*-birds and bows are pictured, hung on standards. They represent enemies from the Delta, who have been conquered by the "Scorpion-king" of Upper-Egypt. Sometimes in the Pyramid Texts [5]) the *rḫy.t* are connected with rebels.

B.20.o. *ḥtrty.w*, see *wḏb.w*.

B.20.p. *ḫrw*, "enemy".

This is a despising word for enemy, also enemy of the gods [6]). Beside a group of condemned ones in the realm of the dead we read: "Oh "enemies", who have no *b3*, who are in the place of destruction" [7]). The picture shows prostrate and fettered men.

B.20.q. *Ṯmḥ.w*, see *Nḥś.w*.

B.20.r. *d3ty.w*, denizens of the *d3.t*.

This denomination has an unpleasant meaning in certain passages. "The *d3.t*-denizens have no power over me" (continuation: "Their fish do not eat me, their birds do not alight on my head") [8]). Here the *d3.t*-denizens have become demoniacal gods.

B.20.s. *ḏwy.w*, enemies.

This is a term for enemies of Osiris, who are punished [9]).

[1]) Zandee, *De Hymnen aan Amon van Papyrus Leiden* I. 350, pp. 76. 77. Leiden I. 344. Verso III. 3, *wʿ wʿty ḏ.t.f m ḥḥ*, All-one, whose body is identical to an infinity of many.

[2]) Pun of *ḥḥi*, to look for and *Ṯmḥ.w*.

[3]) See under *ḫśf*, to keep off, B.1.f.

[4]) Drioton-Vandier, *L'Égypte*[3], Paris 1952, p. 130.

[5]) Pyr. 1837.c.

[6]) Wb. III. 321. 8.

[7]) L.Q. XXIV. 8-9.

[8]) C.T. V. 332.a.

[9]) Book of Gates VIII, lower register, B.S. Pl. XIV, 19.

B.21. *Sundries.*

Among these various terms are dealt with, which refer to an unhappy fate of the dead in the hereafter, as far as they cannot be classed in one of the above-mentioned rubrics.

B.21.a. *3r*, to press hard.

The dead says: "I am not pressed hard by my enemies" [1]).

B.21.b. *ii r*, to come towards somebody in a hostile way.

Demons approach somebody in the realm of the dead with a hostile intention. The term may also mean "to come (in order) to (fetch) somebody". "He has come against you, when he thought of slaughtering you" [2]). "Hey, hey, do not come against me" [3]). The dead says to a demon: "Have you come in order to fetch my heart?" [4]). Those who might come against N.N., as one who puts himself in the way, come to him, come to him" [5]).

B.21.c. *iw*, to be without a ship.

In the Pyramid Texts the dead king has to cross a stream first before beginning at his ascension. He utters the wish not to be without a ship. "Horus, do not let N.N. be without a ship" [6]). Also in later texts the thought occurs that the dead has to cross a water, a.o. in order to reach the *Ḥtp*-fields. There are separate spells to influence the ferry-man or to know the parts of the boat. In such a spell it says about the ferry-man [7]): "Let me not be without a ship" [8]). In a text for bringing the ferry-boat it reads: "I am not one without a ship" [9]). A passage in the *Zweiwegebuch* reads: "I am not without a ship. I am not repelled from the *3ḫ.t.* I am Re. I am not without a ship in the great passage" [10]).

B.21.d. *iri r*, to act against.

This term circumscribes how demons act against the dead in a hostile way. About four demons, who are in the West, it is said [11]): "When you bend yourself against me and you do this against me, what you do against these great ones, whom you know . . . I'll chase

---

1) B.D. 189; 493. 9.
2) Pyr. 944.a.
3) C.T. V. 50.c.
4) C.T. V. 54.c.
5) Pyr. 322.a; cf. C.T. IV. 89.j. k.
6) Pyr. 1030.b. Cf. 1742.c.
7) C.T. V. 174.d.
8) Cf. C. T. V. 188.g.
9) C.T. III. 76.h.
10) B.D. 130; C.T. VII, Spell 1099; B 1 L. 490.
11) C.T. VI. 152.j-153. f.

away evil, I'll bring justice." The dead is stronger than those who treat him inimically or he makes sure of the assistance of a god against them. "You have power over those who act against you in the realm of the dead" [1]). "You have power over him who commands to act against you in the realm of the dead" [2]). "You (Re) save him (Osiris N.N.) from him who acts against him" [3]).

Sometimes it concerns being at law with the dead. "To me justification has been given against him, who acted against me, before Osiris, the bull of the West" [4]). The dead wins the suit of his opponents. "N.N. has risen against those (male and female) who act against him" [5]).

A spirit of a dead may harm somebody, who still lives on the earth. A son complains in a letter to his deceased father, that his deceased brother set somebody against him to rob his possession [6]). "In your presence there is hostile acting against me by my brother, (although) I have buried him". In a letter to a mother about a hostile brother we read: "Why does he act against this son of yours" [7]).

B.21.e. *ih*, to suffer.

A gate in the realm of the dead, which is full of flames and inflicts wounds, is one "along which one does not pass from fear of the suffering caused by it" [8]).

B.21.f. *iśḳ*, delay.

"Delay for your shadows" is promised as a punishment in the netherworld to sinners [9]). The shadow of the dead may be tied and be hindered in its movements like the *b3*.

B.21.g. ʿ, document.

The dead feels threatened by the magical word of a document or spell directed against him.

"There is nobody who drafts a document against me with something evil" [10]). Compare with this the places where a book (*mḏ.t*) is mentioned, the contents of which are detrimental to the dead. "Your pen is broken, your book is rumpled on account of this

---

1) C.T. III. 230.c.
2) C.T. III. 232.a.
3) B.D. 136 A; 298. 10.
4) C.T. III. 328.a.
5) B.D. 172; 445. 8.
6) Gardiner-Sethe, Letters to the dead, Pl. II. A. 4.
7) Op. cit. III. A. 5.
8) B.D. 146; 353. 6; 8th gate.
9) Am Duat VII, 35.
10) C.T. II. 252.g. h.

painful thing you thought to do against me" [1]). The dead says to a demon: "May I escape your stylus, may I tear your books apiece, on account of this painful thing you thought of doing against me" [2]). Is here perhaps thought of a deed with counts of indictment? [3]). Also in a Pyramid Text a rejection of spells bad for the dead occurs: "When N.N. becomes conjured, then Atum becomes conjured" [4]).

B.21.h. *ʿw3*, robbery, outrage.

The dead rejects that this action, detrimental to him, is perpetrated against him. "If they exercise some evil outrage against Osiris N.N., then Osiris N.N. will make the upper ʿ like the bottom ones" (?) [5]). "My robbery is not in the council" [6]). "Some people, gods, etc. do not exercise any robbery against me" [7]). Demons are called robbers: "The fear of him goes behind the robbers" [8]). In the realm of the dead the deceased may be robbed of his possessions by demons [9]) or be taken along himself as plunder [10]).

B.21.i. *ʿnn*, to twist.

In a drawing of the netherworld four women are pictured, standing on their head and with twisted arms. The text says: "Your arms are twisted" [11]). Apparently this is meant as a torture.

B.21.j. *wḫd*, to suffer.

A picture shows goddesses with knives over a division of hell, in which *wḫd.w* are, suffering ones [12]). They are called thus on account of the sufferings, which the goddesses apply to them.

B.21.k. *wd*, to hit.

A demon tries to treat the dead badly, but the latter keeps him off. You shall not hit me" [13]). "Oh you, who comes to hit (me) [14]), I shall prevent you hitting me, I shall hit (you)" [15]).

Wd r is also used in connection with the judgment of the dead [16]). There the dead is taken before the court of justice of Geb together with an enemy. He is acquitted in the lawsuit and no sentence is

---

1) C.T. IV. 385.c-c.
2) C.T. V. 66.f. g.
3) See *gbg3*, B.12.s.
4) Pyr. 492.a.
5) C.T. I. 52. b-53.a.
6) B.D. 40; 110. 2-3.
7) B.D. 42; 113. 7-10.
8) Louvre 3292, ed. Nagel, L. 7-8.
9) C.T. I. 210.b, of his heart.
10) *ʾIṯ m ʿw3*, B.D. 40.
11) L.Q. XXXVI. 8-9.
12) Schmidt, Sark. 871.
13) B.D. 40; 110. 3.
14) Beside *sph*, to catch with the lasso.
15) B.D. 151.d. Naville II, p. 428.
16) C.T. Spell 565; VI. 164.d-e.

pronounced against him. "You shall not hit N.N., you shall not issue an order against him."

In a sun-hymn, resembling B.D. 15, we read that Re lights the netherworld and grants a favourable fate to the just there, but he punishes Apophis as a devil and head of the sinners, "placing evil into the evil one" [1]).

B.21.l. *pnḳ*, to bail out.

The dead rejects tortures in the realm of the dead. "I do not shed water for you with a pot. I do not bail out water for you with a carrying-rod" [2]). This place seems to refer to the work of the Danaïdes. *Nšw* [3]) also occurs in the meaning of a certain measure of capacity. It must refer to a vessel which is unsuitable for bailing out water. There are several Middle-Kingdom versions of this place [4]). T 1 Be, *n śt3.i m sš.w.ṯn*; T 3 Be, *nn śt3.ṯn nwi m šśr.w, n pnn.i n.ṯn m nb3.w*. Perhaps it concerns here actions in weaving. *Śt3* = to spin [5]). *Sš.w*, determined with the pot, may mean "cup" [6]), but could, in connection with the variant, also be a spinning-apparatus. *Pnn* [7]) may be connected with Wb. I. 508. 5, *pn, spindelartig Gerät*. The meaning of the text could be: "I am not spun with your spinning-apparatus, you do not reel me with your reels." All this makes the sense of the New-Kingdom version of B.D. 189 more uncertain.

B.21.m. *pḥ*, to attack.

The dead rejects being attacked by demons. "He has placed . . . behind me, he does not attack me" [8]). In a spell against demons it says: "My magical power is not attacked" [9]).

B.21.n. *m33*, to see.

The sinners in the netherworld have as a punishment that they are not allowed to see Re when he comes. About people punished by beheading it is said [10]): "Who do not see this great god, who do not behold the light of his disk, whose souls do not escape from the earth, who do not hear the words of this great god, when he passes

---

1) Louvre S.N. 173. 17, *w'd ḏw m nik*.
2) B.D. 189; 494. 4-6.
3) Wb. II. 338. 15.
4) C.T. III. 133.a. b.
5) Wb. IV. 355. 4. See C.T. VI. 221.m.
6) Wb. IV. 529. 11.
7) C.T. III. 133.b.
8) C.T. II. 143.a. b.
9) C.T. V. 312.h.
10) L.Q. CXXXV. 2-4.

their cave." A division of Am Duat is the territory of Sokaris [1]). Re is called there: "This great god, who is not seen and not behold." Those who are there, never catch sight of Re. In a division of the *ḳrr.t*-book [2]) the beatified are pictured in the upper register. When Re enters, they see his light, they acclaim him. The people from the lower register, the condemned, do not see Re. Beside four turned upside down it reads [3]): "These are like this: Who do not see Re's light, who do not hear his voice." In a lower register of the Book of Gates [4]) punished ones occur. Atum says to them: "You do not see Re in his shape, when he sails through the netherworld." To condemned women in the realm of the dead it is said: "You shall not see the light, you shall not have the disposal of my beams of light" [5]). About Re it is said that he is the one "whom those who are in the *d3.t*, do not see,whom the dead (those not ritually buried) do not see" [6]).

B.21.o. *mr*, painful.

Demons are "painful of fingers" [7]). To a demoniacal bird it is said: "Your pen is broken, your book is rumpled on account of this painful thing that you thought of doing against me" [8]). Dangerous places, which one has to pass, are painful, e.g., "the house of this *b3*" [9]) or *š wr* [10]). Painful in this connection means that somebody may receive bodily injuries.

B.21.p. *mdś*, sharp, painful.

This is an attribute of beings in the netherworld, who may injure the dead. In a Pyramid Text [11]) "the knives, which are on the two arms of Thoth, the painful one, who has sprung from Seth" are mentioned. Here Thoth is a demon, who tortures his victim with knives. Thoth may also be thought of as the crescent [12]). A gatekeeper is called "painful of face" [13]). The determinative is a knife.

---

[1]) Am Duat V. 1.

[2]) L.Q. XXVI. 7, 3rd *ḳrr.t*.

[3]) L.Q. XXXIII, 9, 3rd *ḳrr.t*, lower register.

[4]) Book of Gates I, lower register, B.S. Pl. III. 38-40.

[5]) L.Q. XXXIV. 6.

[6]) Book of Gates VII, middle register, Budge, The Eg. Heaven and Hell, II, p. 195; E. Lefébure, *Le Tombeau de Séti Ier*, II. 11.

[7]) C.T. IV. 303.b.

[8]) C.T. IV. 385.c-e.

[9]) Pyr. Neith 762.

[10]) Pyr. Neith 761.

[11]) Pyr. 1999.c.

[12]) Cf. Pyr. Neith 667; C.T. I. 289.c; Pyr. 962.a.

[13]) B.D. 144 and 147; 328. 15; 361. 8.

To the dead it is wished: "May you not go on the roads of the painful who utter roaring, who do damage" [1]). A guard in the *Zweiwegebuch* is called "painful of rage" [2]). About another guard it is said: "It is the guard of the twist of this pool. Painful of face, is his name. It is a flame, which is on him" [3]). In a passage of Am Duat the stem *mdś* is used as a verb [4]): "A knife is on them, that it may cut them to pieces." This refers to a horned god (devil's shape with horns!), who belabours beheaded ones with knives.

B.21.q. *nḥm*, to take away.

What is of importance for the dead may be taken away from him [5]). Certain spells have to check this. "Not to take somebody's head away from him" [6]). "Not to take somebody's magical power away from him" [7]). "Spell in order not to have somebody's heart taken away from him in the realm of the dead" [8]). Other spells must prevent somebody's sepulchral linen being taken away from him [9]) or his soul [10]). Demons are summoned to aid against enemies, who take away the bread: "Oh devourer of millions, oh ass, put yourself in the way of these enemies of Osiris N.N. who come to meet her in order to take away her bread from her" [11]). This is a very great danger indeed. For without food-offerings the dead cannot continue his existence in the hereafter. Therefore the robbers of offerings are threatened in several spells. "Who takes food away from me, while I am longing for it" [12]). "Truly, those do not exist who take food away from N.N." [13]). The dead, on his part, threatens a demoniacal god, who puts himself inimically in the way by taking away the latter's food offerings. Without offerings the god cannot exist: "His bread will not exist, his white bread will not exist" [14]).

B.21.r. *nḳʿ*, to cut out (the heart).

The heart is cut from the body and pulled out by a demon. "Oh you, who takes away hearts, who cuts out hearts" [15]). The C.T. [16]) here

---

1) C.T. I. 226. d. e.
2) C.T. VII, Spell 1144; B 1 Be. 191; B 5 C. 525.
3) C.T. VII, Spell 1168; B 1 Be. 242.
4) Am Duat VII. 23.
5) Cf. *ʿwꜣ*, B.21.h.
6) C.T. V. 60.a.
7) C.T. V. 66.a.
8) B.D. 29; idem. C.T. V. 54.a.
9) C.T. IV. 369.a. b.
10) C.T. V. 49.a; B.D. 61; 132. 3.
11) C.T. Spell 656; VI. 276.l-p.
12) C.T. VI. 233.m.
13) C.T. VI. 238.o.
14) C.T. Spell 769; VI. 403.j.
15) B.D. 27; 90. 10.
16) C.T. VI. 344.k. p.

read *ḏbʿ*, to rebuke, C.1.s. "Who makes the hearts (of the dead) rebuke (them), (that is to say accuse them in the judgment of the dead)." L. Keimer [1]) connects *nḳʿ* with *nḳʿw.t* [2]). According to him the latter are the maturing sycamore-fruits, which are cut into in order to make the insects, which are in them, die. Only by this procedure the fruit will ripen and get a good taste. Keimer gives reproductions of such fruit with incisions. He has made the meaning "to cut out" of the heart from the body plausible. Beside B.D. 27 he also cites B.D. 175 (Pap. Ani) [3]), *rdì.tw ḫfty.w.ì m nḳʿw.t*, where it consequently relates to a situation in which the enemies are, apparently, that they are cut.

B.21.s. *nkn*, damage.

This term is used for bodily injury being done by demons. "Let him, who does me damage, not attack me" [4]). About a happy sojourn in the *Ḥtp*-field the dead says: "I live. My damage (masculine and feminine) does not exist. Joy is given to me" [5]). He pronounces the wish: "Let no injury be done against me" [6]). To condemned in the realm of the dead it is said: "The destroying one of face injures you" [7]). That it here concerns a bloody and bodily torture appears from a passage dealing with the punishment of Seth: "Truly, his injury is done, his slaughter is made" [8]).

B.21.t. *rmn tp*, to take the head away (?).

"May you not permit my head being taken away from me" [9]).

B.21.u. *h3ì*, to be brought down, to land in.

This verb is used for landing in dangerous places in the netherworld. "I do not land in their cauldrons" [10]). "To land in the net" [11]). It is also used alone in the sense of "to be brought down", e.g., of the destruction of Apophis: "Apophis, the enemy of Re, is brought down" [12]).

B.21.v. *ḥp*, to hurry.

This refers to undue fatigue, which the dead suffers in the hereafter as a consequence of toil (cf. *k3.t*). "Osiris N.N. does not hurry, he does not get tired in this land to all eternity" [13]).

---

1) AcOr VI, p. 300.
2) Wb. II. 343. 10.
3) Pap. Ani 29/25, Budge, Translation, p. 326, 327.
4) C.T. IV. 69.g.
5) C.T. V. 368.e. f.
6) B.D. 96, 97; 202. 3. 4.
7) L.Q. L. 3, 4th *ḳrr.t*, lower register.
8) C.T. I. 227.h.
9) B.D. 105; 217. 4. 5.
10) C.T. IV. 305.b; B.D. 17. Cf. IV. 323.d.
11) C.T. IV. 348.a.
12) B.D. 39; 106. 7.
13) B.D. 133; 290. 3-5.

B.21.w. *ḥsỉ*, to come to meet inimically [1]).

"He who comes to meet me inimically, does not come" [2]).

B.21.x. *ḥk3*, to charm.

The dead rejects being charmed by his waylayers. "I am a competent spirit, who does not obey magical power" [3]), that is to say who is not subjected to charms [4]). He has the disposal of "a spell to ... destroy all evil magical power" [5]). Apophis, the enemy of Re, is punished by being charmed. This occurs in some passages of the Book of Gates. "May you be charmed so that you are powerless." "These gods say, while they charm Apophis ..." [6]). About those who protect Re against Apophis, it is said: "They charm Apophis for him." "They charm you" [7]).

B.21.y. *ḫḏ*, to damage.

A gate in the realm of the dead "damages the enemies" of Osiris [8]). There is a demon, "who destroys the *k3.w*" [9]). The dead asks Thoth: "Let me not be affected by destruction" [10]). He knows how to prevent a demon damaging him: "He has prevented another damaging him" [11]).

B.21.z. *ẖbẖb*, to trample down.

The first of a series of gates in the realm of the dead is called: "Mistress of trampling down" [12]).

B.21.aa. *ḫpr r*, to happen to.

"Nothing happens to me. The evil is kept off. There is no disturbance against me" [13]).

B.21.bb, *ḫr*, to fall.

This term indicates that the dead is abandoned to eternal destruction. He hopes that this will not happen to him. "May I not fall on account of your knives", he says to demons [14]). The enemies of the sun-god in the realm of the dead perish. "Your enemies fall for you under your feet" [15]). "Hail to you, you are very great, your enemies have

1) Wb. III. 159. 6.
2) C.T. IV. 128.a. Cf. *ḏ3ỉ*, *ḫśf*.
3) C.T. V. 224.e.
4) Idem. C.T. II. 53.g; VI. 132.n.
5) C.T. III. 213.b. c.
6) Book of Gates II, lower register, B.S. Pl. II. 35-37.
7) Book of Gates IX, middle register, B.S. Pl. XIII. 18; XII. 35. 36.
8) B.D. 146, 4th gate.
9) C.T. V. 41.i; 287.b; VI. 206. 1; 207.c. n; 208.a.
10) B.D. 175, A. de Buck, *Pro Regno Pro Sanctuario*, pp. 79-85.
11) C.T. I. 38.a.
12) B.D. 145-146, 1st gate.
13) B.D. 42; 114. 8-10.
14) C.T. IV. 322.d.
15) Am Duat VII. 19. 20.

fallen in their places of judgment. Hail to you, your rebels are punished for you. Apophis is destroyed for you" [1]).

B.21.cc. *ḫśf*, to approach.

This is sometimes used in the meaning of going to meet somebody with inimical intentions, to injure somebody. "There is nobody, who comes to meet me" [2]). "As regards each prosecutor who is going to meet me" [3]).

B.21.dd. *sbn*, to be brought down.

"Apophis, the enemy of Re, is brought down" [4]). "His gang (of Seth) is brought down for me" [5]).

B.21.ee. *śḫ3*, to remember (somebody in an evil way).

A punishment for tomb robbers: "Their remembrance will be bad in the realm of the dead" [6]), that is to say there they will be thought of as being bad.

B.21.ff. *śḫm m*, to have power over.

In the funerary texts it is denied that evil beings have power over somebody. "The messengers of Osiris have no power over me" [7]). "The *d3*.t-denizens have no power over me" [8]). "Their (of demons of Osiris) knives have no power over me" [9]). "The light has no power over me" [10]). About Osiris: "May he not have power over your heart" [11]). "May no enemies have power over me" [12]). "Your powers have no power over him" [13]).

B.21.gg. *śḏ*, to break.

This usually regards the breaking of bones. One of the 42 judges of Osiris is called: "Who breaks the bones" [14]). In a passage concerning the punishment of Apophis it reads: "Your bones are broken" [15]). Executioners in the realm of the dead are called: "The breakers of Osiris" [16]).

B.21.hh. *śḏb*, calamity.

"I am free of all calamity, which comes from the mouth of any

---

[1]) Louvre S.N. 173, VIII. 14-15, *ỉnḏ ḥr.k wr ṯw ˁ3 ṯw ḫfty.w.k ḫr m nm.t.śn ỉnḏ ḥr.k bḥn n.k śbỉ.w.k śḥtm n.k ˁpp.*

[2]) C.T. II. 252.f.

[3]) C.T. IV. 126.f.

[4]) B.D. 39; 105. 14.

[5]) C.T. IV. 105.f.

[6]) Urk. I. 263. 12.

[7]) C.T. V. 331.g-i.

[8]) C.T. V. 332.a.

[9]) C.T. IV. 305.a.

[10]) C.T. II. 112.g.

[11]) Pyr. 145.b.

[12]) B.D. 72; 160. 11. 12.

[13]) C.T. VI. 288.o.

[14]) B.D. 125; 253. 12.

[15]) B.D. 39; 106. 14.

[16]) B.D. 28; 92. 2; cf. *śḏty.w*, C.T. I. 182.d.

god" [1]). Consequently *śdb* may be a word spoken to the detriment of the dead. "Avert calamity going out from the mouth of any god or goddess in an evil way, what men, gods, spirits, dead think of doing against me" [2]). "I am not delivered to this calamity, which comes from your mouth" [3]).

Śdb is the punishment to which sinners, enemies of the god, are delivered. At the end of his journey through the netherworld Re says: "I have passed the cave of the destroyed. I have delivered them to their calamity after I have passed *'Igr.t*" [4]). "Oh behold me, I make my entry at yours. I do damage to you. I assign you to the place of destruction. Your souls do not go out" [5]). The close relation to *ḥtmy.t* shows that *śdb* is a torture in a division of hell. The same in the passage: "I deliver you to your calamity. I count you out to your destruction" [6]).

In a text which deals with the free passage of the *b3* in the ascension *śdb* gives the impression of being an obstacle put in somebody's way. "He has reached the *3ḫ.t* as a great falcon. His obstacle is removed in the *3ḫ.t*" [7]).

B.21.ii. *špt*, annoyance.

This term expresses that a god has objections against the dead, so that he does not receive him kindly. In the Middle-Kingdom version of B.D. 14, C.T. Spell 719, it reads [8]): "To chase away annoyance with a woman from the heart of a god . . . Behold, a word is said to this N.N. by a god, who is annoyed with her . . . May you unite grace with N.N. [9]). To chase away all annoyance, which is in your heart with her."

B.21.jj. *šnṯ*, to fight.

"Oh . . . who has appeared, that he may give orders against these enemies, who will fight Osiris N.N., who will do something against Osiris N.N. in an evil way" [10]).

B.21.kk. *ḳnḳn*, to strike.

A place full of demons is called the house where the "striking ones" are [11]).

---

1) C.T. III. 7.b; 8.a.
2) C.T. VI. 92.p-93.a.
3) B.D. 96, 97; 201. 10. 11.
4) L.Q. CXXXVI. 4.5.
5) L.Q. XXV. 4-5.
6) L.Q. CXXXIII. 9.
7) C.T. VI. 76.j. k.
8) C.T. VI. 347.a. d. l. m.
9) *Ḥtp* and *špt* are each other's opposites.
10) C.T. I. 45.b-46.c.
11) C.T. V. 41.i.

B.21.ll. *ḳ3* (*ʿn.t*), to stretch (the nail).

A Pyramid Text deals with bodily punishments after a judicial sentence [1]). "N.N. is one of that great body which was born in the beginning at Heliopolis, who are not led away to a king, who are not pulled before high officials, who are not sentenced, who are not condemned . . . N.N. is not impoverished. His finger-nails are not stretched. No bone of N.N. has been broken."

B.21.mm. *ḳ3.t*, toil.

The dead fears that he has to toil in the hereafter. Spells must protect him from this. "Not to toil in the realm of the dead" [2]). In the Book of the Dead the "Ushabti"-texts deal with this. The "ushabti" has to do the work for the dead [3]). "Spell to make the "ushabti" work for somebody in the realm of the dead. If I am summoned, if I am assigned to performing some work . . . then obey me there, like a man in his duty. You shall place yourself at my disposal, at all times, to plant the plots," etc. [4]). C.T. Spell 472 is the Middle-Kingdom version of B.D. 6 [5]). "If N.N. is assigned to . . . (here all kinds of work for the cultivation of land follow) . . . to cultivate new land for the contemporary king (so to perform *corvées*), then you will say in his place: "Behold, here I am," to each messengers, who will come for (against) this N.N." "If this N.N. is counted out to that which is done there, to cultivate new land (just deposited after the inundation), to plant the banks, to sail sand from the West so that it is placed in the East and vice versa, then you will say to him regarding this: "Behold, here we are" [6]). The inscription above this spell reads: "Spell to make an "ushabti" work for his master in the realm of the dead" [7]).

B.21.nn. *thi*, to affect.

This is a term for effecting bodily decay. In the Book of the Dead [8]) a spell occurs "to make his flesh and his bones be saved from the worms and from any god, who affects in the realm of the dead." The conclusion is: "He is not bared by the messenger, who affects" [9]).

---

1) Pyr. 1041.a-1043.b.
2) C.T. Spell 210; III. 164.a. Idem V. 280.b; 281.b; B.D. 5; 28. 3.
3) B.D. 6.
4) Idem B.D. 151; 384. 6-15.
5) C.T. VI. 1.f sqq.
6) C.T. VI. 2.e sqq.
7) C.T. VI. 1.a.
8) B.D. 163; 411. 3-5.
9) B.D. Budge, p. 414. 11.

B.21.oo. *ḏꜣi*, to put oneself in the way inimically.

This term is used of evil beings in the realm of the dead, who approach men with evil intentions. Four winds hinder the dead king in his ascension [1]. "Recommend N.N. to these four raging ones, who are round you (Re), . . . that they may not thrust their hand in the way, when (the face of) N.N. directs itself to you." In an ascension text gods, who keep the dead off, are threatened with taking away their offering loaves [2]: "As regards any god, who will put himself in the way of N.N. inimically, his bread shall not exist, his white bread shall not exist."

Those who want to do evil to the dead are averted. "As regards any god, any spirit, any dead, who will put themselves in the way of these dignities of you, while they are together with this gang of *Nḫꜣ-ḥr* (= Seth), Thoth, place your hand against them" [3]. The dead himself renders a god, who wants to do him evil, harmless: "It is N.N. who hacks off the rage of any god, spirit and dead, who will put himself in N.N.'s way inimically in these shapes of his" [4]. The dead calls in the protection of a god against others, who waylay him: "He who guides the hearts of the gods, may protect me, so that I am strong in heaven among the spirits. As regards any god and any goddess, who will put him- or herself inimically in my way, he is counted out to those who are before the year" [5]. The dead may exercise his bodily and spiritual functions unhindered. "Nothing is put in the way of his foot, his wish is not refused" [6]. Also gatekeepers may refuse to let the dead pass. About them it is said: "Let them not put themselves inimically in my way" [7].

In the chapters of the trap-net *ḏꜣi* is used for the manner in which the fowlers and fishermen waylay the dead: "Oh these four catchers of the net . . ., do not put yourselves inimically in the way of N.N. with this net of the trap-net" [8].

C.T. Spell 502 is a resurrection-text [9]: "He has gone away yesterday, he has returned today." The dead has a happy fate in the *Ḥtp*-field [10]. He is able to satisfy all his wishes there. He rejects any god

---

1) Pyr. 498.b. Cf. 978.a.
2) C.T. Spell 769; VI. 403.i. j; cf. Pyr. 1027.a. b.
3) C.T. I. 207.e-208.b.
4) C.T. VI. 300.i. j; Spell 672.
5) B.D. 124; 244. 12-15.
6) Pyr. 311.d.
7) C.T. V. 333.i.
8) C.T. VI. 20.e. h.
9) C.T. VI. 89.a. b.
10) C.T. VI. 88.g.

who would hinder him in this [1]). "There is no god, who will put himself in the way of what he likes." In Spell 506 an opponent is thought of in a lawsuit before a court of justice in the hereafter [2]). "I go up and down against this enemy. He is delivered to me . . . He has the worst of me . . .; his lawyer, who is in the council; anybody who puts himself in my way inimically." To *ḏ3i* belongs the substantive *ḏ3y.t*, enmity. A wish in behalf of the dead is: "May they exercise no enmity against you in their name of enemies" [3]).

B.21.pp. *ḏw.(t)*, disaster, evil.

Disaster or punishment in a general sense, which might happen to somebody in the hereafter, are indicated with this word. It may refer to a punishment, executed by the court of Osiris. "Nothing evil will happen to me in this country, in this hall of the double truth, for I know the name of these gods, who are in there, who follow the great god (i.e. Osiris)" [4]).

Disaster means *ḏw.t* in the following places: "Save me from all evil things" [5]). "Nothing evil happens to me" [6]). The beatified condition of the *Ḥtp*-field is circumscribed as follows: "There is not a single evil thing there" [7]). The goddess of heaven Nut protects the dead: "She saves you from all evil things" [8]). The decay of the body is *ḏw.t*. "The evil which is on N.N. is undone" [9]). Thereupon the collecting of the bones, the joining of the head etc., follow. A punishment for sinners is called *ḏw* [10]): "This great god (Re) passes the place of destruction (*ḫtm*). He inflicts evil to those who are in there as enemies of the lord of the netherworld." It here concerns tortures in hell.

Excursus: *To escape and to be saved from dangers.*

Introduction: that the Egyptian fears to be exposed to all kind of dangers after his death, also appears from the spells which must help him to escape from these dangers. Actually the whole literature of tomb texts provides him with this knowledge. He should know especially what he must say to charm a demon, whom he passes.

---

[1]) C.T. VI. 89.c. d.
[2]) C.T. VI. 91.g-j.
[3]) C.T. I. 284.j; 285.a.
[4]) B.D. 125; 252. 7 sqq.
[5]) C.T. V. 224.b.
[6]) C.T. V. 224.d.
[7]) C.T. V. 350.a.
[8]) Pyr. 638.c.
[9]) Pyr. 843.b.
[10]) L.Q. CI. 8.

Not the least essential is that he knows the name of the demon. Then he has power over him. "Who hacks off heads, who cuts off necks ... who makes a slaughter ... I know you, I know your name" [1]). "He who knows the name of this god ..." [2]). After that a formula follows not to suffer any trouble from him. The dead makes sure that he passes demons, dangerous places and gates with their guards (*św3*, *pḫr*, *nhi*). In the Pyramid Texts the king, in his ascension, passes the house of an inimical *b3* or an extensive sea.

When, on his journey through the hereafter, he approaches a hostile being, he commands him: "Recede, shrink back, be far" (*nwḏ*, *ḥm*, *ḥrtiwny*). In this way he frightens the enemy and the latter does not harm him. He asks gods, who are well-disposed to him, that they save him from the danger (*nḥm*, *nḏ*), or states that he is saved by his own magical word.

The dead is urged to be on the alert. The tomb text warns him for an approaching danger (*s3 ṯw*). Finally he states that he has escaped it like a bird the clap-net of the fowler (*pri*). This is not in the last place owing to the spell which has given him protection (*śśḏ3.t*).

a. *wb3*, to open.

The dead is locked up in the netherworld, but he knows how to set himself free. "Spell to go out into the day and to open the netherworld" [3]).

b. *pri*, to escape.

In the spells of the net which catches the dead, the deceased says, that he escapes it. About the net it is said: "N.N. has escaped from it" [4]). To a catcher it is said: "Oh catcher of the traps, powerful by his voice (or "who has the disposal of his voice"), ... N.N. does not go for you, N.N. does not come to you. He has escaped her trap, appeared as *Śbk*" [5]). It here concerns a trap "of which men, gods and spirits say ... there is no escaping it" [6]).

c. *pḫr*, to go round (something).

In the *Zweiwegebuch* the dead goes round dangerous pools with demons along the pathway. "Spell to go round them in the daytime, since somebody knows this spell. He reaches this pool. He does not die" [7]).

---

[1]) B.D. 71; 158. 7-10.
[2]) C.T. V. 375.c.
[3]) B.D. 72; 159. 12.
[4]) C.T. VI. 21.m.
[5]) C.T. VI. 21.a-d.
[6]) C.T. VI. 35.a.
[7]) C.T. VII, Spell 1062; B 2 L. 536. 537.

d. *nwḏ*, to recede.

A demon is kept off: "Recede, oh *snṯ*, fall into the pool (?) of the Destructor" [1]). "Recede" is here said by the dead to a demon. Sometimes the dead himself is the subject of this actions. He escapes a danger: "N.N. has receded today from the guarding of "Him with the grey hair" [2]).

e. *nhỉ*, to escape.

The dead evades a dangerous place. "He has escaped the rage of *š wr*" [3]). With regard to "the house of this *b3*" it is said: "You escape it an escaping" [4]). Also the reverse is said, not only that somebody escapes a danger, but also that the danger escapes him: "My death has escaped me" [5]).

f. *nḥm*, to save.

The dead wants to be saved from the dangers of the realm of the dead. He says: "I know the depth of the serpents, so that I am saved" [6]). "Save me from this god, hidden of shape" [7]). "Save me from this god, who takes away souls" [8]). "Save me from these inspectors" [9]). He wants to be "exempt from the corvée of Seth" [10]). The gods are invoked that they may save the dead from all kinds of dangers in the realm of the dead: "Oh fathers of the gods, oh mothers of the gods, who are on earth and in the realm of the dead, save N.N. from all bad obstacles, from all evil sorrow, from this fowler, painful of knives, from all bad things, invented to be done against me by men, gods, spirits and dead, on this day, in this night, in this month, half month, this year and its offerings" [11]).

g. *nḏ*, to save.

The second gate of the *Livre de la Nuit* is that "from which one cannot be saved" [12]).

h. *ḥm*, to recede.

By the imperative of this verb the dead keeps evil beings at bay, who threaten him in the realm of the dead. "Recede, backwards, raging one! I know you. I know the name of your boomerang,

---

1) C.T. V. 315.i.
2) C.T. Spell 766; VI. 397.h.
3) Pyr. 334.a.
4) Pyr. Neith 763.
5) C.T. VI. 96.a.
6) C.T. V. 375.a. b.
7) B.D. 17; C.T. IV. 298.a.
8) C.T. IV. 319.e.
9) C.T. IV. 321.e.
10) C.T. II. 151.e.
11) B.D. 148; 365. 5-366. 3.
12) *Le Livre du Jour et de la Nuit*, ed. A. Piankoff, p. 39.

which you throw. Back! On your face! Let your arm go down" [1]). To a crocodile he says: "Backwards! Recede!" [2]) He puts a serpent off with the words: "Recede on account of what you have seen, miserable one!" [3]).

i. *ḥrì*, to be far.

Also this verb serves for keeping demons at bay. "Go away from me" [4]). C.T. 173 is a spell not to eat excretion products. At the end it reads: "You whom I have named [5]), be far from me. Who are you? I am Horus" [6]). The dead identifies himself with Horus and so he is stronger for deterring the *rḏw*. In a similar spell [7]) it says: "My bed of vegetables is in the *Ḥtp*-field, my spoils of the chase (?) are in the *'I3r.w*-field. Be far from me, you, who brings ordure" [8]). The dead puts a demon off, who wants to let him eat ordure. He sets against it that he eats normal food in places, where there is plenty of it. In a spell not to go on the head and not to eat digestion products it reads: "Oh you, who praises the ordure in Heliopolis, be far from me" [9]). C.T. Spell 492 is a spell which prevents the *b3* being locked up. He has to enter unhindered to Re. This text, which has in view the ascension of the soul, dissents from Osiris as god of the netherworld. Helpers of Osiris are deterred from locking the soul up. "Oh guards of the mysteries of Osiris, go away from this soul of mine, do not lock it up!" [10]). Also Spell 493 must deter demons who want to lock the *b3* up. "Oh old one, pave the way for me, save my *b3* from the setters of bird-traps, who take away souls, who lock up shadows, who put in the slaughter-place . . . Be far from this *b3* of mine" [11]). Spell 495 begins with saying that the dead has snatched himself away from earth and ascends to heaven. "He has moved quickly together with *'Iḥy*. He has reached the *3ḫ.t* as a great falcon" [12]). "He saves himself from the criminals, the slaughterers, strong of arm. Be far from this *b3* of mine" [13]). So

---

[1]) *Zweiwegebuch* C.T., VII, Spell 1102; B 1 L. 515.

[2]) B.D. 31; 97. 10.

[3]) C.T. V. 289.b.

[4]) C.T. V. 211.d.

[5]) The "*rḏw*" of III. 58.e.

[6]) C.T. III. 59,a-c. Text B 3 C reads *ḥr.tìwny* = Be you far from this N.N. Perhaps *ḥr.tì ḏd.n.ì r.ì.* is a corruption there of the two other texts.

[7]) C.T. Spell 193.

[8]) C.T. III. 111.a-c.

[9]) C.T. III. 130.c. d.

[10]) C.T. VI. 72.e. f. g.

[11]) C.T. VI. 73.d-h.

[12]) C.T. VI. 76.i. j.

[13]) C.T. VI. 77.a. b.

ḫrtiwny has become a usual expression for deterring demons. "Be far from me, slaughterers of Osiris. You have no power over these feet of mine" [1]). This is a determent of demoniacal gods, who execute sentences in the service of Osiris.

j. *ḫśf*, to put off (demons).

B.D. 31-37 form a series of spells to put off demons. B.D. 39 is a spell "to put off a *rrk*-serpent". "I have put off the trembling for you, great *k3*-serpent" [2]).

k. *s3w*, to beware.

The formula for drawing somebody's attention to dangers is: *S3 ṯw*, beware. It occurs a.o. in the passage: "Oh N.N., beware for *Mḫnty n irty*" [3]).

l. *św3*, to pass.

The dead must try to pass unhindered all sorts of demons in the netherworld. For this purpose there are some spells, which are sent along with him. In the Pyramid Texts the deceased king meets, on his way to heaven, several dangers, which he must try to escape. "Oh she-baboons of him, who cuts off the heads. N.N. may pass you in peace, after he has tied his head to his neck" [4]). "N.N. has passed the house of his *b3* (read "this" *b3*). The rage of the wide sea has escaped him. His passage-money has not been taken away from him on the big ferry-boat" [5]). The verb *św3* often occurs in the *Zweiwegebuch*. For the blue waterway and the black pathway serve to lead the dead safely along dangerous places. The two roads are usually drawn on the bottom of a coffin, on which the mummy lies. So the dead lies on it. The text written beside is "a spell to pass it" [6]). There is a drawing of a chapel, along which the blue road leads. From the inscriptions going with it [7]) it appears that in this chapel there are evil beings, whom one has to pass. "Make the way for me (= let me pass), that I may pass there" [8]). On the blue road there is written: "Spell to pass them who are in front." The dead

---

1) C.T. III. 305.c. f.

2) C.T. V. 286.c; see also 283.b; 286.a; 287.a; 303.a.

3) Pyr. 771.a.

4) Pyr. 286. b. c; C.T. VI. 237. s-u. Wb. IV. 60. 13, *vorbeigehen an einem Tore = es passieren*, 60. 9; *bes. auch bei bösen Wesen im Jenseits vorbeigehen können*; *auch mit dem Zusatz m ḥtp, glücklich, unversehrt* (10).

5) Pyr. 334.a. b.

6) C.T. VII, Spell 1036; B 2 L. 483.

7) C.T. VII, Spell 1149; B 1 Be. 233.

8) C.T. VII, Spell 1148; B 1 Be. 226.

wants to pass the keepers of the doors of the *3ḫ.t*. He knows their name, which is written in the text. He who does not know their words, lands in a dangerous valley [1]), but as regards everyone who will know their words, he passes there. He sits on the side of the great god" [2]). "That which is before him [3]), is a spell to pass it" : "I am one with many faces, etc." [4]). To a serpent it is said: "May you let N.N. pass" [5]). "Wolf, do not enter its territory. Back, lion, backwards *Pḥwy*! May you let the god pass" [6]). The dead passes evil beings, while the latter stand before him with amazement. "My soul passes them in silence" [7]). "Let N.N. through. Then N.N. passes those "who are before their caves", the guards of the house of Osiris ... Pass beautifully, they say, the gods of the *d3.t* with regard to N.N." [8]). "I pass the valley" [9]). "Make ... me pass the hidden gates of the West" [10]). In the realm of the dead there is a fiery gate, "which one does not pass from fear of the suffering caused by it" [11]).

The dead wants to be able to sail to heaven safely and to pass doors without a demoniacal gate-keeper keeping him off. "The two doors of heaven are opened ... Let N.N. through, that this N.N. may pass alive, safely and in good health. Nothing in the bad way is done against N.N." [12]).

The dead passes demons. "N.N. has passed this *ḥnʿ*, who is in Nun. N.N. has passed this raging one, who is within reach of the *3ḫ.t*, who hits each god" [13]). The dead passes safely a dangerous river of fire [14]), in which the following dialogue takes place: "Let me pass ... Then he will say: On which of these roads do you pass safely? Then you will say: The middle one is the right one. Then he will say: Pass along the one you like. I shall go. Beware of what he will say to you."

---

1) C.T. VII, Spell 1131; B 1 Be. 9.

2) See also C.T. VII, Spell 1055; B 2 L, 526; C.T. VII, Spell 1171; B 1 P, 363.

3) I.e. the text written before the monster with the hippopotamus' head.

4) C.T. VII, Spell 1179; B 1 Be. 282; 281. Idem for 3 pools of fire, C.T. VII, Spell 1180; B 1 Be. 283.

5) Pyr. 679.b; *św3* transitive.

6) Pyr. 1351.a-c.

7) C.T. I. 398.c; 399.a.

8) C.T. IV. 84.e. f. m.

9) C.T. IV. 366.k.

10) B.D. 126; 269. 14-270. l.

11) 8th gate B.D. 146; 353. 5-6.

12) C.T. Spell 637; VI. 259.k. o. p. q.

13) C.T. VI. 149.e. f.

14) C.T. Spell 650; VI. 272.f. i-p.

m. *ššḏ3.t*, protecting spell.

The text which is sent along with the dead and which he has to know, enables him to charm evil beings and to pass them unscathed. "As regards everyone, who knows this protecting spell, he is more *3ḫ* on account of it, than Osiris. He passes all councils of judges" [1]).

C. Judgment and execution.

C.1. *To lodge a complaint.*

C.1.a. *iṯi*, to bring (into court).

In the Pyramid Texts a spell occurs which must prevent the dead being brought into court and being condemned. "N.N. is one of that great body which was born in the beginning at Heliopolis, who are not led away to a king, who are not pulled before high officials, who are not sentenced, who are not judged" [2]).

C.1.b. *ʿ3p*, rebuke.

The dead speaks about somebody who treats his grave well as about "him about whom I shall not let arise any rebuke against him with the god" [3]). The dead will not lodge a complaint against him with a divine judge.

C.1.c. *bṯ*, to let down.

Certain spells must prevent somebody's heart giving evidence against him in the judgment of the dead. "This heart of mine does not let me down" [4]). "Hail to you, this heart of mine, this my mind of my kas and of my body. May it not let me down" [5]).

C.1.d. *mtr*, to give evidence.

A bad evidence of his waylayers may harm the dead. About fowlers, who take souls away and lock shadows up, it is said: "Who look for an evidence, when he approaches . . . may your evidence have no power over him" [6]).

C.1.e. *rḳi*, to rebel.

This term indicates that somebody's heart causes an unfavourable

1) Lacau, Sarc. I. 217. 27; C.T. VII, Spell 1117. Cf. *śḏ3.w*, Wb. IV. 379. 14, *Bewahrung o.ä.* This term is used C.T. II. 266.b: "To know what Thoth knows, as guarding." See also C.T. V. 293.b.

2) Pyr. 1041.a-d.

3) Urk. I. 174.6.

4) C.T. II. 128.d.

5) C.T. Spell 459; V. 332.f. g.

6) C.T. VI. 76.b. e.

result in the psychostasy. In this case it has the meaning of "to give evidence against". "Do not rebel against me before the weigh-master" [1]); "You shall not rebel against me" [2]), somebody says to his heart.

C.1.f. *ḥwi mtr r*, to give evidence against.

One of the lower registers of the Book of Gates [3]) deals with a punishment of *ḏ3ty.w*, enemies of Re [4]). Their sins are enumerated. Here it also belongs that they are the ones, who threw an evidence and poured out their voices against *3ḫty* (= Re). In the judgment the same thing is done to them as they have committed. Atum repays them: "The giving of your evidence belongs to you in a bad way. Your slanders belong to you in a bad way. The supervision of my father (Re) belongs to you."

C.1.g. *ḥmśi r*, to testify against.

Also this term belongs to the spells in order not to let somebody's heart testify against him in the realm of the dead. "Spell not to make a man's heart testify against him" [5]). "This heart of mine which testifies against me, it mourns for itself" [6]).

C.T. Spell 587 mentions a judgment of the dead before Re in Heliopolis. The dead hopes for a favourable issue, so that he receives his offerings regularly. He threatens that, if excrements are given to him to be eaten, chaos will not be removed and that Seth eats the eye of Horus. He also invokes Thoth, who plays a part in the judgment [7]). He pronounces a threat in case Thoth testifies against him in the judgment. "Hail to you, Thoth ... when the great council sits to judge and when you (as a witness) sit before them against me, I am not the one, who receives heads of piebald cattle for them after judging in the great house of the judge, which is in Heliopolis" [8]).

C.1.h. *śi'r*, jemds. böses Tun berichten dem ... [9]).

The dead says to the 42 judges of Osiris: "May you not bring my

---

[1]) B.D. 30 B; 96. 3. 4.

[2]) Louvre 3148, V. 2, to *ib*, the heart, *nn rḳi.k..*

[3]) Book of Gates I, lower register, B.S. Pl. IV. 29-33.

[4]) Of *ḏ3i*, to put oneself inimically in the way.

[5]) C.T. II. 126.d.

[6]) C.T. II. 127.e. Idem C.T. VI. 164.j-k; 227.a.

[7]) In the psychostasy he takes the issue down; he reconciles Horus with Seth.

[8]) C.T. VI. 209.d-i. As to *ḥmśi r* with a juridical meaning cf. Hebrew יָשַׁב נֶגֶד 1 Kings 21,v. 13.

[9]) Wb. IV. 33. 12.

guilt to this god, behind whom you are" [1]). The dead asks the judges that they may not lodge a complaint against him with Osiris.

C.1.i. *śiw*, to accuse.

The dead threatens an opponent: "As regards each plaintiff, who will put himself in my way . . ." [2]).

In C.T. Spell 38 it is described that the father of the dead, deceased before the latter, instead of being his intercessor, has accused him before the judgment of the dead and has caused his premature death. "This father of mine, this helper of mine, this advocate of mine, this assistant of mine, this one to whom I have descended, who is in the West, who is in the realm of the dead, he has accused me in the council, he has said that I should be taken away at your command, that my days in the land of the living should be shortened" [3]).

Śiw is a causative of *iw*, to complain [4]). It is used in civil procedure a.o. in the Wisdom of Ptahhotep [5]): "Do not rob the house of a neighbour, do not take away the possessions of one who is near to you, let him not lodge a complaint against you."

C.1.j. *sʿḥʿ*, to set up.

According to the Wb. [6]) this verb also has the meaning: *Jem. hinstellen, belasten, überführen vor Gericht.* To the judgment of the dead the following passage relates: "Not any judgment is set up against him" = not a single complaint is lodged against him [7]).

C.1.k. *śmi*, to accuse.

Properly speaking the meaning is to announce, but according to the Wb. [8]) it may also be *Klage gegen jem. führen.* In B.D. 125 [9]) the dead says to the 42 judges: "May you not lodge a compalint against me." In the *Buch vom Atmen* [10]) it reads: "No complaint is lodged against him before all gods. Behold, he enters the *d3.t* without him being kept off."

C.1.l. *śrḫw*, plaintiff [11]).

In a spell for the ferry-man it is stated that the dead cannot be accused of anything, on account of which he might not be ferried

---

1) B.D. 125; 260. 2.
2) C.T. IV. 126.f; see also 126.b.
3) C.T. I. 158.a-d.
4) Wb. I. 48. 17-19.
5) Prisse XIV. 2.
6) Wb. IV. 54. 4.
7) B.D. 163; 414. 8.
8) Wb. IV. 128. 11.
9) B.D. Budge, p. 261. 6.
10) B.D. Budge, p. 516. 8-10.
11) Causative of *rḫ* = to make known.

over. "There is no plaintiff on account of a living one against N.N., there is no plaintiff on account of a dead . . . etc." [1]). At the beginning of C.T. Spell 40 the dead says that he is not guilty and goes clear in the judgment. "There does not exist any evidence against me. My sin does not exist. My injustice does not exist, my deviation does not exist. My trespass does not exist. My enemy does not exist. My plaintiff does not exist. He against whom I have done anything (bad) does not exist. He whom I have thwarted in an evil way, so that he may speak evil of me in the council, does not exist" [2]). So somebody, whom he has treated badly during life on earth, may put this forward against him in the judgment of the dead.

C.1.m. *śḫśf*, to oppose.

One spell has the title: "Not to let somebody's heart oppose to him in the realm of the dead" [3]).

Also the non-causative *ḫśf* occurs with the same meaning [4]). "Spell to prevent the heart of N.N. opposing him in the necropolis. Oh my heart of my mother, do not raise against me as witness in the presence of the owners of offerings. Do not say with an eye to me: He really has done it, with regard to what I have done. Do not bring about things against me in the presence of the great god, the lord of the West." This spell must prevent somebody's heart reminding Osiris, the judge of the dead, of his evil deeds.

C.1.n. *śḫnš*, to make stinking.

This term occurs in B.D. 30 B, a spell not to let somebody's heart testify against him in the judgment of the dead [5]). The heart should function as somebody's tutelary spirit [6]). It is said to the heart: "Do not make my name stinking with the court, which makes men standing ones" [7]). The text further says: "He who examines rejoices; the judge is pleased."

C.1.o. *śḏwi*, to slander.

In connection with the judgment the dead says: "May I not be slandered" [8]).

---

[1]) Pyr. 386.a. [2]) C.T. I. 173.c-g. [3]) C.T. II. 130.a.
[4]) B.D. 30 A and B; A. de Buck, J.E.O.L. no. 9, pp. 22-23.
[5]) A. de Buck, J.E.O.L. no. 9, p. 23; B.D. Budge, p. 96. 6.
[6]) *kꜣ*.
[7]) Cf. *śʿḥʿ*; it regards judges who indict man.
[8]) Louvre 3283, VI. 7, *nn śḏwi.i*.

C.1.p. *šn ḫ.t r*, to be at law with.

"There is not a single god, who will be at law with you, there is not a single goddess, who will be at law with you on the day of counting the characters before the great one, the lord of the West" [1]. This spell must prevent a god lodging a complaint against the dead in the judgment before Osiris.

C.1.q. *grg*, lie.

In a spell for preventing somebody's heart lodging a false complaint against him in the judgment of the dead [2] it reads: "Do not speak a lie against me in the presence of the great god."

C.1.r. *ṯsi bt3*, to reproach with guilt.

In the Book of the Dead [3] is "a spell not to . . . permit that he is reproached with his guilt, which he had on earth." In an autobiography the passage occurs: "I have done nothing wrong against men, that which their gods rebuke" [4].

C.1.s. *ḏbʿ*, to reprimand.

To beings in the hereafter the dead says: "do not take this heart of mine away from me. Do not reprimand my heart. Let this heart of mine not give rise to this bad reprimand" [5].

C.2. *The judgment.*

C.2.a. *wpi*, to divide [6].

This term is used for pronouncing a judgment by a judge of the dead in the hereafter. The wisdom of Ani [7] says that on earth one may litigate before the judge with somebody, from whom one has experienced something inequitable, although he has to appear later before the judge of the dead. "Be at law with him who trespasses unjustly against you, but god judges the just, when his fate has come to fetch him." They are four baboons in the boat of Re, which function as judges of the dead and "who divide the unhappy one from the bully" [8]. Also here *wpi* is used of a judicial judgment. A place of the Book of the Dead mentions judges of the dead "who divide right from wrong" [9].

---

1) C.T. I. 192.f-h. 2) B.D. 30 B; 96. 9. 10. 3) B.D. 163; 411. 2. 3.

4) Turin 154, stele of Beki, cited, J. Spiegel, *Totengericht*, p. 72; Wb. V. 408. 6.

5) B.D. 27; 90. 10-91. 2.

6) S. Morenz, *Rechts und links im Totengericht*, Z.Ä.S. 82 (1957), p. 66.

7) Wisdom of Ani VII. 11. 8) B.D. 126; 269. 7. 9) B.D. 168 A; 422. 4.

A son asks his deceased mother, whether she wants to pronounce a judgment about his brother, also deceased, who lets his inheritance be robbed. "May you judge between me and Sebekhotep" [1]). A mother writes to her husband in behalf of her daughter, who is treated unjustly [2]): "Execute your judgment on him who does what is painful for me, as I am justified towards any male and female dead who does this against my daughter." So the spirit of the dead can judge dead and alive on account of an evil deed. Somebody alive can be at law with a dead, which is adjudged by a god [3]). "There will be judged between you and me," the living husband says to his deceased wife, to whom he ascribes bad influence.

C. 2. b. *wḏ*ʿ (*mdw*), to judge.

In the period of the Old Kingdom this term is often used in tomb inscriptions, which must prevent the tomb being desecrated. The dead threatens the tomb robber that he will litigate with him before the great god. This great god may be thought of as being the king, Osiris or Re. There is some evidence to prefer the last mentioned [4]). "As regards everything that will get lost from that which I have given to them (the priests of the dead), I shall go with them to the judgment in the place where the judgment is" [5]). Nothing must get lost from the offerings of the tomb. If this happens all the same, the owner of the tomb shall litigate about it with the tomb priests in the judgment of the dead [6]). To desecrators of the graves it is said: "The god will judge him who will do something against it (i.e. the tomb)" [7]). "As regards all men who will take something away from this grave of mine, I shall be judged with them by the great god in the realm of the dead, while I am in the West. The memory of them will be bad in the realm of the dead" [8]). The result of the judgment of the dead is that the desecrators of the grave are dispatched in the realm of the dead. "As regards anyone who will do

---

[1]) Gardiner-Sethe, Letters to the dead, III. A. 4.

[2]) Op. cit., IV. A. 4-6.

[3]) Leiden 371; Letters to the dead, VIII. 38.

[4]) J. Zandee, *De hymnen aan Amon*, p. 122. J. Spiegel, *Die Idee vom Totengericht*, *Leipziger Ägyptologische Studien*, II, 41, "*Die Lehre für Merikare sowohl, wie die im Zusammenhang mit ihr herangezogenen Texte aus dem Anfang des Mittleren Reiches setzen Re als denjenigen voraus, vor dem die Verantwortung im Jenseits stattfindet.*

[5]) Urk. I. 14. 9-10.

[6]) Idem Urk. I. 35. 3; 49. 3; 30. 13.

[7]) Urk. I. 226. 6.

[8]) Urk. I. 263. 9-12.

something against my children, I shall be judged with them by the great god in the place where such a thing is judged" [1]. "I shall be judged with them by the great god, the lord of the West, in the place where there is justice" [2]. The West points to the realm of the dead as a place of judgment. Judgment takes place by the standard of *m3ʿ.t*. "As regards any nobleman, any high official and any man, who will break any brick out of this tomb, I shall be tried with him by the great god. I will seize his neck like that of a bird. I will make all who live on earth fear the spirits which are in the West" [3]. While his enemy is still alive on earth, the deceased may already be successful before the judge of the dead and afterwards he may haunt his opponent. "He who will take away one brick from this grave, I shall be tried together with him by the great god (gap, but if you will treat my grave with respect), I will defend you in the realm of the dead" [4]. *Wḏʿ* regards a lawsuit against an opponent. Appearing before a judge is supposed here.

In a lawsuit before a court of gods in the hereafter not only dead, but also those who still live on earth, may be implicated in the trial. A son, Shepsi, writes a letter to his deceased father, in order to provoke an action against his dead brother, Sebekhotep, who has instigated a robber of the inheritance against him. Consequently this robber and the injured one are litigants as still living on earth. "Go with him to judgment as your scribes are with you in one town" [5]. The following passage deals with a lawsuit between the dead and the living enemy of his son: "You know him who comes to you, here, going into court with Behesty and Ankhiry the son of Ai" [6].

Sometimes there is the conception that somebody is involved in a civil procedure with an enemy and might lose his case [7]. Some spells have to prevent this. "Not to let somebody be judged with an enemy in the realm of the dead" [8]. Here *wḏʿ mdw* sounds unfavourably. There is thought of the possibility of losing the case. In another version [9] of the latter passage the meaning is favourable to the dead:

---

1) Urk. I. 150. 9. 2) Urk. I. 256. 3. 4. 3) Urk. I. 260. 12-18.
4) Urk. I. 261. 6-8. Cf. Urk. I. 122. 12: (Who pronounces the offering formula), "I will defend you." 5) Gardiner-Sethe, Letters to the dead, II. A. 9.
6) Op. cit. I. A. 10, 6th dyn. 8) C.T. Spell. 565; VI. 163.i.
7) See B.17.b. 9) C.T. VI. 164.i, ms. B 1 Bo.

"That there may be a judgment for somebody with an enemy in the realm of the dead." He gets even with his enemy. Here Geb is the dreaded judge of the dead. The text is a charm not to come under the judgment of Geb. "N.N. shall not be judged . . ., when judgment takes place on N.N. by Geb, then . . . (follows a threat)" [1]). In a Pyramid Text it is said about an inimical god [2]): He will not be judged like an inhabitant of this town." The foreigners had less rights than the inhabitants. An unfavourable judgment was passed on them.

In the Pyramid Texts the dead king is not judged, but he himself participates in the administration of justice of the gods. It is said to the king at his ascension: "Sit down on your wonderful throne, that you may judge with the two Enneads" [3]). "N.N. lands among the stars which do not set, he does not go under . . . N.N. sits down between the two great gods, who judge among the gods" [4]). About the dead king it is said that he judges on the living ones in the territory of Re [5]). In the Pyramid Texts co-judging with the gods is the privilege of the king. In the Coffin Texts this is applied to the dead. "I sit down among the great gods, to judge" [6]). In the *Livres* of the New Kingdom it is a common view that the just also judge on the sinners.

The dead is acquitted in the judgment before Osiris. "You are justified on the day of judgment in the council of the master of weakness" [7]). "I do not forget this name of mine on the side of the lord of judgment" [8]). "N.N. cites his spells before the judges" [9]). The result is that he returns to life. The dead knows how to find the right word in order to exonerate himself.

"King, ruler of *'Igr.t*, high official, great of *Wrr.t*-crown, great god, hidden of place, lord of judgment, overlord of his council" [10]). "It is Re who rests like Osiris" [11]). Many texts assign the part of judge of the dead to Re as well as to Osiris. Re is meant in the passage[12]): "On the day of the judgment in the great house of the judge, that is in Heliopolis."

1) C.T. VI. 163.j; 164. b. c.
2) Pyr. 485.c.
3) Pyr. Neith 765.
4) Pyr. 1760. b-1761.a = Pyr. Neith 2.3.
5) Pyr. 273.b.
6) C.T. V. 159.e.
7) C.T. I. 268.d. e.
8) C.T. V. 238.f. See also under *rn*, B.8.d.
9) C.T. V. 262.d.
10) B.D. 180; 471. 8. 9.
11) B.D., Budge, p. 470. 14.
12) C.T. IV. 94. 1.

In the later *Livres* the judgment of the dead is repeatedly mentioned. It is said of Re: "King N.N., he judges on those who are on earth. He judges on king N.N." [1]). A judgment takes place according to what one deserves. Sinners are condemned as enemies of Osiris. "The enemies of Osiris, who are in the place of destruction, on whom the great council, which is in the netherworld, has judged before Osiris, he gives them their bad place in the region of destruction on account of these things which they have done in the hidden room" [2]). *Wḏ' mdw* is a *vox media*, the issue may be favourable or unfavourable. "Oh gods of the *d3.t*, who follow Re-Osiris, who judge souls, who divide right from wrong" [3]). "To sail through this great god . . . to judge in the West, to make the great one a little one among the gods, who are in the *d3.t*" [4]). With this a passage of the Book of the Dead may be compared [5]): "For them a great one is made a little one." This thought also occurs in the wisdom literature. The proud one is humuliated. The text (Book of Gates I) continues "to put the spirits in their places and to deliver the dead to their sentence, to destroy the corpses of the evil-doers to be punished, to lock up their souls." It here concerns a twofold judgment. The *3ḫ.w* have a happy fate, the *mt.w* are sentenced. *Mt* is a term here especially for condemned dead. The just are usually pictured in the upper register, the sinners in the lower register. This classification is applied not quite consistently, for in the 7th hour of Am Duat the upper register deals with a punishment of enemies of Osiris and beheaded ones are pictured there. In view of the fact that the course of navigation of Re's boat is from right to left, the just come to stand on his right side and the godless on his left side [6]). Here sentence, *wḏ'.t*, has an unfavourable meaning. It regards the sentence on the unjust. In another connection, on the other hand, *wḏ'* has a favourable meaning. It is said of Re to the denizens of the netherworld: "He judges you (which in this connection means: he acquits you), he destroys for you your enemies" [7]).

1) L.Q. XL. 3. 2) L.Q. CXX. 4-6. 3) B.D. 168 A; 422. 3.
4) Book of Gates I, middle register, B.S. Pl. IV. 8. 9. 14-17.
5) B.D. 175; 457. 15.
6) S. Morenz, *Rechts und links im Totengericht*, Z.Ä.S. 82 (1957), pp. 62-71.
7) Book of Gates VI, middle register, E. Lefébure, M.M.A.F.C. III, 1, Pl. XXXIII. 5-7.

"They (the beautiful spirits, to whom funerary offerings are regularly made) are the ones who judge at this gate, who hear those who are in there. Re says to them: Hail to you, gods, council of judges, which judges the dead, but saves the divine son (Horus), so that he is placed on his throne. Your justice belongs to you, oh gods" [1]). The just are rewarded with a favourable fate in the hereafter. They are allowed now to take place themselves in the council of judges and judge on the dead. *Wḏʿ mt.w* has an unfavourable meaning. The *mt.w* are the condemned. The *3ḫ.w* answer: "We execute the sentence on the dead, we protect the spirits [2]), so that they become (the ones) . . . to them offerings are made as to a judge in the council." So the just themselves form part of the council of judges. The same thought also occurs in the Book of Gates IV [3]): "Who spoke the truth on earth . . . your seats belong to you (in order to be) a council, in which those who are in me, judge." The dead judges with Re in the latter's boat: "I judge in the *mʿnḏ.t*-boat as the crew of Re" [4]).

C.2.c. *wśḫ.t*, hall.

This is the place where the judgment is held. B.D. 125 is "a spell to enter the hall of the double truth" [5]). As something favourable it is said of the dead: "Your character is praised in the hall before *Śḫm-ỉrw.f*" [6]).

C.2.d. *mḥy*, counsel.

Before the court of justice the dead also has a counsel [7]). The term *mḥy* is derived from the verb *mḥ* = to attend to, to care for [8]). The deceased father is somebody's counsel in the realm of the dead [9]). This thought occurs in a spell in order to make somebody who is in the realm of the dead, well-disposed to his descendant on earth [10]). The father performs his part of "counsel" badly, for he threatens to make the descendant die a premature death. "Behold, this father

---

[1]) Book of Gates VI, lower register, E. Lefébure, M.M.A.F.C. III, 1, Pl. XXXIV. 31-37; Cenotaph Seti I, Vol. II, Pl. LX.

[2]) Proleptically, it concerns people who will be *mt* or *3ḫ* after the sentence, Book of Gates VI, lower register, E. Lefébure, M.M.A.F.C. III, 1, Pl. XXXIV. 39-46.

[3]) Book of Gates IV, middle register, B.S. Pl. VI. 31, 32, 38, 39.

[4]) C.T. II. 140.b. [5]) B.D., Budge, p. 246. 4. [6]) C.T. I. 205.g.

[7]) Cf. p. 220, where also his opponent in the lawsuit has a counsel.

[8]) Sethe, *Lesestücke*, 45. 9, where the soul gives the advice of "*carpe diem*" to the *Lebensmüde*: forget to "fret" (*mḥ*). In Pyr. 1761.b = Neith 3 we find the causative: he recommends N.N. to the care (*śmḥ*) of his brother.

[9]) C.T. Spell 38. [10]) C.T. I. 157.e.

of mine, this defending counsel of mine, this solicitor of mine, this protector of mine, this one to whom I betake myself, who is in the West, who is the realm of the dead, he has accused me in the council" [1]). In another spell [2]) the son invokes the father. "Truly, this father of mine, who is in the West as my counsel, who is in the council of the gods" [3]). The son himself, in his turn, is the "counsel" of his father among the living. It is of interest to the father that his son takes good care of his funerary cult. "I shall be there as your counsel, who is in the council of men" [4]).

C.2.e. *mḫ3.t*, scales [5]).

In the judgment of the dead Anubis and Horus weigh the heart of the dead in a pair of scales against justice. They should be in equilibrium. This scene is pictured in B.D. 125 and in the scene of judgment before Osiris in the middle of the Book of Gates [6]). The dead hopes that his heart will not testify against him before the weigh-master [7]). He fears a demon [8]), whose eyebrows are the arms of the scales [9]). At the end of B.D. 125 [10]) the dead says: "I have come here, that the truth may be established and that the scales may be put into the right position. Judges of the dead are called: "who weigh with the scales" [11]).

C.2.f. *nhp*, to judge.

The dead king is put on a par with Osiris. Osiris was not judged, when Seth killed him, but he himself judges as king in the realm of the dead. In the same way it happens to the king: "If he lives, N.N. lives, if he does not die, N.N. does not die, if he does not go under, N.N. does not go under, if he is not judged, N.N. is not judged. If he judges, N.N. judges" [12]).

C.2.g. *ḥśb*, to count.

The dead is acquitted in the judgment. "Your sin is chased away. Your guilt is wiped off by those who weigh with the scales on the day of counting the characters" [13]). *Hrw ḥśb ḳd.w* [14]) is a variant of

---

[1]) C.T. I. 158.a. b. [2]) C.T. Spell 39. [3]) C.T. I. 171.j.
[4]) C.T. I. 172.e. [5]) Wb. II. 130. 9.
[6]) About the scales, J. Spiegel, *Totengericht*, p. 63 sqq.
[7]) B.D. 30 B; 96. 3. 4.
[8]) The scales personified into a demon. J. Spiegel, *Totengericht*, pp. 48, 49.
[9]) C.T. IV. 298.b; B.D. 17. [10]) Naville II. 319. [11]) C.T. I. 181.d.
[12]) Pyr. 167.b-d. [13]) C.T. I. 181.c-e. [14]) Cf. J. Spiegel, *Totengericht*, p. 48.

ḫrw wḏꜥ mdw [1]). Should it perhaps be assumed that this judgment takes place at once on the day of death? "There is not a single god, who will be at law with you. There is not a single goddess, who will be at law with you on the day of counting the characters before the great lord of the West" [2]). The dead has to fear no complaints on the day of judgment before Osiris. About Isis, who protects the dead, it is said: "She mentions your beautiful name in the boat on the day of counting the characters" [3]). In B.D. 125 it is said of the 42 judges that they gorge down the blood of the evil ones on the day of counting the characters before *Wnn-nfr* [4]). A passage from B.D. 17 reads: "Save me from this god, hidden of shape, whose two eyebrows are the arms of the scales on the day of settling accounts with the robbery [5]) before the Lord of the Universe" [6]). The judgment of the dead is enacted before Re. The dead remains secure from a sentence: "No slaughter is made by the two great ones of the account" [7]). The following passage cannot but relate to a judge of the dead: "Oh he who measures out the universe, who counts the characters, he counts the characters (takes into account), who knows what is in the hearts" [8]). J. J. Clère has devoted a study to the term *ḥśb.t ꜥꜣ.w* [9]). He translates the term by "*L'évaluation de l'excès*". It concerns calculating the overweight of the heart in the judgment of the dead before the divine court of justice, which is registered by Thoth. In the passage of Antef it is written: "He is justified at the calculation of the difference. You speak and your guilt is chased away by everything you say." The term also occurs in the Coffin Texts [10]): "The gate of the *ꜣḫ.t* is the calculation of the difference (the surplus)." A passage from Am Duat reads: "He is justified in the council on the day of calculating the surplus" [11]). Some places, which Clère does not mention, yet, are the following. "I have joined the high gate of the courtiers on the day of the calculation of the surplus" [12]). In this

---

[1]) E.g. C.T. IV. 94.l. [2]) C.T. I. 192.f-h.

[3]) C.T. I. 211.g-212.a. [4]) B.D., Budge, p. 249. 12. 13.

[5]) J. J. Clère, BIFAO XXX, p. 438, "*examen du voleur*" different reading *ḥśb.t ꜥꜣ.w*. [6]) C.T. IV. 298.a-300.a.

[7]) Louvre 3283 VII. 4, *nn šꜥ.tw in wr.wy nty ḥśb*.

[8]) C.T. VI Spell 768; 400.b.

[9]) BIFAO XXX, pp. 425-447. *Un passage de la stèle du général Antef*. Cf. J. Spiegel, *Totengericht*, pp. 48. 68. [10]) C.T. I. 253.d.

[11]) Am Duat IX. 3. [12]) C.T. III. 314.a.

spell [1] there is a connection with Osiris [2], so psychostasy might be meant here. Spell 241 deals with a big wall, which protects Osiris [3]. "You open a way for the tired one of heart (Osiris) to the region of the calculation of the surplus . . . open to me, I am Osiris." Also here there is a connection with Osiris and there may be thought of the judgment with the psychostasy.

C.2.h. *ḫmʿ*, extirpating of sin [4].

To the judges of the dead it is said: "Drive away my evil, extirpate my sin" [5]. Compare with this a place from the Coffin Texts: "N.N. has drive naway his evil, N.N. has extirpated his sin" [6].

C.2.i. *ḥśr*, to drive away, to dispel.

To judges of the dead a request is made of purifying the dead. "Drive away all evil which is on me" [7].

C.2.j. *śpḫ3*, to acquit [8].

"N.N. is acquitted from all sins, which he has done to see the face of the gods" [9].

C.2.k. *śm3ʿ ḫrw*, to justify.

This term is used of acquittal in the judgment of the dead [10]. It is said of the dead: "He is justified in the great council" [11]. A lawsuit with another party, against whom judgment is given, is thought of here. "Oh Thoth, justify Osiris N.N. against his enemies in the great council of Heliopolis" [12]. The prototype is the justification of Osiris against Seth [13]. The opposite of *m3ʿ ḫrw* is *ḫbn ḫrw*. "N.N. is one of that great body which was born in Heliopolis at the beginning . . ., who are not sentenced, who are not condemned" [14].

---

1) C.T. Spell 273.
2) C.T. III. 313.c.
3) C.T. III. 325.g-i.
4) Literally: "to seize", Wb. III. 282. 2.
5) B.D. 126; 269. 12.
6) C.T. Spell 296; IV. 49.k.
7) B.D. 126; 269. 13.
8) Cf. J. Spiegel, *Totengericht*, p. 55.
9) B.D. 125; 249. 4. 5. In Piankhi (Urk. III. 51. 8) *śpḫ3* stands beside *śwʿb* = to purify from sin.
10) S. G. F. Brandon, *A problem of the Osirian judgment of the dead*, NVMEN V, 1958, p. 113, 116, 117, 123.
11) B.D. 127 A; 272.l.
12) C.T. IV. 331.a.
13) E.g. C.T. IV. 94. d. J. Spiegel, *Totengericht*, p. 43: Osiris is acquitted before the judgment in Heliopolis and in imitation of him the dead. By the term *m3ʿ ḫrw* Osiris is connected with the judgment of the dead. Spiegel mentions several places, where *m3ʿ ḫrw* is used of the dead in the original meaning of acquittal in the judgment of the dead.
14) Pyr. 1041.a. d.

C.2.1. *śḏm mdw*, to hear the case.

Evil gods are punished by not sailing to heaven. "He does not sail up to the house of Horus, which is in the heavens, on this day of hearing the case" [1]). Compare: "You live in the palace next to the southern one of his wall (Ptah) on this day of the hearing" [2]). *Hrw n śḏm mdw* is to be compared with *hrw ḥśb ḳd.w* and *hrw wḏʿ mdw*. In an ascension text it is said of the king: "He hears the people" [3]). He takes part in the judgment of the dead. The desecrator of a pyramid is condemned by a court of gods. "Ah! *nḫḫ* for him who will stretch his finger to this pyramid and temple of N.N. and of his *k3*. He has stretched out his finger against Hathor in *Ḳbḥ* . . . he is heard by the gods. His possession does not exist . . . He is one who is punished. He is one who eats himself" [4]). The dead stands before a court together with his opponent. "I am heard together with him" [5]). He gains the lawsuit. "I am acquitted with regard to him" [6]). The beatified dead themselves perform a judicial function. "They are the ones who judge at this gate, who hear those who are in there" [7]). The heart is asked not to accuse somebody in the judgment of the dead. "That is good for him who hears the case" [8]).

C.3. *Denominations for judges of the dead.*

C.3.a. *iʿn*, baboon.

A text of the Book of the Dead [9]) mentions four baboons, represented in a drawing and sitting near a pond of fire. They are seated in front of the boat of Re. They bring him *m3ʿ.t*. They detest evil. The dead asks of them: "Drive away my evil . . . Let my slaughtering be undone . . . Let me not be punished." These baboons, which act as maintainers of *m3ʿ.t*, are judges of the dead. They dispose of sentence and acquittal. The pond of fire is a place of judgment.

C.3.b. *ʾInp*, Anubis [10]).

Anubis counts the hearts of the followers of Seth [11]). He delivers

[1]) Pyr. 1027.c.

[2]) C.T. V. 292.f. g.

[3]) Pyr. 1168.c.

[4]) Pyr. 1278.a. b; 1279.a-c.

[5]) C.T. II. 57.c.

[6]) C.T. II. 57.d; 58.a.

[7]) Book of Gates VI, lower register, E. Lefébure, M.M.A.F.C. III, 1, Pl. XXXIV. 31-33; Cenotaph Seti I, Vol. II, Pl. IX.

[8]) B.D. 30 B; 96. 8.

[9]) B.D. 125-126, papyrus Nsikhonsu, ed. E. Naville; cf. B.D. 126, ed. E. Naville, II, 336, 7-10.

[10]) According to J. Spiegel, *Totengericht*, p. 55 in the judgment of the dead secondary as regards Thoth.

[11]) Pyr. 1287.a.

somebody's enemies to him [1]). In Papyrus Jumilhac he executes the sentence on Seth. In this way he fills the function of judge of the dead.

C.3.c. *nb.w m3ʿ.t*, lords of the truth.

To a council of judges of Osiris it is said: "Hail to you, lords of the truth, college which is around Osiris, which makes a slaughter among the evil-doers who are behind *Ḥtpś Ḫw.ś*. Behold, I have come to you, that you chase away the evil which is on me" [2]). They are implored to acquit the dead in the judgment. They are called to aid by the dead [3]) to avert a raging demon. There they are called "free from evil". Compare with this *m3ʿty.w*, just ones, said of beatified dead, who are near Re and participate in his council, so that they judge together with him [4]). "Re says to this god: Oh great one, who calls for the souls of these just, who is at the head of his council. May it be given that they rest in their places near the council of those who are in myself."

C.3.d. *nb.w ḫ.t*, lords of the offerings.

They form a college of judges. "Spell not to let somebody's heart oppose against him in the judgment... Do not rise against me as witness before the lords of offerings" [5]). A variant is *nb.w ḫr.t* [6]). "Extol him (Re), *d3.t*-denizens, oh council, which is in the *d3.t*, which judges in behalf of Akhte. Re says to them, oh council, which is in the *d3.t*, lords of foods in the West: Judge me by your judgment . . ." [7]) In this connection it is said of them: "To them offerings are made on earth in the retinue of the owners of offerings." [8]) In the Book of the Dead [9]) it is said of the god of the *Ḥtp*-field that he is the one "who takes food to the lords of foods." So the lords of offerings are the just dead, who regularly receive their offerings of the dead [10]), who are acquitted in the judgment and who in their turn now co-judge on the other dead.

---

1) Pyr. Neith 730.

2) C.T. IV. 252.c; 254.a-256.c. B.D. 17. For this passage cf. J. Spiegel, *Totengericht*, pp. 46, 47.

3) Louvre 3148, IX. 24 = B.D. 72; 159. 13. 14.

4) Book of Gates IV, middle register, B.S. Pl. VI. 46-V. 49.

5) B.D. 30 A; 94. 15-95. 3.

6) Book of Gates VI, middle register, E. Lefébure, M.M.A.F.C. III, 1, Pl. XXXIV, 39. 40.

7) Idem 15-22.

8) Idem 38-40.

9) B.D. 110; 226. 15.

10) Those of the unjust are disturbed

C. 3. e. *Ḫnty 'Imnty.w.*

He acts as judge of the dead. In the Pyramid Texts [1]) demoniacal dead and spirits are mentioned, who will lead the dead to *Ḫnty 'Imnty.w*. To the enemies of Re, the children of *Bdš.t*, who are punished, it is said: "Beware of the judgment of *Ḫnty 'Imnty.w*" [2]). Of dead, who are punished, it is said: "The dead are placed in his circle at the gate of *Ḫnty 'Imnty.w*" [3]).

C. 3. f. *śr*, high official.

This is a title for a judge. "The blaze is extinguished, the wrath before the council of the god is cooled (?), when it sits [4]) to judge for Geb. Hail to you, judges of the gods. May Osiris N.N. be justified with you today" [5]).

C. 3. g. *šny.t*, courtiers.

This term is also used as denomination of a bench of judges. In a spell to the heart not to accuse its owner in the court, it reads: "Do not make my name stinking with the courtiers" [6]).

C. 3. h. *ḳnb.t*, council.

The dead is acquitted in the judgment. "He enters the council, while he leaves it justified" [7]).

Those who were just on earth are rewarded in the hereafter with a happy fate. They themselves are acquitted in the judgment. They are allowed to belong to a bench of judges and in this way contribute in judging the dead. "The souls of the people who are in the *d3.t*; who spoke the truth on earth, who respected the way of life of the god. Re says to them: Well-being to your souls! breath for your noses! Landed property belongs to you of the *'I3r.w*-field. Your towns belong to you of the just. Your seats belong to you (to be) a council, in which those who are in me, judge" [8]).

C. 3. i. *ḏ3ḏ3.t*, council.

This is also a term for a court of justice in the hereafter, before which the dead have to justify themselves.

Already in the Pyramid Texts the *ḏ3ḏ3.t* occurs. "N.N. does not

---

1) Pyr. 1999.d.
2) Book of Gates X, upper register, B.S. Pl. X. 48. 49.
3) Book of Gates X, upper register, B.S. Pl. XI. 38-40.
4) Different reading, "they sit".
5) C.T. I. 21.b-22.b.
6) B.D. 30 B; 96. 6. 7
7) B.D. 163; 414. 14. 15.
8) Book of Gates IV, middle register, B.S. Pl. VI. 31-39.

sit in the council of the god" [1]). According to the explanation of Sethe this means: he need not pass a judgment of the dead. "(gap) . . . in his council, on account of the right spell which has gone out of his mouth" [2]). Apparently the deceased king has first justified himself before a court of judges and now he may sail to heaven.

Somebody who enters the tomb structure unauthorized, is threatened as follows [3]): "I shall be judged with him in this glorious council of the great god. But everyone who will enter this grave, pure, while people are satisfied with him, I will be his protector in the realm of the dead in the council of the great god." The dead litigates with the desecrator of his grave in a council of the gods [4]). If he gains, the gods will punish the desecrator of the grave on earth. The dead stands as accuser of his opponent before the court of justice of the lord of the realm of the dead: "I have dealt with him in the council of *Ḫnty ʾImnty.w*" [5]). After the latter is condemned by the court he is said to have got the worst of it [6]). That it here concerns a formal procedure appears from a passage already cited [7]), in which the dead litigates with his enemy before a court of justice, while each of them is assisted by a counsel. The latter, who pleads in behalf of the dead in the court of justice, is also mentioned in C.T. Spell 741 [8]). "The counsel who is in the council . . . he has taken care of Osiris N.N. [9]). He has complained for her as a man in power . . . Backwards, mischief-maker [10]), who says what he has seen [11]) . . . there is a father near you, who is in the council [12]). My protector triumphs over you . . . Your slaughter is before his shape . . . A great one stands by his power, extending his arm to you . . . Your bread is not there, your cakes are not in the realm of the dead. Your offering does not go out from him in eternity" [13]).

There is thought of a bench of judges of Osiris, as in 125, in the following passage: "Orders are given in the great council in the

[1]) Pyr. 309.d. [2]) Pyr. 1776.a. [3]) Urk. I. 202. 9-11.
[4]) J. Sainte-Fare-Garnot, *Le tribunal du grand dieu sous l'ancien Empire égyptien*, *Revue de l'Histoire des Religions*, Tome CXVI, No 1, Paris 1937, pp. 26-33. S.G. F. Brandon, *A problem of the Osirian judgment of the dead*, NVMEN V, 1958, p. 117.
[5]) C.T. II. 233.b. [6]) C.T. II. 66.d.
[7]) Pp. 220 B.17.b; C.T. Spell 149; II. 234.a-235.a.
[8]) C.T. VI. 368.f-369.r. [9]) Cf. Spell 742; C.T. VI. 370.l.
[10]) By this Seth is sometimes meant. [11]) Witness for the prosecution.
[12]) See C.T. I. 174.i, the dead has his deceased father as his helper.
[13]) Menace of an opponent.

cave of Osiris, there is repeating beside the double truth" [1]). Also other gods than Osiris may have their council. "Thoth will justify me against my enemies in the council of Re and of Osiris and in the council of any god and goddess" [2]). The council of Re is mentioned in C.T. Spell 205 [3]): "I am better provided than they [4]), I am the one who is divided from them and joined to them on this day of going to the council of Re. I live on what they live." Thereupon utterances about the eating of normal offerings follow.

The son, who still lives on earth, invokes his deceased father as his counsel in the council of the gods. As in punishing the tomb robbers this presumes that not only may the council decide in the realm of the dead, but that it may also interfere in the world of the living. The son expresses the fear that his deceased father accuses him and may do him damage. He wishes that his father is his counsel in the judgment. "Behold, this father of mine, who is in the West, is my advocate, who is in the council of the god" [5]). "This father of mine complains, who is in the council, to whom I have descended" [6]). "Behold, you are in this country, while you are content, as my intercessor, who is in the council of the god. Behold, I am here as your speaker, who is in the council of men. I fasten your boundary-stone" [7]). The father interferes with the gods in behalf of his son. The son champions his father's cause on earth, a.o. by the care of the funerary offerings and the maintenance of the grave. The son wishes that his deceased father will not testify against him, so that he does not suffer from injurious consequences. "You are here in this isolated country where you are as my intercessor, who is in the council of the god. Behold, I am here in this country of the living as your intercessor, who is in the council of men till I come to you ... Let not ... your heart rise against me" [8]).

The dead wishes that a fair judgment is pronounced on him. "Never is N.N. judged biased ... Never is he heard in the palace,

---

[1]) C.T. II. 249.d-250.b.

[2]) C.T. IV. 333.c. f. See also Spell 337, where time and again a *ḏ3ḏ3.t* of another locality is invoked. For Re as president of a bench of judges, cf. J. Spiegel, *Totengericht*, p. 18. Together with his Ennead he forms the court of justice, op. cit., p. 54.

[3]) C.T. III. 149.c. e.

[4]) Demoniacal spirits, *3ḫ.w*.

[5]) C.T. I. 171.j.

[6]) C.T. I. 174.i.

[7]) C.T. I. 175.i-l.

[8]) C.T. I. 176.d-i.

... when the whole council speaks. The two comrades are satisfied with what N.N. has said in the judgment. N.N. is never repeated ... The court of justice of 6 is made for him, that of 30 belongs to him" [1]). The dead identifies himself with Thoth. As such he has passed the right sentence in the lawsuit between Horus and Seth. In virtue thereof he himself also wants to be treated justly by the judgment of the dead. The dead also puts himself on a par with Horus, who succeeded in his action against Seth. "Go out justified in this council of the gods of P, Dp and Heliopolis, as Horus went out, justified against Seth before this council of the lord of weakness" [2]). B.D. 172 describes how the dead conquers his enemy, who is his opponent in a litigation. "N.N. has risen against those who act against him, male and female. Your enemy has fallen. Ptah has felled your enemy. You triumph in order to have power over them. You are heard. What you have ordered, is done. You are exalted. You are justified in the council of any god and goddess" [3]).

In the Book of Gates [4]) nine figures are pictured, which stand before Atum and the punished Apophis. According to the inscription near it this is "the council which averts Apophis". They regularly receive funerary offerings. They are beatified dead, who now form part of the bench of judges of a god. The same representation is found in another passage from the Book of Gates [5]) "Extol him (Re), denizens of the *d3.t*, oh council, which is in the *d3.t*, which judges in behalf of Akhte. Re says to them: Oh council which is in the *d3.t*, lords of foods in the West, judge me by your judgment. Assign evil to my enemies, as I have given you my truth." The just dead form a bench, which acquits Re and condemns the latter's enemy, Apophis. "It is the council which destroys the enemies. Their offerings consist of justice [6]) ... They are the ones who assign destruction, who write down time of life for the souls which are in the West. Your destruction is against my (Re's) enemies, whom you write down for the destruction" [7]). This council justifies those who served Re and condemns the godless to destruction. The

---

[1]) C.T. IV. 20.d-21.b. [2]) C.T. I. 42.c-43.b. [3]) B.D. Budge, p. 445. 8-13.

[4]) Book of Gates II, lower register, B.S. Pl. III. 12-26.

[5]) Book of Gates VI, middle register, E. Lefébure, M.M.A.F.C. III, 1, Pl. XXXIII. 15-25. [6]) Immaterial food.

[7]) Book of Gates IV, lower register, B.S. Pl. VI. 38-45.

ḳrr.t-book [1]) knows a bench of judges of Osiris [2]): "Oh Osiris, lord of the council which judges the Western ones, hear N.N." In a register with condemned ones [3]) it is said of four figures with knives, who behead the enemies of Osiris: "You are the gods of the great council, who judge." So the judges also execute the sentence.

C.4. *To condemn and to sentence.*

C.4.a. *ip*, to count; *šip*, to assign.

The verb *ip* is used for examining the heart. Sethe circumscribes it as *das Durchschauen der Gesinnung* [4]). It is the judicial inquiry which may lead to acquittal or condemnation. Often the latter possibility is thought of and this is feared by the dead. "Geb has brought Horus to you, that he may count their hearts for you" [5]). Counting also means having power over it. The hearts of the enemies of Osiris are meant. The hearts of the followers of Seth are counted by Anubis [6]) "Anubis, who counts the hearts, he does not reckon N.N. any more among the gods of the earth, but among the gods who are in heaven"[7]). About Osiris it is said: "He does not count your heart" [8]). In his commentary Sethe here remarks: "*Zählen des Herzens*" *bezeichnet sonst das Totengericht* (*Totb. 125 von dem Abwägen gebraucht*). *In den Pyr. wird es als feindlicher, wenn auch wohl als geistiger Akt an den getöteten Feind vollzogen* (*von Anubis 1523. c, an den Feinden des Osiris*)." In the psychostasy before Osiris Anubis stands near the scales [9]). So *'ip* is the investigation whether a man's heart is just. As is the case with *ib*, *ip* also occurs with *b3* as an object. "The boat of Re, in which the souls are counted" [10]). "May he see the great god in his chapel on the day of counting the souls" [11]). *'Ip b3.w* is a judicial inquiry by Re after the moral quality of the dead. The dead says to the 42 judges of Osiris: "Save me from Baba, who lives on the intestines of the great ones on this day of the great reckoning" [12]). The inquiry, the "reckoning", may result in somebody being assigned to the

---

1) L.Q. XXII. 4.

2) S. G. F. Brandon, *A problem of the Osirian judgment of the dead*, NVMEN V, 1958, p. 121.

3) L.Q. XXIV. 6-7, 5th register.

4) Commentary on Pyr. 590.b.

5) Pyr. 590.b.

6) Pyr. 1287.a.

7) Pyr. 1523.c.

8) Pyr. 145.b.

9) Papyrus Jumilhac V. 10.

10) B.D. 92; 195. 8.

11) B.D., Budge, p. 195. 13. 14.

12) B.D. 125; 260. 10-12.

demon Baba. *'Ip 3ḫ.w* is parallel with *ṯnw.t mt.w* [1]). *'Ip* is the inquiry which precedes the execution of the sentence: "You are not counted, you are not locked in, you are not imprisoned . . ., you are not put into the place of judgment" [2]).

'Ip is used for the assigning to an unpleasant situation, e.g., in the text of the ushabtis: "If N.N. is counted out to what is done there (that is to say doing agricultural work) . . . " [3]). More often the causative *śip* is used in this meaning. The following passage relates not to the hereafter, but to a punishment of the enemies of Egypt by Amon: "Assigning (*śip*) them to the damage, which they have destined (for him) (or: "Which they have thought out themselves") [4]). The two sick eyes of the great one have fallen on you. *M3'.t* counts you out to the judgment (*śip*)" [5]). Re says to Apophis: "We count you out (*śip*) to your destruction" [6]).

Also in the following passages *śip* is used. The sinners, as enemies of Re, are delivered to their punishment in the netherworld [7]): "Oh enemies, may you be counted out to the hacking off, as Re has ordered against you, when he founded *'Igr.t* for his corpse and created the netherworld for his body." In the *krr.t*-book enemies of Osiris are given up to total destruction. This is called there "to be counted out to non-existence" [8]). About the sentence on Apophis it is said: "He (Osiris) counts you out to Aker" [9]). *Śip*, in the meaning of revision, check, also refers to exercising judgment. "Save me from these inspectors, to whom the Lord of the universe has given glory, in order to detain his enemies" . . . [10]). Further all kinds of tortures are mentioned. Consequently the *iry.w śip.w* are tormenting devils, who execute tortures. About a gate, which is dangerous for the dead it is said: "It has the inspection for "Who hides the tired one" [11]). A demon in the *Zweiwegebuch* is called: "The anxious one of voice,

---

1) C.T. IV. 336.e. 2) C.T. I. 70.b-d. 3) C.T. VI. 2.e.
4) Urk. IV. 269. 16. 5) C.T. V. 39.a. b.
6) Book of Gates II, lower register, B.S. Pl. III. 22. 23.
7) Book of Gates V, middle register, B.S. Pl. XVIII. 29-31; E. Lefébure, M.M.A.F.C. III, 1, Pl. XXXI. 35-39.
8) L.Q. XXV. 2. 9) B.D. 39; 106. 15.
10) C.T. IV. 321.e-322.a; B.D. 17.
11) B.D. 146; 354. 14. *Ḥbś b3gy* is a demon, who has the supervision of the gates of the realm of the dead. He also occurs in Pap. Westcar (Sethe, *Lesestücke* 30. 6): "May your soul know the ways which lead to the gate of *Ḥbś b3gy*."

the inspector" [1]). The picture shows a demon with a knife in his hand. Cf. B.D. 17 [2]), where the Phoenix is called "the inspector of what has been". Horus visits several necropoles and performs a judicial function there. "Horus, lord of life, you sail to the north, you sail to the south as *ʿnḏty*. You inspect those who have to be inspected in Mendes. You ascend and descend into *R3-śṯ3.w*. You open the face for those who are in the *d3.t*" [3]). About gate-keepers it is said [4]): "Along whom one passes when they inspect the place of judgment." *Śip* here practically means that they themselves execute the judgment. A bench of judges executes the judgment on the godless: "Great council, which is on the roads of the gods in this night of maintaining the inspection" [5]); "inspecting the have-not" [6]). *Śip* is usually used in an unfavourable sense of counting out to judgment. It sometimes occurs in a favourable sense. About the just in the realm of the dead it is said: "Their justice is counted out to them" [7]).

C.4.b. *wḏ*, to assign.

Re executes judgment on his enemies in the realm of the dead in accordance with their deeds. "He assigns them to your slaughtering, he counts you out to what you have done in the great hall of Re" [8]). *Wḏ* is parrallel to *śip*.

C.4.c. *niś*, to call.

In connection with the judgment of the dead this verb is also used of calling somebody to punishment or reward. In an upper register of the Book of Gates [9]) we read about the just: "They are called to this gate-structure." In the lower register we read about the condemned: "Being called to evil belongs to you."

C.4.d. *rdi*, to deliver up (to a punishment).

The dead asks that he may not be given up to a sentence in the realm of the dead. "May I not be delivered up to him who eats those

---

1) C.T. VII, Spell 1038; B 2 L. 490; Lacau, Sarc. I. 190. 9.
2) Urk. V. 16. 12. 3) C.T. I. 255.a-d. 4) B.D. 127 A; 272. 4.
5) C.T. IV. 332.f. 6) C.T. IV. 337.a.
7) Book of Gates V, upper register, B.S. Pl. XVIII. 19. 20; E. Lefébure, M.M.A.F.C. III, 1, Pl. XXXI. 27. 28.
8) Book of Gates V, middle register, B.S. Pl. XVIII. 37-42; E. Lefébure, M.M.A.F.C. III, 1, Pl. XXXI. 39-43.
9) Book of Gates I, upper register, B.S. Pl. IV. 31. 32; lower register, B.S. Pl. IV. 26. 27.

cut to pieces" [1]). A Pyramid Text mentions "to give up to the fire" [2]). The dead wishes not to be exposed to the tortures of a demon. "Who executes his order . . . may you not deliver me up to his fingers" [3]). About the dead king in the Pyramid Texts it is said, that he is with Re in the heavens and does not fall into the hands of the god of the netherworld. "Atum has not delivered me up to Osiris" [4]). Somebody says of his enemy: "He has been delivered up to me. He is not taken away from me" [5]). Re punishes those who rise against him. "Then the children of *Bdš.t* were given up to him (Re) as gods, who are in Hermopolis" [6]). In these passages *rdì* is to deliver up somebody to be punished or, as in Pyr. 145.b, to give up to an unpleasant situation. A special meaning of *rdì* is "to retaliate". "This evil spell, which I have said, this sin which I have committed, may it not be retaliated upon me, for I am this green stone, which is on the neck of Re, which is given to those who are in the *3ḫ.t*" [7]). "Hail to you, gods, lords of the necropolis, who do not neglect the excellence of the words, who give justice to him who comes forward with it and put the evil in its place" [8]). "Who give justice" = who reward justice. *Rdì* is "to give back", to repay someone, and in a special case it gets the sense of "to retaliate". Also Dévaud has pointed to this fact [9]) and he cites the following places: "Giving the lie to him who says it, the truth to him who comes forward with it" [10]). "He gives evil to him who does it, truth to him who comes forward with it" [11]). "The god gives evil to him who does it, truth to him who comes forward with it; then truth is given to me, because I have done it, to me the good is repaid in all valuable things" [12]). *Ḏb3* is parallel with *rdì* and the meaning is about the same.

C.4.e. *š3m*, to cover.

Messengers of Osiris are beings "who are not lenient", literally "whose cover of face does not exist" [13]). This is an epitheton, which expresses that they want to deliver somebody up irrespective of the person.

---

1) C.T. V. 41.d.
2) Pyr. 323.d.
3) B.D. 154; 401. 2. 3.
4) Pyr. 145.b.
5) C.T. II. 62.c.
6) B.D. 17; Naville II. 33.
7) B.D. 105; 216. 13-217. 1.
8) Louvre 3292, ed. Nagel, D. 2-4.
9) Z.Ä.S. No. 50, pp. 129-130.
10) Cairo 20539. I. 8.
11) B.D. 17. 6 (Naville).
12) Urk. IV. 492. 5-8.
13) B.D. 125; 262. 6. 7.

C.4.f. *ṯnw.t*, counting.

In a spell to be united with one's relatives, it reads: "N.N. has saved them from the corvée of Isis, from the counting of Nut" [1]). *'Irw* and *ṯnw.t* are used here promiscuously. *'Irw* = that which must be done, burdening, here labour services, corvée [2]). *Ṯn*, to count, is also to have power over something. "You count the *ḫ3ty.w*-stars" [3]) = you have power over them. The *ḫ3ty.w*-stars are of a demoniacal nature. He who counts out the dead has power over them, may use them for services. Thus *ṯn*, to count, also becomes a verb for counting out to a judgment. "This night of counting the dead" [4]). This is parallel with *śip 3ḫ.w* [5]).

C.5. *To punish.*

C.5.a. *iss*, to punish.

In the Pyramid Texts this verb is used for the punishment of Seth. The body of Seth is cut to pieces and decomposes. "They have punished him, so that he is cut to pieces and his smell is bad" [6]). "He punishes the followers of Seth, they are seized, their heads are chopped off, they are slaughtered" [7]). *'Iss* refers to a bloody punishment of the unjust. It has the same meaning in the tombs of the kings of the New Kingdom. There the term *ssy.w* occurs as a denomination for sinners punished in the netherworld, without doubt derived from the verb *iss*. "Oh punished ones, whose arms are taken away from them, who have no power over their forearms, great transgressors, mourning ones, whose evil is against them, whose blood is on their flesh, when they are slaughtered" [8]). The picture shows eight persons, put on their heads, four of them with hands fettered and four beheaded ones. Just as was the case in the Pyramid Texts with Seth and his followers, it here concerns a bloody punishment and a bodily mutilation.

C.5.b. *nik*, to punish.

According to the Pyramid Texts the king experiences no annoyance of demons. "Who do not know of being punished on account of

---

[1]) C.T. II. 203.b; 204.a; II. 151.e.

[2]) Heerma van Voss, *Pro Regno Pro Sanctuario*, p. 231. note 7.

[3]) Pyr. Neith 660. [4]) C.T. IV. 336.e.

[5]) Cf. 338.g, "the pool of counting the dead".

[6]) Pyr. 643.c. [7]) Pyr. 1285.c. [8]) L.Q. XXXV. 9-XXXVI. 1.

their enemies, N.N. is not punished on account of his enemies" [1]). Sinners, enemies of Osiris, are punished in the netherworld. "Your substance is punished" [2]). Horus chastises them. "He glorifies you, he punishes your enemies" [3]). The punishment of Osiris' enemies consists of deprivation of liberty. "The punisher punishes you with his punishment. You do not escape his guarding to all eternity" [4]). A picture shows sinners in a division of hell of the netherworld. A goddess stands beside it with a knife. The inscription near it reads: "Punishment for your corpses with knives" [5]).

Nik is particularly used in connection with Apophis as the chief enemy of Re and therefore the head of all sinners. The Book of Gates calls them "who punished the evil one of face (Apophis)" [6]). About Apophis it is said: "He is punished, but Re stands in time, while he rests" [7]). About beings with staffs in their hands we read: "Their staffs are in their hands. They have received their knives. They punish Apophis. They are the ones who make his slaughter" [8]). *Nik* refers to a bloody punishment, the cutting to pieces of Apophis. Re says: "I appear. I chase away my enemies, the gods. They punish the evil one of face (Apophis), who is in the *d3.t*" [9]). About uraei it is said: "They have punished Apophis for him in heaven" [10]). Four goddesses with knives are pictured, who cut Apophis to pieces. "They are the goddesses, who punish Apophis in the *d3.t*, who avert the enemies of Re. They are like this: carrying their knives. They punish Apophis in the *d3.t*, each day" [11]). The punishment of Apophis is the destruction of the power of chaos, so that Re may rise and life goes on. "The two very great gods say to Re: Oh behold us, we charm the evil being to be punished (*nik*, determined with the snake). We cut the *b3* of him who surrounds you, that you may become a becoming, oh Re" [12]). In this way *nik* becomes a denomination of Apophis as a serpent inimical to Re, which must be punished. Also those in the

---

[1]) Pyr. 1468.a. b.

[2]) L.Q. CXVIII. 5.

[3]) Book of Gates III, lower register, B.S. Pl. VIII. 17. 18.

[4]) Am Duat VII, 36-38.

[5]) Am Duat XI, 76.

[6]) Book of Gates VII, upper register, Budge, The Eg. Heaven and Hell, II, p. 204; E. Lefébure, *Le Tombeau de Séti Ier*, II. 11.

[7]) Book of Gates X, upper register, B.S. Pl. XI. 17. 18.

[8]) Book of Gates XI, middle register, B.S. Pl. X. 19-23.

[9]) L.Q. CXXIX. 1-2.

[10]) Am Duat XII. 8.

[11]) Am Duat VII. 84-89.

[12]) L.Q. CXXVIII. 4-5.

netherworld condemned to the torturing-post, are called *nik̦y.w* [1]).

C.5.c. *nḏ*, to punish.

Beings in the realm of the dead "punish the rebel" [2]). "Punish the enemies" is said to them [3]).

C.5.d. *ḫśf n*, to punish somebody.

This verb is used of what Anubis does to the gang of Seth, which has sinned against Osiris [4]).

C.5.e. *śswn*, to punish.

The original meaning of this verb is to destroy. In this way it occurs in the wisdom of Ptahhotep for "undoing a dream" [5]). The deceased renders his enemies in the realm of the dead innocuous. "This N.N. makes himself see with his two complete eyes, with which he punishes his enemies" [6]). The dead says of his enemies: "I have punished (destroyed) their dignities" [7]). "I punish those who are not there" [8]).

In the tombs of the kings of the New Kingdom *śswn* is a term often used for the punishment of the godless. Just as in the case of *nik̦* this chastisement implies bodily injury and even total destruction. "We breathe (the beatified say) when you punish the evil ones and ruin them" [9]). "You are punished *Śśy*" [10]). I make the gods content with my rays. I punish the enemies who are in them in the place of destruction. I count them out to the controllers, whose guarding one does not escape" [11]). It here concerns a two-fold judgment. The good are rewarded by the sun-god, the wicked are punished. On the nightly journey of the sun through the realm of the dead Thoth punishes the enemies of Re. "Thoth is permanent in front of your boat, to punish all your enemies who are in the *d3.t*" [12]). Atum says to Apophis: "I chase you away (*dr*) for Re; I punish you for Akhte" [13]).

---

1) B.D. 180; 473. 9.

2) Am Duat III. 25.

3) Am Duat V. 43-44.

4) Papyrus Jumilhac XVIII. 13.

5) Wisdom of Ptahhotep, ed. Dévaud, 359.

6) Pyr. 1240.a.b.

7) C.T. I. 401.c.

8) C.T. II. 252.e. Parallel with it is: "I drive away (*dr.i*) who are there." Cf. the parallelism between *śswn* and *dr* in the Book of Gates II, see note 13.

9) L.Q. XLI. 7.

10) Book of Gates IX, middle register, B.S. Pl. XII. 37. 38. *Śśy* is an inimical serpent.

11) L.Q. XXXVII. 8. 9.

12) Louvre SN 173, VIII. 5 (B.D. XV, 40. 15), *Ḏḥwty mn m ḥ3.t wi3.k r śswn ḫfty.w.k nb.w imy.w d3.t.*

13) Book of Gates II, lower register, B.S. Pl. III. 14. 15.

C.5.f. *ḏw.t*, evil.

To do something evil = to punish him. Re punishes the enemies of Osiris. "I put evil in the enemies" [1]). "Your evil is done to you" [2]). Horus punishes the enemies of Osiris: "Horus, he orders their evil against them" [3]). The dead sentences Apophis for Re: "He places evil into Apophis" [4]). "Do evil in them who must be punished" [5]). Re says on his journey through the realm of the dead: "I have come here . . . to do evil against my enemies," that is to say to punish my enemies [6]).

C.5.g. *ḏ.t*, eternity.

The punishment of the sinners is everlasting. It is said to unjust punished in the netherworld: "You do not see those living on earth to all eternity. They are in the *d3.t* thus: Their slaughter is ordered every day by the majesty of Harakhte" [7]). The punishment is repeated incessantly. The tortured cannot escape it. "Their souls do not escape" [8]). Re says: "I count them out to the place of destruction, where there is no escape" [9]). In the realm of the dead Re's enemies are tied to the torturing-posts of Geb. About them it is said: "Let them not come from under your hands. Let them not escape from your fingers" [10]). Something similar is said of the punishment of Seth by Osiris: "Let him not escape from your hand" [11]). In the netherworld there are punishing demons "whose guarding one does not escape" [12]). The netherworld is "of a lasting nature" [13]), that is to say what is arranged in the netherworld, is irrevocable, everlasting. To Apophis it is said: "You do not escape, you do not get off, Apophis, enemy of Re" [14]). To enemies of Osiris in fiery divisions of hell it is said: "You do not get off and do not escape the fire" [15]).

---

1) L.Q. XXVI. 1. 2) L.Q. CXX. 1.

3) Book of Gates VIII, lower register, B.S. Pl. XV. 11. 12.

4) B.D. 127 A; 271. 10. 5) Louvre SN 173, VIII. 17, *wd ḏw m nik*.

6) Book of Gates IV, lower register, B.S. Pl. VI. 45-V. 48.

7) Am Duat XI. 78.

8) L.C. CXXXIII. 7. 8.

9) L.C. CXXXIII. 9-CXXXIV. 1.

10) Book of Gates V, middle register, B.S. Pl. XVIII. 22-26.

11) Pyr. 1337.b.

12) B.D. 17; C.T. IV. 322.c.

13) Book of Gates VII, middle register, Budge, The Eg. Heaven and Hell, II, p. 194; E. Lefébure, *Le Tombeau de Séti Ier*, II. 10.

14) B.D. 39; 106. 10.

15) Am Duat XI. 77.

C.6. *Sin.*

C.6.a. *iw*, sin [1]).

In the meaning of sin, guilt, this word occurs on the Hyksos-stele [2]): "I will not leave anything of Avaris on account of its guilt". The dead is acquitted of guilt in the judgment of the dead. "Your sin is driven away, your guilt is wiped out by those who weigh with the scales on the day of counting the characters" [3]). Something like it is meant in B.D. 17 [4]): "The evil is driven away from me". On his passage through the netherworld the dead has to pass gates, at which judgment is passed on him. At one of these gates "hearing on account of sin" is mentioned [5]).

C.6.b. *iwy.t*, sin.

The dead states that he is not guilty. "I have done no sin in the place of the truth" [6]).

C.6.c. *iri r*, to act against.

This term is used for sinning against a god. Osiris instructs his son Horus to take care that they who sinned against him, are punished in hell. "Come to me, my son Horus, save me from those, who act against me. Assign them to him who is set over the destruction" [7]). Re says to Osiris with regard to those who have sinned against him: "Have power over those who act against you" [8]).

C.6.d. *isf.t*, sin.

The Wb. gives the following meanings for *isf.t*: wrong doing, sin, in contrast with *mꜣʿ.t* disorder instead of order; the king and the sun drive *isf.t* away, when they appear [9]); lie, parallel with *grg* [10]); in politics, revolution (cf. *sbi rḳw*) [11]). The dead states that he is free of sin. "The evil which is on me is driven away, for I have purified myself in these two big ponds" [12]). In the so-called "negative con-

---

1) Wb. I.48.6.
2) Kamose, line 17, Ch. d'Eg. XXX, n. 60, *juillet* 1955.
3) C.T. I. 181.c-e.
4) C.T. IV. 208.c.
5) B.D. 146, 14th gate.
6) B.D. 125; 250. 2.
7) Book of Gates III, lower register, B.S. Pl. VIII. 20-22.
8) Am Duat VII. 21.
9) Wb. I. 129. 9.
10) Idem 10.
11) Idem 13.
12) C.T. IV. 210.a. b. (B.D. 17), cf. *iw*, *ny.t*. See also *dr iw*, by the ritual purification the dead frees himself from the moral evil which he has done.

fession" the dead says to Osiris: "I bring you *m3ʿ.t*, I chase *isf.t* away for you. I have not done *isf.t* against men," that is to say done something unjust [1]). *M3ʿ.t* and *isf.t* are also opposites in the following passages: An official says in his autobiography that he is somebody, who loves the truth, who despises sin" [2]). The dead states: "I am the one who does justice, I detest the evil for Atum" [3]). "He purifies himself from sin: "N.N. has seized his evil" [4]). "N.N. has loosened the evil that is in him" [5]). About the owners of food offerings, who are behind Osiris, it is said: "Who are without sin, owners of offerings in the West, peaceful ones, lords of the truth, who have the disposal of spells, while they fell the enemies" [6]). These are those who have been morally just and who now may participate themselves in the judgment of the dead.

C.6.e. *ʿw3*, robbery.

Punishing a sin in the netherworld is called "to square accounts with robbery" [7]).

C.6.f. *ʿb*, mischief, sin.

In a passage about the ideal age we read: "He spends 110 years of life, while there are 10 years outside his harm and mischief, outside his guilt and lie" [8]). Perhaps *ʿb* has, in parallelism with *śḏb*, a non-moral sense, while *ḫbn.t* and *grg* do have an ethical meaning. The dead asks not to be punished for his sins. "This evil spell, which I have said, this sin, which I have done, may not be retaliated upon me" [9]). *ʿb* here is moral wrong, bad deeds, beside bad words.

C.6.g. *wn*, guilt [10]).

Wn = something which may be criticized. The dead protests his innocence: "Neither my guilt nor any evil which is on me, is found" [11]).

C.6.h. *wš3 ḫrw*, to pour out the voice.

In the Book of Gates opponents of Re are pictured in the lower register among those punished. During their life on earth they have done wrong against the sun-god. They are the ones "who threw an evidence and poured out their voices against Akhty (= Re)" [12]).

---

1) B.D. 125; 249. 16.
2) Urk. IV. 529. 13-14.
3) C.T. Spell 566; VI. 165.e. f.
4) C.T. IV. 49.k, parallel with *dr ḏw.t.f.*
5) C.T. IV. 60. p.
6) L.Q. XLIV. 4. 5.
7) C.T. IV. 300.a; B.D. 17.
8) C.T. III. 293.a. b.
9) B.D. 105; 216. 14.
10) Wb. I. 314, *Fehler*, *Schuld*, *Tadel*; 7 beside *śrḫ*, rebuke.
11) B.D. 127 A; 273. 11.
12) Book of Gates I, lower register, B.S. Pl. III. 38-43.

Later they are paid back in their own coin. An injurious evidence is also given against them. *Wš3 ḫrw* here points to speaking blashphemous words to Re. It is the opposite of *wš3 ḥknw*, to extol [1]).

C.6.i. *bỉn*, bad [2]).

In the meaning of guilt, crime, it occurs in the "negative confession". The dead says to the 42 judges: "May you not take my guilt to this god, behind whom you are" [3]). "Oh Nefertem, who comes from Memphis, my sin does not exist, I have done no evil" [4]). *Bỉn* in a moral sense occurs in the wisdom of Ptahhotep: "You will belittle evil speaking" [5]). In the wisdom of Ani we read: "Do not fraternize with somebody else's servant, whose name is stinking on account of his bad character, although he is a great nobleman" [6]).

Just as *ỉsf.t* stands in opposition to *m3ʿ.t*, *bỉn* is opposed to *nfr*, e.g., in Ptahhotep: "Good has become evil, all taste has disappeared" [7]). In this connection it concerns the infirmities of old age. The idea is: the pleasant has become unpleasant. Sometimes the contrast may be rendered as "beautiful" and "ugly".

Bỉn may also refer to unhappy circumstances: "Be not in a bad condition on account of your enemies" [8]).

Applied to sin *bỉn* typifies evil as something which is "ugly" or "depraved".

C.6.j. *nỉ.t*, sin.

This occurs in a passage from B.D. 17 [9]): "My sin has been put away" [10]). Might there be a connection with the verb *nỉ*, to reject? *Nỉ.t* = that which must be rejected.

C.6.k. *nḏy.t*, wickedness [11]).

In an autobiography it reads: "I thought I wanted to go to the realm of the dead, without there being any wickedness to which my name was connected [12]).

---

1) Wb. I. 369. 11; Urk. IV. 1095. 6; 1208. 12.

2) Wb. I. 444, *das Böse, das man redet* 1, *oder tut* 2. *Gern neben nfr*: *Gutes und Böses* 3.

3) B.D. 125; 260. 2.

4) B.D. 125, confession 34, Naville II. 305.

5) Prisse V. 12.

6) Ani V. 15.

7) Prisse V. 1.

8) C.T. VI. 217.e. f.

9) C.T. IV. 208.d.

10) Cf. *ỉw*, C.6.a.

11) Wb. II. 369.9.

12) Turin 154, *Rec. de Trav.* IV, 1883, 131, stela of Beki, see J. Spiegel, *Totengericht*, p. 72. The same term also Ptahhotep, 92 and Peasant 66 beside *ʿwn ỉb*.

C.6.l. *ḫww*, wicked actions, sin.

The term is used in the "negative confession". "N.N. is acquitted of all sin he has done, to see the face of the gods" [1]). "I am free from sin" [2]). Compare with this the passage from Ptahhotep. "Sin is seized, until the exemplary things remain" [3]).

The term *ḫww* is etymologically connected with *ḫwi* = to protect. Applied to gods it means "to be venerated" [4]). *Śšm ḫw* = sacred statue [5]). *Ḫw* is what is "protected", put apart. In *ḫww* as term for sin we might think of that which is "protected", which man may not touch. This tallies with the idea of taboo.

C.6.m. *ḫbn.t*, crime.

At his arrival in the other world the dead wishes to be free from guilt. "Your sin is chased away, your guilt is wiped out" [6]). *'Iw* and *ḫbn.t* are parallel here and must have about the same meaning. In another place *ḫbn.t* is parallel with *grg*, lie [7]). The term also occurs in the "negative confession": "My crime does not exist" [8]). The Evil one incites man to evil things: "The devil (*ḫfty*) seduces to commit sins" [9]).

A passage about a premature death deals with somebody's enemies, "who hasten your going away, who say to the god: "Fetch him on the day of judgment" [10]). Compare for this meaning of *ḫbn.t* the verb *ḫbn* "(*den Verbrecher*) *bestrafen*" [11]). *Ḫbn ḫrw*, to be condemned, is the opposite of *m3ʿ ḫrw*, to be justified.

From *ḫbn.t* is derived, as nisbe-form, *ḫbn.ty*, criminal. This occurs in the passage [12]): "Osiris N.N. does not enter the pool of the criminals." This is a place, where sinners in the realm of the dead are punished. The *ḫbn.ty.w* may be demons, who waylay the dead. He flies to the *3ḫ.t* as a falcon, without his *b3* being hindered. "He saves himself from the criminals, the slaughterers, strong of arm; . . . I am the one, whom the criminals have respected" [13]).

After the study of E. Dévaud [14]) the reading *ḫbn* (and not *ḫb n* with

---

1) B.D. 125; 249. 4. 5.
2) B.D. 125; 266. 12.
3) Ptahhotep 496.
4) Wb. III. 245. 5.
5) Wb. III. 245. 8; Urk. II. 29. 14.
6) C.T. I. 181.c.
7) C.T. III. 293.b.
8) B.D. 125; 260. 13.
9) Ptahhotep 292.
10) C.T. I. 73.a. b.
11) Wb. III. 254. 3.
12) B.D. 130; 279. 16.
13) C.T. VI. 77.a. e.
14) Kêmi I, 138.

Sethe [1]) may be considered definitely established. The *itm.w ḫbn ḫrw.śn* are "*ceux qui ne sont pas damnés*". Dévaud quotes some places from Edfu, for instance "I give you justification on the day of judgment, condemnation to your enemies." *Ḫbn* is determined with the bent arm. Etymologically it means "what is crooked", as against *m3ʿ*, "what is straight".

C.6.n. *ẖ3b.t*, sin.

"My sin does not exist" [2]), the dead says in a sequence in which he protests his innocence before the court [3]). He wants to be put in the right by judges in the hereafter towards his opponent. "May I be granted admittance to the council on account of the injustice which has been done against me by my enemy" [4]). In the realm of the dead the just have a favourable fate, but the sinners have not [5]). "They have the disposal of their libations, those who were water in the fire against the sinners and the evil-doers (*iry.w ẖ3b.t*)."

In an autobiographical text from the Old Kingdom we read: "I have never said anything in a bad, sinful and wicked way against any man" [6]). Here *ẖ3b* is determined with the sickle, which points to the original meaning of „being crooked" [7]). Compare *ẖ3b.t*, the thread of the red crown, on account of the curled shape. This is also derived from *ẖ3b*, to be crooked. The term *ẖ3b.t* indicates sin as the "crooked".

C.6.o. *ẖ3k*, to rebel.

The enemies of Osiris are punished in the netherworld. They are "those who rebel against the overlord of the *d3.t*" [8]). "The rebels" [9]) are slaughtered. Sin is rebellion against a god.

C.6.p. *sp*, guilt.

The dead says to the 42 judges: "I am blameless with you" [10]). Of the weighing-scene in the judgment of the dead it is said: "The scales were free from my guilt"; "my guilt was not found" [11]). At a funeral procession the attendants say: "Not a single guilt is found with him" [12]). Compare for the meaning of *sp* = guilt a passage from the wisdom of Ptahhotep: "One passes over his "case" (= guilt)" [13]).

---

[1]) Pyr. 462.b; 1041.d; with commentary of Sethe.
[2]) C.T. I. 173.d. [3]) See also *try.t* and *ḏ3y.t*. [4]) C.T. II. 228.b; 229.a.
[5]) Book of Gates I, upper register, B.S. Pl. IV. 35-III. 38. [6] Urk. I. 204. 9.
[7]) Wb. III. 361. 13. [8]) Am Duat VII. 30-31. [9]) Am Duat X. 2.
[10]) B.D. 125; 260. 3. Wb. III. 435. 9, "*nicht war er zu tadeln*".
[11]) B.D. 1, 30, Naville II. 15. [12]) Urk. IV. 1024. 9.
[13]) Wisdom of Ptahhotep 586.

C.6.q. *sḥ3i*, to denude.

This term is used of making the divine mysteries known, this being a sin. Those who have trespassed against Osiris, are punished by Horus. "You have despised the mysteries. You have handed over the essence of the secret house to publicity. My father Osiris is justified towards you . . . You are those who have profaned the thing hidden" [1]).

C.6.r. *šnṯ.t*, slander.

The dead protests his innocence before the court. "I have guarded myself from slandering those who are in their day (a phyle of priests)" [2]). The sin consists of slandering persons, who are involved in sacred actions.

C.6.s. *ḳn*, "*Böses, Schaden*" [3]), "*Ubeltat*" [4]).

Those who have sinned against the sun-god, are punished in the realm of the dead. "You are those who perform bad deeds (to do damages), who do evil in the West. You are enemies. You are not and you will not be" [5]). In the meaning of crime *ḳn* occurs in a passage about the Instruction of the Vizir. It there concerns transgressions, of which somebody has not known to purge himself and of which deed has been drawn up. "The affairs should be pronounced, on account of which they are inserted into the book, in accordance with their crime" [6]). A nomarch says in his autobiography that he has retaliated transgressions. "He is the one who does harm to those who do harm" [7]). With a view to a famine *ḳn* may mean "dearth" [8]). According to the etymology *ḳn* indicates sin as damage of the order, shortage.

C.6.t, *ḳni*, to be dissatisfied.

D3ty.w, opponents of Re, are punished in the realm of the dead. They are "the opponents in the hall of Re, who were dissatisfied with Re on earth, who called in an evil way to him who was in the egg (Re)" [9]). It here concerns defamatory language, speaking discontented words about the sun-god. In the same passage it is said of

---

[1]) Book of Gates VIII, lower register, B.S. Pl. XIV. 24-31.
[2]) B.D. 125; 266. 12.
[3]) Wb. V. 48. 2. 3.
[4]) Wb. V. 48. 8.
[5]) L.Q. XXV. 3. 4.
[6]) Urk. IV. 1109. 7-8.
[7]) Urk. IV. 968. 15.
[8]) Wb. V. 48. 11-12.
[9]) Book of Gates I, lower register, B.S. Pl. IV. 15-37.

these *d3ty.w*: "Your evil belongs to you. Your slaughter is against you. Your dissatisfaction belongs to you (that is to say is counted out to you). Your summons to evil belongs to you. Your inquiry with Re belongs to you." Their sins are retaliated to them.

Compare for the meaning yet another passage: "The one was not evil towards the other" [1]).

C.6.u. *try.t*, sin [2]).

The dead states to be pure before the court: "My sin does not exist" [3]). Here there is parallelism with other terms for sin, *isf.t*, *ḫ3b*, *d3.t*. *Ṯry.t* is determined with the man standing with his arms raised. In virtue hereof there might be an etymological connection with *twr*, to hold in respect. In that case sin is indicated as something from which one has to abstain, which one has to respect. Thus the thought of taboo might be present also here.

The term also occurs in the Book of Gates [4]) where it concerns the just, *m3ʿty.w*, who have a favourable fate, "who told the truth on earth, who were not close by the sin. They are invited to this gate."

C.6.v. *thi*, to trespass [5]).

The dead protests his innocence: "I have not trespassed" [6]). About a fiery pond in the realm of the dead, in which there is a uraeus, it is said: "Your fire, your glowing breath and your flame are against the souls, when they approach in order to trespass against Osiris" [7]).

C.6.w. *ṯmś.w*, evil, crime, injustice [8]).

The sin of the dead is extirpated: "Your guilt is wiped out; ... your damage is driven away with Hathor" [9]). About four women in the realm of the dead, who are near the punished enemies of Osiris, it is said: "They are like this: they are near the evil among the enemies of Osiris in the *d3.t* of him who is at the head of his cauldrons as guard of this cave" [10]). In this connection it is not quite clear whether

---

[1]) *Stèle de mariage*, Ramses II, ed. Ch. Kuentz, Ann. du Serv. XXV, p. 218.
[2]) Wb. V. 317. 10-12, *Schlechtes im moralischen Sinne, Parallel zu isf.t.*
[3]) C.T. I. 173.c. [4]) Book of Gates I, upper register, B.S. Pl. IV. 30-32.
[5]) Wb. + r = *Böses tun gegen*; Wb. V. 319. 10, *gegen einen Gott freveln*; + *Objekt*, 20, *jem. antasten.* [6]) B.D. 125; 254. 4.
[7]) Book of Gates VII, lower register, Budge, The Eg. Heaven and Hell, II, pp. 215, 216; E. Lefébure, *Le Tombeau de Séti Ier* II, 12, 13.
[8]) The word is connected with *ṯmś*, red.
[9]) C.T. I. 183.h; 184.a. [10]) Am Duat XI. 79.

ṯmś.w is the punishment for sinners or the evil which they have done. In the sense of evil as a punishment it occurs in a passage [1]), where the dead says to Osiris: "Save me from your messengers, who do damage, who cause punishment." A place in the Book of Gates reminds one of the quotation from Am Duat [2]). Near four women, who are involved in the punishment of godless ones, it is written: "They are the ones who fix the duration and who give rise to the years for those who belong to the evil in the *d3.t* and for the living in heaven." This refers to a different fate for just and unjust. The first are in heaven, the second in hell. In a text from the Book of the Dead somebody protests his innocence. "My sin is not in the hand of the scribe of injustice" [3]). The meaning is: the judge of the dead or Thoth as scribe of Osiris cannot note down my guilt.

C.6.x. *ṯs ḏw*, bad spell.

The dead asks not to be punished on account of sins by word and deed, which he might have committed. "This bad spell which I have said, this sin, which I have done, may not be retaliated upon me" [4]).

C.6.y, *ḏw*, evil in a moral sense, sin.

Sinners are punished in the netherworld [5]). Those who have done evil "they belong to the destruction which is in the netherworld among the evil-doers." The dead is purged of guilt. "N.N. has come, that he may chase the evil away which is in his heart" [6]). "Chase away the evil which is on me" [7]). About those punished by Atum in the netherworld it is said: "You are these who have done evil, who have made a slaughter in the great hall" [8]). Punished sinners in the netherworld are called *ḏw.w*. "Re says to this cave: Oh *Spsy*, oh *Spsy.t*, who are in the place of destruction, under whose guard the evil are, who do not escape their cave . . . I count you out to the seizers . . . you are the enemies, evil of character" [9]). The dead protests his innocence: "My evil does not exist" [10]).

---

[1]) B.D. 125; 262. 5.
[2]) Book of Gates XI, lower register, B.S. Pl. IX. 34-38.
[3]) B.D. 40; 110. 1-2.
[4]) B.D. 105; 216. 13-14.
[5]) C.T. I. 208.d.
[6]) C.T. IV. 60.o.
[7]) C.T. IV. 256.c.
[8]) Book of Gates I, lower register, B.S. Pl. IV. 34-36.
[9]) L.Q. CXXXIV. 5-9.
[10]) B.D. 125; 260. 13.

C.6.z. *ḏ3.t*, transgression [1]).

In an enumeration of terms for sin, of which the dead is not guilty, it reads: "My transgression does not exist" [2]).

C.7. *Sinner.*

C.7.a. *isfty.w*, sinners.

They are punished by the council which is behind Osiris [3]). They are chastised by a demon, "who throws a lasso around the evil-doers in order to fetch them to his slaughtering-block" [4]). In the realm of the dead there is a tormentor "who devours evil-doers" [5]).

C.7.b. *ʿpp*, Apophis.

C.T. Spell 414 [6]) is a spell to avert Apophis. "Behold, a fire has gone out from heaven into the cave of the rebel. He thought of rebelling against Re, of committing robbery against him, but his head is broken by the great destroyer, a flame is kindled against him in the houses of Sepa. His ropes are fastened by the gods." Here Apophis is a rebel against Re, who is punished with the same punishments as are applied to human sinners, e.g., with being fettered and burnt. The same is the case in the Book of Gates [7]). He is the devil, the chief sinner, who is sentenced like all other evil-doers. As a sinner he is called *ḏw ḳd*, malicious one [8]). Apophis is represented on a stela from a late period. He has been fettered and he has been bound to a pole before the place of slaughter, where he will be killed. Here he is in the form of a donkey. The context mentions that he is punished on account of his enmity to the sun-god [9]).

C.7.c. *mś.w Bdš.t.*

They are punished as enemies of Re together with the sinners. "The children of *Bdš.t* atone for what they have done" [10]). "The heads of the children of *Bdš.t* (determined as snake) are chopped off" [11]). In the Book of Gates they are also pictured as snakes, as well as in B.D. 17 and they are punished together with the *W3mmty*-snake:

---

1) Cf. *ḏ3ty.w*, C.7.i.
2) C.T. Spell 40; I. 173.d.
3) C.T. IV. 254.a; B.D. 17.
4) C.T. IV. 300.b; B.D. 17.
5) B.D. 40; 109. 15-110. 1.
6) C.T. V. 244.d-245.c.
7) Book of Gates II, lower register.
8) Papyrus Louvre 3292, ed. Nagel, H. 4.
9) H. P. Blok, *Eine magische Stele aus der Spätzeit*, AcOr VII, 109, Pl. II.
10) C.T. IV. 290.a.
11) B.D. 140; 316. 7. 8.

"Destruction on you, oh children of *Bdš.t*" [1]). "They have applied the fetters of the children of *Bdš.t*" [2]).

C.7.d. *nik*, the evil being to be punished.

This is a denomination of beings, who offer resistance to a god, especially Apophis, and who must be punished in the realm of the dead. C.T. Spell 572 is a spell to make somebody get his magical power back in the realm of the dead. Messengers of Osiris are mentioned there, who restore his magical power to him and who do the same for the dead. The *ḥkꜣ* is called the eye of Horus. The enemies of the eye of Horus are punished and are burnt. They are demons who may also waylay the dead. They sin against Horus and are punished as sinners. Their name and their part is to be compared with that of Apophis, the enemy of the sun, in the *Livres* of the tombs of the kings. "You (the messengers of Horus) take the eye of Horus to him, the waylayers of which (who waylay it, the eye of Horus), fall into the fire. Its waylayers are made permanent in the fire. Its waylayers are made permanent on its sinews (with which they are bound)" [3]). Of Apophis *nik* is used in a passage, where two gods say to Re: "Behold, we conjure the evil one" [4]). Criminals are renamed. Instead of a theophoric name they are called after Apophis, the enemy of the sun, the devil and typical sinner. They are punished as enemies of the god [5]). One of the criminals obtains the name *pꜣ nik*. Statuettes, used in magic to injure an enemy, bear, beside the name of the owner, also that of Apophis. In virtue hereof the punishment inflicted on Apophis may be compared with the punishments of sinners. Names like *mśḏ św Rʿ*, Re hates him, or *pꜣ Rʿ kꜣmm.f*, Re blinds him are also given to criminals or enemies. About desecrators of a grave it is said: "They will be treated like *nik*" [6]). Thus sinners are punished like Apophis, the enemy of the sun.

C.7.e. *rḳw*, enemy.

According to the Wb. [7]) "*Gegner der Götter*". *Rḳi* is to rebel. Sin is rebellion against deity.

---

[1]) Book of Gates X, upper register, B.S. Pl. XI. 42.

[2]) B.D. 17; Naville II. 33.

[3]) C.T. VI. 175.g-j.

[4]) L.Q. CXXVIII. 4; determinative serpent. See also C.5.b.

[5]) G. Posener, *Les criminels débaptisés et les morts sans nom*, *Rev. d'Eg.*, V, 1946, p. 53. [6]) Op. cit. 54. [7]) Wb. II. 456. 18.

C.7.f. *ḫfty*, enemy.

See B.17.d.

C.7.g. *śbi*, rebel.

The sinners are called "rebels". Their sin is rebellion against the divine order. "Oh rebels, whom I have placed there (in a division of the realm of the dead) (Re says), you are the enemies of Osiris, who did damage in the hidden country. I count you out to the earth-snakes. You do not escape their guarding" [1]). In the lower register of the 1st *ḳrr.t* 8 beheaded and 8 imprisoned figures are pictured beside it. A "rebel" [2]) is punished as enemy of Re [3]). *Śbi* is also a denomination of Apophis [4]). As sinners against the divine world-order the *śbi.w* occur in the following passage: "I am this big tomcat (Re), on whose side the *'Išd.t*-tree was cleft in Heliopolis in this night of the fight and of the guarding of the rebels on this day, on which the enemies of the Lord of the universe were destroyed" [5]). From the parallelism with *ḫfty.w* it appears that it here concerns rebels against the Lord of the universe.

C.7.h. *ḳywy*, the others.

The Wb. here says: "*Belegt Sp.*; *Gr. die Feinde*" [6]). The term also occurs before. In C.T. Spell 572 it stands as a variant of *niḳy.w* [7]), the enemies of the eye of Horus. In C.T. Spell 316 it occurs beside *ḫfty.w*. There the dead identifies himself with the Horus eye and kills his enemies, just as the Horus eye destroys its waylayers: "Great is your fear, great is your terror, great is your rage, great is your magical power in the belly of your enemies. The *ḳyw* have fallen on their faces for you" [8]). In C.T. Spell 312 the *ḳyw* occur as enemies of Nut [9]). In C.T. Spell 37 *ḳyw* is parallel with *śbi.w* and *ḫfty.w* [10]).

C.7.i. *ḏ3ty.w*, opponents.

As condemned sinners they occur in the Book of Gates, "the opponents of the hall of Re, who were dissatisfied on earth with Re . . ." [11]). Further their punishment is spoken of. Perhaps this word is connected with *ḏ3i*, to put oneself inimically in the way.

---

1) L.Q. VIII. 7. 8.
2) *Śbi*, determined by the snake.
3) Book of Gates VII, upper register, Budge, The Eg. Heaven and Hell II, p. 201; E. Lefébure, *Le Tombeau de Séti Ier* II, 11.
4) Book of Gates IX, middle register, B.S. Pl. XIII. 26. Cf. C.T. V. 244.a. d. e; 247.a. b. See C.7.b.
5) B.D. 17; C.T. IV. 282.a-284.b.
6) Wb. V. 116. 6.
7) C.T. VI. 175.h, see C.7.d.
8) C.T. IV. 98.i-99.b.
9) C.T. IV. 83.c.
10) C.T. I. 156.b.
11) Book of Gates I, lower register, B.S. Pl. IV. 15-30.

CHAPTER THREE

REPRESENTATIONS OF THE NETHERWORLD IN DEMOTIC LITERATURE

An important source of information is the Setne-novel, especially the passages where Setne's son, Si-Osire, shows his father the secrets of the netherworld. The name *ʾImn.t* or *ʾImnt.t* [1]) is retained [2]) and also *twꜣ.t* [3]) occurs, the latter, e.g., II Setne II, 22 "that which you have seen in the netherworld of Memphis (*twꜣ.t*)." The just and the unjust (the poor and the rich man in II Setne [4])) are both in the netherworld. There the one receives a favourable, the other an unfavourable fate. This tallies with the representation of the tombs of the kings, where the just are rewarded by Re and Osiris and the sinners are punished. Si-Osire wishes his father the happy fate in the realm of the dead which the poor man has: "To you shall be done in the West like one will do to this poor man in the West" [5]).

Setne sees the just in their beatification and the godless in their punishment: "They entered the fifth hall and Setne saw the noble spirits, who stood according to their manner of standing" [6]). The term *ꜣḫ* is a *vox media* and may be used for beatified as well as for punished ones. The *Zweiwegebuch* [7]) speaks of a *ꜣḫ ʿpr*, which goes to the heaven of Re and of a *ꜣḫ*, which remains in darkness. In the Book of Gates III, lower register 1st figure, *ꜣḫ.w* occur, which are punished and fear Osiris. However, it also occurs that the *ꜣḫ.w* obtain a favourable fate and the *mt.w* are punished [8]). In the Egyptian texts *wśḫ.t* is the hall where judgment is pronounced [9]). In the Setne quotation *wśḫ.t* answers the use of a word like *śbḫ.t* in the Egyptian texts [10]).

---

[1]) Erichsen, *Glossar* 31. [2]) A.11.b; e.g., II Setne I. 20.

[3]) *Twꜣ.t* = *dꜣ.t*, Erichsen, *Glossar* 613.

[4]) About the poor man: "They took him to the netherworld" (*twꜣ.t*), II Setne II. 10. Idem of the rich one II, 13. Their good and bad deeds are weighed against each other. [5]) II Setne I. 20.

[6]) II Setne II. 2; Erichsen, *Glossar* 69, *rt.ṯ n ʿḥʿ*, *Art des Stehens*.

[7]) Cairo 28085, Lacau, Sarc. I. 216-217, 20 sqq.; C.T. VII, Spells 1115, 1116; See p. 89. [8]) Book of Gates I, middle; C.2.b. [9]) C.2.c. [10]) B.1.h.

It is a division of the realm of the dead. Also the numbering of these divisions tallies with the Book of Gates and Am Duat.

Judgment takes place according to works. The position of men in the realm of the dead agrees with their behaviour during life on earth: "He who has been excellent on earth, will do well in the West, while the bad is treated badly" [1]). This judgment according to works also occurs in the Egyptian texts. The dead are treated in accordance with what they have done (*ỉr.t.n.śn*) on earth [2]).

Also the wording tallies. In the Setne-novel the *mnḫ* in the hereafter answers the being *mnḫ* on earth. Thus it is said in the Book of Gates: Those who have done *m3ʿ.t*, will receive *m3ʿ.t* [3]). Also the interchange of fate of rich and poor occurs in the Book of Gates: "To make the great one a small one among the gods" [4]).

The favourable fate of the just is connected with the realm of the dead as well as with heaven [5]), "but when it is judged that his good deeds are more numerous than his bad deeds, he will be taken among the gods of the council of the Lord of the West and his soul goes to heaven together with the (other) noble spirits." Just as in the Egyptian texts it is especially the *b3*, the element moving freely, which is connected with heaven [6]). In the Egyptian sources the fear is uttered that the *b3* is locked up [7]).

The favourable fate of the dead is also represented as a sojourn with Osiris in the West [8]): "The doors of the West are opened to you, the gates of the netherworld are opened to you, that you may adore Osiris and his sister Isis, who is with him. Cf. B.1.a. p. 115, C.T. Spell 228, where the dead asks the gate-keeper of Osiris to be admitted. The favourable fate here is to be in the netherworld with Osiris, to belong to those who are behind Osiris [9]). The West is taken as the normal realm of the dead, where one wants to be, B.D. 181: "He who knows this spell, is not kept off from the gates of *ʾImnt.t*" [10]). The Papyrus Rhind says that the dead enters the West. There he sees Osiris [11]), "you are admitted among the rewarded".

---

1) II Setne II. 21.
2) Chapter I, Par. 11, pp. 35-37.
3) C.4.d, p. 281.
4) C.2.b, p. 267.
5) II Setne II. 7.
6) B.8.c.
7) B.2.h, *ḫnr*.
8) Rhind, Totenpap., p. 26.
9) Chapter I, Par. 11, *ỉmy.w ḫt Wśir*, p. 40.
10) B.1.j, p. 124.
11) P. 30.

As in the Egyptian texts the dead has to pass gates [1]). They open to him and he enters the realm of the dead [2]) "the *ḳrty*-gods, who guide the netherworld, come to you in order to lead you along a beautiful road of the netherworld; they open the gates of the netherworld to you in the horizon, which is in the West, that you may go in and out." See also B.1.f.j: the dead does not want to be kept off from the gates [3]).

Setne also sees the punished in the realm of the dead. In the fifth hall he sees the spirits of the just in the place destined for them, but also the punished sinners, "those who had been accused on account of [4]) taking with injustice [5]) stood at the door and wailed" [6]). Apparently these sinners are not admitted to a beatific region. This tallies with the representations of gates in the Book of the Dead. Unjust are not admitted. For *śmi* = to accuse cf. C.1.k. For the wailing of the wretched cf. A.16.

Another punishment is that the condemned serve as hinges of the door, "the pivot [7]) of the gate of the fifth hall was fixed in the right eye of a man, who wailed and uttered loud lamentations" [8]). This representation is known from Quibell. Hieraconpolis I, 6, a door-socket with a man's head. Quibell points to enemies under the gate of the realm of the dead in the Book of the Dead and to heads of enemies as props in the palace of Ramses III in Medinet Habu. An alabaster cosmetic-jar from the tomb of Tutankhamen rests on heads of four hostile peoples. About other punished ones the following is said [9]): "These people whom you have seen, who twist rope, while their asses eat it, they are the picture of mankind on earth, who live under the curse of the god. Night and day they are in great pains for their subsistence, while their wives take it away from them, so that they find no bread to eat. They also went to the West and it was found that their bad deeds were more numerous than their good

---

[1]) B. 1. [2]) Rhind, p. 50.

[3]) For the *ḳrty*-gods, see Erichsen, *Glossar* 566, derived from *ḳrr.t*, see B.7.q.

[4]) Erichsen, *Glossar* 432. [5]) Erichsen, *Glossar* 542.

[6]) II Setne II. 2. [7]) See *ḳl3.t*. Erichsen, *Glossar* 545.

[8]) II Setne II. 2-3, idem II. 14. *Abh. Königl. Preuss. Ak. der Wiss.* Jahrg. 1918, *Phil. Hist. Kl.* Nr. 7, *Vom reichen Mann und armen Lazarus*, H. Greszmann-G. Möller; Conjuration of demons, which are to be warded off from the threshold.

[9]) II Setne II, 17 sqq.; *Abh. Königl. Preuss. Ak. der Wiss.* Jahrg. 1918, *Phil. Hist. Kl.* Nr. 7, *Vom reichen Mann und armen Lazarus*, H. Greszmann-G. Möller; Hellenistic influence; rope of Orcos.

ones. They have experienced that the way of living they had on earth has also fallen to their share in the West." The punishment is akin to the sin committed. It here concerns people who only worked for material gain, while their wives were insatiable. Just as these wives squandered the gains, the asses eat the twisted rope and the condemned must continue to work infinitely like Sisyphus or the Danaids. A similar thought occurred in Ptahhotep 99 sqq. [1]): "Do not worry as a man, god punishes with the same." In Book of Gates I a bad evidence is lodged against those who have also given a bad evidence about Re [2]). As regards a punishment with work that is never finished, cf. B.21.l, the meaning of which perhaps is that the condemned has to bail water (*pnḳ*) endlessly.

Unhappy also is the fate of those who must suffer a tantalization [3]), „whose food, bread and water, were hung above them and when they straightened themselves to bring them down, others dug holes under their feet in order not to let them reach it. They are the picture of men who are on earth, whose subsistence belongs to them, but the god digs holes under their feet, so that they cannot reach it. They have come to the West again and the way of living they had on earth again falls to their share in the West. Their soul has been taken up in the *dꜣ.t*. Lay it to heart, my father." These people were predestined to disaster already during their life on earth. They never had any result of their work. Also for them this fate is kept up in the hereafter. Just as in the case of the rope-makers from the previous passage it does not so much concern here a punishment as a consolidation of the situation during life on earth in eternity. Fear of hunger already occurs in the Egyptian texts of the dead [4]). The *Ḥtp*- and *'Iꜣr.w*-fields should provide food in the hereafter. In a work like the Book of Gates it is repeatedly assured that the dead have the disposal of their food offerings. That the situation in the

---

[1]) Chapter I, Par. 11, p. 38. [2]) Chapter I, Par. 11, p. 38.

[3]) II Setne II, 19 sqq. *Abh. der Königl. Preuss. Ak. der Wiss.* Jahrg. 1918, *Phil. Hist. Kl. Nr.* 7, *Vom reichen Mann und armen Lazarus*, H. Greszmann-G. Möller; The mummy-covering, Berlin 11651, shows a gloryfied dead person drawing water for himself by means of a shadûf and one out of four doomed persons, represented as little dark figures, trying to drink from it. See also S. Morenz, *Staatliche Museen zu Berlin, Forschungen und Berichte*, 1. Band, 1957, pp. 55, 60: The doomed ones are, also according to the Setne-story, naked.

[4]) A.5.b. n.

hereafter is a continuation of the one on earth also occurs there. Justice is counted out to those who had *m3ʿ.t* on earth [1]).

The demotic texts also know of a council [2]) of judges of the dead: "But when it is found that his good deeds are more numerous than his bad deeds he is taken among the gods of the council of the lord of the West" [3]). "They entered the sixth hall and Setne saw the gods of the council of the denizens of the West, who stood according to their rank, and the servants of the West, who stood there and propounded spells" [4]). In the Book of Gates the just in the realm of the dead are also called *nṯr.w*, gods, but they are men (*rmṯ*). The just become more favourably situated in the realm of the dead. They are acquitted in the judgment and are going to form part of the bench of judges themselves. This thought which here occurs in the Setne novel, is also found already in Egyptian sources [5]).

The judgment of the dead before Osiris with the psychostasy and with the assistance of Thoth and Anubis still occurs in demotic literature [6]): "They entered the seventh hall. Setne saw the shape of Osiris, the great god, who was sitting on his throne of beautiful gold, crowned with the Atef-crown, with Anubis, the great god, on his left side and Thoth, the great god, on his right side, while the gods of the council of the dwellers in the West stood on his left and right." The just again play the part of the *imy.w ḫt Wśir* from the Egyptian texts. Thoth performs a task in the psychostasy. In B.D. 125 he notes down the issue (B.16.o). For Anubis see C.3.b. In the scales the good and the bad deeds are weighed against each other. So it does not concern the heart and *m3ʿ.t*, although the idea is the same: "The scales were put in the middle (cf. C.2.e) before them and the bad deeds were weighed against the good ones. Thoth, the great god, wrote it down. Anubis proclaimed the words to his comrade" [7]). If the weighing gives an unfavourable issue a punishment is waiting: "When they find that his bad deeds are more than his good ones he is delivered up to *ʿm* [8]) of the lord of the West" [9]). It is the same monster, *ʿm mt.w*, which also occurs in B.D. 125 in a similar function [10]).

---

1) Chapter I, Par. 11, p. 37.
2) *Ḳnb.t*, cf. C.3.h.
3) II Setne II. 7.
4) II Setne II. 3.
5) Chapter I, Par. 11 p. 39.
6) II Setne II. 4.
7) II Setne II. 5.
8) The "swallower", Erichsen, *Glossar* 60.
9) II Setne II. 6.
10) B.6.a.

The sinner is totally destroyed: "His soul is destroyed together with his body and it does not let him breathe" [1]). The term *ḥtm b3* also occurs in the Egyptian texts [2]). It regards a complete destruction of the personality. In the Egyptian texts also it is said of *b3* and *ẖ3.t* both that they are destroyed: "His corpse is burnt, his *b3* does not exist" [3]). As a term for punishing *tb3* [4]) is used, the Egyptian *ḏb3* [5]), to repay, which may also mean to punish [6]).

Death is circumscribed as a going away to the West: "An evil day of going away to the West" [7]). Here the West is considered to be unfavourable in contrast with life on earth [8]). For *šm*, to go away in the meaning of to pass away, cf. A.2.i.

Summarising it may be said that the demotic texts do not show great differences with the Egyptian sources in the representations of the fate of the dead in the hereafter, on the contrary, sometimes even details tally. That the justified dead participate in a bench of judges, that the essential parts of the personality, like the *b3* and the *ẖ3.t*, are destroyed, all this already occurred in the tombs of the kings. The ethical element in the judgment of the dead is slightly more developed, but also this is nothing new with respect to the older Egyptian literature. Even the terminology is maintained for the greater part.

---

[1]) II Setne II. 6.
[2]) B.8.c, p. 177.
[3]) B.8.c. p. 178. See also B.10.b, p. 189 as a cumulation of punishments *śḥtm b3.w*; *śk ẖ3.t*.
[4]) Erichsen, *Glossar* 619.
[5]) Wb. 5. 555. 10.
[6]) Cf. C.5, terms for punishing and *rdi*, to retaliate, C.4.d.
[7]) Rhind, p. 14.
[8]) Cf. A.11.b.

CHAPTER FOUR

PUNISHMENT IN THE HEREAFTER ACCORDING TO THE COPTIC TEXTS

In the Coptic texts treatises in detail occur about punishments of the godless in the hereafter. A.o. the latter are described in the style of the Divina Commedia. A saint is taken round the cosmos by an angel and on his journey also sees the places where sinners are punished. This same motive occurs in the Jewish Apocalyptic, e.g., in the book Enoch. In Coptic it is found in the apocalypse of Paul [1]). An angel shows him the spheres of heaven, paradise and hell. Now and again Paul poses the question: My Lord, what is this? To that the angel explains what sinners have to suffer. Also Pachomius is taken away in the spirit and a guiding angel shows him the places where sinners are punished [2]). The hellish punishments are described in detail. Here the Coptic texts go into details much more than the Bible.

In the literature about these Coptic representations of hell it is an ever recurring point of discussion as to how far ancient Egyptian motives have continued to survive in the Coptic texts. The Egyptian denomination for the realm of the dead *'Imn.t* recurs in Coptic ⲁⲙⲛ̄ⲧⲉ. The term ⲛⲟⲩⲛ also occurs. This fosters the thought that together with the name also the contents of the Egyptian ideas have passed to the Copts. Some authors go very far here, for instance E. A. Wallis Budge [3]). He enumerates twenty items where he sees reminiscences of Ancient Egypt in the Coptic apocrypha, to wit (1) The name ⲁⲙⲛ̄ⲧⲉ. (2) Gates and gate-keepers. (3) Burning of souls. (4) Demons. (5) Abaddon as an equivalent of Seth. (6) Snakes. (7) Lamentation like that of the denizens of the netherworld in Am Duat after the departure of the sun. (8) The worm which does not sleep. (9) Earthquake at the resurrection of Christ like the one at the

---

[1]) Budge, Miscellaneous Coptic Texts, London 1915, no. XVIII, 534 sqq.

[2]) L. Th. Lefort, *Les Vies Coptes de Saint Pachôme*, Louvain 1943, 148.

[3]) Coptic Apocrypha in the dialect of Upper Egypt, London 1913. Introduction, lxi sqq. Egyptian mythology in Coptic writings.

resurrection of the king in the Pyramid Texts. (10) Magical names of Christ (cf. B.D. 163-165). (11) The twelve virtues of the saviour are to be compared with the *ḥmśw.t*-spirits. (12) The use of the magical word by Christ to open the seven heavens. (13) The river of fire as in the Book of Gates III. The sinners are punished by it, but the just pass unhindered. (14) The Cherub carries a soul on his wing to heaven, like Thoth does in the Pyramid Texts. (15) God the Father sits over the waters like Osiris on his throne. (16) The representation of the primeval ocean before creation. (17) The Father makes a grain of corn from his own body and that of his Son, to be compared with Osiris as the corn-god. (18) The earth rests on 4 pillars, to be compared with the 4 columns of Shu. (19) Seven stars in the North of the heavens like the *iḫm.w śk*. (20) John the Baptist ferries souls across the river of fire in a golden boat and is to be compared with *Ḥr-ḥ3.f*.

At first reading it is already striking that some comparisons are far-fetched, e.g., no. 9, the earthquake at Christ's resurrection, which goes back to Matth. 27 : 51 and 28 : 2. Indeed, the earth-quake at the resurrection of the king is found in the Pyr, but does not play such an important part any more afterwards.

Also Morenz sees many traces of Egyptian thought in the Coptic texts [1]): "*Das Achtergewicht liegt auf den beträchtlichen* survivals *der ägyptischen Religion, wobei deutlich wird, welche Bereiche daraus sich lebenskräftig, ja unentbehrlich erwiesen.*" 26 Epep as the date of Joseph's death is connected with the festival of the inundation of the Nile. Joseph = Osiris = the Nile. *Geschichte von Joseph dem Zimmermann*, II, 6 "my father will measure you with a right pair of scales" goes back to the psychostasy before Osiris. XIII, 6 Joseph, when dying, prays that he may be saved from demoniacal angels on the roads of the hereafter. These angels have the heads of animals. Gatekeepers threaten to keep him off. Streams of fire rage against the dead. XXII, 1 the seven dark aeons which Joseph has to pass, make one think of the seven in the Egyptian "*Jenseitsgeographie*". XXVI, 1 Jesus's prayer for his father to check the decay of the body reminds us of similar Egyptian spells like, e.g., B.D. 45 and 154. According to Morenz [2]) the ancient Egyptian religion penetrated Christianity

---

[1]) S. Morenz, *Die Geschichte von Joseph dem Zimmermann*, Berlin 1951 = *Texte und Untersuchungen zur Geschichte der altchristlichen Literatur*, Bd. 56, IX.

[2]) P. 113 sqq.

via Hellenistic syncretism. The trinity Joseph, Mary, Jesus is formed in analogy with Osiris-Isis-Horus. Especially in gnosticism ancient Egyptian elements come into play. The views of Morenz have been combatted by H. de Meulenaere [1]) who remarks that much of what Morenz considers typically Egyptian, is generally oriental or even generally human. Hieronymus Engberding [2]) rejects Morenz' view that Joseph would be Osiris.

O. H. E. Burmester deals with this matter in an article "Egyptian Mythology in the Coptic Apocrypha" [3]). He deems borrowing from Ancient Egypt in Coptic texts improbable, because the Christian Copts consider paganism to be an invention of the devil. That God the Father makes part of his body a grain of corn [4]) can be traced back to Apocrypha of the O.T. and is further derived from ideas of the eucharist. The gates of hell are not borrowed from Egypt, but from Matth. 16 : 18. Abaddon [5]) is not connected with Seth, but with Apoc. 9 : 11 and Job 28 : 22. John as a ferry-man and the gate-keepers on the other hand, may be borrowed from Egypt. About the punishing angels with animal's heads he says [6]): "This dread of encountering the accusers and avengers of wickedness in the Lower world is certainly Egyptian, and we have parallels in the Book of the Dead." In the Apocalypse of St. Paul the bad smell of the well of the abyss occurs. The same is found in the Book of Gates II, where an unpleasantly smelling pool is avoided by birds. Burmester's conclusion is: "That there are definite traces in the Coptic Apocrypha of direct borrowing from Ancient Egyptian Mythology seems to be clearly established by the foregoing examples. These examples are, it is true, practically all concerned with account of Amente, or the Coptic hell, but this is only what we should expect, if we bear in mind the attitude of the Egyptian Christians towards the religion of Ancient Egypt." That birds avoid the bad smell of the netherworld occurs for that matter also in the Aeneis of Vergilius [7]): "A deep cave lay there with an immense gorge, surrounded

1) BiOr X, 182-184.

2) *Oriens Christianus*, Bd. 37 (1953), *Der Nil in der liturgischen Frömmigkeit des Christlichen Ostens*, 56-88.

3) *Orientalia* VII, 355-367.

4) Budge, item 17.

5) Budge, item 5.

6) PP. 365, 366.

7) VI. 237 sqq. H. L. W. Nelson, *Saturnalia van Macrobius*, 20.

by pointed stones, safely hidden behind the dark lake and the shade of the forest, above which birds were never able to hover on their wings unpunished; such a pestiferous vapour rose from the black opening and spread to the vault of heaven."

M. Cramer [1]) deals with a prayer from the Coptic funerary ritual and says about it [2]): "*Die in diesem Gebet enthaltenen furchtbaren Vorstellungen vom Zugang zum Paradiese sind ganz gewisz altägyptischen Ursprungs.*"

M. Kropp [3]) sees in the Coptic magical texts a mixture of Egyptian religion, Greek syncretism and Jewish-Christian elements [4]). "*Mit den alten Unterweltsgöttern und -Dämonen glaubten unsere Zaubertexte die Jüdisch-Christlichen Vorstellungen vom Reiche des Satans vereinigen zu können. So erklärte sich das ungestörte Fortleben der ersteren*" [5]). In the representations of hell Kropp deems Egyptian influence possible: "*Die Ausmalung eschatologischer Orte ist seit alters her eine Lieblingsbeschäftigung der Ägypter. So ist es nicht zu verwundern, wenn sie auch in Christlicher Zeit in dieser Art ein reiches Schrifttum entwickelten*" [6]). Fiery punishing angels, however, are borrowed from the Jewish-Christian apocalyptic. The Acheron, a stream which the dead have to cross to reach the hereafter, occurs in Greek mythology [7]). Tartaruchos as a guard may be a re-shaping of an Egyptian figure [8]).

Louise Dudley [9]) sees Egyptian remnants in apocryphic homilies [10]): "These beliefs are, in the main, but Christianized remnants of the religion of Ancient Egypt." The view that the godless are burnt is Christian. That this takes place in fiery wells is borrowed from Egypt, just as the hellish monsters who execute these punishments. Angels of death in the shape of animals, who come to fetch the soul, the decani of the Coptic texts, bear resemblance to cruel servants of an Egyptian god, who do the same [11]). The Coptic texts mention that the soul has to go along dangerous roads on the way to eternity. This resolves itself immediately to the religion of Ancient Egypt [12]). "These Christian modifications are numerous and obvious. They

---

[1]) *Die Totenklagen bei den Kopten*, Wien 1941, *Ak. der Wiss. Phil. Hist. Kl., Sitzungsberichte* 219 Bd. 2 *Abh.* [2]) P. 73.

[3]) *Ausgewählte Koptische Zaubertexte*, Bruxelles Bd. III, *Einleitung*.

[4]) P. 3. [5]) P. 13. [6]) P. 89. [7]) P. 89. [8]) P. 95.

[9]) The Egyptian elements in the legend of the body and the soul, Baltimore, 1911, Bryn Mawr College Monographs, Monograph Series, Vol. VIII.

[10]) P. 3. [11]) P. 47. [12]) P. 69.

are, however, only modifications. The foundation and much of the superstructure remain Egyptian" [1]. In the Pistis Sophia the netherworld is a snake with its tail in its mouth, divided into twelve sections, with gates above, through which the godless enter. "This is undoubtedly a survival of an Ancient Egyptian belief" [2]. Louise Dudley investigates further, how Coptic ideas have worked themselves out in later ecclesiastical literature.

F. Zimmermann [3] does not want to go as far as J. Leipoldt [4], who sees a great many Egyptian elements in Coptic texts. Nevertheless he agrees with Robinson in that the Coptic texts, in the concrete description of the punishments for the godless, borrow a great deal of traits from Ancient Egypt [5]. He enumerates quite a series of them [6] a.o. "the hidden place" (Egyptian *štꜣ*) as circumscription of the netherworld; "who are at their gates", a denomination of gate-keepers etc. "*Andererseits bot der Strafort des Jenseits gerade für den ungebildeten Christen ein beliebtes freies Feld dar für die ausschmückende Tätigkeit seiner Phantasie*" [7]. "*Dagegen kann allerdings nicht geleugnet werden, dasz das einseitige Hervortreten und die Stärke dieser religiösen Richtung ein geistiges Erbteil der heidnischen Vorfahren der Kopten ist*" [8]. Thus Zimmermann sees the remnants of Egyptian paganism only in the popular belief, not in the official theology!

These authors differ in their judgment how far ancient Egyptian elements still play a part in Coptic texts. They agree, however, in that the Egyptian survivals, especially in the representations of hell, are rather strong. In the following we will examine for some of the most important terms and representations, how far Egyptian influence is possible.

The river of fire, ⲓⲉⲣⲟ ⲛ̄ ⲕⲱϩⲧ̄, ⲓⲁⲣⲟ ⲛ̄ⲭⲣⲱⲙ.

When dying man has to cross a river of fire. This holds good for everyone, just and sinners [9]: "There is a river of fire on this path, which makes its waves beat very highly and its waves are higher

---

[1] P. 73. [2] P. 102.

[3] *Koptisches Christentum und altägyptischer Religion*, *Theologische Quartalschrift*, No 94, 1912, Tübingen, 592-604.

[4] *Die Entstehung der koptischen Kirche*, in *R. Haupts Katalog für Ägyptologie und koptische Sprache und Literatur*, Halle, 1905, V.

[5] P. 597. [6] Note 5. [7] P. 601. [8] P. 602.

[9] Robinson, Coptic Apocryphal Gospels, 95, Life of Mary.

than any mountain. For everyone has to cross it, either just or sinner." This river of fire streams before the throne of the judge [1]): "And mostly the big fright of this nature and the great constraint [2]) of the river of fire, which carries wave after wave, which nobody will be able to escape and its fire and its burning, for either just or sinners, they will be immersed in the river of fire, before they reach the terrible throne." Jesus gives to John the Baptist the charisma of putting souls across the river of fire [3]) in a golden boat: "Those who will remember you on earth, you shall ferry them across that river of fire in it." On the Mount of Olives Jesus makes the measurement of the river of fire known to his disciples: "When they arrive at the end of the waves, I am in the habit of baptising them in the river of fire" (Matth. 3: 11). If somebody invokes the name of John, "the river of fire becomes like the water of the bath" [4]). The river of fire flows before the throne of the divine judge and performs a critical function. The sinners are burnt by it, the just are not. Mary prays to Christ immediately before dying [5]): "May the river of fire be quiet, when I come to you." From this it appears that also the just have to pass the river of fire, but that they are not affected by it. A saint is invoked for protection against the dangers of the river of fire [6]): "Oh saint martyr ..., be with me, till I have crossed this river of fire, which flows before Christ, for the fright of that place is great ... Who is the man who manages to escape getting acquainted with that river of fire?" Also a believer must cross the river of fire after his death. A saint may assist him in this. Christ is the judge, before whom the river of fire flows. Kropp [7]) speaks here of a purgatory. He quotes a text, where it says that just as well as sinners are examined in the river of fire (δοκιμάζειν) [8]). Vycichl [9]) does not see a purgatory in it, for everyone has to pass this stream and the

---

1) Budge, Miscell. 148.
2) Crum, 529.a, constraint?
3) Budge, Apocrypha, 140.
4) Budge, Apocrypha, 141.
5) Budge, Miscell. 70.
6) E. Amélineau, *Etude sur le Christianisme au Septième Siècle*, Paris 1887, 160.
7) *Ausg. Kopt. Zaubertexte*, Par. 159, 92.
8) Mary prays to Jesus (Robinson, Coptic Apocryphal Gospels, 38): "Let the river of fire, in which the two parts of the just and the sinners are examined, be quiet, till I pass it." This passage reminds one of a fire test.
9) *Der Feuerstrom im Jenseits*, von W. Vicichl, *Wien*, *Archiv für Ägyptische Archeologie*, I Jahrg., 1938, 263, 264.

unjust go to eternal judgment in any case. Burmester [1]) also calls the river of fire, which everyone has to pass, a purgatory. Morenz translates in the Story of Joseph XIII, 9: "*Lasse die Fluten des Feuerstroms nicht wild gegen mich werden in dem alle Seelen gereinigt werden, bevor sie den Ruhm deiner Gottheit sehen.*" Nevertheless the denomination provisional judgment fits better than purgatory, for the godless are harmed by the fire and the just are not. Burmester [2]) as well as Kropp [3]) rightly point to the fact that the river of fire, beside a provisional judgment, also inflicts an eternal punishment upon the godless. „What great oppressions are those which are incumbent on those who are in the darkness of the realm of the dead and the worm, which does not sleep and the outmost darkness and the river of fire, which flows before the just judge" [4]). It here concerns an eternal judgment on the unjust. A passage, which deals with eternal punishments reads [5]): "I, Paul, saw a vast river of fire, which carried waves after waves, while a crowd of men and women was immersed in it." Some are in it up to their knees, others up to their neck. They are the sinners, who have refused to give a cup of cold water. Also here it concerns an eternal punishment.

Does this notion of the river of fire reach back to Egypt? In the *Zweiwegebuch* the middle road is a red strip, a pool of fire, which the dead should avoid. In the tombs of the kings fiery ponds occur, which injure the godless. The ferry-man, who has to take the dead across a stream to a beatific region, e.g., the *Ḥtp*-fields, is also known.

On closer inspection, however, there are marked differences with the Coptic texts. The function of the fire in the Egyptian texts is the total destruction of the dead, not the eternal torture [6]). The river, which the ferry-man *Ḥr-ḥ3.f* crosses, is not a river of fire, but only an obstacle on the way to the *Ḥtp*-field. In the Book of Gates II we read, it is true, that the just pass the river of fire unhindered and the godless do not, but for the rest it appears nowhere that the fire has a critical function. Therefore it is out of the question that it here concerns a clear survival of the Egyptian religion.

The apocryphal apocalypses tend to agree with the biblical ones.

---

[1]) Egypt. Myth. in the Coptic Apocrypha, 359.
[2]) P. 359.
[3]) Par. 160.
[4]) Budge, Apocrypha 99.
[5]) Budge, Miscell. 538.
[6]) Chapter I, Par. 6.b.

Burmester [1]) and Kropp [2]) are right when they say that the stream of fire goes back to Daniel 7 : 9 and 10, where it also flows before the throne of God. Also the "pool of fire", Rev. 20 : 14 will be in the background here. Kropp [3]) quotes a place from the Slavonic Enoch [4]), where a similar punishing river of fire occurs. According to Cumont [5]) the Greeks knew the Pyriphlegeton, a river of fire in the netherworld, which could be either purifying or be an eternal punishment. This double function shows similarity to the Coptic texts. Further Cumont points to the river of fire in Jewish apocrypha [6]) and thinks of the influence of Mazdaism. Persian religion knows a stream of metal. This river of molten metal plays an eschatological part. The world is purged in it, but the godless Drug-adherents perish in it [7]). The similarity between these notions and those of the Coptic apocrypha is much stronger than those between Egypt and the Copts. The river of fire of the Coptic texts does not spring from Egypt, but from Persia. The influence of Persian eschatology on the Jewish-Christian one has been considerable. Further Hellenistic syncretism made already felt its influence so strongly that we must not think in the first place of that of Egypt. Even the element that the river of fire does not harm the just occurs in Persian religion [8]). When Gôcihar (a meteor?) falls from heaven on earth, there will be distress on earth, like when a wolf has surprised a sheep, then the fire will melt the metals in the mountains and they will flow over the earth like a stream. Then all people will go through the molten metal and will be purged. For him who is just, it will be as if he went through luke-warm milk, for the bad one, however, as if he went through glowing metal [9]).

The realm of the dead, ⲁⲙⲛⲧⲉ.

As the Coptic texts frequently use the Egyptian denomination ⲁⲙⲛ̄ⲧⲉ = *imn.t*, the West, for the realm of the dead, the thought has occurred that not only the name but also the Egyptians notion

1) P. 359.
2) P. 91.
3) Par. 160.
4) 10. 2.
5) Lux Perpetua, Paris 1949, 224.
6) Pp. 226-228.
7) Art. J. H. Kramers in Van der Leeuw, *De godsdiensten der wereld* [1], (The religions of the world) Part I, 406-407.
8) *Pehlevi-writing Bûndahiš* 30. 18.
9) Lehmann-Haas, *Textbuch zur Religionsgeschichte*, 1922[2], 172.

had been preserved. Judas tells us about the descent of Christ [1]: "And I preceded him to the realm of the dead (ⲁⲙⲛ̄ⲧⲉ) and he descended to this place and he carried all these souls away and he disturbed the realm of the dead, except my soul only. And the gate-keepers of the realm of the dead cried before the devil." The realm of the dead is beneath the earth, for Christ descends into it. This also appears from the following passage [2]: "Then Jesus called Michael, whom he had taken down with him, to the realm of the dead." The realm of the dead is situated beneath the sea. When Paul descends in the latter texts into the realm of the dead, he jumps into the water (ⲛⲟⲩⲛ), in the middle of the sea and in this way lands in ⲁⲙⲛ̄ⲧⲉ. The realm of the dead lies in the interior of the earth [3]: "Go away now to the depth of the realm of the dead, throw yourselves now into the heart of the earth." Christ comes to the earth in order to release sinners and goes to the realm of the dead afterwards, in order to set some of those who are there free too [4]: "Those who are below in the realm of the dead, wait for you, that you may come and redeem them." According to the ⲙ̄ⲡⲉⲥⲏⲧ the realm of the dead is conceived as a subterranean place. Contrary to heaven the earth is connected with the realm of the dead [5]: "He on whom the seven heavens and the firmament and the earth and the realm of the dead depend, was hung on a wooden cross." Also according to Pachomius [6] the realm of the dead is below: "He saw an opening down there, which was near the gate of the realm of the dead."

ⲁⲙⲛ̄ⲧⲉ is thought of as a subterranean realm of the dead. This tallies with the Egyptian notions [7]. Also there *imn.t* is not always the West. In the tombs of the kings, for instance, *imn.t* and *d3.t* are used promiscuously. It is the earth or the subterranean, through which the sun passes from West to East. However, the notions of a subterranean realm of the dead are not limited to Egypt. The Greek-Roman conceptions also know a hell in the middle of the earth, where demoniacal gods bear sway over shadows. Around the earth are seven spheres of heaven [8], but within the earth is "*une*

---

1) G. Steindorff, *Koptische Gramm.*, 53. 2) P. 54.
3) Budge, Apocrypha 161. 4) Budge, Miscell. 82. 5) Budge, Hom. 125.
6) Th. Lefort, *S. Pachomii vita bohairice scripta*, Paris 1925, C.S.C.O.; *Scriptores Coptici*, Ser. 3, 7; p. 100.
7) A. 11. 8) Cumont, *Lux Perpetua*, 5.

vaste caverne s'étendant à l'intérieur de notre globe" [1]). In Greece they also know of a "*katabasis*", a descent into the netherworld and a description of what is found there, a.o. the Nekyia of the Odyssey [2]). With this the journeys of Paul and Pachomius, the precursors of Dante's journey are to be compared. The Pythagoreans considered the Tartarus a dark abyss, equally far from the disk of the earth as heaven, while the disk of the earth itself in its thickness contained the Hades [3]). The Coptic conceptions of the netherworld here show a more exact resemblance to the Hellenistic data than to the Egyptian ones. The term Tartarus also occurs as the deepest part of ⲁⲙⲛ̄ⲧⲉ, where the heaviest punishments are suffered. The Tartarus-conception is non-Egyptian [4]): "At that hour the angels of wrath, who are set over the punishments are in the habit of tying the souls of the sinners and of throwing them into the Tartarus (the deepest) of the realm of the dead and they increase their punishments all the more."

Also with the biblical data the localisation of ⲁⲙⲛ̄ⲧⲉ agrees more exactly than with the Egyptian ones. In LXX ᾅδης is the rendering of שְׁאוֹל, according to the O.T. the dark realm of the dead lying below the ocean [5]). That Paul descends into ⲛⲟⲩⲛ, in order to reach ⲁⲙⲛ̄ⲧⲉ, does not necessarily reach back to an Egyptian example, but may do so to an O.T.-one. The description which Kittel's dictionary gives of the N.T. conception of ᾅδης, tallies with what the Coptic texts say about ⲁⲙⲛ̄ⲧⲉ. The Hades is thought of as being in the interior of the earth [6]). Contrary to heaven this means the greatest depth. It is "the heart of the earth" [7]). One "descends" into it. As a subterranean prison of the godless it is called φυλακή [8]). Also the πύλαι ᾅδου and the keys of the realm of the dead fit in with the ancient-oriental picture of the world.

ⲁⲙⲛ̄ⲧⲉ is sometimes connected with the Jewish-Christian Gehenna-notion [9]): "Let them not throw us into hell" (ⲉⲧⲕⲉⲅⲉⲛⲛⲁ). Some lines further on it is said that punishing angels throw the souls of sinners into the deepest of ⲁⲙⲛ̄ⲧⲉ. Kittel's dictionary points to a

---

1) P. 55. 2) Pp. 64 and 65. 3) P. 193.

4) Budge, Hom. 71. 5) Kittel, N. T. Dict. I, 146, 33 sqq.

6) Cf. Aeth. Enoch 90: 26 sqq, where Gehenna is an abyss in the middle of the earth. 7) Matthew 12: 40.

8) Cf. ϣⲧⲉⲕⲟ in the Coptic texts. Kittel, Dict. I. 148, 23 sqq.

9) Budge, Hom. 71.

certain ambivalence of the Jewish-Christian notions of the Hades. According to the older view the souls of the sinners and of the just all remain in the Hades, the first in a place of punishment, the second in a favourable region. According to the younger view the just go immediately after death to the heavenly beatitude, the godless land in a place of punishment in the realm of the dead.

It agrees with the old Jewish conception that in the realm of the dead there are also favourable places for the just [1]): "I saw yet a vast place on a beautiful side of the realm of the dead and I asked: What is that? And he said: "That is the place of the soul of Abraham, Isaac and Jacob and all the prophets." There are also places in the realm of the dead, which Christ did not visit in his descent. There are those who have committed unpardonable sins [2]): "They told me: These are places which the Lord did not visit after having descended into the realm of the dead, which is the place of crying and the grinding of teeth." Pisentius comes to a tomb where there are many mummies. They are in ⲁⲙⲉⲛϯ, where they are punished on account of their sins, but some are in a place of rest (ⲙ̄ⲧⲟⲛ), on account of their good deeds [3]).

In Aeth. Enoch, chapter 22, various spaces in the netherworld are distinguished. Three of them are dark, one light. The light space, with a well in it, is for the pious [4]). Enoch sees this, when he makes a journey to the netherworld, with Raphael as a guide. Herewith the journeys of Paul and Pachomius in the Coptic texts tally. They also go with an angel as their guide. So what the Coptic texts say about favourable and unfavourable places in the netherworld need not necessarily reach back to Egyptian examples, like the texts of the tombs of the kings, but rather corresponds with Jewish-Christian apocalyptic.

According to certain notions in the Jewish-Christian apocalyptic the Hades is thought of as temporary, a provisional situation before the final judgment [5]). The same situation occurs with ⲁⲙⲛ̄ⲧⲉ in the Coptic texts [6]): "Give the soul in the hand of the jailer of the realm

---

[1]) G. Steindorff, *Koptische Gramm.* 55. [2]) Idem., p. 55.

[3]) Amélineau, *Etude*, pp. 144, 145.

[4]) M. A. Beek, *Inleiding in de Joodse apocalyptiek* (Introduction to the Jewish Apocalyptic), Haarlem 1950, 94, 95.

[5]) Kittel, N.T. Dict. I, 148, 1-3. [6]) Budge, Miscell. 560.

of the dead, that he may torture it until the day of the great judgment." In ⲁⲙⲛ̄ⲧⲉ the godless undergoes a provisional punishment, which apparently changes into a definite and eternal one on the day of judgment. Something similar is meant in the passage [1]): "May the sinners return to the realm of the dead." Thereupon biblical texts follow as: "Go away from me, cursed ones, into the eternal fire" [2]). At first the sinners are in the realm of the dead as a place of punishment immediately after their death only temporarily, after the final judgment they return to it, now for ever.

Some descriptions of the realm of the dead are of such a nature that it does not concern here a temporary, but an eternal punishment. When Paul in the realm of the dead visits a lonely region where the punishment of the godless takes place, it is said to him [3]): "Who will write down the words of this apocalypse, which you have seen in the heavens, he will not relish torture in the punishments which you have seen in the realm of the dead" [4]). Pachomius is taken to the West of the realm of the dead by his guiding-angel [5]). He sees an opening near the entrance of the realm of the dead. The realm of the dead itself gives heat like a fire. It is the prison of the Lord. Here are the people who have not served the God who has created them. This gives the impression of a definitive punishment for the godless.

Sometimes the conception occurs that the just do not get in touch with the realm of the dead at all, consequently also not as a temporary sojourn before the final judgment [6]): "And someone who will remember you on earth, truly I say to you, my relative John, I will never let him know the realm of the dead." This tallies with the later Jewish notion that the souls of the just did not come in the שְׁאוֹל, but went directly to the beatitude of heaven [7]).

The western part of the realm of the dead is considered particularly unfavourable. Apa Isidorus takes Apa Moses along [8]) and shows him devils and angels: "Look to the West and he looked and saw a lot of demons, who were in commotion and who were in a stir as if they waged war." The sequel says that they are the ones who seduce saints. In the East he sees angels who help the saints. In the Apo-

1) Budge, Apocr. 161.
2) Matthew 25: 41.
3) Budge, Miscell. 552.
4) Cf. Rev. 22: 18 and 19.
5) Pachomius, Boh. 100.
6) Budge, Apocr. 140.
7) Kittel N.T. Dict. I. 147. 14-19.
8) Zoëga, 318, 27 sqq.

calypse of Saint Paul [1]) Paul comes to the West, "he took me to the places where the sun sets." Then a detailed description follows of all kinds of hellish punishments, "I saw nothing in that place but grief and sighs." Here ⲁⲙⲛ̅ⲧⲉ is not used but ⲙⲁⲛϩⲱⲧⲡ. One could think here of the Egyptian use of the West (*ỉmn.t*) as an unfavourable region [2]). In Enoch 26 : 1-27, however, also the West as a zone of heaven is considered unfavourable and the East favourable. Enoch goes to the middle of the earth. Towards the East lies the Mount of Olives, to the West the mountain of the bad council with deep abysses and steep rocks. So for the Coptic texts also we rather have to think here of concordance with the O.T. apocrypha.

Sometimes we might think of an Egyptian background. Lazarus says to Jesus: "You for whose voice the realm of the dead trembles. ., the light of whose divineness all those want to see who are in the realm of the dead" [3]). This resembles conceptions of the Book of Gates, where the dead revive for a moment, when they see the light of the sun. But also here the Bible may be the background, where Christ is called a light a.o. in the Gospel of John and the realm of the dead is associated with the outer darkness, which expression the Coptic texts also frequently use.

A clause like [4]) "The realm of the dead itself is very deep and dark" resembles the well-known description of B.D. 175 [5]), but the text immediately continues with the description of a fiery hell and that is why we need not hink here of an Egyptian example.

The Pistis Sophia [6]) mentions as localities of the realm of the dead ⲁⲙⲛ̅ⲧⲉ, ⲭⲁⲟⲥ and ⲡⲕⲁⲕⲉ ⲉⲧ ϩⲓ-ⲃⲟⲗ, the outer darkness. The terms are borrowed from Egypt, Hellenism and the Bible respectively. The outer darkness is represented by a serpent with its tail in its mouth and divided in 12 rooms [7]). "These archons of these twelve chambers are in the dragon of the outer darkness." Stricker rightly says [8]): "There follows a description of the twelve apartments which could have been cut out from the book Am Duat." But here we have arrived at gnosticism, which is of a much more syncretical character than the Christian apocrypha.

---

[1]) Budge, Miscell. 538. [2]) A. 11.b.
[3]) P. Lacau, *Fragments d'apocryphes coptes* (M.I.F.A.O. IX, 1904), 85.
[4]) Pachomius, Boh. 100. [5]) A.10.c. [6]) P.S. 321.
[7]) P.S. 319. [8]) *De grote zeeslang* (The big sea-serpent), 18.

Summarising it may be said that ⲁⲙⲛ̄ⲧⲉ of the Coptic texts has only its name in common with Egypt. The conceptions, associated with it, are the same as those of the O.T. שְׁאוֹל or the N.T. ᾅδης. Apart from that the conception of the realm of the dead as a subterranean space is so general that one need not think of Egypt exclusively on this account.

Gates, ⲣⲟ, ⲡⲩⲗⲏ.

In the realm of the dead there are divisions closed by gates. Paul tells Andreas of the descent of Christ. He shows a splinter of wood from the gates which Christ has smashed [1]): "I saw streets in the realm of the dead, which were deserted and in which there was nobody, with all the doors, which the Lord had smashed to pieces and had made into very small fragments. You see, oh my brother Andreas, this morsel of wood which is in my hand and that I have taken with me upwards. This is a threshold of the gates of the netherworld, which the Lord has smashed." According to another text [2]) these doors are of copper. There we read about the descent of Christ: "He destroyed the copper doors and he broke the iron bolts and he led the souls which were in the realm of the dead upwards to the Father." Idem [3]): "They will put him (Jesus) in a new grave and he will rise from the dead on the third day; and he will descend into the realm of the dead and he will smash the copper doors and he will break the iron bolts. And he will raise you (Adam) with all the prisoners who are with you." Death is alarmed by the descent of Christ and he says to his son, the Plague: "Hurry downwards (the realm of the dead lies under the earth) to the realm of the dead, . . . till I may discover who has deceived me . . . all its doors have been broken and their thresholds have been removed, and their bolts have been broken" [4]). Also in Apoc. Elias gates of hell occur [5]):

---

1) G. Steindorff, *Kopt. Gramm.* 55.

2) Budge, Hom. 129.

3) Budge, Martyrdoms, 240.

4) Budge, Apocr. 9; ⲉⲣⲉ ⲛⲉϥⲣⲟ ⲧⲏⲣⲟⲩ [ϩⲟ]ⲣϥ̄ ⲁⲩⲱ ⲉⲣⲉ ⲛⲉⲩⲙⲉϣϯⲃⲥ̄ ⲛⲛϩⲉ ⲉⲃⲟⲗ [ⲉⲣⲉ ⲛⲉⲩⲙ]ⲟⲭⲗⲟⲥ ⲟⲩⲱⲡ̄; variant Lacau, Fragm. 46, line 5: ⲉⲣⲉ ⲛⲉϥⲣⲟ ⲟⲩⲟⲱⲡ̄ ⲉⲣⲉ ⲛⲉϥⲙⲉϣϯⲃⲥ̄ ⲛⲛϩ ⲉⲃⲟⲗ ⲉⲣⲉ ⲛⲉϥⲙⲟⲭⲗⲟⲥ ϩⲟⲣϥ̄.

5) Achm., ed. Steindorff, 7, 3.

"I saw before me bronze gates, which ejected fire." In the Pistis Sophia the dragon of the outer darkness, which reminds us strongly of Am Duat, is divided into twelve chambers, which have a gate each, opening upwards [1]): "And each of these twelve chambers has a gate opening upwards." Each of these gates is guarded by an angel. On his journey through the cosmos Pachomius sees the gate of hell [2]): "He saw a gate which was down there, which was situated at the entrance of the realm of the dead." Matth. 16 : 18 is quoted in a homily [3]): "He is the one who has said: The gates of the realm of the dead shall not prevail against her."

The gates of the realm of the dead are watched by guards. They become confused by the descent of Christ [4]): "And the gate-keepers of the realm of the dead cried before the devil." Three angels guide the dead in the hereafter, that the dangers may be overcome there [5]): "May the gate-keepers, the terrible speakers, flee for him (the dead)." When Christ descends the gate-keepers flee from him [6]): "The gate-keepers of the realm of the dead saw him, became confused and fled."

The gates and the gate-keepers of the realm of the dead also occur frequently in the Egyptian texts [7]). However, the gates of the realm of the dead are also known in the Bible. A text mentioned above quoted Matth. 16 : 18. For the πύλαι ᾅδου the dictionary of Kittel refers to Jes. 38 : 10 and other places from the Jewish literature [8]). Also outside Egypt the gates of the realm of the dead occur in the ancient East. On her descent into hell Ishtar has to pass seven gates which are watched by guards. According to Greek view souls of sinners were locked up in subterranean spaces and watched there by demons [9]). Vergilius mentions monsters as guards of gates of hell [10]). Cumont ascribes the conception of hell as a subterranean region of punishment and imprisonment under the supervision of devils to Persian influence [11]). Also between the spheres of heaven gates were supposed to be, at which there was an ἄρχων, keeping off evil ones, or a customs-officer, τελώνης, who examined somebody's

---

1) P.S. 319.
2) Pachomius, Boh. 100.
3) Budge, Hom. 133.
4) G. Steindorff, *Koptische Gramm.* 53.
5) Cramer, *Totenklage*, 72.
6) Budge, Hom. 129.
7) B. 1.
8) Kittel, N.T. Dict. I, 148, 28 sqq.
9) Cumont, *Lux Perpetua*, 216.
10) Idem., p. 221.
11) Idem., p. 232.

moral luggage [1]). The conception of the gates of the realm of the dead is so wide-spread in the oriental world, that we need not think exclusively of Egypt for its origin. Perhaps there might be Egyptian influence when especially the figures of the gate-keepers are worked out in detail. For these play in the Egyptian texts a more important part than anywhere else, e.g., in the tombs of the kings. It is possible that, when describing the descent of Christ, the Coptic texts mention the chasing away of the gate-keepers with some stress and that also in the funerary ritual the fear of the gate-keepers is pronounced. Vignettes in the Book of the Dead picture them in a terrifying shape, armed with knives. The Copts may have thought of this, when they prayed to be able to escape these demoniacal gate-keepers. In the description of putting the gate-keepers to flight, when Christ descends into the realm of the dead, there might have been thought of the flight of the keepers at Christ's grave.

Realm of the dead, netherworld, ⲛⲟⲩⲛ.

In the Egyptian texts the primeval ocean, *nwn*, is also realm of the dead. A well-known term for the dead is *imy.w nwn*, who are in *nwn* [2]). The same use occurs in the Coptic texts. Paul tells Andreas about his descent [3]): "Forgive me, my brother, I have gone and I have visited the places of the netherworld [4]), where our Lord has gone to and I have seen, how they were. And it happened, after I had gone [5]) into the primeval ocean [6]) that I saw the dwelling-places of all souls and I saw Judas . . ., while he was in a heavy punishment." In the Apoc. Pauli [7]) Paul narrates the following about his descent into hell: "Then he took me with him to the place of all punishments, he took me along up to the pit of the netherworld and I found it sealed with seven seals of fire." This pit of Nun is the deepest part of earth. It is full of fire, in which those are burnt, who have said that the Son has not come in the flesh. The thought of water is quite gone here in contrast with representations like those in the Egyptian tombs of the kings, where those who are in Nun, are still pictured in the water. Nun has become a name for the netherworld and there

---

1) Idem., p. 299.
2) A.11.d.
3) G. Steindorff, *Koptische Gramm* 51.
4) ⲡⲛⲟⲩⲛ.
5) Paul dives to the bottom of the sea.
6) ⲡⲛⲟⲩⲛ.
7) Budge, Miscell. 545.

may even be conceptions of hell connected with it. Also in the Apoc. Elias [1]) the term ⲛⲟⲩⲛ occurs. Elia is taken to the netherworld and there he sees a punishing angel who says about himself: "I am the great angel Eremiel [2]), who is down in the netherworld [3]) and the realm of the dead, in whose hand all souls are locked up from the end of the deluge . . . this is Amente . . . this great angel, he is the one, who accuses men before the Lord." The angel Eremiel has a scroll, on which the sins of men are noted down. In the latter text ⲛⲟⲩⲛ and ⲁⲙⲛ̄ⲧⲉ are used promiscuously. Both terms indicate the subterranean realm of the dead, where punishments are executed on sinners. Here the original meaning of primeval ocean does not come into play any more. In the descent of Paul, where he jumps into the sea to reach the netherworld, it is still possible to think of the meaning primeval water, world-ocean.

Tartarus, ⲧⲁⲣⲧⲁⲣⲟⲥ.

This Greek-Jewish term is used in the Coptic texts for the worst place of punishment of the netherworld. Jesus orders the soul of Judas to be brought to the Tartarus of the netherworld again, because he has adored the devil [4]): "Take the soul back to the Tartarus of the realm of the dead." Jesus says to Judas: "You will be in the Tartarus until the day of the judgment which the Lord will pronounce over you." In accordance with certain Jewish שְׁאוֹל-conceptions the sojourn in the Tartarus is of a temporary nature, it is a being preserved till the day of judgment. About a sinful soul it is said [5]): "It revolves from one side to the other until it arrives in the Tartarus of the netherworld." So the Tartarus is not quite ⲁⲙⲛ̄ⲧⲉ, but a certain part of it, apparently the most horrible one. In a Homily of Theophilus, bishop of Alexandria, it reads [6]): "At that hour the angels of wrath, who are set over the punishment, are wont to bind the souls of the sinners and they throw them into the Tartarus of Amente and they increase their punishments all the more. And when we suffer, while we cry, who will hear us?" Here the Tartarus is the deepest and most terrible place of the realm of the dead, where the heaviest

[1]) Ed. Steindorff, 10, 8 sqq.
[2]) IV Esra 4: 36.
[3]) ⲡⲛⲟⲩⲛ ⲙⲛ̄ ⲁⲙⲛ̄ⲧⲉ.
[4]) G. Steindorff, *Koptische Gramm.* 54.
[5]) Budge, Apocr. 148.
[6]) Budge, Hom. 71.

punishments are meted out. In that same connection also the Gehenna is mentioned with about the same meaning: "May we not come into the hands of the merciless and suffer. When we call they do not hear us. May they not throw us into the Gehenna." In contrast with ᾅδης, which has a temporary character, the γέεννα in Jewish literature means the eternal punishment. With the Tartarus we are outside the Egyptian world of thoughts. The Egyptian texts do not know more and more terrible divisions of hell in deeper sections. The Greek texts, on the other hand, do know the Tartarus as the deepest and most terrifying place of the Hades. When the gods have sinned, they are also punished, still deeper than the Hades, in the Tartarus, which lies below the Hades [1]). Also in the Coptic texts the Tartarus is the pit or the deepest place of the netherworld, where the heaviest punishments are meted out.

The hell, ⲅⲉϩⲉⲛⲛⲁ.

Jewish-Christian influence appears from the use of the term γέεννα [2]). In contrast with ᾅδης as provisional place of punishment γέεννα is the place of eternal punishment by fire. Also in the Coptic texts Gehenna is thought of as a fiery hell. The wish is pronounced that the fire of hell will be extinguished [3]), which happens after the descent of Christ. John prays [4]) to Christ when dying: "And·may the hell be extinguished."

We read the same in a prayer for the dead [5]): "May the fiery hell be extinguished." In the Gehenna an everlasting fire is burning [6]): "Remember at all times and do not forget the flame of hell, which is not extinguished." A daughter sees her mother in the hellish fire [7]): "Again she exclaimed while crying: My daughter, help me and do not forget the tears of your mother. Remember the pains and do not forget that I perish in the fire of the Gehenna."

Fire, ⲕⲱϩⲧ, ⲥⲁⲧⲉ.

Hellish punishment by burning often occurs in the Coptic texts. The meaning of it is not, as is the case in the Egyptian texts, des-

---

1) Porphyrius after Cumont, *Lux Perpetua* 371.
2) See for New Testamentary use Kittel, Dict. I. 655, 656.
3) Budge, Apocr. 3. 4) Budge, Apocr. 57. 5) Cramer, *Totenklage*, p. 72.
6) Budge, Hom. 35. 7) Zoëga, 331.

truction of the soul [1]), but an everlasting painful torment in accordance with the Jewish-Christian notions. The conceptions of a hell-fire are so universal, that we must certainly not think of an Egyptian influence exclusively. The Egyptian texts mention certain places in the netherworld where fires are burning. Beside these punishments by fire also other ones occur. In the Jewish-Christian texts the hell is a region which is full of fire as a whole. The Coptic sources are closer to the latter.

After Christ's descent the fire of ⲅⲉϩⲉⲛⲛⲁ is extinguished [2]). As Gehenna is mentioned here, the background is a Jewish-Christian one. A fragment from the doctrine of Apa Psote reads: "When he dies, his soul is wont to be taken away and it is made into material for the fire and into food for the worms on account of the sins which he has committed in the time when he was in the world" [3]). That fire and worms are mentioned here together reminds us of Mark 9 : 48 (Jes. 66 : 24 resp.): "... in the hell, ..., where their worm does not die and the fire is not extinguished." On the other hand, in the Coptic texts it usually concerns burning of the soul. This tallies with Hellenistic and Egyptian conceptions (burning of the *b3*). In the Jewish-Christian world of thoughts also the body is exposed to the punishment by fire ("with two eyes thrown into the hell"). The skull describes to Apa Macarius the infernal punishment as follows [4]): "Thus the fire is beneath us and above us, while we are standing in the middle of the fire." This is a Gehenna-conception. The fire is not in certain places, but surrounds men on all sides. In the life of Mary [5]) we read: "They informed me also ... that there is an unquenchable fire, whose flame cannot be cooled by the waters of the sea." Cf. Matth. 3 : 12: He will burn the chaff by inextinguishable fire. On his journey through the cosmos Pachomius sees the hell like a large building [6]): "He was shown yet a kind of great house of stone, the length, the width and height of which were considerable and this house was full of fire." This was the place of punishment for the young people that have abused themselves. In the *Zweiwegebuch*

---

[1]) Chapter I, Par. 6.b.

[2]) ⲁⲧⲥⲁⲧⲉ ⲱϣⲙ̄ = Egyptian *śḏ.t*, Budge, Apocr. 3, Cf. Apocr. Elias, 7, 10, ⲥⲉⲉⲧⲉ.

[3]) Budge, Misc. 153, 154.

[4]) Zoëga, 339, 25.

[5]) Robinson, Coptic Apocr. Gospels, 96.

[6]) Pachomius, Boh. 101.

such fiery spaces occur [1]). Also in the Jewish apocalyptic Gehenna is thought of as being in a certain place. In Enoch 90 : 26 Gehenna is an abyss in the middle of the earth. In this kind of literature the supposed author also beholds various divisions of hell for different kinds of sinners. With Pachomius we are in a fully biblical climate [2]): "When I have finished observing all this that has been ordered to me, I shall be hardly worthy to live and to be saved from the unquenchable fire and the worm that does not die on account of the punishments" [3]).

Beside these places, which have a biblical or generally oriental background, there are some where we may think especially of Egypt. A daughter sees her father in paradise and her mother in hell (ⲅⲉϩⲉⲛⲛⲁ!) [4]). "He who had taken me along to that place, drew me into his grasp, saying: Come and behold also your mother, who is burnt in the fire. And he showed me a fiery oven, which completely burnt and seethed, while some who were very terrifying were standing near it" [5]). Oven, ϩⲣⲱ, is the Coptic form of *ḥry.t* [6]). The context, however, is a description of the Gehenna with a quotation from Matth. 8 : 12 [7]). The fiery oven also occurs elsewhere [8]): "Behold, some who are tied like weeds and are thrown into the fiery oven." Without doubt here the representation of Matth. 13 : 30 is in the background. The Greeks connected the thought of the subterranean oven with the darkness of the Hades [9]). Although ϩⲣⲱ tallies with *ḥry.t* we need not necessarily think of Egypt [10]).

Also there where fiery pits or canals are mentioned, in which sinners are tortured, we might think of Egypt. Pisentius speaks with a mummy who describes to him the horrors of the realm of the dead [11]). He mentions the biblical term "outer darkness". He sees others in fiery pits [12]), still others in pits and canals filled with fire.

---

1) E.g. C.T. VII, Spell 1036; B 2 L, 489, *ʿrr.t n.t śḏ.t*, gate of fire.
2) Boh. 146. 3) Cf. Luc. 17: 10, Mark 9: 48.
4) Zoëga, 329, 35 sqq. 5) Zoëga, 330, 4 sqq. 6) B.4.f.
7) A house of darkness and obscurity, altogether, full of the gnashing of teeth and confusion. 8) Budge, Hom. 36. 9) Cumont, *Lux Perpetua*, 227.
10) Cf. yet Budge, Apocr. 57; John prays to Christ before his death ⲛⲧⲉ ⲧⲉϩⲣⲱ ⲛ̄ⲥⲁⲧⲉ ϣⲱⲡⲉ ⲛⲁⲧϭⲟⲙ, and may the fiery oven become powerless. 11) Amélineau, *Etude*, 144, 145.
12) ϣⲏⲓ, Egyptian š, also used for pond of fire, B.7.n.

In the Pistis Sophia torturing pits full of fire occur [1]), ϩⲓⲉⲓⲧ ⲛ̄ⲕⲱϩⲧ̄ ⲛ̄ⲁⲣⲓⲏⲗ, fiery pits of Ariel. ϩⲓⲉⲓⲧ is the Coptic form of *ḥ3d.w* [2]), the fiery torturing places of Am Duat. The name Ariel, however, points to the Jewish apocalyptic. In another place, where ϩⲓⲉⲓⲧ occurs, although it does not concern there pits with fire, we must certainly not think of Egypt. This passage is to be found in the Apoc. Pauli [3]). Paul is led by an angel to a desolate region "and I saw a wide desiccated field which was terrible to look at, full of pits and depths [4]). And there was a pit, which had been dug to a depth of a hundred cubits." Also Enoch is led to such a desolate region [5]). He sees deep clefts there and steep rocks, on which no tree has been planted. Uriel says: "This cleft is intended for those who are doomed for ever." ϩⲓⲉⲓⲧ of the Coptic texts is evidently the same as these clefts from the book Enoch and not borrowed from Egypt.

In the life of Mary [6]) it is said that bad souls are pursued by evil powers: "They grind their teeth and send forth flames of fire from their mouths into its (the soul's) face." One may think here of representations like those of the Egyptian Book of Gates, where a serpent blows his glowing breath in the faces of the enemies of the sun-god. Summarising it may be said that in the conception of punishment by fire sometimes perhaps the Egyptian background may have been of influence, but that the imitation of the Jewish-Christian apocalyptic prevails, a.o. because the context quotes passages from the Bible.

Prison, ϣⲧⲉⲕⲟ.

Sinners are locked up in a prison in the netherworld. They cry and call to God [7]): "Good and merciful God, have mercy upon us, for we are locked up in prison and send your beloved son to us, that he may have mercy upon us." In a sermon ascribed to Athanasius [8]) it reads that the devil waged war against man. He brought him under the power of death and he locked him up in the prison of the realm of the dead. "That is why the (bound) soul could not . . .

---

[1]) Edition Schmidt, 257.
[2]) B.7.i.
[3]) Budge, Miscell. 538.
[4]) ⲉⲥⲟ ⲛ̄ϩⲓⲉⲓⲧ ϩⲓⲉⲓⲧ ⲉⲥⲟ ⲛ̄ϣⲓⲕϩ̄ ϣⲓⲕϩ̄.
[5]) 26: 1-27, see M. A. Beek, *Inl. t. d. Joodse Apocalyptiek* (Introd. to the Jewish Apocalyptic), 95-97.
[6]) Robinson, Coptic Apocr. Gospels, 96.
[7]) Budge, Apocr. 4.
[8]) Budge, Hom. 123.

escape the place where the dead are locked up." (That is why the Father sent his Son to earth). About the realm of the dead as region of punishment it is said [1]: "For that place is the prison of the Lord." Also the Egyptian texts know of a being locked up in the realm of the dead [2]. In the Book of Gates the dead stay behind closed doors and lament when the sun leaves them. Nevertheless we must think of a biblical background for the Coptic texts. Compare the quotation from the Homily ascribed to Athanasius with Ef. 4 : 8 and 1 Petr. 3 : 19: Christ comes to save at his descent those who are locked up in a prison in the Hades. See also a passage in Lacau [3]: "The saviour arose from the dead and brought the prisoners of war upwards".

Also the Persians know of a subterranean place of punishment as a prison under the supervision of a tyrant [4]. Proclus, following Plato, knows of a prison beneath the earth, in a place removed from the gods as far as possible [5].

Darkness, ⲕⲁⲕⲉ.

The realm of the dead is a dark place. John prays to Jesus for salvation from the darkness of death [6]: "May the darkness recede . . . Let the archons be destroyed and let the powers of darkness recede and fall upon the earth." In a Homily ascribed to Athanasius about the separation of body and soul [7] it reads: "This one (the spirit, ⲡⲛⲉⲩⲙⲁ, of man) was seized in a dark place, after it had died, in the place which is called Amente." He who lights a candle for Saint John and before his image, will be put across the river of fire in a golden boat [8] "and these lamps will burn for them, while they light for them, till they pass the ways of darkness and are brought to the third heaven."

Also the Egyptian texts know the realm of the dead as a place of darkness [9] and in the *Zweiwegebuch* there are paths which lead through the darkness. But also the Romans imagined the Orcus as being a complex of dark grottos and further everywhere in the East the conception of the realm of the dead as a dark place is known.

---

1) Pachomius, Boh. 100.
2) B.2.h.
3) *Fragm*. 47.
4) Cumont, *Lux Perpetua*, 232.
5) Idem., p. 216.
6) Budge, Apocr. 57.
7) Budge, Hom. 116.
8) Budge, Apocr. 143.
9) A. 10; A. 10.c, *kkw* = ⲕⲁⲕⲉ.

In the Coptic sources also in this respect biblical influence is perceptible. The biblical term "outer darkness" is frequently used [1]). "When they had taken me to the outer darkness, I saw a vast place, which was more than 200 cubits deep, full of snakes" [2]). "They will give it (the soul) in the hand of Aftemelouchos, the angel, who is over the punishment and he will throw it into the outer darkness, where there is crying and gnashing of teeth, until the day of the great judgment (Matth. 8 : 12)" [3]). According to a certain שְׁאוֹל-conception the souls of the godless were preserved in the netherworld until the day of judgment. In the ᾅδης they received a provisional punishment. With the last quotation we are in the sphere of the Jewish-Christian Hades-conceptions. A Jewish-Christian Gehenna-notion is also present in the following passage [4]): "Some are tied hand and foot and thrown out into the outer darkness, some are delivered to the worm, that does not sleep and the gnashing of teeth." This reminds us of Matth. 22 : 13 (the royal wedding-banquet) and Mark 9 : 48. Mary prays to Christ for protection against the dangers of death [5]): "May the powers of darkness be ashamed." In the Paulus-apocalypse they are described [6]): "And the powers of darkness; some with a lion's head, while iron breast-plates full of fire are laid on them, while there are broadswords in their hands." The description of these demons reminds us of Egyptian representations, gate-keepers with animal's heads and swords in their hands. The denomination, however, tallies with Lucas 22 : 53, ἡ ἐξουσία τοῦ σκότους.

A sinner's body or soul are dark. Apa Paul [7]) sees people enter a church. He is able to distinguish just from sinners. The believers are accompanied by their ⲁⲅⲅⲉⲗⲟⲥ. A sinner is in darkness. Demons are on his hands. "He saw somebody who was black, whose entire body was in darkness, while the demons surrounded him." About a sinful soul it is said [8]): "Your sins put a stamp on your soul, while it is black like a bag." There may be thought here of Egyptian representations, where the dead is drawn in black, especially when he belongs to the condemned [9]), in the tombs of the kings and in

---

1) Matthew 8 : 12; 22 : 13; 25 : 30.
2) Amélineau, *Etude*, 148.
3) Apoc. Pauli, Budge, Miscell. 558.
4) Budge, Hom., 36, see 35 ⲕⲉϩⲉⲛⲛⲁ.
5) Budge, Miscell. 70.
6) Budge, Miscell. 556.
7) Zoëga, 320.
8) Budge, Apocr. 161.
9) A.8.f; B.20.i.

vignettes of the Book of the Dead. But also the Bible, especially the Gospel of John, connects σκότος with sin. On his cosmic journey Pachomius arrives in the realm of the dead. It is deep and dark "... the great darkness of that place and they do not recognise each other on account of the darkness" [1]). In the Pistis Sophia the outer darkness is described as a big snake [2]), which is divided into twelve apartments.

Generally it may be said that what the Coptic texts say about the realm of the dead as a region of darkness, does not necessarily reach back to Egypt. The frequent use of the term "outer darkness" rather goes in the direction of the Bible.

Punishment, ⲕⲟⲗⲁⲥⲓⲥ.

This term is often used for the punishment of sinners in the netherworld, usually for a provisional punishment, which precedes the last judgment. Paul tells us about his descent [3]): "It so happened, after I had gone into the realm of the dead, that I saw the residences of all souls. And I saw Judas, the apostle, who went with our Lord, while he was in a great punishment, which was full of distress." Pisentius speaks to a pagan mummy, which is chastised in the netherworld [4]). The latter says to him: "Pray to the Lord for me, that I may be released from these punishments." There is a possibility of escaping this provisional punishment. These punishments, which are usually of a bodily nature, remind us of the scenes which occur in the Egyptian tombs of the kings. But these punishments may also be seen against a biblical background. The terms κολάζω and κόλασις occur in the LXX and in the N.T. [5]). In the LXX it concerns a punishment of idolaters. So it regards there also a punishment of sinners by God. In the Apoc. Pauli [6]) it concerns God's judgment on the soul of a sinner: "They will give it (the soul) into the hand of Aftemelouchos, the angel who is over the punishments and he will throw it into the outer darkness where there is crying and gnashing of teeth until the day of the great judgment." This refers to a provisional punishment of the godless, preceding the eternal punishment

1) Pachomius, Boh. 100.
2) P.S. 317; ⲡⲕⲁⲕⲉ ⲉⲧ ϩⲓ-ⲃⲟⲗ ⲟⲩⲛⲟϭ ⲛ̄ⲇⲣⲁⲕⲱⲛ.
3) G. Steindorff, *Kopt. Gramm.* 51.
4) Amélineau, *Etude*, 146.
5) Kittel, N.T. Dict. III, pp. 815-817.
6) Budge, Miscell. 558.

after the last judgment. This tallies with Jewish-Christian Hades-conceptions and with 2 Petr. 2 : 9, "The Lord knows how to preserve the unjust till the day of judgment, while they are punished (κολαζομένους)." It concerns the time between death and the final judgment.

That the Coptic texts reach back to the Bible appears from the appeal to the Scripture [1]: "For there are lots of sinners who die quietly, without their having had any grief to endure in this world on account of the oppressions and the punishments which are prepared for them, as it is written", there follows a quotation of Prov. 16 : 4.

Another term for torment is ⲃⲁⲥⲁⲛⲟⲥ. In the LXX this word is used for punishment of the godless [2]. In the conversation between Macarius and the skull the first says [3]: "There is no punishment worse than this one." "The skull said to him: The greatest punishments (ⲛⲛⲟϭ ⲛ̄ⲃⲁⲥⲁⲛⲟⲥ) are beneath us." Those who have known God but have despised him, obtain a worse punishment than those who have not known him at all. The more heavy the sins the deeper the punished are to be found in the realm of the dead. Pachomius saw on his cosmic journey also the punishment of sinners. Punishing angels pull the soul out by the mouth with a hook [4]. After that they throw the soul deep into the netherworld [5] "and in this way they take it along and throw it into the punishments or down into the realm of the dead in proportion to its deeds." So the worse the works the deeper the soul is thrown into the realm of the dead.

In the Book of Gates and the *ḳrr.t*-book the souls of the sinners are pictured in the lower register, which consequently represents the worst place. Also in the Jewish Apocalyptic the thought occurs that the worst sinners stay very deep in the netherworld. In Enoch 27 a deep cleft is the place for those doomed for ever. In Enoch 90 : 26 Gehenna is an abyss in the middle of the earth. The deeper in the earth the worse the punishment is. As regards the hellenistic

[1]) Pachomius, Boh. 92.

[2]) Dict. Kittel, I, 560, 39 sqq; In the N.T. a.o. in the Rev. for the calamities of the final time which come over the world, idem. 561, 27.

[3]) Zoëga, 339.

[4]) Is this a remembrance of pictures of the ceremony of the opening of the mouth, where a priest touches the mouth of the mummy with a chisel? Or is it the Greek representation that the psyche leaves the body by the mouth?

[5]) Pachomius, Boh. 92.

world: According to Porphyrius the gods who have sinned, are punished in the Tartarus, a place deeper than the Hades [1]).

Demons and punishing angels.

In the Coptic texts the netherworld is populated with a lot of demons or angels, sometimes satellites of the devil, sometimes servants of God, who punish sinners.

The devil is considered king (ⲣ̄ⲣⲟ) of the netherworld, where he rules with all his powers [2]). John asks Jesus that he may escape the punishments of the hereafter [3]): "May the devil be ashamed, may Satan be mocked, may his wrath be extinguished." The devil is called opponent. In a prayer for the dead we read [4]): "May the advice of the opponent (ⲡⲓⲁⲛⲧⲓⲕⲓⲙⲉⲛⲟⲥ) be defeated." Also the Jewish apocalyptic knows Satan as slanderer of man with God [5]). The Jewish literature and the N.T. know [6]) the devil as head of a realm of darkness and as accuser, but not as king of the realm of the dead, although the devil and death are sometimes connected [7]). In the conception of the devil as king of the realm of the dead a recollection of Osiris might survive. On the other hand the Jewish apocalyptic knows of a king of the netherworld [8]).

Connected with the devil are demons of death, who in a terrifying manner snatch man away from life on earth. Also the Jewish-Christian 'Αβαδδών-representation is used here [9]). In the O.T. אֲבַדּוֹן (from אבד) is a name for the netherworld, sometimes also personified, Job 28 : 22. Thus in the N.T. 'Αβαδδών has become a king of scorpion-spirits, which vex man during the last times. The Coptic texts adopt this idea [10]). Joseph fears the demons of death: "Then I looked and I saw that Abaddon had come, followed by the realm of the dead,

---

1) Cumont, *Lux Perpetua*, 371.
2) ⲡⲇⲓⲁⲃⲟⲗⲟⲥ ⲙ̄ⲡⲉⲙⲧⲟ ⲉⲃⲟⲗ ⲛ̄ⲛⲉϥⲉⲛⲉⲣⲅⲓⲁ ⲧⲏⲣⲟⲩ, G. Steindorff, *Kopt. Gramm.* 53.
3) Budge, Apocr. 57.
4) Cramer, *Totenklage*, 72.
5) M. A. Beek, *Inl. t. d. Joodse Apocalyptiek*, 101.
6) Dict. Kittel, II, 70 sqq.
7) Hebrews 2: 14.
8) Aeth. Enoch 20 : 2, N.T. Dict. Kittel I, 4, 18.
9) N.T. Dict. Kittel I, 4, 9 sqq.; Rev. 9 : 11.
10) Lefort, *Le Muséon*, No 66 (1953), 220.

which is a friend and satellite of the devil from the beginning, while a host of servants with all kinds of faces followed him, wrapped in fire and from whose mouth smoke same." In the background is the biblical thought that through the devil death has come into the world, that is why Abaddon is called a satellite of the devil. The helpers of death have various heads. Here there has been thought of the Egyptian demons with animal's heads. But a book like the Revelation itself, to which the name Abaddon points, knows of demons in animal shape. As the term ϣⲁⲃⲉϩⲟ occurs more than once, the Egyptian representation of demons with animal's heads may have been here of influence too. Thus e.g. in the doctrine of Psote [1]): "Beside those with different heads, who are on the roads and the relentless punishers and the dekans who have no shape, who are set over the punishments, while they torture everyone relentlessly and in great wrath." With the beings with various heads who are on the roads, one is inclined to think of representations like those of the *Zweiwegebuch*. In the life of Pisentius [2]) an Egyptian mummy tells about the netherworld: "Oh how many wild beasts I saw on the road, oh how many powers which tortured." These demons in animal shape also occur in the Apocalypse of Paul [3]): "Some with the heads of wild animals with tongues of fire sticking out of their mouth, with teeth of iron." The animal shapes of these demons are further circumscribed: "Some with the head of an ibis, with tails to it like those of these scorpions, who were able to sting the souls and who tortured them relentlessly." "Some with the head of an ass, clad with black breast-plates, with fiery spears in their hands, who surrounded the souls in wrath; some with a crocodile's head, with big knives in their hands, with which they secretly cut off the parts of the body of the soul." One thinks here of autochthonous Egyptian representations, a.o. because Egyptian animals like ibis and crocodile are mentioned. Demons with an animal's head and knives in their hands occur in the *Zweiwegebuch* and in the vignettes of B.D. 145-147. In the life of Mary [4]) the fear of these demons is expressed as follows: "And there are therin (the paths of the realm of the dead) merciless avengers, their faces being very diverse, whom God has set to teach

---

[1]) Budge, Miscell. 154.

[2]) Amélineau, *Etude*, 148.

[3]) Budge, Miscell. 557.

[4]) Robinson, Coptic Apocryphal Gospels, 96.

the lawless in the way." In the description which the Pistis Sophia [1]) gives of the twelve chambers of punishment of the outer darkness which remind us strongly of the twelve divisions of Am Duat or of the Book of Gates, twelve "archons" occur at the head of these divisions, who have different animal's heads, a.o. 1/ϩⲟ ⲛ̄ⲙ̄ⲥⲁϩ crocodile's face, 3/ϩⲟ ⲛ̄ⲟⲩϩⲟⲣ dog's face, etc. See also Pistis Sophia 257 in a description of the realm of the dead and the punishments meted out there by beings with animal's heads, "The fire river of the dog's face", 258, "the lion's face", 259, "the archon with the crocodile's face". In the syncretistic-gnostic literature there is more preserved of non-Christian representations and there might be Egyptian influence. But also elsewhere, e.g., with the Etruscans, we find representations of demons of the netherworld with monstrous shapes [2]).

Other terms for punishing angels are the following: ϩⲩⲡⲏⲣⲉⲧⲏⲥ, servant. Christ destroys the realm of the dead when descending. About this it is said [3]): "The servants were destroyed" [4]). These powers are helpers of the devil.

ⲁⲅⲅⲉⲗⲟⲥ. Judas [5]) is punished by angels, who are in the retinue of the Lord. So they are not helpers of the devil but of God. "The angels, who follow the Lord [6]) threw him down. They pulled his tongue out. They took away the light from his eyes. They plucked out the hair of his head. They . . . filled (?) . . . his mouth with 30 snakes . . ., that they would eat him." These 30 snakes answer to the sins Judas has committed. A mummy tells about punishments in the realm of the dead [7]): "They took my unhappy soul from my body, that is to say the merciless angels, they tied them under a black spiritual horse and they pulled me to the West." An apocryphon mentions: "They will deliver you to the hands of merciless angels and they will flog you with fiery scourges to all eternity" [8]). In the apocalypse of Elia we read [9]): "There I saw a place, thousands and ten thousands of angels, who entered there, whose faces were like those of a panther and whose fangs came outside their mouth like those of the boars,

1) P.S. 317.
2) Cumont, *Lux Perpetua*, 60-62.
3) Budge, Apocr. 3.
4) Beside this: [ⲁ]ⲛⲁⲅⲅⲉⲗⲟⲥ ϫⲱⲱⲣⲉ ⲉⲃⲟⲗ, the angels are dispersed.
5) Budge, Apocr. 7.
6) Compare *imy.w ḫt Wsir.*
7) Amélineau, *Etude*, 148.
8) Budge, Apocr., 166.
9) Apoc. Elias, ed. Steindorff, 4. 15 sqq.

whose eyes are mingled with blood and whose hair was let down like that of a woman, in whose hands are flaming scourges . . . These are the servants of the whole creation. They are the ones who go to the souls of the godless men and they take them and lay them down in this place. They spend three days, while they go about in the air, before they take them and place them in their eternal punishment." These punishing angels are of animal shape. For the rest their shapes and the actions they perform tally less with the Egyptian texts than with the Jewish-Christian apocalyptic, as in Daniel 7, where apocalyptical animals in the shape of a panther and a bear appear with iron teeth in their mouths. See also Apoc. Elias 8, 3-14, where an angel appears with hairs like those of a lion, with teeth in its mouth like those of a bear. Pachomius describes them as follows[1]): "The punishing angels were very glad . . . because the Lord had created them merciless, so that they have no mercy with the godless men who will be delivered to their hands to punish them." These punishing angels are consequently in the service of God and are no helpers of the devil. We need not think of Egyptian survivals with these punishing angels. Jewish popular belief had connected the biblical angelology with the belief in spirits and demons [2]). The N.T. describes how angels co-operate in the final judgment [3]). The Greeks know ἄγγελοι καταχθονίοι and demons of death.

ⲇⲁⲓⲙⲟⲛⲓⲟⲛ. John prays that the horrors of hell may not threaten him [4]), and that the demons may not strike terror into him. These demons are apparently satellites of the devil. Also the Jewish apocaliptic knows Satan's angels [5]).

ⲧⲓⲙⲱⲣⲓⲥⲧⲏⲥ. An Egyptian mummy narrates to Pisentius [6]): "to the hands of how many merciless executioners (ⲇⲓⲙⲱⲣⲓⲥⲧⲏⲥ) they delivered me while the shape of everyone was different." It here concerns punishing-demons.

ⲧⲁⲣⲧⲁⲣⲟⲩⲭⲟⲥ. In a description of hell it reads [7]): "The brother looked and he saw the hell-servant (ⲧⲁⲣⲧⲁⲣⲟⲩⲭⲟⲥ) of Amente, who came with a burning pike in his hand with three points." It her concerns a Greek term. Also the Greeks knew punishing demons

---

[1]) Boh. 99.
[2]) N.T. Dict. Kittel, I, 80, 10, ἄγγελος.
[3]) N.T. Dict. Kittel I, 83, 25.
[4]) Budge, Apocr. 57.
[5]) Dict. Kittel, II, 14, 45 s.v. δαίμων.
[6]) Amélineau, *Etude*, 148.
[7]) Zoëga, 334, 21.

in the netherworld. Later these are connected with Persian conceptions of the helpers of Ahriman [1]). From the Apoc. Pauli [2]): "Give the soul in the hand of the hell-servant (warder, ταρταρουχος) of Amente, that he may torment it (the soul) until the day of the great judgment." The hell-servant is in the service of God, to punish sinners in the Hades provisionally before the last judgment. This tallies with the Jewish notion of Hades.

δεκανος, properly speaking "police-officer" [3]), also occurs in similar texts as a punishing angel [4]). These decanoi also have heads of various animals.

ϐαϊϣινε, messenger. About Pachomius it is told [5]): "It happened that he became ill once and very sad that the messengers who had been sent out on account of him, took away his soul from him and he died." These demons are the tools of death, who take somebody away from life. They call to mind the Egyptian *wpwty* [6]), but may just as well reach back to the Greek psychopompe, who takes somebody to the Hades [7]).

The conceptions of demons mentioned above are not exclusively typical for Egypt. Also the Greeks knew that the condemned in the realm of the dead were threatened by wild beasts [8]). They knew categories of various torturing and punishing demons [9]). Also Persian influences are present, the punishing demons of Ahriman, who torture the godless [10]). Beside perhaps a single recollection of ancient Egypt the influence of the Greeks and of the Jewish-Christian apocalyptic prevails in Coptic demonology, with the Persian eschatology in the background.

Enemy, ϫαϫε.

The Coptic ϫαϫε (*ḏ3ḏ3*) is connected with Egyptian *ḏ3i*, to put oneself in the way inimically [11]). In the Egyptian texts the term *ḫfty*, enemy, takes a special place [12]) as denomination of waylayers in the hereafter.

---

1) Cumont, *Lux Perpetua*, 228, 229. 2) Budge, Miscell. 560.
3) Lefort, *Le Muséon*, no. 66, p. 220, note 39.
4) Story of Joseph, XXI, 1, H. Hyvernat, *Les Actes des martyrs de l'Egypte*, I, Paris, 1886, p. 56.
5) Pachomius, Sah., 17. 6) B.14.i. 7) Cumont, *Lux Perpetua*, 228.
8) Cumont, op. cit., 193. 9) Op. cit. 216.
10) Op. cit. 217. 11) B.21,oo. 12) B. 17.

In Coptic texts ϫⲁϫⲉ is a denomination of the devil: "Your enemy, ... who is the devil" [1]). Pachomius is tempted in the desert by Satan in the form of a serpent (ⲇⲣⲁⲕⲱⲛ), clearly a parallel of the temptation of Jesus. He prays and thereupon "the enemy" becomes powerless [2]): "The enemy is apt to become weak towards me with all his spirits." In descending Christ redeems souls from the netherworld. They are a.o. those who, after the death on the cross, are resuscitated and appear in the streets of Jerusalem. He snatches the devil's prey away from him [3]): "He made the enemy vain and tied the strong tyrant" [4]). "For after our Lord had destroyed the realm of the dead, ... he got the enemy into trouble" [5]). To the descent also refers: "He cured the sons of Adam, the enemy had struck" [6]). It is not necessary to think of Egyptian influence for the term ϫⲁϫⲉ. For it is always a denomination of the devil and borrowed from the Bible as such [7]). In the O.T. pseudo-epigraphists ἐχθρός often means devil [8]). Consequently the use of the term "enemy" for devil in the Coptic texts goes back to the Jewish-Christian world of thoughts. The devil as ἀντίδικος [9]) is close to the ⲁⲛⲧⲓⲕⲓⲙⲉⲛⲟⲥ of the Coptic texts, with regard to whom it is said in a prayer for the dead [10]): "The advice of the opponent may be frustrated."

As regards the Egyptian *ḫfty*, in Coptic it has the form ϣⲁϥⲧⲉ. The meaning in "iniquitous, impious" [11]), the rendering of the Greek ἀσεβής [12]). It answers to the Egyptian use of *ḫfty*, in the meaning of sinner, as enemy of Re or of Osiris, who is punished in the netherworld (B.17.d).

Serpent, ⲇⲣⲁⲕⲱⲛ, ϩϥⲱ, (*ḥf3w.t*).

In the Egyptian texts the fear of threat by serpents in the hereafter plays a considerable role [13]).

Demons in the shape of a serpent threaten the dead. Elia [14]) sees a

---

1) Budge, Apocr. 159.
2) Budge, Apocr. 149.
3) Budge, Hom. 127.
4) Cf. Mark 3: 27.
5) Budge, Hom. 129.
6) Lacau, *Fragm.* 43, line 17.
7) Luc. 10; 19, the "enemy", who sows weeds among the corn, Kittel, N.T. Dict. II, 814, 27.
8) Op. cit. 813, 14.
9) I Peter 5 : 8.
10) Cramer, *Totenklage*, 72.
11) Crum, 611, b.
12) W. Till, *Kopt. Gramm.*, Par. 78 = *gottlos*.
13) A. 12.
13) Apoc. Elias, 8. 13.

punishing angel "whose body was like that of serpents, which wanted to eat me." A mummy tells Pisentius of the realm of the dead [1]: "When they had taken me along to the outer darkness, I saw a big place, which was more than 200 cubits deep, full of snakes." This reminds one slightly of descriptions in the Book of Gates, where also pools with snakes occur. In the Apoc. Pauli [2] we find the following description of the netherworld: "Further I saw men and women, who had been hung by the hair of their heads, under whose faces large fiery torches were burning, while snakes, which ate them, were tied around their bodies." Powers of the darkness, which torment man during and after his death, are described as follows [3]: "Some with snake's heads, while smoke came from their mouths and vapour and fire, with irons in their hands, provided with saw-edges with which they tortured these souls." This description reminds one partly of a snake as it occurs in the Book of Gates, which, with its fiery breath, blows sinners in the face. Paul sees [4] men and women being immersed in a river of fire, where worms eat them: "But I looked and saw pits near the river of fire, in which men and women were immersed, while worms were eating them and they were sighing and crying." ϥⲛ̄ⲧ is not a serpent here, but a worm, which devours the dead. ⲇⲣⲁⲕⲱⲛ is also imagined as being the devil. The devil comes to Judas in the shape of a snake, to tempt him [5]: "Lord, he came to me in the shape of a snake, while his mouth opened, while he wanted to devour me." Pachomius is tempted in the desert [6]: "I had not strength to stand firm on account of the menace of the snake." Also here a temptation of the devil is mentioned. In a prayer for the dead it is said [7]: "The wrath of the snake be vain." Cramer [8] thinks of the Apophis-dragon. In such prayers it rather concerns protection against the devil. Compare with it similar prayers uttered by Mary when dying [9]: "May the dragon flee for me." "Let the dragon hide himeself before me, as he sees me coming boldly to you, the only true God" [10]. It seems as if Rev. 12 has had also something to say here.

---

1) Amélineau, *Etude*, 148, 149.
2) Budge, Miscell. 543.
3) Budge, Miscell. 556, 557.
4) Apocr. Pauli, Budge, Miscell. 541.
5) G. Steindorff, *Koptische Gramm.* 54.
6) Budge, Apocr. 148.
7) Cramer, *Totenklage*, 72.
8) Op. cit., p. 73.
9) Budge, Miscell. 70.
10) Robinson, Coptic Apocr. Gospels, 38.

The representation of the snake as a chthonic animal is so generally spread that we must not think exclusively of Egypt. In the Jewish apocrypha and the pseudo-epigraphists the snake is connected with Hades-representations. In the Slavonic Enoch 42.1 snakes are guards of gates of the Hades [1]). Sometimes the Hades itself is a dragon or a worm, which devours the evil. Later the snake is considered the tool of the devil and finally completely identified with him [2]). These are further elaborations of the theme of the snake of paradise. Further we may think of texts like II Cor. 11 : 3 [3]) and Rev. 12 : 9 [4]). In the Rev. the snake (δρακών) is the common image of the devil [5]). For the Coptic texts we must far more think of this biblical background than of Egyptian origin. Also the Greeks knew of a netherworld populated with snakes [6]). In Parsism Aži-Dahaka is a snake inimical to the head-god in primeval and final times.

We find a direct quotation from the Bible there where "the worm that does not die" is mentioned [7]). Mary fears it when dying: "There is also in that place the worm that does not die, which eats the lawless more than any cancer" [8]). "Confusion and grief in the place of the crying and the grinding of teeth, the place of sighing and confusion and the worm that does not die" [9]). Entirely after Mark 9 : 48 is Pachomius, Boh. 146, where the fear of the unquenchable fire is pronounced and of the worm that does not die.

To seize, ⲁⲙⲁϩⲧⲉ (*mḥ*, B.9.c).

Death is a being seized and snatched away by evil powers. "But this was it he said to you: I beg you, do not forget to come to meet me, that the ones under the earth in the netherworld may not hold me" [10]). "The shadow of those who suffer from thirst, and the spirit of the men who have been taken by force, will bless you "[11]). The dead are those who have been taken away by force [12]). The six sons of death are called ⲥⲟⲛⲉ and ⲕⲁⲕⲟⲩⲣⲅⲟⲥ, robbers and malefactors [13]).

---

1) Kittel, Dict. V, 40 sqq.; cf. Egyptian Book of Gates.
2) Kittel, Dict. V, 577, 15 sqq.
3) As the serpent has cheated Eva.
4) The old serpent, which is called devil.
5) Kittel, Dict. II, 284, 2-4.
6) Kittel, Dict. V, 568, note 15.
7) Mark 9 : 48 and Jes. 66 : 24.
8) Robinson, Coptic Apocr. Gospels 96.
9) Budge, Apocr. 10.
10) G. Steindorff, *Koptische Gramm.* 48.
11) Budge, Apocr. 152.
12) Cf. *ṯ3i*, A.9.g. The Coptic text has ⲉⲧϫⲏⲩ.
13) Budge, Apocr. 2, cf. A.g. e.

The Coptic as well as the Egyptian texts know death as a being snatched away of man, but it need bot be a borrowing here. The metaphor is due to a comman human experience. Also the Bible knows death as a being snatched away of the soul [1]).

Grief, ϩιϲⲉ (*ḫsy*).

The tortures of the netherworld are described as grief. Paul descends into the Hades and sees there a.o. Judas, who is punished [2]): "I saw Judas, . . . while he was in a heavy punishment full of grief." A mummy prays to Pisentius to be released from punishments in the netherworld, "for I have suffered much" [3]). "If we forget the sorrow of this punishment one is wont to bring us into another, which is still more painful" [4]). Punishing angels throw sinners into the deepest part of the netherworld and increase their punishments, "and when we suffer, while we cry, who will hear us?" [5]).

The term "to suffer" is so universal that we must not think of Egyptian influence in particular.

To cry, ⲣⲓⲙⲉ (*rmi*, A.16.c).

Michael leaves Judas in the Tartarus of the realm of the dead [6]), "Judas cried, saying: "Will you go away and leave me in this punishment?" Those tortured in the realm of the dead cry on account of the sorrows they endure. Relentless punishing angels do not pay any attention to the crying of those they torment: "When you cry they will not accept your crying" [7]). Pisentius hears a mummy cry, who suffers from the punishments of the netherworld [8]): "He heard somebody who cried and beseeched my father (Pisentius) in great distress." Souls in the netherworld call for redemption [9]). "They cry, they exclaim: Good and gracious God, have mercy on us." An angel describes to Pachomius the punishments in the netherworld [10]): "When one takes men along, one throws them into it; they utter loud cries: Woe is me that I have not known God, who has created me." This crying in the realm of the dead might remind one of Egyptian

---

1) II Sam. 14 : 14.
2) G. Steindorff, *Kopt. Gramm.* 51.
3) Amélineau, *Etude*, 146.
4) Amélineau, *Etude*, 150.
5) Budge, Hom. 71.
6) G. Steindorff, *Kopt. Gramm.* 54.
7) Budge, Apocr. 161.
8) Amélineau, *Etude*, 146.
9) Budge, Apocr. 4.
10) Pachomius, Boh. 100.

examples, like the Book of Gates, where people cry, when the sun leaves their division and they are in darkness as before. But there are also biblical examples, like the place, often quoted in the Coptic texts, Mark 9 : 48 [1]), where in connection with eternal punishment crying and grinding of teeth is mentioned.

To devour, ⲱⲙⲕ̄ (cf. B.6).

The devil approaches Judas in the shape of a snake [2]) and threatens to devour him, "with his mouth open, while he wanted to devour me." In the Apoc. of Elias [3]) an angel occurs in the shape of a snake, which threatens to devour his victim, "whose body was like that of the snakes, while they wanted to eat me." The Egyptian texts mention the being eaten by demons [4]). In biblical apocalyptic, Rev. 12 : 4, however, a δρακών also occurs, which threatens to devour a woman's child. In a sermon of Theophilus, bishop of Alexandria [5]), terrifying demons occur, who pursue their victims and about these it says: "They want to devour us."

The sun in the netherworld.

There are a few places which remind one of the journey of the sun through the netherworld in accordance with the Book of Gates. Certain sinners never catch sight of the sun [6]): "And I heard a multitude exclaim and cry in other places, but I did not see them. I asked: What places are those? They told me: Those are places which the Lord did not visit, after he had descended to the realm of the dead, which is the place of the crying and the grinding of teeth, where the murderers are and magicians and the people who have thrown little children into the water." The greatest sinners do not catch sight of Christ at all when he descends. Lazarus says of Christ after his resurrection [7]): "Blessed are you, Jesus, you for whose voice Amente trembles, this one, who has called me from death [8]). The light of whose deity all those want to see, who are in Amente." One is inclined to think here of the Book of Gates, where the dead want to see the light of the sun.

---

1) Budge, Apocr. 10.
2) G. Steindorff, *Kopt. Gramm.* 54.
3) Apoc. Elias 8, 13.
4) B. 6.
5) Budge, Hom. 72.
6) G. Steindorff, *Kopt. Gramm.* 55.
7) Lacau, *Fragm.* 85.
8) ⲙ̄ⲙⲟϥ, read ⲙ̄ⲙⲟⲩ ?

To count, ηπε (*ip*, C.4.a).

Death says to his son, the Plague [1]): "Has this soul that died the other day, been taken to you to the West? ... Have you counted it in the large number?" Compare with this *ip* and *śip* (C.4.a), to count out to a judgment. The Coptic text does not have this meaning. There it is only to count in a number.

To tie up, ϲωνϩ̄ (*śnḥ*), ⲙⲟⲩⲣ (*mr*), cf. B.2, particularly B.2.k.

Christ descends to the realm of the dead [2]), "he destroyed him, he tied the devil up." The term *śnḥ* is used in the Egyptian texts as a punishment for sinners. As it here concerns the devil, we may also think of Rev. 20 : 2. Punishing angels tie sinners up and throw them into the worst infernal tortures [3]): "Then the angels of wrath, who are set over the punishments, are wont to tie the souls of the sinners up and they throw them into the deepest part of Amente."

For the biblical background the thought of the tying of the strong one [4]) and of the man without a wedding garment [5]) occurs. As regards the latter compare a description of Gehenna [6]): "Some are bound hand and foot and thrown out in the outer darkness." The soul which is in the realm of the dead may be bound [7]): "The soul, which is strong (in contrast with the body, which decays) is bound in the darkness." "But the soul is not only bound by ties, but with its own sins as fetters" [8]). Here tying has got a more spiritual meaning.

To shorten, ϲⲃⲟⲕ.

Judas is punished by the reduction of his time of life. Also in Egypt the thought occurs that one gets more or less than what is determined by fate; see A.5.q. *śʿr.t*, reduction of the time of life. About Judas it is said [9]): "His days were reduced, his time of life was at an end like something that does not remain; grief came to him." This regards the premature end of Judas, who commits suicide. In the Bible the thought also occurs that God punishes by reducing life: Prov. 10 : 27: "The years of the godless are reduced" (cf. Ps. 102 : 24).

1) Budge, Apocr. 2.
2) Budge, Apocr. 6.
3) Budge, Hom. 71.
4) Matthew 12 : 29.
5) Matth. 22 : 13; bind him hand and foot.
6) Budge, Hom. 36.
7) Budge, Hom. 117.
8) Budge, Hom. 118.
9) Budge, Apocr. 7.

Trident, ϣⲗⲓϫ.

A spear or fork with three points is made red-hot and used as an instrument of torture. A mummy tells of the punishments in the netherworld [1]) and describes tormenting devils: "There were iron tridents in their hands and also iron pikes, which had seven points like lances, which they thrust into my sides, while they ground their teeth at me." A brother sees how a sinner dies and is treated by guards of hell [2]): "The brother looked and saw the hell-servant of the realm of the dead, who came with a burning pike with three points in his hand and he heard a voice say: Just as this soul has given me not a single hour of rest, do not give it any rest, when you take it from the body. The fiery pike was thrust down into his heart, immediately while they tortured him and led his soul away." A belabouring with the trident also belongs to the punishments, which are meted out in the river of fire [3]): "Then I looked upon the river of fire and I saw an old man, who was led away and pulled and was immersed till his knees and the angel Aftemelouchos came with a tall fiery pike with three teeth and he pulled his intestines out of his mouth."

In the Egyptian texts torturing with a red-hot trident nowhere occurs. On account of the connection with the stream of fire one is inclined to think of Persian origin.

Flogging, ⲙⲁⲥⲧⲓⲅⲟⲓⲛ.

A mummy tells Pisentius of the sojourn in the netherworld [4]). Pisentius has prayed for him and he is redeemed from it. "When you prayed for me the Lord ordered those, who flogged me and they pulled the iron gag (?) from my mouth which they had laid upon me and they released me and I came to you." From an apocryphon [5]): "They will deliver you up to the hands of merciless angels and they will flog you with fiery scourges to all eternity." Pachomius says about death [6]): "When man is on the point of dying, so that he does not recognise anybody anymore, one of the merciless angels will go and stand at his head and the other near his feet and in this way they will compose themselves to flog him, until his poor soul is on

1) Amélineau, *Etude*, 147.
2) Zoëga, 334, 21 sqq.
3) Budge, Miscell. 540.
4) Amélineau, *Etude*, 150.
5) Budge, Apocr. 166.
6) Pachomius, Boh. 91, 92.

the point of rising." Sinners are punished in a river of fire [1]. They are delivered up to punishing angels "with fiery whips in their hands. When some souls, which they torture, raised their heads above the fire, they flogged them all the more and immersed them all the more in the fire." The Son of the Father, who came in the flesh, saves the sinners: "He made the punishments and the floggings stop" [2].

Flogging with fiery scourges as a punishment does not occur in the Egyptian texts. Borrowing from Egypt must be ruled out. In the Greek Tartarus the Erinnyans hit the sinners with whips, as criminals are flogged at the order of a worldly magistrate [3]. In syncretistic periods these Erinnyans were connected with the daevas, the Persian tormenting devils [4]. As it here regards punishments by fire (fiery scourges, river of fire), we must certainly think of influence from Iran for the Coptic representations, possibly via the Jewish apocalyptic.

Scroll, ⲭⲉⲓⲣⲟⲅⲣⲁⲫⲟⲛ.

The names of the just are written in the book of life, those of the sinners in the book of the accuser [5]. "The angels of the accuser (ⲕⲁⲧⲏⲅⲟⲣⲟⲥ), they write all the sins of men on their writing-roll (ⲭⲉⲓⲣⲟⲅⲣⲁⲫⲟⲛ). They are sitting at the gate of heaven. They state to the accuser that he has to note them down on his writing-roll, that he may accuse them, when they come from the world."

This writing down of names in a book of life and a book of sinners is scriptural and is nowhere found in Egypt.

Sword, ⲥⲏϥⲉ.

Infernal punishments by wounding victims with knives are found in the Coptic texts. The devil cannot do evil to Macarius [6]: "And behold, the devil met him on his way, while there was a sickle in his hand. And when he wanted to hit him, he could not." The powers of darkness as tormenting devils in eternal punishment have swords in their hands [7]. "While there are broadswords in their hands." About demons with animal's heads: "With spears in their hands.

---

1) Pachomius, Boh. 97.
2) Gospel of the Truth, 31, 21.
3) Cumont, *Lux Perpetua*, 71.
4) Idem, 228-230.
5) Apoc. Elias, 4. 3. sqq.
6) Zoëga, 297. 6.
7) Budge, Miscell. 556, Apoc. Pauli.

Some with a crocodile's head, with big knives in their hands, with which they secretly cut the parts of the body of the soul." This torture with knives reminds one of a similar use in Egyptian texts [1]. In describing hellish punishments torture with knives and swords is so obvious that this also occurs elsewhere in representations of hell. In Egypt cutting to pieces is a total destruction, in the Coptic texts a mutilation or torture.

Path, ϩⲓⲏ.

In the realm of the dead there are paths, on which the souls are. About demons it is said [2]: "Beside those with various heads, who are on the paths." Here one thinks of the demons along the paths of the *Zweiwegebuch* [3]. Paul speaks about his journey to the realm of the dead [4]: "I saw streets in the realm of the dead, which were deserted, while there was nobody on them." Mary speaks about her nearing end [5]: "Therefore I fear, oh my sons, because of these paths, for they are very narrow."

Also outside Egypt conceptions of paths through the realm of the dead occur [6]. In Vergilius the dead go along a path. At a cross-road the just go to the right to the Elysium, the sinners to the left to the Tartarus.

Bad smell, ⲥϯ ⲃⲱⲱⲛ.

The sinner stands out by a bad smell. The powers of heaven say [7]: "Take it (the soul of the sinner) away, take it away from us, because, since we have seen it, there was a strong bad smell in our midst." The torturing places in the netherworld sometimes have the shape of pits. About one of these it is said [8]: "There was a pit full of worms, which smelt very badly." Compare with this a pond in the Book of Gates as place of judgment, the smell of which the birds cannot bear [9].

---

[1]) B. 5.
[2]) Budge, Miscell. 154.
[3]) Chapter I, Par. 10; The journey of the dead.
[4]) G. Steindorff, *Koptische Gramm.* 55.
[5]) Falling asleep of Mary, Robinson, Coptic Apocr. Gospels, 94.
[6]) Cumont, *Lux Perpetua*, 280.
[7]) Budge, Miscell. 557, 558.
[8]) Budge, Miscell. 538.
[9]) A.3.p; B.7.n. Book of Gates II.

SUMMARY

The Coptic conceptions of the netherworld are often to be found in descriptions of a descent or of a cosmic journey of a saint. This already points in the direction of the Jewish apocalyptic (Enoch). The origin of these conceptions should mainly be sought in Jewish and Christian writings. Only a little, which is characteristic for Egypt, is to be found in Coptic sources. Much reaches back to Iran via the Jewish-Christian writings or directly to the Greek-Roman world of thoughts. For Coptic literature arose after the time of syncretism, in which oriental religions were mingled with the Greek-Roman one. Egyptian survivals are more evident in gnosticism. The latter dissented, on account of its nature, less from paganism than orthodoxy. We cannot speak of a powerful influence of Coptic literature by the ancient Egyptian religion. It may be said at the most that the Copts have given more detailed descriptions of the Hades in consequence of their Egyptian past. What was said, for instance, about demons and tortures, may be supplemented and extended by representations borrowed from the Egyptian religion or Hellenistic syncretism. The biblical datum of "the worm that does not die" develops into the presence of many snakes which threaten man. The original datum, however, is also in this case borrowed from the Bible.

ADDITIONS AND AFTERTHOUGHTS

p. 2 l.28—inexorable
p. 4 l.24—Am Duat
p. 8 l.9, 10—The aversion for Geb is even to be found in the C.T. note 1), l.3—"(His) l.4—down"
p. 9 l.26, 27—oh this great one, oh this distinguished one,
p. 10 l.8—return [1]); may
p. 12 l.30—shake off the dust which is on your flesh"
p. 13 l.27, 28—so that it means going away, dying, and
p. 34 l.8—that this judgment
p. 37 l.1—ordered against you, when
p. 39 l.11, 12—judges [5]), who judge the dead [6]), but put
p. 40 l.12—They also are seated in the council
p. 43 l.27—*šbi* (p. 296).
p. 46 l.31, 32—have bewailed. This
p. 47 l.12—come immediately unto him
p. 50 l.17—these gods, who do
p. 51 l.14—funeral saves from destruction:
l.20—Additional note to A.1.i. *šȝy*, fate: See now: S. Morenz, *Untersuchungen zur Rolle des Schicksals in der Ägyptischen Religion, Abh. Sächs. Ak. d. Wiss. zu Leipzig, Phil.-hist. Kl.*, Bd. 52, Heft 1, Berlin 1960.
p. 52 l.8—this world
p. 64 l.28—Fingers bent
p. 65 l.10—back to him in
l.17—taken from you afterwards.
p. 66 l.20—to me" [5]). "My
p. 70 l.2—not suffer thirst, my lips
p. 76 l.10—You do not go upside
l.11—gate
l.21—nose, etc.
p. 80 l.25, 26—and your chapels closed behind you."
l.27—this great god
p. 82 l.27—"Whom
p. 86 l.3—(= to shorten)" [2]).
p. 90 l.4—go in the valley
p. 94 l.20—to you, Osiris"
l.29—that it rewards him
p. 95 l.29—"The doors
p. 103 l.23—him. Those
p. 104 l.2—made, on which the one
l.4—To uncover the inundation
p. 105 l.29—in its exact
p. 108 l.22—"Your shares belong
p. 109 l.27—"He
p. 110 l.24—of its voice
p. 112 l.8—their "fish-traps"
p. 114 l.35—"He finds for himself
p. 116 l.13—without being kept off, without being turned away from Osiris.
l.28—gates
p. 117 l.6—"The gate . . . to you" [2]). This
p. 120 l.6—heaven [1]). "Geb
p. 122 l.21—"Ways
p. 123 l.12—keeps the raging one off.
l.24—gate: "to approach
p. 126 l.11—The dead are placed
p. 128 l.18—out and in, like
p. 132 l.20—seized by her
p. 133 l.25—Asiatics" [8]). "What
p. 134 l.23—is pulled away. The wings
p. 136 l.28—a fiery hell-pool [11]).
p. 137 l.19—keeps demons at bay.
p. 140 l.16, 17—red strip under
p. 141 l.24—whose corpses are burnt
p. 142 l.2, 3—"Its glowing breath
p. 144 l.20—exterminated and punished in
l.29, 30—one before whom
p. 149 l.18—*ḫnti*
p. 150 l.1—not unknown among
l.29—this slaughter-block
p. 151 l.13, 14—this man by whom there is slaughtered.
p. 153 l.30—be made (literally, that a feast of the rebels may be celebrated with me) like an
p. 155 l.15—"You have left
p. 159 l.6—by enemies
p. 160 l.11, 12—that they may eat and destroy their souls which are on earth
p. 165 l.29—Block the gates for
p. 167 l.7—around the evil-doers in order
p. 169 l.14—of these painful things
p. 176 l.7—mine away from me,
p. 178 l. 7, 8—that they may eat and destroy their souls which are on earth
p. 179 l.18—take this name of mine
l.29—It does not perish
p. 180 l.28—give this heart of mine
p. 181 l.14—take it away
p. 193 l.2—from you, mouths of
p. 194 l.27—"Spell
p. 196 l.11—where he ,just

p. 198 l.30—On his journey
p. 207 l.5—beings which the dead has to pass.
p. 213 l.4—to his slaughtering-block
p. 214 l.12—you, mouths of these
p. 215 l.12—*Šw*
p. 229 l.9—draw me together in it
p. 234 l.33—are grown
p. 241 l.2—Under this heading various
l.13—"Those
p. 243 l.26—off. "You
p. 250 l.24—said against this
l.26—heart against her."
p. 251 l.23—sand of the West
p. 257 l.18—who cut off
p. 258 l.3—"but as regards
p. 262 l.7—have directed anything
p. 265 l.7—any stone and any brick
p. 267 l.11—sail by this
p. 268 l.1—the blessed spirits
l.11—made on earth as to
p. 269 l.19—position".
p. 270 l.5—the great one, the lord
p. 277 l.6—by the judges of
p. 279 l.12—"The two sick
p. 280 l.11—roads of the dead in
p. 284 l.20—"I make
l.21—are in it in the place
p. 285 l.2—To do evil to a person = to punish him.
l.6—"Do evil in him who
p. 287 l.5—"who loves
l.6—Atum" [3]). He purifies
l.23—this evil sin
p. 288 l.27—"I remembered I wanted
p. 293 l.17—this evil sin
p. 295 l.7—Messengers of Horus are
p. 296 l.9—8 fettered figures
p. 298 l. 25—him".
p. 299 l.6—out there".
p. 300 l.14—food, water and bread,
p. 303 l.5—Jewish apocalyptic
p. 305-320—headline—Coptic Texts
p. 305 l.27—accounts
p. 311 l.20—"He on whose word the seven
p. 315 l.24—not think here
p. 319 l.17—Greek-Roman term
p. 322 l.8, 9—the worm of the punishments that does not die" [3]).
p. 325 l.15—does not die and
p. 327 l.27—Jewish apocalyptic
p. 330 l.31—thousands and ten thousand ten thousands of angels
p. 331 l.5—go about with them in the
p. 339 l.27—Lord immediately ordered

See also: Additions and Afterthoughts on pages 343, 344

p. XV,21.f	ỉsḳ, hinder 242
XVI,4.e	ṯ3m, to cover 281
XVII	WORLD IN DEMOTIC LITERATURE 297
XIX,l.11	and line,e.g.,I.235 = 1st hour, line 235. The text of Amduat is now also quoted according to the edition of Erik Hornung, Das Amduat, die Schrift des verborgenen Raumes, Ägyptologische Abhandlungen, Teil I: Text; Teil II: Übersetzung und Kommentar, Wiesbaden, 1963; Teil III: Die Kurzfassung, Nachträge, 1967. Abbreviation: Ho.
XIX,l.18	The text of the Book of Gates is now also quoted according to Charles Maystre et Alexandre Piankoff, Le Livre des Portes, Texte; I, Le Caire 1939-1946; II, 1961, 1962; III, 1962. Mémoires de l'Institut Français du Caire, Tomes LXXIV, LXXV, XC. Abbreviation: MaPi.
XIX,l.32-34	5th division.....XXXI. Maystre-Piankoff 6th division.
XIX,l.35/36	6th division.....XXXIV. Maystre-Piankoff 7th division.
XIX,l.37/38	7th division.....XI seq. Maystre-Piankoff 5th division.
XX,l.31	(add after Oxford 1900. one line white and then) Ho. = E. Hornung, Das Amduat I,II,III, Wiesbaden, 1963-1967.
XXI,l.13	(add before this line, G. Maspero, The Tombs...) MaPi, see Charles Maystre et Alexandre Piankoff, Le Livre des Portes.
XXI,l.17	(add after 3e fasc. 1946) Alexandre Piankoff II, 1er fasc., 1961; 2^{e} fasc., 1962; III, 1962.
1,l.15	taneous life is under the earth in the realm of the dead. Kristensen
1,l.25	on tombs the passers-by are hailed as follows: "You who love life
1,l.26	and hate death" [5]).Also ....
1,note 3	Op.cit.,p.17.Cf. S. Morenz, Ägyptische Religion, Stuttgart, 1960, p.199.

P. 3,l.18	pass gates, the keepers of which may repel him (B.1)[2]. Demons
4,note 3	B 1 Be 237; C.T.VII.508.e.f, Spell 1166.
4,note 4	Lacau,Sarc.L,192,30;C.T.VII.308.a.b,Spell 1055.
4,note 5	B 1 Be 256; C.T.VII.505.a-d,Spell 1159.
5,l.14	of Gates his punishment on the part of Atum is represented (B.17.e).
10,l.14	register, B.S.Pl.III,12-15,MaPi I.90, the gods who ....
12,l.29	your bones, collect your limbs, shake off the dust which is on your flesh"
13,l.25	yesterday and returned today."
15,l.14	against Osiris (B.3.u):"Horus says ⟨to⟩ the ḫty -serpent: "Oh fire,
15,l.16	convolutions ⟨my⟩ children guard, ...
15,note 2	Am Duat VI, 216,217; Ho.I.115.8-9.
15,note 4	Book of Gates VIII, lower register,B.S.Pl.XIV,35-48;MaPi II. 216-219.
15,note 6	Book of Gates II, upper register, B.S.Pl.II,55; MaPi I.116 B.3.aa.
15,note 8	Am Duat VIII.226;Ho.I.152.9.
16,l.12	"Your sacredness arises, which is within the Mḥn-snake. Apophis has been
16,l.27	The dead says about his enemies:"I destroy their glory" (bḥn,
16,note 1	ḥśb;Book of Gates X, upper register,B.S.Pl.XI,14-16. MaPi III. 73.74.
17,l.23	(devourer of souls) and ꜥm šw.t (devourer of shadows) occur (B.6.a).
17,l.29	bath (B.21.s).A sinner is destroyed by breaking his bones (śḏ ḳśw,
17,note 4	Book of Gates IX, lower register,B.S.Pl.XIII,14-16;MaPi III.37.38.

p. 18,note 5	Book of Gates VIII,lower register,B.S.Pl.XIV,20-24;MaPi II 213.214.
18,note 6	Am Duat IX.99;Ho.I.164,notes f,g.
19,note 1	Am Duat XI.77;Ho.I.189.2.
19,note 6	Am Duat III.141;Ho.I.53.9.
19,note 7	Book of Gates VIII,lower register,B.S.Pl.XIV.20-22;MaPi II.213.214.
20,note 2	Am Duat V.45.46;Ho.I.82.1-2.
21,l.23	In the Book of Gates I,lower register,B.S.Pl.IV,18-19, MaPi I.61.62, where
21,l.24	the punished are, it reads:"You are bound (<u>k3ś</u>,B.2.p), your arms
21,l.28	the <u>d3.t</u>,irons for your hands, tying for your bonds" [5]. These
21,.l.34	condemned by king Osiris and their town god." The idea is that in the
21,note 2	Book of Gates III, upper register,B,S.Pl.VIII.11-14;MaPi I.177.
21,note 5	Am Duat VII.29-33;Ho.I.121.2-3.
22,l.3	fettering and after that results in total destruction, appears from C.T.
22,l.6	(B.2.r). In the Book of Gates V,B.S.Pl.XVIII.3;MaPi VIth gate, II.105, enemies of Re
22,l.33	The <u>ḥk3</u> and the <u>3ḫ.w</u>, the magical power and the spiritual strength of
22,note 1	<u>ʾInṯ.t</u>,C.T.V.245.c;Book of Gates X, upper register,B.S.Pl. XI.20;MaPi III.74.
23,note 4	C.T. VII.318.c.d.,Spell 1061;B 1 L,393;B.9.d.Other reading: "My foot is not seized".
24,note 4	C.T.VII.492.a,Spell 1144;B 1 Be 191.
26,note 3	C.T.VII.473.f.g.,Spell 1131;B 1 Be 6.
26,note 4	C.T.VII.284.a,Spell 1036;B 2 L 481.
26,note 5	C.T.VII.506.c.d,Spell 1162;507.b-g,Spell 1164;B 1 Be 259, 260

p. 26,note 6 C.T.VII.362.d-363.a,Spell 1086;B 1 Be 303;cf.B 1 L 448.

27,l.8 C.T.VII.356.d.e,Spell 1085;B 1 Be 311.312:"To go in peace, in order to

27,l.24-26 ceeds. Re's protection is my protection"[6]."....who inherits the 3ḫ.t of Re. I am the heir of the 3ḫ.t. I prepare the way for Re, that...

27,l.29 darkness. I do not enter the pool of the malefactors"[8]. So the result

27,note 1 C.T.VII.365.g-366.a,Spell 1087;B 1 Be 309.

27,note 2 C.T.VII.358.d-359.d,Spell 1085;B 1 Be 315.

27,note 3 C.T.VII.356.d.e,Spell 1085;B 1 L 440.

27,note 6 C.T.VII.509.d-h,Spell 1167;B 1 Be 241;B 5 C 268.

27,note 8 C.T.VII.389.a-390.a;B 1 L 484.

28,l.5 one, who is in his eye, who sits kneeling down in the big boat of

28,note 1 C.T.VII.396.b.c,397.b.f,398.a.b,400.a,403.b,408.a-c,409.b.c,413.d.e, Spell 1099;B 1 L 489-502.

28,note 3 C.T.VII.507.e-g,Spell 1164;B 1 Be 260;nbḏ.w; ỉry.w ʿrr.wt, variant C.T.VII.304.c nb.w ʿrr.wt, lords of the gates.

28,note 4 C.T.VII.318.c.d,Spell 1061;B 1 L 398.

28,note 5 C.T.VII.356.e,Spell 1085;B 1 Be 312.

28,note 6 C.T.VI.101.b.c,Spell 513.

28,note 7 C.T.VII.474.i,Spell 1132;B 1 Be 12.

29,l.9 gates (śbḫ.wt), hidden of name, sacred of places. Save me from each one, who causes me any harm, the most evil one of the powers, who are before you, till I come before

29,l.27 near which it is written[10]:"Spell in order to pass the road of the

29,note 1 C.T.VII.475.a,Spell 1132;B 1 Be 16.17.

29,note 2 C.T.VII.416.a sqq,Spells 1100 sqq;B 1 L 504 sqq.

29,note 3 C.T.VII.436.d,Spell 1107;B 1 L 529.

29,note 4 C.T.VII.436.i-437.a,Spell 1108;B 1 L 534.

29,note 5 C.T.VII.455.d-456.b,Spell 1125.

29,note 6 C.T.VII.480.j,Spell 1135;B 1 Be 69.

p. 29,note 7	C.T.VII.481.g-j,Spell 1136;B 1 Be 77-80.
29,note 8	C.T.VII.509.d,Spell 1167;B 1 Be 241.
29,note 9	C.T.VII.510.b,Spell 1168;B 1 Be 242; ỉry ḳ3b,B.7.p.
29,note 10	C.T.VII.504.a,Spell 1157;B 1 Be 251.
34,note 11	Book of Gates,I, middle register, B.S.Pl.IV.14.15.MaPi I. 30-32.
35,l.12	26-29, MaPi I.280.281. Here beings are pictured,.....
35,l.22	robbed" (nḥm.t ʿw3). The unfavourable....
35,note 1	Book of Gates I, middle register, B.S.Pl.IV.17.18.MaPi I. 32.33.
36,l.12	of Gates I, upper register, B.S.Pl.IV,MaPi I.41. There also they are men who
36,l.21	by this great god to the gods who are in this field, ... the
36,note 1	Book of Gates IV, upper register, B.S.Pl.VII.1-VI.17.MaPi I.252-257.
36,note 2	Ḥtp.w n.ṯn ḥtpy.w ḥtp.n.ỉ m ỉr.t.n.ṯn, Book of Gates IV, upper register,B.S.Pl.VI.12-14.MaPi I.256.
36,note 5	Am Duat VI.7-17;Ho.I .99.7.8;100.3.4.Ḥtpty.w,Ho.II,p.110, "Die vom Opfer".
36,note 6	Book of Gates V, middle register,B.S.Pl.XVIII.12-42;E. Lefébure,M.M.A.F.C.III.1,Pl. XXX.26-Pl.XXXI.43.MaPi II.107-108 (VIth gate).
37,note 1	Book of Gates V, upper register, E.Lefébure,M.M.A.F.C. III, 1,Pl.XXX.1-11.MaPi II.110.111 (VIth gate).
37,note 2	Book of Gates V, upper register, E.Lefébure, M.M.A.F.C. III,1,Pl.XXX.23-XXXI.30.MaPi II.114.115 (VIth gate).
37,note 3	Book of Gates V, upper register, E.Lefébure,M.M.A.F.C. III, 1.Pl.XXXI.30-34.MaPi II.115.116 (VIth gate).
38,l.14	Book of Gates I, lower register, B.S.Pl.IV,28-32.MaPi I.64. 65. The punishment
39,note 2	I Cor.6:2.
39,note 7	Book of Gates VI, lower register, E.Lefébure, M.M.A.F.C. III,1,Pl.XXXIV.31-41;Cenotaph Seti I, Vol.II.Pl.LX.MaPi II

165.166 (VIIth gate).

p. 39,note 9 Book of Gates IV, middle register, 2nd figure,B.S.Pl.VI. 31-39. MaPi I.242-245.

40,l.12 They also are seated in the council that destroys the enemies of Re[2], who

40,note 1 Book of Gates II, lower register,B.S.Pl.III.MaPi I.120.

40,note 2 Book of Gates IV, lower register,B.S.Pl.VI.38-40.MaPi I. 286.

40,note 3 Am Duat III.197;201.202.Ho.I.59.1-3.

41,l.22 do not escape their judges (n prỉ). In the Book of Gates[7] the nether-

41,note 3 Book of Gates V, upper register,B.S.Pl.XVIII.19.20;E.Lefébure,M.M.A.F.C. III,1,Pl.XXXI.27.28.MaPi II.115 (VIth gate).

41 (add a new note) 7) Book of Gates VII, middle register, Budge, The Egyptian Heaven and Hell II,p.194; E.Lefébure, Le tombeau de Seti Ier,II.10.MaPi II.31 (Vth gate).

43,l.22 To this point the terms rḳw (C.7.e) and śbỉ (p.296). In the "Livres"

43,l.26 enemy (of the god,B,17.d), belongs to this category.

47,l.3 In a later text the sojourn as a deceased person in the realm

47,l.10 The summons of death is inexorable[2a]. Therefore he is feared.

47,l.11 Nobody can avert him:"As regards death, 'Come' is his name[2b]

47 (add two new notes)

2a) Dieter Müller, Leipzig,letter from 3-11-1960, Mythus vom Sonnenauge,"Er hat die Macht über alles, was auf Erden ist, wie der Tod, der Vergelter, welcher auch der Hirt von allem ist, was auf Erden ist" (XV.4).

2b) Cf. S. Morenz, Ägyptische Religion, p.201.

48,l. 28 them, he sees their shape. He does not perish through their flame"[9)] .

p. 48,note 6 Book of Gates I, lower register,B.S.Pl.IV.37.III.38;MaPi I.67.

48,note 7 Book of Gates VIII, lower register,B.S.Pl.XIV.33,34;MaPi II.216.

48,note 8 Book of Gates VIII,lower register,B.S.Pl.XIV.20-24;MaPi II.213.214.

48,note 9 Am Duat IX.99;Ho.I 164,notes f,g.

49,note 4 Am Duat XI.77;Ho.I 189.2.

49,note 6 Obadiah 16, וְהָיוּ כְּלוֹא הָיוּ .

51,l.27 appropriate time, nothing is added to it"[13)] . Nevertheless some-

51,note 11 W.Max Müller, Liebespoesie I.2,M.Lichtheim, Songs of the harpers,p.195.S.Morenz,op.cit.,p.19.

53,l.2 father, my being far from you, how is that ?"

53,note 3 C.T.VII.506.c-f,Spell 1162;B I Be 259.

54,l.7 the belief in the funeral ritual, give a pessimistic impression[4a)]

54, (add a new note) 4a) See also S. Morenz, Ägyptische Religion,pp. 197,198, "Zweifel an der rituellen Belebung des Toten".

54,note 5 Lacau,Sarc.I.217.27;C 28085;C.T.VII.449.c,Spell 1117;B 3 C 526.

59,l.6/7 decayed. He perishes. All his bones perish. Oh you, who slaughter bodies, who slacken bones..., behold the bad water (fluid of the

59,note 8 B.D. 154, Budge, p.401.12.

61,note 2 Op.cit. pp.124,144.

61,note 9 "Breath is in his nose".

62,note 4 C.T.VI.332.a-d.

63,note 2 Book of Gates VI, lower register. E.Lefébure, M.M.A.F.C. III,1,PL.XXXIII.3;MaPi II.160 (VIIth gate).

63,note 4 Am Duat VIII.15.16;Ho.I. 136.4.

63,note 6 Am Duat VIII.35.36;Ho.I.138.3.

p. 63,note 7 Idem 182;Ho.I.148.2.

63,note 8 Idem 212;Ho.I.152.4.

69,l.25 Against suffering hunger is set having abundance [6]. In a text[7],

73,l.1 the air. N.N. knows the air in this his name of Seth ꜣIst.ti" [1]. "To

73,l.18 A.6. The world reversed.[6a]

73 (add a new note) 6a) E. Hornung, Nacht und Finsternis,p.52, "das Reich des Toten ist das 'ganz andere', allen Unbekannte, in welchem alle irdische Ordnung verkehrt ist, und man daher Gefahr läuft, auf dem Kopfe gehn und seinen eigenen Kot essen zu müssen."

73,note 9 Book of Gates, 2nd gate, B.S.Pl.III;MaPi I.79.

74,note 1 Book of Gates III, middle register, B.S.Pl.VIII.26-29;MaPi I.162.

75,l.24 is in the Ḥtp-field. My superabundance is with the gods... What I

75,l.29 down. The term occurs only once in the Pyramid Texts. "It

75,note 1 C.T.III.75.i-l.

75,note 5 C.T.Spell 581;VI.196.a.n.o.w.197.a.c.p-s.198.d.j.n.o.p.

75,note 6 Pyr.323.a. The same passage C.T.VI.189.e; Pyr.2155.b, n śhdhd N.

76,note 9 C.T.VI.287.b.g-i.k.l.

78,l.7 of Re...N.N. does not live on that on which Ḥr-t3 lives. N.N.

78,note 4 Am Duat XI.76.Ho.I.191.1;Nr.816.

78,note 5 Book of Gates II, lower register, B.S.Pl.III.10, śhd.k; MaPi I.120.121.

79,note 2 Pyr.2202.a-c.

80,l.24 the dead. Re says to mummies in chapels[8] :"Opening belongs to your

80,note 8 Book of Gates II, upper register, B.S.Pl.III.11-16;MaPi I.104.105.

p. 82,l.17 "How near is sleep, how far is the falling asleep"[9]. Ḳd is favour-

82,l.19 able. "This great (Osiris) lies down, while he has fallen asleep"[10]

82,l.21 down, while he has fallen asleep"[11]

82,note 17 Book of Gates VII, lower register, Budge, The Eg.Heaven and Hell II, p.210;E. Lefébure, Le tombeau de Séti Ier, II. 12.13;MaPi II.67 (Vth gate).

83,note 2 Book of Gates VII, lower register, Budge, The Eg.Heaven and Hell II, p.214;E. Lefébure, Le tombeau de Séti Ier,II. 10;MaPi II.68.69 (Vth gate).

83,note 7 Book of Gates I, lower register, B.S.Pl.IV.14.MaPi I.56.

84,note 9 Wb.IV.391.20, schlafen = tot sein, 21 + m, im Sarge, im Grabe ruhen. E. Hornung, Nacht und Finsternis, p.65.

85,note 1 Livre de la Nuit, 8th gate, lower register.

85,note 2 Book of Gates VII, lower register, Budge, The Eg.Heaven and Hell II, p.21; E.Lefébure, Le tombeau de Séti Ier, II. 10-12.MaPi II. 10;MaPi II.68.69 (Vth gate).

85,note 8 Book of Gates VII, lower register, Budge, The Eg.Heaven and Hell II,p.210;E.Lefébure, Le tombeau de Séti Ier,II. 10-12;MaPi II.67 (Vth gate).

88,l.14 man of the 12th gate in the Book of Gates, is iḥḥy (B.S. 1.IX.3;MaPi III.170).

88,l.15 A.10.b.wš3.w, n i g h t, e v e n i n g, d a r k n e s s[3a].

88,l.23 which watches over them. Re says to them:"Opening belongs to your

88,note 1 See E. Hornung, Nacht und Finsternis im Weltbild der Alten Ägypter (1956),p.48 sqq.

88 (add a new note) 3a) E. Hornung, Z.Ä.S. 86 (1961),p.108.109.

88,note 7 Book of Gates II, upper register,B.S.PL.III.11-16;MaPi I. 104.105.

88,note 8 C.T.V.371.f.g.See further E.Hornung,Z.Ä.S.86,pp.113,114.

89,l.10 spirit, which has fallen into the fire, which opens the darkness, which cannot

P. 89,l.21	to be with Re in heaven. "I come to you, oh eldest Horus among those
89,l.24	not take me away...I open the darkness"[4]. The darkness is the
89,note 2	Cairo 28085, Lacau, Sarc.I.216,217,20-26;C.T.VII.447.b.d, Spells 1115,1116;B 3 C 524.
89,note 3	Cairo 28085, Lacau, Sarc.I.216,17-18;C.T.VII.440.e,441.a, 442.a-443.c;B 1 L, 539-543;B 3 C 511.512.514;Spells 1112, 1113.
89,note 4	Cairo 28085, Lacau, Sarc.I.215.13;C.T.VII.443.d-435.a, Spell 1106;B 1 L 527;B 3 C 507.
89,note 5	Lacau, Sarc.I.212.67;C.T.VII.352.a-353.a,Spell 1080;B 2 L 580.
92,note 1	Book of Gates IV, lower register,B.S.VI.26-29;MaPi I.280. 281.
93,note 3	Book of Gates VI, lower register, E.Lefébure,M.M.A.F.C. III,1,Pl. XXXIII.23-25;Cenotaph Seti I, Vol.II,Pl.LIX; MaPi II.163 (VIIth gate).
93,note 4	Book of Gates V, middle register, E.Lefébure,M.M.A.F.C. III,1,Pl. XXXI.34-39;MaPi II.108 (VIth gate).
94,l.25	Pl.IV.18.19,MaPi I.7, there are represented two men with staffs between
95,note 1	Book of Gates IV, lower register,B.S.Pl.VI.35-38;MaPi I. 284.
95,note 2	Pyr.1713.a;cf. p. 117,note 1.
97,note 6	Book of Gates VIII, middle register,B.S.Pl.XIV.19.20;MaPi II.183.
97,note 8	Book of Gates IV, middle register,B.S.Pl.VI.14.15;MaPi I. 235.
100,l.1	Nḥb k3.w is burnt by the poison of the monster"[1]. These passages agree with other spells...
101,note 7	C.T.VII.484.k,Spell 1139;B 1 Be 122;B 1 P 572;B 5 C 453.
101,note 8	C.T.VII.485.a-c,Spell 1139;B 1 Be 126.
101,note 9	Lacau, Sarc.I.191.24;C.T.VII.304.e,Spell 1052;B 1 C 547.

p. 101,note 10	Lacau, Sarc.I.191.46.47;C.T.VII.331.d,332.a,Spell 1069; B 1 C 565, 566.
105,l.3/4	, shake off the earth which is on your flesh"3)
105,l.28	anew. You are distinguished by an eternal work: the stone statue
106,note 2	Am Duat X.II;Ho.I.171.9-10.
107,l.1	funeral a relative has taken care. I shall make a hiding-place for you
108,l.29	A.7.1;
109,l.16	This is an epithet of demoniacal beings who inspire fear:
109,note 7	C.T.VII.370.k;Spell 1090;B 1 L 466.
110,note 4	Book of Gates III, lower register,B.S.Pl.VIII.10.11;MaPi I.199.
110,note 6	Am Duat II.61, read <u>ššnḏ.t</u>;Ho.I.28.2;nr.134.
110,note 9	<u>Livre de la Nuit</u>, 4th gate;Book of Gates, 9th gate,B.S. Pl.XIII.5.6;MaPi III.7.
111,l.30	division (B.S.Pl.IV.1;MaPi I.26.27).
111,note 1	Book of Gates II, lower register,B.S.Pl.II.52-54;MaPi I. 134.
111,note 2	Am Duat V.238;Ho.I.96.2-4.
112,note 1	Am Duat III.25-27;Ho.I.47.3-4.
112,note 2	Am Duat V.197-199;Ho.I.93.6-7.
112,note 3	Book of Gates XI, lower register,B.S.Pl.IX.42-46;MaPi III. 157.
115,note 8	<u>Zweiwegebuch</u> B 1 Be.12;B 1 P. 468;B 5 C.348;C.T.VII.474. i-k,Spell 1132.
115,note 9	C.T.VII.474.j,Spell 1132;B 5 C 348.
115,note 10	C.T.VII.287.b.a,Spell 1037;B 2 L 289.488.
116,note 2	C.T.VII.356.e,Spell 1085;B 1 Be 312.
117,note 1	Pyr.1713.a,Cf.p.95.
118,l.26	<u>Ỉmnty.w</u> which keep people at bay, are opened to you"4). The <u>rḫy.t</u>,
119,note 2	<u>Zweiwegebuch</u>,C.T.VII.386.a;389.a-390.a,Spell 1099;B 1 L, 482-485;B 3 L 623-626;"<u>Torhütergespräche</u>" B.D. 130.
121,note 3	C.T.VI.67.i.j.

p. 122,l.22 The Zweiwegebuch also knows the passing of gates, "Hail to you, gates, hidden of name, sacred of places. Save me from each one who causes me any harm, the most evil one of the powers, who are before you, till I come before the Lord of the universe" 6)

122,note 6 Cairo 28085, Lacau, Sarc.I.218.40;C.T.VII.455.d-456.b, Spell 1125;B 3 C.539.540.

122,note 7 Idem 41-50;C.T.VII.457.n,Spell 1127;B 3 C.554.

123,l.25 this great god to this gate of entering this division" (B.S.Pl.II.7;MaPi I.75.76).

123,note 8 ....ỉnpw n3 šbḥ.wt n.t t3 d3.t,unedited.

125,l.30 B.2.a. ỉnṯ , t o p u t i n f e t t e r s.

125,l.33 I do not fall into his fetter" 5) . Near destructors of Apophis it is

125,note 5 Zweiwegebuch,B 1 L,474;B 2 L,639;C.T.VII.376.b-377.a, Spell 1094.

126,l.10 is tied. "They watch over the rope of the being to be punished, which

126,note 1 Book of Gates X, upper register,B.S.Pl.XI.11-13;18-20; MaPi III.73.

126,note 4 Book of Gates X, upper register,B.S.Pl.XI.7-14;MaPi III.72.

126,note 5 Book of Gates X, upper register,B.S.Pl.XI.34-44;MaPi III. 79.80.

126,note 6 Book of Gates X, upper register, Champollion, Notices II. 532;MaPi III.79.

126,note 8 Book of Gates XI, middle register,B.S.Pl.IX.29.30;MaPi III.117.

127,note 1 Am Duat VII.32.33;Ho.I.121.2-3.

127,note 2 Book of Gates X, upper register,B.S.Pl.X.45.46;MaPi III. 80.

127,note 3 Book of Gates XI, middle register,B.S.Pl.IX.25-27;MaPi III.116.

128,l.15 up the dead asks free admittance for his soul. "A way is opened for

p. 128,l.23 as enemy of the sun, is watched. "Bull of the ḥḥ-gods, who watches

128,note 8 C.T.I.362.d;364.a.Cf.C.T.I.398.b,n s3w.n.tw b3.ỉ ỉn ḥk3.w šnwt Rʿ.

129,note 1 Cairo 28083;Lacau, Sarc.192.33;C.T.VII.312.b-313.b;B 1 C. 556. Spell 1059.

129,note 3 Zweiwegebuch,B 1 Be.34;B 1 P.491;B 5 C.371;C.T.VII.476.h, Spell 1134.

129,note 4 Book of Gates I,B.S.Pl.IV.20.1-2;MaPi I.24.

129,note 8 Book of Gates III, upper register,B.S.Pl.VIII.30-35;MaPi I.183.184.

130,note 1 Book of Gates V, middle register,B.S.Pl.XVIII.4;E.Lefébure,M.M.A.F.C. III,1,Pl.XXX.23;XXXI.30.31.46.MaPi II.106 (VIth gate).

130,note 8 Am Duat V.54-56.Ho.I.82.4.

131,l.15-16 About a gate in the Zweiwegebuch it is said[5]:"Somebody is there, being bound."

131,note 3 Book of Gates I, lower register,B.S.Pl.IV.15-19;MaPi I. 61-62.

131,note 5 C.T.VII.474.j,Spell 1132;B 1 Be.12;B 1 P.468;B 5 C.348.

131,note 6 Book of Gates X, upper register,B.S.Pl.XI.27-29;MaPi III. 78.

131,note 7 Book of Gates X, upper register,B.S.Pl.XI.30-32;MaPi III. 79.

131,l.20 one of face"[7]. Near half of the 16 gods, who hold the chain of

132,l.10 the North, the West and the East have put him in their irons"[4]. Selkis

132,l.14 "They put his bonds on"[7]. Human sinners and the mythical

132,l.20-21 life. He who is seized by it, does not live. He who has been beaten by it, his head is not tied on"[8]

132,note 1 Book of Gates I, lower register,B.S.Pl.IV.18.19;MaPi I. 61.62.

132,note 5 Book of Gates X, upper register,B.S.Pl.XI.21.22;MaPi III.

77.78.

p. 132,note 7	Book of Gates XI, middle register,B.S.Pl.IX.37.38;MaPi III 119.
133,l.13-14	In the Zweiwegebuch .... is burnt. This is to be cancelled.
133,note 3	This note is to be cancelled.
133,note 6	Am Duat VI.216.217;Ho.I.115.9.
133,note 7	Am Duat VII.22;Ho.I.120.3.
133,note 9	Am Duat V.63;Ho.I.82.7-8.
133,note 10	Am Duat II.192-194;Ho.I.34.1-2.
133,note 11	Am Duat VIII.226;Ho.I.152.9.
133,note 12	Am Duat III.148-150;Ho.I.53.11-54.1.
134,l.11	"The water of this pond consists of flames"[5)]
134,note 3	Am Duat IX.74;Ho.I.165.1;nr.681.
134,note 4	Am Duat XI.77;Ho.I.189.4.
134,note 5	Book of Gates II, upper register,B.S.Pl.II.43.44;MaPi I. 113.
134,note 12	Book of Gates III,lower register, 3rd figure,B.S.Pl.VII. 51;MaPi I.215.
134,note 13	Book of Gates VIII,B.S.Pl.XV;MaPi II.175.
135,note 1	C.T. B 1 L.413;B 1 C.584;VII.335.d,Spell 1071;Lacau, Sarc. I.194.61.
135,note 3	Am Duat IX.100;Ho.I.163.4.
135,note 11	Am Duat III.83;Ho.I.52.6;nr.242; Livre du Jour,...... Piankoff,p.15.
135,note 12	Am Duat II.200.201;Ho.I.34.4.
136,l.20	In the netherworld the fire of the snakes burns those who have sinned
136,note 3	Am Duat VII.49;Ho.I.122.2-3.
136,note 8	Book of Gates III, upper register,3rd figure,B.S.Pl.VII. 49-53; MaPi I.191-192.
136,note 10	Am Duat XI.77;Ho.I.189.5.
137,l.22	occurs with fire-spitting snakes. About one of the four fiery schoinoi

p. 137,1.28-29 no power over him"[14]. Demons are kept at bay:"The red-hot breath of your fury does not take me away".[15] Apophis

137,note 4 Book of Gates VII, lower register, Budge, The Eg. Heaven and Hell II, p.215,216;E.Lefébure, Le tombeau de Séti Ier, II.12;MaPi II.83 (Vth gate).

137,note 6 Am Duat I.176.177;Ho.I.15.3;nr.95.

137,note 9 Am Duat IX.76;Ho.I.165,notes c,d.

137,note 15 B.D.130;283.13.14;C.T.VII.412.a,Spell 1099;B 1 L.501; B 2 L.669.

138,note 1 Book of Gates II, lower register,B.S.Pl.III.21.22;MaPi I. 125.

138,note 12 Book of Gates VIII,lower register,B.S.Pl.XIV.35-48;MaPi II.216-219.

139,1.21 great god passed them"[7]. The name of a snake on the 2nd gate of the Book

139,1.29 the middle, along which the two ways lead, reads[12]: "This is the pool of

139,note 6 Am Duat III.147;Ho.I.53.11.

139,note 7 Am Duat IX.100;Ho.I.163.3-4.

139,note 8 Book of Gates II,B.S.Pl.III;MaPi I.78.

139,note 9 Am Duat III.80;Ho.I.52.3;nr.240.

139,note 10 Book of Gates VIII,B.S.Pl.XV;MaPi II.175.

139,note 11 Book of Gates II, upper register,B.S.Pl.III.9;MaPi I.103.

139,note 12 C.T.VII.508.e-g,Spell 1166;B 1 Be.237.

140,note 1 C.T.VII.489.c.d,Spell 1142;B 1 Be.169.

140,note 2 C.T,VII.484.e,Spell 1138;B 1 Be.116.

140,note 3 Cairo 28085;Lacau, Sarc.I.220.58;C.T.VII.458.m-459.a;B 3 C. 562.

140,note 4 C.T.VII.479.c,Spell 1135;B 1 Be.48;B 1 P.504;B 5 C.385; B 1 L.464.465, etc.

140,note 5 Cairo 28085;Lacau, Sarc.I.215.14-16;C.T.VII.436.h-440.b, Spells 1108-1110; B 1 L.533-538;B 3 C.508-510.

140,note 6 C.T.VII.371.a-c,Spell 1091;B 1 L.470;B 2 L.629.

140,note 7 C.T.VII.504.a,Spell 1157;B 1 Be.251; B 1 P.339.

p. 140,note 8	C.T.VII.503.c.d,Spell 1156;B 1 Be.248.
140,note 9	C.T.VII.439.a.d,Spell 1110;B 1 L.537.538.
141,note 7	Am Duat V, lower register, 238;Ho.I.96.2-4.
142,note 3	Book of Gates II, upper register,B.S.Pl.II.55;MaPi I.116.
142,note 7	Am Duat III.89;Ho.I.52.10;Nr.246;snake of the 4th gate in the Book of Gates,B.S.Pl.VII.61;MaPi I.228.
142,note 8	Am Duat V, lower register,211;Ho.I.92.3.
143,note 3	Livre de la Nuit, VI, 5th register, bottom;ed. Piankoff, p.58.
144,note 12	Am Duat V.45 sqq.;Ho.I.82.1-2.Hornung reads incorrectly mt.w "Toten", instead of wḫ3.wt, "cauldrons". Cf. ḥry wḫ3.wt.f, "he who has authority over his cauldrons", Am Duat XI, lower register, end;Ho.I.191.10,nr.821;II, p.183, "Der über seinen Kesseln ist".
144,note 13	Am Duat XI.79 and 93;Ho.I.191.4;191.10,nr.821.
145,l.3	is nsr-m-ỉr.t.f , who cooks the enemies of Re in the early morning"[1].
145,l.6	Khepri, it is said [3]:"It is what they do in the d3.t, roasting the dead..."
145,note 1	Am Duat XII.98;Ho.I.203.1;nsr-m-ỉr.t.f, "Der mit seinem Auge brennt"? Ho.II.191.192.
145,note 3	Am Duat VI, lower register,222,223;Ho.I.116.2.
145,note 4	Am Duat VII.24,Ho.I.120.4;compare III.140, lower register, ỉr.t mʿḳ;Ho.I.53.9.Hornung, Amduat II,p.127,translates probably better, "er brät sie als Braten für sich".
146,note 7	Am Duat XI.77;Ho.I.189.4;XI.84;Ho.I.190.4;nr. 807.
148,note 2	Am Duat XI.78;Ho.I.189.6-7.
148,note 3	Book of Gates V, middle register,B.S.Pl.XVIII.37-40;E. Lefébure,M.M.A.F.C.III.1,Pl.XXXI.39-43;MaPi II.108 (VIth gate).
148,note 6	Am Duat X.2;Ho.I.167.9.
149,l.24	(of the chapel in the sun-boat) arises, which is in the Mḥn-snake. Apophis
149,note 8	Am Duat XI.76;Ho.I.189.1.

p. 149,note 12 Book of Gates X, upper register,B.S.Pl.XI.14-16.MaPi III.73.74.

150,note 6 Book of Gates VIII, lower register,B.S.Pl.XIV.20.21;MaPi II.213.

150,note 9 Am Duat IX.97;Ho.I.163.8.

151,note 2 Am Duat III.148-150;Ho.I.53.11-54.1.

151,note 3 Am Duat XI.77;Ho.I.189.6.

159,note 9 Book of Gates II, lower register,B.S.Pl.III.17-19;MaPi I.124.

152,note 3 Am Duat V.63.b;Ho.I.83.8.

152,note 6 Am Duat XI.76;Ho.I.189.2.

152,note 7 Am Duat V.52.53;Ho.I.83.8.

152,note 8 Am Duat VI.215;Ho.I.115.9.

152,note 9 Am Duat VIII.223;Ho.I.150.9.

152,note 10 Book of Gates II,B.S.Pl.III;MaPi I.78.

152,note 11 C.T.VII.502.g,Spell 1154;B 1 Be.246.

153,note 4 Am Duat III.41;Ho.I.48.2;nr.260.

154,note 6 Am Duat XI.76;Ho.I.188.8.

154,note 9 Louvre 3283 VII,4, nn šʿ.tw ỉn wr.wy nty ḥśb.

156,note 8 The last line should be read:
tḫś mśk.ỉ nn ỉr.tw ḫ.t nb.t ḏw.t r ẖ.t.ỉ nn śk.ś nn wś.ś r nḥḥ ḏ.t.

157,l.2 In the realm of the dead is a slaughtering-block, "which

157,note 10 Am Duat VIII.219;Ho.I.148,notes u,v.

158,l.4 which captured birds and fish are slaughtered. "This knife, with which

158,l.15 The same occurs in the ḳrr.t-book:"Great of secret, lord of the blood,

158,note 4 Am Duat VI.217;Ho.I.115.9-10.

158,note 5 The second line is to be read: places",cf. w3ḏ.t,Wb.I.268.16, for the red crown.Cf. also w3ḏ.w,raw flesh,

158,note 9 C.T.V.51.e.Idem keeper 4th gate Book of Gates,B.S.Pl.VII.56;MaPi I.226.

158,note 11 Wb.I.184.9.Idem about a demon in Am Duat,II,57.58;Ho.I.27.

9;nr.132.

p. 159,l.24 "gods...who are in R3.śṯ3.w who live on the bodies of..."[14].

159,note 5 ʿm b3, Am Duat VII.152;Ho.I.133.3.

159,note 8 C.T.VII.436.i-437.a,Spell 1108;B 1 L.534.

159,note 15 Book of Gates IX, lower register,B.S.Pl.XIII.14-16;MaPi III.37.38.

159,note 17 Am Duat XI.80.81;Ho.I.191.5-6.

160,note 9 Am Duat VI.153;Ho.I.114.1.

160,note 10 Book of Gates, B.S.Pl.III.3;MaPi I.79.

162,note 1 Zweiwegebuch,B 1 Be.7.8;C.T.VII.473.j-474.b,Spell 1131.

162,note 2 Zweiwegebuch,B 1 L.485;C.T.VII.389.c,Spell 1099.

162,note 5 Am Duat XI, lower register, Bucher,p.77;Ho.I.190.13.

164,note 5 Drawing C.T.VI.386.

165,l.11 plots of the dumpalm...For which purpose do you come here? I come

165,l.20 their walls of fire-stone is in R3-śṯ3.w"[3]

165,note 3 C.T.VII.519.c-g,Spell 1182;B 1 Be.291 sqq.

167,note 4 Book of Gates IX, middle register,B.S.Pl.XIII.29-XII.31; MaPi III.15.

167,note 6 Am Duat XI.77;Ho.I.189.5;XI.87;Ho.I.190.10;nr.813.

167,note 8 Am Duat V.37-39.43.44.Ho.I.81.6-82.1.

168,l.31 "fish-traps"[14]. From what follows it appears that there are flames

168,note 11 Am Duat XI, Bucher Pl.X,XI;Ho.I.,Plate "Elfte Stunde", lower register.

168,note 13 Am Duat III.27;Ho.I.47.3-4.

168,note 14 Am Duat XI.77;Ho.I.189.2-3.

169,note 1 Book of Gates III, lower register,B.S.Pl.VIII.20-25;Pl. VII.44-49;50-52;MaPi I.203.204.

170,note 1 Book of GatesI, lower register,B.S.Pl.III.40-43;MaPi I. 67.68.

170,note 4 Book of Gates IV, lower register,B.S.Pl.VI.26-29;MaPi I. 280.281.

170,note 5 Book of Gates IV, lower register,B.S.Pl.VI.37.38;MaPi I. 284.

p. 170,note 6	Am Duat I.234;Ho.I.20.1.
170,note 10	C.T.VII.513.d-g,Spell 1172;B 1 Be.262.
171,1.28	more than once). The rage of the big lake has escaped him"[10]. Beware
171,note 7	Book of Gates VII, lower register, Budge, The Eg. Heaven and Hell, II,pp.215,216;Lefébure, *Le tombeau de Séti Ier*, II.11-13;MaPi II.79-83 (Vth gate).
172,1.21	pool of the malefactors"[6]. Dangerous ponds are mentioned in the
172,note 6	C.T.VII.390.a,Spell 1099;B 1 L.485.
173,note 2	Book of Gates VIII, upper register,B.S.Pl.XIV.49-53;MaPi II.206.207.
174,note 1	Am Duat VIII.225;Ho.I.151.10.
174,note 2	C.T.III.296.b.
174,note 3	C.T.V.51.g.
175,note 2	C.T.I.80.1-m.
175,note 11	Line 2 ought to be read: *ẖ.t.ỉ nn rḳỉ.k r.ỉ*.Cf.B.D. 27 and 30B;*Buch von Atmen* B.D. Budge,p.513.16;
176,note 1	Am Duat VII.101;Ho.I.128.2;nr.527.
177,1.23	*b3* is on a par with total ruination. "Ruin to your souls, hindrance
177,note 6	Am Duat III.141;Ho.I.53.9.
177,note 10	Book of Gates VIII, lower register,B.S.Pl.XIV.20-22;MaPi II.213.214.
177,note 11	Am Duat VII.34.35;Ho.I.121.3.
177,note 12	Am Duat XI.76, Bucher Pl.X;Ho.I.190.7;nr.810;190.9;nr.812.
178,note 2	Am Duat VII.152;Ho.I.133.3.
179,1.20	commemorated with those who are upon earth (i.e. living). His offerings are not made to him.
179,note 3	Am Duat VI.224.225;Ho.I.116.3.
181,1.14	let this crocodile take it away, which lives on magical power"[6]
181,note 5	Am Duat II.195.196;Ho.I.34.2.

p. 182.note 4	Am Duat, Abr.Thutmoses III,26, Bucher,p.88;Ho.III,p.10: 109.
183,l.16	inscription to it reads:"Destruction for your souls, hindrance for
183,l.31	shadows of those who should be exterminated and who should be
183,note 6	Am Duat VII.34.35;Ho.I.121.3.
183,note 8	Am Duat VI.217;Ho.I.115.9-10.
183,note 9	Am Duat XI.76;Ho.I.189.1.
183,note 11	Am Duat V.45 sq.;Ho.I.82.1-2.
185,note 3	C.T.VII.434b-435.a,Spell 1106;B 1 L.527;Cairo 28085, Lacau, Sarc.I.215.13;B. 3 C.507.
185,note 4	Am Duat III.1;Ho.I.44.8.
185,note 7	C.T.VII.318.c-319.a,Spell 1061;B 1 L.393;Lacau, Sarc. I. 193.35, above the black road;C.T.VII.514.j-515.a,Spell 1175;B 1 Be.270.Idem B.D. 144;330.12.
185,note 9	Book of Gates IV, middle register, B.S.Pl.VI.22-30;MaPi I. 238-240.
186,l.20	B.10.a. <u>mt m wḥm</u>, t o d i e f o r t h e s e c o n d t i m e[6a)]
186,l.30,31	back to him" 10). Consequently the content of the text is that the dead gets his <u>ḥk3</u> back. "Truly, this magical power of mine is brought
186 (add a new note)	6a) E.Hornung, <u>Nacht und Finsternis</u>,p.69, "das Anheimfallen an das "Unsein" und an die "Vernichtung".
189,note 1	Book of Gates VII, upper register, Budge, The Eg. Heaven and Hell,p.201;E.Lefébure, <u>Le tombeau de Séti Ier</u>,II.12; MaPi II.56 (Vth gate).
189,note 4	Am Duat V.44;Ho.I.82.1.
189,note 7	C.T.VII.496.a-l,Spell 1146;B 1 Be.213-219.
189,note 8	C.T.VII.511.i,Spell 1169;B 1 Be.244.
190,note 7	Book of Gates II, lower register,B.S.Pl.III.8.9; MaPi I. 121.

p. 190,note 8	Book of Gates VII, upper register, Budge, The Eg. Heaven and Hell II,p.204;E.Lefébure, Le tombeau de Séti Ier,II. 11.12;MaPi II.55 (Vth gate).
190,note 9	Am Duat IX.93.94;Ho.I.155.8-156.1.
190,note 11	Hornung, Amduat II.98, "bezwingen", "bestrafen".
190,note 12	Am Duat II.256.257;Ho.I.41.3-4.
190,note 13	Ḳn.t , harm,Wb.V.48.14.Am Duat V.38.39;Ho.I.81.6-7;V.63; Ho.I.82.7.
191,1.30	"N.N. is not surrounded by your fury, oh gods"[10). An epithet
192,note 6	Am Duat X.2;Ho.I.167.9.
193,1.6,7	uraei"."They cry out, after Re has approached them. Souls recede, shadows perish on account of hearing the voice of the uraei." In
193,note 2	Book of Gates III, upper register, 3rd figure,B.S.Pl.VII. 46-48;MaPi I.189-191.
193,note 3	Am Duat IX.98;Ho.I.163.11.
193,note 4	L.Q.I,1st ḳrr.t, upper register;L.Q.IV.4.Cf. 16 uraei in the gate of Book of Gates X,B.S.Pl.XII;MaPi III.44.
193,note 5	Book of Gates VII, lower register, Budge, The Eg. Heaven and Hell II,p.215;E.Lefébure, Le tombeau de Séti Ier, II. 11.12;MaPi II.79-81 (Vth gate).
195,1.19	It is a snake on legs. The name is connected with the verb šm =
195,note 8	Book of Gates IX, upper register,B,S.Pl.XII.32-39;MaPi III. 26.
196,note 4	C.T.VII.513.c,Spell 1171;B 1 P.365.
197,1.3	peers at the wayside, "Hippopotamus' head, alert in the attack"[1)
197,note 1	C.T.VII.512.g,Spell 1170;B 1 Be.263;B 1 P.361.
197,note 2	C.T.VII.320.a,Spell 1062;B 1 L.388;Lacau, Sarc. I.193.41; B 1 C.558.
198,1.20	wait for him along the paths of the Zweiwegebuch, "the name of the spirits

p. 198,note 7	C.T.VII.499.c,Spell 1149;B 1 Be.232.
199,l.17,18	pond, in which you purge the gods, to which the souls of the dead do not approach"[6] . Another division deals with jackals, which are in the
199,note 6	Book of Gates III, upper register,B.S.Pl.VIII.36-VII.40; MaPi I.185.
199,note 7	Book of Gates III, upper register, 2nd figure,B.S.Pl.VIII. 26-29;MaPi I.182.183.
199,note 8	Book of Gates I, middle register,B.S.Pl.IV.17-20;MaPi I. 32.33.
200,note 6	Book of Gates IX, middle register,B.S.Pl.XII.31.32;MaPi III.15.Cf.E.Hornung, <u>Das Amduat</u>,II,p.31,nr.106, "<u>Preisender</u>".
200,note 7	Wb.II.84.2 <u>mnḥ</u>, to slaughter.
200,note 9	C.T.VII.511,i,Spell 1169;B 1 Be.244.
201,note 1	Lacau, Sarc.I.192.31;33;B1 C.555.556;C.T.VII.309.b;313.a; Spells 1057,1059.
204,l.9	mothers"[2] . When the dead knows the right spells, he passes them
204,l.13	<u>m3śty.w</u> ,the keepers of the gates"[2a] . It is said about them:"It is
204,note 1	C.T.VII.520.a,Spell 1183;B 1 Be.293.
204,note 2	Cairo 28085;Lacau, Sarc.I.211.58.59;B 3 C 410.411;C.T.VI. 347.b.c,Spell 1076.
204,note 2a	Cairo 28085;Lacau, Sarc.I.212.66,68;B 3 C.430-434;C.T.VII. 354.a.b,Spell 1081.
204,note 3	C.T.VII.351.b-d,Spell 1079;B 2 Bo.155 sq.
204,note 6	C.T.VII.518.g.h,Spell 1181;B 1 Be.287.
204,note 7	Book of Gates X, upper register,B.S.Pl.XI,MaPi III.72.
205,l.21	who are on earth like (the fear of) Horus among the gods ....I have
206,note 7	Book of Gates VI, middle register,E.Lefébure,M.M.A.F.C. III,1,Pl. XXXIV.41;MaPi II.149 (VIIth gate).
208,note 1	<u>Zweiwegebuch</u>,C.T.VII.414.c,Spell 1099;B 1 L.502.503.

p. 208,note 3 — C.T.VII.511.g.h,Spell 1169;B 1 Be.244,Zweiwegebuch,3rd part black road.

208,note 5 — Louvre 3865 III.4,śndm.k n.ỉ ỉb.ỉ m 3.t n.t nbd (2nd century A.D.)

209,l.23 — of Mrś‘nh III, Gizah, on a statue of queen Tỉ‘3 (both unpublished). See now: D.Dunham and W.K.Simpson, The Mastaba of Queen Merysankh III, G 7503-7540, Boston, 1974.

209,note 1 — Book of Gates I, lower register,B.S.Pl.IV.8-10;MaPi I.56.

209,note 2 — Book of Gates V, middle register,B.S.Pl.XVIII.8;MaPi II.106 (VIth gate).

212,l.9 — as they actually were already during their life on earth, and now to be allowed to

212,note 1 — Am Duat III.100;Ho.I.50.5.6.

212,note 2 — Am Duat III.139-150;Ho.I.53.9.

212,note 3 — Am Duat III.197 sqq.;Ho.I.58.3-4.

212,note 8 — Book of Gates III, middle register, 2nd figure,B.S.Pl.VIII.23-25;MaPi I.159.162.

212,note 10 — E.g. Book of Gates II, upper register of twelve mummies in chapels;B.S.Pl.III;MaPi I.102;Wb.II.358.3;359.13.

213,note 2 — Am Duat XI.78;Ho.I.189.8-9.

214,note 4 — Book of Gates X, upper register,B.S.Pl.XI.21;MaPi III.77.78;A.Klasens, A magical statue base,p.104.h.9-10.B.D. 39;105.12;see above p.132,B.2.p,k3ś.

216,l.21 — belabours his victims with a knife, occur in the texts several times[9].

222,l.16 — withdraw opposite you"[5]. "He (Horus) has given the gods, your ene-

223,note 7 — Book of Gates VIII, lower register,B.S.Pl.XV.9.10;MaPi II.211.

224,l.22 — from Akhty. Make a slaughter in the flesh of the malicious one".

224,note 3 — Book of Gates II, lower register,B.S.Pl.III.28-Pl.II.35;MaPi I.128.129.

225,l.20 — judge of the dead. "Sia says to this god, when he

p.	
	approaches
225,l.23	seize the rebels". The wśr.t-post of Geb also occurs in the Book of
225,l.24	the Dead[5] in a context, which is not clear: Mk št3.w śb3.w ḥr
225,note 4	Book of Gates V, middle register, E.Lefébure,M.M.A.F.C. III,1,Pl.XXX.13-26;MaPi II.105-107 (VIth gate). See H.P. Blok,AcOr VII,p.103.104.
226,note 3	Am Duat VIII, middle register, Bucher Pl.VII;Capart, Z.Ä.S. 36,p.125;Ho.I.Plate "Achte Stunde", nr.589-597.
227,l.6,7	B.D.153 A reads:"Spell in order to escape the net...Oh catcher, who catches...Oh catchers,...who catch your prey, who go about in
228,l.29	as well as for the fishing-net. "Le mot ỉ3d.t s'appliquait à tout ce qui
230,l.7	is to say the Beduins" (fish and birds mixed)[3].
230,l.13	four ropes, which are in this bird-trap of Śbk"[5]. Also the ỉbṯ.ty.w
232,l.11	The dead wishes not to get entangled into a lasso on earth lest he should
233,note 5	Am Duat VII,79.80;Ho.I.125.4.
234,note 7	Book of Gates IV, upper register,B.S.Pl.VI.31.32;MaPi I. 262.
236,note 1	Book of Gates VIII, middle register,B.S.Pl.XIV.25-55;MaPi II.187-193.
236,note 2	Am Duat X.79 sqq.;Ho.I.176.6-177.5.
237,note 1	Am Duat V.20;Ho.I.79.3-5.
237,note 4	1st gate, 5th register, ed.Piankoff,p.38;7th gate, kingdom of Osiris, ed.Piankoff,p.61;cf.8th gate ed.Piankoff, p.66.
239,note 1	Book of Gates IV, lower register, 1st figure,B.S.Pl.VII. 1 - VI.II;MaPi I.273-275. In E.Lefébure, Le tombeau de Séti Ier, Paris 1886, II,4-5, the foreigners are pictured with features and cloths, which are caracteristic for them,

	the Nḥś.w as negroes.
p. 239,note 4	Lacau, Sarc. I.,28085.221.59;B 3 C.575.576;C.T.VII.464.g-465.a,Spell 1130.
241,note 10	B.D.130;C.T. VII.397.f-398.c,Spell 1099;B 1 L.490.
242,1.22	B.21.f. íśḳ, h i n d e r.
242,1.23	"Hindrance for your shadows" is promised as a punishment in the
243,1.11	o n e s" (?) [5]. "My robbery is not in the council" [6] "People,
244,note 1	Louvre S.N.173,VIII.17, wd d̲w m ník.
245,1.1-3	A division of Am Duat.....sight of Re. These lines ought to be cancelled.
245,note 1	To be cancelled.
245,note 4	Book of Gates I, lower register,B.S.Pl.III.38-40;MaPi I.67.
245,note 6	Book of Gates VII, middle register, Budge, The Eg. Heaven and Hell II,p.195; E.Lefébure, Le tombeau de Séti Ier, II.11;MaPi II.34 (Vth gate).
246,1.25	god, who puts himself inimically in the way, by taking away the
246,note 2	C.T.VII.492.a,Spell 1144;B 1 Be.191;B 5 C.524.
246,note 3	C.T.VII.510.b-d,Spell 1168;B 1 Be.242.
246,note 4	Am Duat VII.23;Ho.I.120.3-4, Hornung, Das Amduat II,p.127, translates more correctly, "Der 'Gewalttätige an Gesicht' (mds ḥr) ist gegen sie, er metzelt sie nieder."
248,1.12	him". "We charm you" [7]
248,note 6	Book of Gates II, lower register,B.S.Pl.II.35-37;MaPi I.122,130.
248,note 7	Book of Gates IX, middle register,B.S.Pl.XIII.18,XII.35.36;MaPi III.14.15.
248,note 15	Am Duat VII.19.20;Ho.I.120.2.
253,1.27	Excursus:To escape and to be saved from dangers.
254,1.11	(nwd̲ , ḥm , ḥrtíwny). In this way he frightens the enemy and the latter
254,note 7	C.T.VII.320.c.d,Spell 1062;B 2 L.536.537.

p. 256,note 1	Zweiwegebuch, C.T.VII.423.c;424.a-c,Spell 1102;B 1 L.515.
257,l.18	"Oh she-baboons of his, who cut off the heads.N.N. may pass
257,l.20,21	passed the house of his b3 (read "this" b3). The rage of the big lake has escaped him. His passage-money has not been taken away from
257,l.26	lies. So the dead is on them. The text written beside is "a spell to pass
257,l.31	there is written:"A spell to pass him is this which is in front"[9]. The dead
257,note 5	Pyr.334.a.b.I.e. "He has escaped the rage of the big lake".
257,note 6	C.T.VII.285.c,Spell 1036;B 2 L.484.
257,note 7	C.T.VII.499.d,Spell 1149;B 1 Be.233.
257,note 8	C.T.VII.498.g,Spell 1148;B 1 Be.226.
257,note 9	C.T.VII.437.b,Spell 1108;502.b,Spell 1153;509.c,Spell 1167; 512.c,Spell 1169;305.b,Spell 1053.
258,note 1	C.T.VII.474.a-c,Spell 1131;B 1 Be.9.
258,note 2	See also C.T.VII.307.a,Spell 1055;B 2 L.526;C.T.VII.513.a, Spell 1171;B 1 P.363.
258,note 3	I.e. the text written before the monster with the hippo-potamus' head. C.T.VII.517.j,Spell 1179;B 1 Be.282.
258,note 4	C.T.VII.517.a,Spell 1179;B 1 Be.281;idem before 3 pools of fire,C.T.VII.518.d,Spell 1181;B 1 Be.284.
259,note 1	used C.T.II.266.b: "To know what Thoth knows, as guarding". See also C.T.V.293.b.
260,note 3	Book of Gates I, lower register,B.S.Pl.IV.29-33;MaPi I. 64.65.
261,l.26	dead says to the 42 judges:"May you not lodge a complaint against
264,l.26	away from my grave, I shall be judged with them by the
265,l.12	opponent. "He who will take away a brick from this grave, I
267,note 4	Book of Gates I, middle register,B.S.Pl.IV.8.9.14-17;MaPi I.30.32.
267,note 7	Book of Gates VI, middle register, E.Lefébure,M.M.A.F.C.

p.	
	III,1,Pl.XXXIII.5-7;MaPi II.143 (VIIth gate).
268,l.1	"They (the beatified spirits, to whom funerary offerings are regularly
268,note 1	Book of Gates VI, lower register, E.Lefébure,M.M.F.A.C. III,1,Pl.XXXIV.31-37;Cenotaph Seti I,Vol.II,Pl.LX;MaPi II.165.166 (VIIth gate).
268,note 2	Proleptically, it concerns people who will be <u>mt</u> or <u>3ḫ</u> after the sentence, Book of Gates VI, lower register, E. Lefébure,M.M.F.A.C.III,1,Pl.XXXIV.39-46;MaPi II.167.168.
268,note 3	Book of Gates IV, middle register,B.S.Pl.VI.31.32.39; MaPi I.242-245.
270,note 11	Am Duat IX.3;Ho.I.154.6.
271,l.10	has driven away his evil,N.N. has extirpated sin"[6].
271,note 1	C.T. Spell 237.
272,l.2,3	Evil gods are punished by not ascending to heaven. "He does not ascend to the house of Horus, which is in the heavens, on this day of
272,note 7	Book of Gates VI, lower register, E.Lefébure,M.M.F.A.C. III,1,Pl.XXXIV.31-33;Cenotaph Seti I,-Vol.II,Pl.LX;MaPi II.165.166.
273,note 4	Book of Gates IV, middle register,B.S.Pl.VI.46-V.49;MaPi I.248-250.
273,note 6	Book of Gates VI,middle register,E.Lefébure,M.M.F.A.C. III,1,Pl.XXXIV.39.40;MaPi II.145 (VIIth gate).
273,note 7	Idem 15-22;MaPi II.144.145.
273,note 8	Idem 38-40;MaPi II.148.
274,note 2	Book of Gates X, upper register,B.S.Pl.X.48.49;MaPi III.81.
274,note 3	Book of Gates X, upper register,B.S.Pl.XI.38-40;MaPi III. 79.80.
274,note 8	Book of Gates IV, middle register,B.S.Pl.VI.31-39;MaPi I. 242.245.
275,l.5	self before a court of judges and now he may ascend to heaven.
275,note 7	P. 220 B.17.b;C.T.Spell 149;II.234.a-235.a.

p. 277,1.29	Their offerings consist of justification[6] ... They are the ones who assign
277,note 4	Book of Gates II, lower register,B.S.Pl.III.12-26;MaPi I. 120.121.
277,note 5	Book of Gates VI, middle register, E.Lefébure,M.M.F.A.C. III,1,Pl.XXXIII. 15-25;MaPi II.144-146 (VIIth gate).
277,note 7	Book of Gates IV, lower register,B.S.Pl.VI.38-45;MaPi I. 284.288.
278,1.22	psychostasy before Osiris Anubis stands near the scales[9]. So i͗p is
279,1.11	destined (for him) " (or: "Which they have thought out themselves") [4].
279,note 6	Book of Gates II, lower register,B.S.Pl.III.22.23;MaPi I. 125.
279,note 7	Book of Gates V, middle register,B.S.Pl.XVIII.29-31;E. Lefébure,M.M.F.A.C.III,1,Pl.XXXI.35-39;MaPi II.108 (VIth gate).
280,1.19	in accordance with their deeds. "He assigns you to your slaughtering
280,note 1	C.T.VII.287.d,Spell 1038;B 2 L.490;Lacau, Sarc.I.190.9.
280,note 7	Book of Gates V, upper register,B.S.Pl.XVIII,19.20;E.Lefébure,M.M.A.F.C. III,1,Pl.XXXI.27.28;MaPi II.115 (VIth gate)
280,note 8	Book of Gates V, middle register,B.S.Pl.XVIII.37-42;E.Lefébure,M.M.A.F.C.III,1,pl.XXXI.39-43;MaPi II.108 (VIth gate).
280,note 9	Book of Gates I, upper register,B.S.Pl.IV.31.32;MaPi I. 50;lower register,B.S.Pl.IV.26.27;MaPi I.63.64.
281,1.28	C.4.e. t͟3m, t o c o v e r.
281,1.30	"whose cover of face does not exist"[13]. This is an epithet, which
281,1.31	expresses that they want to deliver somebody up to the sentence irrespective of the person.
283,1.12	Gates calls them "who punished the evil one of head (Apophis)"[6].

p. 283,note 3	Book of Gates III, lower register,B.S.Pl.VIII.17.18;MaPi I.202.
283,note 4	Am Duat VII.36-38;Ho.I.121.3-4.
283,note 5	Am Duat XI.76;Ho.I.189.1.
283,note 6	Book of Gates VII, upper register, Budge, The Eg. Heaven and Hell II, p.204;E.Lefébure, Le tombeau de Séti Ier II, 11;MaPi II.54.55 (Vth gate).
283,note 7	Book of Gates X, upper register,B.S.Pl.XI.17.18;MaPi III. 74.
283,note 8	Book of Gates XI, middle register,B.S.Pl.X.19-23;MaPi III.116.
283,note 10	Am Duat XII.8;Ho.I.194.8-9.
283,note 11	Am Duat VII.84-89;Ho.I.126.1-4.
284,note 2	Am Duat III.25;Ho.I.46.7. Hornung, Das Amduat, II.64, translates "zermalmen" and points to Wb.II.370.8-9.
284,note 3	Am Duat V.43.44;Ho.I.82.1.
284,note 10	Book of Gates IX, middle register,B.S.Pl.XII.37.38;MaPi III.16. Śšy is an inimical serpent.
284,note 13	Book of Gates II, lower register,B.S.Pl.III.14.15;MaPi I. 123.
285,l.14	every day by the majesty of Ḥr d3ty " 7). The punishment is repeated
285,note 3	Book of Gates VIII, lower register,B.S.Pl.XV.11.12;MaPi II.211.212.
285,note 6	Book of Gates IV, lower register,B.S.Pl.VI.45-V.48;MaPi I.288.289.
285,note 7	Am Duat XI.78;Ho.I.189.8-9.
285,note 8	L.Q. CXXXIII.7.8.
285,note 9	L.Q. CXXXIII.9-CXXXIV.1.
285,note 10	Book of Gates V, middle register,B.S.Pl.XVIII.22-26;MaPi II.107.108 (VIth gate).
285,note 13	Book of Gates VII, middle register, Budge, The Eg. Heaven and Hell II, p.194;E.Lefébure, Le tombeau de Séti Ier, II.10;MaPi II.31.

p. 285,note 15 Am Duat XI.77;Ho.I.189.3-4.

286,note 7 Book of Gates III, lower register,B.S.Pl.VIII.20-22;MaPi I.203.

286,note 8 Am Duat VII.21;Ho.I.120.2.

287,note 12 Book of Gates I, lower register,B.S.Pl.III.38-43;MaPi I. 57.58.

290,note 7 Wb.III.361.13.Cf.C.T.VII.184.q.r,Spell 971, ỉdr.ỉ š3b.t (= ḥ3b.t) iri.ỉ m3ʿ.t, "I remove sin, I do justice". M3ʿ.t means literally "that which is straight". See Wb.II. 22.15,m3ʿ ʿ, to stretch the arm. That which is "crooked" is the opposite of that which is "straight".

290,note 8 Am Duat VII.30-31;Ho.I.121.2.

290,note 9 Am Duat X.2;Ho.I.167.9.

291,l.13 C.6.s. ḳn , "B ö s e s, S c h a d e n"[3]. "Ü b e l - t a t"[4].

291,l.30 Re on earth, who called in an evil way to him who is in the egg

291,note 1 Book of Gates VIII, lower register,B.S.Pl.XIV.24-31;MaPi II.214.215.

291,note 4 Wb.V.48.8. This is perhaps the same word as Wb.V.44.1 ḳni, or V.44.3,6 ḳn, "bezwingen, prügeln". The original meaning could be "violence", "Gewalttat".Cf. Hornung, Das Amduat II.98, ḳni.

291,note 9 Book of Gates I, lower register,B.S.Pl.IV.15-37;MaPi I 56.57.

292,note 4 Book of Gates I, upper register,B.S.Pl.IV.30-32;MaPi I.50.

292,note 7 Book of Gates VII, lower register, Budge, The Eg. Heaven and Hell II,pp.215.216; E.Lefébure, Le tombeau de Séti Ier, II.12.13;MaPi II.83 (Vth gate).

292,note 10 Am Duat XI.79;Ho.I.191.3-4.

293,note 2 Book of Gates XI, lower register,B.S.Pl.IX.34-38.MaPi III. 154.155.

293,note 8 Book of Gates I, lower register,B.S.Pl.IV.34-36;MaPi I. 65.66.

p. 294,note 7	Book of Gates II, lower register;MaPi I.120.
295,note 1	Book of Gates X, upper register,B.S.Pl.XI.42;MaPi III.80.
296,note 3	Book of Gates VII, upper register, Budge, The Eg. Heaven and Hell II,p.201;E.Lefébure, Le tombeau de Séti Ier, II. 11;MaPi II.55 (Vth gate).
296,note 4	Book of Gates IX, middle register,B.S.Pl.XIII.26;MaPi III. 14.Cf. C.T. V.244.a.d.e.
296,note 11	Book of Gates I, lower register,B.S.Pl.IV.15-30;MaPi I. 56.57.
297,l.22	Book of Gates III, lower register, 1st figure, MaPi I. 199,3ḫ.w occur, which are punished
297,note 7	Cairo 28085, Lacau, Sarc.I.216-217;C.T.VII.447.b-d,Spell 1116;See p.89
297,note 8	Book of Gates I, middle register;MaPi I.33;C.2.b.
299,note 6	II Setne II.2;Erichsen, Demotisches Glossar,p.519.
300,note 2	Chapter I,Par.1,p.38.MaPi I.64.65.
304,l.5	in the Book of Gates III, MaPi I.116.
305,l.22	of the pit of the abyss occurs. The same is found in the Book of Gates II, MaPi I.113.114, where an unpleasantly smelling pool is avoided by the birds.
306,l.13	können. So erklärt sich das ungestörte Fortleben der ersteren"[5]. In the
306,l.25	is Christian. That this takes place in fiery pits is borrowed from
307,note 9	Robinson, Coptic Apocryphal Gospels, 94, Life of Mary.
308,note 9	Der Feuerstrom im Jenseits, von W. Vycichl, Wien, Archiv für Ägyptische Archeologie, I Jahrg., 1938,263,264.
309,l.12	which does not die and the outmost darkness and the river of fire,
309,l.29	an obstacle on the way to the Ḥtp-field. In the Book of Gates II, MaPi I.116.
321,l.16	9:48 (Isaiah 66:24 resp.)....
321,l.27	is an unquenchable fire, whose flame cannot be extinguished by the waters

p. 321,note 2 ⲁⲧⲥⲁⲧⲉ ⲱϣⲙ̄ = Egyptian śd.t , Budge, Apocr.3,cf. Apoc.Elias,7,10, ⲥⲉⲉⲧⲉ .

322,note 1 E.g. C.T.VII.287.a,Spell 1037;B 2 L.488, rr.t n.t śd.t , gate of fire.

324,1.8 from the Homily ascribed to Athanasius with Eph.4:8 and 1 Peter

327,1.2 conceptions and with 2 Peter 2:9, "The Lord knows how to preserve

330,1.19 ⲁⲅⲅⲉⲗⲟⲥ Judas[5] is punished by angels, who are in the retinue of

330,1.22 out. They took away the light from his eyes. They plucked out[6a] the

330 (a new note 6a is to be added)

Read ⲁ[ⲩⲧⲱ]ⲗⲕ̄ , not with Budge ⲁ[ⲩⲱ]ⲗⲕ̄.

331,1.33 came with a burning pike in his hand with three points". It here

333,1.26 Serpent, ⲇⲣⲁⲕⲱⲛ ,ϩϥⲱ ,(ḥf3w.t).

333,note 7 Luc.10:19, the "enemy", who sows weeds among the corn, Kittel,N.T.Dict. II, 814,27.

335,note 7 Mark 9:48 and Isaiah 66:24.

336,1.2 snatched away of man, but it need not to be a borrowing here. The

341,note 9 A.3.p;B.7.n Book of Gates II,MaPi I.113.114.

Aeth. Enoch
20:2 328
22 313
90:26 312
Am Duat, ed. E. Hornung, Part. I
I, lower register
15.3; nr. 95 137
I, final text 170
II, upper register
27.9; nr. 132 158
28.2; nr. 134 110
II, lower register
34.1-2 133
34.2 181
34.4 135
II, final text
41.3-4 190
III, introduction
44.8 185
III, upper register
46.7 284
47.3-4 112, 168
48.2; nr. 200 153
III, middle register
50.5-6 212
52.3; nr. 240 139
52.6; nr. 242 135
52.10; nr. 246 142
III, lower register
53.9 19, 145, 177, 212
53.11 139
53.11-54.1 133, 151
III, final text
58.3-4 212
59.1-3 40
V, upper register
79.3-5 237
81.6-7 190
81.6-82.1 167
82.1 189, 284
82.1-2 20, 144, 183
82.4 130, 190
82.7 190
82.7-8 133
83.8 152
V, lower register
92.3 142
93.6-7 112
96.2-4 111, 141
VI, upper register
99.7-8; 100.3-4 36
VI, lower register
114.1 153
115.8 15
115.9 133, 152
115.9-10 158, 183
116.2 145
116.3 179
VII, upper register
120.2 248, 286
120.3 133
120.3-4 246
120.4 145
121.2 290
121.2-3 21, 127
121.3 177, 183, 242
121.3-4 283
122.2-3 136

VII, middle register
125.4 233
126.1-4 283
128.2; nr. 527 176
VII, lower register
133.3 159, 178
VIII, upper register
136.4 63
138.3 63
VIII, lower register
148.2 63
148, notes u, v 157
150.9 152
151.10 174
152.4 63
152.9 15, 133
Plate "Achte Stunde", nr. 589-597 226
IX, introduction
154.6 270
IX, upper register
155.8-156.1 190
IX, lower register
163.3-4 139
163.4 135
163.8 150
163.11 193
164, notes f, g 18, 48
165.1; nr. 681 134
165, notes c, d 137
X, introduction
167.9 148, 192, 290
X, upper register
171.9-10 106
X, lower register
176.6-177.5 236
XI, lower register
188.8 154
189.1 149, 183, 283
189.2 19, 49, 152
189.2-3 168
189.3-4 285
189.4 134, 146
189.5 136, 167
189.6 151
189.6-7 148
189.8-9 213
190.4; nr. 807 146
190.7; nr. 810 177
190.9; nr. 812 177
190.10; nr. 813 167
190.13 162
191.1; nr. 816 78
191.3-4 292
191.4 144
191.5-6 159
191.10; nr. 821 144
Plate "Elfte Stunde" 168
XII, upper register
194.8-9 283
XII, lower register
203.1 145
"Kurzfassung", ed. E. Hornung, Part III
p. 10:109 182
E. Amélineau, Etude sur les Christianisme en Egypte au septième siècle.

144, 145 313, 322
146 326, 336
147 339
148 325, 329, 330, 331
148, 149 334
150 336, 339
160 308
Amenemhēt (A.H. Gardiner, Tomb of -)
Pl. XXX.c 73
Ani (Wisdom of -)
IV.11, 12 53
IV.13 56
IV.17 sqq. 87, 202
V.2-4 13
V.3 87
V.15 288
VII.11 33, 263
VII.12 13, 51, 86
Berlin 11651 300
Berlin, Papyrus P 3050, IV.8 149
Bible
2 Sam.14:14 336
1 Kings 21:13 260
2 Kings 20:6 52
Job 28:22 305, 328
Ps.61:7 52
Ps.102:24 338
Prov.10:27 338
Prov.16:4 327
Isaiah 38:10 317
Isaiah 66:24 321, 335
Daniel 7 331
Daniel 7:9, 10 310
Obadiah 16 49
Malachi 4:1-3 38
Matth. 3:11 308
Matth. 3:12 321
Matth. 8:12 322, 325
Matth. 12:29 338
Matth. 12:40 312
Matth. 13:30 322
Matth. 16:18 305, 317
Matth. 19:28 39
Matth. 22:13 325, 338
Matth. 25:30 325
Matth. 25:41 314
Matth. 27:51 304
Matth. 28:2 304
Mark 3:27 333
Mark 9:48 321, 322, 325, 335, 337
Luke 10:19 333
Luke 17:10 322
Luke 22:53 325
1 Cor. 6:2 39
2 Cor. 11:3 335
Eph. 4:8 324
Hebr. 2:14 328
1 Peter 3:19 324
1 Peter 5:8 333
2 Peter 2:9 327
Rev. 2:26 38
Rev. 3:21 39
Rev. 9:11 305, 328
Rev. 12 334
Rev. 12:4 337
Rev. 12:9 335
Rev. 20:2 338
Rev. 20:4 38

Rev. 20:14 310
Rev. 22:18, 19 314
Blok (H.P. -. Eine magische Stele aus der Spätzeit; AcOr. VII)
Pl. II 214
p.98 151, 153, 214
pp. 98, 100 134, 149
pp. 98, 103-113 166
p. 103 214
pp. 103, 104 225
p. 105 170
p. 108 214, 215, 217
p. 109 194, 294
p. 110 161
Book of the Dead (quoted according to the edition of Budge, 1898, unless another indication has been given)
p. 16.10 32
chapter page
1 30; Nav.II.15 290
5 28.3 251
6 251
7 29.8 83, 159
8 30.9 48
9 Nav.II.19 147
12 225
14 250
15 36.8 132
15 40.15 284
15 40.15 sqq. 127
15 41.2 125
15 A 36
15 B 36
Chapter 17, see C.T.IV.252-322.
17 6, Nav. 281
17 Nav.II.33 281, 295
17 Nav.II.64 159, 172, 209
17 Nav.II.68 166
17 Nav.II.71 195
17 Nav.II.72 130, 191, 219
17 Nav.II.73, 74 168
17 Nav.II.74 133, 177
25 64
26 89.10-12 95
26 89.12 64
26 89.13 64
27 155, 175, 176, 247
27 90.10 246
27 90.10-91.2 263
28 155
28 91.16 166
28 92.1 201
28 92.2 249
29 246
29 93.4-7 202
30 501.5 181
30 A 94.15-95.3 273
30 A+B 262
30 B 175, 262
30 B 96.3.4 260, 269
30 B 96.6 262
30 B 96.6.7 274
30 B 96.8 272
30 B 96.9-10 263
31 97.10 256
31-37 257
32 98.6.7 194

32	100.3	50	45		11, 58, 304
33		101	45	120.4	58
34		101	45	120.5	82
36		194	46		14
38 A	103.11	72	46	120.11	50
39		224, 257	50 A	121.14-122.10	84
39	105.11	155	55	126.15	73
39	105.12	132	55	127.3-4	62
39	105.14	249	58		73, 68
39	106.4.5	132	59		73
39	106.7	247	63 A		67
39	106.10	285	63 A	133.7.8	135
39	106.13	158	63 B		67
39	106.14	249	65.7, 8	Nav.II.140, 141	193
39	106.15	279	71	158.5-10	151
40	109.7	17	71	158.7-8	147
40	109.7-110.5	160	71	158.7-10	254
40	109.15	158	71,20, 21	Nav.II.153	52
40	109.15-110.1	294	72		124
40	110.1.2	293	72	159.12	254
40	110.2.3	243	72	160.2	191
40	110.3	243	72	160.11.12	249
40	110.5	86	72	160.11-13	125
41	110.9	154	72	160.12	80
41	111.5	72	80	177.9	194
41	111.6	84	80	177.9-10	111
42		12	80	177.11	235
42	113.6	186	80	179.12.16	75
42	113.7-10	243	85	C.T.IV.63.c	189
42	114.8-10	248	85	Nav.II.191.2.3	8
42	114.9	191	85	Nav.II.192	2
42	Nav.II.116	12	89	189.4	178
43	116.15 sqq.	154	89	190.6	178
44	119.13	63	90		62

90	191.12	215	125	252.7.8	24
91		19, 176	125	252.7, sqq	253
92		40, 183	125	253.2	159, 183
92	194.12	103	125	253.4	109
92	195.8	278	125	253.12	249
92	195.11	211	125	253.16	109, 141
92	195.13.14	278	125	254.1	136
92	195.16	211	125	254.4	292
96.97	201.10.11	250	125	254.5	160
96.97	202.3.4	247	125	254.7	160
101		78	125	255.5	171
101	212.16-213.3	78	125	255.11	190
102	214.10-12	75	125	256.10	88, 142
105	216.13.14	293	125	260.1	154
105	216.13-217.1	281	125	260.2	261, 288
105	216.14	41, 287	125	260.3	290
105	217.4.5	247	125	260.10.11	210
110	225.11.12	68	125	260.10-12	278
110	226.15	273	125	260.11	159
110	C.T.V.346.a	51	125	260.13	289, 293
113		168	125	261.1.2	32
124	243.13.14	75	125	261.6	261
124	244.12-15	252	125	262.3-6	202
124	244.15	144, 159	125	262.5	293
125		17, 31, 34, 238, 301	125	262.6.7	281
125	246.4	268	125	266.12	291
125	249.4.5	271, 289	125	268.11	124
125	249.11.12	17, 159	125	Nav.II.277	129
125	249.12	159	125	Nav.II.308; nr. 40	100
125	249.12.13	270	125	Nav.II.319	269
125	249.15-250.9	32	125/126	Nsikhonsu	272
125	249.16	287	126	269.7	34, 263
125	250.2	286	126	269.12	271
125	250.8	33	126	269.13	271

126	269.14-270.1	258	138	314.4.5	221
126	Nav.II.336.7-10	272	140	316.7.8	294
127 A	271.4	189	141	1st gate	110
127 A	271.5	90	144		116, 124
127 A	271.10	285	144	328.11	197
127 A	272.1	271	144	328.15	245
127 A	272.2-6	115	144	330.12	185
127 A	272.3	159, 160	144	331.12	208
127 A	272.3,272.9,273.7	121	144	333.1-3	118
127 A	272.4	280	145,146	334,7	122
127 A	273.8.9	116	145,146	334.9 sqq	123
127 A	273.11	287	145,146	334.11-13	123
130		119, 241	145,146	1st gate	248
130	279.11	191	145	334.10.11	129
130	279.14	90	145	337.11	205
130	279.16	289	145	348.9	205
130	283.13.14	137	145-147		329
130	283.15-284.3	192	146		15
133	290.3	82	146	4th gate	248
133	290.3-5	247	146	8th gate	152
134	292.10-12	162	146	14th gate	286
134	293.1 sqq	152	146	15th gate	35
134	Nav.II.345	216	146	350.9	137
135	295.3	63	146	351.5.6	158
136 A		14	146	351.12 sqq	138
136 A	298.10	242	146	351.14	205
136 A	299.6	116	146	353.3.4	135
136 A	299.8	208	146	353.3-6	137
136 A	299.9	116	146	353.4	135, 142
136 A	300.4	50	146	353.5.6	258
136 B	300.16-301.1	138	146	353.6	242
136 B	302.15	101	146	353.14-354.14	83
137 A	309.5	27	146	354.4	110
137 A	309.6-8	185	146	354.11; 11th gate	134

146	354.14	279	154	399.3	56
146	355.3	190	154	399.11 sqq.	59
146	356.10-12	109	154	399.16-400.1	84
146	357.2.3	225	154	400.12-14	102
146	357.4	148	154	400.14-401.2	16
146	357.7	141	154	400.14 sqq.	153
147		27, 116, 124	154	401.1.2	159
147	360.14.15	197	154	401.2.3	281
147	361.8	245	154	401.5	59
147	362.8 sqq.	116	154	401.6	59
148	365.5-366.3	255	154	401.12	59
148	365.7-11	199	154	401.13	147
148	365.11-14	219	154	401.14	60, 149
149		184	154	402.2	51, 182
149	372.5	205	155	402.14.15	212
149	Nav.II.412	184	163		14, 19, 33
151	382.11	215	163-165		304
151	382.14.15	223	163	410.16	51
151	383.4	233	163	411.1	160, 178
151	384.6-15	251	163	411.1.2	33
151	385.3	60	163	411.2.3	263
151 d	Nav.II.428	243	163	411.3-5	251
153		22, 228, 229	163	411.4	160
153 A+B		227, 229	163	411.14-16	208
153 A	390.5	234	163	411.16	160
153 A	390.5.6	231	163	412.1-6	138
153 A	390.11.12	230	163	412.4-6	106
153 A	391.3.4	216	163	412.11	159
153 A	391.11	83	163	414.8	261
153 B		232	163	414.11	202, 251
153 B	396.1	231, 233	163	414.12	156
154		11, 59, 229, 304	163	414.13	215
154	398.15	56	163	414.14.15	274
154	399.1.2	56	163	414.15.16	109

164	415.4.11.12	214
164	416.14	171
164	418.1.2	133
164	418.3.4	100
165	418.7	65
165	419.7	233
166	421.4 sqq.	65
168 A	422.3	267
168 A	422.4	263
168 A	423.5.6	146
168	430.5	142
168	431.6.7	204
168	431.7.8	212
168	431.13.14	186
168	432.1	50
172	445.8	242
172	445.8.9	23
172	445.8-13	277
173		256
173	452.14	190
175		9, 248, 315
175,	Pap.Ani 29/25, Budge Translation, p. 326,327	247
175	457.15	267
175	458.7 sqq.	90
175	458.11	61
176	460.13-16	161
178	463.14	70
178	466.4	70
178	467.11	221
179		13, 207
179	469.15-470.2	220
180		22
180	470.14	34, 266
180	471.8.9	266
180	472.6	88
180	473.6 sqq.	226
180	473.8	126
180	473.9	284
180	474.2	131
181		124, 298
181	477.13-15	124
182	481.10.11	217
182	481.15.16	217
182	483.5-7	217
183	488.15.16	217
189		77
189	492.7	77
189	493.6 sqq.	115
189	493.9	241
189	494.4-6	244
189	494.8	77

Book of Breathings
(Buch vom Atmen)
(at the end of Budge's Book of the Dead)

	513.16	175
	516.8-10	261

Book of Gates (ed. Maystre-Piankoff)

Introduction

I.7	94

First Gate.

Door

I.24	129
I.25.26	90
I.26.27	111

Middle register

I.30-32	34, 267

I.32.33 35, 199
I.33 297
Upper register
I.41 36
I.50 280, 292
I.52.53 290
Lower register
I.56 83, 209
I.56.57 291, 296
I.57.58 287
I.61.62 21, 131, 132
I.63.64 280
I.64.65 38, 260, 300
I.65.66 293
I.67 48, 245
I.67.68 170
Second Gate.
Door
I.75.76 123
I.78 139, 152
I.79 73, 160
Middle register
I.90 10
Upper register
I.102 212
I.103 139
I.104.105 80, 88
I.113 134
I.113.114 305, 341
I.116 15, 142, 304, 309
Lower register
I.120 40, 294
I.120.121 78, 277
I.121 190
I.122 248
I.123 284
I.124 151
I.125 138, 279
I.128.129 224
I.130 248
I.134 111
Third Gate
Middle register
I.159-162 212
I.162 74
Upper register
I.176.177 131
I.177 21
I.182.183 199
I.183.184 129
I.185 199
I.189-191 193
I.191-192 136
Lower register
I.199 297
I.202 283
I.203 286
I.203.204 169
I.215 134
Fourth Gate
Door
I.226 158
I.228 142
Middle register
I.235 97
I.238-240 185
I.242-245 39, 268, 274
I.248-250 273

Upper register

I.252-257 36

I.256 36

I.262 234

Lower register

I.273-275 239

I.280.281 35, 92, 170

I.284 95, 170

I.284-288 277

I.286 40

I.288.289 285

Fifth Gate

Middle register

II.31 41, 285

II.34 245

Upper register

II.54.55 283

II.55 190, 296

II.56 189

Lower register

II.67 82, 85

II.68.69 83, 85

II.79-81 193

II.79-83 171

II.83 137, 292

Sixth Gate

Middle register

II.105 22

II.105-107 225

II.106 130, 209

II.107,108 36, 285

II.108 93, 148, 279, 280

Upper register

II.110.111 37

II.114.115 37

II.115 41, 280

II.115.116 37

Seventh Gate

Middle register

II.143 267

II.144.145 273

II.144-146 277

II.145 273

II.148 273

II.149 206

Lower register

II.160 63

II.163 93

II.165.166 39, 268, 272

II.167.168 268

Eight Gate

Door

II.175 134, 139

Middle register

II.183 97

II.187-193 236

Upper register

II.206.207 173

Lower register

II.211 223

II.211.212 285

II.213 150

II.213.214 18, 19, 48, 177

II.214.215 291

II.216 48

II.216-219 15, 138

Ninth Gate

Door

III.7 110
Middle register
III.14 296
III.14.15 248
III.15 167, 200
III.16 284
Upper register
III.26 195
Lower register
III.37.38 17, 159
Tenth Gate
Door
III.44 193
Upper register
III.72 126, 204
III.73 126
III.73.74 16, 149
III.74 22, 283
III.77.78 132, 214
III.78 131
III.79 131
III.79.80 126, 274
III,80 127, 274, 295
Eleventh Gate
Middle register
III.116 127, 283
III.117 126
III.119 132
Lower register
III.154.155 293
III.157 112
Twelfth Gate
Door
III.170 88

British Museum (B.M.) 10508
IV.3-5 143
Buck (A. de -), The fear of premature death, Pro Regno Pro Sanctuario, pp. 79-85.
Pl.III.23 70
Pl.III.27 70
Budge, Coptic Apocrypha
LXI sqq 303
2 335, 338
3 320, 321, 330
4 323, 336
6 338
7 330, 338
9 316
10 337
57 320, 322, 324, 328, 331
99 309
140 308, 314
141 308
143 324
148 319, 334
149 333
152 335
159 333
161 311, 314, 325, 336
166 330, 339
Budge, Coptic Homilies
35 320, 325
36 322, 325, 338
71 312, 319, 336, 338
72 337
116 324
117 338

118 338
123 323
125 311
127 333
129 316, 317, 333
133 317
Budge, Coptic Martyrdoms
240 316
Budge, Miscellaneous Coptic Texts
70 308, 325, 334
82 311
148 308
153-154 321
154 329, 341
538 309, 315, 323, 341
539 sqq. 303
540 339
541 334
543 334
545 318
552 314
556 325, 340
556, 557 334
557 329
557, 558 341
558 325, 326
560 313, 332
Cairo 20539
I.8 281
Chester Beatty Papyrus
I.15.5 202
Coffin Texts
I.8.d-9.c 221
I.11.a.b 96
I.12.e-13.d 218
I.21.b-22.b 274
I.37.d 95
I.38.a 248
I.42.c-43.b 277
I.45.b-46.c 250
I.52.b-53.a 243
I.57.b-d 103
I.59.f-60.c 76
I.70.b-d 21, 133, 170, 279
I.71.a.b 105
I.72.b-73.b 52
I.73.a.b 289
I.75.b.h 121
I.80.k 207
I.80.1.m 175
I.90.d 203
I.118.c 203
I.123.b 216
I.137.d-138.a.c 203
I.156.b 296
I.156.d-157.a 218
I.157.e 268
I.158.a.b 269
I.158.a-d 261
I.158.c 85
I.162.g 86
I.164.i 70
I.165.a 70
I.167.a-g 71
I.167.b.c 86
I.171.j 269, 276
I.172.e 269
I.173.c 292

I.173.c-g 262
I.173.d 290, 294
I.173.i 70
I.174.i 275, 276
I.175.i.l 276
I.176.d-i 276
I.181.c-e 35, 269, 286
I.181.c 289
I.181.d 269
I.181.e 34
I.182.d 125, 249
I.183.h;184.a 292
I.188.d sqq. 9
I.188.d-189.b 76
I.189.b 42
I.192.f.h 263, 270
I.193.b-d 222
I.193.d 166, 204
I.196.h 178
I.196.i;197.a.b 172
I.205.g 268
I.207.b 46
I.207.e;208.b 198, 252
I.208.b-d 18, 188
I.208.d 293
I.210.b 176, 201, 243
I.211.g-212.a 270
I.212.d.e 176
I.226.d.e 246
I.227.h 247
I.229.a 110
I.231.e-232.a 222
I.249.b 205
I.249.c-e 214
I.253.d 270
I.255.a-d 280
I.255.d 96
I.265.a.b.e.f 175
I.268.d 34
I.268.d.e 266
I.268.g.i 206
I.269.e-j 231
I.273.c 209
I.280.f 91
I.282.h 207
I.283.h 102
I.284.f-g 162
I.284.f-h 172
I.284.g 2
I.284.i 209
I.284.j-285.a 253
I.289.c 245
I.289.f 118
I.290.h;291.a 205
I.291.f 172
I.292.d 85
I.295.b 11, 57
I.300.b-f 46
I.304.b 58, 59
I.304.b.c 11
I.304.c.d 63
I.306.a 11, 83
I.313.a 111
I.362.d 128
I.363.d-364.a 211
I.364.a 128
I.378.a-380.a 141
I.397.b 184, 194, 195

I.398.a	91, 186	II.73.a	137
I.398.c	258	II.75.a	95, 120
I.399.a	258	II.77.a-d;78.a	58
I.400.a-d	218	II.81.c-83.b	120
I.400.c	103	II.94.d	200
I.401.a-c	218	II.95.g;96.a.b	200
I.401.c	284	II.109.c	206
I.402.a-e	218	II.112.b.c	80
I.402.b	148	II.112.e	184, 186
I.403.a-c	218	II.112.f	148
I.404.a-c	218	II.112.g	249
I.405.a	218	II.114.a	80
II.13.c.d	128	II.115.b	80
II.28.a	91	II.115.c	108
II.42.b	195	II.116.a	193
II.45.c	186, 215	II.116.v	154
II.47.b	186	II.116.v.w	210
II.47.d	217	II.116.w	86
II.49 sq.	99	II.117.k	68, 150
II.50.i	198	II.117.n	190
II.51.d-j	99	II.125.d.e	93
II.53.g	248	II.126.d	175, 260
II.54.j.k	135	II.127.e	260
II.55.b.c;56.b	193	II.128.d	175, 259
II.55.c	128	II.130.a	262
II.57.a-c	221	II.131.d;132.a.c	166
II.57.c	272	II.133.f	156
II.57.d;58.a	272	II.140.b	41, 268
II.60.a	77	II.143.a.b	244
II.62.a-c	221	II.147.f	97
II.62.c	281	II.151.d	66
II.66.c	221	II.151.e	214, 255, 282
II.66.d	275	II.162.d	95
II.72.b	171	II.162.g.h	6

II.191.c.d	81	II.379.a	134
II.196.d	81	II.386.a	126
II.197.a	81	III.111.a-c	256
II.198.b	81	III.116.a-118.g	76
II.203.b;204.a	282	III.117.d	77
II.205.a	150, 166	III.117.e	77
II.213.b	153	III.125.a	77
II.216.a.b	130	III.126.k	77
II.225.c.d	137	III.128.i.j	77
II.228.b;229.a	220, 290	III.130.a	77
II.230.a sq.	21	III.130.c.d	256
II.230.b-e	127	III.133.a.b	244
II.230.c;232.c.d	220	III.133.b	244
II.233.a-235.a	220	III.133.c	77
II.233.b	275	III.139.i	77
II.234.a-235.a	275	III.141.e.f	57
II.236.b.c	220	III.142.d.e	77
II.249.d-250.b	276	III.143.a	77
II.252.a.d.e	199	III.144.d	195
II.252.e	284	III.146.e	77
II.252.f	23, 249	III.148.b	77
II.252.g.h	242	III.149.c.e	276
II.253.d.f	173	III.153.a	77
II.253.g	51, 179	III.154.d	77
II.254.o	64	III.164.a	251
II.254.o.p	160, 178	III.168.e	77
II.254.p	17	III.173.e	77
II.276.a	134	III.194.e-j	76
II.291.j.k	76	III.197.a	77
II.298.a	217	III.201.k	9, 77
II.310.d sq.	77	III.202.h	77
II.351.b.c	168	III.206.d	201, 210
II.353.b.c	168	III.211.a	5
II.373.d	101	III.213.b.c	248

III.230.a-232.a 218
III.230.c 23, 242
III.232.a 242
III.232.b-234.a-c 95
III.248.a-e 105
III.253.a 95
III.255.a 60
III.256.a.b 60
III.256.b 64
III.258.a 209
III.260.g 222
III.268-276 27
III.268.a.b 115
III.270.b.g 115
III.272.d.e 65, 115
III.274.b-276.c 65
III.285.a 200
III.293.a.b 287
III.293.b 42, 289
III.295.h 150, 210, 231
III.296.a.b 16
III.296.a-e 150
III.296.b 19, 160, 174, 177
III.296.e 179
III.296.f 22, 215, 227, 232
III.296.h.i 20
III.296.k 175
III.298.c 72
III.304.f 109
III.304.f-305.b 202
III.305.b.f 62
III.305.e 210
III.305.e.f 201, 257
III.313.c 271
III.314.a 270
III.317.o 185
III.323.a 210
III.325.g-i 271
III.327.a 106
III.328.a 242
III.335.h 167
III.337.a.d.e 141
III.337.e 156
III.337.f 136
III.337.g 157
III.339.a 141
III.349.b.c 82
III.349.b.e 214
III.349.e 46
III.349.f 214
III.350.a 108
III.350.e-g 180
III.359.c 49
III.368.a-c 207
III.371.a 50
III.396.g 186
III.398.a-d 188
IV.11.d 150, 190
IV.12.a 166
IV.12.b 22, 132
IV.20.a-21.b 277
IV.21.b 196
IV.29.p 30
IV.39.c 172
IV.49.k 271, 287
IV.49.s 182
IV.60.o 293
IV.60.p 287

IV.62.q 171
IV.63.c 189
IV.64.b 57
IV.65.b 89
IV.65.j 191, 213
IV.66.d 192
IV.66.n 134
IV.67.h 157
IV.67.o.p.s 213
IV.69.c.e.f 122
IV.69.e.c 96
IV.69.g 247
IV.71.c.d 210
IV.72.c.d 122
IV.72.d 96
IV.72.e 115
IV.73.a.b 82
IV.73.f 96
IV.74.d.e 96
IV.74.f 27, 115, 120
IV.77.a 27, 120
IV.78.a 122
IV.83.c 296
IV.83.f 122
IV.83.i 96
IV.84.a 27
IV.84.e.f.m 258
IV.84.f 173, 210
IV.85.q 147
IV.89.j.k 241
IV.90.g 214
IV.90.l 158
IV.90.m 148
IV.93.p.q 51
IV.94.a 234
IV.94.d 271
IV.94.f.h 127
IV.94.l 34, 266, 270
IV.97.a-g 120
IV.97.g 28
IV.97.i 148
IV.98.i-99.b 296
IV.105.f 249
IV.107.a 137
IV.115.f 205
IV.119.e 127
IV.126.b 261
IV.126.d.e 150
IV.126.f 249, 261
IV.128.a 248
IV.155.f 207
IV.178.m 178
IV.208.c 286
IV.208.d 288
IV.210.a.b 286
IV.252.c 273
IV.254.a 294
IV.254.a-256.c 273
IV.256.c 293
IV.260.c 137
IV.262.a 133, 177
IV.268.c 137
IV.268.d 208
IV.270.b 134, 136
IV.282.a-284.b 296
IV.282.c 128
IV.284.a 128
IV.284.b 223

IV.290.a 294
IV.298.a 255
IV.298.a-300.a 270
IV.298.b 269
IV.300.a 153, 287
IV.300.b-301.a 287
IV.300.b 23, 233, 294
IV.301.a 157, 177
IV.303.a 146, 152
IV.303.b 24, 200, 210, 245
IV.304.b 224
IV.305.a 157, 249
IV.305.b 144, 247
IV.306.a 161
IV.308.b.c 53
IV.309.a 143
IV.309.b 146
IV.311.b 98
IV.311.c-314.a 196
IV.312.b.c 17, 159
IV.313.d 172
IV.313.d-314.a 172
IV.314.a 173
IV.314.b 159
IV.314.c 181
IV.314.d.e 153
IV.315.d 158
IV.316.c 158, 166
IV.319.e 87, 255
IV.319.e-320.d 212
IV.320.a 73
IV.320.d 82, 110
IV.321.e 21, 255
IV.321.e-322.a 279
IV.322.a-c 128
IV.322.b 153, 161
IV.322.c 285
IV.322.d 16, 149, 157, 248
IV.322.f 280
IV.323.a-c 146
IV.323.b 161
IV.323.d 144, 168, 247
IV.324.a 168
IV.327.a.c.g 121
IV.237.b 136, 138
IV.327.c 138
IV.327.d 142
IV.327.h.l 121
IV.327.i 123
IV.327.t-328.b.c 193
IV.329.c-330.e.g.h 122
IV.329.g 125
IV.329.h 135
IV.239.i 138
IV.329.j 141
IV.329.k 137, 214
IV.331.a 271
IV.333.e.f 276
IV.333.f 38
IV.336.e 279, 282
IV.337.a 280
IV.338.g 282
IV.338.m 177
IV.343.a 115
IV.344.c-e 120
IV.346.a-f 194
IV.347.f.g 181
IV.347.g 144, 194

IV.348.a 227, 232, 247
IV.351.c-356.b 227
IV.353.c 171
IV.353.d 162, 231
IV.354.b 232
IV.355.a 22
IV.366.j 171
IV.366.k 258
IV.369.a.b 246
IV.383.d-f 85
IV.385.b 195
IV.385.c.e 243, 245
V.1.a-d 72
V.8.a 68
V.10.g 67
V.12.d 67, 135
V.12.e 209
V.19.a.b 68
V.19.a-d 70
V.22.c.d 68
V.26.a 93
V.26.a.h.i 62
V.26.b 195
V.28.d.e 76
V.29.a 144, 159
V.29.d.f.g 76
V.30.a-e 74
V.31.e 101
V.33.b.c 101
V.33.d.e 72
V.34.a.b 72
V.35.a.k.l.p.q 72
V.38.a 101
V.39.a.b 279
V.41.a.d 100
V.41.d 148, 281
V.41.i 208, 248, 250
V.41.i;42.d.e 184
V.42.f 100
V.44.c 100
V.44.h 100
V.45.a 82
V.49.a 246
V.49.a-c 177
V.49.c 158
V.49.e-50.a 191
V.50.c 23, 241
V.51.a 160
V.51.e 158
V.51.g 19, 174
V.52.b 181
V.54.a 180, 246
V.54.b,55.b 202
V.54.c 241
V.54.c,55.a.b 181
V.57.a.d;58.b 180
V.57.d 166
V.60.a 246
V.62.a 154
V.66.a 246
V.66.f.g 243
V.68.b 30
V.68.e 30
V.79.a 84
V.80.b 30
V.103.e 30
V.103.e-104.a 113
V.105.b.e.h 31

V. 105.b.h 113
V.115.a-d 31
V.115.d.e.f 31
V.121.c.d 30
V.125.a sq. 31
V.151.e.f 113
V.151.f 31
V.154.c 31
V.154.e sq. 31
V.158.e 31, 113
V.159.a-d 113
V.159.e 266
V.166.a.b 165
V.174.d 241
V.175.a.b 20, 186
V.175.g.h 187
V.181.a 121
V.181.b 121
V.182.f 154
V.188.g 241
V.209.n 61
V.211.c 84
V.211.d 256
V.223.g 12, 64
V.224.b 253
V.224.d 253
V.224.e 248
V.224.f 166
V.227.g.h 220
V.234.a-c 179
V.236.e.g;237.a;238.e 179
V.238.f 266
V.244.d-245.c 294
V.245.b 142
V.245.c 126
V.251.a 77
V.252.a-253.a 231
V.254.b.c 231
V.256.b 231
V.257.g 166
V.261.a 186
V.262.d 266
V.263.a 46
V.263.a-c;264.a 187
V.263.c.g 181
V.263.d 199
V.263.d.g 198
V.269.a 195
V.269.a-g 196
V.271.c 181
V.277.a 195
V.280.b 251
V.281.b 251
V.281.c 195
V.283.b 100, 257
V.286.a 100, 257
V.286.c 102, 110, 257
V.286.e 136
V.287.a 257
V.287.a-289.b 100
V.287.b 248
V.287.c 147
V.288.a 102
V.289.b 256
V.290.a 46, 188
V.290.d 188
V.291.i.k 188
V.291.k.n 46

V.292.a	195	V.334.a-c	200
V.292.f.g	272	V.334.j-m	71
V.293.a	195	V.338.a	93
V.297.b	180	V.339.a	30
V.299.b	181	V.343.a.b	198
V.299.d	174	V.346.a	68
V.303.a	257	V.349.f;350.a	111
V.311.e.f	174	V.350.a	253
V.311.f.g;312.a.b.h	181	V.355 X	101, 195
V.312.h	244	V.363.e.f	217
V.315.i	255	V.364.b	64
V.318.a	209	V.368.c.d	64
V.319.a	15, 135	V.368.e.f	247
V.319.n.b	181	V.371.f.g	88
V.321.a.b	225	V.375.a.b	199, 255
V.327.a.b	103	V.375.c	254
V.327.h	61	V.379.a.b	206
V.327.h-m	62	V.380.b	53
V.328.b;329.e	217	V.389.i-k	162
V.328.e	64	V.390.f	207
V.328.f	62	V.396.a-c	156
V.328.h	60	V.396.b	216
V.329.a	215	V.396.d	216
V.330.f.i	71	VI.1.a	251
V.331.d.f-j,jj	187	VI.1.f	251
V.331.g.h.i	202	VI.1.j	203
V.331.g-i	23, 249	VI.2.e	251, 279
V.332.a	23, 240, 249	VI.3.a	228
V.332.b	195	VI.3.e.g	228
V.332.c	192	VI.3.e.g;4.a	84
V.332.f.g	259	VI.3.h-4.c	228
V.332.h	175	VI.4.g sq.	228
V.333.g.h	93	VI.6.f	228
V.333.i	252	VI.7.b.c	230

VI.7.g 229
VI.8.b.c 151
VI.8.c 216
VI.8.d.e 146
VI.8.e 216
VI.9.d 229
VI.10.c 229
VI.10.f 229
VI.13.h-j;14.d-g 77
VI.15.b-d 234
VI.17.c-e 232
VI.17.e 84
VI.17.f 228, 230
VI.17.g 229
VI.17.h 230
VI.18.g 229
VI.19.a 229
VI.19.c 229
VI.20.e.h 231, 252
VI.20.q 231
VI.20.a-d 254
VI.21.i-m 168, 229
VI.21.l 230
VI.21.m 254
VI.21.p 148
VI.22.c 185
VI.22.o 231
VI.23.a 232
VI.23.g-j 233
VI.23.h-o 234
VI.23.i 228
VI.24.m 229
VI.27.a 232
VI.27.b 233
VI.29.b 229
VI.30.b 229
VI.31.g 229
VI.32.c 229
VI.32.e.f 158
VI.32.g.h 146
VI.33.c.d 86
VI.34.a 230
VI.35.a 254
VI.36.g-i 206
VI.37.h 228
VI.37.l.m 232
VI.37.n 84
VI.38.t 229
VI.39.f 229
VI.40.a 229
VI.40.d.e 185
VI.40.h 143
VI.40.h.j.l.n 144
VI.40.p;41.c 185
VI.43.m-44.a 230
VI.43.n 84
VI.44.n.o 230
VI.45.g.h 206
VI.46.g 185
VI.47.b 147
VI.47.c 148
VI.63.a 84
VI.67.g 201
VI.67.g-i 119
VI.67.h 130
VI.67.i.j 121
VI.67.i.k 176
VI.69.a.b 176

VI.69.e-70.b 176, 211
VI.70.a 130
VI.70.b 128
VI.71.a.b.f 176
VI.71.f 211
VI.72.e 211
VI.72.e.f.g 256
VI.72.h.i 64
VI.73.a 128
VI.73.d-h 256
VI.73.e.f 230
VI.73.g 170
VI.74.c 64
VI.74.k 185
VI.74.m.n 142
VI.74.o 218
VI.74.p 205
VI.75.l-n 230
VI.76.d.e 137
VI.76.i.j 256
VI.76.j.k 250
VI.77.a 205
VI.77.a.b 256
VI.77.a-e 289
VI.80.f.g 128
VI.81.b 211
VI.82.a 128
VI.84.e 186
VI.84.g 201
VI.86.c.d 91
VI.86.e-f 52
VI.86.g.h 220
VI.86.i 55
VI.86.j 221
VI.88.g 252
VI.89.a 52
VI.89.a.b 52, 252
VI.89.c.d 253
VI.89.m.n 176, 186
VI.90.i 52
VI.90.j.k 52
VI.91.e 52
VI.91.g.h 221
VI.91.g-j 253
VI.91.j 221
VI.91.m.n 55
VI.92.p-93.a 250
VI.93.a.e 200
VI.93.d.e 154
VI.95.h 96
VI.95.l 119
VI.96.a 255
VI.98.d-99.b 207
VI.100.c.e 52
VI.101.b.c 28
VI.104.b 118
VI.104.j 118
VI.107.e.f 205
VI.107.k;108.b 119
VI.108.g 59
VI.108.k.l 71
VI.119.k-m 221
VI.126.a-h 65
VI.126.j.k 215
VI.132.b.d-g.j.l.m 167
VI.132.d 147
VI.132.d-g 211
VI.132.e 153

VI.132.i 130
VI.132.i.j 177
VI.132.n 248
VI.134.i 47, 51
VI.135.b.d 163
VI.136.k 8
VI.136.s 48, 51
VI.144.a.b 187
VI.144.a.h 161
VI.144.h 86
VI.144.h-145.a.d 153
VI.145.a 161, 187, 206
VI.145.c 86, 161
VI.145.e 187
VI.145.e-146.b 150
VI.145.e-146.d 87
VI.146.e 161
VI.147.b-e 233
VI.149.a 192
VI.149.a-d 26
VI.149.b.c 192
VI.149.e.f 26, 258
VI.149.f 192
VI.149.g;150,a 192
VI.150.b 192
VI.150.h.i 109
VI.150.k 208
VI.152.a 167, 177, 215
VI.152.f 92
VI.152.j 92
VI.152.j-153.f 241
VI.158.e.f 191
VI.161.e 70
VI.161.e.f 57
VI.162.r-u 76
VI.163.h 48
VI.163.i 265
VI.163.j 266
VI.164.b.c 266
VI.164.d.e 243
VI.164.i 265
VI.164.j.k 260
VI.165.b 130
VI.165.e.f 287
VI.165.g 189
VI.165.g.h 79
VI.168.a-e;169.a-i 221
VI.170.a.b 173
VI.170.g.h 104
VI.171.a 104
VI.173.k-n 104
VI.173.m 51
VI.174.h 175
VI.174.h;175.a.b 182
VI.175.c 175
VI.175.f 175
VI.175.g-j 295
VI.175.h 296
VI.175.k.f 182
VI.176.f 175
VI.176.g 175
VI.176.h-j 40
VI.178.j 144
VI.179.g 203, 213
VI.179.h 216
VI.179.i 146
VI.179.l.m 144
VI.181.h.l 201

VI.182.b	183	VI.232.a.e.i.	165
VI.183.f.g	77	VI.233.m	246
VI.184.e.f	77	VI.234.a	61
VI.189.e	75	VI.234.b-e	71
VI.189.e.f	8	VI.237.s-u	257
VI.191.c.e.g.j.l	61	VI.238.o	246
VI.192.a-193.b.e.j.k.m	221	VI.240.k;241.c	207
VI.193.f	87	VI.242.a.b.d.h	164
VI.193.j.m	220	VI.242.d	201
VI.195.a-c,e.f.m.n	78	VI.248.a-d	165
VI.195.i	200	VI.249.q sq.	25
VI.196.n.o.w	75	VI.252.c-e.g.h	73
VI.197.a.e.p.s	75	VI.253.g.h	73
VI.198.d.j.n.o.p	75	VI.255.a-d	73
VI.201.d-f	200	VI.255.k.l	73
VI.203.a	200	VI.259.k.o.p.q	258
VI.205.h	100, 194	VI.261.a	100, 166
VI.205.i.j.k	208	VI.261.e	84
VI.206.d.e.f	146	VI.264.e-j	121
VI.206.l	248	VI.264.p.q	150
VI.206.l.p	184	VI.265.i.n	120
VI.207.c.n	248	VI.266.b-h.k	223
VI.207.c;208.a	184	VI.269.p	190, 200
VI.208.a	248	VI.270.r.s	163
VI.209.d-i	260	VI.270.o.w.x	218
VI.213.k	171	VI.271, Plan of G 1 T	138, 165
VI.217.e.f	288	VI.272.d.f.i.j	138
VI.221.m	244	VI.272.f-p	29
VI.223.i	105	VI.272.f;i-p	258
VI.223.i.j	63	VI.274.e	110
VI.224.u.f.t	141	VI.274.f	138
VI.227.a	260	VI.274.i	141
VI.231.c.d.e.s	165	VI.275.h-j.m.v	96
VI.231.d-k	95	VI.276.a.b	96

VI.276.a.b.h 219
VI.276.l.p 219, 246
VI.277.q-s 224
VI.278.a 224
VI.278.g.o.p.r 182
VI.287.g.i.k.l 77
VI.287.o.p;288.a 194
VI.288.h 77
VI.288.o 249
VI.289.a 72
VI.289.j-l 219
VI.293.n 53
VI.293.o-q 208
VI.293.r.s 87
VI.294.l 174, 203
VI.297.c-e 210
VI.300.i.j 191, 252
VI.302.b-303.r 76
VI.303.o.p 70
VI.304.h.j.m.o 46
VI.305.e 206
VI.315.a-c 101
VI.316.e 231
VI.316.r;317.a 50
VI.317.b.c. 208
VI.318.a-o 196
VI.319.q 156
VI.326.l.m 219
VI.327.d-i 205
VI.332.a-d 62
VI.333.a-j.i 107
VI.335.m 154
VI.342.r.s 138
VI.344.k.p 246
VI.344.n-p.j 176
VI.345.n 175
VI.346.a-g 101
VI.347.a.d.l.m 250
VI.350.f.g.h.q.r 163
VI.353.o.p 114
VI.354.a 114
VI.368.f;369.r 275
VI.370.l 275
VI.377.a 164
VI.377.g 164
VI.378.m 164
VI.379.k-t 200
VI.380.a-e 200
VI.380.e-f 55
VI.380.m 59
VI.381.a-c.y 121
VI.381.p 121
VI.383.h 102
VI.384.h 58
VI.384.k 58
VI.384.o 58
VI.384.p 56
VI.384.q 58, 59
VI.385.d 58
VI.385.e 59
VI.385.f 57
VI.386, drawing B 1 C, beginning of head 164
VI.386.a 58
VI.386.b 57
VI.386.e 58, 59
VI.386.f 149
VI.386.h.j 191

VI.387.b	164	VII.284.a	26
VI.387.c	164	VII.285.c	257
VI.387.e	164	VII.287.a	322
VI.387.j.k	164	VII.287.a.b	115
VI.388.h	164	VII.287.d	280
VI.388.j	164	VII.304.c	28
VI.388.p	164	VII.304.e	101
VI.389.a-d	164	VII.305.b	257
VI.390.k.l	164	VII.307.a	258
VI.391.a	60	VII.308.a.b	4
VI.391.b	60	VII.309.b	201
VI.391.d.e	219, 222	VII.312.b-313.b	129
VI.392.g-n	98	VII.313.a	201
VI.393.b.f.g	163	VII.318.c.d	23, 28
VI.393.g-394.m.n	81	VII.318.c-319.a	185
VI.394.c	57	VII.320.a	197
VI.394.m	57	VII.320.c.d	254
VI.394.o	57	VII.331.d;332.a	101
VI.396.n	58	VII.331.e	214
VI.396.q.r	79	VII.335.d	135
VI.397.h	255	VII.347.b.c	204
VI.399.d.f.g	187	VII.351.b-d	204
VI.400.b	270	VII.352.a-353.a	89
VI.403.i.j	252	VII.354.a.b	204
VI.403.j	246	VII.356.d.e	27
VI.406.o	66	VII.356.e	28, 116
VI.409.f	54	VII.358.d-359.d	27
VI.410.a-c	73	VII.362.a-363.a	26
VI.411.g-n	163	VII.365.g-366.a	27
VI.413.j.k	222	VII.370.k	109
VI.414.j-l	55	VII.371.a-c	140
VI.415.h-q	188	VII.376.b-377.a	125
VI.415.m	190	VII.386.a;389.a-390.a	119
VII.184.q.r	290	VII.389.c	162

VII.390.a 172
VII.396.b.c;397.b-f;398.a.b;
400.a;403.b;408.a-c;409.b.c;
413.d.e 28
VII.397.f-398.c 241
VII.412.a 137
VII.414.c 208
VII.416.a sq. 29
VII.423.c;424.a;425.a-c 256
VII.433.d-435.a;435.e 89
VII.434.b-435.a 185
VII.436.d 29
VII.436.h-440.b 140
VII.436.i-437.a 29, 159
VII.437.b 257
VII.439.a-d 140
VII.440.e;441.a;442.a;443.c 89
VII.447.b-d 89, 279
VII.448.d-449.a 259
VII.449.c 54
VII.455.d-456.b 29, 122
VII.457.n 122
VII.458.m-459.a 140
VII.464.g-465.a 239
VII.473.f.g 26
VII.473.j-474.b 162
VII.474.a-c 258
VII.474.i 28
VII.474.i-k 115
VII.474.j 115, 131
VII.475.a 29
VII.476.h 129
VII.479.c 140
VII.480.j 29
VII.481.g-j 29
VII.484.e 140
VII.484.k 101
VII.485.a-c 101
VII.489.c.d 140
VII.492.a 24, 246
VII.496.a-l 189
VII.498.g 257
VII.499.c 198
VII.499.d 257
VII.502.b 257
VII.502.g 152
VII.503.c.d 140
VII.504.a 29, 140
VII.505.a-d 4
VII.506.c.d 26
VII.506.c-f 53
VII.507.b-g 26
VII.507.e-g 28
VII.508.e.f 4
VII.508.e-g 139
VII.509.c 257
VII.509.d 29
VII.509.d-h 27
VII.510.b 29
VII.510.b-d 246
VII.511.g.h 208
VII.511.i 189, 200
VII.512.c 257
VII.512.g 197
VII.513.a 258
VII.513.c 196
VII.513.d-g 170
VII.514.c-f 27

VII.514.j-515.a 185
VII.515.e 214
VII.517.a 258
VII.517.j 258
VII.518.d 258
VII.518.g.h 204
VII.519.c-g 165
VII.520.a 204
Coffin Texts. Spells
37 296
38 85, 261, 268
39 85, 269
40 262
62 231
84-87 99
88 99
96 58
107 193
131-146 14, 66
158 168
162 72
165 72
173-218 74
173 74
174 74
181 75
202 77
205 276
226 60
228 27, 115, 298
237 271
241 271
242 103, 106, 124
246 156
267 188
273 271
277 196
312 27, 122, 296
316 296
336 121, 123
337 276
341 120
343 22
353 72
355 72
356 72
359 72
361 72
362 72
365 62
373 72
395-398 30
397 113
398 113
402 186
411 20
414 294
423 187
425 196
438 188
455 12
458 187
472 251
473 228, 230
473-481 228, 229, 231, 233
474 168
477 230
480 230

481	230	700	107
491	211	716	175
492	256	717	101
493	256	719	231
495	256	741	275
499	183	747	164
502	252	748	164
506	253	750	200
548	161, 187	752	121
551	192	754	102
553	177	971	290
572	175, 295, 296	1036	26, 257
576	61	1037	115, 322
577	221	1038	280
580	78	1051	28
586	184	1052	101
587	260	1053	257
610	141	1055	4, 258
615	111	1057	201
619	95, 165	1059	129, 201
624	207	1061	23, 28, 185
625	164	1062	197, 254
630-635	72	1069	101, 214
633	73	1071	135
640	166	1076	204
645	120	1079	204
649	165	1080	89
650	29	1081	204
653	110, 141	1085	27, 28, 116
655	96	1086	26
661	77	1087	27
682	99	1090	109
688	195	1094	125
698	62	1099	27, 28, 119, 137,

162, 172, 208, 241
1102 256
1106 89
1107 29
1108 29, 159, 257
1108-1110 140
1110 140
1112, 1113 89
1115, 1116 89, 297
1117 54, 259
1125 29, 122
1127 122
1129 140
1130 239
1131 26, 162, 258
1132 28, 29, 115, 131
1134 129
1135 29, 140
1136 29
1138 140
1139 101
1142 140
1144 24, 246
1146 189
1148 257
1149 198, 257
1153 257
1154 152
1156 140
1157 29, 140
1159 4
1162 26, 53
1164 26, 28
1166 4, 139
1167 29, 257
1168 246
1169 189, 200, 208, 257
1170 197
1171 196, 258
1172 170
1174 27
1175 185
1176 214
1179 258
1181 204, 258
1182 165
1183 204

Cramer, M-, Die Totenklage bei den Kopten, Leipzig, 1941.
p.72 317, 320, 328, 333, 334
p.73 334

Crum, W.E.-,Coptic Dictionary
529.a 308
611.b 333

Dendera
4495, temple of Osiris 156

Ebers (Papyrus)
I.13-16 199
XIX.7 sq. 224

Edfou
VII.124 142

Eloquent Peasant
66 288
B 1, 241 44
Sethe, Lesestücke 20.12 94

Erichsen, W.-,Demotisches Glossar
31 297
60 301

69 297
432 299
542 299
545 299
566 299
613 297
619 302
Erman, A.-, Denksteine aus der Thebanischen Gräberstadt.
1098, Turin, Stele nr. 102 197
IV Esra
4:36 319
Faulkner, R.O.-, The man who was tired of life (Geschichte des Lebensmüden)
41-51 107
52-55 107
55-57 107
58-59 87
61-63 108
63 83
67 47
130-131 46
142-144 41
151-154 107
153 82
Gardiner, A.H.- and K. Sethe, Egyptian letters to the dead
p.11 197
Pl.I.A.8 86
I.A.9-11 198
I.A.10 265
II.A.4 242
II.A.9 265
III.A.4 264
III.A.5 242
IV.A.3-4 198
IV.A.4-6 264
IV.A.5 199
VI.A.2-4 198
VII.1-3 (Leiden 371) 197
VIII.38 (Leiden 371) 264
X.n.2,4-6 197
Gardiner, A.H.-, P.S.B.A.
XXXV.165-170 92
Gospel of Truth
31.21 340
Jumilhac (Papyrus-)
(J.Vandier, Le Papyrus Jumilhac, Paris, 1961)
III.18 131
V.10 278
VIII.19-20 168
X.16 212
XI 225
XIV.23 sqq. 230
XV.20 233
XV.24 106
XV.25 139, 178
XVIII.13 284
XX.6 148
XX.10 223
XXII.9-11 154
Junker, H.-, Gîza
II.58 163
Kees, H.-, Ein Klagelied über das Jenseits
P.76 86, 90, 94, 97

p.78 61

Kittel,G.-, <u>Theologisches Wörterbuch zum Neuen Testament</u>

I.4.9 sqq. 328

I.4.18 328

I.80.10 331

I.83.25 331

I.146.33 sqq. 312

I.147.14-19 314

I.148.1-3 313

I.148.23 sqq. 312

I.I.148.28 sqq. 317

I.560.39 sqq. 327

I.561.27 327

I.655, 656 320

II.14.45 331

II.70 sqq. 328

II.284.2-4 335

II.813.14 333

II.814.27 333

III.815-817 326

V.40 sqq. 335

V.568, note 15 335

V.577.15 sqq. 335

Kropp, P.A.-,<u>Ausgewählte koptische Zaubertexte</u>, 3 vols., 1930/31.

Par. 159.92 308

Lacau, P.-, <u>Fragments d'Apocryphes Coptes</u>

43 line 17 333

47 324

85 315, 337

Lacau, P.-, <u>Textes Religieux</u>

XXIII.A.74 57

Lansing, (Papyrus -)

IX.8 14

Lefort, L.Th.-, <u>S. Pachomii Vitae Bohairice Scripta</u>

91, 92 339

92 327

97 340

99 331

100 311, 314, 315, 317, 324, 326, 336

101 321

146 322, 335

Lefort, L.Th.-, <u>S. Pachomii Vitae Sahidice Scripta</u>

17 332

Leiden

SA.3 71

V.38 54

I.344, Verso, III.3 240

Lichtheim, M.-, The songs of the harpers, J.N.E.S.IV

Pl.I.1-2 45

Pl.III.11-12 51

p.192, 193 47, 49, 55

p.196 56

p.197 92

p.198, Pl.II.9 105

p.203 47, 51, 56

p.206 104

<u>Le Livre des Qererts</u> (ed. A. Piankoff, B.I.F.A.O.XLI-XLIII)

I 193

I, 2nd register 196

III.5 102, 109

III.6 167
III.7.8 109
IV.2 102
IV.4 193
V.3-4 196
VI.4 212
VIII.5 129
VIII.7-8 296
VIII.8-IX.1 170
IX.1 16
IX.1 sqq. 147
IX.4 18
IX.4-6 189
IX.6 131
XI.1-2 129
XI.5 109
XI.6 136
XI.8 23, 233
XXII.3 18, 188
XXII.4 278
XXII.8-9 18, 188
XXIV.6-7 278
XXIV.8 150
XXIV.8-9 240
XXIV.9 78
XXV.1 16, 152, 155
XXV.1-2 18, 49
XXV.2 205, 279
XXV.3-4 291
XXV.4-5 250
XXVI.1 285
XXVI.7 245
XXXIII.3 179
XXXIII.9 245
XXXIII.9-XXXIV.1 182
XXXIV.3 78, 223
XXXIV.3-4 183
XXXIV.4 20
XXXIV.4-5 178
XXXIV.5 67
XXXIV.6 129, 245
XXXV.9-XXXVI.1 282
XXXVI.3 157
XXXVI.7 78
XXXVI.8-9 243
XXXVII.2-3 178
XXXVII.4 20, 182
XXXVII.8 41
XXXVII.8-9 284
XXXIX.1 98
XL.3 34, 267
XLI.7 41, 284
XLIV.4-5 287
XLVII.5 235
XLVIII.5 111
XLVIII.5-7 235
XLVIII.6-7 126
XLVIII.7 194
XLIX.7 152
L.1 234
L.2 223
L.3 247
LI 144, 145
LXV.9 22
LXV.9-LXVI.6 226
LXVI.7 145
LXVII.7 sqq. 145
LXXV.1-4 146

LXXXVII.1 158
XCIV.5 202
XCVII.5-6 225
XCVII.7-8 146
XCVII.8-XCVIII.1 144
XCVIII.2 22
XCVIII.2-3 226
XCVIII.3 126
XCVIII.4 148
XCVIII.5 184
XCVIII.6 146
XCVIII.8 20, 181
XCIX.1 137
XCIX.5 144
XCIX.7 78
CI.5-6 139
CI.6 15, 90, 141
CI.8 253
CV.5 208
CVIII.9 59
CXIV.6 97
CXVII.3-4 177
CXVII.6 144
CXVII.9 168
CXVIII.2 16, 154, 157
CXVIII.3 152
CXVIII.3-4 157
CXVIII.5 283
CXVIII.8 134
CXIX.7 144
CXX.1 285
CXX.2 170
CXX.4-6 267
CXX.5 171
CXX.5-6 34
CXXVIII.3 157
CXXVIII.4 295
CXXVIII.4-5 283
CXXIX.1-2 283
CXXXII.4 151
CXXXII.6 157
CXXXIII.7 131
CXXXIII.7-8 285
CXXXIII.9 250
CXXXIII.9-CXXXIV.1 285
CXXXIV.5-9 293
CXXXIV.9-CXXXV.1 179
CXXXV.2-4 244
CXXXV.7 78
CXXXVI.4-5 250
Louvre
SN.173, VIII.5 284
VIII.6 125
VIII.14-15 249
VIII.17 244, 285
1039 177
3148, III.10-11 116
V.1 175
V.2 260
IX.24 273
IX.b.3 80, 206
3177.b 159
3283, II.3-7 135
V.1 230
V.3 230
V.4-5 230
VI.1 57, 63
VI.3 63

VI.6 57
VI.7 262
VI.13 102
VII.3-5 156
VII.4 154, 270
VII.5 68
3292, D.2-4 281
H.4 294
L.6-7 115
L.7-8 243
N.1-4 117
N.9 109
P.1-7 116
P.7 115
S.15 173
T.15 194
I.3297 136
3865, III.4 208
III.11 123
IV.2-3 99
IV.2-4 47

Lüddeckens, E.-, <u>Totenklagen</u>
pages
21 105
28 92
29 55
66 219
97 55
102 55
104 86, 203
109 53
109, 110 53
110 94
112 45, 67, 79
114 54, 87
116 83
121 54
124 61
130 91
134 68
135 91
144 61
146 66
156 54
171 54

Möller, G.-, Rhind, <u>Totenpapyrus</u>
pages
14 302
26 298
30 298
50 299

Montet, P.-, <u>Les scènes de la vie privée</u>
pages
18-20 231
34 229
152 23
153 149
167 151, 155
169 151
173 151

Müller, W. Max-, <u>Liebespoesie</u>
I.1-2 82
I.2 49, 51
I.6-9 53
I.9 94
I.16 51
I.23 56

XII.4 49
XII.8 55
XII.9 47
XIV.2 47, 55
Naville, E.-, Mythe d'Horus
XVIII.2 156
Naville, E.-, Papyrus Funéraires de la XXI. Dynastie
pp. 37,38,Pl.XXVII,XXVIII 227
Piankoff, A.-, Clère, J.J.-, A letter to the dead on a bowl in the Louvre, J.E.A.XX.pp.157-169 219
Piankoff, A.-, Le Livre du Jour et de la Nuit
Livre du Jour
I 141
1st. register, p. 7 153
2nd. register, p. 10 156
3rd. register, p. 15 135
4th. register, p. 27 142
Livre de la Nuit
2nd. gate 123, 142
3rd. gate 123, 237
4th. gate 110
6th. gate, 5th. register 143
8th. gate 85
9th. gate 110
11th. gate 37
p.35 139
p.35, 1st. gate 123
p.36, 1st. gate 109
p.38, 1st. gate, 5th. register 139, 237
p.39 255
p.42 93
p.46, 3rd. gate, lower register 235
p.51, 5th. gate, 5. and 6. reg. 237
p.61 139
p.61, 9th. gate 237
p.66, 8th. gate 93, 237
p.66 139
p.74, 10th. gate 124
Ptahhotep (Wisdom of -)
Prisse V.1 288
VI.4-5 42
XI.11-12 42
XIV.2 261
Pyramid Texts
16.b 222
75.a 65
134 97
134.a 55
136.a 171
145.b 8, 210, 249, 278, 281
149 51
149.d 50
153.c 14
161.b 99
163.d 217
166.c 94, 237
167.b-d 269
207.b.d 79
208.a 215
211.a 79
229.a-c 99
230.c 226
245.b 145
251.b.c 198

260.b	84, 85	401.a	233
265.c	44	402.a	213
269.b	206	403.a	215
273	41	403.b	145, 146
273.b	266	403.c	144
275.b-f	113	405.a.b	144
278.a	160	405.b	146
285.a	58	407.c	160
285.c	12, 79	410.c	144
286.b	151	413.c	183
286.b.c	257	414.b	201
290.c sqq.	71	417.b	79
298.b	201	425	101
308.b sqq.	85	429.a-c	100
308.b.c	96	430.a	102
309.c	189	444.e	160
309.d	275	445	214
311.a	99	456.b	222
311.d	252	462.b	290
322.a	79, 241	468, 469	25
323.a	8, 75	485.c	169, 266
323.a-d	89	492.a	243
323.d	136, 281	498.b	26, 252
334.a	171, 209, 255	502.a.b	134
334.a.b	257	516.c	210
338.a	180	520.a	114
340.d	30	526	113
349	12	545.a	214
349, 350	80	545.b	215
349.a-350.c	81	551 sqq.	69
349.b-350.a	214	553	69
350.b	46	555.b	69
382.a.b	69	572.c	65
386.a	262	575.b	215, 222

579.b 222
590.b 278
593.b 108
604.e.f 8, 46
617.a 70
635.c 222
637.a 70
638.c 253
639.a.b 65
643.c 282
651.b 222
654 12
654.a-d 105
654.b 65
655.b 118
656.d 97
656.e 203
658.d 91
662.d 159
672.b.c 132
675.b 225
679.b 258
716 102
721.d 11, 85
722 11
722.a-d 58
722.b 59
725.a 70
735.a 82
744.b 203
747 97
748.c 205
748.d 180
749.c-e 113
762.a 157
764.b 14, 50
771.a 257
771.c 162
792.c 5, 46
796.b 91
828.a 65
828.c 174
835.a 65
843.b 253
851.b 207
854.a 209
871.c 10
872.d 172
873 97
885.a 172
894.b 82
903.a 72
908.a.b 180
944.a 152, 241
962.a 245
962.a.b 157
962.a-963.b 216
963.a.b 157
966.e 149
978.a 252
1005.c 207
1013.b 203
1014 10, 96
1021.c 232
1027.a.b 252
1027.c 34, 272
1030.b 241
1041 32

1041 sqq. 24
1041.a-d 259, 271
1041.a-1043.b 251
1041.d 42, 290
1121.c 215
1134 213
1151.a 211
1157.a-c 114
1162.c 30
1168.c 40, 272
1193.b 52
1201.a 114
1207 213
1236.a.b 199
1236.b 79
1236.c 215
1236.d 202
1237.a 202
1237.a.b 23
1240.a.b 284
1252.a 114
1258 213
1264.c 214
1265.c 205
1274.a 205
1278.a.b 272
1279.a-c 272
1283.a.b 11, 56
1283.b 105
1285.c 282
1285.c-1286.c 155
1286.a 157
1286.b 149
1286.c 152
1287.a 272, 278
1299.c 14, 48
1308.a 214
1329.a 169
1336.a.b 222
1337.b 285
1337.b-d 153
1337.d 16
1351.a 194
1351.a-c 258
1351.b 195
1363 81
1363.a-c 105
1376.c 167
1382.a 167
1441.a 167
1454 51
1459.b 13
1459.b.c 86
1464.c 46
1468.a.b 283
1477 46
1484 79
1500.c 85
1501.b 24, 191
1512 sqq. 69
1523.c 278
1525 94
1531.a.b 161
1535.b 205
1541.a 167
1547.b 214
1552.a 215
1557.d 214

1570.b 222
1574.c 167
1607.a-1608.a 222
1610.a.b 191
1632.a 223
1639.c 207
1641 97
1641.a-c 103
1658.b 222
1713.a 95, 117
1726.c 205
1734.b 213
1737.a 167
1747, 1748 13
1749.b 118
1752.c 172
1753 70
1760 50
1760.a 167
1760.b-1761.a 266
1761.b 268
1764 117
1770 215
1772.c 195
1776.a 38, 275
1780.b 60
1786.b 174
1800, 1801 11
1800-1801.c 57
1801.b sqq. 64
1812.c 14, 51
1837.c 240
1878.a 108
1878.a.b 103
1892.a 174
1908.b 64
1931 172
1939, 1940 179
1947.a 203
1953 97
1955 97
1975.a 54
1975.a.b 84
1979.c 222
1986.b 96
1999.b-d 198
1999.c 216, 245
1999.d 274
2008.a.b 104
2009.a 104
2022.a-2023.b 97
2023.a 8
2040.a.b 99
2057, 2058.c.d 58
2061.c 30, 167
2092.a 11, 82
2097.c 174
2114.b 81
2169.a 96
2171.b 96
2172.c 167
2175 10
2175.a 55
2175.a-d 93
2184.b 81
2186.a 50
2186.a.b 218
2202 79, 80

2202.c 91
Spell (Spruch) 216 96
222 79
273 143
274 143
Pyramid of Aba 538 238
561 sqq. 207
Pyramid of Neit
2 167
2-3 266
3 268
6 215
479 64
653 11, 58
659 160
660 282
661 82, 203
664 81
665 17, 159, 207, 214
667 245
668 159
717 100, 102
718 93, 191
729 64
730 222, 273
733, 734 235
736 238
737 82
738, 739 174
742 174
743 81
744 189, 205
746 213
748-751 207
750 79, 201
751, 752 84
753 216
757 117
761 162, 245
761, 762 199
762 209, 245
763 60, 209, 255
765 40, 99, 266
766 65
766, 767 118
767 97
771 166, 179
779 8, 117, 213
807 117
818 114
833 70, 81
833, 834 149
834 95
Quibell, J.E.-, Hierakonpolis
I,Pl.XXVI.c 7
Robinson, F.-, Coptic Apocryphal Gospels
38 308, 334
94 341
95 307
96 321, 323, 329, 335
Sachau, Ed.-, Festschrift Ed. Sachau; A. Erman, Zwei Grabsteine griechischer Zeit
104 67, 71, 85
106 67, 88
108 66, 91
109 68

110 47, 87
Salt (Papyrus Salt 825)
IV.7 161
Schmidt, C.-, Die koptisch-gnostischen Schriften. Erster Band (Pistis Sophia)
257 323, 330
258 330
259 330
317 326, 330
319 315, 317
321 315
Schmidt, V.-, Sarkofager
694 110
697 109
698 97
700 97, 203
871 182, 183, 243
Sethe, K.-, Dramatische Texte
216 44
Sethe, K.-, Lesestücke
30.5-6 184
31.2 239
45.9 268
47.19-48.3 199
48.20 224
II Setne
I.20 297
II.2 297, 299
II.2-3 299
II.3 301
II.4 301
II.5 301
II.6 301, 302
II.7 298, 301
II.10 297
II.13 297
II.14 299
II.17 sqq. 299
II.19 sqq. 300
II.21 sqq. 298
Sottas, H.-, La préservation de la propriété funéraire dans l'ancienne Egypte.
36 sqq. 6
49 179
53 48
93 174
96 6, 130
158 51
161 217
Steindorff, G.-, Die Apokalypse des Elias (Leipzig, 1879; Texte u. Untersuch.N.F.,II,3a)
4.3 sqq. 340
4.15 sqq. 330
7.3 316
7.10 321
8.3-14 331
8.13 333, 337
10.8 sqq. 319
Steindorff, G.-, Koptische Grammatik, 1894
48 335
51 318, 326, 336
53 311, 317, 328
54 311, 319, 334, 336, 337

55 313, 316, 337, 341

Turin

154 263, 288

<u>Urkunden des ägyptischen Altertums</u>

I

14.9-10 264

30.13 264

35.3 264

49.3 264

122.12 265

150.9 265

174.6 259

202.9 38

202.9-11 275

204.9 43, 290

226.6 34, 264

256.3-4 265

256.4 34

260.12 sqq. 34

260.12-18 265

260.17 197

261.6-8 265

261.8 34

263.9-12 264

263.12 249

304.17-305.4-6 174

305.17-18 6, 126, 130

II

29.14 289

III

24.4.6 14

51.8 271

IV

6.14 49

7.6 49

10.9 104

65.1-9 124

113-115 66

113.5-114.1 118

114 66

114.2 178

114.10-115.5 60

115.17-116.12 118

146.17-147.3 51

148.12 sqq. 91

269.16 279

401.16-402.2 106

414.2 105

430.9-15 119

439.12 54

445.9-10 66

446.6-8 183

446.8 105

484.8 44

492.5-8 281

497.11-13 96

518.14 179

520.2-11 119

529.13-14 287

613.15-614.1 133

614.1 157

938.3-6 128

965 54

968.15 291

1014.16-17 124

1024.9 290

1031.9 94

1063.13-1064.3 120

1084.15 31
1085.10 96
1095.6 288
1109.7-8 291
1183.15 103
1193.14-1194.1 128
1200.4-8 103
1208.12 288
1218.1, 9-11 178
1219.15 96

V

16.12 280
57 143
78.15 21
87.13 170

VII

14 54

Vycichl, W.-, _Der Feuerstrom im Jenseits_

263, 264 308

Westcar (Papyrus-)

VIII.17 239

Wörterbuch

I

48.6 286
48.17-19 261
76.1 59
90.20 85
125.13 235
129.9 286
129.10 286
129.13 286
176.15 201
184.9 158
268.4 158
268.16 158
292.11 36
314.7 287
337.3 82
338.7 82
369.11 288
404.8 80
431.2 82
443.1 42
443.9 42
444.1-3 288
508.5 244
583.7 149

II

30.10 79
50.3 145
73.8 225
84.2 200
85.26. 42
130.9 269
132.14 228
213.7 9
234.12 137
234.16 137
266.8 83
266.9 83
291.9 99
338.15 244
343.10 247
358.3 212
359.13 212
369.9 288
456.18 295

III

36.4-6 168
159.6 248
168.4 149
195.3 36
221.21 171
242.9 161
245.5 289
245.5-9 43
245.8 289
252.7 170
254.3 289
282.2 271
321.8 240
343.8 227
354.1 136
361.13 290
363.11, 12 205
416.19 128
435.9 290

IV

33.12 260
40.5 44
54.4 261
60.9 257
60.13 257
128.11 261
176.9 88
355.4 294
379.14 259
391.20 84
391.21 84
401.7 195
463.8 54
529.11 244
561.7 155

V

44.6 190
48.2-3 291
48.8 291
48.11, 12 291
48.14 190
86.13 180
92.18 sqq. 180
116.6 296
251.5-9 64
317.10-12 292
319.10 292
320.12 43
320.14 43
328.4 156
408.6 263
467.12 160
514.14-17 44
518.3 sqq. 44
522.12 142
534 II 233
539.13 233
546.2 41
546.7 41
546.15 41
547.1 41
555.10 302

Zoega, G.-, _Catalogus codicum copticorum manuscriptorum qui in Museo Borgiano Velitris adservantur_, Romae, 1810.

297.6 340

318.27 sqq. 314
320 325
329.35 sqq. 322
330.4 sqq. 322
331 320
334.21 331
334.21 sqq. 339
339 327
339.25 321

GENERAL INDEX

A

accuse 261
acquit 271
act against 241 sq., 286
actions against the dead 17
affect 251
affliction 110
air 72 sq.
alone (be-) 67
animals 192 sq.
annoyance 250
Apophis 294
approach 125, 249
arrest 132
ascension 25
Asiatic 235
asleep 84
ass 194
assign 278
attack 244

B

baboon 272
bad 41 sq., 288
to go bad 59
bad smell 341
bad spell 293
bail out 244
bandage (mummy -) 108
be (not to -) 48
beatification 35 sq.
become (not to -) 49
beings to be feared 192
belly 63
bend 172
bent (to be -) 42, 64
beware 257
big one (a snake) 98
bind 21, 78, 130, 131, 132
bird 192, 195
bird-trap 230
black one of face 208
blind 64
blindness 60

blood 151, 158
boar 195
body 65
bolt 131
bond 80, 81
bones 64
boomerang 231
Book of Gates 123
Böses 291
branding-iron 225
bread 72
break 249
breath 72
breath (glowing -) 137
breath (red hot -) 136
bring into court 259
bring down 247, 249
build 107
burn 14, 133 sqq., 137, 139, 141, 142

C

calamity 249
call 280
carnage 153
carry off 13
case 44
case (to hear the -) 272
cat 194
catch 230, 231 sqq., 232, 234
cattle halter 80
cauldron 143, 145
cave 173
channel 167
charm 248
chop off 147, 149 sqq., 152, 153, 154, 158
close 64, 84
coal-basin 142
combative of face 206
come 52
come to meet inimically 248
complaint 33, 259 sqq.
condemn 39, 278 sqq.
consume 56, 58, 160
contrast (death - life) 45
cook 142 sqq., 144, 145
cooking-pot 145
coptic 303 sqq.
copulate 61
corpse 20, 63, 182
council 274 sqq., 301
counsel 268 sq.
count 35, 269 sqq., 278 sqq., 282, 338
counter-heaven 237
court 38
courtier 274
cover 281
crime 289 sq., 292
crocodile 192, 194
cry 111, 336 sq.
cut 16, 157
cut off 147, 150, 151
cut off breath 68
cut out 149
cut out heart 246
cut to pieces 148, 149

D

damage 17, 43, 247, 248
danger 19 sqq., 173 sqq., 253
dangerous places 24 sq., 160 sqq.
dangers 112 sqq.
darkness 88 sqq., 324 sqq.
dead one 198 sq.
deaf 60
decapitation 226
decay 10 sq., 56, 58, 59
decomposition 56 sqq., 59
delay 242
deliver up to a punishment 280 sq.
demon 21, 200 sqq., 206 sqq., 217 sqq., 328 sqq.
demoniacal animal 194
demotic 297 sqq.
denude 291
desiccate 67
destroy 45, 188 sq., 190, 235, 302
destruction 14 sqq., 45, 169 sq. 186 sqq.
deterioration of the body 60
device of decapitation 226
devil 224
devour 158 sqq., 160, 337
devourer 32
die 45
die for a second time 186 sqq.
digestion products 73
disaster 42, 253
dispel 271
dissatisfied 291 sq.
disturbance 191
divide 263 sq.
document 242
dog 195
door 114
door-keeper 114 sq.
drink 160
drive away 271
drowned 236 sq.
dry up 57, 67, 68
dualistic conception of death 2 sqq., 5 sqq., 104

E

ear 61
earth 96
earth (god of the -) 91, 95
eastern 161
eat 160
encroachment on the continuance of life 66 sqq.
enemies of Re or of Osiris 223 sq.
enemy 206, 217 sq., 238, 295 sq., 332 sq.
escape 253, 254, 255
eternity 285
evidence (to give - against) 260
evil 44, 253, 285, 292, 293
evil begin to be punished 295
evil-doers 201
evil one 208
evil place 171
excrements 74 sq.
execution 259 sqq.
executioner 32
extended (to be -) 83
extinguish 134

extirpating of sin 271

F

face 63
falcon 194
fall 248
far (be -) 52
fat (be -) 256
fate 51, 300
fear 109, 110
fear of death 3
fell 190
ferry 30
fetter 79, 126, 131, 132
fettering 21
fighter 201
fire 134, 135, 138, 139 sqq., 142, 320 sqq.
fire-water 135
fish 195
fish-trap 168
fisherman 232
flame 134 sqq., 139 sqq., 142
flogging 339 sq.
flow away 59
fluid of the corpse 57
foot 62
foot-iron 78
forget 63
fowler 233
fright 110
funeral 102 sqq., 105 sqq.
fury 191

G

gang 205
gaoler 21
gate 28, 114 sqq., 115, 116, 117, 120 sqq., 299, 316 sqq.
Geb 8
give evidence 259
go away 54, 56
go forth 53
go round 254
go upside down 75 sqq.
god 212
gods 209
grasshopper 194
grave 103, 104
great one 206
grief 336
guard 128, 203
guilt 43, 287, 290

H

hall 268
happen 248
head 65
heaper up of corn 201
heart 20, 174 sqq., 180 sq.
heat 141
hell 320
hew 147
hidden of face 208, 235
high of voice 110, 208
hinder 242
hippopotamus 197
hit 243
horror 109
house 103 sq.
hunger 68 sqq.

hunting 21, 226 sqq.
hurry 69, 247

I

ichneumon-fly 195
impregnate 64
imprisonment 78
injure eyeball 65
insect 195
instruments of torture 224 sqq.
iron 125 sq.

J

journey 25 sqq.
journey (cosmic -) 342
judge 33, 264 sqq., 269
judge of the dead 272 sqq.
judgment 31 sqq., 170, 259 sqq., 263 sqq., 298
justice 292 sq.
justify 37, 271

K

keep at bay 118 sq.
keep off 117, 124
keeper of 200
kettle 146
kid 193
kill 190
knife 150, 156, 157

L

lament 111
land 53, 54, 247
lasso 233
law (to be at - with) 263
leave 53
left 161
let down 259
liberty (deprivation of -) 125 sqq.
lick of flame 137
lie 44, 263
light (to be -) 56
lion 195
live on 159
Livre de la Nuit 123
Livres 4, 34
lock in 132
lock up 127 sq.
lodge a complaint 259 sqq.
loosen 81
lord of offering 273
lord of the netherworld 204
lord of truth 273
loss of functions of life 60

M

maggoty 57
magical power 181 sq.
make stinking 262
man 200
men 197, 199 sq., 238
messenger 202 sq.
mischief 287
misery 42
monistic conception of death 1 sqq.
monster 32
mooring-post 225
motionless 11
mourn 112
mourner 207
mouth 62
mutilate 147

mutilation 147 sqq.

N

name 179 sq.
narrow 71
negroes 237 sqq.
net 227 sqq., 231
netherworld 91, 94, 96 sq., 318
night 91
non-functioning of senses and limbs 12

O

ocean (primeval -) 94
offering 147
open 254
opponents 296
opponents in lawsuit 219 sqq.
opponents of Osiris 221 sqq.
oppose 262
Osiris 8, 27, 32, 34, 36, 40, 210 sqq., 301
others 296
outrage 243

P

painful 245
part of the body 60
pass 45, 257 sq.
pass away 13, 52
path 341
penetrate (of knives) 149
perish 14, 49 sq., 57
physical phenomenon 10 sqq.
pierce 156
pig 195
pit (fiery -) 168
plaintiff 261 sq.
pond 171 sq.
pour out the voice 287
power (to have - over) 249
press hard 241
prison 21, 323 sq.
protecting spell 259
psychostasy 301
punish 282 sqq.
punishing angel 328 sqq.
punishment (bloody -) 299, 303 sqq., 326 sqq.
put off (demons) 257
put oneself in the way inimically 252 sq.

R

rage 191 sq.
Re 32, 34, 37, 39, 40
realm of the dead 95, 307 sqq., 318 sqq.
rebel 205, 206, 259 sq., 290, 296
rebellion 43
rebuke 259
recede 255
red 43
relatives 66
remember (in an evil way) 249
remove 157
reporter 124
reprimand 263
reproach (with guilt) 263
retaliation 38
reversed (world -) 73
reward 35

river 30
river of fire 307 sqq.
riverain 235
road 26, 162 sqq.
roast 145
rob 87
robbery 243, 287
rope 126, 127
ruin 186 sqq.

S

sad 68
savage one of face 208
save 255
save (to be saved from dangers) 253 sqq.
scales 269, 301
Schaden 291
scorched (to be -) 68
scroll 340
sealing 131
second (die for a - time) 20
see 244
seize 23, 184 sqq., 335 sq.
sentence 31 sqq., 278 sqq.
serpent 333 sqq.
set up 261
Seth 214 sq.
Setne 297 sqq.
setter of traps 234
sexual desire 61
shadow 20, 182 sqq.
sharp 152, 245
sheol 7 sqq.
ship (to be without -) 241
shorten 338
shortening of time of life 70
shouting 110, 112
silence 93
sin 41 sqq., 286 sqq., 288, 289, 290, 292, 293
sinners 223 sq., 294 sqq.
slander 262, 291
slaughter 148, 149, 150, 151, 152, 156
slaughterer 201, 204 sq.
slaughtering-block 166 sq.
sleep 81 sqq., 82, 83, 84, 85,
smell 59
smell (bad -) 59
snake 97 sqq., 100, 101, 102, 195
snare 130
snatch away 85, 185
soften 84
soul 19, 176 sqq., 184
sound 63
spirit 19, 174, 197 sq.
stiff 61
stranger 206
strap 81, 132
stretch the nail 251
strike 250
strong one 207
subterranean realm 94
suffer 68, 69, 242, 243
sun in the netherworld 337
sundries 241 sqq.
sweat of the corpse 57
sword 340 sq.

T

taboo 43
take away 85 sqq., 246
take away the head 247
take away parts of the body 154 sqq.
tantalization 300
Tartarus 319
tendon 69
terror 109
testify against 260
texts 3 sqq.
thirst 67
those who are not 234 sq.
Thoth 216 sq.
throw down walls 189 sq.
tie 79, 80, 108, 126
tie up 338
tired (to be -) 82, 83 sq.
tired (to make -) 84
toil 251
tomb 102 sqq.
torment 20 sqq.
torture 18, 20 sqq., 161
torturer 200
torturing-post 225, 226
trample down 248
transgression 43, 294
transitoriness 56
trap-net 230
tremble 110
trespass 292
trident 339
twist 243
tying 21

U

Übeltat 291
unfavourable position 234 sqq.
uraeus 192
urine 74

V

valley 161

W

walk upside down 8 sq.
want of breath 67
want (to be in -) 68
warm breath 71
watchman 204
water 68
well 171
West 92 sq., 302
western 235
who are in Osiris 235
who are not there 199
who are there 199
who do their evil deeds 201
wicked actions 289
wickedness 288
wild of face 109
with tumbled hair 207
wolf 194
worm 100
wound 148, 153
wretched one 234

Z

Zweiwegebuch 4, 29, 122, 129

The most important cases are indicated by underlined page numbers

3.t (rage) 93, 191
3.t (moment) 208
3w ỉb 68
3b 225
3b.t (relatives) 66
3b.t (branding-iron) 225
3pd 192
3m (to burn) 133, 169
3m (to seize) 184
3mw.t 133
3r 241
3ḫ 19, 35, 39, 81, 89, 135, 174, 176, 181, 184, 190, 197, 198, 212, 267, 268, 279, 282, 297
3ḫ.w 18, 22, 99, 128, 189
3ḫ.t 26, 27, 28, 47, 79, 81, 114, 118, 120, 162, 163, 187, 188, 192, 204, 205, 207, 241, 250, 256, 258, 270, 281, 289
3ḫ.t-eye 137, 239
3ḫty 260
3śb 139
3ḳ 45
3ḳy.t 45
3kr 8, 10, 91, 95, 96, 117, 119, 232
3d (rage) 24
3d (crocodile) 192
3d.w 191

ỉ 135
ỉ3.t 93, 184
ỉ3y 200
ỉ3y.t 151
ỉ3b 60, 161
ỉ3b.t 161
ỉ3r.w-fields 30, 31, 39, 61, 73, 74, 112, 113, 119, 121, 123, 256, 274, 300
ỉ3rr 60
ỉ3kb 111
ỉ3ṯ 59, 147, 161
ỉ3d 234
ỉ3d.t 227-229, 232
ỉỉ 13, 52, 54, 102, 165, 198
ỉỉ r 23, 241
ỉ'b-sšw 115
ỉʿn 272
ỉʿr.t 192
ỉʿrty 137, 145
ỉw (to come) 55
ỉw r (to come against) 23
ỉw (shipless) 31, 241
ỉw (to chop off) 147
ỉw (sin) 286, 288, 289
ỉw (misery) 42, 43, 76
ỉw (to complain) 261
ỉw Nśỉśỉ 28, 195, 218
ỉwy.t 73, 286
ỉwmś 193
ỉwn 25
ỉwty.w 73, 199, 234
ỉb (heart) 20, 64, 144, 173-175, 185, 208, 260, 278, 288
ỉb (thirst) 67, 135
ỉb3n 82
ỉbw 193

Ỉbk3 193
ỉbṯ.t 22, 228, 230
ỉbṯ.ty 230
ỉp 278, 279, 338
Ỉpỉỉ 69
ỉf 57
ỉm.t 102
ỉmỉ 230
Ỉmỉw 198
ỉmy Nw 236
ỉmy nwn 318
ỉmy rd 78
Ỉmy ḫnt ỉrty 62
Ỉmy-ḫnt Wr 168, 229
ỉmy ḫt 40, 204, 212, 298, 301, 330
ỉmy.w ʿ.t 211
ỉmy.w Wsỉr 235
ỉmy.t 102
ỉmn.w ḥr.w.śn 235
Ỉmn.t 92, 116, 235, 303, 310, 311, 315
ỉmnḥ 200, 210
Ỉmnt.t 124, 298
ỉmnty.w 235
Ỉmḥ.t 28, 111, 112, 118-120, 141
Ỉmś.tỉ 69
ỉmk 10, 56
Ỉn-ʿ.f 213
ỉn.t 24, 161
ỉnỉ 85, 230
ỉnỉn 147
ỉnp 56
Ỉnp.(w) 123, 272
ỉnn.t 162
Ỉnśw 217
ỉnḳ 79
ỉnk 175
ỉnty.w 126
ỉnṯ 79, 125
ỉnṯ.t 22, 79
ỉnḏ ḥr 249
ỉrỉ 21, 28, 36, 37, 116, 123, 128, 298
ỉrỉ r 23, 241, 286
ỉrỉ ḫ.t r 34
ỉry 200, 290
ỉry ỉb 201
ỉry ʿ 79, 176, 201
ỉry ʿ.wt 204
ỉry ʿ.t 40, 200, 211
ỉry ʿ3 114, 123, 201
ỉry ʿrr.t 28, 211
ỉry ʿrry.t 116
ỉry w3.wt 201
ỉry r3 200
ỉry rd 79, 201
ỉry śỉp.w 279
ỉry śbḫ.t 201
ỉry št3.w 211
ỉry ḳ3b 29, 201
ỉrw 135, 282
Ỉrw 77
ỉh 242
ỉḥ 126
Ỉḥy 74, 256
ỉḫm 234, 235
ỉḫm.w śk 304
ỉḫmty.w 235, 236

ỉḫḫy 88
ỉḫḫ.w 88
ỉs 97, 103
ỉsỉ (to be light) 10, 56
ỉsỉ (to pass away) 52
ỉsp 147
ỉsf 44
ỉsf.t 44, 286-288, 292
ỉsfty 201, 294
ỉsfty.w 83
ỉss 282
ỉss.t 228
ỉsṯ.tỉ 72, 73
ỉśś 230
ỉśś.t 230
ỉśḳ 242
Ỉšnw 49
Ỉšd.t 296
ỉḳr 197
Ỉḳnty 140
ỉgr.t 12, 37, 93, 117, 151, 250, 266, 279
ỉtm 290
Ỉtm 209
ỉtmw 67
ỉtrw 29
ỉṯỉ 23, 32, 86, 156, 185, 243, 259
ỉd 12, 60

243
ʿ (document) 242
ʿ.t 60
ʿ3 (ass) 194
ʿ3 (door, gate) 114, 123
ʿ3 (big) 239, 249
ʿ3 ḥry ẖ.t.f 98
ʿ3.w 270
ʿ3b.t 147
ʿ3p 33, 259
ʿ3m.w 235, 239
ʿ3tyw 4, 140
ʿw3 24, 35, 87, 243, 246, 287
ʿwn 288
ʿwg 67, 68
ʿb (mischief) 42, 287
ʿb (heaper-up of corn) 201
ʿb3.t 126
ʿpp 249, 294
ʿpr 89, 297
ʿpš3y.t 194
ʿfn.t 108
ʿm 17, 158, 301
ʿmʿ3.t 231
ʿn.t 251
ʿnn (bandage) 108
ʿnn (to twist) 243
ʿnḫ (ear) 61
ʿnḫ (to live) 14, 17, 46, 50, 116, 224
ʿnḫ m 17, 159
ʿnḫ-ỉrw-snake 133
ʿnnt 126
ʿnḏty 280
ʿr 24, 162
ʿrry.t 89
ʿrr.t 28, 29, 115, 116, 197, 322
ʿḥ 231
ʿḥ3 201, 235

ʿḥ3 ḥr	206
ʿḥʿ	76
ʿḥʿ.w	35
ʿḫ	25, 142, 143
ʿḫm	57, 67, 68, 134, 135
ʿẖm	194
ʿḳ	42, 116
ʿḏ	148
ʿḏ.t	148
ʿḏty	201, 210
w3.t	25, 28, 162, 230
w3ỉ	52, 175
w3w3.t	134
W3mm.ty	126, 294
w3ś	224
w3g	179
w3ḏ	158
w3ḏy.t	191
wỉ3	284
wʿ	240
wʿ.ty	240
wʿỉ	67
wbn	148
wbd	134
wpỉ	33, 34, 199, 263
wpwty	202, 332
wn (to open)	123
wn (guilt)	287
wn (to pass)	45
wnm	17, 160
wnn	19, 40, 48
Wnn-nfr	96, 159, 270
wnš	194
wr	154, 156, 206, 249, 270
Wr.t	193
Wrr.t	266
Wrś	30
wrš	203
wrḏ	11, 82
wrḏ ỉb	82
whm	134
whn	51
wḥ3.t	25, 143, 168
wḥʿ	231
wḥm	14, 20, 47, 186
wḥś	148
wḫd	243
wsf	232
wś	68, 156
Wśỉr	40, 204, 210, 211, 212, 298, 301, 330
wśr	225
wśr.t	22, 36, 225
wśḫ.t	268, 297
wśš.t	74
wš3	38, 287, 288
wš3.w	88
wšr	68
wt	108
wt3.w	108
wd	243, 244, 285
wd r	41, 243
wdp.w	206
wḏ	280
wḏʿ	39, 80, 264, 265, 267, 268, 270, 272
wḏʿ mdw	33, 34, 40, 220, 264

265, 267
wḏʿy 39
wḏʿ.t 267
wḏb.w 235, 236, 240

b3 14, 17-20, 29, 47, 58-60, 64, 66, 85, 96, 103, 106, 115, 117-119, 121, 124, 125, 127, 128, 130, 133, 135, 145, 154, 159-161, 171-174, 176-178, 181-186, 191, 205, 206, 211, 239, 240, 242, 245, 250, 254-256, 278, 283, 289, 298, 302, 321
B3 pf 209
B3b3 61, 159, 172, 209
B3by 134, 219
b3n 82
b3g.w 83
b3gỉ 11, 82
bỉn 38, 41, 42, 171, 288
bỉk 194
bʿbʿ 152
bʿḥ.t 69
bw 44
bnw.t 95
brd 61
bḥn 16, 249
bḫn 148
bḫḫ.w 134
bḫḫy 134
Bśw 135
bśk 149
bṯ 33, 259
Bdš.t 126, 127, 274, 281, 294, 295

p.t 47, 118, 123, 162
p3 143
pʿ.w 135
pf 29, 60, 69, 161, 172
pfś 144
pn 244
pnn 244
pnḳ 244, 300
pr (house) 29, 60, 161
pr (exit) 116
pr wr 64, 179
pr-nśr 64
prỉ 12, 41, 53, 118, 230, 254
pḥ 23, 244
Pḥwy 195, 258
pẖr 25, 254
pśỉ 145
Pḏw 104

fnṯ 57
ftft 232
fd.t 11, 57
fdk 68, 149

M3-h3.f 30
m33 8, 244
m3ʿ (to be extended) 83
m3ʿ (righteous) 33, 271, 289, 290
m3ʿḫrw 40, 42
m3ʿ.t 34, 37, 40, 73, 140, 176, 217, 224, 265, 272, 273, 279, 286-288, 298, 301
m3ʿty 37, 83, 273, 292
m3fd.t 132

m3r 79
m3ś.t 204
m3śty 166, 204
mỉ (come) 47
mỉ (like) 123
mỉ (give) 230
mỉwty 194, 235
mʿb3y.t 196
mʿnḏ.t 268
mʿḳ 145
mʿḏ 24, 166
mw 68, 135, 230, 239
mw n śḏ.t 135
mn (to last) 41, 116, 284
mn (to suffer) 68
mnỉ 25, 53
mnỉ.t 22, 225
mnḥ 200
mnḫ 42
Mnš 208
mr (painful) 24, 245
mr (to bind) 338
mr nḫ3 30
mrỉ 116
mrw.t 135
mrwty 181
mrrwty 135
Mrśʿnḫ 209
mḥ (to seize) 185, 335
mḥ (to care for) 268
mḥ(y).w 83, 236, 237
mḥy (counsel) 268
mḥn 36, 164, 165
mḫ3.t 269
Mḫnty n ỉrty 257
mẖn.t 84
mś 294
mśḥ 194
mśk 156
mśḳ.t 125
mśḏ 295
mśḏr 61, 156
mk 225
mt 13, 14, 20, 35, 39, 45-47, 51, 52, 54,55, 198, 199, 218, 267, 268, 279, 297, 301
mt m wḥm 186
mt.w 16
mt.t 218
mtr 38, 259, 260
mdw 130, 270, 272
Mdw-t3.f 115
mdś 24, 245, 246
mḏ.t 12, 80, 242
Mḏ3.w 237

n 48
n3 123
nỉ 288
nỉ.t 288
nỉś 280
nỉś r 205
nỉk 41, 244, 282-285, 295
nỉky 284, 296
Nỉkt 233
ny.t 286
nʿw 99, 135
nʿẖ 207

Nw.t 99
nwỉ 244
nwḫ 68
Nwn 10, 94, 318
nwn (with tumbled hair) 207
nwḥ 126
nwḫ 135
nwt.k nw 207
nwḏ 25, 254, 255
nb (each) 38, 44, 156, 175, 284
nb (lord) 37, 40, 175, 204, 273
nbʿrr.t 28
nb m3ʿ.t 124
nb ḫ.t 124
nb k3.w 124
nb t3.wy 54
nb3 244
nbỉ 135
nbḏ 28, 208
nfw.t 136
nfr 41, 116, 288
nfr.w 47
npr 72
nm.t 18, 24, 92, 166, 167, 249
nmʿ 83
nmś 140
nmty 157, 167
nn 135
nn.t 9, 94, 237
nnỉ 11, 83, 84, 227
nny 83, 84
Nnmw.t 162
nnty.w 237
nrỉ 109
nhỉ 25, 254, 255
nhp 269
nhm 111
nhś 204
nḥ 136
nḥ3 ḥʿ.w 109
nḥ3 ḥr 109, 252
Nḥb k3.w 47, 98-100
nḥb.t 147
nḥm 24, 25 , 35, 87, 99, 246, 254, 255
nḥḥ 68, 98
Nḥś.w 235, 237, 240
Nḥśy 239
nḫ3 24, 167, 231
nḫḫ 272
nś 136
nś.t 156
nśb 137
nśm 145
nśr.t 137
nš3y 109
nšw 244
nšm.t 203
nšnỉ 191
nšny 35
nḳʿ 246, 247
nḳʿw.t 247
nk 61
nkn 17, 247
nty 199
nṯ.t 80
nṯr 33, 38, 123, 156, 159, 199, 212, 224, 301

nṯr.t 38, 123
nṯṯ 126
nṯṯwy 21
nḏ 25, 254, 255, 284
nḏy.t 288
nḏmy.t 61
nḏḥ 232
nḏr 23, 28, 185

r3 (day) 175
r3 (worm) 100
r3 (spell) 57, 230
r3 (mouth) 62
r3 (gate) 116
r3 n d3.t 116
R3-śṯ3.w 26, 89, 113, 159, 165, 204, 280
Rʿ 224, 295
rw 195
rw.t 117
rw.ty 230
rwỉ 10, 57
Rwty 185
rwḏ 62
rpw 149
rm 146, 195
rmỉ 111, 239, 336
rmy.w 111
rmn 247
rmṯ 39, 199, 212, 237, 239, 301
rn 20, 179, 180, 266
Rnnwt.t 98
rrỉ 195
rrk 100, 257
rḥty 135, 195
rḫ 36, 230, 261
rḫy.t 7, 8, 118, 234, 240
rhś 149
rsf 230
rś 55
rḳỉ 33, 175, 259, 260
rḳw 43, 286, 295
rkḥ 137
rtḥ 232
rd 62
rd.wy 76
rdỉ 41, 47, 57, 247, 280, 281, 302
rḏw 11, 57, 59, 256

h3ỉ 156, 247
hwt (to lament) 111
hwt (fire) 137
hb 10, 58, 149
hmhm.t 112
hny 218
hnhn 236
hry ỉb 156
hrw 34, 269, 270, 272
hh 137
hkỉ 100
Hdd 141

ḥ.t 103, 209
ḥ3 112
Ḥ3 58
ḥ3.t 104, 150, 284
ḥ3p 59

ḥ3m 230, 232
ḥ3ty 20, 155, 173, 180, 185
ḥ3d 24, 134, 168, 212, 323
ḥꜥ 47
ḥꜥ.t 159
Ḥꜥpy 60
Ḥw 72
ḥw3 10, 11, 58
ḥw33.t 11
ḥwỉ 38, 239, 260
ḥwꜥỉb 68
Ḥbś-b3gy 184, 279
ḥp 247
Ḥpỉ 69
ḥf3w 101
ḥf3w.t 333
ḥm 25, 254, 255
ḥm-nṯr 209
ḥm-k3 107
Ḥmn 168
ḥmśỉ r 33, 260
ḥmśw.t 304
ḥn.t 116
Ḥnꜥ 26
ḥnꜥ (preposition) 116, 156
ḥnꜥ (noun) 258
ḥnwy.t 102
ḥnb3 100, 102
Ḥnn 171
ḥnḥn 117
ḥnṯ 204
ḥnṯỉ 149
ḥr 63, 140
Ḥr-ḥ3.f 304, 309
Ḥr ḫnty Ḫmw 212
Ḥr ẖ3ty 63
Ḥr Śmśw 170
Ḥr t3 78
Ḥr d3tỉ 213
ḥr.t 104
ḥrtỉwny 254, 256, 257
ḥrỉ 256
ḥry 172
Ḥry-š.f 166
ḥry.t 25, 145, 322
ḥrw 109
ḥḥ 128, 240
ḥḥỉ 240
Ḥḥw 26
ḥs3 215
ḥsỉ 248
ḥś 74, 76
ḥś3 ḥr 208
ḥśb (to slaughter) 16, 149
ḥśb (to reckon) 34, 35, 154, 156, 269, 270, 272
ḥśb.t 270
ḥśḳ 16, 149, 150, 156
ḥḳr 68
ḥk3 20, 22, 63, 127, 144, 146, 173, 175, 181, 186, 187, 194, 213, 248, 295
ḥknw 288
ḥtp 4, 36, 37, 250, 257
ḥtp k3 74
Ḥtp-fields 3, 26, 30, 31, 51, 53, 68, 69, 75, 88, 101, 111-113, 118, 165, 195,

198, 199, 241, 247, 252, 256, 273, 300, 309
ḥtpy.w 36
Ḥtpś Ḫw.ś 273
ḥtpty.w 36
ḥtm 14, 17, 18, 19, 22, 41, 49, 50, 169, 177, 188, 253, 302
Ḥtm-bird 87
ḥtm.t 41
ḥtmy 23
ḥtmy.t 18, 24, 35, 41, 92, 169, 250
ḥtmty.w 16
ḥtr 12, 80
ḥtrty.w 236, 240
ḥdk 150
ḥḏ 248

ḫ.t (fire) 29, 135, 138, 139
ḫ.t (thing) 156
ḫ.t 40, 273
ḫ3 171
ḫ3-lake 140
ḫ3.w 127
ḫ3 53
ḫ3ty 205
ḫ3ty.w 207, 282
ḫʿ.w 161
ḫʿỉ 161
ḫw 289
ḫwỉ 43, 289
ḫww 43, 289
ḫb 170
ḫb.t 15, 24, 161, 170
ḫb3 16
ḫbn 42, 271, 289, 290
ḫbn.t 287, 289
ḫbnty 289
ḫbḫb 248
ḫpỉ 54
ḫpy.t 54
ḫpp 181
ḫpr 19, 49, 55
ḫpr r 248
Ḫpr 150
ḫprw 102
ḫpš 146
ḫf3 186
ḫft.t 218
ḫfty 32, 33, 43, 205, 217, 218, 224, 247, 249, 284, 289, 296, 332, 333
Ḫfty.wt 223
ḫm 64, 235
ḫmỉ 18, 188, 189
ḫmy 190
Ḫmy.t 182
ḫm 271
ḫmw 104
ḫnp 87
Ḫnm.t wr 222
ḫnr 21, 124, 127, 133, 298
Ḫnsw 213
ḫnś 172
ḫnt 156
ḫntỉ 95
Ḫnty ỉmnty.w 118, 126, 198, 220, 222, 227, 274, 275
Ḫnty ỉrty 62

Ḫnti mnwt.f 117
ḫr (to fall) 51, 248, 249
ḫr (with) 156, 183
ḫr.w 37
ḫr.t 40, 273
ḫry.t 150
ḫrw 38, 42, 63, 240, 271, 287-290
ḫśf 23, 28, 35, 118, 119, 240, 248, 249, 257, 262
ḫśf n 284
ḫśr 271
ḫśḏ 59
ḫty 15
Ḫty 138, 223
ḫty.w 228
ḫtm 62, 80

ẖ.t 63, 156, 175
ẖ3.t 11, 18, 20, 47, 57, 63, 127, 159, 173, 182, 302
ẖ3b 42, 43, 290, 292
ẖ3b.t 42, 290
ẖ3s.t 24, 171
ẖ3k 290
ẖ3k ỉb 205
ẖnw 135, 230
ẖnf.t 25, 145
H̱nmw 166
ẖnn 10, 59
ẖnn.w 191
ẖr 76, 130
ẖr.t nṯr 47
ẖry 42
H̱rty 8, 17, 81, 117, 159, 213
ẖsy 336

s 200
s3 mr.f 107
s3 t3 102
s3 ṯw 254
s3w 21, 116, 123, 128, 129, 257
s3w.t 128
s3b 59
sỉ 50
sỉn 18, 70
sw3 150
swr 160
sbn 249
sp 44, 290
sps 207
Spsy 293
sf 150
sfṯ 151
sm3 t3 25, 54
sm3.wt 205
smy.t 94, 129
sn 16, 151
snw 70
snf 151, 152
snsn 51, 116
snṯ 59, 205, 255
Sḥsḥ 162
ssy 282
sš 244

ś.t 135, 156
ś.t bỉn.t 171
ś3b 58

ś3m 15, 16, 133
ś3r 80
ś3ḥ 47
ś3ḫ 47, 174
śi͗ʿr 33, 260
śi͗w 261
śi͗p 37, 38, 41, 278-280, 282, 338
śi͗pw 21
śi͗sf 44
śi͗ḳ 152
śʿm 158
śʿnḫ 47
śʿr.t 70, 338
śʿḥʿ 33, 261, 262
św3 25, 29, 254, 257, 258
św3ḏ 47, 99
śwʿb 271
śwr 135
śwš.t 130
śb3 37, 120, 225
śb3gi͗ 84
śbi͗ 206, 249, 286, 296
śbḫ.t 29, 35, 39, 115, 121-123, 129, 156, 297
Śbk 168, 230, 254
Śp3 171
Śp3y 78
śpḥ 233, 243
śpḫ3 35, 271
śpd 140, 152
Śpd 9, 76
Śpd.t 162, 191
śfḫ 12, 81
śm3 16, 152, 153
śm3y 16
śm3ʿ 271
śm3ʿ ḫrw 35
śmi͗ 33, 116, 124, 197, 261, 299
śmḥ 268
śmḫ 63
śnḥ 126, 130, 338
śnḥwy 21
śnśn 59
śnk.(t) 88
śnḏ 110
śnḏm 156, 208
śr 274
śrf 71
śrḫ 287
śrḫ.w 33, 261
Śrḳ.t 214
Śrdy 78
śḥ3i͗ 291
śḥtm 44, 135, 188, 189, 249, 302
śḫ.t ḥtp.t 113
śḫ3 249
śḫi͗ 156
śḫpr 239
śḫfḫf 33
śḫm 135
śḫm m 23, 206, 249
Śḫm.i͗rw.f 268
Śḫm.t 134, 149, 151, 214
śḫnš 33, 262
śḫr 18, 190
śḫr (nature) 41, 42
śḫśf 262
śḫt 234

śḫty 232, 233
śḫd 8, 9, 74, 75, 77, 78, 114
śẖb 160
śswn 41, 284
śsf 44
śś 139
śśy 136, 139, 284
śśnḥ 131
śśnḏ 110
śśnḏ.t 110
śśḏ3.t 254, 259
śšm 289
śḳd 84
śk 18
śkỉ 14, 48-51, 98, 156, 302
śkśk 190
śgnn 84
śgr 93
śt3 153, 244
śtỉ 139
Śty 139
Śtš 214
śtỉ 11, 41, 60, 64, 161
śd3 110
śdf 131
śdfy 131
śḏ 17, 249
śḏ.t 29, 89, 139, 140, 321, 322
śḏ3.w 259
śḏ3.t 131
śḏ3y.t 21
śḏwỉ 262
śḏwy 33
śḏb 42, 249, 250, 287
śḏby 129
śḏm 272
śḏm mdw 34, 35
śḏḥ 102
śḏr 11, 55, 84
śḏty 249

š 24, 171, 322
š wr 29, 162, 172, 245, 255
š3 195
š3ʿ.t 172
š3r 99
š3ś 26
šʿ 153, 154, 156, 270
šʿ.t 17
šʿd 154
Šw 26, 215
šw.t 14, 17, 20, 127, 159, 173, 177, 182-184, 211
šp 12, 64
špt 250
šfšf.t 110
šm (to go) 13, 25, 54-56, 63, 230, 302
šm (heat) 141
šmś.t 226
šmty 100, 195
šn ḫ.t r 33, 263
šny.t 274
šnʿ 28, 124, 125
šnṯ 250
šnṯ.t 291
Šsmw 104, 143, 145, 146, 151, 158, 215, 216

šśm 81
šśr 244
št3 97, 161, 225, 307
št3 ḥr 208
štm 42
Štṯ 114
šṯy.t 95, 170
šd 87, 155
šdỉ 154, 166, 174
šdn 164

ḳ3 251
ḳ3 ḫrw 110, 208
ḳ3b 29, 30, 172
ḳ3ḥ 221
Ḳ3ḥ.w 184
ḳ3ś 22, 80, 81, 108, 132, 221
ḳỉ 116
Ḳbḥ 272
Ḳbḥ-śnw.f 69
Ḳbḥw 114, 232
ḳn (damage) 18, 43, 291
ḳn (to kill) 190
ḳn.t 190
ḳnb.t 38, 39, 203, 274, 301
ḳnḳn 24, 250
ḳrf 64
ḳrr 141
ḳrr.t 67, 102, 131, 145, 146, 150, 152, 157, 173, 193, 245, 247, 296, 299
ḳrr.t-book 4, 6, 15, 17, 144, 145, 150, 157, 158, 177, 178, 183, 245, 278, 279, 327
ḳrś 105
ḳś 17, 64, 77
ḳty.t 25
ḳd (character) 34, 35, 269, 272, 294
ḳd (to sleep) 11, 82, 85
ḳd (to build) 107

k3 50, 71, 74, 75, 98-100, 102, 104, 128, 173, 180, 184, 219, 227, 262, 272
k3-snake 110, 257
k3.w 248
K3.t 144
k3.t 247, 251
k3mm 295
kyw 296
kywy 296
kf 156
km ḥr 208
knỉ 291
knḥ.w 88
kkw 88, 89, 324
kty.t 145
ktt 195

g3w 67, 71
G3g3y.t 144
Gb 95, 225
gbg3 195, 196, 243
gmm 136
gr 12, 93
grḥ 91
grg 33, 44, 230, 234, 263,

286, 287, 289

t 72
t3 (article) 123
t3 (earth) 8, 10, 47, 69, 96, 123, 142, 227, 230
T3y.t 235
T3ḫb.t 81
tỉ3 64
Tỉ3.w 63, 64
Tỉʿ3 209
twr 43, 292
tbś 156
tp 65, 113, 156, 247
tm 14, 18, 19, 48, 49, 51, 55, 57
Tm 47
try 47
try.t 290, 292
thỉ 43, 251, 292
tḫnỉ 65
tḫś 156
tk3 142
tkn 125

ṯ3ỉ 87, 335
ṯ3w 72
ṯ3m 281
Ṯb 86, 161
ṯpḥ.t 24, 173
Ṯmḥ.w 240
ṯmś 43
ṯmś.w 292, 293
ṯn 282
ṯnw.t 279, 282
ṯnm 25, 146
Ṯnn.t 233
ṯry.t 43, 292
ṯs ḏw 293
ṯs.t 108
ṯsỉ bt3 33, 263
ṯsty.w 206
ṯṯ 132

d3.t 10, 21, 23, 37, 39, 71, 88, 93, 96 , 104, 106, 109, 116, 119-124, 127, 132, 133, 139, 145, 146, 150, 162-166, 173, 178, 188, 190, 192, 195, 202, 204, 212, 240, 245, 249, 258, 267, 273, 274, 277, 280, 283-285, 290, 292, 293, 297, 311
d3s 226
d3s.wy 22
D3ty 146
d3ty 240
d3ty.w 111
dw3 113
Dw3-mwt.f 69
dwfy 25, 146
Dwn-ʿ.wy 215
db 197
dp 160
dm 156
dn 157
dnyw.t 110
dnm 160
dr 157, 284, 286, 287
dś 16, 157

dšr.w 158
dšr.t 237

ḏ.t (body) 64, 65, 240
ḏ.t (eternity) 68, 116, 285
ḏ3.t 172, 292, 294
ḏ3ỉ 24, 38, 44, 248, 252, 253, 260, 296, 332
d3y.t 44, 253, 290
ḏ3f 142
ḏ3f.t 142
ḏ3ḏ3 332
ḏ3ḏ3.t 38, 39, 274, 276
ḏ3ty 38, 44, 291, 292, 294, 296
ḏʿm 224
ḏʿr 233
ḏw 41-44, 156, 244, 253, 285, 293, 294
ḏwy 240
ḏw.t 24, 253, 285, 289
ḏb3 281, 302
ḏbʿ (finger) 24
ḏbʿ (rebuke) 33, 247, 263
ḏfy.t 83
ḏnd 24, 191
ḏnḏn 158
ḏrḏr 206
Ḏḥwty 216, 284
ḏḥr.t 22, 132
ḏś 175
ḏśf 228, 234
ḏśr 227
ḏd 47, 256
Ḏdw.t 81
ḏdf.t 102
ḏdh 132

3ḫ 297
b3 298, 302
i͗3rw-field 300
Imn.t 291
Imnt.t 297
ʿm 301
ʿḥʿ 297
wśḫ.t 297
mnḫ 298
rt 297
Ḥtp-field 300
ḥtm 302
śmi 299
šm 302
ḳnb.t 301
ḳrr.t 299
ḳrty 299
ḳl3.t 299
tw3.t 297
tb3 302
d3.t 300

COPTIC WORDS

ⲁⲅⲅⲉⲗⲟⲥ 325, 325
ⲁⲙⲁϩⲧⲉ 335
ⲁⲙⲛ̄ⲧⲉ 303, 310, 311, 312, 313, 316, 319
ⲁⲛⲧⲓⲕⲓⲙⲉⲛⲟⲥ 328, 333
ⲁⲣⲓⲏⲗ 323
ⲁⲧⲅⲟⲙ 322
ⲁⲩⲱ 316
ⲁϣ 143
ⲃⲁϊϣⲓⲛⲉ 332
ⲃⲁⲥⲁⲛⲟⲥ 327
ⲅⲉϩⲉⲛⲛⲁ 320, 321, 322
ⲇⲁⲓⲙⲟⲛⲓⲟⲛ 331
ⲇⲉⲕⲁⲛⲟⲥ 332
ⲇⲓⲁⲃⲟⲗⲟⲥ 328
ⲇⲣⲁⲕⲱⲛ 326, 333, 334
ⲉⲃⲟⲗ 316
ⲉⲛⲉⲣⲅⲓⲁ 328
ⲏⲡⲉ 338
ⲓⲉⲣⲟ 307

ⲕⲁⲕⲉ 315, 324, 326
ⲕⲁⲕⲟⲩⲣⲅⲟⲥ 335
ⲕⲁⲧⲏⲅⲟⲣⲟⲥ 340
ⲕⲉϩⲉⲛⲛⲁ 312, 325
ⲕⲟⲗⲁⲥⲓⲥ 326
ⲕⲱϩⲧ̄ 307, 320, 323
ⲙⲁⲛ̄ϩⲱⲧⲡ̄ 315
ⲙⲁⲥⲧⲓⲅⲟⲓⲛ 339
ⲙⲉϣϯⲃⲥ̄ 316
ⲙ̄ⲙⲟⲩ 337
ⲙ̄ⲙⲟϥ 337
ⲙⲛ̄ 319
ⲙ̄ⲡⲉⲥⲏⲧ 311
ⲙⲟⲭⲗⲟⲥ 316
ⲙ̄ⲥⲁϩ 330
ⲙ̄ⲧⲟⲛ 313
ⲙⲟⲩⲣ 338
ⲛⲟⲩⲛ 303, 311, 312, 318, 319
ⲛⲟⲩϩⲉ, qual. ⲛⲏϩⲉ 316
ⲛⲟϭ 326, 327
ⲡⲩⲗⲏ 316
ⲣⲓⲙⲉ 336
ⲣⲟ 316
ⲣ̄ⲣⲟ 328
ⲥⲁⲧⲉ 320, 322
ⲥⲃⲟⲕ 338
ⲥⲉⲉⲧⲉ 321
ⲥⲏϥⲉ 340
ⲥⲟⲛⲉ 335
ⲥϯ ⲃⲱⲛ 341
ⲥⲱⲛϩ̄ 338
ⲧⲁⲣⲧⲁⲣⲟⲩⲭⲟⲥ 331, 332
ⲧⲏⲣ 316, 328
ⲧⲓⲙⲱⲣⲓⲥⲧⲏⲥ 331
ⲟⲩϩⲟⲣ 330
ⲟⲩϭⲡ̄ 316
ⲭⲁⲟⲥ 315
ⲭⲉⲓⲣⲅⲣⲁⲫⲟⲛ 340
ⲭⲣⲱⲙ 307
ⲱⲙⲕ̄ 337
ⲱϣⲙ̄ 321
ϣⲁⲃⲉϩⲟ 329
ϣⲏⲓ 322
ϣⲓⲕϩ̄ 323
ϣⲗⲓϫ 339
ϣⲧⲉⲕⲟ 312, 323
ϣⲱⲡⲉ 322
ϥⲛⲧ̄ 334
ϩⲓⲃⲟⲗ 315, 326
ϩⲓⲏ 341
ϩⲓⲉⲓⲧ 168, 323
ϩⲓⲥⲉ 336
ϩⲓⲧ 168
ϩⲟ 330
ϩⲟⲣϥ̄ 316
ϩⲩⲡⲏⲣⲉⲧⲏⲥ 330
ϩⲣⲱ 322
ϩϥⲱ 333
ϫⲁϫⲉ 332, 333
ϫⲏⲩ 335
ϫⲱⲱⲣⲉ ⲉⲃⲟⲗ 330

THE LITERATURE OF DEATH AND DYING

Abrahamsson, Hans. **The Origin of Death:** Studies in African Mythology. 1951

Alden, Timothy. **A Collection of American Epitaphs and Inscriptions with Occasional Notes.** Five vols. in two. 1814

Austin, Mary. **Experiences Facing Death.** 1931

Bacon, Francis. **The Historie of Life and Death with Observations Naturall and Experimentall for the Prolongation of Life.** 1638

Barth, Karl. **The Resurrection of the Dead.** 1933

Bataille, Georges. **Death and Sensuality:** A Study of Eroticism and the Taboo. 1962

Bichat, [Marie François] Xavier. **Physiological Researches on Life and Death.** 1827

Browne, Thomas. **Hydriotaphia.** 1927

Carrington, Hereward. **Death:** Its Causes and Phenomena with Special Reference to Immortality. 1921

Comper, Frances M. M., editor. **The Book of the Craft of Dying and Other Early English Tracts Concerning Death.** 1917

Death and the Visual Arts. 1976

Death as a Speculative Theme in Religious, Scientific, and Social Thought. 1976

Donne, John. **Biathanatos.** 1930

Farber, Maurice L. **Theory of Suicide.** 1968

Fechner, Gustav Theodor. **The Little Book of Life After Death.** 1904

Frazer, James George. **The Fear of the Dead in Primitive Religion.** Three vols. in one. 1933/1934/1936

Fulton, Robert. **A Bibliography on Death, Grief and Bereavement:** 1845-1975. 1976

Gorer, Geoffrey. **Death, Grief, and Mourning.** 1965

Gruman, Gerald J. **A History of Ideas About the Prolongation of Life.** 1966

Henry, Andrew F. and James F. Short, Jr. **Suicide and Homicide.** 1954

Howells, W[illiam] D[ean], et al. **In After Days;** Thoughts on the Future Life. 1910

Irion, Paul E. **The Funeral:** Vestige or Value? 1966

Landsberg, Paul-Louis. **The Experience of Death:** The Moral Problem of Suicide. 1953

Maeterlinck, Maurice. **Before the Great Silence.** 1937

Maeterlinck, Maurice. **Death.** 1912

Metchnikoff, Élie. **The Nature of Man:** Studies in Optimistic Philosophy. 1910

Metchnikoff, Élie. **The Prolongation of Life:** Optimistic Studies. 1908

Munk, William. **Euthanasia.** 1887

Osler, William. **Science and Immortality.** 1904

Return to Life: Two Imaginings of the Lazarus Theme. 1976

Stephens, C[harles] A[sbury]. **Natural Salvation:** The Message of Science. 1905

Sulzberger, Cyrus. **My Brother Death.** 1961

Taylor, Jeremy. **The Rule and Exercises of Holy Dying.** 1819

Walker, G[eorge] A[lfred]. **Gatherings from Graveyards.** 1839

Warthin, Aldred Scott. **The Physician of the Dance of Death.** 1931

Whiter, Walter. **Dissertation on the Disorder of Death.** 1819

Whyte, Florence. **The Dance of Death in Spain and Catalonia.** 1931

Wolfenstein, Martha. **Disaster:** A Psychological Essay. 1957

Worcester, Alfred. **The Care of the Aged, the Dying, and the Dead.** 1950

Zandee, J[an]. **Death as an Enemy According to Ancient Egyptian Conceptions.** 1960